Race, Ethnicity, and Place in a Changing America

Race, Ethnicity, and Place in a Changing America

edited by

John W. Frazier and Eugene L. Tettey-Fio

Global Academic Publishing
Harpur College, Binghamton University
2006

Library of Congress Cataloging-in-Publication Data

Race, ethnicity, and place in a changing America / edited by John W. Frazier and Eugene L. Tettey-Fio.
    p. cm.
    Includes bibliographical references.
    ISBN-13: 978-1-58684-264-2 (pbk.: alk. paper)
    1. United States--Race relations--History--20th century. 2. United States--Ethnic relations--History--20th century. 3. Population geography--United States--History--20th century. 4. Pluralism (Social sciences)--United States--History--20th century. 5. United States--Social policy. 6. Landscape--Social aspects--United States. 7. Minorities--United States. I. Frazier, John W. II. Tettey-Fio, Eugene.
    E184.A1R284 2006
    305.800973'09045--dc22

2005034926

Distributed by:

Global Academic Publishing
State University of New York at Binghamton
Binghamton, NY USA 13902-6000
Phone: (607) 777-4495; Fax: (607) 777-6132
Email: gap@binghamton.edu
http://academicpublishing.binghamton.edu

Acknowledgments

This book could not be published without the support of many people. Jean-Pierre Mileur, the Dean of Harpur College of Arts and Sciences, financially supported the second "Race, Ethnicity and Place Conference (REP II) in 2004, which was the impetus of this book. We are very grateful to him.

Orlando Taylor, Graduate Dean of Howard University, and Douglas Richardson, Executive Director of the Association of American Geographers, also financially sponsored REP II, which was held on the campus of Howard University, and served with John W. Frazier as co-directors of that Conference. This book could not have come to fruition without their support and the support of their staffs. We thank them, too.

We similarly acknowledge the strong support of our entire Binghamton Geography faculty. In particular, we thank Florence M. Margai, who served on the 2003–2004 REP II Planning Committee and contributed a chapter to this text. Norah F. Henry, Associate Dean for Administration, and Mark E. Reisinger provided constructive criticism on a number of the chapters in this volume. Lucius S. Willis and Kevin Heard contributed many of the original graphics and improved others used in the text. We thank these colleagues for their time and talents.

We also thank all of our authors, who not only agreed to restructure their conference presentations into a form suitable for undergraduates, but responded promptly to our requests and those of reviewers for changes in their manuscripts. We gratefully acknowledge the constructive criticism of several anonymous reviewers; their suggestions improved the volume.

Thanks are also due to Jennifer Fox Frazier, who served as our editorial assistant. Finally, we are especially grateful for the thoughtful guidance, suggestions, and assistance of the entire staff of Global Academic Publishing. We especially express our thanks to Mary Beth Willis, Director of Publications, Angela Hwang, Marketing Director, and publication staff, Lori Vandermark Fuller, Jennifer Winans, and Ashley Rambus.

JWF ELT

Dedication

This book is dedicated to
the memory of our colleague and good friend,

William Dakan,

who passed away unexpectedly on December 3, 2005.

Contents

Part III
U.S. HISPANIC/LATINO GEOGRAPHIES:
CHANGING SPATIAL PATTERNS AND THEIR IMPLICATIONS

Part IV
ASIAN AND PACIFIC-ISLANDER GEOGRAPHIES:
CULTURAL PERSISTENCE AND CHANGING PATTERNS

Contents

Foreword

The human geography of the United States reflects both continuity and change due to a number of global, national, and local forces, one of the overarching themes of *Race, Ethnicity, and Place in a Changing America*. Some patterns, such as the black ghetto, have persisted due to unfortunate circumstances, while new places have taken on special meaning and purpose for groups, such as the Eden Center in northern Virginia for the Vietnamese. As ethnic groups relocate, they reshape inherited landscapes, remaking places to reflect their presence, such as Puerto Ricans and other Latinos. Also, for some native cultures, such as Hawaiians, place is an essential ingredient of cultural identity. Each of these examples reveals the complexity and breadth of issues associated with race, ethnicity and place.

In a world where the media, telecommunications, and the Internet have drastically altered how individuals conceive of themselves and their place in the world, it is essential that scholars, politicians, journalists, and all citizens are aware of the many ways in which the place one lives, works, or visits affects and is affected by race and ethnicity. It is equally important to share research findings related to these topics with students and others. *Race, Ethnicity, and Place in a Changing America* was designed to achieve this goal. Although the concept of this text evolved from a national conference on Race, Ethnicity and Place convened at Howard University in 2004, co-sponsored by the Association of American Geographers (AAG), Howard University and Binghamton University, a substantial effort after the conference resulted in this volume. Editors John W. Frazier (founder of the REP Conferences) and Eugene L. Tettey-Fio requested that authors recast their conference presentations into a format suitable for undergraduates. The authors have met this challenge and the result is a strong text covering such important topics as migration, cultural conflicts over space, place-based identities, changing ethnic and racial landscapes, spatial dimensions of health inequalities, institutional roles in shaping human geography, and racial/ethnic relations.

Because each of these issues is too large for any one scholar or institution to address alone, collaborations and partnerships are increasingly essential for continuing this research agenda. In nearly every case, the essays in this book have an interdisciplinary perspective, spanning disciplines from geography, economics, political science, communications, sociology, social work, history, business, law, and medicine. The research tools of multiple disciplines and their focal points require scholars and other leaders to form partnerships that allow them to address these questions in a holistic way.

Just as disciplines cannot address these issues in isolation, neither can institutions. Higher education institutions, often because of their own location or place, have different missions, thus, the research foci they may bring to a project vary widely. It is essential that these different perspectives be brought together, so that institutions (and the scholars who work there) can share in the future development of these issues. For example, Howard University — one of the co-sponsors of the 2004 conference — is the nation's largest producer of African American Ph.D. recipients in many of the social, behavioral and economic sciences, and a central component of its institutional mission commits addressing issues of African Americans and other groups historically marginalized in the United States. Although Howard does not currently have a geography department, its predominantly African American faculty includes individuals who have focused their careers on issues of race and ethnicity. On the other hand, Binghamton University's geography department has made the study of race, ethnicity and place a special focus of inquiry and its faculty has published widely on this topic and sponsored the first national conference on this topic in 2002. Thus, Howard and Binghamton, because of institutional differences and strengths, can do things together that neither can do alone.

Similarly, organizations like the Association of American Geographers play a critical role not only in organizing diverse individuals in an individual discipline, but also in bringing specific problems or questions to the forefront for national public and disciplinary discussion. Government at all levels, and corporate America as well, must be full partners in these efforts, since in many cases, the solutions to problems require governmental or corporate action.

It would be a mistake to think that issues of race, ethnicity, and place can be confined to one nation, and thus, the partnerships that are necessary to address these issues must be global as well. Migration, for example, often involves movement from one country to another, with resulting effects on both countries. The research questions these issues raise are best addressed by partnerships of universities and scholars that span national boundaries, with perspectives that are influenced by the particularities of the place where they are located.

The Association of American Geographers, Binghamton University, and the Howard University Graduate School have pledged to continue their partnership and to seek other collaborators. The partners have embarked on a variety of related projects, from joint grant submissions to collaborative international research, and these possibilities continue to grow. Additional conferences on the topic of race, ethnicity, and place also are planned for the future. In 2006, Texas State University, under the leadership of Lawrence E. Estaville (local conference director), will join the AAG, Binghamton, and Howard to plan the next Race, Ethnicity and Place Conference to be held in San Marcos, Texas (http://rep-conference@binghamton.edu). As in previous conferences, the program at this next conference will be broadly based. However, it also will take advantage of its location to stress Latino issues from a geographic perspective. Also, within a global context, scholars from Latin America and other regions will be invited to participate in this next conference.

Many of those attending the Race, Ethnicity and Place Conference at Howard University, among them AAG Past-President Larry Brown and Tom Boswell, current Chair of the AAG Ethnic Geography Specialty Group, commented that this event, on the campus of the world's leading historically black university, was among the most significant conferences in which they had participated during their careers. There was indeed a general consensus of something important happening at the meeting, a sense of auspicious beginnings. It will now be up to all of us — working together — to ensure that those beginnings are carried through to real and meaningful endings. The 2006 San Marcos conference will certainly build on previous successes and contribute to this goal.

Race, Ethnicity, and Place in a Changing America provides one of the most rigorous and comprehensive assessments available on racial and ethnic geographies and explains why they are important to all of us.

Orlando Taylor, Graduate Dean, Howard University
Douglas Richardson, Executive Director, Association of American Geographers

THE CHANGING AMERICAN SCENE

Two of the most significant changes occurring in the second half of 20th century America involved racial and ethnic composition of the population and the national focus on civil rights policy (housing, school desegregation, etc.). Debates about U.S. immigration after WWII resulted in profound changes in the magnitude and origins of immigration flows into the country. In the same period, the U.S. was steeped in the conflicts of the Civil Rights Era. The laws that emerged on these two fronts dramatically changed how America would treat immigration and racial issues in the future and also modified American human geography throughout most U.S. regions. Cultural and ethnic landscapes, the visualization of cultural imprints by the occupying group, capture the racial and ethnic changes in particular American places. Some of these landscapes and places illustrate the nature and range of changes that have occurred, and that are likely to continue, in places across the nation in coming decades.

Audrey Singer, in a subsequent chapter, informs us that the public library in Montgomery County, Maryland, "welcomes visitors in 11 languages." The welcomes are not for tourists. Rather, Montgomery County, like other suburban Washington, D.C. areas, is experiencing a rapidly changing population due to recent immigration that has made the nation's capital a gateway city. In the same county, African-American family homes of professional, white collar workers are decorated to reflect ethnic ties — among the decorations are pieces of African art, a Civil Rights era painting, and a colorful poster highlighting a recent jazz festival — and, at the same time, such homes express the achievements of the black middle class (Wiese, 2005). These examples illustrate the increasing suburbanization of the black middle class and the rise of ethnic diversity.

In suburban Minneapolis, black patrons of a barbershop exchange stories. They are not African Americans; they are Africans, "Liberians of War," living their "Liberian Way." Earl Scott (chapter 12) explains the importance of social spaces for Liberian immigrants to reminisce about their homeland. Here in the American Heartland, Liberians have carved out landscapes and remain distinct from the local African-American population, despite their common cultural ties. Liberians are not the only immigrants who have settled in the heartland. Asian ethnic groups also have settled in inconspicuous and perhaps unexpected places, including Minnesota. The Hmong people of Southeast Asia provide a good example. Following the Vietnam War, this culture experienced genocide for their support of Americans. Since receiving refugee status, more than one million Hmong people have immigrated to the U.S. and more than 60,000 have settled in the Minneapolis-St. Paul region, where hundreds of their successful businesses help define the new Hmong landscape there.

The African ethnic scene described for Liberians is repeated in other American cities by other African immigrants, Ghanaians in New York, Somalis in Maine, and Ethiopians in Los Angeles, among others. Meanwhile, black ethnic Caribbeans have created cultural landscapes in various places, including Miami, Florida (Haitian and Trinidadian). Miami also is home to "Little Havana" and became the center of Cuban-American politics and culture after Castro overthrew Battista in 1959. Their position grew even stronger due to subsequent migrations of Cubans of varying social and economic status. The U.S. subsidized "freedom flights" and other efforts contributed to this diversity. Thus, "Little Havana," too, is a distinctive ethnic landscape of a newly emerging America in the last four decades.

No region has changed more during the last generation than the American South. Its booming economy and warm climate have attracted migrants of all backgrounds. Among the newcomers are Mexican immigrants, legal and illegal, who have been attracted by the potential for a better life. Charlotte, North Carolina, once a black-white city, realized a greater percentage increase in its Latino population than any American city of comparable size. It is now classified as an immigrant "gateway" city (Singer, 2004). Atlanta, Georgia, the largest city of the South, also has experienced significant increases in ethnic immigrants and has been a favored destination for the "reverse" migration of African Americans, who for the first time since the Great Migration, have begun returning South in very large numbers (see chapter 7). However, African Americans "returning home" are not only being attracted to the employment opportunities of large metropolitan regions like Atlanta, some are returning to their Southern roots in rural places in North Carolina and are drawn there for non-economic reasons (Cromartie and Stack, 1989 and Stack, 1996), Similarly, Latinos are moving to small towns as well as cities, settling for example in rural Tennessee and Kentucky, as well as other rural southern areas, in their search for a better life (Smith and Fuerseth, in press).

In the south central U.S., other racial/ethnic patterns illustrate change. San Antonio, Texas, has long been the residence of many people of Mexican ancestry. In recent years this community has prospered and become one of America's most rapidly growing metropolitan regions. The established Mexican community of San Antonio has distanced itself from recent Mexican immigrants on the basis of class, and has created an interesting urban geography in that community. Further north, in the Texas Panhandle, other changes are occurring. Once occupied by Anglos, this region has experienced an out-migration of Anglos, who are being replaced by Mexican immigrants who perceive the region's value differently. The region's composition is changing as a result. Both of these examples are presented in more detail in subsequent chapters.

On the Pacific Coast, the influence of the Mexican-American population was significant for most of the 20th century. It remains so today, despite the growing dispersion of Latinos into other U.S. regions. Latinos have become a political and economic force in California. They also have brought controversy. Illegal immigrants, including Mexicans, have brought serious problems to that state, which in combination with Texas, is expected to have 35 million Latinos by the year 2050. Chinese Americans also have created unique geographic places in the United States, including Chinatowns and more recently "ethnoburbs" in California. Wei Li has described them as a novel form of clustered immigrant suburban settlement of ethnic people and their businesses with complete institutional structures. She and her colleagues described the process of their formation:

> "... Waves of new wealthy and middle-class immigrants from the global Chinese Diaspora settled in Los Angeles suburbs, where they strengthened their ties to the Pacific Rim through business activities; their financial resources created the demand for a strong ethnic banking sector — and, indeed, for the second wave of Chinese-American banks ... (which have) been instrumental in creating the San Gabriel Valley ethnoburb by financing new Chinese residential settlements and transforming the local business structure and its landscapes" (Li et al., 2002, p. 792).

Li discusses the racial encounters of Asian Americans later in this text and argues that racial experiences are important to first-generation immigrants' paths both to assimilation and their settlement choices.

Further northward on the Pacific Coast in Oregon, white Europeans have settled in what Susan Hardwick terms "Causcasia," indicating the long-term dominance of the European-white population. She relates a fascinating story in chapter 25 of Russians and Ukrainians, who are refugees and fundamentalist Christians guided to the area by religious networks tied to the former Soviet Union. Her analysis reminds us that not all recent immigrants and landscapes represent non-whites. More importantly, she illustrates the important roles of institutions in shaping geographic settlement patterns and in operating in the political arena, where these groups have attempted to be classified as a "coalition of color," using racial classification as a means to access competitive government funding to address their community needs.

In the country's largest metropolitan area, New York City, a great deal of racial/ethnic change continues to occur. New York City has always been noted for its diversity and as a global city. Manhattan's Lower East Side witnessed a sequence of cultural occupants, including the Dutch, Germans, Jews, Italians, and others. Beginning in the 1950s, Puerto Rican settlement became significant there too. In fact, Puerto Ricans were the dominant Hispanic group in the City for decades. One of the most significant changes in the City in the recent decades has been the diversification of Latino groups, accompanied by continued white flight. There also has been a noticeable out-migration of Puerto Ricans to nearby states, most notably to Connecticut and Pennsylvania. These are topics of two subsequent chapters. Distinctive Latino clusters have arisen in places like Long Island and multicultural neighborhoods have taken form in some city boroughs. Ninety miles away, in southeastern Pennsylvania, small post-industrial cities like Allentown and Reading are being transformed by the arrival of Puerto Ricans relocating from the City and directly from the island. Recently, they have been joined by a wide variety of Central and South American Latinos. Distinct settlement patterns and cultural landscapes are emerging as a result.

These brief examples indicate the increasing racial and ethnic diversity that is changing the composition of the American population and the appearance of landscapes. The newer landscapes are troubling for some Americans who see them as undermining the American culture and leading to the decline of America's position in the world. It is important to note that, as new landscapes appear, the remnants and expansion of persistent geographic distributions remain.

CULTURAL PERSISTENCE OF NON-ANGLO LANDSCAPES IN AMERICAN PLACES

There are places and landscapes that serve as evidence of the perseverance of subcultures who have struggled to successfully retain their cultural identities, despite the hardships resulting from second-class citizenship. These are important reminders of how the dominant culture in a society can restrict the access of subcultures to opportunities. They also speak to the societal failures to improve the living conditions of all Americans and to create policy to eradicate the Black ghettos and other places that exist because subcultures are denied equal access and are restricted in American geographic space. The magnitude and ubiquity of the geographic expression of such places are not well known by most Americans, perhaps because of another American failing, the lack of geographic education at all levels of the U.S. education system. This is why the average American was so appalled by the plight of the inner city New Orleans population that was trapped during Hurricane Katrina. Millions open their wallets to assist and criticized the government's lack of preplanning and poor initial response. Unfortunately, American cities are filled with such places and conditions. Several American regions help us visualize this type of cultural persistence in the shadow of a dominant culture.

The persistence of culture is expressed through ethnicity, which is a deliberate effort to distinguish one's own group from another through strong group self-identity linked to group characteristics, common ancestry, and attachment to a particular place. Sometimes a place shapes culture and other times culture acts as an agent, sculpting a landscape that reflects its presence. Numerous examples exist and discussion of a few illustrates the importance of recognizing these American landscapes and places, which are occupied by American subcultures.

Perhaps nowhere is the bond stronger between place and culture than in the case of native Hawaiian culture and the Islands. Shawn Malia Kana'iaupuni and Nolan Malone make the argument in chapter 21 that, despite the multicultural mixing and sustained Anglo efforts to "dismember" the Hawaiian nation, the natives' sentiment toward place has been the key connection between native Hawaiian people and their heritage and self-determination.

Among other American examples are those of Native American Indians and early immigrant subcultures who have persisted for more than a century. In Tahlequah, Oklahoma, for example, after the "Trail of Tears," the Cherokee nation created and preserved a lasting commercial and cultural center. This place remains a symbol of Native American cultural perseverance, as does the recently opened Native American Museum in Washington, D.C. Other examples include the early Asian immigrants who also left landscape reminders of their earlier American history. In California, which has long been one of America's cultural hearths for Chinese and Japanese Americans, Chinatowns and "Little Tokyo" are thriving examples. Little Tokyo, although never fully recovered from WWII-related depopulation and dispossession by the U.S. government, has persisted as the place of cultural focus for Japanese Americans. James Smith discusses the historical and contemporary importance of this place to Japanese-American identity in chapter 22.

These are specific examples of cultural perseverance. Other less attractive examples speak to American failures to solve the legacy of black slavery, which resulted not only in the division of black immediate families and scattered them across the South, but left a legacy of fear and hatred among many whites who refused acceptance of African Americans as equals and as neighbors, despite a war fought over slavery and later amendments to the U.S. Constitution. Separate schools, unequal access to employment, housing and services, and imposed segregation in northern and southern places resulted in African American landscapes of despair and fear that have persisted as black ghettos in the 21st century. Despite obvious African-American gains in socioeconomic status and their corresponding suburban landscapes, millions of blacks remain trapped in inner city slums. Even successful African Americans routinely must absorb racist behaviors of American society (Cose, 1993). No matter how significant Black progress has been, the daily conditions experienced by too many African Americans should be constant reminders to all Americans that the nation has failed to adequately address its unique race problems.

Part I

Perspectives on American Race and Ethnicity

Section one contains five chapters that provide varied approaches to the study of American race and ethnicity in a place context. Chapter one lays the foundation for the book by providing definitions and context for the basic concepts it presents. The next two chapters examine aspects of race but from very different perspectives. Chapter two provides a stark contrast to Martin Luther King, Jr.'s perception of future American racial landscapes by exploring the racial landscape images of Malcolm X. In doing so, we see how the human condition and state of mind are expressed on the landscape but also how our surroundings shape our consciousness and our possibilities. Chapter 3 illustrates the effects of policies (usually considered abstract) in practice (praxis). School desegregation policies (usually recalled as an across-the-board-positive landmark) are examined for pros and cons and how people were actually affected by institutional decisions.

The final two chapters in this section deal with important perspectives on immigration. Chapter 4 explains "gateway cities," where they emerged and the roles they played in immigrant choices and settlements. It also provides a typology of gateway cities and provides a discussion of the nation's capital as a relatively new gateway, explaining its influence on immigrants and the impact of immigrants on this particular region. Chapter 5 explores the roles of race and place in contemporary immigration. It uses history and compares models of assimilation with the author's own experiences and observations of the U.S. In doing so, the argument is made that "racialized assimilation" occurs among many contemporary first-generation American immigrants and influences their settlement patterns.

In summary, Section One provides the conceptual introduction to the text and illustrates the variety of approaches taken by social scientists to examine aspects of race, ethnicity and place in a changing America.

Chapter 1

Race, Ethnicity, and Place in a Changing America:
A Perspective

JOHN W. FRAZIER

PERSISTENCE AND CHANGE IN AMERICAN HUMAN GEOGRAPHY

Culture, and the human geography it produces, persists over a long time period. However, culture changes slowly, as does the visible landscape it produces and the ethnic meanings imbued by the group that shapes it. That many examples of persistent and new cultural landscapes exist in the United States is not surprising given the major technological, demographic, and economic changes in American society since World War II (WWII). America emerged from WWII as one of two superpowers, developed and embraced technology that took Americans to the moon, created an electronics revolution that greatly modified the ways that Americans work and live, and built a globally unique interstate highway system, new housing stock, millions of additional automobiles, and otherwise increased its production to meet the challenge of nearly doubling its population between 1950 and 2000. The post-WWII baby boom and massive immigration fueled population growth and modified American society in important ways, creating different needs and growing aspirations. A larger African American middle class also emerged during this post-war period. Leadership in a growing global economy enabled unprecedented economic growth that supported these changes.

Some less positive changes occurred during this period as America repositioned itself in global affairs, while experiencing great domestic and global economic, social and political challenges. America fought and lost a war in Vietnam, experienced an energy crisis, and suffered through double-digit inflation and severe economic recession, which contributed to a more conservative mood in Washington, D.C. For many people of color, economic and social disparities with whites were magnified between large inner cities and their surrounding communities. The human geography of the U.S. was modified and reflected some of these major changes. Perhaps the biggest of the geographic changes was the rapid consumption of rural lands, their transformation into thousands of new small communities independent of their nearby large cities, and the relocation of much of the white middle class and economic activities to emerging suburbs. While suburbanization had begun prior to WWII, it intensified in the post-war era and made America a commuting nation dependent on the automobile and foreign oil. While undeniable gains were made by African Americans, suburbanization also increased racial segregation and literally pushed the worlds of blacks and whites farther apart. Americans witnessed the remainder of the Great Migration until 1970, which brought millions of additional African Americans to northern and western cities and, when the economy changed, left millions jobless. Racial strife increased. One of the more obvious results of these culturally-based geographic patterns in American cities has been the unequal distribution of resources that created and concentrated poverty and caused the deterioration of neighborhoods and living conditions. This was true in the early industrial cities, where immigrants were segregated into high-risk ethnic neighborhoods, such as the tenements of New York City or the housing adjacent to the Chicago rail yards and garbage dumps that killed many children. Inner cities since 1950 are no different. Poverty and the risks of infant mortality remain high, despite the national economy being second to none in the world. Poverty begets the crime and the drug cultures, which add to the ills of poor living environments, especially those containing American minorities.

In stark contrast to the outer cities of large, old metropolitan areas, inner cities disproportionately contain areas of poor housing, persistent unemployment, low wages, and a declining tax base. American ghettos persist as landscapes of fear and despair that encompass horrendous conditions, despite a half-century of national growth and prosperity. Typically invisible to middle-America, these conditions became more apparent when Hurricane Katrina struck New Orleans in 2005. Hundreds of thousands of residents evacuated, but the very poor, predominantly black, inner-city residents who lacked resources and access to transportation were left behind to experience one of America's most devastating natural disasters and its aftermath. The conditions and racial distribution of New Orleans is typical of many other American cities, including Detroit, Milwaukee, Chicago, Cleveland, Buffalo, Rochester and others, that experienced ghetto formation generations ago. America's outer suburbs are the antithesis of such conditions, and represent the relatively new, prosperous and spreading American landscapes.

In short, the early industrial cities with sharp class distinctions and contrasting living conditions also provided the basis for the suburbanization of industry, commerce, and the white middle class, while disproportionately restricting those of lesser means, especially non-whites, to declining sections of large cities. The new environments of suburbia, attracted private investment, but were subsidized by federal spending and federal guaranteed residential loans. The dominant (Anglo-American) culture created new geographic forms, but retained its position of privilege. In general, suburbia meant "white suburbia." Despite the power of the white majority, some African Americans struggled and pushed into suburbia, creating their own ethnic landscapes (Wiese, 2004). However, these cultural and ethnic landscapes receive little attention in the social science literature to date.

The black-white settlement geography is only one part of the increasingly complex, post-WWII American landscapes. Immigration and internal migration have greatly complicated most aspects of American life, economy, politics, and geography. More recent patterns from late 20th century immigration overlay pre-existing patterns. The millions of immigrants ("foreign-born") who entered the U.S. since WWII differed substantially from the predominantly European immigrants that entered in the 18th, 19th and early 20th centuries. The most recent immigrants are likely to be from Latin America or Asia. They represent two economic groups: poverty with low/no skills, and those with social and economic capital in hand. These immigrants represent a far more heterogeneous set of Asian and Latin cultures, literally from scores of ancestral homes and speaking numerous languages. Because of this increased cultural and economic diversity, some contemporary immigrants are living in ethnic enclaves. Others are creating places quite different from the general pattern associated with their European predecessors, leading to both practical and theoretical issues concerning their assimilation processes, including non-assimilation or what has been termed "segmented assimilation."

The history of American racism complicates contemporary immigrant assimilation in a number of ways, as will be discussed later, as has the massive influx of illegal immigrants that contribute to the perception that changes in racial and ethnic composition amount to a "siege" of American culture. Others describe it as enrichment. Because American racism is unique in its character and has such a long and complex history, including its geographical imprints, a brief review of race as a widely applied social construct is useful.

RACE AS SOCIAL CONSTRUCT

Many Americans would like to dismiss discussions of race and racism because they are uncomfortable topics that lead to responsibility for racist actions. However, American racism and associated prejudice predate the republic and remain an issue, so we must discuss them. Race is a social construction unsupported by science. A number of recent statements about American racism dismiss the "biological truths" of racial distinctions as scientific inaccuracies (e.g., Bamshad and Olson, 2003; Graves, 2004). After illustrating that science cannot justify America's socially constructed racial schema, Graves, among others, argues that the social construction of the African-American race was rooted in the ideology of "whiteness" for the purpose of social domination that has continued to the present day. His analysis supports the contention that race is significant in America because Americans have made it significant on all levels. There is a long history of racial classification in America that goes beyond black-white schemas.

When considering race, many Americans think of skin color, which is not surprising given the history of American racial relations. Despite the discrimination and wars against native Indian cultures, it was slavery that led to the Civil War and sharpened American focus on skin color. Prior to the Civil War, however, there is no doubt that white prejudice against blacks was nationally ubiquitous and visible to outsiders. One of the best examples was provided by Alexis de Toqueville, nearly a generation prior to that war:

> "The prejudice of race appears to be stronger in the states that have abolished slavery than in those where it still exists, ..." (Reeve, Brown, and Bradley, 1945, quoting A. de Toqueville, 1835).

Post-Civil War activities intensified racial prejudice and Social Darwinist, Herbert Spencer, was "welcomed like royalty" into the U.S. because of his support of capitalism (Kevels, 1985) and his racist ideas flourished. By the early 1900s WEB Dubois spoke of America's color line and the belief of the superiority of one race (white) over another race (black). Racialism had penetrated the popular and scientific realms, leading to the public endorsement of eugenics. The latter involved the "science" of improvement of human stock through selective breeding and other restrictive, racially-motivated policies, including anti-miscegenation laws that avoided the negative results of association with the "darker races." Black-white tensions continued as the basis for repetitive racial conflict throughout the 19th and 20th centuries. Jim Crow Laws and various institutional mechanisms segregated whites and non-whites nationwide.

Because of slavery, the Civil War, and the Civil Rights Era, black-white racial issues were incorporated into high school curricula in the late 20th century, making Americans aware of racial issues and discrimination. However, little effort has been made to dismiss the notion of the biological basis of racial categories or the racial geography that has resulted from the deliberate efforts of various American institutions to restrict African-American living space. It has been the creation of negative images of minority cultures and their concomitant denial of access to equal education, employment, and housing opportunities by white society that has contributed to the continuing perception of the inferiority vs. superiority of cultures. Rather than address the persistence of these patterns and trace the resulting racial geographies associated with them, some Americans are satisfied with generalization and implied explanation that equity differences are explained by the fact that "all cultures are not equal." Certainly, different cultures have different strengths and weakness. However, to suggest cultures are "unequal," unable or unwilling to take advantage of technology or other benefits, and that this explains the "haves" and "have-nots" of the world is a misuse of generalization that dismisses centuries of deliberate social constructions of race and their debilitating consequences for minorities. It is also indicates a return to Social Darwinism. These prejudicial constructions are limited neither to American society, nor to African Americans.

Until recently, high school textbooks largely ignored indigenous cultures, or treated them poorly. American Indian cultures have been portrayed as savages with little human understanding or sentiment. Only in the last quarter of the 20th century did the interactions between colonial and Indian cultures, such as native culture support for the concepts of liberty and self-government, begin to appear in high school texts. This does not deny the influence of Europeans but recognizes the results of other cultural interactions, and casts them in a more accurate light (Loewen, 1995).

The characterizations of American Asian and Latino cultures as non-white "races" with negative characteristics have been largely ignored until recently. Such omissions lead to the impression that the playing field in America has always been level for all racial/ethnic groups. There are many examples of racial constructions of these groups. The U.S. Census Bureau created the "Mexican race" for use in the 1930 Census, and in the 1940s opinion leaders and the media combined to produce a racial image of the "zoot-suiters" (referring to Mexicans in particular dress) that contributed to a 1942 riot. This social construction portrayed all Mexicans as zoot-suiters and all zoot-suiters as criminals.

Most Asians fared no better than Mexicans. Three Asian immigrant groups, who provided essential, inexpensive labor for some of the most difficult and dirty jobs to help develop the American West Coast, were the Chinese, Japanese, and Filipinos. Together, they were classified as "Orientals" who constituted an "Asiatic Coolie Invasion" (Organized Labor, 1906). Each of these three immigrant groups was initially welcomed as hard workers but, after economic stresses occurred for whites, faced later prejudice, discrimination and exclusion (e.g., the 1882 Chinese Exclusion Act). The social construction of the Chinese ethnic group as a "race" is provided in the following paragraphs for clarity.

Kay J. Anderson has argued that racial ideology, rather than prejudice, was the key explanatory variable in the Western construction of "Chinatowns." She illustrated the role of missionaries, traders and opinion leaders of the West in creating stereotypical images of the Chinese as "conscious agents of Satan," who were backward, peculiar, immoral and treacherous (Anderson, 1987, p. 591). This became the foundation for characterizing the Chinese immigrants in North America as undesirable outsiders and a threat to local culture. Anderson used Vancouver to illustrate the role of racial ideology linking social construct to place. By 1886, the Chinese, largely a bachelor society, were already under the control of the government and were geographically concentrated in a small neighborhood of Vancouver. While the Chinese contributed to their self-definition and local cultural landscape, the local white European culture created the essence of "Chineseness" and created the regional image of Chinatown "on capricious grounds" (p. 583). According to Anderson, the Chinese were described as "the same everywhere," dirty, undesirable and a threat. Their "evils" were concentrated in "unsanitary sink{s}," or in their "morally aberrant communit{ies}" (Anderson, p. 586). The local government used this racial classification as a justification for monitoring, restricting and discriminating against Vancouver's Chinatown. Again, Anderson's view was that this was not merely prejudice. It was racial ideology that combined race ("Chineseness") with place ("Chinatown") for the benefit of Western white society, and to justify its discriminatory, and often harsh, actions against an immigrant population.

In the U.S. the Chinese were victimized by white violence and discrimination in "Chinatowns" in San Francisco, Oakland and other cities. The physical appearance of late 19th and early 20th century "Chinatowns" differed significantly from the late 20th century image of bright and colorful landscapes attractive to tourists and diners. Early enclaves consisted of small, crowded, unattractive structures criticized by local whites as despicable, repulsive, and threatening to local geography. This type of social construction allowed the white majority a basis for ridding local society of its problems. Chinatown, a den of inequity wedged into white society, was the place that magnified the shortcomings of this race. Despite the protests of Chinese merchants and leaders, and their efforts to correct these false race-based images, the strength of social construct created by whites prevailed and resulted in prejudicial discriminatory behavior by the white population and its institutions towards the Chinese people. Many Chinese fled eastward to escape prejudice and discrimination and developed Chinatowns in Chicago, Boston, and New York City, or returned home to China (especially after the passage of the 1882 Chinese Exclusion Act).

Before we attribute social constructions of race to "old" American history, consider a different construction of the Post-WWII characterization of American Asian ethnics for a different purpose. In response to the demands of African Americans during the Civil Rights Era for fairer treatment in housing, employment, and education, Asian Americans were elevated to the status of a "model minority" for African Americans to emulate. Like African Americans, Asian Americans had faced prejudice and discrimination. However, unlike African Americans, they were perceived as having family values, a drive for advanced education, perseverance, and other features that allowed them to overcome roadblocks and become highly successful in the American economy. The message to other minorities was "quit whining and emulate the behavior of Asians." Later, many Asian American scholars responded by debunking this image and indicated that it would be more appropriately termed the "model minority myth."

These examples illustrate how race in America is a majority culture social construct that stereotypes a minority group. In a contemporary context, social constructions of others, including other minority ethnic groups, also occur. In this case, one group stereotypes another and demonizes it as an alien group that creates negative impacts on society. Such conditions contribute to poor ethnic relations, rioting and other forms of conflict. Important concepts in social conflict theory and racism are culture and ethnicity.

CULTURE AND ETHNICITY

Culture refers to an entire way of life of a group of people. A culture maintains values, beliefs, practices, and behaviors that help define and differentiate one group from others. These traits are learned, or exchanged within and between groups and are passed from one generation to the next. Many traits are common among cultural groups but cultural identification entails a unique set of individual elements and processes that together create a unique cultural identity. Biological and ideological characteristics, social institutions, and technology are typically used to identify a specific cultural group. Wilbur Zelinsky, in discussing the American culture and its landscapes, observed that certain characteristics, while not uniquely American, were uniquely American in their combination. He also suggested that American culture was linked to northern Europe, especially Great Britain. This implied the importance of the English language, representative government, a focus on the individual, and the preponderance of the Judeo-Christian outlook among its members. However, it involves much more.

Cultural groups may also have an affinity for a particular environment, which can influence cultural identity. Because the host environment provides a range of opportunities for indigenous resources and accessibility to others, it may contribute to cultural identity. An example of the attachment of environmental features to culture identification is the term "mountain people," which implies more than living at high elevation. Such descriptions are meant to help identify cultural groups by location and the influence of environment on the group. Mountain people, for example, live in rough and isolated terrain that keeps them at relatively low levels of economic development and separated from other societal groups, which leads to distinctive qualities. The Hmong people are an example of a culture defined in part as a "mountain people" of South Asia. They supported the U.S. during the Vietnam War, suffered genocide afterwards, and were admitted later into the U.S. as refugees. Perhaps one of the best known perspectives on environmental influence on cultural development is the "Turner hypothesis," which credited the environmental conditions of the North American frontier as a significant force that shaped the "rugged individualism" trait of the American culture (Hofstadter and Lipset, 1968).

Beyond environmental influences, a culture may have a sense of synergy with environment, feeling inextricably linked with nature. This also can be a defining element of that particular cultural group. In such cases, the culture self-identifies using aspects of nature and place. For example, indigenous populations often have a very different association with their environments than those cultures in advanced industrial societies. Examples within the U.S. include American Indian, Eskimo, and native Hawaiian cultures. Their relationships with their environments contribute to their cultural identification and, therefore, helps distinguish their cultural traits. Later in this text, this association of native cultures with place is explored for the case of native Hawaiians.

Culture, then, can be understood to be a set of values, beliefs, technology, and institutions that brings meaning to and preserves a group's existence. Cultural continuity is provided by a common language and cultural history. Both function as powerful sources for strengthening individual ties to the group. Particular social institutions, such as schools and social organizations, reinforce and maintain culture. The cultural system contains individual elements that combine to form a unique set of interrelationships, dynamic in nature, always open and adaptive to new information, ideas, and technology. It also seeks stability through continuity.

Ideology refers to the comprehensive vision of a culture. Cultures encompass strong beliefs, often involving deities or a particular political ideology, or both. This is why a shared sense of the divine is often a component of ethnic identity. Cultural ideology and associated emotions sometimes result in malicious actions toward other groups, including open conflict directed at the destruction of the enemy culture and/or its cultural symbols. Ideology also results in expressions within the culture, such as memorializing a special place or sacred space associated with some event or person important to the host culture. When two cultures value the same land or place, cultural conflict typically ensues due to competition over the depth of beliefs and sentiment toward the place.

Technology refers to the tools available to a society to make its living, to communicate and exchange with others, and to transform its surroundings. As with other traits, technological devices and expertise vary by culture, as does the vision of technology's role in the future of the society and the globe. In America, a constant increase in technology has created a historical framework for discussing progress and development of the nation. By the middle 1850s, canals and railroad systems were both established in the U.S. Their creation attracted numerous ethnic immigrants to work in their development. These technologies allowed for the rapid development of the American Midwest, the stunning transformation of Chicago from trading outpost to the rail center of the nation and one of the leading industrial cities in America. By the 1860s the Transcontinental Railroad connected eastern and western coasts and stimulated even greater growth by century's end. The creation of the automobile industry with its assembly line revolutionized American industry and transportation systems. Air travel followed on the heels of the auto and by WWII America was an air power. Post-WWII saw a rapid development of commercial aviation and the space race that placed a human on the moon by 1969. A person born in the late 1890s literally observed the transformation of American travel. In the early 1900s some workers operated with horse-drawn wagons, such as in the delivery of ice to homes and businesses. In that same lifespan, a human traveled to the moon and safely returned. The electronics revolution during the same lifetime changed the ways that Americans traveled, worked, and played. It also provided global military advantage. It is little wonder, then, that American culture is perceived as different from others on the basis of technology in combination with other distinctive traits.

It should be clear by the discussion thus far that culture also has transforming powers. The group imposes boundaries between its areas and that of others, gives meaning and sentiment to place and objects, and transforms the land by imprinting its cultural presence. While the dominant culture may control the geographic space of a nation, any cultural group can and typically does leave its cultural imprint on the land it occupies. Cultural groups create spaces and places of their own to celebrate and perpetuate their culture. The transformed visible cultural pattern on the earth's surface is called a **cultural landscape**. It therefore is the material expression of the occupying culture, an affirmation of what is valued by that culture. It represents a set of ideas about life — family, the social group and social relations, relations with nature, and the value given to objects that embody its beliefs — present in every culture. The landscape contains cultural markers symbolizing what is important, those deeply embedded values, and what is unique about the group. This is true of American culture. However, changes in the human enterprise are constant and evolving cultural landscapes represent not only the inseparable elements of history and historical geography, as visibly apparent expressions of human occupation of various places, but contemporary expressions that result from recent immigrant settlements. As we will see later in this text, cultural landscapes, one of geography's central concepts, take on many forms but one of the most dominant examples among American immigrant ethnic groups is the clustering of ethnic businesses that serve commercial and cultural functions.

Ethnicity involves a group-constructed identity using one or more of its cultural attributes. Ethnic identity connects group members through a shared sense of what is unique and therefore distinguishes "us" from "them." Common attributes contribute to characteristics that may also make groups distinct from other groups, influencing how others within the larger society see them ("they-ness") (Ringer and Lawless, 1989). The shared traits can involve, for example, language, cultural history, cultural traditions, and religion. There also is a shared sense of aspirations and sometimes vulnerability among those in an ethnic group. National origin may be important but is not synonymous with ethnicity. Ethnicity is a social construct that defines the "we-ness" of group membership and often involves connection to place. Immigrants, by definition residents of a new land, often find it necessary to reaffirm their ethnic identity, which involves preserving cultural value and distinctiveness and preserving ties to a homeland.

Ethnicity, however, is not the equivalent of race. However, racism certainly can cause a shared sense of vulnerability and, therefore, contribute to ethnic identity. This is particularly true when struggle is a part of the group's cultural history, as in the cases of African Americans and Jews. Religious customs and cultural celebrations are two ways that ethnic affinity is strengthened. For example, American Jews celebrate cultural and religious holidays, which strengthen their ethnicity. It is also important to note that "racial" differences within a community, within the context of different skin color, need not preclude a common ethnic identity. Puerto Ricans are a good example. Black and white Puerto Ricans are included in this ethnic group.

Ethnicity also has been defined within the context of ethnic polarization as a "strategic construction" of cultural boundaries, a process driven by economic and political differences and concerns (Ballard, 2002). As such, ethnicity can be a deliberate process of amplifying cultural distinctiveness and "moral solidarity" to protect community interests. This, of course, is not limited to minority ethnic groups. The majority, or host culture, closes ranks to sustain its power base, whereas the minority ethnic group seeks refuge because it feels threatened. Both tend to organize geographic space in ways meaningful to their group. Sometimes, when both groups seek the same spaces, this results in contested space. A simple example involves suburbanization in the 20th century. African Americans sought a place in the suburbs but were rebuffed by the white majority. Despite this, African Americans created their own cultural landscapes and carved out living space in suburbia as "places of their own" (Wiese, 2004).

This notion of physically and economically defending one's ethnic group from discriminatory actions of the host culture is but one dimension of ethnicity. Even among European groups, who have been permitted to assimilate into the broader American culture and economic system without experiencing long-term exclusion, there is a need for belonging, or for ethnic affinity. This is why "Irish-only" enclaves still exist in the Catskills, various ethnic celebrations (German, Italian, etc.) remain popular, and some ethnic groups, such as Greek Americans, retain a sense of ethnicity decades after assimilating into the American culture. Affinity takes on many forms and can even lead to claims for aid by contemporary white, first generation immigrants, as demonstrated by Susan Hardwick in chapter 25 of this text. Important dimensions of culture include prejudice and privilege, which can lead to cultural and ethnic conflict.

PREJUDICE, PRIVILEGE AND CONFLICT

An important understanding related to culture is that the creation of a feeling of "we-ness," while establishing a sense of coherence and wellness within the group, results in that group perceiving its cultural system as superior to all others. Accordingly, although adaptive, each culture seeks preservation of their perspective and goes to some length, including conflict with others, to perpetuate their superior system. The result is power struggles between cultures. In making this argument, Roger Ballard argued that European-based cultural systems, because they emerged from the Enlightenment perspective that elevated personal freedom to the position of a universal value, are particularly given to feelings of superiority. They tend towards "hegemony," the "use of ethnocentric judgments to justify their own position of socioeconomic privilege" relative to other cultures and subcultures (Ballard, 2002, p. 140). A dominant culture also constructs an image of other cultures that is the antithesis of their own positive cultural image. Typically, the dominant culture believes that it should convert others to their superior cultural values. Further, cultural superiority justifies prejudice and discrimination towards others who have not sought or achieved the same universal values.

Prejudice is an attitude that expresses intellectual beliefs about another societal group. It is an inflexible pre-judgment, or bias, against a person or group without cause. While direct contact with that "other" may have some influence in prejudice, it is among the lesser causes of prejudice, which typically occurs prior to contact. Prejudice results from a number of sources; among the most important are historical and socio-cultural. Prejudice passes from generation to generation through social institutions and, therefore, maintains animosity. This is why we speak of long-term ethnic conflict across the globe, including, for example, the ethnic conflict between the Irish and English that has periodically resulted in conflict over two centuries. Other factors, such as persistent negative social conditions, including urban poverty, are credited as sources of prejudice as well.

As noted earlier, prejudice can be due to unfounded suspicion. However, it also is caused by ethnic and racial intolerance and often leads to dislike and even hatred. Obviously, prejudice interferes with the fair treatment of "others" (Allport, 1954). Although an indirect relationship, prejudice is related to discrimination, the behaviors that include the harsh treatment and exclusion of "inferior" groups from access to resources and equality. *Privileges* are extended to those of the dominant cultural group because of their superior qualities and withheld from others. These privileges may be on ethnic or racial grounds. In the case of European-based cultures, like the U.S., the racial construction of *"whiteness"* as descriptive of all things good about Anglo culture (and of those who assimilate with it) amounts to the antithesis of being non-white. That status results in *white privilege*, or a system that provides access to resources and other preferences based on race and culture. Social psychologist Beverley Tatum has discussed the difficulty for some white students in accepting this concept in her college classroom. She spoke of a white woman who, after being presented the unsought benefits of white advantage, concluded that the list of unasked-for advantages was substantial:

> " … she hadn't always noticed she was receiving them. They include both major and minor advantages. Of course, she enjoyed greater access to jobs and housing. But she also was able to shop in department stores without being followed by suspicious sales people.… She could send her child to school confident that the teacher would not discriminate against him.… She could also be late for meetings, and talk with her mouth full, confident that these behaviors would not be attributed to the fact that she was white. She could express an opinion in a meeting or in print and not have it labeled as the 'White' viewpoint" (Tatum, 1999, p. 8).

Together, prejudice and privilege help define what resources are open to societal groups and where they are welcome to live geographically speaking. They place the "us and them" dichotomy into economic, political, and geographic contexts. In particular cases, these occur within a racial context. However, they also become the basis of conflict between minority ethnic groups, too. Such conflicts can arise from economic differences but occur within the context of racial and ethnic stereotyping and end in violence.

In a contemporary context, a good example is the conflict between Latinos and blacks in the U.S. Despite facing some of the same challenges and vast economic disparities, these two groups have exhibited a great deal of mistrust and animosity toward one another in recent decades, especially since the rapid increase in Latino legal and illegal immigration. Notwithstanding occasional collaboration on a common issue, tensions have increased between blacks and Latinos across the U.S., from Miami to Chicago, and from Chicago to Los Angeles and Washington state, and points in between. One dimension of this mistrust and conflict lies in black resentment of the increasing number of immigrant Latinos relocating in formerly predominantly black neighborhoods and the competition they bring to the housing and job markets in those areas. The black perspective is that progress made during the Civil Rights era has been lost, in part by the willingness of Mexican immigrants and other Latinos to work for below market wages. Further, when Latino businesses open in black neighborhoods, selling to largely an African-American market, they refuse to employ blacks. Hispanics are cast by African Americans as criminals and as economic threats. On the other side, some Latinos have characterized blacks as unwilling to perform hard work, favoring government welfare, and as having a tendency toward criminal behavior. Racial stereotyping by both sides quickly antagonizes the other. The actual conflict pertains to scant resources and jobs available for minorities in the urban economy. One of the most frequently quoted perceived racist comments against blacks occurred in 2004 and was attributed to Mexican President Vincente Fox , who indicated that Mexicans in the U.S. were performing labor "that not even blacks want to do in the United States."

Unfortunately, name calling and stereotyping sometimes turn to violence, including in the nation's schools. High Schools in the West, including several in California, have experienced serious conflicts between Mexicans and blacks. Reports from Midwestern, Eastern and Southern states illustrate that tensions are there as well.

Tensions and racial/ethnic problems have taken on various forms and involve contested space and unfair competition. One of the better examples of a controversial urban program occurred in Detroit, a predominantly black city. There an outspoken critic (some say racist), African American Claude Anderson openly criticized Latinos as having motives for non-assimilation into the economy, specifically to undermine the economic position of African Americans. Susy Buchanan reported on the impact of Anderson's economic development plan endorsed by the Detroit City Council:

> "His recommendation was that the city spend $30 million to develop something called 'African Town' — an inner city business enclave for blacks that would keep them from spending money in immigrant businesses.
>
> Anderson and others argued that the city had provided incentives to Mexicantown and Greektown, two neighborhoods marked by ethnic businesses and restaurants. Why shouldn't they do the same for black businesses? ... Anderson went further, Hispanics, he said in the kind of comment that lit up many citizens of Detroit, 'have surpassed Blacks now and make them third-class citizens'...
>
> The blacks-only funding plan outraged many....
>
> Detroit Mayor, Kwame Kilpatrick, who is African American, vetoed.... But the Council overrode his veto, although it did ultimately strike the requirement (for all-black funding)" (Buchanan, 2005, p. 14).

Unfortunately, ethnic and racial conflict over resources and space continue to be a problem in the U.S. When this occurs, ethnic and racial groups turn to social institutions to protect their interests.

SOCIAL INSTITUTIONS AND CULTURE

Social institutions are vehicles that support common cultural goals and objectives. Because ethnicity is a part of culture, they also support the existence of ethnicity, including minority ethnic groups within the dominant American culture. They can influence all aspects of an individual's life from birth to death. They permeate marriage and family, govern financial transactions, guide worship where it exists, and often structure burial ceremonies. They are in the market place and they take on many forms, social, political, and economic, but share the same purpose of supporting and perpetuating the health and strength of the culture they are designed to serve.

Educational institutions, for example, are dedicated to teaching particular knowledge and skills that support cultural interests. Governments and legal institutions create and administer the affairs of culture, including the governing body of law and its interpretation, and the military. Social institutions have great power. Subsequent chapters of this book will have much to say about American institutions because they have shaped American immigration policy, including the numbers and sources of migrants from time to time, the rights of American subcultures in many different ways, and have contributed directly to the settlement patterns of suburbia mentioned earlier. Institutions also serve economic functions (market institutions), such as in lending money for home mortgages and real estate agencies that present available properties to interested buyers. Both of these institutions played major roles in shaping the racial distribution of urban Americans (discussed in detail in later chapters). Finally, social institutions also can be ethnic organizations that seek to support their group in many ways. The Chinese Benevolent Association is an example. It has provided guidance and support to sustain many Chinese immigrants in America and has served as an umbrella organization for their other ethnic institutions as well.

In summary, social institutions appear in many contexts, support members of a group, and perpetuate culture and ethnicity. They are the mechanisms of social structure that, although they change from time to time, are the permanent means of governing and supporting the culture. This leads to a consideration of what constitutes the uniqueness of the Anglo-American culture.

ANGLO-AMERICAN CULTURE

The United States continues to change as a nation yet maintains its central beliefs that guide its behaviors as a culture. This supports the notion that, although the U.S. is a relatively young nation, it definitely has cultural qualities that some social scientists believe constitute an "American culture." Recall the tendency of European-based cultures to see western democracy's individual freedom as a "universal value." This Enlightenment-based concept projected social evolution in a rational manner wherein democracy and personal freedom would be globally achievable (Gray, 2000 and Ballard, 2002). In this vision, individual freedom is a personal right that supersedes group value and association. Personal freedom is the path to a more perfect society. This, of course, ignores the "non-universal" visions of cultures that stress group welfare over individual freedom. The concept also assumes that western democracies have evolved a set of superior cultures. This justifies their political hegemony and messianic desire to "share" ("convert") their superior values with others (Ballard, 2002). As such, the Euro-American approach uses the importance of individual freedom to act superior and to argue that their cultural virtues should be emulated as universals, applicable for all others to follow.

During the post-1950 period chronicled earlier, the U.S. maintained a set of unique cultural motifs that created many of the societal and landscape changes discussed earlier. When discussing American culture, Zelinsky was clear that American cultural history was tied with that of northern Europe, especially with the British. An overall set of American cultural traits evolved under these ties with Great Britain and resulted in an Anglo-dominated U.S. cultural system that had a distinctly American flavor. Zelinsky explained American cultural characteristics as "the basic values and axioms that define aspiration and direction" and as an "ethos — that powerful mood of this and all other distinctive cultures …" (Zelinsky, 1973, pp. 39–40). His American cultural traits included "a reverence for individualism," a high valuation placed on "mobility and change," "a mechanistic world vision" that values "growth and bigness," which also explains America's reverence for technology and its cures, and a "messianic perfectionism" with a drive to share their culture with others. Related to the last trait, Zelinsky stated:

> "… the notion that the United States is not just another nation, but one with a special mission —
> to realize the dream of human self-perfection and, in messianic fashion, to share its gospel and achievement with the remainder of the world. This moral expansiveness (some would call it 'moral imperialism') exists over and beyond the usual flexing of economic or military muscle …" (Zelinsky, 1973, p. 61).

He elaborated the expressions of each of the motifs as American cultural landscapes. Several examples are provided here.

The strongest trait attributed to Americans is the "intense, almost anarchistic individualism" that permeates American society and is expressed in American landscapes. This is American's most dominant value and drives institutional decisions as well as individual behaviors. Having many dimensions, it has transformed American landscapes in diverse and important ways:

> "… the fanatical worship of extreme individualism indeed an almost anarchistic privatism, affects so many phases of our existence so deeply that no one can interpret either the geography or the history of the nation without coming to grips with it … a critical force … in shaping the cultural landscape" (Zelinsky, 1973, pp. 41–42).

Among the numerous patterns attributable to American individualism is American political fragmentation, the notoriously inefficient and costly legal and administrative maintenance of small geographic territories (towns, villages, etc.). These jurisdictions, maintained within larger regional contexts, with duplication of services (e.g., police and fire departments), represent enormous unnecessary costs to local taxpayers. Zelinsky argued that this landscape example of American individualism had resulted in "tens of thousands" of local expensive governments that, despite increasing costs and financial problems, persevere because of Americans' need for autonomy and individualism. He argued that America's "haphazard morphology" of metropolitan regions with their "lack of aesthetic or functional association" with adjacent entities constitutes an additional landscape expression of American individualism. Further, the uniquely American drive for personal autonomy has been "symbolized by the metal-and-plastic bubble around each American," the automobile, which gives uniqueness to another form of human cultural geography, the American transportation and commuting system, where non-auto modes struggle for survival and the auto culture thrives despite increasing costs and periodic fuel shortages. The automobile culture also serves the American drive for secluded living in an ever expanding metropolitan region, whose outer suburbs emphasize the maximum spaciousness and separation that money can buy.

During all of the post-1950 changes noted earlier, the American cultural-political economy guided the organization of space and the creation of American landscapes based on cultural motifs. Meanwhile, a growing number of recently arrived immigrant cultures, as well as the subcultures already occupying the nation, made their cultural marks in various places. The growing volume of immigrants in recent decades, along with their ability to settle in exclusively white American locations, has made contrasting cultural landscapes more visible and cultural conflict more apparent. Several geographic concepts and social science theories relate to these geographic settlement structures, social and economic assimilations, and cultural landscapes.

GEOGRAPHIC CONCEPTS AND SOCIAL SCIENCE THEORY

Human geography is influenced by numerous factors related to the creation, maintenance and changes in geographic patterns and, therefore, they are important to an understanding of American geography presented in this text. A few of the most important of the concepts are discussed below.

Globalization is a term frequently used by the popular media and in academic literature. Academically, it is a hotly debated topic because some see it as the modern-day tool of unbridled capitalism that exploits weak countries by connecting them to a world economy that serves the interest of corporations and lays waste to the global environment. Others use the rapidly expanding economies and declining poverty in China and India as examples of the positive outcomes of this process. Trade agreements between nations are a key part of promoting the globalization of capital and labor. There is no doubt that connecting the world's economies has risks and opportunities, but the big question is for whom. Here we use the term to describe processes that have led to a more interconnected and interdependent world. In this context, globalization has resulted in the restructuring of national and regional economies due to global competition. It has led to the deindustrialization of the U.S. manufacturing base, the rise of the service and high-tech sectors with polarized skill and wage levels, and regional shifts in employment that created internal migrations and therefore the redistribution of the U.S. population since WWII. Perhaps most importantly for this text, it created employment shortages in high and low tech jobs in the U.S. that are increasingly filled by a growing number of immigrants, who not only fill jobs, but also are entrepreneurial in creating new small businesses that support ethnic immigrants.

Three additional geographic concepts are related and are important in subsequent chapters: *movements, gateways,* and *networks. Movement* refers to motion, which implies directionality between an origin and destination. It also recognizes that certain forces (push and pull) influence motion either by impeding it (barriers) or facilitating it (assisting in some way). Various phenomena spread throughout geographic space over time. Innovations are a good example. How they move, the direction they take and the speed with which they travel, are influenced by the nature of the innovation, the support it gets from opinion leaders, and any geographic and cultural barriers that may slow its acceptance. In the context of this text, the key movements influencing changing places and landscapes are *immigration* and *migration.* American history and geography of the 19th and 20th centuries were greatly influenced by both types of movements. More than 30 million immigrants, largely from northern and western Europe, came to the U.S. due to a variety of causes, but generally seeking better living conditions for themselves and their families. Most entered without financial or social capital and settled in the inner portions of American industrial cities, near their work places. In addition to urban ethnic neighborhoods, broader regional patterns also resulted from these processes, such as the Scandinavian logging and agricultural settlements in the Upper Midwest. Internal migrations have continuously reshaped American regions. A few examples include the "Gold Rush," the "Great Migration" that brought millions of African Americans to northern cities, and the more recent mass movement of northern and Midwestern residents to the "Sunbelt" states.

Gateways are cities that serve as entry ports, or receiving areas, for immigrants. However, as Audrey Singer notes, they also are the places that foreign-born enter to live and work. Thus, they are also places influenced by ethnic groups who may be different in terms of language, culture, and ethnicity. Singer states their functions:

> "The word 'gateway' also implies that the region functions as a symbolic destination. Such portals hold out opportunities for newcomers, and beckon to others, as well-known centers populated by significant numbers of immigrants. As such, cities and localities become identified with immigrants, and their reputation itself may generate further settlement as social networks circulate information on employment, housing, and educational opportunities there" (Singer, 2004, p. 4).

A *network* is the path connecting two or more points. In geography, the network concept has multiple applications. For example, in the physical world, a system of networks is highways (termed "edges" or "ties") that connect markets ("points") with services and retail operations ("points") by providing easy access and movement between two or more points. In this context, contemporary applied geographers consider the existence and strength of such linkages when analyzing store productivity or when locating a new facility (a "new point"). Historically, transportation systems ("networks"), including the canals and rail roads, were vital to American economic development and urbanization because they efficiently linked resources ("points") and markets ("points"), while also providing easy access for arriving European immigrants to work in the exploding factory system of the late 19th and early 20th centuries in various cities. The development of Chicago, for example, occurred because of the linkages provided by the canal and rail networks. Chicago became the nation's rail hub and the primary industrial center of the American interior, linking agriculture, timber, meat production, and industrial outputs with various U.S. markets and served as a magnet for European immigrants.

Networks are also important to geography because they represent the social linkages between people and places. The spread of innovations over space and time, discussed above, provides as an example of movement. Diffusion theory was developed to explain the spread of ideas and innovations and utilizes social networks in part to explain the timing of the adoption of an innovation. In this sense, social networks involve influential people, such as opinion leaders, and friends and family, who influence the adoption of a new product or idea by the broader population. These social relationships involve nodes (points) and linkages (ties), or the paths that connect people. The individual actors are points within the network and the linkages are the social ties between them. Social networks are known to be important to immigration and internal migration. Migrants keep connected (tied) to their previous communities and influence future migration decisions. For example, if a migrant communicates to others in the homeland that she has been successful in finding employment and is happy in her new location, then her social contacts at her previous home location are more likely to consider migrating to the same destination. There are other more complicated relationships, such as the "socio-spatial networks" discussed by Marie Price in chapter 16. She examines the ways in which Bolivian immigrants stay connected to their homeland and how these connections and perceptions of place influence their behaviors.

Two central geographic concepts are space and place. These are guiding principles in geographic research. The *spatial theme* of geography emphasizes the importance of location and its linkages, or connections, to other locations. Geographers theorize about locations and about identifiable patterns associated with locations. Geography poses the theoretical questions: What forces create a geographic pattern (why has a particular group clustered in a particular area)? How and why do spatial patterns change (Why have new Latino subregions emerged in Northeastern cities)? This implies that a region with spatial structure exists, i.e., it contains a geographic distribution of points that is non-random. Phenomena are distributed as the result of some process, or set of processes, and assume a spatial form. Accordingly, before WWII, the distribution of U.S. Latinos could be characterized as a region in the borderlands of the American Southwest and California, due to what Haverluk termed the "Mexican Legacy," America's long association with Mexico, the Mexican War, the Mexican Cession, and the Gadsden Purchase, among other factors (Haverluk, 1998). However, this U.S. Latino geography changed significantly with the influx of Puerto Ricans and Cubans. Similarly, the early 20th century distribution of African Americans involved a geographic pattern that reflected the legacy of slavery. The Great Migration changed the nature of African-American geography and the contemporary reverse migration of blacks to the South will likely add a new geographic dimension in the future. These are examples of the application of the spatial theme in human geography. It focuses on the analysis of population distributions and movements at the regional scale that bring spatial variation and spatial structure to the nation. There, of course, are many other examples as well.

Space also is a commodity, something of value. Because space has economic or social value, it can become "*contested space*," desired by more than one group. Space also can be manipulated for a specific purpose, as in the "Chinatown" example presented earlier. A related geographic concept is place. Its meaning overlaps with space but *place* has a more specific connotation. Place is space at a micro-scale, which has been infused with cultural and ethnic meaning. Groups shape space to symbolize what they value and hold dear; in this sense, place becomes a part of their identity. Place is a dynamic concept particularly suited to the study of local geographies. Harner nicely summarized the dimensions of place that make it suitable for the study of human geography:

> "Place is process, continually constructed and transformed.... Place is the interaction between extralocal forces, local histories, cultural constructs, and individual human agency.... Through struggle, meaning is built into inanimate objects that give place symbolic significance. This meaning can become part of social identity" (Harner, 2001, p. 661).

Geographic studies of place are localized and typically field-oriented analyses of landscapes that differentiate an ethnic group and its territory, and sometimes become contested space between two groups.

Because race and ethnicity are distinguishable concepts, it is important to make a distinction between ethnic and racial geography. Both are parts of multicultural geographies.

ETHNIC, RACIAL AND MULTICULTURAL GEOGRAPHIES

Earlier it was noted that race and ethnicity are not equivalent. Both are social constructs but race is a social classification created by another culture, often the culture in control of the broader society in which a minority ethnic group lives. Ethnicity refers to the self-construction of an identity that amplifies particular cultural traits for the purpose of creating a group distinction and a set of common aspirations. Racism and persecution can contribute to feelings of vulnerability. Therefore, racism can contribute to the formation of an ethnic identity. Given this distinction, it is important to clarify the difference between racial and ethnic geography. McKee has defined *ethnic geography* as "the study of the spatial and ecological aspects of ethnicity" (McKee, 2000; Preface, p. xv). Numerous examples of ethnic geography are available, including those dealing with the new Latino geographies (Areola, 2005), emerging Latino settlements in the South (Smith and Furuseth, forthcoming), the creation of ethnic spaces and places in multi-ethnic cities (Chacko, 2003), the formation and evolution of urban and suburban ethnic enclaves (Allen and Turner, 1996; Li, 1997), and the ethnic transformation of places (Miyares, 1997), among others. In all of these cases, ethnic groups are creating new human geographies by their actions, often times due to migration, adjustment, and conscious decisions to create places of their own.

McKee presented the broad ethnic core regions of the U.S., including the broad settlement patterns of African Americans and provided an explanation for the "spatial zonation" of American ethnicity. Such a classification is acceptable for ethnic purposes because it entails group description of common ancestry and the formation of cultural tradition, living as a minority in a larger or "host culture" (p. 41). This broad living area includes the region where the African-American ethos was formed. African-American landscapes emerged there over time. However, this broad classification makes no mention of the processes that resulted in black settlement and restrictions within this geographic zone. Such discussion mandates a movement from ethnic to *racial geography*. Clearly, the factors cited by McKee, distance decay, environmental affinity, and the nature of internal, voluntary migration streams, to explain the formation of other ethnic regions of his classification, did not apply to African-American geography prior to the Great Migration. The discussion of historical and contemporary African-American geography must include the persistent role of racial ideology that shaped their geography and disproportionately the poor and unequal living conditions of many African Americans. Race as a social construct not only created the initial forced migration of blacks, but also guided forced migration streams from the northern section of the South to the plantation agriculture of the Cotton Belt. The same construct would limit housing choice and employment opportunities in the North, lead to three periods of ghetto formation (Rose, 1971) and explode into the Civil Rights movement of the 1960s. Today, that legacy continues to haunt numerous American cities. It would be ludicrous to refer to such racial geographies as "just another set of ethnic patterns."

Racial and ethnic geographies, then, are distinctive by purpose. *Ethnic geography* explores the impact of movements, adjustments and the formation of landscapes and places forged by the actions of ethnic groups. *Racial geography* recognizes the role of the controlling society in the creation of the racial ideology that governs the use of space, often restricting access to places and to resources to preserve the privilege of the controlling group. It is important to note that the creation of racial geography does not preclude the creation of cultural/ethnic landscapes. As Wiese has illustrated, for example, despite white racism and often violent actions to keep African Americans out of white suburbia, blacks struggled and pushed their way into suburban areas, where they created African-American landscapes and "places of their own" (Wiese, 2004).

Thus, racial and ethnic geographies evolve and change, creating new settlement geographies. Quality of life in the places that result is determined by the actions of individuals and agencies, technology, and the resources of the environment. The living quality also depends on the goodwill and fairness of others. This involves power relationships, which sometimes become the most important forces in shaping the quality of life and the geographic patterns in an area.

Multicultural geographies are the study of both racial and ethnic geographies. They consider at several geographic scales the processes that determine the nature of spatial patterns, cultural landscapes, and places. They pay particular attention to spatial inequities and other group differences that result in a particular lifestyle and quality of life. Multicultural geographies examine the processes, particularly the social institutions that influence, control, and transform geographic space. They recognize and interpret the unique attributes of the spaces and places, including their expression and problems, as they influence the groups that occupy them. Multicultural geography courses provide students with perspectives on the importance of complex geographic patterns and the processes that produce them. In the process they inform us about the persistence and changes associated with the American scene. This volume is a compendium of works by geographers and other social scientists who have been working on both the ethnic and racial geographies of the U.S. Together, they inform us of America's multicultural geographies, both past and present.

THE NEED TO REVISIT THE MULTICULTURAL PAST

America, like most societies, is extremely complex. Knowledge of the cultural histories and geographies subsumed within the dominant Anglo-American culture is necessary to understand this complexity in contemporary society and its challenges. While some of the very basic facts related to American subcultures and increasing ethnic diversity are presented in small doses in the secondary education curriculum, a comprehensive context for these issues in contemporary America is rarely provided. Among the historical and geographic stories too infrequently detailed in the American educational system are those of even the broadest ethnic groups that have long been present and contributed to the evolution of the American economy, including African Americans, Hispanics, and Asians.

The United States began as an agrarian society that supported its Southern economy through slavery. The legacy of slavery is a uniquely American racism that maintains a black-white divide. The Great Migration of the 20th century resulted in millions of African Americans relocating to northern and western cities, and in

the formation of a national ghetto system. Despite the rise of an African-American middle class, racial inequalities created by discriminatory institutional practices and white avoidance behavior remain obvious in the nation's segregated metropolitan regions, and disproportionately place blacks and other minorities in schools with much higher poverty rates than their white counterpart schools. These conditions remain a challenge.

The 19th century experienced rapid industrialization and urbanization based on rapid technological change and related transportation improvements that connected the nation by canals and rails. This growth and expansion necessitated a large, cheap labor force, which was provided largely by Western European immigrants. The Northern economy was built on unfair wages and harsh working conditions that led to labor unrest and unionization. Over a period of time, the diverse European groups that provided much of that labor were observed to have assimilated, socially and spatially, into the broader American society and its host Anglo culture. This was the basis of the "straight-line assimilation" model of the Chicago School.

This model was developed to explain urban expansion. It was influenced by physical concepts of the period, especially ecological niche, the social fluidity attributed to the factory system, and rapid changes in transportation technology that permitted relative ease of access to urban core and periphery. A series of concentric zones (ecological niches) containing residents, radiated from a circular central business district and constituted its conceptual diagram. Adjacent to the CBD was the zone of transition, an area of varied uses, including rooming houses for recent poor immigrants seeking factory work. New and old slums mixed with warehouses, factories, and other uses there as well. Subsequent zones contained niches of residential land use, ranging from the adjacent zone of working-class homes, to higher valued and, finally, to even better homes in the commuter zone.

Key to this conceptualization was the desire and ability of immigrants and their decendents to move to a better zone based on their socioeconomic success made possible by the class fluidity of capitalism. This amounted to spatial absorption by the host culture of immigrants who fit the new niche. This process became known as straight-line assimilation.

However, the other American cultural histories and geographies that are less often told and much less understood include Hispanics. The shared border with Mexico and the rapid expansion of western agriculture in the 20th century resulted in a "Mexican Legacy" that shaped early Hispanic and Mexican American settlement geography and interactions between Anglos and Spanish-speaking people in the U.S. Mexicans frequently lost their lands and became part of the lower stratum of the American socioeconomic-political hierarchy by virtue of their changing land ownership and occupational status. Restrictions and guest worker programs became the norm for Mexicans residing in the western U.S. In the early decades of the 20th century, increase in the Mexican population, especially in California, led to low-quality residences in overcrowded barrios for many Mexican Americans. While new colonias were constructed and a modest size Mexican-American middle class emerged, Anglos relocating from the eastern U.S. had become the dominant political, economic, and cultural force in the region. Discrimination and animosity remained and inequality prevailed. Since the 1970s, millions of Latinos have entered the American middle class but millions of other Latinos, including Mexican Americans, remain locked in barrios, living in the shadow of wealth that surrounds them. Also, after the Cuban Revolution that established Fidel Castro's regime, large numbers of Cuban exiles migrated to Florida and were classified as refugees. Many of these early arrivals represented the wealthy fleeing Cuba and, with U.S. government assistance, were able to develop a strong base for future Cuban arrivals. This picture stands in strong contrast to other Hispanic migrant cases, including Puerto Ricans, who are American citizens, and Dominicans, who represent some of the poorest Latinos residing in the U.S. These trends greatly diversified American Latino ethnic groups and created an entirely new set of Latino geographies in Post-WWII America. These are complex scenarios that deserve more than a passing glance in the social studies curriculum.

Asian ethnic groups have a heritage in the American West somewhat similar to Mexicans. Initially praised for their willingness to work hard for a fair wage, they later were attacked as "Coolie labor" and restricted geographically. Their groups were sharply restricted from entering the U.S. after the Great Depression, until immigration laws changed after WWII. Similar to the Mexicans, the Chinese, Japanese, and Filipino groups contributed a great deal to the construction of western infrastructure and to its cheap labor force that built a strong economy. Like African Americans, they were resented, racialized as different and inferior to the Anglo culture, and restricted socially, economically and geographically. Today, Asian immigrants are among the most rapidly growing percentage of the total U.S. population and represent a vast number of ethnic groups of multiple origins. Some come with their social capital in hand and enjoy almost immediate economic success. Others are unskilled refuges with little hope for assimilation or economic success. These groups are forcing a reconsideration of traditional straight-line assimilation theory because many have moved directly to American suburbs (Li, 1998).

The cultural and geographic histories of these important ethnic groups are part of the American heritage and must be incorporated more fully into the story of America's incredible and unprecedented economic and technological gains. These need not replace coverage of traditional accounts of American's founding fathers, which some analysts fear. Rather, such accounts must be more fully and accurately reported. Similarly, social scientists must reconstruct theories of settlement and assimilation to explain the forces of inclusion and exclusion of particular groups in American society, past and present. Finally, given the emergence of new geographic settlement forms, such theory must move away from singular explanations, as though they apply to all and become the basis for political arguments for English-language only and other non-inclusive remedies to America's social problems. One of America's biggest challenges in confronting the legacy of racial and ethnic inequalities lies in transforming educational institutions and the policies that control their well-being. The multicultural settlement patterns, organization of school district boundaries, funding mechanisms, and the curriculum are problems that require attention. The levels of government that are theoretically controlled by the electorate have commandeered the system and made the electorate pawns. The result is a Prussian-style education system that marches lock step through the academic year, in spite of the needs of students, and then tests them each June, in spite of what they have not learned. Such a system has minimized the cultural histories and contemporary issues associated with the legacy of slavery and racial ideologies. It also has not addressed the significance of a rapidly changing ethnic population mix that will dramatically reduce the significance of the historically strong host culture.

Before exploring some of the new patterns emerging across the U.S., it is informative to examine some of the numerical trends in America's prominent minority groups and the growth of particular ethnic groups in recent decades.

IMMIGRATION TRENDS: INCREASING DIVERSITY BY THE NUMBERS

America has been changing from a predominantly white, non-Hispanic nation to a more multicultural and multiracial society. Using the broad racial/ethnic categories of the U.S. Census, this shift is quite obvious between 1940 and 2000. In 1940, nearly 90 percent of Americans were non-Hispanic white. In the year 2000, a half-century later, that proportion had dropped to seventy-five percent. By 2050, whites are likely to be a slim majority of about 52 percent (Frazier, Margai, and Tettey-Fio, 2003). This racial/ethnic diversification is due to a number of factors, especially immigration and birth rate differences between white non-Hispanics and Hispanics.

The major racial/ethnic categories and their changes in the share of the total U.S. population between 1940 and 2000 also are reported in Table 1.1. These data indicate that the African-American population changed little in its proportion of the total U.S. population between 1940 and 2000, especially relative to the other two growing minority groups. The black proportion of the total population increased only 1.3 percent between 1940 and 1970 and only 1.2 percent in the following thirty years, 1970 to 2000. However, the total black population increased from just under 13 million in 1940 to more than 34 million by 2000. Latinos, on the other hand, accounted only for slightly more than 1 percent of the total U.S. population in 1940 but jumped to 4.5 percent by 1970, and to 12.5 percent of the total in 2000. Thus, while the black population experienced very modest gains in the sixty years reported in Table 1.1, the Hispanic total reached over 35 million in 2000 and became America's largest minority group.

The Asian population was relatively miniscule in 1940, when approximately a quarter of a million Asians resided in America, less than 1 percent of the total American population. The Asian total had increased to about 1.5 million by 1970 but still accounted for less than 1 percent of the U.S. total. However, although a relatively small percentage of the total in 2000, at 3.7 percent, Asians realized the largest percentage increase between 1970 and 2000, and therefore were America's fastest growing minority on a percentage basis.

While these numbers indicate the substantial increase in diversity in the American population, they do not express the cultural diversity within each group that contributes to an increasingly multicultural society. Table 1.2 clarifies this within-group diversity by reporting the national origin for each unique foreign-born population in the U.S. with a minimum of a half-million people in 2000. A number of observations are possible from that table.

1. Fourteen different source nations are represented, indicating the diversity of foreign-born in the U.S. in 2000 for those groups with at least one-half million people. These 14 foreign-born groups together account for only about 61 percent of the 31,107,889 total foreign-born population in 2000, suggesting an even greater diversity if all source nations had been listed in the table.
2. Mexico stands out as the chief source nation of the U.S. foreign-born. It alone provided nearly 30 percent of the total in 2000.
3. The sources of the next four largest foreign-born American populations are in Asia and together account for nearly five million foreign-born and about 12 percent of the U.S. total.
4. Of the 14 sources, six are in Latin America and five are in Asia. This illustrates the shift in U.S. immigration policy since 1952 and especially since 1965, when immigrant sources shifted from Europe to Latin America and Asia.

Many of these groups have shaped their new landscapes so that they are reminded of their culture and homeland.

Table 1.1
Major Racial/Ethnic Group Changes in Percentages of the Total U.S. Population, 1940, 1970, and 2000+

Group	Year and Population in Thousands		
	1940	1970	2000*
White, non-Hispanic	116,353 (88.5%)	169,653 (83.4%)	211,460 (75.1%)
Black	12,866 (9.8%)	22,539 (11.1%)	34,650 (12.3%)
Hispanic	1,861 (1.4%)	9,073 (4.5%)	35,308 (12.5%)
Asian/Pacific Islander	255 (<1%)	1,526 (<1%)	10,641 (3.7%)
Totals	131,669 (100%)	203,210 (100%)	281,421 (100%)

+ Source is U.S. Census Bureau and all numbers are rounded.

Not shown in the table are 2.5 million American Indians and Native Alaskans. The 2000 Census data are not directly comparable to previous census years due to a change in the race/ethnicity question in the 2000 Census, which requested respondents to self-identify as being of one-race, two or more races, or some other race. Those reporting two or more races and other race totaled more than 21 million people and do not appear in the table.

Table 1.2
Source Nations of U.S. Foreign-Born, 2000,
with a Minimum Population of 500,000

U.S. Total 31,107,889

Source Nation by Rank	Foreign-born Population
1. Mexico	9,177,487
2. China	1,518,652
3. Philippines	1,369,070
4. India	1,022,552
5. Vietnam	988,174
6. Cuba	872,716
7. Korea	864,125
8. Canada	820,771
9. El Salvador	817,336
10. Germany	706,704
11. Dominican Republic	687,677
12. United Kingdom	677,751
13. Jamaica	553,827
14. Columbia	509,872

Source: U.S. Census 2000.

CHANGING U.S. IMMIGRATION LAW

Immigration Policy Between Two World Wars

As mentioned earlier, social institutions may take the form of legal and political actions designed to protect the host culture, as in the case of the 1882 Chinese Exclusion Act that attempted to eliminate Chinese immigration into the U.S. By the beginning of the 20th century, American labor's dissatisfaction had turned toward the Japanese immigrants who were perceived as flooding the U.S. labor market and unfairly displacing honest Anglo workers. This perception was particularly acute in California and resulted in the Gentlemen's Agreement in 1907 between the leaders of Japan and the U.S., wherein Japan promised to limit Japanese immigration and avoided an international incident (details are provided in chapter 20). By the 1920s, already involved in a period of isolationism, the U.S. had become generally suspicious of involvements with foreign nations, especially in terms of formal agreements in trade and military treaties. Many Americans believed that the U.S. could set the standard for global democracy and peace by its independent example. Isolation did not mean the U.S. would cease its economic and territorial expansion policies, but it would refrain from unnecessary foreign entanglements with European nations. Of particular relevance to the evolution of American culture in this period were the actions by the U.S. Congress related to new immigration policies. As noted earlier, the entry of three waves of European immigrants totaled about 30 million in less than a century. The first two waves attracted cultures from northern and western Europe: Irish, English, German and Scandinavian populations. The third European wave differed sharply from the previous two in that it attracted eastern European and Italian immigrants who spoke different languages and had very different customs and cultural features than the earlier northern and western European groups, many of whom had assimilated into the Anglo-American culture by the 1920s. Various actions by the Congress illustrated their desire to protect Anglo-America from being diluted by those who were culturally dissimilar.

In 1917, Congress passed a law to impose literacy testing as a means to slow unwanted immigration. After nearly another million immigrants entered the country in 1920, Congress passed the 1921 Emergency Immigration Act as an immediate stop-gap action that established the quota system, an annual limit of 350,000 and a 3 percent national limit based on foreign nations share of the U.S. population in 1910. Given the dominance of western and northern European nations during the previous century, this law, by design, provided immigrants from those regions a significant numerical advantage. Congress continued to debate the immigration issue during the early 1920s and, in 1924, passed an even more restrictive act that President Coolidge signed into law. The 1924 Immigration Act had the clear intention of restricting eastern and southern Europeans immediately, and ending the entry of all Asians (especially the Japanese), who were ineligible for U.S. citizenship. The law continued the favorable status of northern and western Europeans. It set the national limit at 2 percent of the 1890 U.S. Census, which further strengthened the position of the Irish, English and other Europeans that had dominated the first two waves of immigration. By 1927, an annual cap of 150,000 was to be instituted. For a period, exceptions were made for the Americas and resulted in Canada and Mexico providing large numbers of immigrants in the 1920s. However, the pattern of immigration remained the same in the 1930s, although annual numbers dropped significantly due to the Depression; Western hemisphere nations of Great Britain, Germany and Mexico provided the most immigrants. The large influx of Mexicans during the 1920s led to the U.S. Census Bureau's initial effort to count those of the "Mexican race" by 1930. Congressional action soon restricted the influx of immigrant Mexican workers.

Immigration Policies Since 1952

American immigration policies changed dramatically after World War II beginning with the 1952 U.S. Immigration and Nationality Act (amended as the McCarran-Walter). America emerged as a superpower after WWII and contributed substantially to the rebuilding of Europe and Japan. The American economy expanded and labor shortages in key fields led to a different attitude toward immigration. The impact of communism also was influential; the "Red Scare" associated with the McCarthy era not only frightened many Americans, it increased their awareness and sympathy for foreigners who had fallen victim to the spread of communism. The new policy established in 1952 recognized both of these forces and also took a more tolerant attitude about admitting the close relatives of existing American citizens. Thus, while maintaining the quota system, the new law established a new preference system for skilled workers (preferred occupations based on employment shortages), and for immediate family members (e.g., unmarried children, siblings, and parents of American citizens), and an emergency entry provision for those fleeing immediate danger related to political crises. The latter led to the admission of refugees, including hundreds of thousands of Latin American and Asian refugees.

Undoubtedly the most dramatic change in immigration law since the establishment of the quota system, however, occurred with the passage of the 1965 Immigration and Nationality Act (Hart-Celler Act), which abolished the quota. By this time, America had entered the Civil Rights Era and was involved in a war in Vietnam. A more liberal element of Congress (including Ted Kennedy, Claiborne Pell, and Philip Hart) argued that the proposed changes associated with this Act would not significantly alter the cost or magnitude of immigration. Of course, history has proven them wrong. The unanticipated impacts of this law were extremely significant. The new law abolished the quota system and replaced it with numerical limits and a multiple category preference system. Under its terms, it mattered less where you were from, and more who you were in terms of skills, family relationships, and refugee status. The new limits were hemispheric as opposed to nationality-based: 170,000 from the Eastern Hemisphere (to compensate for previous biases) and 120,000 from the Western Hemisphere.

All non-refugee immigrants theoretically had an equal chance of admission either in the occupational or family preferences categories, specifically under family reunification or in preferred professionally-based occupations in six categories. Most importantly, however, the new law also created exemptions for immediate relatives (spouses, offspring and parents) from the numerical limits established by this legislation. This caused the number of annual immigrants to increase dramatically, an unanticipated impact of the Hart-Celler Act, especially in the numbers of immigrants from Latin America and Asian countries. The impact has increased cultural and ethnic diversity in the U.S.

There have been other immigration acts passed since 1965 that permit temporary or permanent status to certain immigrant applicants. Not all of these laws are examined here. However, there are many ways for foreign nationals to secure lawful permanent residents status, popularly called the "green card," in America. Among the possibilities are employment, family member, lottery, adoption, business investment, and refugee/political asylum. Decisions related to this status are based on the preference system mentioned previously. Among the modifications in the law are those that address unforeseen bias outcomes. For example, due to the impact of the family reunification clause in the existing law, a "lottery" system was created under a new law passed in 1990. This was to address the fact that the reunification clause favored particular underdeveloped nations, while excluding others. The 1990 U.S. Immigration Act addressed this problem by the addition of 55,000 immigrants drawn by "lottery" from those nations who had been excluded.

The labor market in the U.S. also continues to influence immigration law. There are two general types of visas (permission to enter the country), issued by the U.S. government: immigrant and non-immigrant visas. An immigrant visa recognizes the immigrant's intention to live and work in the country permanently. The non-immigrant visa is for a temporary visitor to work, study, receive training, and engage in other short-term activities. The 1990 Act and subsequent immigration legislation modified existing law and also increased the number of immigrant visas in the occupational/employment category. Also, in recognizing the market needs for high-tech skills and managerial personnel, the new law encouraged non-immigrant visas. This category has L-1 and H-1B visas to promote non-immigrant entry. The L-1 visa supports the establishment of multinational corporation investment through the creation of branch operations with skilled employees. Once non-immigrants hold the L-1 visa, they are eligible to apply for permanent residency after one year of successful operation of the new business. In the same vein, high-tech corporations have lobbied Congress to increase the number of annual H-1B visas for non-permanent immigrants for various skilled and educated foreigners. Congress has responded by raising those limits, which in 2003 reached 195,000 visas. Just as L-1 visa holders are eligible for permanent residency, so too are the holders of H-1B visas during their six-year approved work status.

All of these changes have contributed to the continued growth in the number of annual immigrants entering the U.S. and to an increasing number securing permanent status. Beyond these changes in the laws regulating legal immigration, America has experienced a tremendous influx of millions of illegal immigrants in recent decades. Various efforts to better control the international border have been undertaken but none have had a lasting impact on this problem. Mark Reisinger addresses some of the dimensions of illegal immigration in chapter 14. Legal and illegal immigration have led to major changes in the spatial distribution, settlement, and cultural landscape patterns of the U.S.

RETHINKING APPROACHES AND THEORETICAL CONCEPTS

American society has changed a great deal in many ways since the periods described in the preceding paragraphs. It has welcomed cultures from around the globe as prospective citizens or as temporary workers. Just as American social institutions mistreated and restricted various non-white groups, they changed immigration law in order to permit a broader representation of ethnic groups in the U.S. What remains uncertain is how well the new multicultural diversity will avoid the pitfalls of American history and how well it can fare in an economic and political system that remains dominated by the Anglo perspective. Illegal immigration has reached a magnitude that allows it to cloud the issues surrounding the prospect of national unity under multicultural diversity. Global terrorism has profoundly influenced the average American and the media. A 2005 editorial in a major U.S. news magazine illustrates the conservative perspective on multicultural diversity issues:

> "Multiculturalism is based on the lie that all cultures are morally equal. In practice, that soon degenerates to: All cultures are morally equal, except ours, which is worse. But all cultures are not equal in respecting representative government, guaranteed liberties, and the rule of law. And those things arose not simultaneously and in all cultures but in certain specific times and places — mostly in Britain and America but also in other parts of Europe" (M. Barone, 2005, p. 26).

Multiculturalisms' focus on the treatment of subcultures should not be interpreted as a vote to destroy western democracies. Rather, it is self-criticism and an effort not to perpetuate the wrongs of the past. It also recognizes that a multicultural society will not abide by a narrow set of ideals and restrictions that favor a group whose influence will undoubtedly shrink in coming decades. The data provided in Tables 1.1 and 1.2 clearly illustrated the diversity trends in the U.S. It seems equally clear that, while cultural traits persevere, the American culture will not remain fixed in the face of an increasing multicultural society. The bigger issue for American leadership is how to find a course that supports ethnic and cultural diversity, while keeping the nation bound together by ideals that can be fairly realized by all, regardless of ethnic background. This is a tall order for a society steeped in feelings of Anglo-cultural superiority and white entitlement, as well as by a history of neglect and discrimination of minority cultures.

Perhaps a vital first step, after reviewing the multiple cultural histories and geographies of the U.S., is to examine the nature of ethnic and racial settlements in contemporary America, to understand the processes at work in places where the newest Americans are reshaping regions and landscapes, using their own culture and ethnic identities. At the same time, we can explore the settlement experiences and challenges of these groups as they attempt to "fit" and, change American landscapes into a set of different images. We are likely to unveil places where non-white racial groups, foreign-born, and particular ethnic groups are still unwelcome and experience resentment and discrimination. We may discover where and why conflicts are occurring, or may be likely to occur, and where the types of issues, such as education and health, may provide our greatest challenges. Finally, we may uncover places of success, places where multicultural geographies are a reflection of the future and serve as models for other communities.

In the process of examining the various settlement paths of recent immigrants, social science researchers have found it necessary to recast existing theories and create new theoretical concepts to help explain the complexities of the settlements of the multicultural population. The Chicago School's assimilation model served as a singular concept that explained how European immigrants were absorbed into Anglo society. However, recent critiques and newer formulations recognize both the attributes of the host culture and the non-European mix as important elements requiring different formulations to explain emerging racial and ethnic settlement geographies. More recent approaches have included issues of gender, race, ethnicity and other factors. Among the most cited works are those that emphasize the multiple paths that immigrant assimilation can follow. Collectively, these multiple options are termed "segmented assimilation" (Portes and Zhou, 1993; Portes, 1995; Zhou, 1997). This concept recognizes that, in addition to the possible straight-line assimilation concept discussed earlier, immigrants have the option of other paths that either lead to their partial absorption into the host culture or lead to separate maintenance. Zhou has expressed two options beyond the ecological model's direct spatial absorption, including one involving "downward mobility," which implies immigrants are pushed into a lower socioeconomic status, and another option for middle class absorption by "economic integration," which involves "lagged acculturation" with "deliberate preservation" of the immigrant's ethnicity. These multidirectional paths are due to America's class structure and racial constructs that together influence immigrant options and behaviors. Wei Li will discuss this further in chapter 5 because she believes race has a key role in American settlement geographies.

Zelinsky's text raised the issue of changes in American cultural composition and its implications for landscapes in 1992. He noted the increasing interdependencies between places and cultures, the transnationalization trends due to globalization and its associated mass migrations. He suggested that "America is at a turning point, some sort of crisis of identity" (Zelinsky, 1992, p. 184). He recognized that the changes in American immigrant sources were raising questions about the future of American culture. A few years later, Zelinsky and Lee suggested that the ecological straight-line assimilation model alone no longer adequately explained immigrant settlement patterns, especially those who had entered America with social and economic capital. Termed "heterolocalism," their concept recognized that local settlements by some immigrant populations took on a unique form unlike that of ethnic enclaves of the past. This concept described cases wherein "recent populations of shared ethnic identity … enter an area from distant sources, then quickly adopt a dispersed pattern of residential location, all the while managing to remain cohesive through a variety of means" (1998, p. 281). The relationship of this concept to "segmented assimilation" should be obvious.

The debate over immigration in some ways can be reduced to the same issue of the last century: acculturation and assimilation for the good of American society. However, not all Americans agree that assimilation is necessary to maintain a healthy nation. Further, the rapid change in cultural diversity is unprecedented in American history and is likely to change the position of the white majority. It is unlikely that the nearly one-half of the American population by 2050 will be as eager to tow the Anglo-line of acculturation and assimilation as did their white European predecessors of the last century. A new attitude by the traditional white European population likely will be necessary to meet the demands of a new American populace.

In short, more recent theories and concepts dealing with immigrant assimilation and settlement geography recognize the growing importance of pluralism, multiculturalism, and class in the U.S. As Chacko noted, "race/ethnicity and socioeconomic class" are among the most prominent barriers to the assimilation of first- and second-generation U.S. immigrants (Chacko, 2003, p. 494). These viewpoints also recognize the importance of race as a social construct that shapes the institutional controls of the host culture toward the immigrant group and the importance of ethnic identity in the path of the subculture decisions related to geographic space. As we explore America's increasing cultural and ethnic diversity, it should become clear that the future demands careful and thoughtful attention of all Americans as we look to the future.

RACE, ETHNICITY, AND PLACE: PERSISTENCE AND CHANGE IN AMERICA

This text provides a number of examples of some specific ethnic groups that represent the broad racial/ethnic categorizations provided by the U.S. Census, Hispanics/Latinos, Blacks, Asians and native cultures. Part I of the book serves as an introduction to key terminology and illustrates a broad range of thought on American multicultural geographies, ranging from social criticism to a policy viewpoint, and from ethnic impacts on gateways to the racial ideology that has influenced immigrant settlement geography. Each of the next three sections (Parts II, III, and IV) of the text focuses on some of the major relevant processes and patterns associated with Blacks, Latinos, and Asians living in America. Part II of the book examines patterns and processes that have produced and continue to produce black geographies in America. This section, like the others, contains an overview chapter, followed by case studies that reveal at least one dimension of the persistence or change related to that group's human geography. Ethnic case studies also indicate the increasing diversity within the broadly defined census categorization (Blacks) and the impact of that ethnic group on a landscape or place.

Part III of the book focuses on Latinos in America and is organized in the same fashion as the previous section. Part IV, which follows the same format, examines various Asian ethnic experiences in the U.S., including their settlement geography, using both historical and contemporary examples. We cannot possibly cover all aspects of all groups, but we endeavor to provide some insight into America's broader heritage and changing places over time through several examples.

The final section, Part V, provides perspectives on several dimensions of American ethnic diversity. It begins by reviewing the changing economic development contexts for American Indians. It then examines a few examples of white-European ethnic groups in the U.S., revealing the continuing presence of Europeans as part of America's complex ethnic mix. The first case study looks at the contemporary settlement experiences of Russian immigrants in the Pacific Northwest, while the second explores the persistence of an established group, Greek Americans. As the foreign-born continue to enter the U.S., they find themselves settling in cities where they must compete for employment and housing with established native-born populations. Paterson, New Jersey, has a diverse population, including many foreign-born. Analysis of this group with the established native population illustrates important disparities between groups in a diverse community. Ethnically diverse cities are becoming more common in the U.S., including in the American Heartland. This section uses Louisville, Kentucky, to explore the dimensions of multicultural diversity. Finally, racial and ethnic diversity have led to serious issues related to education and healthcare. The final chapter in this section examines both equity issues and health conditions due to diversity.

Chapter 2

Nightmarish Landscapes:
The Orwellian World of Malcolm X

JAMES A. TYNER

"I have a dream that one day every valley will be exalted, every hill and mountain shall be made low, the rough places will be made plain, and the crooked places will be made straight, and the glory of the Lord shall be revealed.... So let freedom ring from the prodigious hilltops of New Hampshire ... from the mighty mountains of New York ... from the snow-capped Rockies of Colorado.... From the curvaceous peaks of California ... let freedom ring from Stone Mountain Georgia ... from every hill ... of Mississippi ...

... when we let it ring ... from every state and every city , we will able to speed up that day when all God's children, black men and white men, Jews and Gentiles, Protestants and Catholics, will be able to join hands and sing ... thank God Almighty, we are free at last." Speech by M. L. King, Jr., delivered on August 28, 1963, on the steps of the Lincoln Memorial.

INTRODUCTION

"I see America through the eyes of the victim. I don't see any American dream; I see an American nightmare." So argued Malcolm X (1965b, p. 26) in his momentous *The Ballot or the Bullet* speech delivered at the Cory Methodist Church in Cleveland. The speech came just months after Martin Luther King, Jr.'s "I Have a Dream" speech in Washington, D.C. Malcolm X explained that he was not an American. Rather, in his words: "I'm one of the 22 million black people who are victims of Americanism. One of the 22 million black people who are victims of democracy, nothing but disguised hypocrisy. So, I'm not standing here speaking to you as an American, or a patriot, or a flag-saluter, or a flag-waver — no, not I. I'm speaking as a victim of this American system."

The statements of Malcolm X[1] refer directly to concepts articulated within the discipline of Geography, namely national and ethnic identity. But Malcolm X also spoke to the notion of geographical imaginations, of alternative place-making and place-meaning. I take this observation as the starting point of my study. In so doing I contribute to the project of David Delaney (1998, p. 9) who argues that "if we want to understand the historical constructions of geographies of race and racism in the United States, [then] we have to do more than map changing distributions of 'black people'." This paper, therefore, is a convergence of three areas of inquiry: cultural landscapes, dystopian literatures, and jeremiad rhetoric. I argue that through these three components an explicitly *geographic* understanding of Malcolm X is manifest.

As Pierce Lewis (1979) succinctly writes, "If we want to understand ourselves, we would do well to take a searching look at landscapes." This sentiment has been well expressed by geographers whose work is grounded in critical race theory. Peake and Kobayashi (2002), for example, identify a need to understand the historical and geographical specificity of "race" and its durability in influencing human landscapes. Ordinary landscapes are important archives of social experience and cultural meaning (Groth, 1997). Malcolm X was an astute reader of the landscape, for these spaces provided meaning to his political thought.

A second component of this chapter entails dystopian literatures. As indicated by the quote at the beginning of this paper, Malcolm X viewed the American landscape as one of a nightmare. He did not see a Promised Land; America was not a bright "City on a Hill" illuminating the world in all its glory. Rather, America was hypocrisy, a place of dreams deferred and promises not kept. And it was within these spaces that Malcolm X implored his audiences to retain a sense of self within a dehumanizing landscape.

Through my positioning of Malcolm X within the genre of dystopian writings, I am providing a specific and unconventional understanding of his political thought. I cannot claim that he would have approved; to my knowledge, Malcolm X never specifically mentioned his ideas as dystopian. My justifications for such an approach, however, are derived from the arguments advanced by Malcolm X. First, by situating the writings and speeches of Malcolm X within a broader context, namely that of dystopian literatures, I indicate how his life's work contributes in ways not traditionally associated with African Americans. In the conclusion of his autobiography, Malcolm X reflected on his perceived greatest failing in life, specifically his not having an academic education. Malcolm X, I contend, believed that this limited his societal impact and perhaps prevented him from contributing *not* simply to the study of race, but rather to the study of humanity. He concluded:

> "You see, most whites, even when they credit a Negro with some intelligence, will still feel that all he can talk about is the race issue; most whites never feel that Negroes can contribute anything to other areas of thought, and ideas. You just notice how rarely you will ever hear whites asking any Negroes what they think about the problem of world health, or the space race to land men on the moon" (1965a, p. 388).

Elsewhere, I argue that geography and geographers would do well to listen to the voice of Malcolm X for his thoughts on power/knowledge, representations, and our own geographies (Tyner, 2003, 2004, 2005a). This applies likewise for the dystopian style forwarded by Malcolm X.

Second, I situate Malcolm X within the genre of dystopian writings in an attempt to establish his work within a larger tradition of both American and African-American political writings. The fictional works of George Orwell, Aldous Huxley, and Anthony Burgess, for example, serve as warnings of totalitarianism. Malcolm X, however, did not produce a work of *fiction*; rather, he provided a narrative of reality. My coupling "fictional" accounts (e.g., Orwell) with "realist" accounts (e.g., Malcolm X) merits some explanation. Power shapes landscapes. Both Orwell and Malcolm X use their perceptions (in one case fictitious and in one case subjective and "other"-ized) of spaces and places to characterize situations dealing with ill-effects of power hierarchies which are conceptually true. In *Empire of Signs* the literary critic Roland Barthes (1983) discusses the blurring of "true" representations and that of fiction. Barthes explains that just as he is unable to represent a place in its entirety so too is he unable to construct a work of purely original fiction. The fictional writings of Orwell, certainly, are modeled after the Soviet Union. Malcolm X, on the other hand, attempts to represent a particular racialized landscape; he does so, however, not from the position of a social scientist, seeking to empirically document, verify, and describe accurately an authentic landscape. Instead, the realism of Malcolm X — his ground-level reality — was used rhetorically. Malcolm X grounded his political thought in his routine observations, as well as his audience's life experiences. Malcolm X did not try to support his assertions with the kind of evidence that whites would accept, because he was not trying to persuade them; rather, he was speaking from a *black* point of view, and he wanted to identify the enemies of black people so that they would know whom they had to fight against in their struggle for dignity (Cone, 1991). Consequently, Malcolm X constructed composite landscapes, scenes of oppression and exploitation that his African-American audiences would readily understand. It was through this process that Malcolm X was able to fight against social injustice, and it was through this geographing that Malcolm X assumed the role of the jeremiad, the third component of my study.

As Howard-Pitney (1990) explains, the term *jeremiad*, meaning a lamentation or doleful complaint, derives from the Old Testament prophet, Jeremiah, who warned of Israel's fall and the destruction of Jerusalem temple by Babylonia as punishment for the people's failure to keep the Mosaic covenant. Within the United States, the jeremiad has a long and deeply entrenched history. The Puritan John Winthrop referred to New England as a "City on a Hill," a shining example of socioreligious perfection lighting the way for the coming of God's earthly kingdom (Howard-Pitney, 1990). Indeed, Howard-Pitney argues that, "People in the United States have always believed America to be somehow special and uniquely set apart from the rest of the world" (1990, p. 5).

Underlying every utopia is the thought either of the road to perfection or of the return to grace (Porter and Lukermann, 1975). The jeremiad tradition is closely connected with utopian (though not so much dystopian writings). Within the U.S. context, therefore, America is to constantly *become* a utopia; America is a process of nation-building as reflected by the phrases "Manifest Destiny" and "American Exceptionalism."

The American jeremiad has been frequently adapted for the purposes of black protest and propaganda (Howard-Pitney, 1990). This is seen in the nineteenth-century separatist movements, such as "Pap" Singleton — the "Moses of the Negro People" — who led an exodus of African Americans from the Deep South to Kansas. This jeremiad tradition is also evident in the writings of Booker T. Washington, Ida B. Wells, and W. E. B. Du Bois, who employed various guises to chastise white Americans for violating the national ideals and covenant with their racism (Howard-Pitney, 1990). Malcolm X follows in this long tradition of African-American protest.

DYSTOPIAN LANDSCAPES AND THE JEREMIAD

Geography has always been a part of the struggle for political, economic, and social rights. Indeed, as Gilmore (2002) articulates, some geographic imperative lies at the heart of every struggle for social justice. That these struggles are manifest on the landscape should come as no surprise. Groth identifies the term landscape as " the interaction of people and place: a social group and its spaces, particularly the spaces to which the group belongs and from which its members derive some part of their shared identity and meaning" (1997, p. 1).

Landscape studies are often intimately associated with the concept of territoriality. Territoriality may be viewed as the spatial expression of power, an expression that Malcolm X advocated in his writings and speeches (Tyner, 2004). These expressions of power, moreover, were visible on the landscape. And the landscape that Malcolm X perceived was marked by oppressive living conditions in northern urban ghettos and the Jim Crow South. Malcolm X's landscape consisted of police dogs attacking black people, of black babies being blown up in churches, and of lynchings and beatings of black people. These were landscapes of exclusion, whether defined as *de jure* or *de facto* segregation. And it was in these everyday landscapes, of lunch counters and street corners, that discrimination, prejudice, and violence were confronted.

An engagement with Malcolm X thus augments the crucial importance of "everyday" landscapes, for it is these spaces — more so than grandiose monuments with high-styled designs — that are most vital to the formation of human meaning (Groth, 1997). It is within these landscapes that day-to-day activities occur, and social movements are played out.

Dystopian writings are geographical signposts for social movements. Confronting a totalitarian state — the American system — Malcolm X advocated revolution because he believed that fundamental transformations of racism were not possible within such a system. To "integrate" into such a system was to placate a racist hegemony. Malcolm X explained that:

> "... it's impossible for a chicken to produce a duck egg.... A chicken just doesn't have it within its system to produce a duck egg.... The system in this country cannot produce freedom for an Afro-American. It is impossible for this system, this economic system, this political system, this social system, this system, period.... And if ever a chicken did produce a duck egg, I'm quite sure that you would say it was certainly a revolutionary chicken!" (1965b, pp. 68–69).

At this point I want to underscore the role of dystopian literature as a form of social criticism. Following Booker (1994), the construction of alternative geographical imaginations in dystopian literature is always highly relevant more or less directly to specific "real-world" societies and issues. Dystopian fictions are typically set in places or times far distant from the author's own, but it is usually clear that the real referents of dystopian fictions are generally quite concrete and near-at-hand (Booker 1994). The writings and speeches of Malcolm X, as indicated above, were not meant to be read as fiction; nevertheless, as composite representations of landscapes, the geo-graphing of Malcolm X operated as a powerful tool of social criticism. His narratives were minimalist; detailed, in-depth descriptions were not necessary. The realism — and significance — of his words lie in their personal experiential basis, one that his audience would quickly grasp. And it was this construction of concrete landscapes — of places of discrimination, prejudice, and violence with which his audiences were all too familiar — that was most effective. Consider, for example, Malcolm X's discussion of the linkage between urban politics, city-scapes, and riots. Malcolm X explained that:

> "It's the city structure that incites. A city that continues to let people live in rat-nest dens in Harlem and pay higher rent in Harlem than they pay downtown.... Who lets merchants outcharge or overcharge people for their groceries and their clothing and other commodities in Harlem, while you pay less for it downtown. This is what incites. A city that will not create some kind of employment for people who are barred from having jobs just because their skin is black. That's what incites [rioting]. Don't ever accuse a black man for voicing his resentment and dissatisfaction over the criminal condition of his people as being responsible for inciting the situation. You have to indict the society that allows these things to exist" (quoted in Lomax, 1968, p. 239).

Unlike dystopian writers, the American jeremiad's dark portrayal of current society never questions America's promise and destiny (Howard-Pitney, 1990). Howard-Pitney explains that the "jeremiad's unfaltering view is that God will mysteriously use the unhappy present to spur the people to reformation and speedily onward to fulfill their divine destiny" (1990, p. 8). For Malcolm X this was unattainable. Malcolm X did not see that society, as it was presently composed, would ultimately reform and become a utopian world for African Americans.

DEHUMANIZED LANDSCAPES

We should keep in mind the assertion that "If we want to understand ourselves, we would do well to take a searching look at landscapes" (Lewis, 1979). Malcolm X was a teacher-philosopher, one who based his movement for social justice on the everyday realities of his and his audience's experiences. The overarching objective of cultural landscape writing, according to Groth (1997) is to inform the public. It is thus a form of advocacy and, viewed in this light, sits comfortably within both the dystopian genre and the rhetorical style of jeremiad. Gottlieb (2001) writes that dystopian literature, in general, makes us ponder how an originally utopian promise was abused, betrayed, or, ironically, fulfilled so as to create tragic consequences for humanity. Malcolm X is forthright in his accusations that African Americans had been denied to participate in the American Dream. He argued that various Civil Rights Acts were disguised forms of hypocrisy. In 1963, for example, Malcolm X, speaking before an audience in Harlem, assailed President Kennedy for "talking about freedom in Europe when 20,000,000 black [people] have no freedom here" and "Right now representatives of the American government are in Nazi Germany complaining about the Berlin Wall, but haven't done anything about the Alabama Wall" (quoted in Cone, 1991, p. 113). As further evidence, Malcolm X directed attention to the Alabama church bombings that followed the March on Washington.

Malcolm X's nightmarish landscapes were at odds with the rhetoric of both King's "Dream" as well as the larger "American Dream." The north was not a Promised Land for recently transplanted southern African Americans. And America — through its colonial wars fought in Vietnam and the Congo — was not the beacon of hope for humanity. The dystopian world of Malcolm X was not, in this respect, that of the traditional American jeremiad for he did not perceive the U.S. as the Promised Land. In a speech delivered in 1964, Malcolm X asked what kind of country is the United States. His response was a series of questions and answers:

> "Why should we do the dirtiest jobs for the lowest pay? Why should we do the hardest work for the lowest pay? Why should we pay the most money for the worst kind of food and the most money for the worst kind of place to live in? I'm telling you we do it because we live in one of the rottenest countries that has ever existed on this earth. It's the system that is rotten; we have a rotten system. It's a system of exploitation, a political and economic system of exploitation, of outright humiliation, degradation, discrimination ..." (Malcolm X, 1970, p. 46).

He, in short, argued against what he perceived to be the hypocrisy of integration attempts: it is not enough to sit at the table, if one is not allowed to eat. The Civil Rights Movement, to be effective, required a complete remaking of the American system.

Relatedly, dystopian writings attempt to de-familiarize the familiar: by focusing their critiques of society on spatially or temporally distinct settings, dystopian fictions provide fresh perspectives on problematic social and political practices that might otherwise be taken for granted or considered natural and inevitable (Booker, 1994). Malcolm X, through his writings and speeches, was attempting to de-familiarize the ghetto. He argued that the living conditions of African Americans were *not* natural; squalid conditions in the ghetto were neither normal nor inevitable. But as it currently existed, the ghetto was certainly alienating. Malcolm X observed that there existed, in 1964, thirty-five council members in New York City. He asked his audience if they knew how many were Black, then explained:

> "... there's only one black one, and he's a councilman-at-large.... And many of our people don't even know who the black councilman is. How would you expect to change our miserable situation when we have a council that the black man can't even get into? He's not even represented there. We're not represented in the city government in proportion to our number. We're not represented in the state government in proportion to our number. And we aren't represented in the federal government in proportion to our number" (1970, pp. 94–95).

Through their acquiescence to a racist (but supposedly democratic) system, African Americans remained alienated. African Americans were linguistically defined by white society, and remained marginalized materially. A first step was to de-familiarize the "Negro" landscape. An example of this is seen in Malcolm X's deconstruction of the meanings of the term "Negro" itself.

Malcolm X began with a simple declarative statement: "One of the main reasons we are called Negro is so we won't know who we really are" (2001, p. 25). He then proceeded to emphasize the spatiality inherent in the term "Negro." Malcolm X explained, "Negro doesn't tell you anything. I mean nothing, absolutely nothing. What do you identify it with? ... Nothing.... It's completely in the middle of nowhere. And when you call yourself that, that's where you are — right in the middle of nowhere." In a manner reminiscent of Franz Fanon's (1967) rhetorical question, "Where am I to be classified? or, if you prefer, tucked away?," Malcolm X understood the interconnections of self and place. The term "Negro," for Malcolm X, was a term used to negate the physical presence of African Americans. This is made possible because, according to Malcolm X, "Negroes" do not exist as people. Rather, they "were scientifically produced by the white man" (2001, p. 25). In other words, we would say that "Negro" is a social as well as spatial construction, one perpetuated through the reiteration of the term "Negro" in our studies, classroom teachings, and other activities. Malcolm X firmly understood the linkage between "self" and landscape: it is a matter of who we are through a concern with where we are (Tyner, 2005b).

Dystopian literature highlights the sense of alienation that emerges within a totalitarian system. This idea conforms readily with Malcolm X's spatial understanding of the term "Negro." Within a racist totalitarian system that was the United States, he implored his listeners to make the connection between institutional racism and the suppression of African-American individuality. Malcolm X explained that Negro "doesn't give you a language, because there is no such thing as a Negro language. It doesn't give you a country, because there is no such thing as a Negro country. It doesn't give you a culture — there is no such thing as a Negro culture, it doesn't exist. The land doesn't exist, the culture doesn't exist, the language doesn't exist, and the man doesn't exist. *They take you out of existence by calling you a Negro*" (2001, p. 26; italics added). African Americans, defined by others as "Negroes," were existentially removed from the American landscape. They became, to paraphrase Orlando Patterson, socially-dead and spatially-dead. Accordingly, the segregated landscapes of Jim Crow and the concentrated urban ghettos of the north, were sites emptied of humanity, a dark spot on the mental maps of a racist society.

To counter these representations, and reflecting the influence of Marcus Garvey[2] on his thinking, Malcolm X attempted to introduce his African-American audiences to a sense of self. The crux of Malcolm X's view was his insistence that African Americans were worthy independent of their association with whites. Whites were not needed as a yardstick to measure the value of blacks. He used the example of desegregated schools to make his point: "If we can get an all-black school, that we can control, staff it ourselves with the type of teachers that have good at heart, with the type of books that have in them many of the missing ingredients that have produced [an] inferiority complex in our people, then we don't feel that an all-black school is necessarily a segregated school." This comment was made in response to debates regarding the 1954 Supreme Court decision, and particularly King's comments that it was important for black children to interact with white children. From Malcolm X's point of view, black children should not be defined by their relation to white children; nor should the sense of worth of black children be based on an association with whites. He concluded:

> "I just can't see where if white people can go to a white classroom and there are no Negroes present and it doesn't affect the academic diet they're receiving, then I don't see where an all-black classroom can be affected by the absence of white children. If the absence of black children doesn't affect white students, I don't see how the absence of whites is going to affect the blacks" (1970, p. 17).

Moreover, conforming to a jeremiad tradition, Malcolm X stressed the personal responsibilities that were required to negate the dehumanizing elements of a racist state. As Howard-Pitney (1990) recounts, Malcolm X addressed jeremiads to African-American audiences, urging them to atone for their sins (e.g., drug addiction, promiscuity, family instability, lack of thrift and enterprise). He called on the people to repent so that they may fulfill their destiny. For whites, Malcolm X — before his split from the Nation of Islam — held no possibility of salvation. Whites were *not* the chosen people; they were to incur the wrath of Allah for their sins. This, incidentally, would justify further Malcolm X's intonement to *not* integrate with a doomed society.

CONCLUSIONS

Much dystopian literature — particularly that of the twentieth-century — has concentrated on socialism, fascism, and totalitarianism. Malcolm X directs attention to the racial underscoring of dystopian worlds and the interconnections of self and landscape. Conforming to the American jeremiad tradition in part, Malcolm X encouraged his African-American audiences to resist the dehumanizing tendencies of a racist society. The revolution advocated by Malcolm X was not reducible to violence. Rather, Malcolm X forwarded a revolution in thinking and learning. He encouraged his audiences — and especially the younger members — to observe their landscapes and to draw insight into the workings of society. Malcolm X, in this respect, was a landscape geographer. He understood that landscapes said much about how people behaved and interacted.

For Malcolm X there was an immediate and practical dimension to the reading of landscapes and the production of knowledge. As he explained in a 1965 interview, students must learn to think for themselves, instead of accepting racist language. He explained:

> "... if the students in this country forgot the analysis that has been presented to them, and they went into a huddle and began to research this problem of racism for themselves, independent of politicians and independent of all the foundations (which are a part of the power structure), and did it themselves, then some of their findings would be shocking, but they would see that they would never be able to bring about a solution to racism in their country as long as they're relying on the government to do it" (1991, p. 89).

I relate this statement of Malcolm X to Orwell's approach to political writing. Arguably the most noted of twentieth-century dystopian writers, Orwell explained that "Every line of serious work that I have written since 1936 has been written, directly or indirectly, against totalitarianism and for democratic socialism, as I understand it ... I write ... because there is some lie that I want to expose, some fact to which I want to draw attention, and my initial concern is to get a hearing" (1981, p. 314). Malcolm X sought to expose the "lie" of the American Dream, to highlight the oppressive and exploitative landscapes of a racist society. And it is because of this form of social criticism — this alternative geo-graphing — that I situate Malcolm X within the realms of landscape studies, dystopian literatures, and the jeremiad.

NOTES

[1] Malcolm X (1925–1965) was a prominent spokesperson and activist in the Civil Rights Movement. Born Malcolm Little in Omaha, Nebraska, Malcolm X emerged as the most influential member, other than Elijah Muhammad, of the Nation of Islam. In 1964 Malcolm X separated from the Nation of Islam and formed his own Civil Rights organization, the Organization of Afro-American Unity (OAAU). He was assassinated, most likely by members of the Nation of Islam, on February 21, 1965. A good starting point to understand Malcolm X is to read his autobiography. Additionally, there are many good biographies of Malcolm X, including Lomax (1968), Goldman (1979), Perry (1991), Wolfenstein (1993), Dyson (1995), and Natambu (2002). Other books focus on selected aspects of Malcolm X's life, including religion (DeCaro, 1996, 1998) and his post-Nation of Islam period (Breitman, 1968; Sales, 1994). Malcolm X's contributions to geographic thought can be found in Tyner (2003, 2004, 2005a). Family memoirs provide a more personal angle to his life (Collins and Bailey, 1998; Rickford, 2003).

[2] Marcus Garvey was a Jamaican-born black nationalist. During the first decades of the twentieth-century Garvey developed a broad Pan-African nationalist movement. He argued that African-American oppression was linked to the European colonization of the Caribbean and Africa. Scholars agree that the ideas expounded by Garvey influenced the political thought and internationalist focus of Malcolm X.

Chapter 3

Public Policy Impacts on School Desegregation, 1970–2000[1]

John R. Logan, Deirdre Oakley, and Jacob Stowell

Public schools have struggled with their response to the 1954 U.S. Supreme Court ruling in the case of *Brown* v. *Board of Education*. More than 700 separate court cases involving several thousand school districts have dealt with the requirement to desegregate. Yet court decisions in the 1990s paved the way for releasing districts from desegregation orders in many cases even if whites and minorities were again becoming more separate. School districts that voluntarily sought to retain desegregation plans became subject to lawsuits from groups that opposed those plans (as in the famous case of *Swann* v. *Charlotte-Mecklenburg, North Carolina*).

School researchers from Coleman (Coleman, Kelly, and Moore, 1975) to the present have judged that mandated desegregation is effective in those school districts where sufficient force is brought to bear on school authorities. The evidence from individual districts seems strong indeed. Welch and Light (1987) identified nearly 50 major districts where desegregation orders were implemented during 1968–1984, and where the Index of Dissimilarity between white and minority students declined by as much as 75 points.[2] But the corollary is that desegregation policies would wither away without external pressure. This is the perspective reflected in Orfield and Yun's (2001) report on the effects of "resegregation decisions" — a series of court decisions and changes in the political climate in the 1990s that allowed many districts to be freed from desegregation orders.

We take a different position, suggesting: 1) that the adoption of desegregation policies diffused widely after 1970 to encompass parts of the country where there was never much risk of court action, and 2) that because the policy of desegregation was so strongly legitimized in the decades after the Brown decision, court mandates had already lost their relevance when they were being withdrawn in the 1990s. Certainly desegregation occurred in districts where it was not required by court or federal enforcement actions. Rossell and Armor (1996) report that many desegregation plans were voluntary, though perhaps often defensive, and in the long term they were about as effective as mandatory plans. We believe that the combination of Supreme Court decisions, highly visible public battles over their implementation, and the commitment of the federal government to enforce court actions created a national climate in which desegregation orders could be effective. Equally important, they may have created conditions for desegregation even in the absence of court or federal mandates.

At the same time, because courts and other agencies made the policy decision to reject inter-district remedies, metropolitan-level segregation, including separation both **within** and **between** school districts, declined much less over these three decades. White flight from districts with larger black populations has reduced the inter-racial contact generated by within-district desegregation. Desegregation *within* districts has left large disparities in poverty concentration for black and white students *across* districts in the same metropolitan region. In fact, a large share of overall segregation, possibly more than half, is attributable to racial disparities **between** districts (Rivkin, 1994; Clotfelter, 1999; Reardon, Yun and Eitle, 2000). Accounting for segregation between districts is critical for assessments of the effectiveness of desegregation policies, because desegregation cannot increase interracial contact if it motivates white families to abandon racially mixed school districts. Many analysts from the 1960s to the present have viewed white flight as the Achilles heel of desegregation plans.

SCHOOL ENROLLMENT DATA SOURCES

School enrollment data for this study were culled from two sources. School enrollment data from the late 1960s are drawn from the Franklin Wilson and Karl Taeuber Desegregation Study data file, from which findings were published in Wilson (1985). These data were originally obtained from the Office of Civil Rights (OCR) of the U.S. Department of Health and Human Services. Between 1968 and 1976, OCR produced a data file containing school enrollment by race and segregation indices for a large sample of the nation's school districts. For those districts that were not surveyed in 1968, we substitute data from either of the two subsequent years (1969–70; 1970–71). For more recent years we rely on the National Center for Education Statistics (NCES) Common Core Data.

For convenience in the following text and tables, "1970" refers to one of the years in the 1968–70 period, "1990" refers to the 1989–90 school year, and "2000" refers to the 1999–2000 school year. NCES files categorize students as non-Hispanic white, non-Hispanic black, Hispanic, Asian, Native American, and other. The Wilson/Taeuber file categorizes students as non-Hispanic white, non-Hispanic black, Hispanic, and other race. In the following text, the terms white and black refer only to non-Hispanic students. Because the *Brown* v. *Board of Education* decision and its implementation primarily dealt with black students, this study focuses mainly on white-black segregation.

MEASURING METROPOLITAN SCHOOL SEGREGATION

To ensure comparability over time, we have applied consistent 2000 definitions of metropolitan regions. Individual schools were assigned to metropolitan regions based on the zip code in which they were located or (for 1970) the zip code of the school district office.

To measure segregation, we rely mainly on the Dissimilarity Index developed by Duncan and Duncan in 1995. This index measures the extent to which two groups, in this case blacks and whites, live in different areas of a city. The index ranges from 0 to 100, giving the percentage of children in one group who would have to attend a different school to achieve racial balance — one where every school replicates the group composition of the city. A value of 60 or above is considered very high. For example, a D score of 60 for black-white segregation would mean that 60 percent of either group must move to a different school for the two groups to become equally distributed. Values of 40 to 50 are usually considered moderate levels of segregation, while values of 30 or less are considered low.

INVENTORY OF DESEGREGATION CASES

The desegregation case inventory used in this study was compiled from multiple sources. These include case dockets and bibliographies concerning desegregation court orders from the Department of Justice, NAACP Legal Defense Fund, and the U.S. Department of Education. Other published sources are *From Brown to Boston: Desegregation in Education 1954–1974* (Jones, 1979); *Desegregation in Education: A Directory of Reported Federal Decisions* (Wise, 1977); and *New Evidence on School Desegregation* (Welch and Light, 1987). Every case has been checked through legal databases, including Westlaw, to determine the name of the case, the school districts involved, whether the case actually included the issue of school segregation, whether there was a court-mandated desegregation plan, and the year of the initial court order.

Aside from formal court cases, we also treat as "under a desegregation order" those school districts that implemented desegregation plans in response to federal pressure from the U.S. Department of Health, Education, and Welfare (HEW). Our analysis incorporates partial information on those plans, based on lists compiled by HEW for the years 1977 and 1978 (*School Desegregation: A Report of State and Federal Judicial and Administrative Activity*, by the National Institute of Education, HEW 1977, 1978.).

A webpage has been developed to present information on court cases and demographic data for all of these districts (http://www.s4.brown.edu/schoolsegregation). Users can select a state, and then a school district within a state. The webpage lists court cases (if any) that involved this district, and provides a link to the Westlaw text of the court decision. It also provides information on racial and ethnic composition of the elementary student population for available years, and summary indices of school segregation. The webpage includes data on Hispanic and Asian students; this report deals only with white-black segregation.

COURT-ORDERED DESEGREGATION: HOW MANY DISTRICTS, WHEN, AND WHERE?

Since the 1950s there have been many court cases in which some aspect of equal educational opportunity across racial groups has been at issue, involving many districts, sometimes challenging statewide practices that affect every school district in a state. This report deals with only those cases where assignment of students across schools was directly at stake. This line is not always easy to draw. A case regarding North Carolina's statewide law prohibiting busing to achieve school desegregation is treated as a segregation case; a case challenging a state's financial support to private schools created in the wake of desegregation is not. We treat districts as having a "mandated desegregation plan" if a case results in a court decision requiring or affirming steps to reduce school segregation, regardless of whether the decision was later reversed. A plan was sometimes reached through an out-of-court settlement between the parties that was later ratified by a court. We found 358 such court cases. In addition, some districts implemented a voluntary desegregation plan (where "voluntary" may have been in response to external pressure and perhaps to a lawsuit). Unless we could identify a specific court decision requiring or affirming the plan, we treat the district as having no plan. We also code districts as having a "mandated desegregation plan" if there was no court case, but the district implemented a plan after having been targeted for compliance by HEW.

The cases we have identified since 1950 that mandated a desegregation plan, plus the HEW administrative actions, involved a total of 1,094 school districts. This represents about one in ten districts in the country. A single school district is party to the majority of cases, but a few cases cast their net much more widely. Some Southern cases mandated desegregation plans for dozens of districts within a state. These include *Alabama NAACP State Conference of Branches* v. *Wallace*, *Coffey* v. *State Educational Finance Commission*, *US and Ridley* v. *State of Georgia*, and *Lebeauf* v. *State Board of Education of Louisiana*.

Table 3.1 summarizes the number of districts in cases resulting in a mandated desegregation plan, categorized by the date of the initial decision. This table demonstrates the very strong focus on Southern states (787 districts) compared to the North (307 districts). Although school segregation has always been a national concern, it was particularly in many Southern states that public policy mandated that white and black student attend different schools. Many early political and legal battles therefore focused on districts in the South. Note that the cases affecting most Southern districts were decided in the period 1963–1970. Only 94 non-Southern districts had been involved in such cases through 1970. But desegregation plans ordered after this time were concentrated outside the South.

Although only 1,094 districts were directly affected by these cases, they represent a very large share of the black elementary school population. In the South, 74.8 percent of black elementary students in 2000 (out of a total 2.6 million) were enrolled in districts that had been mandated to desegregate at some point during the 1950–1994 period. In the remainder of the country the figure is lower but still substantial: 61.9 percent (out of a total two-million black students).

Table 3.1

Cumulative number of districts with mandated desegregation, by year of decision and region

	Total U.S.	South	Non-South
1955	14	10	4
1960	76	71	5
1965	331	311	20
1970	778	682	96
1975	925	752	173
1980	1080	785	295
1985	1082	787	295
1994	1094	787	307

Source: All tables are adapted from Logan and Oakley (2004)

Table 3.2

Average levels of segregation (D) in school districts (black students > 5% in 2000)

	Segregation plan	1968	1990	2000
South	No	72.2	26.5	29.8
	Yes	86.9	47.6	47.3
	All districts	83.8	43.5	43.7
Non-South	No	59.3	36.2	33.1
	Yes	80.0	58.5	62.6
	All districts	76.2	53.8	56.2
Total	No	67.0	30.6	31.1
	Yes	83.9	51.9	53.3
	All districts	80.5	47.6	48.6

Table 3.3

Segregation: overall metropolitan total and average school district in the metropolis (mean by region)

	Overall metropolitan region					Average district
	1968	1990	2000	1968	1990	2000
South	83.4	53.3	56.2	83.0	42.5	43.0
Non-South	81.5	70.7	70.7	74.4	49.3	48.7
Total metro	82.4	61.8	63.3	79.4	45.4	45.5

TRENDS IN SCHOOL SEGREGATION: THE IMPACTS OF DESEGREGATION PLANS

What difference did this legal struggle make to the separation between white and black students? We address this question first by comparing data from 1968 (constituting the "base year," before implementation of a desegregation plan in most cases) with data from 1990 and 2000. The analysis focuses on elementary school students, since elementary schools tend to be smaller than middle schools and high schools, and if a school district is segregated, this is most likely to show up in the elementary grades.

Many school districts especially in rural areas have very few black students and only one elementary school. For this part of the study we select only those districts that meet the following criteria: they had two or more elementary schools in 2000 and at least 5 percent of the student population was black in that year. A total of 1,608 districts meet these criteria, and they enrolled 83 percent of all black elementary students in 2000.

Table 3.2 summarizes the trends over time, contrasting districts in the South and non-South, and districts that ever were subject to a desegregation order with those that were not. The average values in this table, are weighted by the number of black students, in the district in a given year (so that a district with a large black enrollment counts more heavily than one with few black students). Hence these values reflect the "typical" experience of the minority student population over time.

This table reveals both the extent of school segregation nationally prior to 1970, and the trends since that time. We begin with the base year of 1968. In 1968, segregation was very high nationally, at a level that social scientists would consider extreme. By this measure, 80.5 percent of black students would have had to change their enrollment to a school where they were previously under-represented in order to achieve total racial balance. At this time segregation was somewhat higher in the South than elsewhere, although the regional difference was not as large as one might have expected. In some Southern districts there had already been modest progress toward integration by 1968. Segregation was substantially higher in districts that came under desegregation orders at some point in the 1950–1994 period, suggesting that successful litigation was highly targeted.

Then what changes occurred through 1990? By 1990 levels of segregation had declined dramatically to a national average below 50. Segregation at this time was actually lower in the South than elsewhere and by a substantial margin — clearly stronger efforts had been made in the **South** than in the North during the 1970s and 1980s. A key finding is that **even more progress** was made in Southern school districts that had not been party to a desegregation order.

We would have expected some overall improvement at a national level, and perhaps particularly in the South, but the degree of change here is stunning. And most important, change occurred throughout the country, not only in districts that were successfully sued. What explains this counter-intuitive result? A principal factor is that successful legal action was only one of the forces for change in this period. Considerable federal government resources had been marshaled, including close scrutiny of many districts by the Office for Civil Rights in the Department of Health, Education, and Welfare. As the law evolved and it became clear that many state and federal courts would ultimately demand an end to separate school systems for white and black students, potential vulnerability to litigation made a difference in many cases. There were also many school districts whose administrators and elected officials believed that desegregation was a desirable goal for social and educational reasons.

Certainly, however, such change would not have been possible without the remarkable shift in the legal environment created by the *Brown* v. *Board of Education* decision, the willingness of the nation's political leaders to enforce it, and the continuing and persistent efforts by many participants in the legal and political battles that maintained the pressure for new policies. Logan and Oakley (2004) list 25 districts where one would expect desegregation to face great obstacles: these are large districts (more than 10,000 elementary students in 2000) with at least 5% black enrollment. None of these districts was required by a court order or HEW action to implement a desegregation plan. But they achieved very significant changes between 1968 and 1990, and in most cases they have managed to protect their gains. These include districts like Grand Prairie, TX (13.2 percent black in 2000), where segregation declined from 97.7 in 1968 to 20.4 in 2000, and Hayward, CA (16.9 percent black), where segregation declined from 57.5 to 18.9. In an era when legal trends may jeopardize the legacy of *Brown* v. *Board of Education*, these districts are a reminder that much still depends on local decisions.

Nevertheless progress stopped in the 1990s. Nationally there has been a slight upward drift in school segregation, as experienced by the average black student. This was expected as a result of Supreme Court and other decisions in the 1990s that facilitated the dismissal of desegregation orders. But, if dismissal of segregation orders is the source of this upward tilt, the table shows that this phenomenon applies primarily outside the South. On average segregation did not rise in Southern districts that had implemented a desegregation plan.

QUALIFYING THE PROGRESS:
THE FAILURE TO DESEGREGATE ACROSS DISTRICT LINES

The preceding analyses show that much progress has been made in the struggle against segregated schools. Although this movement was brought to a halt in the last decade, there has been no return to the pre-*Brown* status quo. But the assessment of progress needs to be qualified in three major ways, all of which are tied to the failure to reach across school district lines in most desegregation plans.

Preserving Segregation at the Metropolitan Level

The gains achieved by plans that have been implemented within districts, under court order or not, have been undermined by white families' withdrawal from public schools or residential mobility to communities to which minorities have not yet gained full access.

Although some court cases sought interdistrict remedies, especially linking central city school districts with surrounding suburbs, constitutional law has mostly been interpreted to bar such action. The key legal case in this respect was for the Detroit metropolitan region, decided by the U.S. Supreme Court (*Milliken* v. *Bradley 1974*). In this decision, the Supreme Court blocked efforts for interdistrict, city-suburban desegregation remedies as a means to integrate racially isolated city schools. The Court prohibited such remedies unless plaintiffs could demonstrate that the suburbs or the state had taken actions that contributed to segregation in the city. A high bar was set to prove such collusion.

To demonstrate the impact of this constraint, Table 3.3 provides information on the average levels of segregation in metropolitan areas (rural schools are omitted in this part of the analysis, but this part of the analysis includes all districts regardless of black enrollment). Segregation is calculated in two ways. The first is the level of segregation in the metropolitan region as a whole, including separation both **within** and **between** school districts. The second is the level of segregation in the average school district (weighted by the number of black students in each district). This tells us the degree of separation **within** metropolitan school districts (necessarily limited to districts with more than one school).

Much rests on understanding the distinction between these two averages. If all school districts in a metropolis had the same racial composition, then there would be no "between-district" segregation. Metropolitan segregation would be entirely due to separation between children within districts. At the other extreme, if there were no segregation at all within districts, but whites in a given metropolitan region tended to be concentrated in some districts and blacks in others, then there could still be considerable metropolitan segregation, but now entirely due to segregation between districts.

In Table 3.3, the "average district" columns represent segregation within districts. District-level segregation has been averaged for all districts in every metropolitan region, and then the metropolitan averages have been brought together in a South, non-South, and total metro mean. The "overall metropolitan region" columns include this within district segregation as well as segregation between districts (Averages are weighted by the number of black students enrolled in each year).

Table 3.3 shows that in 1968 there was little difference nationally between these two measures — both were close to 80, a level that is similar to what was reported in Table 3.2. Outside the South, though, average district segregation was only 74.4, about seven points below average metropolitan segregation. This means that between-district effects were already visible outside the South. This is to be expected, given regional differences in how school districts are organized. In much of the South school districts encompass an entire county, including a central city and many suburbs. Elsewhere there are typically one or more large central city districts and many suburban districts, often with very unequal racial composition.

By 2000, there had been very sharp reductions in within-district segregation, similar to the 30–40 point drop that was reported in Table 3.2. But metropolitan segregation had declined by less than 20 points, and outside the South the decline was only about 10 points.

Hence, especially in Northern and Western metropolitan regions, the great progress made toward racial balance within school districts was largely undermined by continued imbalance between districts — about two-thirds of the potential gain was not realized for this reason.

An important example is Boston, where the average district had a segregation level of only 35.2 (in large part as a result of a history of desegregation policies in the City of Boston and a few other districts). But the overall metropolitan segregation was 70.2 — almost the same as it had been in 1968. It is ironic that this particular region endured a traumatic struggle over busing within Boston, achieving substantial changes in city schools, but the broader impacts of this effort have been negligible because of what happened beyond the city's borders.

Limited Inter-Racial Contact Despite Desegregation

In many school districts, desegregation was accompanied by a substantial flight of white students to private schools or to other school districts (often in the suburbs) where desegregation's impact would be limited. If desegregation were accompanied by massive white flight, it is possible in theory for "segregation" to decline but for black students to be integrated with relatively few white classmates remaining in their schools.

Some studies focus exclusively on this question: what is the racial composition of schools that students of different races attend, and how has it changed over time? For example, Frankenburg, Lee and Orfield (2003) show declines in the last decade in black exposure to white students, and an increase in the proportion of blacks attending majority-minority schools.

To examine this aspect of the process, we employ different measures of segregation than used above. These are called "exposure indices," and they calculate the proportions of white, black, and other students in the school that the average child attends. Table 3.4 displays the average values of two such indices for white students. These are average values, weighted by the number of white students in each district for a given year. For this analysis, all school districts are included (even those with a single school) if data are available for all three time points.

Nationally whites have experienced steadily growing diversity in their schools over time. In 1968, 85.9 percent of the average white student's classmates were white; this dropped to 79.3 percent in 2000. Much of this change is due to increasing exposure to blacks, which grew from a modest 4.2 percent in 1968 to 9.3 percent thirty years later. These changes at the national level certainly are small, suggesting a very different magnitude of change than we found in within-district segregation scores. To a large extent this result is due to the fact that many white students were already concentrated in school districts, including suburban school districts, that were predominantly white in 1968, and white students shifted toward such districts in subsequent years.

Table 3.4 also allows us to see where change occurred. Overall the greatest shift was in the South, and particularly in Southern school districts that were subject to desegregation plans. The racial composition of the average white student's classmates in those districts changed from 91.4 percent white and 6.1 percent black (in 1968) to 67.8 percent white and 22.7 percent black (in 2000).

Outside of the South change appears **only** in districts with desegregation plans. The racial composition of the average white student's classmates in those non-Southern districts changed from 83.0 percent white and 8.6 percent black in the base year to 59.9 percent white and 18.3 percent black three decades later.

These findings show that the impacts of the *Brown* v. *Board of Education* decision on inter-racial contact in schools were more limited than was the progress toward desegregating individual school districts. And effects were greatest within districts that were subject to legally mandated desegregation.

Table 3.4

Changes in average white students' exposure to white and black students in their elementary school

Region	Segregation plan	White to whites			White to blacks		
		1968	1990	2000	1968	1990	2000
South	No	85.5	82.3	78.8	6.3	10.5	11.0
	Yes	91.4	70.7	67.8	6.1	23.0	22.7
	All districts	88.7	76.9	73.8	6.2	16.3	16.3
Non-South	No	85.1	88.8	85.2	1.9	3.1	3.8
	Yes	83.0	64.9	59.9	8.6	18.7	18.3
	All districts	84.6	85.6	82.2	3.3	5.2	5.5
Total	No	85.2	87.1	83.6	2.8	4.9	5.6
	Yes	87.4	68.7	65.2	7.3	21.5	21.2
	All districts	85.9	82.5	79.3	4.2	9.1	9.3

Table 3.5 reports similar indices from the perspective of black students. Black children now attend schools with a higher share of white classmates than was true thirty years ago. Nationally the percent white in the average black student's school increased from 19.1 percent in 1968 to 33.6 percent in 1990, but then it declined to 29.1 percent.

Our 1968 data source does not provide the percent black in the school attended by the average black student; these cells are left blank in the table. However, knowing the percent white in these schools allows us to infer the percent minority (including blacks, Hispanics, and children of other races). During the last decade and at the national level, there was almost no change in black exposure to black classmates (it increased only from 56.4 percent to 56.8 percent, and indeed there was little change in category of school district). The 4-point drop in exposure to whites, then, resulted from growing exposure to other racial and ethnic groups. The growth of the Hispanic and Asian populations in most regions of the country is becoming an important ingredient in school composition, affecting schools attended by both whites and blacks.

Table 3.5 allows us to determine where black exposure to whites was more likely to increase. First, change occurred mainly in the South, where there is a net 17-point increase over the three decades; the net change in the rest of the country was minimal. Second, whether there was a segregation plan made a small difference in the South; exposure to whites increased more in districts without a plan in the first twenty years, but then also declined more in the next decade.

Do these trends constitute widespread re-segregation of black students, seen in terms of intergroup contact? Here in brief are the findings: 1) whites slowly but steadily are attending schools with a more diverse racial composition, 2) whites' exposure to blacks grew significantly in the 1970–90 period before coming to a halt, 3) blacks' exposure to whites increased substantially during 1970–90 and was still substantially higher in 2000 than it was in 1970, and 4) most of the last decade's reduction in white students' and black students' exposure to whites occurred due to growing Hispanic and Asian populations.

Bringing together all of these elements of the situation leads away from the conclusion that the United States is now resegregating its schools. As we saw with the earlier measure of racial balance, the Index of Dissimilarity, desegregation made the most progress in the 1970–90 period, and has halted or reversed since then. Changes in intergroup contact have been smaller and more specifically focused in the South and in districts with desegregation plans than have changes in within-district racial balance. But on balance the exposure indices show that most of the gains since 1968 were preserved in the last decade of the 20th century.

Table 3.5

Region	Segregation plan	Black to whites			Black to blacks		
		1968	1990	2000	1968	1990	2000
South	No	29.7	55.0	47.8	NA	34.6	32.9
	Yes	10.5	31.2	26.3	NA	63.7	65.7
	All districts	14.9	36.7	31.5	NA	54.6	54.0
Non-South	No	48.4	48.5	44.3	NA	37.0	38.6
	Yes	17.4	20.8	15.6	NA	63.8	65.6
	All districts	24.5	29.4	25.8	NA	57.6	59.0
Total	No	37.7	51.8	45.9	NA	35.8	35.6
	Yes	13.5	27.1	22.1	NA	63.8	65.6
	All districts	19.1	33.6	29.1	NA	56.4	56.8

Changes in average black students' exposure to white and minority students in their elementary school

Metropolitan Segregation and Concentrated Poverty

For many participants in the struggle for desegregated schools, the end goal was not integration for its own sake, but equality in educational opportunity. Indeed current policy discussions now focus almost exclusively on school outcomes. To what degree has "less separate" in public schools translated into "more equal?"

Considerable information on school performance (test scores, identification of failing schools, and other measures) is becoming available. At this time the only national measure is the degree of concentrated poverty in schools that white and black students attend. This is a valid measure because considerable evidence has accumulated to show that high levels of poverty undermine the educational process, creating additional barriers that have to be overcome by teachers and students.

The National Center for Education Statistics collects annual reports on the numbers of students who are eligible for free or reduced-price lunch programs, an indicator of the number of poor or near-poor students in the school. Long-term trends cannot be analyzed because no data are available for 1968 and reporting was still very incomplete in 1990. We analyze data for schools in metropolitan regions (that is, in cities or suburbs) for 2000, including all states except Arizona, Illinois, Tennessee, and Washington, states that did not report lunch program participation. Results are summarized in Table 3.6.

Table 3.6

Poverty rates in the school attended by the average student, 2000

	Poverty rate in average school	Disparity with black students
Black students: national average	64.3%	
White students: national average	29.6%	34.7%
White students: comparing within metropolitan regions	32.5%	31.8%
White students: comparing within school districts	48.8%	15.5%

The average black elementary student in a metropolitan school district attended a school where 64.3 percent of classmates were poor. This contrasts with 29.6 percent in the average white student's school. Such a vast disparity in the class composition of schools seems inconsistent with the reductions in segregation that have been achieved. But it is a natural result of the fact that white and black students are concentrated in different school districts, even if they are now less segregated within districts.

The table provides two other average figures for white students. "Comparing within metropolitan regions" is the white average for a mix of metropolitan areas identical to those where black students are enrolled. Another way to describe it is "white exposure to poverty in the metropolitan area of the average black student." The value is 32.5 percent, almost identical to the national white average. This means that the disparity between whites and blacks is mostly not due to **cross-metropolitan** differences in racial composition.

"Comparing within school districts" provides the white exposure to poverty in the school district of the average black student — much higher at 48.8 percent. This shows that more than half of the disparity between whites and blacks is due to segregation **between districts** in the same metropolitan region. The remaining disparity (64.3 percent vs. 48.8 percent) is due to segregation within districts.

This point can be reinforced by looking at the data for the largest metropolitan regions in the country (more than 30,000 black students in 2000). Table 3.7 (in the "metropolitan averages" columns) shows that in the Detroit metropolitan region the average white student attended a school that was only 21.1 percent poor, compared to 76.2 percent for the average black student, a disparity of more than 55 points. But we can look only at differences within school districts by calculating the white exposure to poverty in the school district attended by the average black student — and it is almost as high as blacks', 74.4 percent. In other words, in Detroit nearly all of the disparity in attending schools with concentrated poverty is due to differences between districts, rather than within them.

Other districts near the top of the list are similar — disparities within districts are all less than ten points in Newark, Milwaukee, Cleveland, Boston, Kansas City, and St. Louis, but disparities across the metropolis are greater than 40 points. These are all areas with a traditional fragmented structure of school administration, with deep divisions between cities and suburbs.

Table 3.7

White and black exposure to poverty in selected metropolitan regions in 2000

	Metropolitan averages			Within district averages		
	White	**Black**	**Disparity**	**White**	**Black**	**Disparity**
Detroit, MI	21.1%	76.2%	55.1%	74.4%	76.2%	1.9%
Newark, NJ	12.4%	69.2%	56.8%	60.5%	68.8%	8.3%
Milwaukee-Waukesha, WI	19.6%	66.9%	47.3%	66.9%	66.9%	0.0%
Cleveland-Lorain-Elyria, OH	25.2%	74.1%	48.9%	68.1%	72.5%	4.5%
Boston, MA-NH	15.6%	61.5%	45.9%	58.8%	61.3%	2.5%
Kansas City, MO-KS	22.3%	64.3%	42.0%	56.6%	64.0%	7.4%
Philadelphia, PA-NJ	17.7%	67.1%	49.4%	51.4%	67.0%	15.5%
St. Louis, MO-IL	26.6%	67.0%	40.4%	57.4%	66.9%	9.5%

At the other end of the table, the Tampa-St. Petersburg-Clearwater metro is made up of just five countywide school districts, and almost all of the disparity between white and black exposure to poverty is within these districts rather than between them. Other metros near the bottom of the list are similar both in the predominance of countywide (or parish) school districts and in the very small role that cross-district segregation plays in assigning black students to high-poverty schools.

The clear conclusion is that the failure to achieve more even racial balance across school districts in much of the country has sharply limited progress toward equal educational opportunity by placing black students disproportionately in high-poverty schools.

What Difference did Brown v. Board of Education *Make?*

Litigation over segregation embroiled many of this country's school districts during the decades since the *Brown* v. *Board of Education* decision. Our results demonstrate that the nation does have something to show for all of this effort.

It is often debated whether court rulings have any real effect on major social divisions. In the *Brown* v. *Board of Education* case, it is not only the Supreme Court decision but also decades of continuing effort by federal and state courts, public officials at every level, and national and local organizations that made the difference. There was real progress in reducing segregation, and it extended to every part of the country and to school districts that were not party to mandated desegregation plans as well as those that were.

There are concerns that the country has begun to experience a sharp reversal of these gains in the years since 1990. The analysis documents that no further progress was made during the 1990s. There is evidence of actual resegregation in some school districts, and in some cases (e.g., Cleveland) this seems to have coincided with dismissal of court-ordered desegregation plans. On average, however, there has been very little change in black-white segregation in this later period.

A shift in the overall racial and ethnic composition of the student population is now adding large numbers of Hispanics and Asians into the schools. In some cases, like Boston, large geographic concentrations of black and Hispanic school children result as shown in Figure 3.1 In the last decade the growth of these new groups has combined with the continuing decline of the white share of enrollment to change patterns of intergroup exposure in public schools. Both whites and blacks are now more likely to be in schools with falling percentages of white students, stable percentages of black students, and growing percentages of Hispanics and Asians. In many parts of the country the issues of segregation and educational opportunity increasingly involve these new groups.

If desegregation has made considerable progress, we must also remember that much is yet to be accomplished. Racial imbalance between whites and blacks has been cut nearly in half, but it remains large. In some of the nation's most important metropolitan centers there has been very little change. Current 2000 segregation levels in a number of school districts are as high as, or even higher than, the national average value thirty years earlier. These include the District of Columbia, Chicago, Newark, Atlanta, New York City, Baltimore, New Orleans, Philadelphia, Detroit, Houston, Los Angeles, Cleveland, and Miami. There are also limitations that were built into the strategy of carrying out desegregation almost entirely within school districts. Especially outside of the South, public officials, lawyers, and others involved in these cases were always reluctant to think about the problems in regional terms. Supreme Court's *Milliken* v. *Bradley* decision for Detroit ratified this approach, making it very difficult to deal effectively with segregation in the North and West.

We have shown that segregation across schools in the metropolis overall has remained much higher than segregation in the average school district. Consequently dramatic improvements in racial imbalance within the average school district have had only modest impacts on intergroup contact. As long as blacks do not gain equal access to the full range of communities in the metropolis, desegregation within districts can have only a limited impact on contact between white and black students.

In addition, black students attend schools with more than double the poverty rate of the schools that white students attend. We have shown that disparities across school districts within the same metropolitan region account for about half of this difference. Even if desegregation within districts had run its full course, black students would still be educated in very different and more difficult school settings than white children.

The public discourse on education is in a post-*Brown* phase. In the 1950s segregation was understood as a key element in the problem of unequal educational opportunity for black and white children. Today segregation is treated as a lesson of history, and current policy options disregard the persistence of racial imbalance within and between school districts. This report shows that much progress has been made, but that the approach to desegregation in the aftermath of the *Brown* v. *Board of Education* decision inherently limited its impact. Future efforts to "leave no child behind" will have to address the strong connection between continued segregation at the metropolitan level, limited intergroup contact in children's formative years, and extreme racial disparities in concentrated poverty among children's classmates.

Figure 3.1

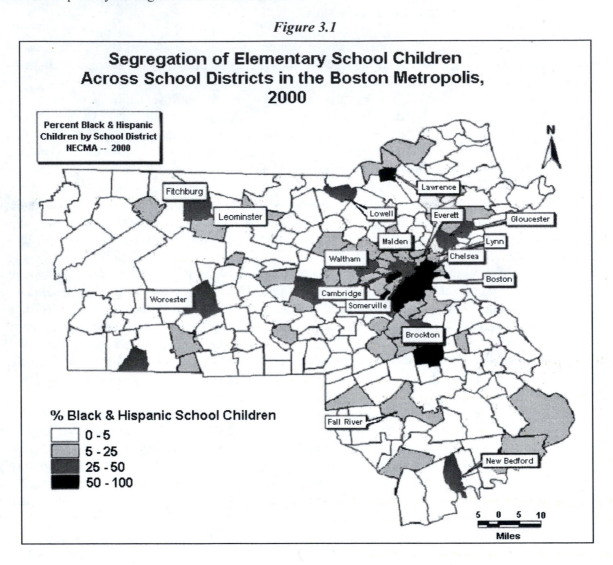

NOTES

[1] This research was supported by a grant from the American Education Research Association which receives funds for its "AERA Grants Program" from the National Science Foundation and the U.S. Department of Education under NSF Grant #REC-9980573. Opinions reflect those of the authors and do not necessarily reflect those of the granting agencies. The authors thank Dr. Franklin Wilson, University of Wisconsin at Madison, for providing the school segregation data for 1968–1970 on which part of this analysis relies.

[2] Readers unfamiliar with the calculation of the index of dissimilarity should see note 2 in Chapter 13.

Chapter 4

The New Metropolitan Geography of Immigration:
Washington, D.C. in Context

AUDREY SINGER

The front door of the Long Branch public library in suburban Montgomery County in Washington, D.C. welcomes visitors in 11 languages. This is not a symbolic gesture meant to embrace multiculturalism, but a reflection of the clientele served by this branch library. Inside, library visitors can find print, audio, and visual materials in major world languages and a language lab to sharpen their English language skills. A telephone interpretation service is offered in 140 languages.

As the nation's capital, Washington, D.C. has long been an international city. However, it has only recently joined the ranks of major metropolitan immigrant destinations. In 1970, only 4.5 percent of greater Washington's population was born outside the United States. By 2000 one-in-six persons or 17 percent of metropolitan Washington's population was foreign-born.[1] While the entire metropolitan area population, 1970–2000, grew by 54 percent, the immigrant population has quintupled during the same period. Greater metropolitan Washington now ranks as the 7th largest metropolitan concentration in the U.S. Region wide, 21 percent of the region's population communicates in non-English languages at home.

Washington fits into a class of metropolitan areas that have recently emerged as new immigrant gateways. Places like New York and Chicago have long held an attraction for immigrants throughout the 20th century, and large metropolitan areas such as Los Angeles and Houston rapidly gained foreign-born residents after World War II. However, in the 1980s and 1990s, settlement patterns began to shift away from more traditional settlement areas to many places with little history of immigration. Washington along with places like Atlanta and Las Vegas have in the last decades of the 20th century, become significant destinations due to burgeoning job markets, particularly in the construction, services, and technology sectors.

Although in absolute numbers the majority of immigrants are still going to the established destinations, rates of growth of the foreign-born have been fastest in the newest destination areas. The changing metropolitan geography of immigrant settlement is transforming many new cities into emerging gateways as well as continuing to change the character of more established ones.

This chapter describes this new geography of immigration, and highlights how immigrant destinations in the 1980s and 1990s differ from earlier settlement patterns. Drawing on a growing body of research on immigration to Washington, D.C., trends are examined in detail to illustrate an immigrant gateway that has recently emerged as a major destination.

TWENTIETH CENTURY IMMIGRATION AND SETTLEMENT TRENDS

During the last century, immigration to the United States has ebbed and flowed (see Figure 4.1 which shows both the number of immigrants and the share of the population that is foreign born by decade). The foreign-born population increased between 1900 and 1930, from 10.3 million to 14.2 million; however, as a percentage of the population, the foreign-born peaked in 1910 at 14.7 percent, dropping to 11.6 percent of the total population.

During the depression in the 1930s, the worldwide movement of people was curtailed and immigration to the United States stalled. Immigration levels were low during the period between WWII and the late 1960s due to restrictive immigration laws that resulted in a diminishing of the number of immigrants, 11.6 million in 1940 to 9.6 million in 1970. At the same time, lower levels of immigration coincided with the "baby boom" when fertility rates were high, producing lower proportions of the total population that were born outside the U.S. This percentage dropped to a low of 4.7 percent nationally in 1970. By 1980, the immigrant share of the population began to climb as the less restrictive immigration laws enacted in 1965 brought fresh waves of immigrants numbering 4.5 million during the 1970s. This policy change, together with the mobility fostered by economic growth in many developing nations, brought about an immigration boom of unprecedented proportions in the 1980s and 1990s. By 2000, the foreign-born population numbered 31.1 million or more than 11 percent of the population.

Figure 4.1

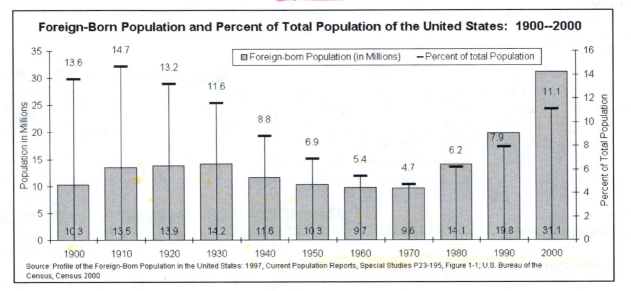

Foreign-Born Population and Percent of Total Population of the United States: 1900--2000

Source: Profile of the Foreign-Born Population in the United States: 1997, Current Population Reports, Special Studies P23-195, Figure 1-1; U.S. Bureau of the Census, Census 2000

In addition to the swings in immigrant entries, the origins of immigrants have changed considerably during the course of the 20th century. Today most immigrants come from Latin America, the Caribbean, and Asia, but for most of the 20th century, they came largely from Europe. For example, during the first two decades of the century, 85 percent of the 14.5 million immigrant newcomers arrived from Europe, the majority from Southern and Eastern European countries. However, the last two decades saw the same percentage arriving from non-European countries.

For American cities that developed during the 19th and early 20th century, immigration was the primary driver of population growth. In addition to domestic workers arriving from rural areas, many Northeastern and Midwestern cities attracted workers from abroad to fill the burgeoning industrial job market.

The beginning and the end of the 20th century share a similar story regarding changes to the national economy. Both were periods of great industrial transformation. In the earlier period, the shift was from an agricultural to an industrial economy. At the end of the century, America's economy moved away from an industrial base to services and information technology. Similarly, the demand for workers in high-growth sectors during both periods of economic restructuring was met in part by immigrants.

As cities began to decentralize after WWII due to the development of highways and the suburban construction boom in housing, cities began to lose population, especially those in the industrial core in the East. By the 1970s, those places were overshadowed by economic and population growth in the West and the Southwest. While some of the older Eastern and Midwestern cities have maintained their status as immigrant gateway cities through the century, others have more recently become destinations.

In research on the changing trends in immigrant destinations, I have analyzed the changing destinations of urban immigrant settlement during the 20th century. I identified six major types of U.S. immigrant gateways among 45 large metropolitan areas (see Singer, 2004). *Former gateways*, are places such as Buffalo and Pittsburgh, which once attracted immigrants in the early 1900s but no longer do. *Continuous gateways*, such as New York and Chicago, are long-established destinations for immigrants and continue to receive large numbers of the foreign-born. *Post-World War II gateways* like Los Angeles, Miami, and Houston began attracting immigrants in large numbers only within the past 50 years. Places with very fast immigrant growth in the past 20 years alone, such as Washington, D.C., Atlanta, and Dallas stand out as *emerging gateways*. Other areas such as Minneapolis and Seattle, began the 20th century with a strong attraction for immigrants, waned as destinations during the middle of the century, but are now *re-emerging gateways*. Finally, there are places with the newest fast-growing immigrant populations as of the 1990s, such as Raleigh-Durham and Austin that may continue to grow as destinations. They are designated *pre-emerging gateways*.

These 45 metropolitan areas house nearly three-quarters of the entire foreign-born population in the United States and had an average growth of their foreign-born populations of 55.4 percent between 1990 and 2000. Eight metropolitan areas are in the *former gateways*, 9 in the *continuous gateways*, 7 in the *post-WWII gateways*, 7 in the *emerging gateways*, 9 in the *re-emerging gateways*, and 5 in the *pre-emerging gateways* (see Table 4.1 for a list of all 45 metropolitan areas used and their gateway designations and Singer, 2004 for how the gateways were defined). I will refer to this classification in the remainder of this chapter.

Immigrants have largely been urban settlers in the United States. In 2000, 94 percent lived in metropolitan areas (Census, 2000). Calculations by the Louis Mumford Center for Comparative Urban and Regional Research show that 48 percent lived in central cities, while the remaining 52 percent resided in the suburbs. This distribution reflects a slight tipping toward suburban residence from the previous census when immigrant residence was almost exactly evenly split between central cities and suburbs.

This trend marks a new development. The classic European immigrant assimilation model formulated by the Chicago School and mentioned in a previous chapter, suggested that immigrants settled close to the factories, shops, and institutions that employed them, often clustered in ethnic neighborhoods (e.g., Park and Burgess, 1921). Immigrants (and more often perhaps their offspring), as they established themselves economically, were able to improve their living conditions by moving to the more spacious suburbs with more desirable housing. This city-to-suburb movement was a historical move that was made millions of times over and certainly not limited to the foreign-born.

This earlier description has been further elaborated by social scientists who have found empirical support for the "spatial assimilation" of immigrants (see Massey, 1985; Alba et al., 1999a and 1999b). However, more recent research on the suburban residential patterns among immigrants shows that contemporary settlement is different. Alba and colleagues, using data from the 1990s census, found that immigrants were already a growing presence in the suburbs, that suburbanization was more related to education and income than to English language speaking ability, and that immigrant suburbanization reflected idiosyncratic metropolitan growth patterns. Furthermore, newer waves of immigrants were not necessarily clustering by ethnic groups as they often did in the past (Alba et al., 1999b).

Therefore, several distinctive patterns of immigrant settlement have emerged in metropolitan areas, some of it due to the differential development history of areas. For example, and most notably, although the city-to-suburbs movement among the foreign-born has been prevalent in the historical immigration gateways, the same patterns are not observed in places that began receiving immigrants only recently. The central cities of *continuous* and *former* gateways, (as well as some of the *re-emerging gateways*) developed their central cities during an era that was before the preeminence of the automobile. Metropolitan areas such as Baltimore, New York, and San Francisco developed dense urban cores earlier in comparison to the more sprawling nature of many of the *post-WWII* and *emerging gateways*. Houston, Los Angeles and Washington, D.C., by contrast, are dominated by highways and suburban density. Thus, immigration to the newer destination metropolitan areas took place entirely in the era of population and job decentralization and suburbanization. Consequently, many immigrants, particularly in the new destination areas are moving directly to suburban areas, without touching down first in the central city.

Table 4.1

Six Immigrant Gateway Types, Metropolitan Areas, 2000

FORMER	CONTINUOUS	POST-WWII	EMERGING	RE-EMERGING	PRE-EMERGING
Baltimore	Bergen-Passaic	Fort Lauderdale	Atlanta	Denver	Austin
Buffalo	Boston	Houston	Dallas	Minneapolis-St. Paul	Charlotte
Cleveland	Chicago	Los Angeles	Fort Worth	Oakland	Greensboro-Winston-Salem
Detroit	Jersey City	Miami	Las Vegas	Phoenix	Raleigh-Durham
Milwaukee	Middlesex-Somerset-Hunterdon	Orange County	Orlando	Portland, OR	Salt Lake City
Philadelphia	Nassau-Suffolk	Riverside-San Bernardino	Washington, DC	Sacramento	
Pittsburgh	New York	San Diego	West Palm Beach	San Jose	
St. Louis	Newark			Seattle	
	San Francisco			Tampa	

Table 4.2

Top Thirty Countries or Regions of Birth, Washington Metropolitan Area, 2000

		Number	Percent of Foreign Born
1	El Salvador	104,960	12.6
2	Korea	45,835	5.5
3	India	45,610	5.5
4	Vietnam	37,223	4.5
5	Mexico	32,391	3.9
6	China (including Hong Kong)	32,035	3.9
7	Philippines	31,701	3.8
8	Peru	20,304	2.4
9	Guatemala	20,015	2.4
10	Bolivia	19,558	2.4
11	United Kingdom	18,915	2.3
12	Jamaica	18,310	2.2
13	Iran	17,389	2.1
14	Germany	17,295	2.1
15	Pakistan	16,908	2.0
16	Ethiopia	15,049	1.8
17	Honduras	13,727	1.6
18	Nigeria	13,670	1.6
19	Canada	11,950	1.4
20	Other Eastern Africa	11,442	1.4
21	Ghana	11,043	1.3
22	Other Western Africa	10,336	1.2
23	Taiwan	10,116	1.2
24	Colombia	9,910	1.2
25	Trinidad and Tobago	9,648	1.2
26	Nicaragua	8,404	1.0
27	Japan	8,223	1.0
28	Russia	8,036	1.0
29	Other Northern Africa	7,880	0.9
30	Dominican Republic	7,858	0.9
	Total Foreign Born	832,016	76.4

Source: US Census Bureau, 2000

WASHINGTON, D.C.: A NEW KIND OF IMMIGRANT GATEWAY

Metropolitan Washington is the best example of this new era of immigrant settlement. The region has a strong and stable economy, due in large part to the presence of the federal government and associated institutions. With a mixed economy tending toward the highly skilled as well as the lack of a manufacturing base, Washington attracts immigrants with heterogeneous backgrounds. Due to various headquarters of international organizations and embassies, there has been a noticeable presence of foreign-born residents in the region for most of the second half of the 20th century. However, Washington's international character has changed considerably in recent decades, in part due to global transformations that have altered economies and politics abroad and induced mass movements of people across national borders. In short, Washington has absorbed many people from around the world who have been unsettled by international strife or attracted by the abundant opportunities in the U.S.

Washington's increasing internationalization, which began largely with professionals and students, has continued to grow through several different processes. In particular, there has been a continuation of a professional class of international residents, including students seeking higher education. In the past three decades, large waves of refugees have been resettled in the region, particularly from Southeast Asia and Africa. Many social networks are firmly in place that entice immigrants to join family members and friends already living in the Washington region.

The total population of Washington, D.C. grew by 51 percent between 1980 and 2000. It is currently the fifth largest metropolitan area in the U.S. Like many southern cities, the region's population growth excludes a rich history of immigration, but relatively recently this has changed. Unlike many immigrant destination areas with long established streams of arriving immigrants, Washington's immigrant population has grown markedly only recently. During the same twenty-year period, the foreign-born in greater Washington increased by 228 percent.

One of the most important characteristics of the small historical presence of immigrants in Washington is that residential ethnic enclaves, in the traditional sense, do not exist. In the central cities of many of the *continuous gateways*, there are longstanding immigrant and ethnic neighborhoods such as the Lower East Side in New York, Chinatown in San Francisco, and Pilsen/Little Village in Chicago, which have housed, employed, and otherwise incorporated immigrants for most of the entire 20th century. Although the immigrant groups may have changed over time, these places have served the same function: they provide a port of entry for immigrant newcomers where they can associate with others who have common origins and a common language, and where commercial establishments and stores cater to the group. Immigrant enclaves serve to anchor and establish immigrant groups, economically and residentially. However, they also have their limitations and while they are places where immigrants often land, they also become places from which to launch.

In more established immigrant gateways, these neighborhoods have primarily existed in central cities. Washington did have some early immigrant residential enclaves such as Swampoodle, a neighborhood presently located near the U.S. Capitol and Union Station. This area first housed Irish workers in the 1800s followed by Italian immigrants in the 1900s. However, few traces are left of these ethnic neighborhoods as the work that brought the immigrants there in the first place eventually diminished and people moved on. These early settlements in Washington tended to be temporary especially due to the fact that workers located there to be close to the job, but housing conditions were poor, overcrowding was a problem, and crime was high (Cary, 1996). Ironically, it was the temporary housing that facilitated the settlement of workers; but people found other more desirable places to live as their circumstances allowed. And in the case of Swampoodle, when projects like the U.S. Capitol finished, immigrants moved on to the next opportunity, whether it was in Washington or elsewhere (Singer and Brown, 2000; Cary, 1996).

The lack of long-standing immigrant neighborhoods has a direct bearing on the contemporary settlement patterns of immigrant newcomers. As we will see, many neighborhoods, particularly in suburban areas, have foreign-born populations of very mixed national origins. As a result, there are many implications at the local level regarding the integration of immigrants and for policies related to their incorporation.

JURISDICTIONAL DISPERSION OF THE FOREIGN-BORN IN METROPOLITAN WASHINGTON, D.C.

More than half a million immigrants settled in the Washington metropolitan area between 1980 and 2000, representing an increase of 228 percent. In 2000, 17 percent of the metropolitan population was foreign-born. Washington's foreign-born population does not yet approach the scale of the three largest metropolitan immigrant destinations, indeed Los Angeles, New York and Chicago house one-quarter of the nation's immigrant population. Nonetheless, the increase in its immigrant population represents nearly half of all population growth in greater Washington, with consequences for many local jurisdictions. And, the size of its foreign-born population is on par with Houston and Orange County, CA and considerably larger than the Riverside-San Bernardino, San Diego and Dallas metropolitan areas.

The Washington metropolitan region is large (includes 25 separate jurisdictions) and politically complex because it includes counties in two states, Maryland and Virginia, as well as the capital city of Washington, D.C.[2] The region's growth and change in the distribution of immigrant residence is shown in the following figures. Figure 4.2 shows that the foreign-born population has shifted from being highly concentrated in the inner core jurisdictions of the District of Columbia (26%), Arlington County (9%) and Alexandria (4%) in 1970s, to a more regionally dispersed population by 2000. Whereas the inner core areas housed nearly 40 percent of the foreign-born in 1970, by 2000 only 19 percent of all immigrants resided in these same areas. However, in absolute terms, the numbers rose. During this same period, the proportion of the region's immigrants residing in the inner suburbs (the three largest inner counties of Fairfax, VA, Montgomery, MD and Prince George's, MD) increased from 59 percent to 71 percent.

Gains were also evident in the outer suburbs, where immigrants comprised 9 percent of the total metropolitan area's foreign-born population, up from 2 percent in 1970. The far suburbs also just began to register immigrant residents in 2000. Bear in mind that although some of the jurisdictions decreased in their share of the region's immigrants, they all increased in absolute terms.

The two spatial trends can also be seen by comparing Figures 4.3 and 4.4, which display the share of the total population of the region that is foreign born in 1990 and 2000. In 1990, immigrants were relatively residentially concentrated in the inner core of D.C., Alexandria, and Arlington County as well as the inner suburbs of Fairfax, Montgomery, and Prince George's counties, particularly in the areas inside the Capital Beltway. The remainder of the region's residents was primarily native-born.

By 2000, immigrant residents were even more densely concentrated in the inner areas, and over the same period, they also fanned out further in the region, taking up notable residence in the next ring of suburbs, including Prince William and Loudoun counties. Maryland suburbs of Langley Park, Silver Spring, Wheaton, and Virginia suburbs of Bailey's Crossroads, Seven Corners, and Annandale have some of the highest shares of their population that are foreign-born. These trends notwithstanding, it is important to note that the residential patterns shown in these maps also reflect the general population trends of outward growth in the 1990s.

NATIONAL ORIGINS AND TRENDS IN NEIGHBORHOOD SETTLEMENT

One of the most prominent characteristics of Washington's immigrant population is the wide variety of national origins from which the foreign born come. In an earlier study using INS admissions data, legal permanent immigrants in the 1990s were identified as coming from 193 countries (Singer, Friedman, Cheung, and Price, 2001). Table 4.2 reveals that the entire foreign-born stock is composed of immigrants from all corners of the world, and that the 30 largest country groups comprise three-quarters of the immigrant population. Five of the groups on this list represent contemporary refugee-sending countries or regions (Vietnam, Iran, Ethiopia, other Eastern Africa, and Russia).[3] By and large, these particular five groups are comprised of refugees mixed with other foreign-born from those source countries. They are distinguished by these origins, which may have implications for their incorporation into the U.S.

Figure 4.2 a

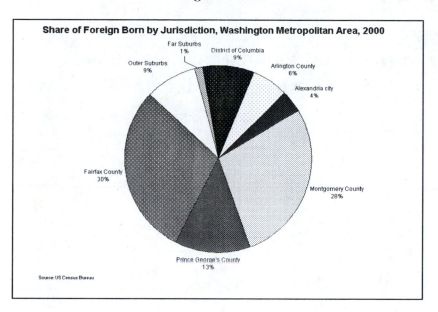

Figure 4.2 b

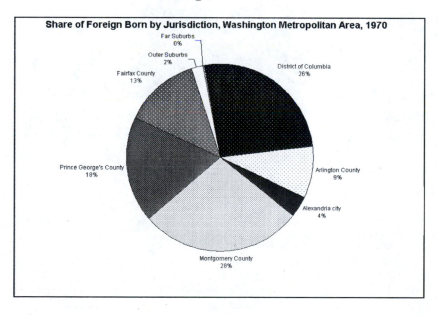

Figure 4.3

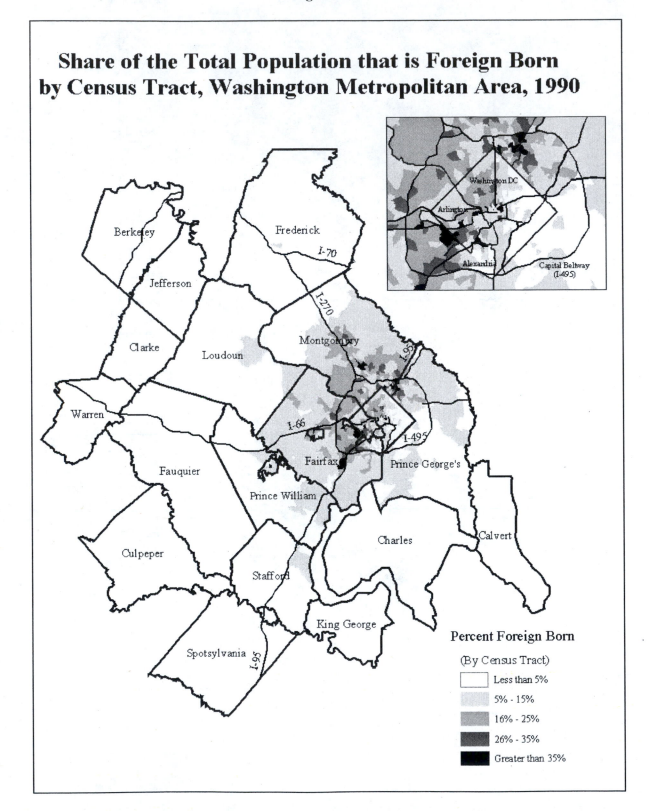

Share of the Total Population that is Foreign Born by Census Tract, Washington Metropolitan Area, 1990

Figure 4.4

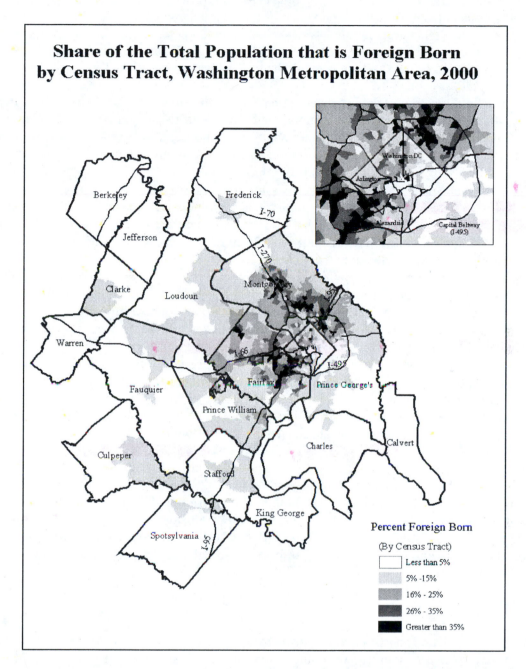

Share of the Total Population that is Foreign Born by Census Tract, Washington Metropolitan Area, 2000

Percent Foreign Born
(By Census Tract)
- Less than 5%
- 5% -15%
- 16% - 25%
- 26% - 35%
- Greater than 35%

The largest of Washington's origin groups is from El Salvador, with more than 100,000 residents, but even as the largest group, they are only 12.6 percent of the total. Nationally, Washington's Salvadoran population is second in size only to Los Angeles', which had twice the number of Washington's population.

Salvadorans are an important feature of the immigrant portrait not just for their size, but for their reasons for coming to Washington and for the legal status that many hold. A civil war beginning in the early 1980s drove thousands of Salvadorans out of their home country, many reuniting with an already established community in the Washington, D.C. area (Repak, 1996). When a series of natural disasters hit El Salvador including several devastating earthquakes in 2001, migrants naturally flocked to the region. Many Salvadoran residents are permitted to stay in the U.S. under *temporary protected status* (TPS), visas that allow them to live and work in the U.S. but will likely require them to return to their home country if conditions improve.

The next three largest immigrant origin groups are from different parts of Asia: Korea and India have nearly identically sized populations, with approximately 46,000 immigrants each, or 5.5 percent of the total. Following these groups are Vietnamese immigrants who come in at 4.5 percent. Immigrants of Mexican origin are ranked fifth, and are one of the newest groups to arrive in the region. The next five groups — China, Philippines, Peru, Guatemala and Bolivia — together with the first five groups mentioned, comprise nearly one-half of the region's immigrants.

Another defining feature of the immigrant population is the large number of immigrants from the African continent. More than 11 percent of Washington metropolitan area's immigrants are African, as compared with less than 3 percent of the national foreign-born population. The region's 93,000 Africans are second only to New York City, however, New York's African immigrants are less prominent at only 3 percent of the metropolitan area's total (see Wilson, 2003 and Chacko, 2003).

Price, et al. (2005) observed three types of residential patterns among the major immigrant groups in Washington. "Highly dispersed" groups such as immigrants from India, Mexico and the United Kingdom; "dispersed with areas of concentration" such as the Salvadorans, Koreans, and Ethiopians; and "concentrated" such as the Vietnamese, Somalian and Bolivian populations. They found that although there are areas where immigrants tend to cluster, such areas are seldom the exclusive territory of a particular group.

Singer (2003) also found at the neighborhood level there are few places that are predominantly foreign-born, and furthermore, even those that have a high share of the population that are immigrants, rarely are they a majority from the same origin country. However there are many places where from 20 percent to 35 percent of the residents are immigrants. Two inner suburbs stand out as areas with a majority immigrant population. Langley Park in Prince George's County and Seven Corners in Fairfax County are both nearly two-thirds foreign-born. The distributions by national origin, however, are widely different. In terms of the largest source countries, Langley Park is dominated by Salvadorans, coming in at 39 percent of the foreign-born and 31 percent of all immigrants originating from Guatemala, Mexico and Honduras, providing a very definitive Latin American bent. Seven Corners is more mixed, but Salvadoran immigrants also predominate (30%). However, the next largest group are Vietnamese (16%) followed by Guatemala (7%), Bolivia (6%), and India (3%).

Other suburban areas are even more diverse. For example, Silver Spring in Montgomery County had the largest number of immigrant residents of all the suburban neighborhoods, with 35.2 percent foreign-born. Although Salvadorans were again the largest country group (22%), the four next-largest groups were from a diverse set of origins: Ethiopia (6%), Vietnam (5%), other West Africans (4%) and Guatemalans (4%). The five largest groups totaled only 41 percent of Silver Spring's entire foreign-born population. Fairfax's Annandale was 35 percent foreign-born and the distribution is different altogether. Vietnam and Korea both contributed about 15 percent of the foreign-born, followed by Bolivia and El Salvador (8% each), and India (4%).

CONCLUSION

Long-held assumptions about immigrant settlement based on a 19th- and 20th-century European model of immigration may no longer hold true regarding the latest wave of immigration to the U.S. The growth and development of metropolitan areas in the second half of the 20th century have yielded metropolitan areas with greater suburban form than in the past, even at their core. This development, in turn, has produced greater suburban settlement of urban immigrant newcomers. In emerging gateways such as Washington, D.C., many newcomers are bypassing the cities and moving directly to suburban areas.

The growth and change of the immigrant population in the Washington metropolitan area has been substantial in the past 30 years. In part, both national and international transformations have produced a greater movement of people abroad as well as changed the economy and character of the local region. Washington appears to have emerged as one of the newest large metropolitan immigrant gateways.

Several distinctive attributes of the region appear to have an impact on the residential choices made by the foreign-born in the Washington metropolitan area. The first is that the immigration to the region has been recent, fast, and diverse in its origins. The second is that immigrants have taken up residence primarily in the inner suburban areas, with more limited but fast growth also occurring outside the inner ring. Third, there are some areas that are becoming immigrant-dense, but they are generally not ethnically uniform and tend to be quite mixed in terms of national origins.

One implication of these overall patterns is that arguably, immigrants are finding their way into the labor market and contributing to the local economy. They are part of both ends of the hourglass economy, with high-skilled workers in area hospitals, high-technology firms, and international agencies as well as lower-skilled workers in the abundant construction, service, and hospitality sectors.

It is also clear from their dispersion around the region that many immigrant newcomers may not be able to rely on established immigrant enclaves, because there are few. Part of the dispersion observed may be due to the fact that most foreign-born newcomers are making residential choices based on the housing market, access to transportation, school choices, and family and social ties, just as the native born largely do.

Therefore most local jurisdictions and school districts are dealing with the challenges brought on by such rapid and heterogeneous change. New residents have widely varying educational backgrounds, experiences and skills. For those with limited English language proficiency, policymakers continue to be challenged in both serving this population and in raising proficiency levels. For the large groups in the region who arrive as refugees or are living with *temporary protected status*, gaining English proficiency may be a hurdle. Even their U.S.-born children may be disadvantaged despite their education in U.S. schools; indeed currently about 15 percent of metropolitan Washington's limited English proficient population was born in the U.S. (Singer and Wilson, 2004).

It appears from recent trends that immigration to the national capital region will continue, and the need for programs and policies to assist in their economic, social, and political incorporation will continue to put demands on area institutions and local governments.

NOTES

[1] Data from the Census Bureau used in this chapter refer to the *foreign-born* population, however, the terms *immigrant* and *foreign-born* are used interchangeably. The *foreign-born* population encompasses all persons born outside the United States, including legal permanent residents, temporary immigrants, refugees, asylum seekers, and to the extent to which they are counted, undocumented immigrants.

[2] The Washington, D.C. metropolitan area used for this study is the 1999 census-defined Primary Metropolitan Statistical Area (PMSA): the District of Columbia; the "inner core" (Arlington County and Alexandria city); the "inner suburbs" (Fairfax County, VA and Montgomery and Prince George's Counties, MD); the "outer suburbs" (Calvert, Charles, Frederick Counties, MD and Loudoun, Prince William, Stafford Counties, VA); and the "far suburbs" (Clark, Culpeper, Fauquier, King George, Spotsylvania, Warren Counties, VA and Berkeley and Jefferson Counties, WV).

[3] The Census (at the summary level) only produces tabulations for six African countries, therefore most are aggregated regionally. Among the largest African refugee groups in the region are two that are not identified individually: Somalia and Liberia. Somalians comprise a large share of the "other East African" group.

Chapter 5

U.S. Immigration and Racialized Assimilation

Wei Li

- *Scene1: San Francisco International Airport: March 1, 1988 — the first day the author landed in the U.S. as a junior exchange scholar from Peking University, China.*
  Airport employee: **"Miss, your English is so good; where did you learn it?"**
  Author (felt flattered): **"No, not at all. My English is not good. I learned it in China."**
- *Scene 2: San Francisco International Airport: March 11, 2005 — 17 years later and the author is an Associate Professor at ASU.*
  Airport solicitor: **"Miss, may I ask you a question? Do you understand English at all?"**
  Author (felt offended): **"I do not appreciate the way you asked me this question. Why don't you speak to me in English first then see if I understand or not? Don't assume any Asian-looking person does not understand English."**

When these experiences are related to my undergraduate classes, a typical response from them is: "Wow, you are SO Americanized in the way you answered the question in 2005!" While I certainly agree with this assessment, the above two scenes also prompted me to think beyond the experiences themselves. Yes, I have become Americanized in some ways, but in what specific ways? My answers to the questions about my English, 17 years apart, indeed revealed part of my "acculturation" process; I have become more assertive and outspoken. But at a broader and deeper level, I realize that the second question was asked in a manner that results from a misguided perception of many Americans of minority cultures living in America. They are often viewed as "outsiders," foreigners who can neither understand nor speak English. Many Asians, despite being native-born Americans, or living in America for a considerable period as U.S. citizens, face the same questions that I did because they are still ill-perceived by some white Americans due to their non-European features. My airport experience may not seem like a serious offense to some but I believe it is indicative of a serious American problem, one of creating racial categories based on perceived differences from the white American mainstream. Many Americans simply make categorical judgments about people who are different culturally or by appearance. The results range from insulting and insensitive remarks like the one I experienced, to ethnic/racial slurs, or worse, overt discriminatory behaviors. The use of "FOB" ("fresh off the boats") is an example of a racial slur, a derogatory term, used to describe new immigrants. This type of slur is hurtful and unwarranted. It also ignores the fact that immigrants are contributing to America and many have worked diligently to learn English.

Perpetual negative white images of non-whites and stereotyping result not only from recent immigration trends that have brought millions of new immigrants from Asia and Latin America, but from the racism that has deep roots in American history and has shaped important parts of its geography. This also results in a full range of mistreatments of non-whites in the workplace, public areas like airports, and other places in American society. The persistence of these racial classifications and white attitudes influence the ability of immigrants to be accepted fully into American society. This chapter briefly focuses on social science theories that have attempted to explain the absorption, or assimilation, of ethnic groups into American society. It begins with a brief discussion of the classical acculturation/assimilation theory of the Chicago School, including its spatial components. More recent work is discussed, including the ethnic pluralism and multicultural approaches, as the basis for challenging the use of traditional explanations of the immigrant experience in contemporary analyses of immigrant settlement patterns. This has become increasingly important given the growing number of non-white cultures in the U.S. and the projections for non-whites in America in the coming decades.

Some recent research has argued that immigrants assimilate in multiple ways that are best characterized as forms of "segmented assimilation." In this chapter, I extend this argument to explain more specifically how racial constructs are instrumental in the ways immigrants assimilate or remain separate from the dominant American white culture. This "racialized assimilation" results in various racial/ethnic geographies. Historical examples demonstrate that the use of racial categorization resulted in a number of geographic patterns that are racial geography. Contemporary examples of racial categorization and their impacts also are provided and help explain the variety of suburban ethnic forms in America. The chapter closes with a discussion of some relevant issues for racial/ethnic research in geography.

THEORIES OF U.S. IMMIGRANT SETTLEMENT AND ASSIMILATION

Assimilation, Acculturation and the Chicago School

During and after the mass European immigration to the U.S. in the 19th and 20th centuries, the prevailing public and academic views of Anglo-American culture emphasized acculturation and assimilation of newcomers. Immigrants, often poor, uneducated, and sometimes lacking English-language ability, climbed the socioeconomic ladder with the passage of time and merged into American society. Developed by "Chicago School" in the early 20th century, this "straight line" *assimilation/acculturation* model suggested that ethnic immigrant groups gradually become acculturated by yielding their distinctive ethnic identity in favor of that of the host culture (*acculturation*). Attitudinal and behavioral changes, shifts in cultural referents, community association, and intermarriage dissolve any value and power conflict between immigrant ethnic origins and that of the host (Park, 1950; Gordon, 1964). *Assimilation*, or the absorption of a minority ethnic group into the majority culture, occurs with time and acquiescence. Among the important aspects of acculturation/assimilation theory is the idea of **spatial assimilation** (Aldrich, 1975; Ward, 1971). Inner-city ethnic ghettos and enclaves are ports of entry for temporarily poor ethnic immigrant groups, whose advancement hinges on their ability to be absorbed socioeconomically and spatially into host societies. Remaining in the inner city's poorer geographies is the spatial antithesis of merging with the host culture. It carries the disadvantage of being isolated from the more successful mainstream. Immigrants and their descendants eventually realize economic success and merge into the American middle or working-class mainstreams, launched from their temporary inner city geography to better neighborhoods farther away. Thus, according to this model, socioeconomic success is coupled with geographic space and spatial mobility, which ultimately leads to a place in the middle-class suburbs. A vast body of academic studies, including those by geographers, measures spatial assimilation as evidence of successful immigrant integration into the American host society, or suggests that spatial separation hampers such processes (Kearns, 1977; Peach, 1980; Raitz, 1979; Roseman, 1971).

More Recent Theoretical Formulations of Immigrant Experiences:
Segmented Assimilation and the Geography of Immigrant Settlement

A number of observations led to the reconsideration of this traditional straight-line assimilation theory during the last quarter century. Both the academic world and the public media in the United States reconsidered their premises due to international independence movements, the U.S. Civil Rights era, and massive U.S. immigration since 1965. Alternatives have been offered that challenge the adequacy of the European-based explanation of ethnic groups "melting" into a single harmonious culture of "Americans."

Alternative frameworks include pluralism and multiculturalism, which have common features. Pluralism has emphasized the persistence of ethnicity, rather than a tendency toward acculturation. It also recognized the value of ethnic and racial diversity to American society and stressed the need to differentiate the experiences of specific ethnic groups. This rethinking of ethnic assimilation in favor of maintaining diversity is important when considering the recent dramatic changes in American immigration sources. Geography has paid attention to these changing racial/ethnic streams and what they mean for settlement patterns and cultural landscapes. The work of Clark and his colleagues, for example, illustrated that America's diverse ethnic groups have a broad set of experiences, a clear sense of identity based upon a shared tradition (including a language), a sense of racial or biological descent, and a shared territory. More recently, texts have appeared to support coursework in ethnic and racial geography (McKee, editor 2000; Frazier and Margai, editors, 2003). As noted in chapter one of this text, both pluralism and multiculturalism emphasize ethnic diversity and retention of ethnic traits by immigrant groups. Multiculturalism goes further, not only emphasizing the differences in cultural experiences in the U.S., but by highlighting the roles of social and economic institutions that shaped and maintain racial and ethnic geographies. It also seeks exposure and redress for the social ills created by institutional actions (such as the internment of Japanese Americans during WWII). Thus, newer theoretical approaches to inter-ethnic and inter-racial relations have moved away from the traditional European-based model of acculturation/assimilation by raising questions about race, gender, ethnicity, sexual orientation, and other issues. They also recognize that multiple spatial forms are emerging due to a variety of circumstances related to race and ethnicity, including those dealing with dimensions of a concept termed **"segmented assimilation"** (Portes, 1995; Portes and Borocz, 1988; Portes and Zhou, 1993), which identifies multidirectional patterns of assimilation due to the fragmented and unequal segments of American society. This concept recognizes the existence of the time-honored acculturation and assimilation of some immigrants into middle-class America as one of a number of possible paths immigrants pursue. However, two others recognize the theoretical importance of structural factors in placing limitations on some immigrant groups and the strength of ethnicity and ethnic ingenuity in shaping new forms of partial assimilation, while preserving cultural identity. Zhou characterizes the two other types as:

> "… the downward-mobility pattern, in the opposite direction (to "straight-line"), dictates the acculturation and parallel integration into the underclass; and economic integration into middle-class America, with lagged acculturation and deliberate preservation of the immigrant community's values and solidarity" (Zhou, 1997, p. 894).

Recognition of these patterns represents the newer pluralism and multiculturalism approaches by emphasizing the economic polarization of American society and the entrapment of some groups in particular places due to their class and race.

While this conceptualization of segmented assimilation of immigrants is new, the reality of segmented assimilation based upon race and highly segregated settlements is not new to African Americans. The historical and contemporary experiences of African Americans in these contexts follow in the next section of this text. The persistence of racism and its social constructs coupled with the increasing ethnic diversity in the U.S., have resulted in a range of black geographic patterns across America. For example, traditional African-American ethnic geographies are found within racialized spaces of American suburbia. Other recent cultural landscapes have emerged due to the recent immigration of other black ethnics. Examples of contemporary economic integration by non-white and white immigrants into middle-class America without yielding racial/ethnic identity also exist. Settlement forms vary considerably among these diverse groups, from ethnic enclave to ethnoburb and from ghetto to other emerging spatial forms. Examples are provided throughout this text. In each of these cases immigrants from diverse cultural backgrounds create landscapes of their own within localized contexts, which sometimes are racially charged and other times are embracing of newcomers. Understanding the increasingly diverse American society, its racial contexts and its resulting geographies, is important to establishing a constructive dialogue about America's future. The next section examines the significance of the persistence of race in America, especially as a social construct.

RACIALIZATION OF THE AMERICAN IMMIGRANT: A HISTORICAL PERSPECTIVE

Recent research has emphasized the long-term, historical importance of race and ethnicity in shaping American views. The persistence of racism and ethnocentrism are not uniquely American. Despite America's image as the global leader of freedom and democracy, these unfortunate traits have persisted for centuries. The Irish, Jews, Italians and eastern European immigrants, along with blacks, Latino and Asian ethnics, provided necessary hard and dirty labor in building the agricultural and industrial sectors of American industry for little compensation, yet experienced prejudice and discrimination within the Anglo-American political economy. For example, the Irish were instrumental in building the Erie and Chicago Canals that completed the link between the Mississippi River and the Great Lakes. Asians and Latinos worked on western railroads and in agricultural production and food processing in the western states. Each was scorned by the white majority. Despite this, however, many white ethnics, like the Irish, were able to assimilate into middle-class America over time, and leave their ethnic neighborhoods behind.

European immigrant experiences provided the rationale to support the traditional acculturation/assimilation model (Ignatiev, 1995; Roediger, 1991). However, this model conveniently ignored the importance role of race in non-assimilation, despite substantial evidence to the contrary (Frazier, 1932). The use of race as a social construct dates practically to the beginning of the republic, if not before. The use of whiteness and the distinction of "race" in America begins as early as 1790, when the "Nationalization Law" declared that only "white persons" were eligible for citizenship. Following this law, a continuous process of redefining race, especially who should be excluded from the "free white" category, emerged. Mexicans, for example, after the U.S. takeover of California, were considered "semi-civilized" and, although eligible for citizenship, were never treated as the equal of whites when employment, housing and service provision were considered. Similar constructs contributed to the exemption of American Indians, African Americans, and Asians from citizenship; such groups may have been valued for their cheap labor for a period but were considered "heathens" and personal property, and unacceptable as white equals (Almaguer, 1994; Barrera, 1979; Saxton, 1995).

White Americans have used race not only to differentiate groups by color or some other physical feature, they have used it as an evaluative mechanism to categorize non-white groups for political and economic reasons. As such, a racialization process imposes social structure for the purpose of shaping and maintaining power relationships in society. Omi and Winant introduced the term *racialization* to specify the extension of racial meaning to a previously racially unclassified relationship, social practice, or group (emphasis added); they underscored the notion that "racialization is an ideological process, a historically specific one" (1986, p. 64; also see Omi and Winant, 1994). Hence, race is not just a way to differentiate people, but a means to deliberately classify groups for the purpose of shaping power relationships and social practices.

One of the clearest examples of racialization of a non-white group in North America was provided by K. Anderson, who illustrated how native Canadians and European immigrants constructed "Chineseness," an image of negative characteristics created by various means, and linked it to a negative perception of place, "Chinatown" (Anderson, 1987, 1988, and 1991). The purpose of this deliberate process was control and elimination of the Chinese from an Anglo community. This was accomplished through discriminatory institutional practices that regulated Chinese place and justified illegal treatment of Chinese people and their businesses. This is but one research example that reveals the role of racial dynamics in constructing a negative image of groups by using "whiteness" to define their negative attributes (Bonnett, 1997; Hoelscher, 2003). Of course, such social constructions of the Chinese and other Asian immigrants led to their exclusion or extremely limited their numbers in the United States until 1965, first by the 1882 Chinese Exclusion Act and later by other methods until 1965.

Some international geopolitical events also yield a modified perception or changing fate of a particular group. The fate of racial minority groups often varied during critical moments in U.S. history. The experience of the oldest Asian immigrant group in the U.S., Chinese Americans, illustrates how American racial dynamics and international geopolitical-triggered events altered their fate in the U.S. Initially welcomed as an indispensable labor force in building California in the mid- to late-nineteenth century, the Chinese also were the first group to prompt a federal anti-immigration legislation and turned the U.S. into an immigrant "gate-keeping" country

(Lee, 2003) because of their race. Their fate did not change again until WWII, when China became a U.S. war ally against Japan, at the same time Japanese Americans were interned and lost their rights, despite being long-term American citizens. After WWII, however, due to the communist take over of mainland China, Chinese Americans again faced scrutiny and mistrust as they were often suspected of supporting Communist China. Such suspicions and treatment resulted in anxiety and frustrations among this group (Zhao, 2002). During the Civil Rights Movement, Chinese Americans were labeled as a "model minority" by mainstream media. This suggested that their culture was worth emulating by other minority racial groups. To this day, however, the perceptions of Chinese Americans vary from a "model minority" group of academic overachievers, to mistrusted suspects targeted for hatred and racial backlash. Because of these continuing racially-based incidents, Chinese Americans, both first- and later-generations, have become increasingly aware of their racial "place" in the American society (Wu, 2003), one that is subservient to the white majority.

RACIALIZATION IN CONTEMPORARY AMERICA

Results from empirical studies strongly support the resiliency of racism in contemporary America. Research also indicates that the experiences of "dark-colored" immigrants and their offspring often resemble those of African Americans. However, racism and racialization are not limited to black ethnics from Africa and Caribbean, nor is it a matter of simply being reduced to skin color and other features. Olsen (2001) has argued that the contemporary Americanization process generally includes the racialization of immigrants. Latinos and Asians routinely face American racism and are subject to the same processes long faced by African Americans and contemporary black immigrants. Hirschman (2001), for example, investigated immigrant children school enrollment and found that those of Hispanic-Caribbean and Mexican (1.5 generation) origins often lagged behind the achievement levels of native-born Americans. Despite the influx of numerous Asian ethnics since the liberalization of U.S. immigration laws, the racialization and concomitant discrimination against Asian American groups has not disappeared. A few contemporary examples make the case.

A successful California developer, originally from Hong Kong but now residing in the San Francisco Bay Area, thought little about his "Chinese American" identity during his long U.S. career. He had been involved in many "mainstream" economic development projects, such as golf courses and hotels. In the mid-1990s, however, he renovated and redeveloped a rundown mall into an upscale "Asian-theme mall" in City of Cupertino, Ca. He initially thought of this as just another typical business deal that made good financial sense. That was until the negative attention and publicity surrounded the project. Specifically, the developer was heavily criticized because of the perception that the mall was to serve Asian customers. Whites were very troubled by the rumor that the mall's signage would appear in Chinese language only, rather than in English. This charge was untrue. The developer had requested all his tenants to use English-language signs. The city manager later confirmed this statement. The public scrutiny and criticism of "catering to a Chinese-only audience, while living in America" (in the absence of accurate information) made this immigrant developer keenly aware that he is a Chinese American developer, who because of his "race," is subject to a different kind of scrutiny and criticism than are his white peer developers (author interviews, 2000, B6 and C13).

Another case involved the 1999 Wen Ho Lee case.[1] Mr. Lee was accused of being a spy for China without sufficient evidence and prior to a thorough investigation. For many first-generation Chinese and Taiwanese American scientists and entrepreneurs living in the Silicon Valley area, this was an awakening to the realization that their integrity was open to racial interpretation and that they too could become easy targets with unwarranted accusations of espionage. As a result, the Chinese became the most vocal group in seeking justice for Wen Ho Lee. The Wen Ho Lee case had an impact on first-generation Chinese immigrants similar to that of the 1982 Vincent Chin murder case, which affected native-born Asian Americans. They, too, realized they could easily become victims of racial hate crimes. Vincent Chin, a native-born Chinese American, was murdered by two laid-off white autoworkers because he was misidentified as being Japanese. This occured during the peak of anti-Japanese sentiment due to the influx of Japanese cars to the American market (author observation; Ling-chi

Wang, personal communication). These brief examples illustrate that race matters in contemporary America and suggest that racialized assimilation of immigrants is a concept worthy of special attention for complementing the theory of segmented assimilation.

RACIALIZED ASSIMILATION AND SEGMENTED ASSIMILATION: A THEORETICAL PERSPECTIVE

Although segmented assimilation theory considers class, "color," racial status, and "places more emphasis on the effect of continuing racial discrimination," (Zhou, 1997, p. 989) the three options for assimilation, as presented earlier in this chapter, do not explicitly address the issue of racial impacts on first-generation immigrants. It would be extremely helpful to our understanding of assimilation processes endured by various immigrant groups to overtly consider what might be termed "racialized assimilation." By this concept I am suggesting the explicit study of identity transformation and assimilation trajectory of first-generation adult immigrants in response to a racial dimension not previously explicitly explored. The contention is that first-generation adult immigrants, despite a lengthy U.S. residency, may not experience an identity transformation to the mainstream non-Hispanic, white "American," as prescribed in the classical straight-line assimilation theory. This may be explained in some cases by the rejection of first-generation immigrant groups by members of the "white American mainstream." This approach complements segmented assimilation theory by suggesting that the racial dynamics created by the American racial reality play crucial roles in the way first-generation immigrants have responded to American society and its dominant culture. First-generation adult immigrants may become "racialized Americans." By being subjected to this process, some first-generation immigrants make an effort to protect their group identity and lack the desire to interact with mainstream America, while others have a different experience. Therefore, the assimilation trajectory taken by any group is contextual and may differ from that of other groups.

Factors Influencing Racialization and Assimilation

INTERNATIONAL EVENTS

International events can have tremendous impacts on the host culture's perception and treatment of a minority subculture. This may lead to a sense of nativism on the part of the host and influence its tendency to racialize a minority. Such treatment, of course, negates a minority group's ability and interests to integrate with the host culture. In the most dramatic cases, racialization results in geographic separation of immigrant ethnics on the basis of their race. Among the most dramatic historical examples is the American treatment of Japanese Americans after 1941. During the early 20th century, Japanese Americans tried very hard to fit into the American culture, especially after the exclusion and treatment of the Chinese. Despite continuous discrimination by the white majority, Japanese Americans worked hard and became successful financially. Even after Japanese immigration was restricted, the Japanese living in America attempted to assimilate to the best of their ability. The 1941 attack on Pearl Harbor and Executive Order 9066, however, dramatically changed the lives of American Japanese. Citizenship and loyalty were not considered as some 120,000 Japanese Americans were collected and sent to internment camps on barren and remote lands away from the Pacific Coast. Their properties were seized, their jobs were lost, and their family lives were left in shambles. Many were American-born, second-generation. Nativity and citizenship, however, did not matter. Their race/ethnicity and residential location did. More than five billion dollars in property and other forms of wealth were taken from Japanese Americans. Their release came in 1946 and, after more than forty years, those who survived were eligible to receive $20,000 from the U.S. government as redress.

It would be easy to assign generational fear and ignorance as the only motives for such behaviors. However, a somewhat similar fate, since September 11, 2001, has befallen Arab Americans and Muslims (even their look-alikes, especially Sikh Americans), who have faced increasing hostility, anger and frustrations in the workplace, neighborhoods and other public settings, and have been subjected to profiling and other forms of discrimination. Being a law-abiding citizen who speaks English and holds a professional job (or owns a business) is not always sufficient to avoid racial classification in the U.S. even today. Fear and ignorance surely prevail and are heightened by some media and governmental reports. However, a deep historical racial prejudice also must be credited with American actions against non-white groups (Frazier, Margai and Tettey-Fio, 2003). Negative racial experiences have and continue to bind immigrant ethnic groups together, despite their many ethnic differences (Clemetson, 2004). In some cases, it also has influenced their settlement geography.

ECONOMIC GLOBALIZATION AND TRANSNATIONAL CONNECTIONS

American racial and immigration dynamics increasingly have become more complicated by economic globalization and transnational migration patterns in recent decades. Global economic competition makes major immigrant receiving countries in the world more selective in their shifting immigration policies with biases in favor of the highly-skilled immigrants and investors, while at the same time accommodating low-skilled and poor immigrants, both legal and undocumented, to meet domestic labor needs. As a result, new immigrant streams contribute to the existing domestic bifurcation of socioeconomic differences created by economic restructuring and changing U.S. demographics. They also complicate the potential paths taken to assimilate into American society. Also, global flows of goods, information, technology, people, and capital have resulted in greater awareness of international events and their impacts on America and places of immigrant origin. Today, some immigrants still come to the U.S. with racial naiveté, but increasingly others have become aware prior to arrival that many Americans harbor negative racial images. These immigrants adjust their perceptions of the U.S. accordingly. Some of this awareness is based on feedback from other immigrants and reports from the international media.

There are other complicating factors shaping racial relations in the United States. Transnational elites and other transmigrants contribute to the complexity of assimilation in America. Their economic and sociocultural activities occur across national borders, making them indispensable parts of international trade and important contributors to the American economy and society. Rather than be molded by American culture, however, some of these influential ethnics often retain their ethnic identity and actually may be contributing to a slow cultural transformation of America. In short, because of the global economy in which all nations must participate, more and more Americans are being exposed to other cultures and their strengths. As a result, many immigrants are not forced to integrate into a unilateral assimilation process. In some cases, power derived from economic position and international awareness result in such immigrants having control over the parts of American culture they wish to absorb and how much ethnicity they will retain. Not all immigrants, of course, enjoy this choice. But, for those who do, alternative paths to assimilation are open. Their perceptions of American racial dynamics and other factors likely will influence their decision and their settlement geography. As we have seen in the case of the Asian developer and my personal experience, socioeconomic status does not exempt one from exposure to American racialization on the basis of class status.

RACIALIZED ASSIMILATION AND SEGMENTED ASSIMILATION: SOME ISSUES TO BE EXAMINED

Racial awareness and negative experiences serve as a reality check for many first-generation immigrants. Also, over time many immigrants learn more about the racial history of America. Some acknowledge that they will never be truly equal to native-born citizens, and retreat within themselves or their families and locate in ethnic communities. Others capitalize on the economic globalization trends by seeking opportunities overseas, including their countries of origin. Yet others, who have lived in the U.S. for a long time and have become more politically active through alignment with American "people of color" (racial minority groups), have joined the pursuit for equal opportunities and rights for all Americans.

The concept of "racialized assimilation" argues that the immigrant assimilation process is very complex and cannot be fully considered in the absence of American racial dynamics because white Americans routinely classify other people on the basis of white privilege. The process yields various outcomes for people of different ethnic backgrounds, regardless of their class status or other individual characteristics. In fact, longer U.S. residency provides more exposure to American race relations and results in increased awareness of racial dynamics among first-generation adult immigrants. Recent scholarly work indicates that contemporary immigration has prompted changing American racial dynamics beyond the traditional black-white dichotomy that characterized previous decades of American history. Immigration has resulted in a recasting of racial identity politics, especially in immigrant gateway cities (Clark and Blue, 2004; Wu, 2003). The resulting outcomes of racialized assimilation may be summarized as follows:

- Upon exposure to American racial dynamics, some first-generation ethnic identities may change due to a transformation into a racialized minority;
- Culturally disadvantaged immigrants — linguistically isolated and relying on ethnic network for survival and information exchange — are likely to tune into homeland politics more than American politics, despite increasing racial awareness;
- Economically disadvantaged immigrants are more likely to participate in community grassroots politics by seeking workers' and immigrants' rights, rather than participating in electoral politics, especially beyond voting;
- Middle- or upper-class professional immigrants are likely the most vocal groups to seek political clout and be involved in both grassroots and electoral politics as candidates, campaigners, and/or financiers, as they have the time, financial and other resources to do so;
- Among different locales, those immigrants who live and work in large metropolitan areas with pre-existing or newly-emerged ethnic neighborhoods and networks are likely to be aware of American racial dynamics, active and organized in seeking racial, economic and civic/political equality for minority groups.
- The experiences of immigrants who live and work in a dispersed pattern in urban and rural areas likely vary along class-lines as described above. The better one's economic position, the more likely she will be civically and/or politically involved. Economically disadvantaged immigrants are likely in a much more isolated situation.
- The racialization experience results in a number of reactions by immigrants. It may lead to confrontation and protest. It also may influence immigrants' self-perception and identity, individually and collectively, which may influence how they interact with the host society. Specifically, whether or not an immigrant group is exposed to the racialization process may well dictate their social responses and settlement decisions related to the host culture. For example, in the absence of racialization, a first-generation ethnic might simply be absorbed, or assimilated more quickly than one with the opposite experience. On the other hand, immigrants who are met with negative racial stereotyping and mistreatment, may seek to withdraw from the host society entirely, while still enjoying some of the benefits of being located in an advanced economy. In some cases, this may explain the differences in the settlement geography of a recently arriving immigrant populations. This is not to suggest that racialization alone encourages geographic separation, or clustering of a particular group. However, it does suggest that one cause of ethnic solidarity involving geographic concentration may involve segmented racialization.

Among the above observations, the geographic dimension involves the intertwining dynamics of race and place within the changing contexts of globalization and transnationalism. Geographers are in a good position to examine how race and place matter in the immigrant assimilation process, including where racialization is involved. Geography has emphasized the examination of the influence of local factors on settlement and urban geography, such as in the investigation of immigrant settlement patterns and economic integration (Li, 1998; Skop and Li, 2003; Zhou, 1998). For instance, Newbold (2004) found that the Chinese assimilation process across three U.S. metropolitan areas, over two decades varied significantly over space and persisted over time. More work needs to be done at multiple geographic scales and should be comparative in nature: (inter-) national, regional, metropolitan area, municipality, neighborhood, household, and individual scales must be explored in terms of immigrant assimilation patterns and American racial dynamics. Not all assimilation of first-generation immigrants results from American racial dynamics but where it is a significant influence, it must be exposed.

CONCLUSION

Ellis and Wright (1998) denounced the use of "balkanization" to describe immigrant-induced ethnic fragmentation and its implied metaphor of immigration-driven dangers for U.S. society. In this chapter, I have addressed the continuing importance of race in assimilation within American society by providing contemporary examples and revisiting some historical lessons. Our understanding of immigrant integration in a changing American society is incomplete without explicit recognition of the role of race on the well being of minorities, including first-generation immigrants. The racialized assimilation concept recognizes the role of the changing dynamics of globalization and transnationalism and the historical context of American racism that has regularly applied race as a social construct for the benefit of Anglo-America. This concept complements "segmented assimilation" theory by crystallizing the overarching roles of race in assimilation, especially in terms of options that create human geography in contemporary America. Much more work remains for adequate empirical testing of this concept.

NOTE

[1] For both Wen Ho Lee case and Vincent Chin murder, please see Wu, 2003.

Part II

U.S. African American, African, and Caribbean Geographies

This section continues the overarching themes of the text, including racial discrimination against minorities, the perseverance displayed by minorities, movement, ethnic diversity, and how racial and ethnic geographies are created. It illustrates how African Americans and more recent black migrants, including first-generation immigrants, have carved their respective niches in order to have a community and a support system. Black cultural landscapes are illustrated for African Americans and more recently arriving ethnic groups. Another overriding theme of this section is the attachment people form to place, and how humans and their environments affect one another in a cyclical way. These chapters also deal with the politics of movement, and explain why and how migration patterns occur. Finally, this section illustrates the critical importance of American social, political, and economic institutions to the creation of human geography.

Section Two opens with the broad perspective in chapter 6 of the obstacles, progress, and current status of African Americans in the United States. It also illustrates the growing black ethnic diversification in the U.S. Chapter 7 provides more detailed information about waves of African American migration and settlement patterns, including blacks' treatment by white Americans as they sought life in the suburbs and better status, surroundings, and opportunities. It also explores the contemporary "reverse migration" to the South by African Americans from all other regions and illustrates the importance of scale and place in understanding black migrant streams.

The next three chapters deal with spatial inequities. Chapter 8 follows the thread of living conditions and the geography of settlement to describe what African Americans are now facing in the less affluent communities where many of them live, and uses two case studies to illustrate predatory lending techniques and their effects on the geography of settlement. Chapter 9 examines predatory lending from a less social and more legal perspective, discussing the possibilities of anti-predatory legislation. This chapter also examines a real difference in policy and law, weighing the political climate, the severity of the situation, and the racial makeup of local politicians and population, to give the reader a clear understanding of how predatory lending works, and how society can be changed to protect people against it. Chapter 10 deals with the injustices or inequities of location by illustrating that it takes Blacks longer to get to work than Whites.

Chapter 11 shifts the focus to black immigrants and their ethnic settlement patterns. It describes in positive terms the ethnic enclave of Little Ethiopia, describing how a group of immigrants has created an "ethnic enclave" in Los Angeles that helps them to preserve their customs and way of life, and to share a support system with people of their own ethnic background. The chapter examines the pros and cons of this situation.

Chapter 12 focuses on a different kind of black ethnic community, the "new" Liberian refugees who have come to America, and how they are integrating both with Americans and the Liberians who came over in an earlier immigration wave. The chapter focuses on how place unifies them — they are able to share food, customs, and language — as well as how their proximity to one another and to other African Americans also highlights minor cultural divides — differences in some foods, languages (Gullah), or customs.

Finally, chapter 13 looks at the geographic distribution and corresponding socioeconomic status (SES) of West Indians living in the U.S. It charts their distribution across the country, compares their respective SES by state/region, and then compares SES statistics between the regions listed and other groups in the U.S., including the white majority.

Thus, this section begins with the general to establish context, then follows specific threads to provide insights into what is happening with race relations and racial and ethnic settlement patterns in the United States, and to explain broader historical and sociocultural understandings based upon previous events and policies.

Chapter 6

Black American Geographies:
A Perspective

EUGENE L. TETTEY-FIO

INTRODUCTION

Until recently, blacks constituted the largest minority population in America. The U.S. Census 2000 reported about 34 million blacks and approximately 35 million Latinos. Even though Latinos have surpassed blacks as the largest minority group, the token minority status of blacks remains in social focus. This is partly the result of the better assimilation of other minority groups and the persistence of Dubois' "color line" in the United States.

Highly segregated, inner city black American neighborhoods have become symptomatic of all the negative perceptions of life in the U.S. Pervasive poverty, persistent low-income jobs, infrastructure deficiency, and above average crime rates are a few of the characteristics of neighborhoods that many blacks inhabit. Black spatial clusters are often islands of social isolation and physical and "moral" decay. These clusters were formed in response to historical, social, economic and political processes. Since 1970, however, improvements in black class status and a rapid increase in black suburbanization have contributed to changes in U.S. black geographies.

This chapter examines the processes that have controlled and channeled black settlements in America from a historical perspective, as well as in terms of more recent trends and geographic patterns emerging on urban and regional bases. Despite white resistance, African Americans have persisted in the search for opportunities to create better living conditions in new places. That struggle has become part of African-American self-identity and ethnicity. As will be shown in future chapters, this and other ethnic characteristics have resulted in African-American cultural landscapes within the boundaries of racial geography created by white power.

The history of U.S. black settlements has involved black migrations in response to changes in the American political economy and the motivation of black people to improve their unequal living conditions with white Americans. This chapter briefly examines the geographic distributions of blacks in specific time periods of American history and explains the processes that underlie those distributions. Particular attention is paid to the migrations and the roles of institutions in creating particular black geographies. In addition to examining the creation of the national black ghetto system associated with the Great Migration and white institutional responses to the growing number of new black migrants to northern cities, the change in black socioeconomic status and increased black suburbanization are discussed. The chapter closes with a brief discussion of two important black trends at the end of the 20th century: increasing reverse migration and black ethnic diversity.

HISTORY OF BLACK SETTLEMENT AND MOVEMENT

Africans were among the first non-indigenous permanent settlers of what is now the U.S. They were among the settlers who came to America, 1607–1700. They came initially as indentured servants and as refugees from Spanish colonies. However, the need for hard physical labor to work in subtropical and tropical conditions resulted in slavery. Virginia's slave code of 1705 ushered blacks into slavery in colonial America. Soon after, Maryland, the Carolinas, Georgia, the Middle colonies and New England replicated Virginia's code. The first African slaves shipped across the Atlantic Ocean arrived in North America in the early 17th century. By 1650 there were 1,600 blacks in America, about three percent of the estimated population of the colonies. Over all, an estimated 10 million slaves were brought to the Americas (Farley and Allen, 1987).

Forced black migration to America resulted in 757,208 (19.2 percent) people of African descent by 1776 of which 697,624 (92.1 percent) were slaves. The population of free blacks had reached 25,000 by 1776 and 60,000 by 1790. In 1787 the U.S. Constitution was adopted and the Free African Society was founded, a precursor to the first independent black church, the African Methodist Episcopal Church. In 1790, natural increase accounted more for black population growth than importation and the percentage of foreign-born blacks was small by the end of the 18th century.

The invention of the cotton gin in 1793 dashed any hope for black emancipation because it dramatically increased the demand for slaves. Prior to the gin, one-half of the labor required to make cotton ready for market was in separation of the hull and seed (the other half was in planting and harvesting). The gin dramatically reduced the labor required after harvest and freed additional slaves for planting and harvesting. At the same time, cotton had become the fabric of choice in the U.S. and in England. The increased demand required many more slaves for production and harvesting than the existing population could supply. The result was a rapid growth in the slave trade and in the number of black slaves in the U.S. In short, the Southern economy became dependent on cotton production and the growing American economy needed cotton products and the cotton trade, a crucial synergy that inextricably linked slavery to the Southern and national economies. Regional patterns of black distribution had been established by 1900 but would undergo fundamental changes in the decades to follow.

Pre-1910 Distribution of Blacks

Before the beginning of the 19th century, most blacks resided in the Chesapeake Bay area. Virginia and Maryland were the primary black concentrations and the Carolinas were secondary centers. Between 1790 and 1860, the number of blacks increased dramatically from about 700,000 to four million (Rose, 2000). This demographic development was associated with the establishment of the cotton plantation economy of the South. Plantation agriculture was the major determinant of the distribution of blacks until the beginning of the 20th century. The increasing demand for black labor in the expanding cotton-growing economies of the South initiated regional and interregional distributions of the black population from the Upper South to the Lower South. Black migration at this time was from east to west. Alabama, Mississippi, Louisiana and Texas, all primary cotton-producing areas, received major increases of black labor. At the onset of the Civil War a black cultural hearth had formed with clear boundaries overlapping the states of the Confederacy. The black cultural hearth included all counties with at least 33 percent black in 1910 and included states from Texas to North Carolina (Hart, 1960; Lewis, 1969). At that time, Mississippi and Georgia each had more than a million blacks. Most of other southern states from Virginia to Texas had over one-half million blacks (Rose, 2000). It is within this spatial and social context of restricted movement and bondage in the American South that Africans of diverse ethnic backgrounds became integrated, or "Americanized" into a single cultural unit.

Blacks in bondage had little control over their movements in America. Their settlement was confined to places designated by plantation owners. Demands for forced labor dictated where and how blacks could reside. The Civil War over states rights and slavery began in 1861. During the war, Lincoln's 1863 Emancipation Proclamation freed all slaves. However, Post-Civil War emancipation of blacks did little to alter their settlement patterns and interregional movement was absent, except for minor movements to Kansas and some northeastern states. A more remarkable trend is the movement of blacks to small towns and cities in the South at the incipient stages of southern urbanization process. By 1910, one-fifth of the southern region's blacks resided in urban areas and most still resided in the rural South. In spite of additional freedom, most blacks continued working in the agricultural sector. Before 1910, black settlement geography was relatively fixed, concentrated in the South and a few urban neighborhoods in Boston, New York City and Philadelphia, which Dubois characterized as areas of poor and overcrowded housing that were rented to African Americans at higher prices than that of similar quality housing rented to whites (Dubois, 1901).

Post-1910 Distributions

By the beginning of the 20th century, one generation of free blacks had occurred. Freedom, however, did not come with full protection under the law. Oppressive measures were instituted in the South to perpetuate white supremacy, while retaining black labor for the agricultural tenancy system. Economic options and social choice for blacks were extremely limited and, in some places, non-existent. Jim Crow laws, which legally separated blacks from whites from birth (separate hospital accommodation) to death ("white only" cemeteries), also excluded them from economic, social and housing opportunities. In spite of the continued practice of a slave culture, blacks shaped a new subculture in the core areas of black concentration in the South.

In the second generation after the Civil War, blacks started moving from the South to other regions in the country. The Great Migration, massive movements northward and westward between 1910 and 1970, resulted in the largest internal migration in American history. Movements northward between 1910 and 1920 were directed to particular northern cities, such as Chicago (Rose, 2000). This migration occurred at a time when war in Europe had stemmed European immigration to America. However, the more massive movements of blacks northward were driven by the 1920s quota system and labor shortages associated with the two world wars. Positive information from blacks and labor agencies in the North coupled with dismal economic and social conditions in the South, served as pull factors for their interregional migration to the northern industrial belt. The states with the highest out-migration flows were Alabama, Virginia, Georgia, North Carolina and Mississippi. These early movements were directed to a few urban centers in the Middle Atlantic and East North Central census divisions. With these movements, major redistribution of the black population was underway.

At the start of this migration, one-third of the South's blacks were concentrated in densely settled rural counties in Georgia, Mississippi, Alabama and South Carolina. These concentrations contained one hundred counties with 50 percent or more black residents in 1910 (Hart, 1960). These areas were located in a belt of continuous good cotton and tobacco growing soils. From these origins, over one-half million blacks departed to the northern states, 1910–1920. These movements became the vehicles for the diffusion of black culture from its southern core. There was also a concurrent rural to urban movement in the South. Even larger migration streams would follow.

BLACK GHETTO FORMATION AND DEVELOPMENT

Earlier Black Concentrations and Black Ghetto Development, 1910–1920

Tremendous commercial and industrial growth and associated rapid urbanization led to rural-to-urban movement of blacks from the South and produced pre-ghetto communities. Poverty and the absence of economic opportunity in the South also caused these regional movements. In 1910, few southern cities had less than 25 percent black population. Fifteen major black concentrations existed by this time. Most southern cities that grew at this time were port cities. Birmingham, Alabama was one of the few non-port cities that also underwent urban and economic growth. New Orleans and Baltimore were the most populous black urban centers in the region in 1910. Their numbers exceeded those for New York and Philadelphia.

The growth of southern cities provided a spatial context for examination of the southern black settlement system. According to Rose, the absence of Eastern European type clusters and the physical characteristics of southern black urban concentrations help explain the delay in the application of the ghetto in the South (Rose, 1971). However, he considered the lack of an appropriate social construct for defining these settlements to be the key reason for the absence of "ghetto" terminology there. Kellogg's work also explained that the location of black communities in the post-bellum South did not fit the locational and physical characteristics of the quintessential Eastern European ghetto of the North (Kellogg, 1977). The northern central city ghetto was the first place of residence for many immigrants serving as a transient rather than permanent zone of residence. However, for black migrants this same zone became a permanent ghetto, a racial geography produced by prejudice and discrimination.

In the South, black enclaves contained black-controlled institutions and black culture flourished. In addition to the largest cities, black urban villages of ten thousand or more people existed in places such as Little Rock, Augusta, Macon, Lexington, Charlotte, Columbia, Chattanooga and Portsmouth. In the North, on the other hand, black centers emerged only after black migration streams to particular cities, mostly in the Midwest. To better understand the national settlement pattern, Rose utilized a 25,000 black threshold to identify "ghetto centers," which applied to Chicago, Cincinnati, Pittsburgh and St. Louis during the first generation of the national ghetto system, 1910–1920 (Rose, 1971). In addition to these ghetto centers, seven southern and Atlantic seaboard cities also met the criterion.

The Great Migration and Second Generation of Black Ghettos, 1920–1950

During World War I and the Great Depression that followed, America experienced limited immigration but tremendous black interregional migration from the South to northern urban centers. Migrants moved to northern and western cities seeking employment in manufacturing. First generation ghettos grew and expanded rapidly in these cities. The populations of blacks in Chicago, Cleveland and Detroit had doubled in ten years between 1910 and 1920 while others, like New York, Philadelphia, St. Louis, Cincinnati and Indianapolis, grew by one-half. Houston was the only large southern city that experienced black population growth in this period. Others, like Nashville and Louisville, lost blacks and by 1920 the largest concentrations of blacks were in New York, Philadelphia and Chicago rather than Washington, D.C., New Orleans and Baltimore. This period also witnessed the movement of both rural southern whites and blacks to the cities. Within twenty years, the number of blacks in cities exceeded those in rural areas for the first time. This movement was sustained, despite continuing employment in the low-wage sectors of the economy, because of rural poverty and repression.

Movement of blacks to the Middle Atlantic and Great Lakes region accelerated in the 1920s and continued until the Great Depression, when it slowed but remained steady in spite of some southern return migration. By 1940, 1.7 million blacks had relocated to the North. By southern black standards, it was the Promised Land. However, in spite of less severe social constraints and better-paying jobs in the North, blacks faced rampant prejudice and housing accommodation difficulties in the North (Rose, 1971).

By the 1940s, southern black migration resumed in response to the WWII induced labor shortages. Black migration to the industrial belt where industries were converted from peacetime production to wartime manufacturing, accounted for much of this relocation. In addition to the North, the West experienced sizable gains in their black population. Before 1940, Los Angeles was the only western city with more than 25,000 blacks. War-related employment opportunities influenced the numbers of migrants moving to western cities. While blacks with skills could not find jobs in the South, they competed with whites who migrated in larger numbers than blacks to northern and western cities. New black ghetto centers included Dallas, Los Angeles, Cleveland, Detroit and Newark. In addition to the new second-generation centers in the North, western cities such as San Francisco and Oakland also qualified for black ghetto status for the first time.

Agricultural change was a major factor in black out-migration from southern states. Less acreage in production and the mechanization of farms resulted in surplus agricultural labor in the rural South. Tobacco producing areas, which were slow to mechanize, were an exception and retained black agricultural labor during this period. Generally, however, declining economic opportunities in the South, complemented by expanding industrialization and war production in the North and West, became the push and pull forces that led blacks to migrate. Northern recruiters also played an active role in convincing southern blacks of opportunities in the North. By 1950, a generation of black migrants had established themselves in the Northeast and North Central regions and lived in significant spatial concentrations. Two million black migrants, originating from eight southern states moved to the North (Rose, 2000, p. 89), making this relocation one of the most prominent migrations in American history.

Ghetto Development 1950–1970

In the third period of national ghetto formation, 1950–1970, blacks continued to move from the South to the North and West. By the 1970s the South's national share of black population was 53 percent, down from 77 percent in 1940. The black population urbanization rate had grown from 50 percent to 75 percent in the same period. While the black population continued to move in this period, a net increase in the southern black population occurred due to natural increase. Two million blacks were added to the population in the South between 1940 and 1970.

Between 1950 and 1970, even though the number of destinations of southern black migrants had increased, first- and second-generation ghetto centers were the primary destinations for black migrants. These large cities had the resources to best accommodate the large numbers of new blacks. Unlike the previous period, however, when much of the black migration skipped southern urban centers in favor of northern cities, black migration in this period included relocations to southern cities such as Washington, D.C., Baltimore, Houston, Norfolk and New Orleans. These secondary black destinations surpassed earlier black urban concentrations in Birmingham, Jacksonville, Richmond and Louisville. Also in this period, black origins and destinations were altered. In addition to the South Atlantic states, the east South Central region, primarily Alabama and Mississippi, generated migration streams. Also among the west South Central states, Arkansas and Louisiana contributed to migration streams.

Both New York and Chicago had more than a million blacks by the end of this period. For first- and second-generation ghetto cities, the black population represented one-third or more of the city's population. Los Angeles, the only exception, had one-fifth. The changing proportions of blacks in these third-generation cities were related to the rate at which whites were abandoning the city for suburban communities. Because the numbers of blacks entering these older central cities were lower than the number of whites leaving, declines in population occurred. In the North, major economic changes occurred before the end of this era in black settlement history. The national economy was in a transition stage, moving from manufacturing to service provision, bad timing for blacks moving to major industrial centers seeking manufacturing jobs. In addition, jobs were leaving central cities either for the suburbs or for entirely different regions.

Northern blacks acquired housing through racial residential succession in the 1950s and, by the 1960s, a construction boom enabled some blacks to secure better quality housing. By the mid-1960s, blacks had started moving beyond the confines of the central city core into surrounding area and eventually to selected suburban areas. In the same period and unlike the northern model, blacks in southern cities were seldom involved in residential succession in the 1950s. Housing construction was undertaken to meet race-specific demand. Southern cities at this time contained pockets of black residential development, which expanded on an as-needed basis. The ghettoization process in the South was delayed until the 1950s, when economic and social changes led to a modification of the housing allocation process. This process involved filling-in the spaces between black settlements and racial residential succession ensued. Sharing of urban space by blacks and whites in the South became similar to the situation in the North. Residential segregation patterns identical to that of the North began to emerge in the South. Over time there was a transition from construction of new non-white housing to white-black residential succession. Today both types of housing access, new construction and racial residential succession, are responsible for meeting housing demand in the South.

Rose reported third-generation ghetto centers were geographically widespread on a national basis and were related to "white flight." These included Boston, Buffalo, Rochester, Milwaukee, Denver, San Diego, and Seattle. By 1970, twenty-eight ghetto centers existed by Rose's definition. More than one-half were outside the South.

Metropolitan Centers and Hypersegregation

By 1970, most blacks lived in urban centers. America's national ghetto system had many cities with more than 50,000 blacks. In addition to north-south migration, movement was occurring between U.S. metropolitan areas by non-southern blacks as well as by whites. For example, in New York and Chicago, non-southern migration represent only one-third of the total but in cities like Columbus, Ohio and Kansas City, Missouri, non-southern migrants dominated the relocating black population (Rose, 2000). The proportion of non-southern migrants in urban centers was as high as 80 percent of the southern migrant numbers.

What started as the formation of black enclaves within these cities, evolved into hyper-urbanization and hyper-segregation in large central cities. Chicago is an example. Prior to 1920, black Chicagoans numbered fewer than 50,000. However, by 1940, approximately 300,000 were counted by the U.S. Census. By 2000, more than 1 million blacks resided in that city. The relocation of blacks in mass numbers shocked northern communities like Chicago. While Jim Crow laws legally separated blacks and whites in the southern states, institutional mechanisms — restrictive deeds, redlining, loan denials and steering, became the tools of northern whites to restrict the living spaces of black Americans. As a result, black segregation rates became extremely high and ghettos were preserved. In some cases, extreme segregation levels occurred, as in the case of East St. Louis, which was more than 95 percent black by 1990, and plagued with infrastructure and social problems. This extreme segregation persisted between 1940 and 1980 in the entire St. Louis metropolitan area, and was termed "hypersegregation" by Denton and Massey (1989).

Emerging ghettos formed new cores of black urban culture and sanctuaries for new immigrants. The continuous flow of blacks, the refusal of whites to share social space, and codified covenants restricted black settlement options and turned the ghetto into a permanent feature of the American urban landscape. In this period, older central cities experienced overall population declines and an erosion of their tax bases. Jobs shifted to the suburbs and the national highways system provided easy access to smaller cities for whites, while lower-income blacks were trapped and middle-class blacks were limited to housing access largely in adjacent areas of their cities, thus extending the highly segregated ghetto to contiguous areas. By 1980 postindustrial changes left many black migrant dreams unfulfilled. The economic trends that emerged in the 1970s and 1980s caught many blacks unprepared for the changing labor market. Employment instability triggered other interregional migrations. At the same time, however, black suburbanization, which had begun early in the 20th century, had reached new heights, totaling more than 4.6 million African Americans by 1978 (Clark, 1979). By 2000, African American suburbanites reached approximately 12 million. Much of this suburbanization resulted from the improved status of African Americans in the last three decades preceding the 2000 U.S. Census counts.

EVOLUTION OF THE BLACK MIDDLE CLASS

The Great Migration moved millions of blacks to northern cities and provided hope for escaping poverty and other consequences of the Jim Crow laws. By World War II, jobs were plentiful both in northern and western cities. Many early black migrants found work in a variety of manufacturing and service industries as well as wartime work in large cities, such as Chicago and Detroit. Early black migrants sent word of the new-found opportunities back to their original rural southern communities. Consequently, thousands of additional blacks, as noted previously, migrated to Chicago, New York, Detroit, and other growing cities over the next several decades. Many blacks suffered the consequences of discrimination, but over time, many other black Americans improved their economic standing. The result was a growing black working class.

Some black Americans prospered before and especially during the Civil Rights Era. A new black entrepreneurial class had been born and the number of black businesses increased in the 1960s and beyond. Affirmative action opened up several job opportunities for blacks in the government sector. As many new black families found stable employment, they achieved middle-class status and moved into former white neighborhoods, becoming renters and homeowners in what soon became new black neighborhoods. In the 1970s, African Americans realized economic gains that even reduced their earnings gap with whites. By 1979, Clark claimed that about one-fifth of all African Americans had reached the American middle class (Clark, 1979). As a result, black suburbs expanded and blacks with resources pushed into previously all-white areas. The black middle class had undeniably emerged on the American scene.

Over the years, however, a number of analysts have come to question the success of the black middle class to reach equity with their white counterparts. Questions have been raised about the definition of the "Black Middle Class," especially their ability to earn equal pay for equal work, achieve equity in education and health, and sustain the stability of their achievements under poor economic conditions and the persistence of geographic isolation. This chapter will not address all of these questions. However, the issues of class definition, education and residential segregation are touched upon briefly.

Analysts such as A. J. Robinson (1997) have addressed the question of economic status and well being by confronting the empirical definition of the black middle class. He argued that the positive contemporary assessments of the black middle class, such as its doubling from 1965 to the present and the fact that it is the most rapidly expanding black segment, are at best misleading. His first problem was the 1994 definition of the black middle class as persons earning $15,999 to $50,000, which suggested that nearly one-half of all black families had achieved middle class status. Robinson found the definition flawed and suggested an alternative.

"I believe a more accurate definition of the black middle-class places the income range between $25,000 and $49,999. I say this because the poverty line for a family of four, in 1995, was $15,569 ($15,141 in 1994). It seems disingenuous to categorize those making slightly more than the poverty line as members of the black middle class. Using this income range puts the number of black families in the middle class at 31.9% of all black families in 1994. (Keep in mind that 32.2% of all black families earned incomes below the poverty line during the same period — 1994)" (Robinson, p. 2).

Robinson noted the following points about black incomes and the black middle class:

1. Nearly one-third of black families of the period lived below the poverty level.
2. Among black income groups, the upper quintile, the wealthy has grown most rapidly since 1965.
3. A "squeezing effect" occurred between 1970 and 1990, wherein some middle-income blacks have been elevated to high income blacks without squeezing the poor income groups to middle-income status. The obvious result is movement towards bifurcation in black "haves" and "have-nots."

The modest gains by African Americans were echoed regionally in the 1990s. For example, Jack Norman of the *Milwaukee Journal Sentinel* wrote in 2000:

"Despite a strong economy and a flood of diversity programs and rhetoric from businesses, Milwaukee's middle-class African Americans saw only limited progress during the 1990s in their quest for equality . . . " (p. 2).

He reported research findings related to employment and mortgage data during a decade of prosperity when unemployment was relatively low.

"Thirty-two-to-one. That's the ratio of white men to black men holding white-collar jobs in Milwaukee area's 1,833 largest firms in 1998 … one hundred and six to one. That's the ratio of white households to black households with incomes of $40,000 or more who applied for home loans in Milwaukee's suburbs in 1998 …" (p. 2).

The increases in white-collar employment growth for blacks also were modest, especially when compared to whites:

"For example, African-American white-collar employment at area firms required to file EEOC reports jumped 78% from 1990 through 1998. But the increase was only 1,549 jobs, from 1,981 to 3,530. Meanwhile, the number of whites in the same white-collar categories — officials, management and professional — grew by 15,399, to 84,482 in 1998" (p. 3).

Perhaps the best summation of the black middle class is made by a black executive who told Robinson, "There is a healthy black middle class, but there aren't enough of us" (p. 5).

Additional issues affecting the long-term viability of African Americans and their neighborhoods include the consequences of persistent residential discrimination and segregation. Small progress has been made on a national basis in reducing black-white segregation rates and they remained high in 2000. On a national basis, the Lewis Mumford Center reported that:

" … at the national level … the extent of segregation (between suburban whites and blacks) is little changed, remaining very high for African Americans, moderate for Hispanics and Asians …

On the whole, black residential enclaves have been maintained at about the same level as in 1990 … lagging behind (Asians and Hispanics) are African Americans" (Logan, 2001, pp. 1–2).

The Mumford Center, in a separate publication, examined income and quality of life along racial lines and found that "separate translates to unequal even for the most successful black and Hispanic minorities" (Logan, 2001, p. 1). The report noted that African Americans, the most highly segregated racial group, not only had the lowest income levels during the prosperous 1990s but also experienced an actual widening of the income gap "in absolute dollars" (Logan, 2001, p. 33). Logan suggested that "black neighborhoods are separate and unequal not because blacks cannot afford homes in better neighborhoods, but because, even when they achieve higher incomes they are unable to translate these into residential mobility" (Logan, 2001, p. 33).

Perhaps one of the most disturbing pieces of news about segregation is that after decades of civil rights and desegregation efforts directed at public education, segregation of black, Latino and Asian children from white children increased in 1999–2000; this is after remaining virtually unchanged for the last decade (Stowell and Oakley, 2002). This trend flies in the face of post-WWII efforts to overcome a "separate but equal" American education system.

Notwithstanding these spatial and economic inequalities, the persistent struggle by African Americans has yielded progress on economic, social and geographic grounds. One area into which blacks have pushed is America's suburbia. This has been a long-term process involving contested spaces.

BLACK SUBURBANIZATION

The U.S. black population distribution changed regionally at different scales between 1910 and 1970. At one level, the Great Migration redistributed millions of blacks from South to North. At another scale, blacks changed from a rural to a largely urban population. Black residential developments in the urban north largely involved black central city settlement. However, some early black movement was to northern suburbs too, as early as the 1920s. The suburbanization of blacks, which will be discussed more fully in the next chapter, also changed black population distribution. Thus, black suburbanization throughout the 20th century also created new black geographies at a different geographic scale. This became most pronounced by the 1970s, a period that Thomas Clark called a "watershed" of African American suburbanization (Clark, 1979).

By the 1970s, as black populations increased in selected large cities across the country, a concurrent non-central city suburban ring settlement of African Americans also was occurring. Rose (1976) showed that the largest metropolitan centers experienced black settlements in the suburban ring in 1960–1970. While the number of suburbanized blacks was impressive (3.5 million) during the decade, it was overshadowed by an even greater number of whites who were fleeing to suburbia. An important geographic observation about black suburbanites is that they were concentrating in a few metropolitan areas. By 1970, thirty-five percent of all blacks resided in 12 large metropolitan areas; a comparable percentage of whites were concentrated in the 20 largest metropolitan areas of the country. Because of the black "preference" for older metropolitan regions, most African Americans moved within the same region in which they resided. Many blacks left behind politically independent black cities to relocate to suburbia, which tended to be of various types, including dormitory and industrial suburbs. Most of the emerging black suburbs had existing black settlements, or were directly adjacent to existing urban black neighborhoods that expanded geographically. Most of the new black suburbs in the North involved racial struggles over contested space, or resulted from abandonment of fleeing whites. Rose saw existing black settlements as magnets for black suburbanization that resulted in geographic extensions of urban ghettos. He termed them "ghettolets" (Rose, 1976).

Two types of black suburban ring settlements occurred in the North during the mid-late 20th century. One, as described above, involved spatial spillover of blacks from the central city into adjacent suburban jurisdictions, such as the case of East Cleveland, Ohio, into its adjacent communities (see next chapter for details). The other form resulted from the development of vacant land surrounding historically black communities already in existence, as was the case of Prince George's County, Maryland, near Washington, D.C. Suburbanization in the South took a form uncharacteristic of western and northern industrial cities. Southern cities housed relatively middle-class and higher status whites. Poor whites and blacks resided in adjacent segregated rings, where new developments provided much needed housing for all black communities and accommodated the white power politics requirement for racial separation. This racial geography resulted in a "checkerboard" pattern of suburban racial settlement. Not surprisingly, black suburbs, whether industrial or dormitory, lacked amenities and conferred suburban ring status that differed from the high status and good living associated white suburban living.

The existence of an early 20th century black suburban ring was noticed by urban scholars. Taeuber discussed this ring, for example, and noted that by 1950 twenty-five percent of the black population in northern urban areas was located outside the central city. She stated that "the growth of negro population outside the central city of the SMSA cannot be identified with a movement of the lanes of suburbia," implying a difference in quality and experience between white and black suburbia (Taeuber, 1958). Black suburbanization rates steadily increased from 4.05 percent in 1950 to 7.14 percent in 1980, and were higher than that of whites.

Black suburbanization accelerated in the 1960s, as white-black relations changed in response to civil rights legislation. Large numbers of blacks moved to the suburbs but usually to places where black populations already existed. A new black suburban form emerged in this period. This involved black ghettoized suburbs that developed in declining white areas described by Rose (1972) as "leapfrog" suburbs. These are areas of older housing and declining white population. Stahura (1986) attributed black access to these places to lower white demand for their aging housing, the civil rights climate, and potential specter of civil unrest.

In the 1970s, overall U.S. suburbanization growth slowed due to decreased central city fringe movement by whites and a reverse movement by some white suburbanites to the central city in response to the gentrification (renewal) of inner city neighborhoods to upscale housing and amenities. Growth in the suburban fringe areas during this time still outpaced central city growth, as employment continued to decentralize to industrial parks, office parks, and shopping centers far away from the troubled inner cities (Muller, 1981). At the same time, although black suburbanization was on the rise, African Americans found their choices largely limited to the inner ring, older suburbs adjacent to their central cities and adjacent to nearby black neighborhoods. According to Logan and Schneider (1984), as black suburbanization accelerated in the 1970s, greater residential choice emerged. However, they also noted that racially parallel developments occurred: blacks moved to black suburbs and whites to white suburbs in the 1970s. There was less racial invasion and succession in the 1970s than in 1960s.

During and after the 1980s, two trends became apparent. First, blacks were moving into suburban communities close to the central city. These suburbs generally had lower median incomes than other suburbs and were characterized as having low infrastructure expenditures. African Americans were inheriting suburbs with less public investments in goods and services than nearby white suburbs. In fact, the highest infrastructure-expenditure communities contained the least number of blacks (Schneider and Phelan, 1993). The second trend speaks to the bifurcation of the black community on economic and class terms. At the same time that blacks with lower status increasingly inhabited communities with low infrastructure investments, a growing class of wealthy blacks, although relatively small, has made its way to wealthy exclusive suburbs.

Pattillo-McCoy (1999) has placed the consequences of black-white urban-suburban geography into the proper context in her study of Chicago's Southside. In her analysis of the urban geography of the black middle class in "Graveland," Pattillo-McCoy illustrated how racial segregation and concomitant disproportionate poverty, along with structural changes in the economy, have significant impacts on blacks living there. She showed that racial segregation shapes black residential boundaries, resulting in middle class and poor blacks sharing neighborhoods. Despite expansion of the black middle class and geographic expansion of black residential space, "black flight" never results in complete separation of the two economic classes. Rather, the middle-class black residences serve as buffer zones between whites and poor blacks and middle-class blacks continue to interact with poor blacks that are adjacent to their living space. Eventually, the poor blacks push into middle-class black neighborhoods, which cannot expand freely into white neighborhoods. This is no different than Harold Rose's observation in 1976 that the ghetto was expanding with all of its negative consequences. The black middle and poor classes may inhabit different spaces but they are adjacent and overlapping, forcing black middle class encounters with the crime culture and often being stereotyped as part of it. The most negative aspect of this unique urban geography is the potentially profound effect the negative perceptions can have on all black groups.

REVERSE MIGRATION AND CULTURAL DIVERSIFICATION: TWO RECENT TRENDS IN THE BLACK POPULATION

In 2000, blacks constituted 12.3 percent of the U.S. population, or 34,658,190 persons. Some interesting trends and patterns have emerged among this population due to the legacy of slavery, the Great Migration, reverse southern migration, and black immigration during the past three decades.

One legacy of the Great Migration is large black urban populations in the North. Some American "inner cities" continued to see major increases in their black proportions after 1970 (e.g., Cleveland, Newark, Washington, D.C., and New Orleans). Some cities even became "black majority" cities (see Table 6.1). By 2000, the four American cities with the largest black populations were located in the North. New York City and Chicago each had more than one million blacks, while Detroit and Philadelphia had approximately three-quarters and one-half million blacks, respectively. However, the legacy of slavery and a current return migration to the South also have resulted in the majority of American blacks being located in the southern U.S. by 2000.

The "reverse migration" of blacks refers to the relocation of blacks from other major U.S. regions to the southern states, which began in the 1970s and accelerated in the decades of the 1980s and 1990s. During the decade of the 1990s, just over 3.5 million blacks moved to the South from other regions, more than doubling the number from the previous decade. These "reverse migrants" moved disproportionately to five southern states: Florida, Georgia, Texas, Maryland, and North Carolina (Frey, 2001a). Although the four largest black urban centers were in the North in 2000, five of the next seven largest were in the South: Houston, Memphis, New Orleans, Dallas, and Atlanta. It is also noteworthy that among the cities with the largest black populations, nine are "majority black" cities.

Demographer William H. Frey reported data for twenty U.S. metropolitan regions that met one of two criteria: a minimum of 200,000 blacks in 2000 or a minimum black population increase of 20 percent during the 1990–2000 period. By rank, the top five metropolitan areas were: Orlando, Atlanta, Miami-Ft. Lauderdale, Tampa, and Charlotte. The black population growth rates of these five southern metropolitan regions ranged from 35 percent to 62 percent. Fifteen of twenty metropolitan areas that met Frey's criteria were located in the southern U.S. (Frey, 2001a).

A final trend among the U.S. black population examined here is its increasing ethnic diversity over the past thirty years. Because the U.S. Census does not differentiate blacks by national origin, it is necessary to examine the "foreign born" category reported in the census tabulations. The percent of foreign-born blacks in 1970 was 1.3 percent. However, by 2000, that percentage had increased to nearly 8 percent (Frey, 2001b). Not surprisingly, a geographic pattern is associated with this trend. The greatest number and concentration of foreign-born blacks occur in the immigrant gateways of New York, New Jersey, Florida, and California (Frey, 2001b). The leading origins of these immigrants include Haiti, Jamaica, the Dominican Republic, Trinidad and Tobago, Ghana, and Nigeria.

Table 6.1

Black Population and Percent Black in Selected U.S. Cities, 2000

South	Number of Blacks, 2000	Percent Black, 2000
Birmingham. AL	178,372	73.5
Miami, FL	80,858	22.3
Orlando, FL	49,933	26.9
Tampa, FL	79,118	26.1
Jackson, Miss	130,151	70.6
Charlotte, N.C.	176,964	32.7
Memphis, IN	399,208	61.4
Dallas, TX	307,957	25.9
Fort Worth, TX	108,310	20.3
Houston, TX	494,496	25.3
Northeast		
Washington, D.C.	343,312	60.0
Boston, Mass	149,202	25.3
Newark, NJ	149,250	53.5
Buffalo, NY	108,851	37.2
Philadelphia, PA	655,824	43.2
Midwest		
Chicago, IL	1,065,009	36.8
Gary, IN	86,340	84.0
Indianapolis, IN	199,412	25.5
Detroit, MI	775,772	81.6
Minneapolis, MN	68,818	18.0
Kansas City, MO	137,879	31.2
West		
St Louis, MO	178,266	51.2
Cincinnati, OH	142,176	42.9
Cleveland, OH	243,939	51.0
Pittsburgh, PA	90,750	27.1
Milwaukee, WI	222,933	37.3
Los Angeles, CA	415,195	11.2
Oakland, CA	142,460	35.7
San Diego, CA	96,216	7.9

DIVERSIFICATION OF U.S. BLACK POPULATION

Diversification of the black population in the U.S. has increased over the last three decades. Much of this increase reflects two major changes in immigration law, 1965 Hart-Celler Act, which dramatically increased immigration from Latin America and Asia, and the 1986 Immigration Reform and Control Act and its subsequent 1988 Amendment, aimed at "under-represented" countries. The latter targeted visas for relatives of people already in the U.S. legally or people with skilled jobs needed in the U.S. The 1990 Immigration Act was designed to diversify the U.S. immigration pool. It is sometimes referred to as the Diversity Visa. Under this Act, 55,000 visas are set aside for people from countries with less than 50,000 in the previous five years. The U.S. black foreign-born is 2.8 percent African and 5.2 percent non-Hispanic Caribbean. Together they constitute 8 percent of the total U.S. foreign-born population (U.S. Census, 2000). This percentage excludes South American blacks from Brazil and other countries. Table 6.2 reports data for the period 1970 through 2000 and demonstrates the impact of the Diversity Visa. Besides Egypt, most of the African foreign-born in the U.S. are of sub-Saharan origin. Since the 1990s, Ghana (totaled 65,570 in 2000) and Nigeria (totaled 134,940 in 2000) have taken most advantage of the Diversity Visa with annual rates of 900 from Ghana (had 5 percent of awards in 1990s) and 800 from Nigeria.

Table 6.2 also illustrates the substantial increases in the numbers of Africans and Caribbeans entering the U.S. between 1970 and 2000. In the 1990–2000 period, the number of African foreign-born entering the U.S. more than doubled (142%) and the Caribbean total increased by nearly 600,000 (a 57% increase). A similar pattern involving the African foreign-born occurred in New York City in the same period, where the African total increased by nearly 50,000.

In 2000, the Caribbean foreign-born accounted for 5.28 percent of the U.S. total. However, four nations contributed more than 80 percent of the Caribbean total: Jamaica (553,825), Guyana (211,190), Haiti (419,315) and Trinidad and Tobago (197,500). Recent immigration trends, then, indicate a gain in immigration to the U.S. from Africa and the Caribbean.

At the metropolitan level, New York City is a place where black population diversification is best observed since the 1970s. While the African foreign-born is 3.2 percent of the total New York City foreign-born, non-Hispanic black Caribbean foreign-born is 20.6 percent of the total. Caribbean countries rank among the top twenty contributors to the foreign-born in New York City with Jamaica and Guyana ranked 3 and 4, respectively, and Haiti and Trinidad and Tobago at 7 and 8. With more than a fifth of the New York foreign-born population being black, a strong black ethnic quilt has emerged. Clearly, immigration has diversified the "native" African-American ethnicity by introducing an increasing number of black foreign-born immigrants.

Table 6.2

U. S. Foreign-Born Population, 1970–2000				
Foreign-Born Population	1970	1980	1990	2000
U.S. (Africa)	61,463	199,723	363,819	881,300
U.S. (Caribbean)	183,692	530,010	1,004,174	1,603,862
New York City (Africa)	13,029	23,360	42,481	92,435
New York City (Caribbean)	113,892	282,980	410,532	591,660
Source: The City of New York, Department of Planning, p. 13.				

SUMMARY AND SOME OBSERVATIONS ABOUT BLACK ETHNICITY

As we begin the 21st century, the U.S. faces increasing multicultural and racial diversity. The black-white dichotomy remains pervasive and issues remain unsolved. Black Americans remain highly segregated from whites, especially in particular places. Black poor neighborhoods continue to be plagued by the consequences of disproportionate poverty, inequitable access to quality education, employment, fair housing and services.

Despite these enormous challenges and inequities, a black middle class has emerged and has grown significantly since World War II. Its current status, relative to the white middle class, remains unsatisfactory and black living space, which defines daily contacts and quality of life, remains too restricted.

The perceived opportunities that led millions of blacks out of the American South, became real for some African Americans, changing their class status and allowing black suburbanization. The same hope has brought an increasing number of foreign-born blacks to America in recent decades and has attracted millions of blacks to the American South during the last quarter of the 20th century. African Americans and other black ethnic groups are establishing new geographic patterns across America as they reshape its regions and landscapes.

Despite undeniable progress, many racial issues confront America as we begin a new century. Unfortunately, many of these issues remain black and white, although immigration and racialization have increased their complexity. Racial issues will require attention to avoid serious civil problems in future decades. Some of these issues are discussed in more detail in the following chapters after a closer examination of the two most recent black migrations in America, suburbanization and the reverse migration.

African American ethnicity evolved in early clusters of African slaves, who exchanged beliefs, speech, cooking and other cultural attributes and, then to shape a self-view and subculture with distinctive southern U.S. traits. For example, food staples such as beans and greens were boiled and meats were deep fried in a seasoned batter. Gumbo and thick soups became standards, as did rice. Also, African Americans prepared and displayed several major dishes simultaneously at meal time.

As African American culture evolved, a unique music genre also evolved, including that of the jazz era. Similarly, uniquely African American dialects and slang language evolved over time and became distinctive from white America. While other traits define African American ethnicity, perhaps the most striking is the shared vision of struggle inherent in their culture due to American racism and the legacy of slavery.

African American geographies have resulted at least in large part from white racism that limited residential choice and segregated blacks from whites. The color-line established in early American history has persisted and now also influences the plight of immigrant blacks. Despite the growing black diversity presented in the previous section and the strong sense of ethnicity among Caribbean and African immigrants, the racial categorization, or racialization discussed by Wei Li earlier in this text, results in a generalization of a "black" population when black immigrants are discussed. For example, there is no distinction between Ghanaians and Jamaican Americans when census descriptors are tabulated. This makes it impossible to study these ethnic blacks groups, which represent very different origins and cultures. Rather, all such groups are simply classified as "black." This construction of race creates what Laporte (1972) described as "invisible immigrants." Further, the settlement geographies of black ethnic groups can be very different.

As Wei Li also noted earlier, straight-line assimilation theory does not apply to many new immigrant groups. Racialization leads to segmented assimilation. Despite strong ethnic identities, immigrant blacks are stereotyped as being equivalent to poor African Americans, a racially-loaded perception. Waters' (1994) work on the Caribbean community in New York City underscore this identity construction within the context of social racialization in the U.S. She examined the differences between first- and second-generation Caribbean immigrants and explored how their ability to assimilate into the larger black society is facilitated or hindered by their perception of the American-born black and the extent to which they buy into the black stereotypes. Taking into consideration social backgrounds and social networks of parents, type of school and family structure, she described Caribbean youth as creating three mutually exclusive self-identifiers, the American-identified, the ethnic-identified, and immigrant-identified. She suggested that segmented assimilation results.

The broad range of black immigrant groups are settling in and changing American places. As noted earlier, some black foreign-born groups are concentrating their settlements in particular places. Ghanaians were cited as an example. There are numerous examples in the U.S. Two chapters in this section of the text (by Earl Scott and Elizabeth Chacko) report the adjustments and sculpting of cultural landscapes by immigrant Africans, the Ethiopians in Los Angeles and the Liberians in metropolitan Minneapolis-St. Paul. Another chapter, by Tom Boswell and Terry Ann Jones, illustrates the patterns of black Caribbeans in Florida and New York.

Chapter 7

People on the Move:
African Americans Since the Great Migration

JOHN W. FRAZIER AND ROGER ANDERSON

"During the Great Migration of the 1910s and 1920s, one in six African American migrants to the urban north moved to a suburb ...

By 2000, more than one-third of African Americans — almost 12 million people — lived in suburbs" (Wiese, 2004, p. 1).

"The South ... never ceased to represent home to many.... The years have not changed conditions at home so much as they have changed the people who once left home so urgently..." (Stack, 1996, pp. xiv–xv).

African Americans have been people on the move since the period of American Reconstruction. Their movements have been shaped by choices confined in part by the racial boundaries imposed by white-controlled American institutions. Racial geography, therefore, contains African American cultural landscapes that reflect unique cultural history and ethnicity, and the controls of white America. This chapter examines briefly two major movements since the Great Migration and discusses some of their dimensions from a geographic perspective. One is black suburbanization during the 20th century. We address race, class, and ethnicity, as they have influenced African American suburban geography and landscapes. The second and most recent movement is the "reverse migration" of blacks to the South from other U.S. regions. We briefly examine the rural and metropolitan migration streams and some explanations for them.

BACKGROUND

The previous chapter discussed the multiple reasons that eight million African Americans left the South during the Great Migration. African American migration was motivated by the hope for a new and different life, one that provided family and economic stability through employment and land ownership. The importance of World War I and subsequent changes in immigration law (1910s–1920s) led to labor shortages during the period. African Americans were recruited as laborers in steel, munitions, and other factories, and the railroads. African American social networks quickly nullified the need for further recruitment. Reports sometimes exaggerated, told of job opportunities and the existence of a climate in which blacks might even talk back to white people. As a result, millions of African Americans made their way to the perceived "Northern Promise Land" (and later to the West). Tettey-Fio summarized some of the impacts of this movement in America's largest industrial cities, where black populations expanded rapidly, especially after 1960. However, a less discussed movement also was underway prior to WWII and accelerated afterwards. This was the suburbanization of African Americans.

TWENTIETH CENTURY AFRICAN AMERICAN SUBURBANIZATION: RACE, CLASS, AND ETHNICITY

Geographers have classified America's diverse suburbs on the basis of employment type and commercial activities (Harris, 1990, 1991; Hartshorn and Muller, 1986). Although the growth of African American suburbs received some attention in the 1970s (Rose, 1976), more recent studies examine suburban geography along racial and ethnic lines (Harris, 1996; Darden, 2003; Li, 1998; Skop and Li, 2003). Recent studies also offer valuable insights into some of the details of African American suburbanization, both in terms of process and as places where African Americans shaped their cultural landscapes. One important dimension of evolving black suburbs receiving attention is socioeconomic status.

The Blue-Collar Basis for the Rise of the Twentieth Century Black Working Class

African Americans desire for permanent employment and land ownership preceded their entry to the working and professional classes, as indicated by their formation of new communities in Texas, Oklahoma, and Kansas in the 19th century. Few blacks, however, could afford home ownership at the beginning of the 20th century. Improved economic status was necessary for accumulation of capital sufficient for home ownership. Despite remaining an elusive goal for many, the twentieth century expanding industrial complex and labor shortages provided sufficient opportunity for some blacks to secure working-class status by the 1920s. Richard Harris demonstrated the importance of this status and its link to home ownership. He maintained, based on a study of eight U.S. metropolitan regions, that by 1940 working-class Americans "seem to have valued property ownership more highly than other occupational and class groups, notably the middle class" (Harris, 1990, p. 63). He also demonstrated that many working-class Americans actually built their own homes in unplanned suburbia prior to 1940. This occurred due to the decentralization of industrial employment, inexpensive lumber, and the shorter workday won by labor, and the cessation of suburban annexation by central cities which resulted in the absence of strict building codes (Harris, 1990). These working-class "home builders" were blue-collar workers who did so out of economic necessity.

These and other observations led Andrew Wiese to examine the nature of African American suburbs in the early 20th century and, specifically, the relationship between working-class black status and home self-construction (Wiese, 2004). Although African Americans accounted for less than five percent of all suburbanites by 1940, their total number outside the South had reached approximately one-half million and they were clustered in particular northern communities. Like their white counterparts, African Americans of the period constructed their homes out of economic necessity. Wiese made some important observations about early Northern black suburbs, including the fact that, rather being dormitory in nature, they were working-class communities containing the jobs and the homes of their African American residents. Although various types of African American suburbs existed in northern areas, the factory-induced black suburb was the most common form. In these suburbs, black housing ranged in quality from substandard units located in poor physical environments to stock that equaled white working-class suburban housing of the period. According to Wiese, compared to their urban black counterparts, black suburbanites had less education and tended to be employed in lower-skilled jobs.

Industrial suburbs had emerged as part of America's changing urban-industrial geographic structure. During the Pre-Depression Era of industrial expansion, factories were being built on the periphery of cities, often miles away from the old inner city core where factories had previously located. These decentralized factories became magnets for those seeking entry into growing industrial employment. African Americans became increasingly aware as a group that they were able to secure industrial employment in Northern cities. This access to working-class status attracted additional black migrants to large industrial Midwestern cities that were experiencing growth and spatial expansion, including into newer outlying areas. In Chicago, for example, where industry was booming, the African American population grew fivefold to 25,000 in less than a generation (1910–1940). The same was true in cities like Pittsburgh and Detroit.

The Detroit region is a good example of industrial decentralization that spurred the growth of industrial working-class suburbs during that period. While many black migrants continued to move into that city, auto plants became new nuclei for suburban Detroit. Dearborn, for example, grew exponentially in the 1920s due to this industrial decentralization; some other nearby communities at least doubled in size. Most of these were all-white communities that did not welcome black migrants. Despite this, blacks made their way into nearby areas and created African American suburban landscapes (Wiese, 2004).

Much has been written about Henry Ford's impact on the organization of labor and the consumption patterns of Americans. He doubled the daily wage of the time, changed the nature of labor and management, and thereby increased production efficiency. He also made the factory a magnet for the poor and unskilled seeking the security and promise of working-class status. Thousands of European immigrants and white Southern migrants flooded Detroit's emerging suburbs for such factory jobs. So did 10,000 blacks, but only into places acceptable to whites, specifically the nearly all-black working-class areas found "Downriver" (Wiese, 2004). In these suburban places, African American migrants constructed homes made possible by their new class status.

The Rise of the Black Middle Class and Suburbanization After World War II

The U.S. black population grew by more than two million during the 1940s and added another three million in the 1950s. By 1960, the total black population had reached nearly nineteen million. The second wave of the Great Migration was in full swing by 1960, bolstered by an expanding U.S. economy. At the same time, African American soldiers returning from WWII experienced discrimination in housing and were unwilling to settle for second-class citizenship. Civil disobedience and, later, urban riots, provided white America a wake-up, indicating that African Americans were no longer willing to accept white racism. Despite great resistance and delay, the 1965 Civil Rights Act and the Fair Housing Act of 1968 were passed and signaled a different federal view of black rights in America. Greater federal attention to affirmative action and greater success in admission to and graduation from college by African Americans followed. Improved black economic status increased dramatically as a result.

Important racial changes occurred in metropolitan America during and after WWII. Despite the increase in wartime black employment and the rapid growth of large central cities during the 1940s, few northern communities had large percentages of African Americans by 1950. Even the South, although containing more than one-half the nation's black population, had no city with a black majority population in 1950. Washington, D.C., which had the highest percentage of any U.S. city, counted slightly more than one-third (35%) of the city as black, followed by Baltimore (24%). But in the next twenty years, 1950–70, a tremendous influx of blacks associated with the second wave of the Great Migration dramatically changed American cities. A relatively small number of large northern cities received the bulk of black migrants. Although the national percentage of blacks in the U.S. changed little during the second wave of migration (about 10% in 1950 and about 11% in 1970), the total number of African Americans in the country increased from nearly 13 million to 22.5 million during this time. Particular cities, such as Philadelphia, Pittsburgh, Newark, Chicago, Detroit, Cleveland, St. Louis, Cincinnati and Indianapolis, at least doubled or tripled their black populations in the 1950–70 period.

Thus, from the beginning of the 20th century until the end of the Great Migration in about 1970, regional and local black geographies dramatically changed. In 1900, less than one in four African Americans resided in urban America. By 1960, for the first time, nearly three of every four African Americans lived in urban environments and blacks became more urbanized than whites. In the North, this meant increasing black-white segregation, particularly in large metropolitan regions.

By 1970, the nation's capital had become a majority black city and several others (Baltimore, Detroit, New Orleans, and Birmingham) were not far behind, with black percentages in the 40–46 percent range. Still others had gained sufficient African American numbers to boast one-third of their total population as black, including Chicago, Cleveland, Philadelphia, and Memphis (Clark, 1979). It was indeed a period of rapid ghetto formation and expansion (Rose, 1971), but this was only half the story. Blacks also had pushed their way into suburbia, building on pre-existing black settlements in the North and moving into newly constructed suburban housing in southern communities.

American urban history was being made in 1970 because the U.S. suburban population exceeded that of the central cities for the first time. Not surprisingly, this meant that more African Americans were making their way to America's suburbs. Thomas A. Clark referred to the 1970–78 period as a high-water mark of black sub-urbanization. He noted that the net migration of blacks to the suburbs in the period increased their total to 4.6 million. According to his analysis, 52 percent came from a central city within the same metropolitan region, while 22 percent entered from different areas (Clark, 1979). He also reported the black economic gains over two decades. In 1955, black men working full-time, for example, had earned less than two-thirds the average income of their white counterparts. By 1975, black men's incomes rose to 77 percent of that of white males of the same full-time employment. For African American women, who had always been important partners in supporting black households, earnings rose to 57 percent of white female full-time workers during the same period (Clark, 1979). In both cases, African Americans made important strides in closing the earnings gap with white workers in America. Also, service employment became more available to African Americans and white-collar blacks replaced blue-collar blacks as the mainstream moving to suburbia in the post-1960 period.

The median income of black suburban families in constant dollars rose 12 percent and the number of black families earning over $15,000 per year doubled between 1970 and 1976. This signaled an emerging and growing black middle class economically prepared to flee the increasing ills of aging cities for suburbia. By then, the black middle class included about 20 percent of all African Americans, who shared the motivations often attributed to the white middle class, a secure and attractive environment that their incomes would allow. As black status improved, these motivations resulted in continued rapid black suburbanization, which by 2000 resulted in approximately 12 million black suburbanites, about one-third of the total African American population. Between 1960 and 2000, American suburbs received about nine million African Americans, nearly equivalent to the number participating in the Great Migration. Metropolitan America was evolving with the addition of new suburbs and, at the same time, black geography was undergoing changes.

Racial Geographies: White Institutions and White Avoidance

It would be easy to celebrate the socioeconomic and suburban successes of African Americans were it not for their constant struggle for acceptance in most urban and suburban white neighborhoods. Despite black economic gains, white Americans remained in control of African American living spaces during black suburbanization. The 20th century was marked by constant battles for contested space between black and white Americans. Blacks won some battles, but white political and economic institutions largely prevailed in limiting the choices of African Americans. When institutional practices failed to achieve the preservation of all-white neighborhoods, the wholesale turning over of white neighborhoods to blacks (white flight) maintained black-white segregation. Black culture, coupled with white institutional discrimination and white avoidance, created discernable patterns of black ethnic geography within the bounds of racialized space.

Post-WWII Southern black suburbanization was unique. To meet the growing demand for black housing and to maintain the color line, southern white institutions politically accommodated blacks by providing new housing in acceptable but separate suburbs at the edge of existing cities. The North, on the other hand, provided stiff political and economic resistance to "black intrusion," which took on a number of forms. Wiese explained the white control of the earliest black suburbs, settings typically characterized by the poorest and often "nuisance-type" lands separated from whites by barriers that made them seem non-existent. He used the Detroit region to describe the inscription of racial geography across its pre-WWII landscape:

> "For the black southerners who had moved to … 'Mr. Ford's place,' the River Rouge-Ecorse community represented a familiar social environment. By the early 1940s, the N.Y. Central tracks marked the end of one world and the beginning of another, as though the color line had been scrawled across these suburbs with a steam shovel" (Wiese, p. 50).

Restrictions

Unwelcome in all-white communities, African Americans were relegated to particular places that were unattractive to whites. These became the locations of the early northern black suburbs. Geographically, the process involved spatial expansion by blacks replacing whites in particular neighborhoods. Some new construction also was permitted on available and unwanted land.

Violence was not uncommon in northern cities after WWII, but less overt discriminatory actions came by way of well-documented institutional methods. Institutional discrimination restricted black settlements and directed its geographic extension into areas nearly adjacent or contiguous to existing black neighborhoods. Some federal and local methods were based on the erroneous assumption that black presence in a neighborhood led to property devaluation. This misconception frightened white homeowners and stimulated unfortunate actions by government and private institutions. At the local level, various land-use controls were favorite mechanisms of white community leaders. Restricted deeds, which forbade selling a property to non-whites, and exclusionary zoning regulations, including such actions as banning public housing developments from white communities and assigning public housing units on the basis of race. These were favorite mechanisms for maintaining black-white segregation and racial geography. Some communities also used urban renewal as a mechanism to remove unwanted black settlements, claiming improvement through the removal of visual blight. Additional government restrictions included local land use and zoning regulations, including overly restrictive building codes that required excessive lot sizes or expensive construction elements, which by design prevented blacks and other poor people from residing in some residential communities.

At the federal level, the Federal Housing Authority's role in local lending guidance after WWII resulted in almost total exclusion of African Americans from home ownership in the rapidly expanding suburbs. The Federal Housing Authority (FHA), which guaranteed home mortgages, provided guidance to local lenders whose deposits were federally insured. Believing that mixed-race neighborhoods would spell investment disaster, the FHA directed local lenders to provide low ratings to "high risk" loan applications that would lead to transitional neighborhoods and ultimately property devaluation. The FHA's *Underwriters Manual* explicitly stated:

> "If a neighborhood is to remain stable, it is necessary that properties shall continue to be occupied by the same social and racial classes" (quoted in Jackson, 1985, p. 208).

The FHA also supported restrictive covenants that forbade the sale of properties to non-whites to prevent "infiltration" of blacks into white neighborhoods.

Other institutional methods also deliberately reinforced black-white segregation and contributed to the evolution of racial geography in northern cities. Some unscrupulous practices were rooted in greed. For example, realtors and mortgage lenders conspired to create rapid turnover of white housing to blacks seeking home ownership in white neighborhoods through a process termed "blockbusting." These businesses sought high profits that rested on their ability to create panic selling through the use of a blockbuster and erroneous information to prospective white sellers. A blockbuster was the first African American family to enter an all-white neighborhood. Realtors would work the black-white border areas of communities looking for a white homeowner who would believe their emotionally-charged sales pitch that "blacks were looking to buy in the neighborhood" and certainly would cause a loss of property values for those who waited too long to sell. The story line was that the first white seller would preserve his investment before property values fell dramatically. When successful, the realtor paid a fair price to the first white seller and then created panic among the remaining homeowners who sold below market. Then, African Americans, who replaced the departing whites, paid above market prices, resulting in more business for lenders and large profits for the realtor, while at the same time lending support to the institutional myth that "black presence results in white property devaluation."

Other institutional practices denied blacks access to white neighborhoods and led to disinvestments in neighborhoods. "Steering" is an example. It refers to the private realtor practice of directing potential homebuyers to different neighborhoods on the basis of race; African Americans were "guided" to "appropriate neighborhoods" where they would feel "most comfortable," and were steered clear of price-appropriate homes in white neighborhoods. "Redlining," another institutional mechanism, was based on the institutional assumption that black presence could be equated with the generation of urban blight and neighborhood decline. To protect against bad loans, credit institutions employed "red ink" to carve neighborhoods on city maps that were simply "too risky" for investment. The result was few or no loans, which resulted in neighborhood disinvestments; money required for repair and neighborhood improvements was unavailable and urban decline followed. Also, black buyers sometimes turned to non-conventional speculative lenders with predictable results. Racial geography, then, was the results of actions designed to deny civil rights and to mandate the separation of blacks from whites through racist policies and behaviors by public and private institutions. However, there is no doubt that racial geography was supported by individual white behaviors. When institutional policies failed to keep African Americans out of white neighborhoods, whites simply abandoned their neighborhoods to blacks and fled to new communities that would maintain black-white separation. This process of "white flight" occurred across the North and helped create the two worlds described by Andrew Hacker as different on the basis of race and status (Hacker, 1992). These racial geographies have been maintained by white power relationships over time.

One of the best visual examples of the geographic results of these multiple processes at work over time is in the Cleveland, Ohio metropolitan area. The patterns of black population in that region (Cuyahoga and adjacent counties), 1970 to 2000, are provided in Figures 7.1 and 7.2. The data have been spatially standardized for the two census periods, making the geographies directly comparable. Figure 7.1 shows the high concentration of blacks on Cleveland's eastside by 1970, when the Great Migration had reached its completion and African American suburbanization had begun in Cuyahoga County. About a generation later, in 2000, Cleveland's Westside remained practically devoid of blacks, while the highly segregated Eastside added significantly more African Americans. African Americans pushed out of the inner city in a wedge-like fashion, predominantly in a single direction over a 30-year span. At the same time, the city's middle-class black population had pushed farther into suburbia, like a wedge driven from the inner city's Eastside. Comparing the two maps shows that an almost one-dimensional expansion occurred on the city's Eastside, spilling over into adjacent and nearby communities. This process and pattern not only represents a geographic extension of Cleveland's earlier black settlement, but an experience repeated in other large northern cities like Philadelphia, Detroit, and Chicago, among others. In the case of Cleveland, the expansion of African American settlement outside the city boundaries involved discrimination, racial struggle, and white flight. The institutional processes described earlier took place, including blockbusting and panic selling, followed by redlining and its consequences. Wiese detailed this transition in the Cleveland area, which began in the 1960s when slightly more than 23,000 African Americans replaced a nearly equal number of whites fleeing the "invasion":

> " … in urban neighborhoods such as Hough and Glenville, where aspiring black families had once replaced departing whites, blockbusters and unscrupulous landlords taxed the newcomers' resources…. Area banks redlined … and the local commercial district suffered … owners fled…. As a result the municipal tax base plummeted … and the city was forced to curtail services" (Wiese, p. 252).

It is important to note that the early black migrants into these all-white Cleveland suburbs had stable families and middle-class status, but nonetheless white avoidance and panic selling prevailed. As suburbs nearest the city declined, however, lower-income blacks replaced middle-class blacks, who pushed farther into adjacent suburbs, creating more white flight. This process continued with the growth of the black population and their desire for home ownership. The patterns of ghetto expansion and the spread of the black middle class into nearby white suburbs, followed the spatial limitations imposed by white society. Whites defined the process of African-American residential expansion and established the borders of racial geography. Although black middle-class families relocated in a process of "black flight," they could not separate themselves spatially from the working and lower economic African-American classes that were pushing out of the inner cities. As a result, middle-class status meant different things for blacks and whites; achievement of class status did not provide African Americans the same freedom of residential choice. Despite improved socioeconomic status, middle-class blacks remained linked to blacks of lower status. This led Harold Rose to describe black suburbanization as "the spatial extension of the ghettoization process with all that implies regarding the quality of life" (Rose, 1976: 263). This situation remained intact at the close of the 20th century (Pattillo-McCoy, 1999).

Figure 7.1

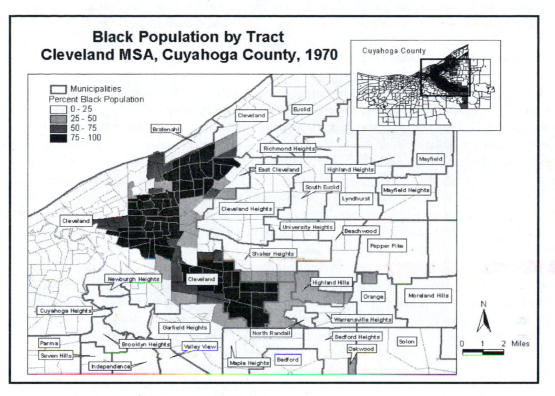

Figure 7.2

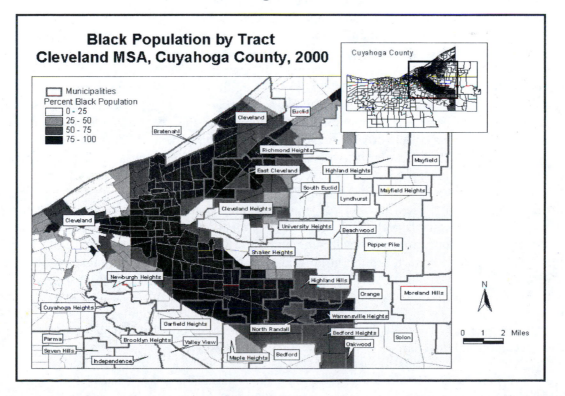

In summary, institutional mechanisms and white avoidance behavior created racial geography in metropolitan America. Institutional greed combined with misplaced white fear and racism have resulted in a uniquely American racial geography that continues to disadvantage millions of black Americans.

African American Ethnicity: Cultural Imprints

Where poor African Americans remain highly concentrated and trapped in inner city ghettos, landscapes are characterized by visual blight, crime, and other maladies associated with poverty and the loss of hope. Such landscapes also reflect the values, power, and willingness of the controlling white society to tolerate structural inequalities rooted in racialization. These landscapes are perceived by many whites as being associated with "blackness," or the flaws of black people, such as their unwillingness to work or stay in school, rather than being due to structural problems in the American economic system. Such a narrow vision ignores the earlier black landscapes of pride and contemporary African Americans landscapes. Just as class and race have shaped the evolution of black racial geographies, African-American ethnicity has shaped other discernable African-American places. When provided the freedom of choice, African Americans, like other cultures, have constructed landscapes of their own.

Wiese's *Place of Their Own* is rich with examples. When discussing early 20th century black suburbs, he noted that, within the confinement of racial geography, there exists a "sociocultural place" and distinctive African American cultural landscapes (Wiese, 2004). While similar to white, low-cost residential subdivisions, such places were distinctly black — dotted with black churches, recreation venues, restaurants, and other commercial shops, entertainment venues and services — and signaled their distinctive ethnic existence, while solidifying their cherished place-based self-identity. Those familiar with Brownsville and other early northern black settlements are aware of the existence of similar African American landscapes associated with black pride and dotted with African American cultural institutions. They also are knowledgeable about the provision of black news and cultural information through black newspapers like *The Chicago Defender*.

Wiese described early African American northern suburbs fashioned by black migrants. These blended rural southern traditions with a newer urban existence within the racialized spaces permitted by the white majority. Black home plots, which together formed black landscapes, contained gardens and livestock representative of their Southern experience. Together these attributes and low-cost dwellings in a semi-rural setting provided a "rustic landscape" that stood as distinctly African American (Wiese, 2004).

The uniqueness of African American landscapes and the preservation of their ethnicity did not disappear with more recent black suburbanization. Although blacks share the class aspirations of most middle-Americans to purchase a home in a safe, attractive environment, many suburban African Americans have remained thoughtfully connected to the broader African American community and its culture. A strong desire to retain ethnicity may seem somewhat ironic given the drive to escape the spatial confinement of America's worst racial geographies. However, African Americans residing outside a black residential concentration have undertaken important actions to retain their ethnic identity. They have sought the security of black solidarity for their children and achieved it in at least two ways. First, some African Americans residing in predominately white neighborhoods, while enjoying their class achievements and the benefits of integrated, upscale neighborhoods, regularly reach out to other African Americans through black social institutions located outside of their residential community. They deliberately interact in a variety of black community institutions — churches, clubs, and other venues — for the purpose of reinforcing racial/ethnic identity and providing a secure, nurturing environment for their children. Second, like other cultures, African Americans have attached ethnic-cultural meanings to their neighborhoods and homes. Contemporary suburbs tend to be homogenous in many ways, including appearance. Therefore, it is not surprising that material expressions of African-American culture appear as "housescapes," home décor inside, rather than outside the home. Wiese effectively demonstrated this when describing homes in a new black residential subdivision:

"While its class emblems were obvious, the development also reflected attempts to reinforce a racial identity for its majority.... Contemporary jazz filtered into the room.... The decor in the adjoining room resembled a Pottery Barn store with an African American accent — leather armchairs, early American prints, and a potted lily, plus African masks on the wall…. On the walls, framed art posters depicted Cuban cigars, an advertisement for the Montreux Jazz Festival, Miles Davis cradling a trumpet, and a gathering of mid-century civil rights leaders on the stoop of a Harlem brownstone, suggesting a man with cultural and political commitments…." (Wiese, 2005, pp. 274–75)

African-American ethnic geography exists, in part, because of the desire to express African American identity. While there is no doubt that, as a group, African Americans have made economic and social progress since WWII, it has come only through continuing racial struggle. As a result of racial conflict, struggle has become an essential ingredient of the ethnic glue that binds African Americans together. Thus, struggle is a component of African-American self-identity sometimes expressed in their homescapes.

We now turn to the third black movement, or migration, of the 20th century, the black "reverse" migration of the last generation.

A CONTEMPORARY BLACK MOVEMENT FLOWS SOUTHWARD

Carol Stack recognized the complexity of the most recent significant black movement within the United States. For most of the 20th century, blacks left the South for the promise of a better life in other regions. However, in the 1990s, more African Americans migrated to the South from the Northeast, Midwest, and West than departed the South for those regions. This "reverse migration" represented a 35-year trend reversal and a net gain of black migrants from all three other U.S. regions by the South. John Cromartie and Carol B. Stack identified the importance of social factors in explaining this geographic process based on 1975–80 census data and ethnographic fieldwork. They showed how social ties linked northern blacks to their southern roots from generation to generation. Cyclical movements between places for a variety of reasons (visits, long-stays with relatives, etc.) have resulted in young blacks strengthening social ties with southern relatives and friends. They also have increased their familiarity with and sentiment toward particular southern places. Such familiar places constitute a small set of destination choices considered by black migrants. The result is migration streams that "follow well-worn paths back to home places or other locations where relatives have settled" (Cromartie and Stack, 1989, p. 309).

Carol Stack's more recent work in rural North Carolina is an example of ethnographic research. Her in-depth interviews with African Americans returning to rural North Carolina revealed that black migrants were answering a *Call to Home* for a variety of non-economic reasons: the attraction of the physical setting, the needs of aging parents, retirement, the economic instability of northern states, the desire to avoid northern urban ills that threatened their children's future, and a desire to rebuild southern places using skills learned outside the South (Stack, 1996). Discussing the uncertainty and internal struggle faced by many of these migrants, including the racial climate and a fear of not "fitting in," Stack emphasized that returning African Americans are "no fools." She suggested through black migrants' stories that, although some returning migrants may come back for the growing professional opportunities, most subjects were drawn home to poor rural communities largely by non-economic factors only the South and home can offer.

Southern black history and the rural, rustic places served as attractions. She also argued that black return migrants particularly are drawn by "personal and family ties" — the bonds "never broken between people never entirely departed" — to particular places (Stack, 1996, p. 16). They return, however, armed with skills learned outside the South and with the realization that the "New South" does not necessarily mean new racial attitudes. Returning African Americans recognize that white politicians and bureaucrats still often provide barriers to improvements for black people. Thus, black migrants are prepared to take risks, fight the establishment, and apply their skills with the intention of modifying southern places during their own lifetimes. Such changes, in the eyes of those interviewed, will come only through entrepreneurship and struggle that means confrontation with the white-controlled system. Thus, returning black migrants are far from being naïve. Rather, in Stack's words, they come to "create another place in that place you left behind" (p. 199).

It is necessary to look empirically at black return migration at a different scale to better understand origins and destinations and perhaps some of the implicit macro reasons for African Americans departure for other regions. William H. Frey has termed the black migration to the South the "new Great Migration" and reported broadly on its origins, destinations and the attributes of black migrants between 1965 and 2000 (Frey, 2004). He noted that destinations have differed between white and black migrants over the past generation. Black destinations represented a narrower choice set than those destinations chosen by white migrants. In particular, metropolitan Atlanta and Washington, D.C., represented the preferred destinations of blacks, while whites were more likely to migrate to Los Angeles, Phoenix, and other southern communities. Another observation is the large loss of black migrants to the South from certain large northern metropolitan regions, such as New York and Chicago. Finally, Frey suggested that black college graduates are leading the "reverse" migration and are migrating selectively, including to places like Texas, Georgia, and Maryland, while being drawn disproportionately away from states like New York (Frey, 2004). Frey also offered some potential explanations for this migration reversal, including southern economic prosperity, family ties, social networks, and an improved racial climate.

The most recent black migration data reported by the U.S. Census are the county-to-county migration files for the period 1995–2000. Table 7.1 includes gross and net migration data for U.S. census-defined regions. A number of observations can be made from these data. First, nearly one million blacks (gross migration) moved between the South and these three other regions during this five-year period, indicating that the reverse migration continued at the close of the 20th century. Second, the highest gross black migration total (the number of migrants moving in and out of regions combined) occurred between the South and the Northeast regions (393,436), followed closely by the South-Midwest gross migration total (347,453). Third, the net migration (the difference between the totals moving into and out of a region) amounted to a combined loss of 334,237 blacks from the three regions to the South in just five years. The Northeast accounted for about 60 percent of this overall loss. In fact, more than a quarter million blacks departed the Northeast for the South, while only 95,640 southern blacks moved to the Northeast during the five-year period.

Despite the fact that the net migration between the West and South amounted to a relatively modest numerical loss (58,202) for the West, this trend has created concern among California's college administrators. The black out-migration may represent a brain drain of the youngest and brightest out of that region, and has already contributed to a decreasing number of African American college applications, which already are "alarmingly low" (Pikman, 2005).

One final observation must be made regarding the use of U.S. Census data. The Census contains a "race" variable. In short, respondents must declare their "race." For migration purposes, all blacks are treated as a single group, despite black ethnic diversity. Thus, when we speak of the black reverse migration, we cannot differentiate native African Americans from black natives of Caribbean or African ancestry. The only distinction possible using the migration flow files is by nativity, which indicates foreign-born or native-born status. We will return to a discussion of nativity in our analysis.

MIGRANT SELECTIVITY, REGION AND PLACE

Migration literature has emphasized that the migration process is selective (Long, 1988; Tobler, 1995; and Schacter, 2001). Rather than a pool of migrants representing a cross-section of the population at an origin, push and pull factors at the origin and destination exert differential impacts on certain residents who decide to migrate. Generally, migrant selectivity theory argues that individuals with certain characteristics are more likely to migrate than others whose attributes are different. For example, individuals who acquire human capital (education, job skills, etc.) are more likely to become migrants than those without the same advantages. Thus, migration operates as a selective process. Of course, other factors, such as age, also come into play and are part of migrant selectivity theory. The theory suggests that younger people, from the teenage years through their thirties, are more likely to be migrants than older persons (although those of retirement age are more likely to move than those in their 40s and 50s). Migrant selectivity theory, then, argues that individual characteristics influence the decision to migrate and, therefore, determine the nature of a migrant stream from place to place.

Table 7.1

U. S. Black Regional Migration, 1995–2000						
In/Out Regional Flows Between Regions			Gross Migration Flows Between Regions		Net Migration Flows	
Origin	Destination	Flows	Regions	Flows	Regions	Flows
Northeast	South	297,796	Northeast-South	393,436	Northeast-South	-202,156
Midwest	South	210,666	Midwest-South	347,453	Midwest-South	-73,879
West	South	154,388	West-South	250,574	West-South	-58,202
South	Northeast	95,640	Total	991,463	Total	-334,237
South	Midwest	136,787				
South	West	96,186				
Source: U. S. Bureau of the Census, 2002, Flow Files.						

Implicit in the migrant selectivity framework is that one potential destination may hold a stronger attraction than another destination for a variety of reasons. The collective attraction of a location has been termed place utility. Given the differential attraction among places, migrant flows between places should emerge and attract migrants with particular characteristics. The scale used to portray and analyze such migrant flows is guided by the purpose of the researcher. Many are interested in regional flows of migrants that suggest ways in which the U.S. is changing. This scale of analysis revealed the reverse migration of blacks from other U.S. regions to the South. However, this regional scale does not permit examination of flow characteristics between places of these regions. Given the arguments of migrant selectivity theory, we might expect different flows to sets of places within the destination region from the same city of origin. For example, we might expect differential flows between southern cities and New York City based on the various attractive qualities of each place to New York City migrants.

New York City has experienced a great deal of migration, in and out of the five boroughs. Where do migrants out of the City locate within the South? Frey indicated that the Northeast lost a large black migrant population to the South and especially to the Atlanta metropolitan region in recent decades. This raises any number of questions related to migrant selectivity theory. Addressing a few such questions contributes to our understanding of differential black migrant streams between places. Our focus is on New York City (the five boroughs) and the South.

Before examining migrant flows between New York City and three southern metropolitan areas, it is informative to examine a single variable at various geographic scales to illustrate the importance of scale choice. Nativity refers to the location of birth, either as native-born or foreign-born migrant. In the case of black Americans, it determines whether one is an American by birth or is an immigrant. Any number of questions can be raised about nativity and migration at different geographic scales. For one, we may simply be interested in what proportion of the regional black migration stream between the Northeast and South is by American blacks. Calculations from U.S. Census data show that 84.3 percent of the black migrants leaving the Northeast for the South between 1995 and 2000 (for those providing location of their birth data) were native blacks. The reverse flow, South to North, was even slightly higher; 90.5 percent were native black Americans. However, if we change geographic scale, and pose the same question about New York City migrant streams from and to the South, the answer changes somewhat. Those percentages drop to 76 percent and 85 percent, respectively. This illustrates the role of New York City as a an immigrant gateway and explains why nearly one in four black southbound migrants from New York City, 1995–2000, were foreign-born. In terms of migrant selectivity, the South holds a differential attraction to New York City foreign-born blacks than it does from other northern origins.

If we change our scale again and consider places within the South, we should also expect that some places are disproportionately more attractive than others. For example, larger metropolitan regions likely to have a greater range of employment opportunities than smaller areas. Similarly, certain communities will have disproportionate numbers of members of specific ethnic groups than other communities. If ethnic affinity is important to some migrants, then southern ethnically diverse communities will hold an advantage as potential destinations, when all other factors are equal. These are only a few examples of characteristics that make particular places more attractive than others. Our focus is on three southern metropolitan areas, Atlanta, Miami, and Houston, in relation to black migrant flows with New York City.

Frey noted the differences in destination choices between northern blacks and whites and the disproportionate attraction of Atlanta over other southern communities for black reverse migrants in recent decades (Frey, 2004). A corollary is that the flow of black migrants from New York City to Atlanta was larger than the black flows to either Miami or Houston in the 1995–2000 period. Similarly, we should expect that Georgia attracted more black migrants than any other southern state. Figure 7.3 portrays the flows between New York City and the southern states and illustrates that Florida had the highest flow, followed by Georgia. The "Atlanta" hypothesis is tested and the results portrayed in Figure 7.4, which illustrates the magnitude of the flows between New York City's five boroughs and the three southern MSAs. The flow maps support acceptance of the hypothesis; Atlanta attracted more black migrants than Miami and Houston in the 1995–2000 period.

Figure 7.3

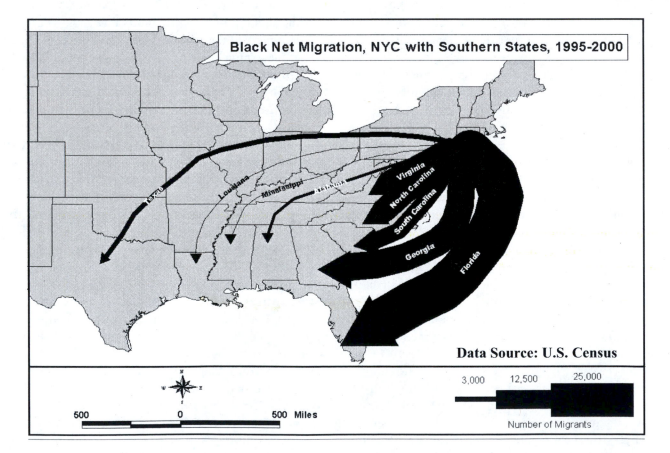

Figure 7.4

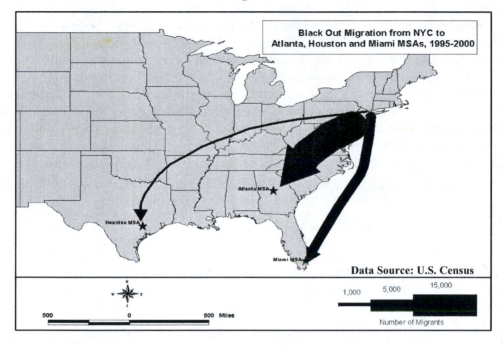

Table 7.2 reports a cross-tabulation of the same flows by nativity. The table addresses the question of whether or not an interrelationship exists between migrant flows and nativity. The data reveal a significant relationship. Nearly nine of ten (87%) black migrants moving from Atlanta to New York City were native-born blacks, while nearly seven of ten (69%) leaving New York City for Atlanta also were native blacks. However, the pattern changes significantly when New York City-Miami flows are considered. In contrast to the Atlanta flows, slightly more than 57 percent of the black reverse migrants (NYC to Miami) were foreign-born blacks, compared to only 31 percent of the same stream for the Atlanta case. The same foreign-born factor was present in the Miami to New York City flow; slightly more than 44 percent were foreign-born blacks, compared to only 12.9 percent in the Atlanta-NYC black migrant stream. These findings illustrate clearly the importance of place in defining migrant selectivity. Atlanta is a traditional African American city where many northern native blacks have a sense of cultural history, family, or friends. Miami, on the other hand, is an international metropolitan region with stronger ties to the Caribbean than Atlanta and, thus, would naturally hold a greater attraction for migrating foreign-born blacks from New York City.

Table 7.2

Black Migrant Streams by Nativity, NYC * and Atlanta and Miami MSAs, 1995–2000			
Migration Flows	Nativity		
	Native-Born	Foreign-Born	Totals
Atlanta to NYC	1,855 (87.1 percent)	274 (12.9 percent)	2,129 (100 percent)
NYC to Atlanta	9,409 (69.0 percent)	4,233 (31.0 percent)	13,642 (100 percent)
Miami to NYC	935 (55.7 percent)	745 (44.4 percent)	1,680 (100 percent)
NYC to Miami	1,520 (42.8 percent)	2,034 (57.2 percent)	3,554 (100 percent)
Totals	13,719	7,286	21,005
Chi Square= 1394.4 for 3 degrees of freedom. Significant at the .001 level of confidence.			
* Data represents migrants to and from the five boroughs.			

As Cromartie and Stack noted, census data can capture place-related macro structural factors, such as climate, employment opportunities, and educational levels, but they cannot substitute for detailed individual case histories that explain in depth micro factors typically not included in macro-economic models. Such factors include but are not limited to intricate social ties, the health of aging parents, "topophilia," or the sentiment toward place, and the desire to make social and economic change in places one cares about. They also will not capture the meanings of emerging cultural landscapes that millions of black migrants inevitably will infuse.

Such observations and insights will be crucial to developing an understanding of the newest black movements and their impacts on specific southern places. The complexity of migration patterns should not be lost on generalized findings of macro data alone. Black Americans are changing the demographic, ethnic, and racial dimensions of particular southern places. There may be a new racial climate, but this does not negate the reality of the continued racial struggle noted by Stack's findings. The nature of individual migrant streams between specific places and their impacts beg further analysis. So do the reinvented African American landscapes emerging across the South. A great deal of work remains for a better understanding of the various dimensions of this complex movement and the newly emerging black geographies. Hopefully, students will meet this challenge.

Chapter 8

Lending and Race in Two Cities:
A Comparison of Subprime Mortgages, Predatory Mortgages, and Foreclosures in Washington, D.C. and Akron, Ohio

DAVID H. KAPLAN AND GAIL SOMMERS

A new form of housing finance has emerged within the past 10 years. Up until the mid 1990s, studies of mortgage lending were more concerned with whether mortgage lenders avoided loans in the inner city. The volume of loans in poor, predominantly African-American, inner city neighborhoods was disproportionately small and denial rates were disproportionately high. In the extreme form of "redlining," such neighborhoods were considered too risky and excluded from all mortgage investment. In response to this, several fair housing protections were put into place in the 1970s. Still, residents of poorer neighborhoods enjoyed limited access to mortgages of any kind. The banks were not physically present, the volume of loans was small, and those applicants who did apply for a mortgage were more likely to be denied. This was especially true among African-American applicants, where denial rates were roughly double that of white applicants, assuming that they had access to mortgage lenders in the first place.

During the 1990s, there was an explosion in so-called "subprime" lending — lending that assessed higher interest rates and fees for some prospective homeowners. At their best, subprime loans allow households to enter a mortgage market from which they would otherwise be disqualified. Subprime lenders are attracted to lower- and moderate-income households while these same households are interested in what these lenders had to offer. While the supply and demand for subprime lenders is found throughout the metropolitan areas, income segregation has led to a concentration of subprime lending activity in specific neighborhoods. Subprime loans are also much more likely to occur in African-American neighborhoods than in white neighborhoods.

There is a further problem with several of these mortgage instruments in that some impose an undue financial burden on households by forcing debts that far exceed assets. In the worst case, the result may be foreclosure. In other cases, it means that households are paying more than they should in debt servicing. These types of loans have been termed "predatory" and have become the focus of a great deal of recent community activism.

There are several ways to study the phenomenon of predatory lending. One approach is to examine the activities of a known lender. A geographical study would explore the degree to which lender activities are unevenly distributed or where the spatial distribution of this lending covaries with other neighborhood aspects. A second approach would be to examine the distribution of all loans, noting in particular the incidence of foreclosures, subprime loans, and (if information is available) predatory loans. This chapter utilizes both approaches to compare the racial geography of subprime lending in both Washington, D.C. and Akron, Ohio. These two cities, very different in size and importance, reflect the widespread nature of the predatory lending phenomenon.

SUBPRIME LOANS, PREDATORY LENDING, AND FORECLOSURES

In 1995, there were approximately 21 subprime lenders making 24,000 loans (not including refinances). By 1998, some 256 subprime lenders were making 207,000 loans (Hong and Sommers, 2000). This rapid increase far outstripped the overall mortgage market, to the extent that subprime lending went from being a tiny fraction of the "prime" market — about one percent — to a substantial proportion that some estimate has closed in on ten percent (Engel and McCoy, 2001).

Subprime loans are those loans made available to customers who do not enjoy the credit qualifications necessary to secure a "prime" mortgage loan. In mortgage lending terminology, prime borrowers are rated as "A." This rating is determined largely on the basis of a credit score and entitles the borrower to the lowest rates and often fewer fees. It may be up to the borrower to pay additional points (each representing one percent of the total cost of the loan) but in return (s)he can expect even lower interest rates.

Those borrowers that do not meet the credit criteria to secure a prime loan need to settle for a subprime loan. These borrowers are divided into categories of "A–," "B," "C," and "D," with nearly two-thirds falling within the A– rating and another one-quarter included as "B" (CRA-NC, p. 3). This has been a large potential market that became much more attractive in the 1990s for several reasons (Engel and McCoy, 2001).

Most studies have noted the extent to which mortgage lenders avoided loans in the inner city and focused instead on suburbs and affluent city neighborhoods. The volume of loans in these poorer neighborhoods was disproportionately small. In its extreme form, this was a practice known as "redlining." What made this practice especially pernicious was that such neighborhoods tended to have a large African-American population. To address this and other issues, the 1975 Home Mortgage Disclosure Act (HMDA) mandated that banks over a certain size report the number, location, and disposition of loans by race and sex. These data have continued to be used by researchers and public advocacy groups to disclose gaps and disparities within the mortgage market. Moreover, the 1977 Community and Reinvestment Act (CRA) required that banks retain a presence in LMI (Lower- and Moderate-Income) neighborhoods. In some instances, lawsuits were successfully filed against banks that evaded their CRA responsibilities. Such fair housing efforts still did not fill the void.

Subprime loans became a way for many borrowers to qualify for mortgages that would have previously been out of reach. Subprime lenders tended to focus on LMI borrowers and neighborhoods, those same neighborhoods that lacked prime lenders. Increases in housing prices nationwide affected many poorer neighborhoods, increasing property values and therefore home equity. Homeownership rates increased among the poor, which meant more opportunities for refinancing. In fact, many poorer households found themselves in trouble with credit card, automobile, and other forms of debt, while maintaining significant equity in their homes. Mortgages that offered debt consolidation could be very attractive to such households, offering a way out of immediate credit difficulties. Refinancing represents about 80 percent of the subprime mortgage market (HUD, 2000). As far as lenders were concerned, subprime loans offered a way to make more money through higher interest rates in a mortgage market where prime rates were falling to record lows.

In brief, subprime lenders were attracted to lower- and moderate-income households, while lower- and moderate-income households were interested in what these lenders had to offer. While such households — and the demand for subprime lenders — were found throughout the metropolitan areas, income segregation led to a concentration of subprime lending activity in specific neighborhoods. An analysis by the Department of Housing and Urban Development concluded that a disproportionate percentage of subprime loans occurred in low-income neighborhoods — representing about one-quarter of all loans made in poor neighborhoods (HUD, 2000). In fact, subprime loans were three times more likely to occur in low-income compared to high-income neighborhoods. The analysis further pointed out a racial dimension to subprime lending. Subprime loans were five times more likely to occur in African-American neighborhoods than in white neighborhoods. Part of this could be attributable to income disparities, but much occurred independent of income. In fact, the HUD analysis showed that high-income black neighborhoods reported twice as many subprime loans as *low-income* white neighborhoods.

On the face of it, subprime loans offer a valuable service to those households that would not be able to enter into the conventional mortgage market. As such, they could be viewed as falling in a long line of efforts to facilitate homeownership and similar in certain respects to loans offered by the Federal Housing Administration (FHA) that make mortgages available for households that cannot afford a higher down payment. But this service comes at a price. Subprime loans stipulate higher loan rates, greater fees, or other elements — like prepayment penalties. Subprime lenders often maintain that these additional charges are necessary to defray the costs of making a riskier loan. Advocacy groups suggest that the pricing of subprime loans is out of proportion to the risks. Interest rates on subprime loans, for instance, are generally greater than the rates charged for automobile loans, although the risks are smaller. Subprime loans are generally quite profitable, with returns estimated at six times that of banks (Coalition for Responsible Lending, 2001).

In addition, there is the prospect that certain households and those living within some neighborhoods end up with a subprime loan even when they may qualify for a prime loan. Studies conducted by Freddie Mac and Standard and Poor indicated that about one-half of the A-rated borrowers would qualify for a conventional, prime loan (Conference of State Bank Supervisors, 2000). Given that these A-borrowers are about two-thirds of the subprime market, this means that one-third of subprime borrowers should be able to acquire the better terms of a prime loan. Also, given the preponderance of subprime loans among the poor and minority populations, it might follow that this slippage has a discriminatory effect.

The distinction between subprime lending and predatory lending is difficult to draw. In the very recent literature on predatory lending, much of the effort goes towards attempting to create working definitions, but it can be a matter of degree rather than kind. To take a case in point, subprime lenders would understandably seek higher interest rates in return for the greater degree of risk. In this case, their situation is analogous to bond issuers. Those issuers with a lower credit rating must offer a higher interest premium. But when do these rates become predatory? Subprime lenders may also seek more fees to compensate for the higher costs of servicing the loan. The absolute size of the loan is often smaller — as expected with lower income properties — and the fees in percentage terms are usually greater. When does this otherwise legitimate practice become predatory?

Several manuals offer methods of defining predatory lending. One of the most comprehensive comes from Sturdevant and Brennan (2000), who mention the following predatory practices:

- Overly onerous interest rates, sometimes falling in a range between 19 and 25 percent, when conventional mortgage rates were less than 8 percent.
- High points, which may account for 20 percent of the total loan cost. This is especially noteworthy because conventional mortgage points are 1 to 3 percent, and work to reduce the interest rate. In predatory lending, no such trade-off occurs.
- Misrepresentation of loan terms to the borrowers that hide many of the fees assessed. There is also misrepresentation of the applicants to capital markets. Lenders may overstate applicant income or debt burden, for example, in order to place them in loans that they could not realistically afford.
- Equity stripping through negative amortization, which reduces rather than builds equity, and through balloon payments that demand an amount at the end of a period that is sometimes equal or greater than the original loan.
- Excessive prepayment penalties that lock borrowers into a predatory loan and make it impossible for them to refinance with another company.
- The promotion of loan-to-value ratios in excess of 100 percent, or more than the cost of the property. This is done through the addition of unsecured debt, like credit card bills, into the loan or even the addition of the loan fees themselves. Either way, it puts the borrower at great financial peril.
- "Flipping" the loans several times through frequent refinancing at the instigation of the mortgage company. This may allow for short-term payment reduction, but in effect reduces the amount of equity and adds layers of additional fees.
- "Packing" the loan with lots of unnecessary fees and items like excessive insurance.
- Steering the borrower into higher interest loans when they probably qualify for lower interest loans. Sometimes this is accompanied by a kickback to lenders for bringing in the borrower at a higher rate.

These practices are unethical. They charge people more than they need to. They end up stripping away equity from households and assets from poor neighborhoods. They often end in foreclosure; sometimes this is the goal. Because predatory loans are found disproportionately in poorer neighborhoods they end up cheating people least able to protect themselves. And because they are found disproportionately in African-American neighborhoods, they end up as racially discriminatory, at least in outcome. They may or may not be illegal, however.

While many subprime lenders do not engage in these practices, some do. One advocacy group estimated that, among borrowers of subprime lenders, about one-half experience some degree of predatory lending (Conference of State Bank Supervisors, 2000). At the same time, it is important to note that these practices are not just confined to the subprime market. There are examples of predatory practices found in FHA and Veterans Administration (VA) sponsored loans (Fishbein and Bunce, 2000).

Because predatory lending is relatively recent, government actions have taken some time to catch up. North Carolina probably has the most progressive predatory lending statute. It defines what are considered high-cost loans and limits the ability of lenders to modify the rates and fees through flipping and other mechanisms. A New York law passed in 2002 explicitly prohibits flipping and packing and requires counseling. Illinois requires consumer counseling for high-risk loans. The types of action that can be taken are limited, however, and must be careful not to result in elimination of subprime lending altogether.

For a household, the worst possible outcome of a mortgage is a foreclosure. The process of residential foreclosure occurs when a mortgage holder is legally separated from the property to which s/he holds title and thereby loses all claims to the property. Foreclosures are a sign of severe economic distress, and are generally the last step in a process of increasing indebtedness.

The relationship between residential foreclosure and subprime or predatory lending is intuitive but largely untested. Sometimes foreclosure may be the goal among unscrupulous lenders. More often, we suspect, it is an unfortunate outcome of a process whereby financially vulnerable borrowers are led to take on too much debt with terms that are overly onerous.

While foreclosures can occur in any situation, from a financial standpoint, more non-conventional, non-prime-level mortgaged properties end up as foreclosures. In our analysis of the Akron area, 34 percent of foreclosures originated with subprime lenders, while only about seven percent of all loans were subprime. Foreclosures and subprime/predatory lending also coincide geographically. Again in our Akron study, among "high foreclosure" block groups, 16.1 percent of loans were from subprime lenders, compared to only 3.7 percent among "low foreclosure" block groups. In American metropolitan areas, geographic location is an important barometer of one's income, race, and lifestyle — so much so that companies like Claritas have been established to exploit this relationship for marketing purposes — so the geographic coincidences strongly suggest relationships at the scale of the household. Finally, from an analysis standpoint, foreclosure data are often the most precise data series we have available in our tool kit. As our previous discussion made clear, predatory lending is difficult to identify. Sometimes, we need to rely on foreclosures in order to infer other geographic patterns.

RACIAL TARGETING IN WASHINGTON, D.C.

The first example of predatory lending comes from activities conducted by a Washington, D.C. area subprime lender (Kaplan, 2004). The Lender — not identified because the case has been settled — was alleged to be engaged in the practice of predatory lending to poorer families and churches, which resulted in foreclosure. These loans were generally refinanced to help consolidate debt. Interest rates were set at 24 to 30 percent. There was a significant amount of misrepresentation of the loan terms themselves. Additional and unreasonable charges were assessed. Balloon payments at the end of a short period were often as high as the original principal. These loans were structured to fail and, in fact, "The Lender" initiated foreclosure proceedings on about one-half of the loans, successfully foreclosing on about one in five. In most cases, The Lender would take these foreclosed properties and resell them.

As is evident in Figure 8.1 most of the loans were made in the District itself and in Prince Georges County in suburban Maryland. These areas also correspond with neighborhoods whose majority is African American. Moreover, The Lender appeared to be targeting African-American borrowers. The intent of this analysis was to demonstrate the extent to which targeting occurred. The properties securing loans from the "The Lender" were found predominantly in census blocks with a large percentage of African Americans. Figure 8.2 illustrates that the vast majority of the properties securing loans from "The Lender" were in majority black (86 percent) neighborhood. Also, a substantial majority of the loans (59 percent) were located in census blocks that had a proportion of 90 percent black or more.

The distribution of loans (see Figure 8.2) is far more skewed towards predominantly African-American census blocks (skewed to the right) than the population as a whole. The figure also shows the distribution of population among all 22,763 Washington, D.C. area blocks by percent black. This line graph represents the divided racial geography of the D.C. area. Very few blocks and people are found in the middle of D.C.'s racial spectrum. Over 50 percent of all people live in blocks with fewer that 15 percent black and this represents about 62 percent of all census blocks (see line graph). At the same time, about 14 percent of the population, and 12 percent of all blocks, were found to be more than 90 percent black. In this case, clearly the population skew is towards the left, in those blocks with a negligible black population.

Figure 8.1
Distribution of Loans in D.C. Region, 2001–2003

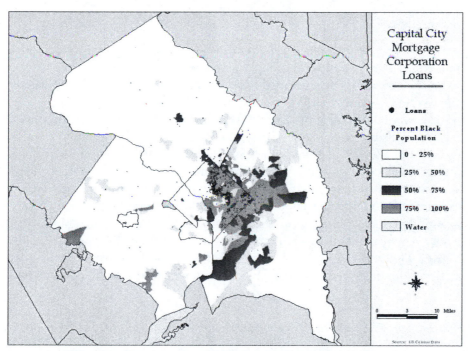

The distribution of loans is statistically different from the distribution of population. A two-tail t-test indicates that there is less than a 0.6 percent probability that the distribution of loans made by The Lender in predominantly or majority black census blocks was attributable to chance. Put another way, there is a 99.4 percent probability that the distributions are different (whereas the standard statistical threshold that has to be met is 95 percent probability). Another measure that can be used is the index of dissimilarity. This is a measure of "unevenness." The number indicates what percentage of loans would need to be relocated so that their distribution matched that of the population. An analysis of dissimilarity indicates that 60.6 percent, or 644 of the 1063 loans, would have to be redistributed to match the distribution of the population.

Figure 8.2

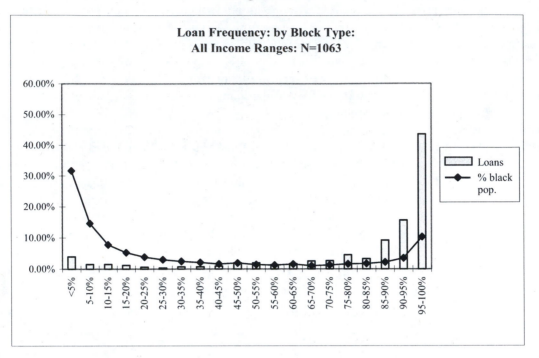

The statistically significant difference was found when considering loans made in the District of Columbia as well as in the suburban counties. In other words, the apparent targeting of African-American neighborhoods was not a consequence of The Lender focusing loan activity only within the central city. So racial targeting occurred both within Washington, D.C. and its surrounding suburbs.

Moreover, the skewed distribution of loans to African-American blocks is independent of the effects of income (Table 8.1). The census blocks were classified into three ranges according to median household income: less than $20,000, $20,000 to $40,000, and more than $40,000. The distribution of loans continued to be different from the distribution of population within these three income bands. The table compares the number of loans made in black majority blocks compared to the population distribution. For example, nearly 87 percent of the population in low-income blocks are also in black-majority blocks, pointing out the correspondence between these two measures. But more than 96 percent of all loans are made in low-income, black-majority blocks — an even higher percentage. About one-half of the population in moderate-income blocks is also found in black-majority blocks, but over 93 percent of all loans were made there. For those wealthier neighborhoods, about 11 percent of the population is found in black-majority blocks, but almost 62 percent of loans occurred there.

Table 8.1
Distribution of Loans to African Americans in Washington, D.C. by Block

	Majority Black Blocks		Two-Tail Probability
	Loans	Population	of Similarity
<$20K	96.69%	87.14%	13.5%
$20K – $40K	93.70%	49.73%	0.01%
Over $40K	61.98%	11.09%	0.04%

The last column shows the probability that there is a statistical similarity between the distribution of loans and population. Statistical significance is often held at the 5 percent level. For those loans made in census blocks where the median income was over $40K and for those loans made in census blocks where the median income was between $20K and $40K, the results were statistically significant. For those loans made in census blocks under $20,000, the difference did not meet the threshold of statistical significance (partly because the sample size was only 181 and partly because there is a strong correspondence between these neighborhoods and predominantly African-American neighborhoods).

FORECLOSURES AND SUBPRIME LENDING IN AKRON, OHIO

This second case study focuses on the racial geography of recent subprime and predatory lending activity in Summit County, Ohio — a county that includes Akron and surrounding suburbs. Public property records, foreclosure files, and federally collected banking data determine where these lending activities take place, whether particular practices or outcomes correspond with certain neighborhood characteristics, and the extent to which some neighborhoods are affected by the practices of subprime and predatory lending.

Answers to these questions require the assembly of a number of large data sets. Chief among these is a foreclosure file that was compiled from individual foreclosure records stored in the County Recorder's Office. Other information assembled included all residential property transactions in Summit County, including by borrower, lender, size of loan, property value, and a list of subprime lenders from the Department of Housing and Urban Development, as well as block group level census data from 2000 and 1990.

Subprime and Predatory Lending

The extent of subprime lending can be shown with two maps (Figures 8.3 and 8.4) and a table (Table 8.2). The first map shows the percentage of loans that are subprime loans throughout Summit County. Here, it is clear that the proportion of subprime loans falls sharply away from the central city. Subprime loans are more than twice as likely in Akron than in the suburbs. Subprime loans are also focused within a few neighborhoods, as this second map makes clearer. What this means is that particular neighborhoods bear the brunt of subprime lending — and these are often neighborhoods that have been underserved by the conventional mortgage process.

The difference between a prime and a subprime loan often shows up in the interest rate. A proportion (about one-tenth) of the loan records indicated the interest rate and allowed us to calculate averages, although fees are not available. Generally, the interest rate charged on a subprime loan was about two percentage points higher than on a prime loan. Subprime loans were also smaller than prime loans.

The geographic correlates of subprime lending indicate a pronounced tendency for subprime loans to be found in neighborhoods with high percentages of minorities, lower socioeconomic status, greater vacancy rates, and higher levels of housing stress, as demonstrated by mortgage payments over 30 percent of income and loan-to-value ratios over 100 percent (see Table 8.2).

If we examine the mortgage data for each individual transaction, more subprime loans are built on a shakier financial foundation, as over one-quarter of subprime loans exceed the value of the property. Nearly 18 percent of subprime loans originated with loan amounts greater than the value of the property, compared to 11 percent of all loans.

Unlike our Washington, D.C. study, where "The Lender" was alleged to have made predatory loans throughout the metro area, incidences of predatory lending are more difficult to gauge in this Akron area study. A set of alleged predatory lenders was assembled, on the basis of previously published lists (Stocks, 2002) and court cases, but we are not necessarily comfortable with using the results of this list because it paints an entire bank or mortgage company as "predatory" when only the tiniest fraction of this company's activity may even be alleged to be predatory.

Figure 8.3
Subprime Loans in Summit County, Ohio, 1999–2001

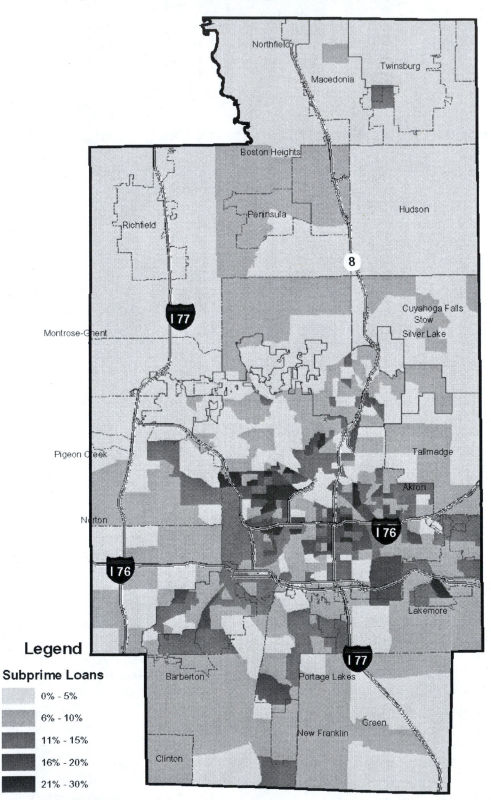

Figure 8.4
The Concentration of Subprime Loans in Akron Area Neighborhoods, 1999–2001

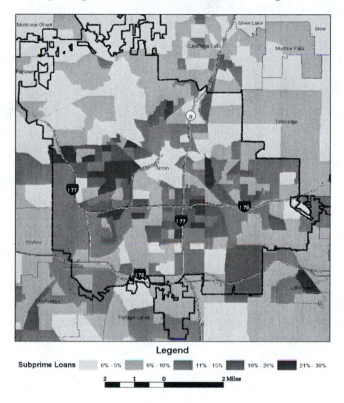

Legend

Subprime Loans 0% - 5%   6% - 10%   11% - 15%   16% - 20%   21% - 30%

2   1   0   2 Miles

Table 8.2
Geographic Correlates of Subprime Lending

Variables	Sub Prime Pct.
Women 65+ Percent	**-0.15**
Black Pct 2000	**0.48**
Black Pct Change 1990–2000	0.08
Minority Pct 2000	**0.48**
Minority Pct Change 1990–2000	**0.12**
Unemployment Pct 2000	**0.34**
Median HH Income 2000	**-0.50**
Vacant Pct 2000	**0.27**
Vacant % Change 1990–2000	0.02
Mortgage Payment over 30%	**0.31**
Loan to Value > 100% Pct	**0.36**
Loan to Value > 80% Pct	**0.38**
Percent Not in residence in 1995	0.06
Poverty Percent 2000	**0.37**
Poverty % Change 1990–2000	**-0.19**
Significant at 5% level	

When our list of predatory lenders is used in the analysis, it indicates that: 1) Akron originates a larger number of loans from these identified predatory lenders than do the suburbs; 2) predatory lenders tend to originate higher interest rates and lower mortgage amounts, although the difference is slighter than in comparing subprime with prime lenders; and 3) the set of correlations with neighborhood variables presents a picture similar to that of subprime loans, albeit in most cases the association is weaker.

Analysis of Foreclosures

The incidence of foreclosures is geographically concentrated. First, the city of Akron accounts for about 64 percent of County foreclosures, despite containing much smaller percentages of population and housing units. Second, certain parts of Summit County account for most of the foreclosure activity; about 25 percent of all census tracts account for half of the foreclosures and half of all tracts account for more than three-fourths.

We standardized the foreclosure numbers by dividing them by the number of housing units within each block group. Countywide, there were 12 foreclosures during our period of analysis for every 1000 block groups, varying from a low of zero for 29 block groups to a high of 77 foreclosures per 1000 units.

The geography of foreclosures indicates a strong linkage between where foreclosures occur and where subprime lending occurs. This is apparent in the subprime percentages found within each of the foreclosure categories. The correlation between subprime percentage and the foreclosure index (see Table 8.3) is likewise high (r = 0.59). The set of correlations with the same neighborhood level variables we have used for subprime and predatory lending also indicates that there is an association.

One question might be raised as to extent to which the correlation between foreclosures and subprime lending explains much of the relationship with the other variables, particularly race. As Table 8.3 indicates, there is some indication of this, but certain variables exert an effect independent of subprime percentage.

Racial variables hold up even with the foreclosure controls. Most other variables also continue to have some effect, although generally a weaker effect. The one variable that is most affected is median household income. A simple bivariate correlation indicates that foreclosure incidence decreases with an increase in median household income. After controlling for subprime percentage, the effect is the opposite. Lower income neighborhoods are more likely to have a larger subprime presence, which in turn leads to higher foreclosure rates. But there is no independent effect.

Among the sample of foreclosures we compiled, there is clear evidence that among those lenders involved in many foreclosures, a much higher proportion tend to be subprime and identified as predatory.

The Significance of Race

The information so far suggests a strong racial effect. One way to gauge the extent of this effect is to look at the differences between neighborhoods categorized by income and racial characteristics.

Table 8.4 examines the differences between neighborhoods categorized by household income. What is clear from this view is that wealthier neighborhoods have far fewer foreclosures, a low foreclosure index, and fewer foreclosures that were originated by subprime lenders, and far fewer subprime loans in general. The only exception to that trend lies in those very poor neighborhoods where the median household income is under $20,000 a year. Fewer people can afford to enter into the mortgage market, and about 80 percent of occupied units in these neighborhoods are renter occupied, and so foreclosure rates are lower. Subprime lending rates are also lower — a finding that is more surprising.

We also looked at the Home Mortgage Disclosure Act database that reports loan application outcomes at the census tract level. This does not cover all lenders, but only those with higher level of assets, but it does give a sense of the degree to which denial rates vary by neighborhood type. It also points out the market for subprime lending has thrived largely in those areas underserved by prime lenders. The prevalence of loans from identified predatory lenders is likewise skewed. Not surprisingly, denial rates in poorer neighborhoods (see Table 8.4) are about double what they are in the wealthiest neighborhoods.

Table 8.3
Correlations Between Standardized Foreclosures and Neighborhood Variables

	FCLS Index	Control for Subprime Pct
Sub Prime Pct.	**0.59**	
Black Pct 2000	**0.58**	**0.42**
Black Pct Change 1990-2000	0.01	-0.04
Minority Pct 2000	**0.59**	**0.43**
Minority Pct Change 1990-2000	**0.15**	**0.09**
Unemployment Pct 2000	**0.35**	**0.20**
Median HH Income 2000	**-0.42**	**0.17**
Vacant Pct 2000	**0.33**	**0.22**
Vacant % Change 1990–2000	0.01	0.00
Mortgage Payment over 30%	**0.33**	**0.20**
Loan to Value > 100% Pct	**0.41**	**0.26**
Loan to Value > 80% Pct	**0.27**	**0.05**
Women 65+ Percent	**-0.19**	**-0.13**
Pct Not in Residence in 1995	0.00	-0.04
Poverty Percent 2000	**0.36**	**0.19**
Poverty % Change 1990–2000	**-0.23**	**-0.14**
Significant at 5% level		

Table 8.4
Denial Rates by Income

Income	2001–2003 Foreclosures	FCLS Index	Subprime Pct	Subprime Foreclosures	HMDA Deny Rate
Under $20K	162	1.17%	11.86%	34.57%	37.7%
$20K–$30K	824	2.60%	14.26%	40.90%	39.3%
$30K–$40K	870	1.70%	9.99%	34.94%	33.8%
$40K–$50K	607	1.00%	6.52%	27.68%	27.2%
Over $50K	479	0.65%	3.61%	25.89%	18.6%

The next table (Table 8.5) examines the differences between neighborhoods categorized by minority composition. The figures show a clear pattern: neighborhoods with at least 50 percent minorities have more than triple the foreclosure incidence as neighborhoods that are over 90 percent non-Hispanic white. Subprime and predatory rates are likewise much higher in minority neighborhoods, and more foreclosures occurred from loans made by subprime lenders. Denial rates for HMDA registered loans are greater in majority-minority neighborhoods.

Putting together income and minority composition shows that both variables are important and operate somewhat independently. Within the $20,000 to $30,000 set of neighborhoods, majority-minority neighborhoods have more than double the incidence of foreclosure and a far higher subprime presence than do small minority neighborhoods. Similarly, wealthier neighborhoods with a substantial minority presence have a lower foreclosure incidence and a slightly lower proportion of subprime loans than do poorer neighborhoods. In regard to the proportion of foreclosures that originated with a subprime lender, there are some similar trends here as well.

Table 8.5
Denial Rates by Neighborhood Composition

Minority Composition	Foreclosures	FCLS Index	Subprime Pct	Subprime Foreclosures	HMDA Deny Rate
Small Minority	1301	0.94%	5.82%	28.67%	25.0%
Minority 1/10 to 1/4	470	1.05%	5.83%	34.04%	28.5%
Minority 1/4 to 1/2	360	1.74%	11.26%	35.83%	36.2%
Majority Minority	811	3.05%	15.33%	40.32%	43.0%

In general, our data indicate that the racial geography of the Akron area plays an enormous role in structuring the geography of foreclosures and of subprime lending. Socioeconomic status — manifested through household income, poverty rates, and unemployment rates — also exerts a powerful effect. Yet, the racial effect is independent and a way to graphically illustrate this is through an examination of both foreclosure incidences and subprime percentages among the reasonably affluent.

The next two figures (Figures 8.5 and 8.6) assume a household income of $40,000 — generally a population with reasonable credit and the ability to afford a mortgage. The foreclosure incidence is low, less than 6 percent of all housing units in any event. Yet, the level of foreclosures is quite sensitive to the minority composition, as calculated by a simple regression model. All white block groups have roughly half the incidence of foreclosures as do all minority census block groups. The same dynamic applies when looking at the percentage of loans that are from subprime lenders. Only about one of eight mortgages in all-white neighborhoods — both in Akron city and in suburban Summit County — are from subprime lenders. In all-minority neighborhoods, closer to one out of five mortgages are from subprime lenders.

COMPARING THE TWO CASES

The two cases mentioned above differ by location, method, and units of analysis. The Washington, D.C. case tracks the activities of a single lender — alleged to be engaged in predatory practices — in order to assess the extent to which loans made by this lender target particular neighborhoods. The Akron, Ohio, case examines the universe of all loans made for home purchases (not including refinances and home improvement loans) between 1999 and 2001, and then considers all foreclosures for a period of 16 months between 2001 and 2003. From these data, it is possible to examine the distribution of loans from subprime lenders, lenders alleged to be predatory, and the pattern of foreclosures.

There are several points of agreement between these two case studies that reflect common aspects of today's lending environment. First, the geographical distribution of all of this loan activity — from individual lenders alleged as predatory, to all subprime loans, to foreclosures — cannot be attributed to chance. It differs markedly from the general distribution of houses and mortgages. Second, the loan activity reported here is correlated with the minority composition of neighborhoods and this is especially apparent for African-American neighborhoods. Third, this predisposition of subprime loans, predatory loans, or foreclosure outcomes towards minority neighborhoods exists independently of the socioeconomic status of those neighborhoods. Income matters a great deal, of course, but race matters above and beyond the effects of income. Fourth, given the racial geography of American metropolitan areas and our use of small spatial units (blocks or block groups), we feel that we can reasonably infer that the geographical targeting demonstrated in these analyses corresponds to the racial targeting of specific households.

Figure 8.5

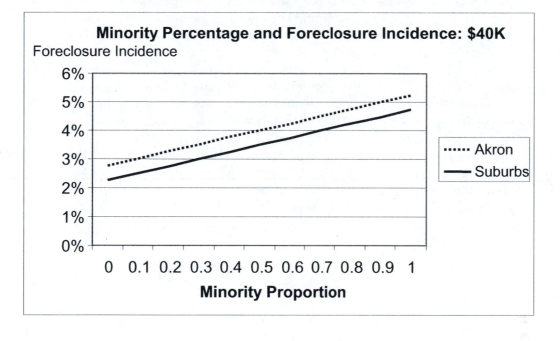

Figure 8.6

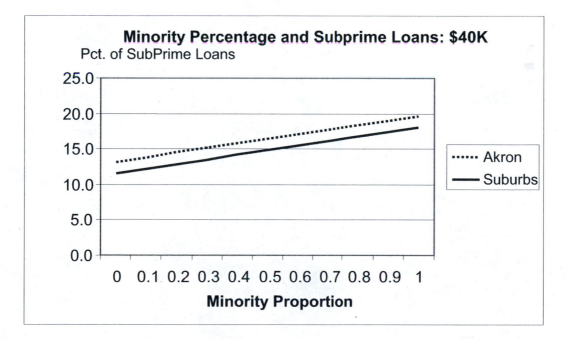

Subprime lending provides an option to those households that could not otherwise qualify for a mortgage. Moreover, borrowers in the subprime market represent higher degrees of risk and so may be more likely to foreclose. In this respect, the growth of subprime lending since the early 1990s represents a positive development and it would be a shame to go back to a period where many households were shut out of the mortgage market. Ironically, neighborhoods with a high percentage of subprime lending are those neighborhoods previously ignored by conventional mortgage lenders. According to current data, they continue to suffer lower rates of conventional loans and higher denial rates among residents who do apply for a loan. This makes the issue of subprime lending less one of affording a choice to those who may not qualify for prime loans, and more one of constraints imposed by living within a neighborhood that many mortgage lenders ignore.

The racial geography of subprime lending, predatory lending, and foreclosures is most disturbing, and such targeting continues to be confirmed by our aggregate analysis. It could be the case that there are other factors at play, including below-average credit scores that reflect past payment histories. Micro-level information, based on the credit histories of individual households, is the only way to uncover whether this contributes to the discrepancies reported here. In any event, it is essential to provide greater levels of protection to these households, in order to make sure that they are not penalized for being poor or for being black.

Chapter 9

Concentrated Poverty, Race, and Mortgage Lending:
Implications for Anti-Predatory Lending Legislation

JOE T. DARDEN AND LOUISE JEZIERSKI

INTRODUCTION

The differential access to mortgage loans based on race, class, and residential location of population groups is a serious public policy issue. It appears from reports that populations that are black or Hispanic and reside in areas of concentrated poverty are more likely to be denied prime loans and forced to obtain subprime loans (U.S. Department of Housing and Urban Development, 2000 and 2002). While prime loans are made to borrowers at the prevailing interest rates, subprime loans have interest rates that are less favorable. Indeed, some community groups consider interest rates of many subprime loans so unfavorable to the borrower that they have been called "predatory" (see National Community Reinvestment Coalition, 2002). Although the concepts of subprime and predatory lending are related, there are some slight differences. A subprime loan is made to a borrower with less than perfect credit. In order to compensate for the additional perceived risk associated with subprime loans, some lending institutions charge excessively high interest rates. Such excessively high interest rates make the loan a predatory loan.

THE CONCEPT OF A PREDATORY LOAN

A predatory loan is an unsuitable loan designed to exploit vulnerable and unsophisticated borrowers. Predatory loans are a subset of subprime loans. Thus, predatory loans are subprime, but not all subprime loans are predatory. A predatory loan has one or more of the following features: (1) charges more in interest and fees than is required to cover the added risk of lending to borrowers with credit imperfections, (2) contains abusive terms and conditions that trap borrowers and lead to increased indebtedness, (3) does not take into account the borrower's ability to repay the loan, and (4) often violates fair lending laws by targeting women, minorities, and communities of color (National Community Reinvestment Coalition, 2002, p. 4).

Targeted Groups by Subprime and Predatory Lenders

African Americans, Hispanics, and low-income residents in concentrated poverty neighborhoods are disproportionately targeted by subprime lenders in the home mortgage market. High levels of subprime mortgage lending indicate markets where borrowers are paying unusually high costs for credit. While some subprime lenders may perform a useful service by making credit available to high risk borrowers who could not otherwise borrow money, other lenders seem to be exploiting uninformed borrowers and borrowers who could otherwise qualify for conventional loans (ACORN, 2003).

Exploitation can occur in one of three ways: (1) equity stripping, i.e., charging borrowers exorbitant fees that are routinely financed into the loan, (2) rate-risk disparities, i.e., charging borrowers a higher rate of interest than their credit histories would indicate is justified, or (3) excessive foreclosures, i.e., making loans without regard to a borrower's ability to pay (Immergluck and Wiles, 1999). Some states have tried to address this practice through "anti-predatory lending" legislation.

As of March 2003, eleven states had passed anti-predatory lending legislation. Thirty-two states had introduced legislation, and seven states had not taken action to address the problem. This chapter: (1) determines the variation in subprime lending, and (2) explores the factors that may be related to the passage of anti-predatory lending legislation.

DATA AND METHODS OF ANALYSIS

Data from the 2000 U.S. Census on population by race, loan data from the Center for Community Change (Bradford, 2002), and information on state anti-predatory lending legislation were analyzed as follows. Metropolitan areas were divided into: (1) states that have passed anti-predatory lending legislation, (2) states that have introduced anti-predatory lending legislation, and (3) states that had not introduced such legislation as of March 2003. Variation in subprime lending was analyzed by computing the mean percent of subprime loans received by blacks, Hispanics, and Asians and the loan disparity ratio by race. Only refinance loans, which are prevalent in the subprime market, were used. Certain demographic and political variables were examined to determine which factors might have contributed to state variations in the passage of anti-predatory lending legislation.

CONCEPTUAL FRAMEWORK

It is hypothesized that predatory lending is inherently a problem of geography in terms of neighborhood characteristics by race and class. Thus, predatory lending follows other patterns in American society, such as residential segregation. Residential segregation among America's 330 metropolitan areas reveals a pattern of racial stratification. Blacks are the group most residentially segregated from the white majority population, followed by Hispanics. Asians are the least residentially segregated group (Iceland, Weinberg and Steinmetz, 2002). Blacks are more likely than any other group to reside in neighborhoods of concentrated poverty (Jargowsky, 2003). Blacks are followed by Hispanics, while Asians are least likely among racial minority groups to reside in concentrated poverty.

Among all racial groups, blacks are more likely to be victims of subprime lending. Hispanics are less likely than blacks to be victims and Asians are least likely to experience subprime lending, in part because they are least likely to live in areas of concentrated poverty. Since mortgage lenders are reluctant to make any loans in areas of concentrated poverty, subprime loans emerge as more competitive in such neighborhoods than are prime loans. Since blacks are more likely than any other racial group to reside in neighborhoods of concentrated poverty, they are most victimized by predatory lending.

THE CONCEPT OF CONCENTRATED POVERTY

Unlike the poverty of individual families, which is defined merely on the basis of income, concentrated poverty has a geographic or spatial dimension. It is defined as the percentage of metropolitan-wide poor individuals in each racial category living in census tracts (neighborhoods) with poverty rates of 40 percent or higher. Such neighborhoods increased between 1970s and 1990, especially among blacks (see Wilson, 1987; Massey, Gross, & Shibuya, 1994). However, between 1990 and 2000, there was a substantial decline in high poverty neighborhoods. According to Jargowsky (2003), the number of people living in high poverty neighborhoods where the poverty rate was 40 percent or higher declined in the 1990s. Concentrated poverty declined among all racial groups, and especially among blacks. Despite the decline, in 2000, blacks remain the one racial group with the highest percent of the population living in concentrated poverty. While 19 percent of the black population lived in concentrated poverty, only 6 percent of the white population did so, making blacks three times more likely than whites to live in concentrated poverty.

Of the total concentrated poverty population, 39 percent were blacks, 29 percent were Hispanics, and 24 percent were whites. Asians constituted only 4 percent of the concentrated poverty population (Jargowsky, 2003). Thus, Asians are expected to receive fewer subprime loans than blacks and Hispanics.

RELATIONSHIP OF CONCENTRATED POVERTY TO SUBPRIME LENDING

Subprime lending is clearly related to concentrated poverty. This is evident when blacks and Hispanics are compared in the 20 largest metropolitan areas. While 15 percent of blacks on average reside in concentrated poverty neighborhoods, only 9 percent of Hispanics do. This is reflected in a higher average rate of subprime loans — 48.5 percent for blacks, compared to 29.1 percent for Hispanics. The percent of subprime loans was determined by dividing the total number of loans made to applicants by race, by the number of subprime loans × 100. The black vs. white mean racial disparity ratio was 2.73 and the Hispanic vs. white mean racial disparity ratio was 1.61. The racial disparity ratio compares the percent of subprime loans to whites and blacks, and to whites and Hispanics. A ratio of 1.00 is equivalent to racial equality. A ratio greater than 1.00 indicates more subprime loans to blacks or Hispanics.

THE IMPACT AND POLICY IMPLICATIONS OF SUBPRIME LENDING

A study by Bradford (2002) concluded that subprime lending is widespread and growing. High levels indicate markets where borrowers have unusually high risks of losing their homes. The sheer geographic concentration of these loans, therefore, may have a significant negative impact not just on individual borrowers, but on entire neighborhoods. The subprime market is fertile ground for predatory lending (Bradford, 2002). Moreover, the prevalence of subprime loans with abusive characteristics has been devastating to families and neighborhoods (U.S. Department of Housing and Urban Development, 2002; Immergluck & Wiles, 1999; Stein, 2001). Yet, Fannie Mae argues that up to half of all subprime borrowers could qualify for lower cost conventional financing (Zorn, 2000).

Stein (2001) estimated that U.S. borrowers lose $9.1 billion annually to predatory lending practices. Clearly, predatory lending has become one of the most critical policy issues facing the financial services industry, particularly mortgage lending (Carr & Kolluri, 2001). Despite the need to take action via legislation to combat predatory lending, such action thus far has been limited. Moreover, it is not known what factors influence some state legislators to pass anti-predatory lending legislation while other states do not. The next section addresses this question and provides knowledge about the patterns of anti-predatory lending by states.

RACE AND VARIATION IN SUBPRIME LENDING BY STATES

States That Have Passed Legislation

Subprime lending varies by race and by state. The results presented in Table 9.1 reveal the variation in subprime lending to blacks, Hispanics, and Asians in states that have passed anti-predatory lending legislation. Table 9.1 shows the variation by race in the mean percent subprime loans and the mean racial disparity ratios.

Among the eleven states that had passed anti-predatory lending legislation as of 2003, seven states had sufficient populations of each racial minority group (blacks, Hispanics and Asians) for comparison purposes. In California, Colorado, Florida, Michigan, New York, Georgia, and Pennsylvania, the mean percent of subprime loans was highest for blacks, lower for Hispanics and lowest for Asians. Such high mean percentage of subprime loans to blacks is reflected in the black-white disparity ratios. In these seven states, the mean disparity ratio ranged from 2.35 in New York to 3.48 in Georgia. In other words, blacks were more than three times more likely than whites in Georgia to receive subprime loans. Among Hispanics, the mean Hispanic-white disparity ratios ranged from a high of 2.20 in Pennsylvania to 1.45 in New York. The disparity ratios were lowest among Asians, ranging from 1.21 in California to 0.61 in Georgia.

Table 9.1

Racial Variation in Percentage Subprime Loans and Racial Disparity Ratios in States that Passed Anti-Predatory Lending Legislation										
States	Date of Passage	Mean Black Percent Sub-prime Loans	N Black	Mean Hispanic Percent Subprime Loans	N Hispanic	Mean Asian Percent Subprime Loans	N Asian	Mean Black/White Disparity Ratio*	Mean Hispanic/White Disparity Ratio*	Mean Asiasn/White Disparity Ratio*
California	10/01	39.6	12	27.7	22	19.7	14	2.45	1.68	1.21
Colorado	6/02	46.4	2	27.6	6	18.5	1	2.74	1.77	1.07
Connecticut	6/02	45.3	4	28.0	3	+	+	2.76	1.91	+
Florida	3/02	55.4	16	35.9	10	25.1	3	2.46	1.50	1.00
Georgia	4/02	48.5	7	23.5	1	9.0	1	3.48	1.59	0.61
Kentucky	3/03	40.7	2	+	+	+	+	2.95	+	+
Michigan	12/02	41.8	8	26.2	4	8.4	1	3.14	1.98	0.55
New York	10/02	56.6	4	33.8	2	20.8	2	2.35	1.45	0.88
North Carolina	7/99	50.4	9	+	+	+	+	2.72	+	+
Pennsylvania	6/01	53.6	3	38.1	1	19.9	1	3.15	2.20	1.15
Virginia	3/03	48.7	5	+	+	+	+	2.52	+	+

N = number of metropolitan areas

+ Data on Hispanics was insufficient for analysis for Kentucky, North Carolina and Virginia. Data on Asians was insufficient for analysis for Connecticut, Kentucky, North Carolina and Virginia.

* A ratio of 1.00 equals racial equality. A ratio greater than 1.00 equals a higher rate of subprime loans to blacks, Hispanics, or Asians.

Source: Computed by the authors from data obtained from Bradford (2002).

Among the 11 states that have passed anti-predatory lending legislation, the mean percentage of black subprime loans ranged from a low of 39.6 in California to a high of 56.6 in New York. However, New York State had the lowest black/white disparity ratio among states that have passed anti-predatory lending legislation. The ratio ranged from 2.35 in New York to 3.48 in Georgia (Table 9.1). Georgia was one of three states where black applicants received more than three times the percentage of subprime loans than whites. The other two states were Michigan (3.14) and Pennsylvania (3.15).

States That Have Introduced Legislation

In addition to the eleven states that had passed anti-predatory lending legislation as of March 2003, 32 states had introduced such legislation in the House or Senate. A sufficient black population existed for analytical purposes in 24 of the 32 states, which included 78 metropolitan areas. In those 24 states, the mean percent of subprime loans to blacks was 47.2 percent and the mean black-white disparity ratio was 2.80. In other words, blacks were more than twice as likely as whites to receive subprime loans.

Among Hispanics, a sufficient population existed for analytical purposes in 19 states, which included 48 metropolitan areas. The mean percent of subprime loans was 30 and the mean Hispanic-white disparity ratio was 1.73. This is lower than the mean disparity ratio for blacks vs. whites.

Concerning Asians, a sufficient population existed for analysis in 12 states that included 16 metropolitan areas. The mean percent of subprime loans to Asians was 19 percent, and the mean Asian-white disparity ratio was 1.08. This is lower than the mean ratio for blacks vs. whites, and Hispanics vs. whites. In fact, the Asian-white ratio almost reflected equality with whites in terms of the percent of subprime loans received.

In general, the percentage of subprime loans and disparity ratios varied by race in states that had introduced legislation. The case was similar to states that had passed legislation — blacks received the highest percentage of subprime loans, followed by Hispanics. Asians received the lowest percentage of subprime loans.

States That Had Not Introduced Legislation

A sufficient number of blacks existed for analysis in three states that contained four metropolitan areas. In those three states, the mean percent of subprime loans received by blacks was 51, and the mean disparity ratio was 2.70. Caution is advised in interpreting the results for Hispanics and Asians, since the analyses were based on a single state and metropolitan area. The percent of subprime loans for Hispanics was 32.4 percent, and the disparity ratio was 1.92. This is lower than the ratio for blacks. The percent of subprime loans to Asians was 19.0 percent, and the Asian-white disparity ratio was 1.50. This is the lowest ratio among the three racial minority groups.

In sum, regardless of the status of anti-predatory lending legislation, the percent of subprime loans to blacks was the highest, followed by Hispanics. Asians were least likely among the three racial groups to receive subprime loans. Asians also had the lowest disparity ratios when compared to whites.

FACTORS RELATED TO PASSAGE OF ANTI-PREDATORY LENDING LEGISLATION

In this section, we explore some factors that may be related to the passage of anti-predatory lending legislation. Although exploratory, this discussion may shed more light on the question as to why some states had passed legislation, while other states had introduced it, and some states had not considered such legislation, as of March, 2003. The factors explored are as follows: (1) the severity of the problem, (2) the percent Democratic control of the legislature, (3) the percent of black legislators, and (4) the percent of metropolitan population in the state.

Severity of the Problem

The problem of subprime lending varies among states and among racial groups. In the previous section, we revealed that blacks had a higher percent of subprime loans in states that had not introduced legislation, although the black/white disparity ratio was lower. On the other hand, Hispanics and Asians had higher racial disparity ratios in states that had not introduced legislation. We applied a statistical method, analysis of variance (ANOVA) to test whether or not statistically significant differences exist between the percentage of black subprime loans and black/white disparity ratios, in states that had passed and in states that had not passed anti-predatory lending legislation. The results of ANOVA revealed no statistically significant differences between the states. The number of cases for Hispanics and Asians was too small for statistical analysis. Thus, the severity of the problem of subprime lending was not the significant contributing factor to explain why some states had passed anti-predatory lending legislation as of March of 2003 and other states had not.

The Percent of Democratic Control of the Legislature

In most states, the Democratic Party is more likely to have a higher proportion of racial minority constituents than the Republican Party. The Democratic Party, we assume, would be more responsive to the needs of racial minorities. Thus, whether the Democratic Party or the Republican Party is in control of the state legislature may influence the passage of anti-predatory lending legislation. Table 9.2 presents the mean percentage of Democratic control of the state legislatures in 2002. Although states that had introduced legislation had a higher percentage of Democratic control than states that had passed legislation, the key difference is revealed when states that have not introduced legislation are compared. The Governor, the Senate, and the House show low Democratic control, constituting only 28.5 percent among Governors, only 40.8 percent in the Senate, and 34.2 percent in the House. ANOVA results revealed no significant differences between the states in the percentage of Democratic control of the Senate. However, the percentage of Democratic control of the House was significant at a .005 level between states that had not introduced anti-predatory lending legislation and states that had introduced or passed such legislation.

Table 9.2

ANOVA Results Mean Percentage of Democratic Control of the State Legislature as of 2002			
States That Have Passed Legislation			
	Governor	Senate	House
Mean	45	48.1	50.3
States That Have Introduced Legislation			
Mean	50	55.5	56.3
States that Have Not Introduced Legislation			
Mean	28.5	40.8	34.2*
*Percentage Democratic control significant at the .005 level.			
Sources: Computed by the authors from data obtained from state assembly Web sites and www.worldalmanac.com			

The Percent of Black Legislators

Since blacks are the group most targeted by predatory lenders, it is logical to expect, therefore, that black legislators would be more likely than other legislators to support passage of anti-predatory lending legislation. However, ANOVA results revealed that, while the percent of black legislators was indeed higher in the Senate and the House in states that had passed legislation, the results were not statistically significant (Table 9.3).

The Percent Metropolitan Population in the State

It is reasonable to expect that the higher the percent of metropolitan population in a state, the higher the likelihood that the legislators will be influenced by those population groups who are more likely to experience subprime loans. Blacks are disproportionately resident in metropolitan areas. Thus, states with the highest percentage of metropolitan residents are expected to be among those that have passed anti-predatory lending legislation. Metropolitan populations, in general, have a higher proportion of racial minority groups and groups that are more concerned about fairness in lending patterns.

ANOVA results revealed that states that had passed anti-predatory lending legislation had average populations that were 81 percent metropolitan. This was a significant difference at the .05 level from those states that had not introduced legislation. These states had an average metropolitan population of 50.6 percent (see Table 9.4).

Table 9.3

ANOVA Results Percent Black Legislators				
	N	Mean	SD	NS
Senate				
States That Have Passed Legislation	11	9.9	6.13	NS
States That Have Introduced Legislation	31	3.14	7.39	NS
States That Have Not Introduced Legislation	7	6.48	3.07	NS
House				
States That Have Passed Legislation	11	10.81	6.11	NS
States That Have Introduced Legislation	31	8.12	8.75	NS
States That Have Not Introduced Legislation	7	3.28	3.54	NS

Note: Nebraska has a unicameral legislative body that runs on anon-partisan ballot.
　　Thus, only 49 states are included.
SD= Standard Deviation
NS= Not Significant
Sources: Computed by the authors from data obtained from state assembly Web sites and www.worldalmanac.com

Table 9.4

ANOVA Results Percent Metropolitan Population				
	Mean	SD	N	Significance
Legislation Passed	81.0	14.5	11	*
Legislation Introduced	67.1	20.1	32	
Legislation Not Introduced	50.6	18.2	7	

*Significant at the .05 level.
Sources: Computed by the authors from data obtained from state assembly Web sites and www.worldalmanac.com

SUMMARY AND CONCLUSIONS

The data and analyses presented in this chapter revealed that mortgage lending (prime or subprime loans) varies by race and neighborhood characteristics. It follows spatial patterns in American society similar to those of racial residential segregation and concentrated poverty. An examination and analysis of demographic and mortgage lending data led to the conclusion that among racial groups, whites are least likely to live in neighborhoods of concentrated poverty and least likely to receive subprime loans.

Among racial minority groups, blacks are most likely to live in neighborhoods of concentrated poverty and most likely to receive subprime loans. Asians, on the other hand, are least likely to live in neighborhoods of concentrated poverty and least likely to receive subprime loans. The status of anti-predatory lending legislation to address the problem also varies by states.

Although the percent of subprime loans received by each racial minority group varied between states that had passed and states that had not passed anti-predatory lending legislation as of March, 2003, the difference was not statistically significant. Regardless of the status of anti-predatory lending legislation, blacks received the highest percentage of subprime loans, followed by Hispanics. Asians received the lowest percentage of subprime loans. The mean percentage of loans received by blacks was higher in those states that had not introduced or passed anti-predatory lending legislation. However, the difference was not statistically significant.

Four factors were explored for their relationship to state passage of anti-predatory lending legislation. Those factors were: (1) the severity of the problem, (2) the percent of Democratic control of the legislature, (3) the percent of black legislators, and (4) the percent metropolitan population in each state.

Although race clearly matters in explaining the pattern of subprime lending, ANOVA results revealed no significant difference between the percentage of black subprime loans and black/white disparity ratios between states that had passed anti-predatory lending legislation and other states. Since anti-predatory lending legislation is very recent, possibly not enough time has passed for the legislation to have had an impact.

The percent of Democratic control of state legislatures matters in explaining state passage of anti-predatory lending legislation. The percentage of Democratic control of the House was higher and statistically significant in states that had passed or introduced legislation, compared to states that had not.

While the percent of black state legislators matters in explaining passage of anti-predatory lending legislation, the strength of its influence was not statistically significant. Finally, the higher the percentage of metropolitan population in a state, the more likely it is that the state will have passed anti-predatory lending legislation.

While this study has explored four factors related to state variation in anti-predatory lending legislation, the explanation is clearly more complex. Future research should consider important qualitative factors. Among these is the factor of local neighborhood consumer group mobilization. Whether the Association of Community Organizations for Reform Now (ACORN) or other neighborhood groups were actively involved in various communities in the states probably had an impact that contributed to passage of legislation. Clearly, more study is needed to better understand this very important policy issue, which is deeply linked to race and the concentrated poverty of neighborhoods.

Chapter 10

Race, Location and Access
to Employment in Buffalo, N.Y.

IBIPO JOHNSTON-ANUMONWO AND SELIMA SULTANA

Differences in the residential, employment, and household characteristics of African Americans and European Americans as well as racial differences in the journey to work are well documented. There are many studies about the commuting behavior of non-whites, but the specific impact of the exodus of jobs to suburban locations on African American men and women who live in inner cities is still widely debated. An earlier study of Buffalo, N.Y. which, examined racial differences in commuting focused only on women (Johnston-Anumonwo, 1995); and in a follow-up study, men were included in the analysis (Johnston-Anumonwo, 1997). The purpose of the present study then is to examine the question of racial differences in locational access to jobs in Buffalo, N.Y. by presenting new data for the year 2000. The study retains the critical inquiry on whether suburban employment imposes longer commute times on African Americans than on European Americans. The results strongly complement those for 1990 and also 1980 by highlighting the fact that many African American men and women continue to endure relatively long commutes to get to work in spite of transportation, locational, and socioeconomic hindrances. Following a review of the background literature of the journey to work for African Americans, a brief description of the study area and data is provided, and then the findings are presented followed by the conclusions reached.

THE JOURNEY TO WORK FOR AFRICAN AMERICANS

Inquiries about racial disparities in employment accessibility are central to the spatial mismatch hypothesis (Kain, 1968). When it was first proposed in the 1960s, the hypothesis emphasized that employment opportunities are expanding in suburban locations, but because of continuing segregation of blacks in inner cities, there exists a spatial mismatch, such that black inner-city residents face difficulties in reaching the growing job opportunities in suburbs (see Holzer, 1991; Kain, 1992; McLafferty and Preston, 1997; Ihlanfeldt and Sjoquist, 1998; and Preston and McLafferty, 1999 for some comprehensive reviews). There has been little change in the residential segregation of blacks between 1960s and now (Darden, 1990; Denton, 1994; Massey and Hajnal, 1995), and this is true for Erie County New York (with Buffalo as its central city). A sharp pattern of disproportionate representation of Blacks in the central city prevails in Erie County. Erie County was 7 percent black in 1960 and 10.1 percent black in 1980 with 94.7 percent and 92.4 percent of the black population respectively living in the central city in both time periods (U.S. Dept. of Commerce, 1963; 1983). By the year 2000, the county was 13 percent black (U.S. Census Bureau, 2004 — Quick Facts), and the 2000 census tract map of the residential distribution of blacks in the County displays persistent central city concentration and limited suburban presence.

Early research on the effect of the exodus of jobs to suburban locations on the workplace accessibility of inner city African Americans rarely included female workers even though African American women have historically had high levels of labor force participation. There are now more studies that have investigated spatial mismatch concerns and commuting constraints of women (e.g., Sultana, 2003; Thompson, 1997; McLafferty and Preston, 1992; Johnston-Anumonwo, 2000). The available studies on the journey to work of female workers highlight two key trends. First, black women have longer travel times than white women. Second, unlike white women who typically have shorter commutes than white men, the journey-to-work time of black women is generally as long as those of Black men (McLafferty and Preston, 1991, 1992 and 1996). For example, McLafferty and Preston (1991) report that in 1980, African American women in metropolitan New York spend 10 minutes longer on the average for their home-to-work trip than European American women. Many early studies reported longer commuting times for African American men than European American men as well (e.g., Greytak, 1974; Ellwood, 1986). The research finding that being black is associated with longer work-trip times can readily be attributed to racial differences in the use of a private automobile, but racial differences in other locational and socioeconomic variables that are known to affect journey-to-work time are also relevant. Holzer et al. (1994) found less automobile ownership among central city residents and greater reliance on public transportation. Blacks are affected more than whites by these mobility constraints since they live disproportionately in central cities.

The journey-to-work literature is replete with findings that workers who use public transportation usually spend a longer time getting to work than those who use a private car. Similarly, those earning high incomes have longer work-trip times than those who have low incomes (e.g., U.S. Department of Commerce, 1982; Pisarski, 1996; Ihlanfeldt, 1992; McLafferty and Preston, 1992).

Although the spatial mismatch hypothesis specifies the growing trend of workplaces in suburban locations, there are still insufficient empirical inquiries of the impact of suburban workplace destination on the commuting behavior of African American men and women. One study of race and commutes in Detroit found that in 1980, blacks who worked in the Central Business District worked closer to home than whites, but for suburban destinations, blacks commuted longer than whites (Zax, 1990). This different commuting pattern, according to Zax, suggests that racial residential segregation restricts black suburbanization and contributes to longer commutes for blacks who have to work in suburban Detroit (see also Zax and Kain, 1996).

Other studies have examined the role of suburban residence versus inner city residence on the labor market outcomes of blacks and whites (e.g., Jenks and Mayer, 1990; Fernandez, 1994; Ihlanfeldt and Young, 1994; McLafferty and Preston, 1996; Stoll, 1999; Sultana, 2005). These, and the findings of more recent studies on large cities about racial differences in access to transportation, employment location, residential mobility, and unemployment levels (e.g., Stoll, 1996; Mouw, 2000; Martin, 2004) all support the spatial mismatch hypothesis which posited that African Americans suffer from distant suburban employment.

But for a variety of reasons, including methodological ones about appropriate measures of accessibility (e.g., Hodge, 1996; Perle et al., 2002, disagreement persists about whether or not African American workers in U.S. metropolitan areas are more distant from centers of employment than European Americans are. This chapter reports on an empirical inquiry about the question of the spatial mismatch of African Americans resident in Erie County (Buffalo) New York. Using data from the 2000 census, the study investigates whether African American working men and women in Buffalo experience greater commuting difficulties than European Americans while taking into consideration racial differences in key factors that affect work-trip length — namely, automobile use, location, occupation, and income.

In Buffalo, the majority of African Americans still live in segregated neighborhoods. In fact, Buffalo remains a city with one of the highest levels of racial residential segregation in the United States, ranking third according to the 2000 census. Buffalo is a representative example of a city that experienced massive de-industrialization starting in the 1970s when manufacturing jobs slumped in the urban economy, and moved out of the central city to the suburbs. The prevalent trend was one of job decentralization. One can expect to find evidence of journey-to-work constraints for inner city African American residents of Buffalo.

A specified set of research questions is examined. Do African American men and women in Buffalo spend a longer time commuting than European American men and women? Does unequal access to private automobiles lead to differences in the journey-to-work time of African Americans and European Americans? If differential access to private automobiles is responsible for longer commute times among African Americans, then there should be no racial difference in the work-trip times of private auto users. Is location of the workplace responsible for any racial difference in commuting? Finally, is there any difference in the commute times of African American and European American workers with similar occupation or income?

DESCRIPTION OF THE DATA

The range of factors necessary for a full understanding of racial disparities in commuting means that detailed data about working individuals are preferred. The Public Use Microdata Samples (PUMS), which is a database with information on individuals' socioeconomic characteristics and their locational and work-trip attributes, meets this requirement. The 2000 five percent Public Use Microdata Samples (PUMS) for Erie County, New York, is used for this study. In 1980, for the first time, the census included information on journey-to-work time (i.e., the time spent traveling from home to work), so it is now possible to conduct some longitudinal analysis about changes in the length of work trips over a period of 20 years. Travel time, the actual number of minutes spent from home to work as reported by the respondent, is the measure available for work-trip length. The travel mode is the means of transportation that the worker uses to get to work, e.g., public transportation or private automobile.

While socioeconomic and demographic information provided in the PUMS is quite detailed, detailed information about location is not provided in these public use data sets in order to protect the confidentiality of respondents. Only two very broad locational categories are used for this study — central city location and non central city location. In other words, locations outside the census-designated central city limits are classified simply as non central city locations (i.e., suburb). Income, the worker's personal earnings in 1999, is divided into two categories: (a) below $25,000 or (b) $25,000 and above. Only employed white and black (based on respondents' self-classification of "race") males and females who are sixteen years old and older are selected for the study.

The five percent PUMS is used so that the sample size for the study would include a large number of black workers in this predominantly white upstate New York county. Because the focus is on the journey-to-work, the sample selected for the study consisted of a total of 18,083 respondents who worked outside the home. This comprises 15,971 whites (88.3%) and 2,112 blacks (11.7%). Of these, there are 977 African-American men, 8,254 European-American men, 1,135 African-American women and 7,717 European-American women. These then are the four race-sex groups that constitute the basis of much of the comparisons in the study. Racial differences in journey-to-work time are assessed using simple t-test statistics and analysis of variance. Only racial differences that are significant at 95 percent level of confidence and above are reported. The results are presented next starting with racial differences in means of transportation used for the work trip.

FINDINGS

Blacks Rely More on Public Transportation

Black workers in Buffalo continue to use public transportation more than whites do in 2000. Out of the total sample of workers reporting a work trip, about 95 percent of whites used a private car compared to 78.4 percent of blacks (Table 10.1). Indeed, 16 percent of blacks ride the bus, compared to only 1.8 percent of whites (see Figures 10.1 and 10.2). This greater reliance of black Americans on buses conforms to well-documented patterns, and it is expected to increase their average work-trip time since public bus transportation is typically a slower and more time consuming mode of travel.

Table 10.1

Racial Differences among Private Automobile Users and Bus Riders Erie County 2000 PUMS			
	Auto Users	Bus Riders	Total Sample
BLACKS	1,655	338	2,112
%Blacks	78.4%	16.0%	
WHITES	15,145	286	15,971
% Whites	94.8%	1.8%	
note: total sample includes all other modes (not shown on this table — see Figs. 1 and 2)			

Figure 10.1

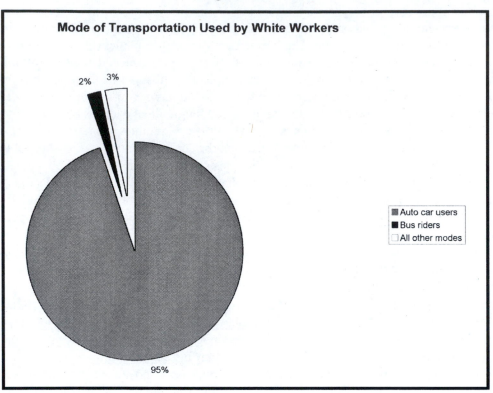

Figure 10.2

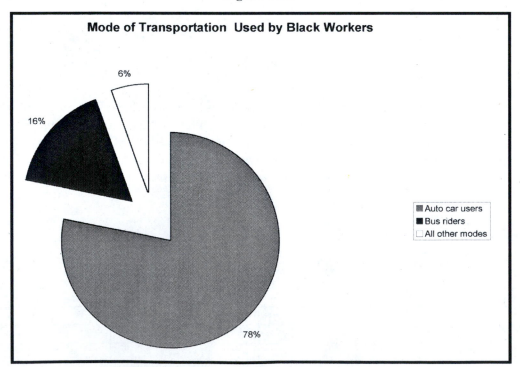

Blacks Spend More Time for the Work Trip

The overall average work-trip time of the 18,083 respondents in the sample is 21.3 minutes (this is similar to the value reported in the aggregate data set, Census Transportation Planning Package — CTPP 2000, and it represents a slight increase from the reported mean travel time of 19.7 minutes in 1990 (U.S. Bureau of Census)); but the work trips of blacks are longer than for whites. Blacks spend 23.7 minutes versus 21 minutes for whites (significant at $p = < 0.01$). This means that African Americans spend almost 3 minutes longer on the average for their work trip than European Americans. Table 10.2 displays racial differences in commuting time.

Table 10.2

Racial Difference in Mean Travel Time by Travel Mode Erie County 2000 PUMS	
FULL SAMPLE 18,803	21.31 minutes
Blacks 2,112	23.74 minutes
Whites 15,971	20.99 minutes
difference	2.75 minutes
BUS RIDERS 624	37.38 minutes
Blacks 338	38.72 minutes
Whites 286	35.81 minutes
Difference	2.91 minutes
AUTO USERS 16,800	20.89 minutes
Blacks 1,655	20.97 minutes
Whites 15,145	20.88 minutes
difference	0.09 minute

Since more African Americans use public transportation, and since research consistently confirms the pronounced lengthening effect of public transportation on workers' commute times (e.g., U.S. Department of Commerce, 1982; McLafferty and Preston, 1992; Holzer et al., 1994; Taylor and Ong, 1995), one should make allowance for this, and examine only workers with the same mode of travel.

Among bus riders, blacks spend almost 3 minutes longer than whites (38.7 versus 35.8 minutes); but this difference is not statistically significant. When the work-trip times of private automobile users are examined, there is no overall racial difference in Erie County in 2000 (20.97 versus 20.88 minutes). By the year 2000, black and white auto users in Erie County in general more or less spend the same time for their commutes (Figure 10.3). Greater dependence on public transportation does not offer much explanation for continuing longer work-trip times of many blacks because when the sample is examined further by workplace location or by occupation, and income status, significant racial differences persist in the travel time of many auto users.

For the remainder of the study, all comparisons about racial differences in work-trip time are restricted to respondents who use a car. We find that in spite of the use of a private automobile, some black commuters spend a longer time than white counterparts. The continuing racial differences in travel time among auto users with similar locational and socioeconomic profiles are reported below. We start with those with the same residence-workplace location.

Black Central City Residents Spend a Longer Time Than Whites

If a work trip begins and ends in the same area, it is likely to take a shorter time than if the trip starts in one area and ends in another area. For instance, trips that begin in the central city and end in the central city may take a shorter time than those that start in the central city and end in the suburbs. That is, intra-area trips typically take a longer time than opposite direction trips (Hanson and Johnston, 1985; Johnston-Anumonwo, 1995). Racial differences in geographic location of the home and workplace are likely to contribute to racial gaps in commute times, so it is more accurate to compare workers with the same home and work location.

Figure 10.3

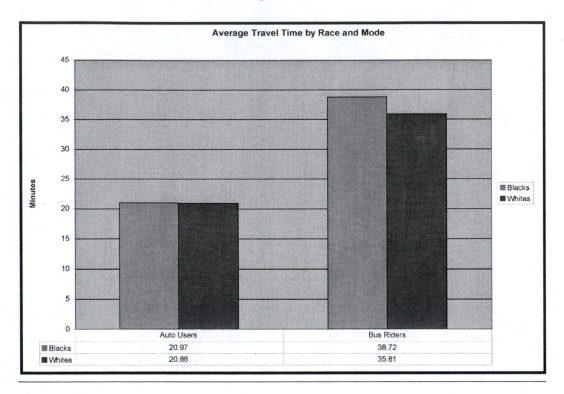

We find that black male and female auto users who live in the central city and whose workplaces are in Buffalo central city spend longer times than white counterparts (Table 10.3). In Figure 10.4, black respondents who reside and work in central city locations are seen to spend a longer time than the white respondents. Also, among those workers with non central city destinations (i.e., reverse commuters), black women spend three minutes longer than white women and black men spend four minutes longer than white men (significant at $p = < 0.01$ in Table 10.3; see also Figure 10.5). This finding is consistent with the argument of the spatial mismatch hypothesis that inner city blacks have long commutes to suburban work destinations. Based on these findings therefore, there is evidence of continuing commuting constraints for Buffalo inner city African American men and women in the year 2000. In fact this study also finds that suburban black women have longer commutes than white counterparts with suburban jobs.

Black Women With Suburban Work Destinations Spend a Longer Time Getting to Work

When we focus on those workers with non central city destinations (i.e., to concentrate on suburban destinations in general), we find that whether they live in the central city or outside the central city, black women spend 3 minutes longer than white women if they work in suburban locations (significant at $p = < 0.01$). Generally therefore, in the year 2000, all black *women* auto users with work destinations in the suburbs of Erie County spend more time commuting to work. Primarily because of insufficient sample sizes for blacks who reside outside the Buffalo central city, and precisely because the spatial mismatch hypothesis is concerned with the situation of inner city workers, we restrict some of our conclusions of the remaining racial comparisons to respondents with central city homes.

Central City Blue-Collar African Americans Spend a Longer Time Getting to Work

The two socioeconomic factors examined are occupation and income. The common expectations are that low-status, low-wage workers will be less able to afford long commutes. Black and white workers usually differ in socioeconomic status. Black workers should have shorter commutes if their lower earnings disallow long commutes.

Table 10.3

Racial Differences in Journey to Work Time (minutes) Erie County 2000					
N=18,803					
MEN 9,231			**WOMEN** 8,852		
Blacks	Whites		Blacks	Whites	
977	8,254		1,135	7,717	
23.8	**22.4**	*	**23.7**	**19.5**	**
AUTO-USERS					
792	7,846		863	7,299	
21.6	**22.4**	ns	**20.4**	**19.3**	*
City-to-City Commuter					
284	690		374	685	
17.6	**15.2**	**	**17.1**	**14.9**	**
Reverse Commuter					
207	633		232	553	
26.1	**21.9**	**	**23.7**	**20.7**	**
Suburb-to-City Commuter					
100	1,738		82	1,515	
23.3	**24.6**	ns	**25.0**	**24.9**	ns
Suburb-to-Suburb Commuter					
169	4,274		150	4,283	
19.8	**20.9**	ns	**20.4**	**17.3**	**
Reverse Commuter Only					
Service					
40	104		69	118	
23.9	**24.3**	ns	**21.1**	**17.8**	ns
Manufacturing					
92	201		41	36	
31.2	**23.5**	*	**30.3**	**23.9**	ns
note: **=significant at p=<.01; *=significant at p=<.05; ns=not significant					

Figure 10.4

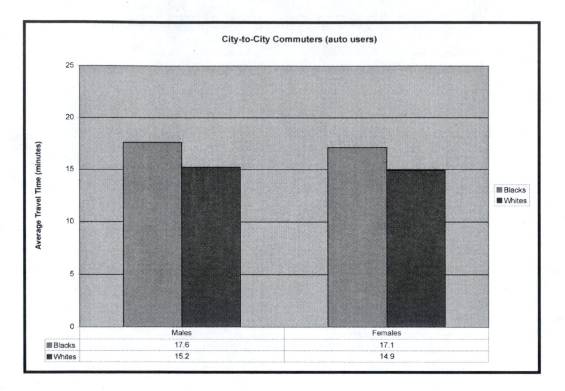

Figure 10.5

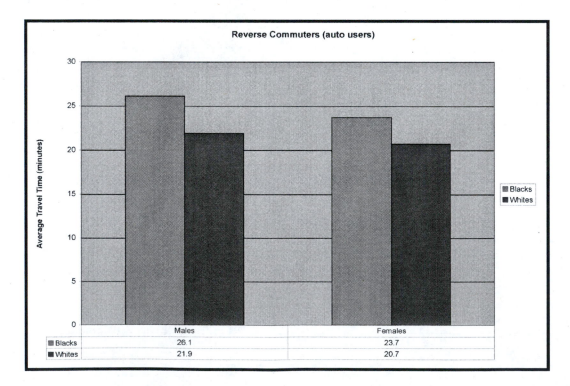

First, we examine racial disparities in work trip length of workers in two occupation groups — services and manufacturing. As shown in Table 10.3, black male service workers and white male service workers spend almost the same time (23.9 and 24.3 minutes) getting to work; but black male manufacturing workers spend a considerably longer time getting to their jobs in suburban locations than do their white counterparts (31.2 versus 23.5 minutes). The racial differences among women, while present, are not significant statistically (this could be because of small sample sizes). The substantial racial difference in commute time among male manufacturing workers (over seven minutes) is noteworthy. It is indicative of a central tenet of the spatial mismatch hypothesis, as it applies to inner city minorities with long commutes to manufacturing jobs in decentralized locations.

Next, we examine differences by earnings. Although a positive relationship between wages and journey-to-work length is widely reported in the literature (e.g., Madden, 1981; Rutherford and Wekerle, 1988; Ihlanfeldt, 1992; Ihlanfeldt and Young, 1994; Hanson and Pratt, 1995), it is not necessarily a simple relationship. Gordon et al. (1989) and Johnston-Anumonwo et al. (1995) discuss varied effects of earnings on commuting across race and gender categories.

For our purposes, we simply categorize workers based on travel time and income. Four types of commutes are identified on the basis of short versus long commutes, and low versus high incomes (Table 10.4). Since the average travel time for auto users in the sample is just over 20 minutes, work trips shorter than 20 minutes are considered short. Also, this comparison on commute length and income excludes part time workers; thus full-time workers with reported personal earnings below $25,000 are considered low-income workers. It is necessary to examine only full-time workers (those who worked 35 hours or more a week) in order to remove the effects of reduced income due to part-time employment.

The typology differentiates commutes labeled as "convenient" and "compensatory" from those labeled "compromised" and "constrained," the former pair being commutes to high-wage jobs. Compromised commutes are those in which either the worker forgoes a higher income for a shorter commute or the worker's low income makes a long commute uneconomical. Compromised commutes differ from constrained commutes that are typified by long commutes to low-wage jobs. Rutherford and Wekerle (1988) present a similar combination (long commutes and low wages) for "disadvantaged commutes." Convenient commutes combine the advantages of short trips and high wages, and are considered the best of the four possibilities; therefore in a sense these are the "choice" commutes (Johnston-Anumonwo, 1997). We maintain our focus on central city residents in the first section below as we compare the extent to which blacks and whites differ in their commute times relative to their personal earnings.

Table 10.4

Typology of Commutes		
	short commute (<20 mins)	long commute (=>20 mins)
high income (=>$25,000)	**Convenient**	**Compensatory**
low income (<$25,000)	**Compromised**	**Constrained**

Central City Black Women With Low Incomes are More Likely Than White Women to Have Long Travel Times

Among central city residents, white men and women have fewer compromised trips than black men and women. Vice versa, white men and women have more convenient trips than black men and women. For example, whereas around 38 percent of white women have convenient trips, only about 28 percent of black women do. In addition, black women have *more constrained trips* than white women (14.6% versus 10.9% — Figure 10.6).

Suburban Residents With Long Commutes: Racial Differences in Earnings

As expected, suburban residents generally have higher incomes, and we find that in 2000, about the same fraction of suburban black men and white men have convenient trips (this is true of black and white women also). But suburban black men have fewer compensatory trips and more compromised commutes than do white men (Figure 10.7).

Figure 10.6

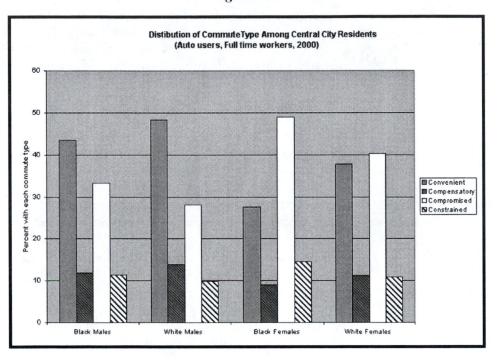

Figure 10.7

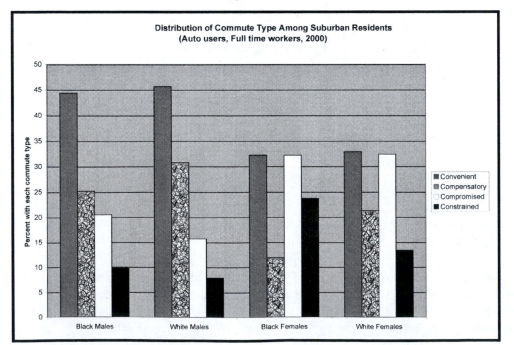

There is remarkable similarity in the distribution of suburban black and white women with short commutes — about 32 percent each of the black and white women have convenient and compromised commutes. The glaring difference among suburban women is the substantially lower proportion of black women with compensatory commutes vis-à-vis the substantially higher proportion of black women with constrained commutes compared to the white women.

Because of some of the low numbers of black men and women with long commutes in the suburban sample (i.e., only 23 black men with constrained trips, and only 21 black women with compensatory trips), we believe that it is more accurate to conclude from this study that suburban black men are less likely than suburban white men to have compensatory trips, while suburban black women are more likely than suburban white women to have constrained trips. Findings from the Multi-City Study on Urban Inequality by Ihlanfeldt and his colleagues show that long commutes by whites who live in suburbs are compensated by higher wages, while this is less likely to take place for inner city blacks (Ihlanfeldt, 1992; Ihlanfeldt and Young, 1994).

For both central city and non-central city (suburban) locations, the gender differences are as important as are the race differences (Figures 10.6 and 10.7). Men have the highest proportions of convenient commutes (i.e., the "best" commute types). Women are more likely than men to have compromised commutes. Among suburban residents, women are more likely to have constrained commutes than are men. These findings fit the well-known wage gap associated with the gender-segregated labor force. This cursory look at associations between earnings and commute length reveals primarily that commutes of women are similar in their disproportionate concentration in the two low-income commutes.

Our analysis thus shows that many black women are enduring relatively long commutes to low-waged jobs. This finding runs contrary to common expectations that low status workers earning low incomes will have shorter commutes. In spite of the constraints, low-income African American women put up with longer commutes than their European American counterparts. In part, the results counter the welfare queen stereotype of black women since the women in the analysis are all employed. In the final section of the paper, we elaborate on the implications of these findings on racial differences as well as on the notable gender differences.

CONCLUSIONS AND DISCUSSION

According to the findings of this study, black workers in Erie County, as a group, still have longer commutes than do white workers. As expected, the reason lies largely in the greater reliance of African Americans on public transportation. Once travel mode is taken into account, the racial difference in commuting time among most auto users is negligible. Taylor and Ong (1995) note that among workers with automobiles, there is reduced racial gap in trip time.

By failing to conduct race-specific and sex-specific comparisons, many previous studies masked continuing significant differences among sub-groups of workers, and by ignoring the impact of workplace location on the duration of the work trip, racial disparities in locational access to jobs are understated. Hence, one main contribution of this study is to demonstrate that taking into account the workplace location provides a clear assessment of the existence and nature of commuting difficulties that African Americans face when they live in central cities and/or work in suburbs. In addition, by differentiating central city residents from suburban residents, the findings from the specific analysis on commute type, highlight the important connection between race and place.

Most of the African Americans in Erie County do live and work in the Buffalo central city (and these work trips are shorter than the overall county average trip duration). But the more striking finding regarding African Americans is the significantly longer commuting time of reverse commuters. A central line of inquiry in the study is the specific impact of suburban employment on the commutes of African Americans. The need to work in suburban destinations (i.e., outside the central city) of Buffalo in the year 2000 imposes a disproportionate commuting time burden on inner-city blacks than on whites. This study thus provides support of a spatial mismatch in black workers' geographical access to employment in Erie County in 2000.

Keeping in mind that since most of these comparisons are conducted only for auto users, the findings show that even when access to an automobile is not a hindrance, many African-American workers in Buffalo still bear a bigger time cost than European Americans. Also, although the time differences may appear small, the time cost for African-American workers is not trivial. For instance the cumulative time of the two-way work trip is quite considerable, and it amounts to time lost from other tasks. Lastly, the findings on constrained commutes validate the very early conclusions of McLafferty and Preston (1991) that many African-American women experience a very insidious form of spatial mismatch and face significant transportation and locational barriers in traveling to work. In fact, the results for this Upstate New York city corroborate those of other cities using PUMS data. For example, Cooke and Shumway's (1991) study of three large Midwest cities — Chicago, Cleveland and Detroit — revealed that central city residents experience constrained access to employment.

The slightly longer times spent by black workers may be expected to decrease if black workers continue to have more access to private automobiles. However, the longer commutes of African Americans who reverse commute suggest that it is reasonable to speculate that as employment opportunities expand more in suburban locations and less in central city locations, African-American men and women (even those who use a car) are still likely to suffer the inconvenience of significantly longer commutes to suburban workplaces than European Americans.

There is reason to believe that concerns about spatial mismatch remain in U.S. cities. For example, a study of Detroit presents evidence of spatial mismatch as well as evidence of the negative treatment of blacks by suburban police officers and white residents as testimony of the multiple barriers facing African Americans in gaining access to employment opportunities in suburban Detroit (Turner, 1997). Similarly, in Buffalo, the current validity of both an automobile mismatch and a spatial mismatch for African American women proved tragically true in the case of a black woman who was killed while crossing an expressway in suburban Buffalo on her way to the shopping mall where she was employed. This particular case had racist underpinnings because the management of the suburban mall seemed to have pursued explicit policy decisions preventing buses coming from inner city Buffalo from stopping at the mall.

If more jobs were available in central cities, there would be less need to reverse commute to reach suburban jobs. Alternatively, if blacks had unhindered access to suburban housing, the racial disparity in locational access to jobs would be lessened. It is inaccurate to minimize the importance of locational access to black employment outcomes (see for example, Martin, 2004), and it would be premature to abandon inquiries about the possible role of location in the mismatch of workers and jobs.

Apart from difficult access to suburban work destinations, the study also finds evidence of other travel time constraints for black women. Specifically, it is low status black women who have relatively long commutes. Clearly, not all African American women face the constraints of long journeys to low-paying jobs. But the emerging profile of black women with suburban job destinations who earn low wages but endure long commutes, suggest that policy makers need to recognize the efforts of these working women and reward their diligence with remunerative job opportunities.

It is essential to stress that, like all studies that use commuting data, this study understates the general problem of access to jobs since it excludes the unemployed, many of whom are unemployed probably due to locational constraints. However, the use of journey-to-work data and the focus on travel time in particular, is appropriate. Time is a resource. In some instances, time is money; therefore lost time is lost money. Much of the extra time that African Americans in Erie county spend longer than European Americans can be extrapolated into over 25 hours a year — the equivalent of a sizeable fraction of a work week. Cast in this light, the longer commute times of African Americans can be interpreted as constituting a race tax burden.

In conclusion, this analysis of work trips in Buffalo complements and expands the empirical literature on racial differences in commuting patterns. The study has shed additional light on analyses about racial differences in commuting by highlighting the significance of several factors — race, means of transportation, residence, workplace location, income, and gender — in the job access constraints of groups of African Americans. These factors have to remain central in more detailed data analyses particularly for informing contemporary policy debates such as welfare reform. The findings at the beginning of the twenty first century about the journey to work of black workers in Buffalo counter prevailing stereotypes of welfare dependent African Americans, but also underscore the continuing significance of race and place in locational access to jobs.

Chapter 11

The Formation of a Contemporary Ethnic Enclave:
The Case of "Little Ethiopia" in Los Angeles

ELIZABETH CHACKO AND IVAN CHEUNG

INTRODUCTION

The urban enclave is popularly characterized as an area of strong residential concentration and clustering of an ethnic population. The presence of ethnic businesses such as restaurants and retail stores, as well as services that cater to various other needs of area residents, add to the distinct ethnic feel of these enclaves (Ward, 1968, 1971; Sowell, 1981). While ethnic enclaves may be in part an outcome of racism and prejudice (Tchen, 1985 cited in Hayden, 1995; Abrahamson, 1996), they can also be a sustaining force as communities cluster for greater visibility, political influence, security, status, and empowerment (Clark and Morrison, 1995; Clark, 1998; Kaplan and Holloway, 2001).

In this chapter, we investigate the creation of a contemporary ethnic enclave (Little Ethiopia) by a relatively new immigrant group (Ethiopians) in Los Angeles in 2002. The sprawling metropolis houses a plethora of ethnic, racial, and nationality groups; minorities add greatly to the diversity of its population. Although immigrant groups in the U.S. now tend to exist both within cities and in suburban locations (Zelinsky and Lee, 1998; Zelinsky, 2001; Singer, 2003), ethnic neighborhoods of distinct groups can be found scattered in many U.S. cities (Allen, 1996; Bobo et al., 2000; Hayden, 1995). Among the ethnic neighborhoods that are recognized and marked on L.A. city maps are Chinatown, Little Tokyo, Koreatown, Little Armenia, Thai Town and Little Saigon. Little Ethiopia in Los Angeles is the first city-designated Ethiopian enclave in the U.S.

METHODOLOGY AND DATA

We focus on the central city and inner suburbs of the primary metropolitan statistical area (PMSA) of Los Angeles, the city with the second-highest population of foreign-born Ethiopians in the U.S. To understand the characteristics and pathways to achieving enclave status, we examine the concentration and clustering of the foreign-born Ethiopian population and their businesses and institutions, the potential exposure of this ethnic population to other immigrant groups, and the political activities and activism of Ethiopians in the city. Using a multi-pronged approach that includes the use of descriptive statistics and geostatistics, as well as insights obtained from media reports and members of the community, we highlight the salient features involved in the designation of "Little Ethiopia" along a segment of Fairfax Avenue in Los Angeles.

We use the measures of concentration, clustering and exposure, to understand the spatial patterns exhibited by foreign-born Ethiopians in the Los Angeles PMSA and their implications for the formation of the ethnic enclave. Using Massey and Denton's (1988) definitions, we characterize *concentration* as the relative amount of physical space occupied by the group. *Clustering* is the extent to which the tracts occupied by Ethiopians are adjacent to each other in space. E*xposure* refers to the degree of potential contact between this ethnic group and members of other groups. We use data from the U.S. Census 2000 STF (Summary Tape Files) 3 on foreign-born Ethiopians to investigate the strength of these three dimensions, employing the census tract as the unit of analysis. Statistics on Ethiopian businesses and their locations were obtained from the Ethiopian Yellow Pages for Los Angeles (*Ethiopian Yellow Pages*, 2002–2003). Data on political activism and efforts of Ethiopian immigrants to demarcate ethnic space and gain greater recognition as a significant and growing population were gleaned from print media coverage of such activities and from communications with local community leaders.

Using a threshold of 100 Ethiopian foreign-born persons per square mile, we identified clusters of the ethnic group through visual interpretation of density maps in the Los Angeles PMSA. We computed the Entropy Index,[1] a diversity index defined by Theil and Finezza (1971) and Theil (1972), to evaluate the degree of diversity at the local level. The Entropy Index assumes that maximum diversity occurs when each immigrant group has an equal share, implying even distribution within the geographic unit (Massey and Denton, 1988; Iceland, 2002; Wong, 2002).

We also computed the Exposure Index,[2] an asymmetrical measure devised by Lieberson (1981), to evaluate the level to which Ethiopian foreign-born persons within the clusters were exposed to selected groups of foreign and native-born populations. This index incorporates the spatial interaction process because it is determined for clusters that are made up of contiguous census tract areas.

ETHIOPIANS IN THE UNITED STATES: FLOWS AND DISTRIBUTION

Ethiopian immigration to the U.S. was prompted by civil unrest and drought and aided by Congress' historic 1965 changes in immigration law that would herald the influx of populations from non-European countries in the following decades. Early Ethiopian immigrants were largely the educated elite and university students, who arrived on temporary visas and eventually remained as professionals in the U.S. (Ungar, 1995; Selassie, 1996). The trickle of immigrants in the late 1960s and early 1970s became a flood during the 1980s in the aftermath of the Refugee Act of 1980 (Bigman, 1995), which permitted many of these fleeing dictator Mengistu Haile Mariam's repressive regime to find safe haven in the U.S.

Approximately 93 percent of African refugees to the U.S. between 1982–1991 were from Ethiopia and Eritrea, although in subsequent years the flows from these two countries were surpassed by those from neighboring Sudan and Somalia. During the period of 1983–1990, California was overwhelmingly favored for the initial resettlement of Ethiopian refugees, drawing approximately 22 percent of this population (Levinson and Ember, 1997). As immigrants moved from the status of permanent residents to that of U.S. citizens, they sponsored the entry of their immediate relatives, setting into motion the process of chain migration. The establishment of Diversity Visas (also known among the immigrants as the Lottery) by Congress in 1990, which provided work permits to professionals from countries that had traditionally sent few immigrants to the U.S., further stimulated immigrant flows from Ethiopia.

By official U.S. Census 2000 counts, there are 69,531 foreign-born persons from Ethiopia living in the U.S. These Ethiopians are overwhelmingly concentrated in the Washington, D.C. PMSA, numbering 15,049 and accounting for approximately 22 percent of this population in the entire U.S. In the Los Angeles-Long Beach (LALB) PMSA, Africans comprise less than 3 percent of the foreign-born. Hispanics and Asians are the more significant elements in the ethnic mosaic of the city. Still, the Ethiopians have a significant presence in Los Angeles, where a recorded 4,501 Ethiopians form the second largest urban cluster of this immigrant group in the U.S.

RESIDENTIAL PATTERNS OF FOREIGN-BORN ETHIOPIANS IN LOS ANGELES

Concentration and Clustering

The demographic attributes of an immigrant group can have a profound effect on its social, economic, and political future (Clark, 2003). Claiming urban space for a single ethnic group is no easy task in multicultural cities, especially in neighborhoods with multiple minorities and no clear ethnic majority (Allen and Turner, 1996; Allen, 1999). The immigrants' spatial concentration relative to that of other groups can determine their ability to carve out ethnic space within the city. Therefore, residential clusters may be considered incipient sites for the marking and development of ethnic identities through the creation of ethnic enclaves.

Figure 11.1 shows the density of the Ethiopian foreign-born population in graduated tones, while concentrations of all foreign-born persons are depicted via outlined polygons. Using density thresholds of >100 Ethiopians per square mile, we identified two small Ethiopian clusters in Los Angeles. These two clusters form a northeast-southwest-oriented polygon straddling the Santa Monica (I-10) Freeway. The cluster to the north of I-10 is centered on the intersection of West Pico Boulevard and Western Avenue. The cluster to the south of the freeway is in the Crenshaw/Baldwin Hills neighborhoods.

Ethiopians make up a very small percentage of all non-Mexican foreign-born in the Los Angeles PMSA, and even in the two clusters identified, tracts with high densities only have between 100 and 150 Ethiopians per square mile. The West Pico/Western cluster, north of I-10, overlaps the largest of the three foreign-born clusters located near downtown Los Angeles, to the west of the intersection of I-10 and U.S. 101. The other Ethiopian cluster does not coincide with the distribution of the foreign-born population in the city.

Figure 11.1
Clusters of Ethiopian and Foreign-born Persons in Los Angeles

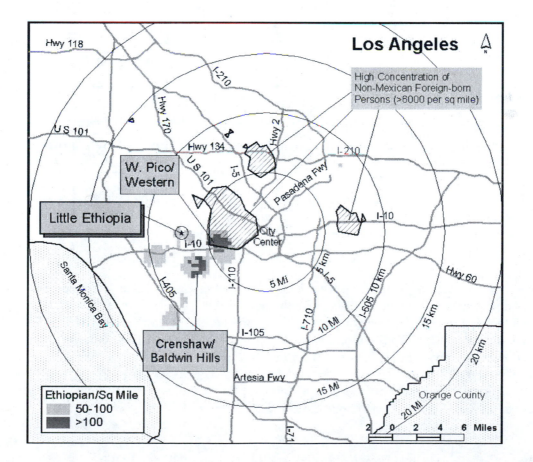

Entropy and Exposure — Local Level Characteristics of the Clusters

There is also a need to understand the social chemistry of inter-ethnic interactions in multi-group neighborhoods. Such groups negotiate space, positioning themselves physically and politically as discrete entities in relation to other immigrant populations in the area. Especially in neighborhoods with multiple groups, each with a separate cultural and visual presence, the demarcation of ethnic space may be problematic (Clark, 2002; Logan et al., 1996; Logan et al., 2002). For example, in south-eastern Los Angeles, efforts to place "Little India" exit signs on Artesia Freeway have met with opposition. Artesia's multiethnic population includes those of Latino heritage and residents from a number of Asian countries, none of which has an absolute majority. Asian-Indian merchants, whose stores make a strong visual statement along Artesia's Pioneer Boulevard, continue to face resistance from fellow immigrants in their efforts to claim ethnic space there (Fellers, 2003).

Table 11.1
Scaled Composite Entropy and Exposure Indices for Los Angeles PMSA

	ENTROPY INDEX	EXPOSURE INDEX						
		FOREIGN BORN				NATIVE		
		OTHER AFRICAN	ASIAN	EUROPEAN	LATIN AMERICAN	LATIN AMERICAN (EXCL MEXICAN)	NATIVE	NATIVE (INCLUDING MEXICAN)
LOS ANGELES	0.78	0.01	0.10	0.02	0.19	0.09	0.66	0.78
Clusters								
1. West Pico/Western Ave.	0.49	0.01	0.08	0.00	0.38	0.21	0.51	0.70
2. Crenshaw/ Baldwin Hills	0.61	0.01	0.01	0.00	0.13	0.08	0.83	0.91
Clusters 1 + 2	0.51	0.01	0.05	0.00	0.27	0.15	0.65	0.80

To address the issue of interaction, we calculated the entropy index of each Ethiopian cluster to evaluate the degree of diversity within them. The second column of Table 11.1 shows the scaled entropy index, which ranges from 0 to 1.0. For comparative purposes, we also provide the overall entropy indices for the metropolis. As Table 11.1 indicates, the overall entropy index is 0.78 in Los Angeles. Both clusters in Los Angeles have substantially lower entropy indices (0.49 for West Pico/Western and 0.61 for Crenshaw/Baldwin Hills), when compared to the overall entropy index for the metropolitan area. Although it is obvious from its high entropy index that Los Angeles is a highly diverse city, within the Ethiopian clusters identified, entropy indices are low because these areas are dominated by persons from a particular ethnic group.

To further understand the ethnic nature of these clusters, we computed the exposure indices of the Ethiopian population to selected population groups (Columns 3 through 9 in Table 11.1). The exposure indices suggest that potential interactions overall with groups such as foreign-born Asians, Europeans and Latin Americans is fairly low. However, considerable variations also occur in localities within the metropolitan area. Los Angeles' West Pico-Western area has an exposure index of 0.08 to Asians, probably due to its proximity to Koreatown, while the index drops to 0.01 in the nearby cluster of Crenshaw/Baldwin Hills (Figure 11.1). A fairly large difference also exists between the two clusters in their exposure to Latin Americans. West Pico-Western has an exposure index of 0.38, whereas the index is only 0.13 in Crenshaw/Baldwin Hills.

From the above analyses it is evident that the distribution of foreign-born Ethiopians across the Los Angeles PMSA reflects a general trend of residential scattering. Nevertheless, distinct residential clusters crystallized in the central city and in the inner suburbs of the city. Ethiopians are not in the majority in any of the foreign-born clusters identified in Los Angeles. However, their ability to create well-defined enclaves is partially dependent on the mix of groups within the clusters, on potential interactions with other ethnic/racial groups in the area, and the possibility of skirmishes over the claiming of city space.

In the West Pico-Western cluster, Salvadoran and Korean immigrants make up 50 percent of the foreign-born, while Ethiopians are only the 8th largest group. In the more diverse Crenshaw/Baldwin Hills cluster, 50 percent of all immigrants come from five countries, namely, El Salvador, Guatemala, Ethiopia, Korea, and Jamaica. However, it is important to note that 17.5 percent of all foreign-born Ethiopians in the Los Angeles PMSA live in the aggregated cluster even though they comprise only 2.6 percent of the total foreign-born in the combined unit (U.S. Census, 2000).

Sociocultural, Commercial and Political Factors

The manifestation of cultural expression in geographic space and its preservation are powerful functions of the ethnic enclave. In highly diverse metropolitan areas in the U.S. today, ethnic groups do not merely retain their heritage and identities, but are permitted to emphasize them in increasingly pluralistic environments. One of the means by which tendencies for distinction find geographic expression is through the partitioning of space. This partitioning creates separate ethnic areas within the urban mosaic. The purposeful carving out of marked ethnic territory in a multicultural city through the efforts of immigrant groups points to their territorial necessity.

Traditionally, enclaves, besides having residential concentrations of immigrant groups, afforded protected niches for ethnic businesses that supplied jobs to workers who were locked out of the mainstream labor market by their lack of occupational and language skills (Aldrich and Waldinger, 1990; Light, 1984, 2002; Logan et al., 1994; Zhou, 1992). Today, retail establishments that cater to the special needs and preferences of the immigrant community, and restaurants and cafes that serve ethnic food form dominant elements of ethnic enclaves. Clearly ethnic physical elements of the Ethiopian landscape include ethnic institutions and socio-commerscapes, settings where the community gathers to celebrate festivals and life events but also to shop and eat (Chacko, 2003). Because their street frontage and signs make them visually compelling facets of the local cultural landscape, we use Ethiopian restaurants and cafes as a proxy for ethnic enterprises in our examination of the coincidence of Ethiopian enterprises and Ethiopian foreign-born populations.

Los Angeles' primary Ethiopian enclave was introduced to a larger audience of Los Angelinos and Californians via Public Broadcasting Service (PBS), when Huell Howser's popular show, "Our Neighborhood," focused on Little Ethiopia. The show led to a heightened local awareness of Ethiopian culture and cuisine, and presented the neighborhood both as a semi-exotic locale and as a space of interaction between the immigrant group and other residents of the city. During the late 1980s, a few Ethiopian restaurants and specialty stores located their businesses along South Fairfax Avenue in Los Angeles. Located in the mid-Wilshire district, this stretch of Fairfax Avenue had many qualities that attracted Ethiopian entrepreneurs. Commercial properties that were offered at modest rents provided the initial locus for settlement, while good access to the Santa Monica (I-10) freeway was an additional draw. Ethiopian commercial enterprises along the street grew in number and density, and in less than a decade the area was transformed into a visually prominent ethnic enclave. Ethiopian restaurant owners also drew co-ethnics from the Los Angeles area and beyond by organized performances by prominent Ethiopian singers and musicians in their establishments (Demissie, 2002). The strip soon came to be known in common parlance as "Little Addis" after the national capital, or "Little Ethiopia."

The transformation of a collection of ethnic stores and restaurants on Fairfax Avenue into a thriving Ethiopian enclave was no accident. Key business owners, who established their ventures on the street in the 1980s and continue to anchor the ethnic strip today, disclose that they made a concerted effort to replicate in Los Angeles the well-known Ethiopian enclave in the Adams Morgan neighborhood of Washington, D.C. (personal communication with restaurant owners). The growth of the enclave was not effortless or uncomplicated. In the early years, although good location and low rents were very helpful, small businesses faced financial hardships here, especially during the state-wide recession of the early 1990s and in the wake of the 1992 city riots, forcing some to shut down operations. But over time, failed stores and restaurants were replaced by new Ethiopian establishments. Today, 14 Ethiopian-owned businesses (six of them restaurants), are located on Fairfax Avenue between Olympic Boulevard and Whitworth Drive (Figure 11.2). Six more are found on Pico Boulevard. This concentration of commercial enterprises while not contiguous with the residential clusters of foreign-born Ethiopians is close to them and provides the population with a variety of services.

Figure 11.2
The Merkato Restaurant and Market on Fairfax Avenue in Little Ethiopia, Los Angeles

In the endeavor to create officially sanctioned ethnic space, factors such as the educational attainment of the group, its fluency in English, and its ability to partake in and influence the local political process are critical to the immigrants' success in carving out official ethnic neighborhoods. Like other immigrants from Africa, who are known to have substantially higher levels of educational attainment than both native-born and other immigrant populations (Arthur, 2000; Ashabranner, 1999; Anonymous, 2000), foreign-born Ethiopians are well educated. Their store of human capital facilitates the Ethiopians' greater involvement in issues in the larger American sphere. Moreover, proficiency in the language of the host country helps these immigrants understand the American political process and become more quickly involved in it, unlike fellow cohorts from non-English speaking countries.

In the case of the Ethiopians in Los Angeles, political assertiveness and the immigrants' ability to garner support from elected state and city officials also were decisive factors in the official designation of the ethnic enclave. A large proportion of immigrants who left Ethiopia during the 1970s and 1980s did so because of political repression. These persons often had a history of political activism and may even have been coerced to emigrate from Ethiopia because their political affiliations and the danger such associations posed to themselves and their families. The roles of human agency and the utilization of host country political processes have been palpable in the generation and solidification of the concept of a "Little Ethiopia" in Los Angeles.

The Ethiopian-American Advocacy Group (EEAG), an organization whose mission is to spearhead and facilitate the involvement of Ethiopian immigrants in U.S. political practice, was established in Los Angeles. The EEAG lobbied key political figures at city and state government levels, pushing for the official designation of the ethnic enclave. Finally, on August 7, 2002, the Los Angeles City Council approved the naming of the strip as "Little Ethiopia," officially acknowledging its Ethiopian signature (City News Service, 2002). The visual and spatial separation of the ethnic neighborhood from the larger mid-Wilshire area was further established when a large street sign was erected at the intersection of Fairfax Avenue and Pico Boulevard, designating the area as "Little Ethiopia" (Figure 11.3). The ethnic enclave and its establishments are the primary cultural hub for a dispersed society of Ethiopian immigrants in Los Angeles, while offering ethnic experiences to the larger community.

Figure 11.3
Sign Marking Little Ethiopia on Fairfax Avenue in Los Angeles

DISCUSSION AND CONCLUSION

The ethnic enclave continues to be an area where group identity and urban space coalesce. But successes in gaining official endorsement of ethnic enclaves vary according to the demographic concentration, economic configurations, culture, and political activity of new immigrant groups.

Common interest and affective ties based on ethnic grouping are a source of strength for minority immigrant groups like the Ethiopians, who wish to build community and mark their special territory in the fragmented spaces of America's cities. Although prejudice and involuntary segregation should not be underestimated as factors that trigger the spatial congregation of minority populations (Frazier et al., 2003), group desires, and pride in national origins are instrumental in the creation of the new ethnic enclave and its transformation into a positive place for immigrant populations. Always a distinctive locale because of its conspicuous cultural expression, the enclave, once a site of segregation and discrimination, is progressively becoming one of group ownership and pride.

The Ethiopian community in Los Angeles appears to be a scattered one held together mainly by interactions and shared activities rather than by spatial closeness. Nevertheless, residential clusters of the ethnic group can be found in the zone between the central city and the outer suburbs. The bulk of foreign-born Ethiopians live in neighborhoods with a mix of other ethnic groups. This co-location with other immigrant populations poses a challenge for the official designation of an Ethiopian enclave. Success is more likely in locations where some degree of demographic concentration/clustering occurs in the same broad vicinity as the prospective enclave.

Measures such as the entropy index and exposure index offer insights into the current and latent interactions between co-located ethnic groups in the city and the probability of creating ethnic enclaves in multi-ethnic settings. Concentrations of businesses with a clear ethnic stamp are equally important in presenting visual evidence of a strong ethnic presence. In Los Angeles, areas with residential clusters of foreign-born Ethiopians and those with Ethiopian businesses overlap or are in close proximity to each other. These ethnic demographic and commercial concentrations emerge as islands; discrete areas rising from a multi-ethnic sea. However, even in areas with demographic and commercial ethnic concentrations, the possibility of creating city-approved ethnic enclaves is restricted to locales where claims to space are not likely to be contested by other ethnic or racial groups.

Ethiopians today make effective use of imagery and identity to project the idea of the enclave as a site of authentic ethnic and cultural experience. Neon and painted signs outside restaurants and commercial enterprises in Ethiopian neighborhoods announce their national and ethnic heritage through the use of the bright red, yellow, and green of the Ethiopian national flag, cartographic representations of Africa and Ethiopia, and signage in Amharic, national language of the country (Chacko, 2003). Visual references to Ethiopia and its culture continue inside the establishments. Sometimes the *gojo*, a type of Ethiopian thatched roof is incorporated into the décor or patrons are seated around *messobs*, traditional dining tables made of goat skin stretched over drums. Portraits of Ethiopian personages such as the late emperor Haile Selassie or marathon runners Abebe Bikila and Fatuma Roba hang alongside pictures of familiar natural and manmade landmarks in the home country.

The creation of a city-authorized enclave produces space that, in addition to its usual complement of ethnic signatures, is marked on city and neighborhood maps and identified on street signs, making it difficult to ignore or erase. We believe that even if all other vital elements are present, the odds of achieving official status for an ethnic enclave hinge on an additional factor: the political influence of the group. It is largely through the political efforts of recent immigrant groups and their quest for self-determination that new enclaves have been formally demarcated in urban space. These ethnic enclaves form distinct geographic patterns impressed on the urban fabric. Given the processes of suburban migration and succession in ethnic enclaves (Burgess, 1925; Funkhouser, 2000), whether these configurations will fade or intensify will depend on the trajectory of the immigrant community in the years ahead. Nonetheless, one of the ways in which immigrant groups preserve a sense of identity and bequeath a legacy of commitment to an ethnic heritage is through the creation of officially acknowledged and named ethnic spaces such as "Little Ethiopia."

NOTES

[1] The **Entropy Index** (ENT) is computed as follows:

$$ENT_i = -\sum_{j=1}^{M}\left[\left(\frac{P_{ij}}{P_i}\right)\ln\left(\frac{P_{ij}}{P_i}\right)\right] \tag{1}$$

where ENT_i is the Entropy Index for the *ith* cluster; M equals the numbers of countries of origin included in the analysis; P_{ij} is the immigrant flow to the *ith* cluster from the *jth* country; and P_i is total immigrant flow (from all countries) to the *ith* cluster. This index ranges from 0, indicating complete domination by one group, to the natural logarithm of M, indicating maximum diversity. To facilitate easier interpretation, the index was scaled to a range of 0 to 1. The Mexican foreign-born population was excluded from the analysis to minimize the bias introduced by the Mexican foreign-born, who make up over 40 percent of the foreign-born population in Los Angeles. Therefore, M is 72 (countries of origin) in Los Angeles.

[2] The **Exposure Index** was computed as follows:

$$EXPOSE_i = \sum_{k=1}^{G}\left(\frac{E_k}{\sum_{k=1}^{G}E_k}\right)*\left(\frac{A_k}{P_k}\right) \tag{2}$$

where $EXPOSE_i$ is the Exposure Index of Ethiopians to group A for the *ith* cluster; G is the number of census tract areas within the *ith* cluster; E_k is the numbers of Ethiopians in the *kth* census tract area; A_k is the numbers of persons from group A in the *ith* cluster; and P_k is the total population in the *ith* cluster.

Chapter 12

The New African Americans:
Liberians of War in Minnesota

EARL P. SCOTT

Landscapes reflect cultural and socioeconomic imprints of the societies that occupy the land. Discernible landscape features give meaning to human-environment interaction over time. Understanding the culture and experiences of the societies that occupy a land leads to better interpretation of any landscape including slightly modified, "nuanced" landscapes. These landscapes must be understood from the perspective of the people who gave them functional and emotional meaning (Tuan, 1979, p. 387). Because America is still open to immigrants, its landscapes are constantly under modification as new arrivals imprint the land surface. The four goals of this chapter relate to the Liberian immigrant settlements in Minnesota. First, it examines the formation and distribution of Liberian communities in the Twin Cities metropolitan area in Minnesota. The second goal addresses the question: What cultural elements are shared by Liberians and African Americans? The third goal is to analyze the extent to which shared traits influence Liberian-African American interactions and promote cultural solidarity and convergence between the two groups. The final goal is to examine the nature of landscapes and the reconstruction of Liberian ethnic spaces in the Twin Cities. The chapter concludes with a discussion of the future cooperation of these two ethnic groups with a common heritage.

THE FORMATION OF LIBERIAN COMMUNITIES IN MINNESOTA

The "Established" Liberian Immigrants: Pre-1996 Arrivals

Recent strife brought global attention to Liberia and Liberian immigrant flows to the U.S. However, a relatively small number of Liberians immigrated to the U.S. before 1996. Given its interior location, harsh winters, and predominately northern European population, Minnesota appears to be an unlikely destination for such African immigrants. Still, a small number of African and Liberian immigrants made their way to Minnesota in two waves. The pre-1996 period is considered the first wave and the immigrants are termed the "established" Liberians. These immigrants, like others, sought better education, job opportunities, and generally, hope for a better life that America could offer. While a small number of these original Liberians settled in small farm towns and university communities, the vast majority settled in the Twin Cities Metropolitan Area. Generally, like local African Americans, the established Liberian immigrants continue to reside near the inner city. However, Liberian immigrants of the second wave are mainly suburban residents. These are referred to as "recent Liberian immigrants," because they came after 1996. They also are mainly refugees of war and subsequent reprisals.

Recent Immigration Process: Liberian Families of War

The recent Liberian immigrants comprise by far the larger of the two waves, and continue to arrive in Minnesota. Often, entire families ultimately reassemble in Minnesota. The Lutheran Social Services and other service agencies assist refugees in their resettlement because Minnesota requires agency or family sponsorship. For most refugee immigrants, the journey from war-torn Liberia to Minnesota was long, hard, and unbelievably frightening. Most came to escape the civil unrest and violence of the 1990s. One family's story illustrates what immigrants have endured to reach safety and freedom. Members of this family, who lived and worked in Monrovia, escaped arrest and possibly death moments before the soldiers arrived at their door. The family abandoned its home, valued possessions and other properties, and with grandparents and children, waded through mosquito-infested swamps. The family hid with friends and acquaintances until they reached their traditional vernacular region. After days of uncertainty, fear, and harassment by rogue elements, the family managed to cross the eastern border (i.e., the Cavally River), and found shelter and food in a refugee camp in northern Ivory Coast. They stayed in the camp for more than two years, until the father, who had attended the University of Minnesota, became established with friends in Minnesota and met the requirements of the Lutheran Social Services. Then the entire family reassembled in Minnesota.

The Lutheran Social Services assists such families in settling into permanent homes, obtaining proper identification cards, and employment. However, Liberian-organized agencies, such as the Pan-African Social Services and the Liberian Community of Minnesota Corporation, now have assumed the same responsibilities. These service organizations are social institutions providing multiple functions. They not only support recent arrivals in their settlement, they have become vehicles through which recent immigrants speak, criticizing American-Liberian policy and their desire to return to Liberia to change their home nation.[1] Meanwhile, these immigrants of war make their homes in America, including the Twin Cities, reshaping the streetscapes and expressing their ethnic identity.

Estimating the Liberian Community

The number of Liberians residing in Minnesota and the Twin Cities Metropolitan Area is not known. The U.S. Census undercounted Liberians in Minnesota. This is due to the use of social constructs to classify non-white Americans, including immigrants. Liberians become invisible when they are racialized as "African" and placed into "Black" or "African Other" categories. This, unfortunately, obscures the number of Liberians living in Minnesota and America. For example, according to the U.S. Census 2000, the total number of African immigrants in Minnesota is over 43,000. Of that total, only 3,126 are Liberian, the third largest African immigrant population in the state. However, according to federal statistics, 43 percent of immigrants in Minnesota also were classified as "African Other" in 2000, meaning that Africans of different ethnicities and national origins in small countries were lumped into one category.

Thus, in order to better estimate the actual Liberian population in the Twin Cities region, other sources had to be consulted. The Twin Cities School District was one source. The school districts count the number of students who speak a language other than English at home, plus they include two parents in their estimates. This approach revealed that eighty-plus foreign languages are spoken in the Twin Cities School Districts. However, the districts mistakenly count Liberians as African American because they speak English in the home, which is another data limitation. In addition, the INS, the U.S. Census, and local social service agencies, all fail to account for secondary immigrant residents, those Liberians immigrants who subsequently move to Minnesota from other cities. It seems apparent that all agencies have underestimated the total Liberian immigrant population. Estimates range between 10,000 and 30,000. This makes it very difficult to analyze the distribution of Liberians in the region.

Despite the severe data limitations related to establishing the total Liberian population and its geographic distribution, another data source provides a reasonable surrogate for their local settlement geography. The best available data for Liberians in the Twin Cities are the location of birth by ancestry and address of parent, which are maintained by the Minnesota Department of Health's Center for Health Statistics (Sechler, 2002). These data, which contain the number of births by year, are presented in maps in the next section.

The Suburbanization of Post-1995 Liberian Immigrants

The Lutheran Social Service (LSS) operates one of the largest resettlement programs for Liberians in Minnesota. Between 1997 and 2002, the LSS assisted 816 Liberian immigrants, mostly families, assisting their settlement in several municipalities of the Twin Cities Metropolitan Area (Walen, 2002). Liberian immigrants in the Twin Cities Metropolitan Area initially settled in the inner cities of Minneapolis and St. Paul. Liberian residential concentrations were areas near existing African-American neighborhoods. However, in recent years, a noticeable shift of Liberians has occurred with the resettlement of recent immigrants in nearby suburbs of the Twin Cities. Personal communication with a LSS representative confirmed this observation that recent Liberian immigrants were now being placed in the suburbs, although Minneapolis and St. Paul also receive immigrant refugees as well (Walen, 2002). To verify this observation, the Department of Health births data mentioned above were mapped at the zipcode level for the Twin Cities metropolitan area. This map of Liberian births between 1989 and 2000 (Figure 12.1) suggests that the primary locations of recent Liberian immigrants are likely in the Twin Cities and certain suburbs. Figure 12.2 is a map of Liberian births that occurred in the year 2000 only, and helps further clarify the distribution of Liberians in the metropolitan region. Besides the Twin Cities, four particular suburbs located to the west and northwest of the Twin Cities appear to have a high number of Liberian births. The total number of Liberian births in suburbs exceeded total Liberian births in the Twin Cities.

One can infer from this distribution of births and from information provided by LSS that Minneapolis was the early core and remains an important center of the established Liberian community and their families. However, the data on births clearly indicates the increasing importance of the Twin Cities suburbs for Liberian settlement. The largest concentration of recent Liberian births is in suburbia, where a wedge extends from the inner city core out to the northwest selected inner suburbs of New Hope and Brooklyn Center, on to Brooklyn Park and Crystal, to the outer suburbs. The maps of Liberian residential distribution reflect a process of spatial inertia, with expansion occurring on the edges of the established Liberian communities toward the suburbs. The "established" Liberians lived mainly in the cities of St. Paul and Minneapolis, but the suburbanization of recent Liberian immigrants has shifted away from the African-American inner city residential areas. This residential pattern of Liberian Community members seem to confirm that there are differences in place of settlement by established Liberians and recent Liberian immigrants of childbearing age. The suburbanization of recent Liberian immigrants is unusual for some immigrant black groups, but not uncommon for other recent ethnic immigrants in America (*The Economist*, 2004). The changing areas of settlement of recent Liberian immigrants, who will be among the newest African Americans, have cultural and socioeconomic implications for possible ethnic solidarity and community development with the native-born African Americans and their communities.

LIBERIANS AND AFRICAN AMERICANS: SHARED HERITAGE AND CULTURE

As noted earlier, African Americans and Liberian immigrants share a common heritage forged by the common history in America. They developed a subculture, including an acquired language and modified African food traditions, including taboos, preparation methods, and preferred food staples. Each of these components of that heritage is briefly described below.

Common Cultural Heritage

Africans were first brought to America and initially concentrated in the Charleston area, the Chesapeake Bay region, and later along rivers to produce tobacco, rice, sugar cane, and cotton in the Mississippi Delta.

Figure 12.1

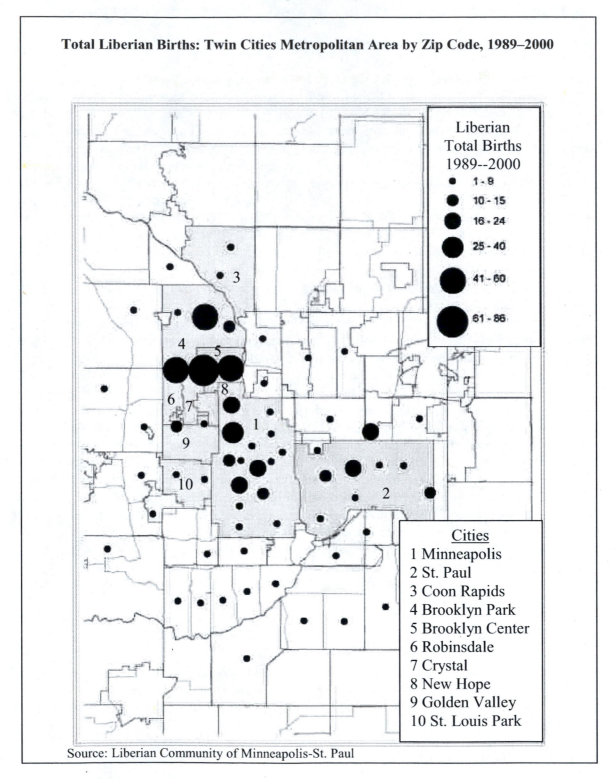

Total Liberian Births: Twin Cities Metropolitan Area by Zip Code, 1989–2000

Liberian Total Births 1989--2000
- 1 - 9
- 10 - 15
- 16 - 24
- 25 - 40
- 41 - 60
- 61 - 86

Cities
1 Minneapolis
2 St. Paul
3 Coon Rapids
4 Brooklyn Park
5 Brooklyn Center
6 Robinsdale
7 Crystal
8 New Hope
9 Golden Valley
10 St. Louis Park

Source: Liberian Community of Minneapolis-St. Paul

Figure 12.2

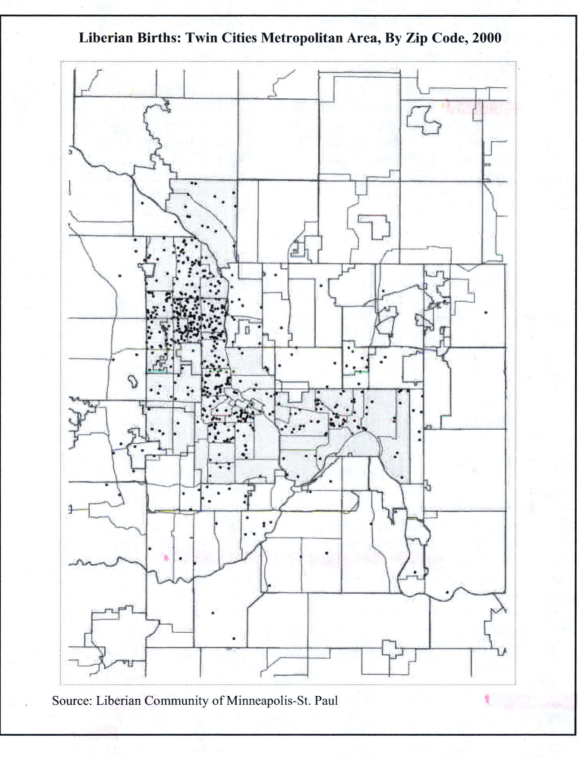

Liberian Births: Twin Cities Metropolitan Area, By Zip Code, 2000

Source: Liberian Community of Minneapolis-St. Paul

This clustering accounts for the development of an African-American folk culture in a society otherwise dominated by its white population (Gomez, 1998). Close proximity ensured extensive interactions and fostered continuity and retention of an ethnic culture through sharing of ideas, beliefs, cooking methods, and farming techniques (Gomez, 1998). This culture was further reinforced through mixed marriages between African ethnic groups and slave laborers, especially those who cultivated and harvested rice in the Carolinas, Mississippi, and Louisiana.

The critical fact is that African slaves from several parts of Africa constructed their own subculture. They achieved a "self-view" in opposition to the image prescribed by European power and authority (Gomez, 1998). Gomez argued that the transformation of the African into the African American actually began on African soil. African captives quickly discovered that they held in common their "blackness." They were literally in the same boat, facing the same problems as intended slave laborers. The Middle Passage for the first time brought intended slaves together and provided the opportunity to experience their differences, especially in language and staple foods. Being together for a long period, Africans then devised methods of speech and cooking that evolved into elements of unique African-American slang language and cuisine as we today know it.

Language as Cultural Identity

Similarities in speech of Liberian immigrants and African Americans evolved from the founding of Liberia. Initially, African Americans from Louisiana, Mississippi, and elsewhere lived as American expatriates in that African colony, permanently away from home. Indeed, these expatriates carried their Southern, and specifically, their African-American cultural heritage with them. Once there, they recreated an American society and constructed a new "American" cultural landscape in a new place. Huffman (2004, p. 159) argued "… the history of the Mississippi colony and of Liberia as a whole is both a transplanted African-American story and an African experiment with Western culture." Liberians, like African Americans, valued their shared, American-informed culture. This common heritage is reflected in Liberia by their beliefs, dress, tastes, house types, and place names, including newly established residential communities. The long-term geographical and cultural isolation of these freed slaves, limited cultural exchange or assimilation, and thus preserved their African-American heritage and culture. Although a minority group in Liberia, Americo-Liberians assumed political and economic power and an aristocratic status in their new home. Their isolation from native Liberians was important in preserving their new culture. It fostered the preservation of their language and their cultural identity. Americo-Liberians used their African American-based language to preserve their cultural identity in a dominate culture, which is similar to the way African Americans use language in America. While English is the official and formal language in Liberia (i.e., the language of instruction and parliament and of professional speech), the common or everyday language is *pidgin*. Pidgin is "broken" or "shorten" English, which means that English words are literally shortened and speech is very rapid, making it unintelligible to the untrained ear. Liberians consciously use dual speech under certain circumstances to obscure issues under discussion or to clarify their meaning. This purposeful, functional use of language to preserve ethnic identity is steeped in traditional African-American culture as well. In Minnesota, this dual language capability facilities communication and understanding and ameliorates tension between Liberians from different vernacular regions and between Liberians and African Americans.

The best example of African American use of language to preserve cultural identity is found on the Sea Islands (Gullah Islands). Among African slaves, English ultimately became the *lingua franca* or trade language in America with regional dialects and accents. On the more isolated Gullah Island, located off the Carolinas and Florida coasts, and on the coastal mainland, Africans developed a unique language called *Gullah*, a language that is a combination of Caribbean and West African languages (e.g., Yoruba, Ibo, Sierra Leone, and Liberian, specifically the Vai). *Gullah*, sometimes derogatorily called *Geechee*, "is an important reason why Sea Islanders have preserved a way of life that remains African in some of its essentials" (Blockson, 1987, p. 735). Because *Gullah* is a combination of English, Caribbean and West African languages, it is virtually incomprehensible to non-speakers, including mainland African Americans. The two communities, African Americans and Americo-Liberians, enjoy marked advantages in using both formal English and modified English in speaking. Just as in Liberia, English is the official and formal language used for instruction and professional speech on the Sea Islands. However, Sea Islanders also use dual speech to avoid stereotypes and embarrassment as country bumpkins. More importantly, *Gullah* (in America) and Pidgin (in Liberia) function to define a small, mainly isolated group and have had the effect of preserving a culture that is curiously similar in food preferences and preparation.

Staple Foods as Cultural Identity

Like language, Americo-Liberians retained their acquired American food ways and eventually reconstructed Liberia's cultural landscapes based on their preferred staple crops and foods. African-American expatriates introduced a staple crop, the long-grained, Carolina gold rice, into Liberia's interior. Carolina gold rice symbolizes the Liberian's curious Diaspora; wherever Liberians settle they maintain their preference for this specific rice.

> "The circle of rice history in the Atlantic basin thus closes with the introduction of the Carolina rice of U.S. slavery to Sierra Leone and the West African rice region via freed men and Christian missionaries. Through another African Diaspora (i.e., the voluntary repatriation of the thirty-five surviving Amistads or the Mendi Mission], this one based on freedom and voluntary return to the continent by some of its descendants, Carolina rice reached into the heart of Africa all the way to the floodplains of the Niger River in Mali…. A cereal and a knowledge system that left West Africa on ships with slaves and became established in the Americas under bondage, returned once more to African shores in freedom through the agency of black missionaries, freed and recaptured slaves. Known as Méréki, (note: name is drawn from America) the rice drew its name from America, the continent of human bondage. But this time the history of those who brought it would not be forgotten" (Carney, 2001, p. 174–77).

Minnesota Liberians have brought the American-based Carolina rice nearly full circle, locationally speaking, by returning it to the U.S.

Food preferences also modify existing landscapes. Americo-Liberians transformed Liberia's cultural landscape by introducing Carolina rice, and retaining the methods of food preparation developed in the American Southeast. Most prepared meals included the use of rice as the staple. Curiously enough, this aspect of the African American-based cultural transformation is a distinctive cultural signature of the Liberian Diaspora. Liberian staple food dishes are explicitly of African-American origin, evidence of the African-American cultural influence in Liberia. More importantly, rice, like language, helped to preserve the African American-based culture that recent Minnesota immigrants have brought with them. This curious but unique cultural phenomenon among recent Liberians migrating to America, not only informs our understanding of the common cultural heritage of Liberians and African Americans, also demonstrates that these cultures have not diverged significantly over space or throughout generations of time.

It is useful to examine Liberian and African-American food traditions in some detail because inspection reveals strong similarities. African-American and Liberian staple dishes have diverged in terms of the ingredients used, but they remain similar in the method of preparation and, in some cases, even the actual name of the dish (Table 12.1). While these popular dishes link African Americans in America and Americo-Liberians in Liberia, the method of food preparation is greater evidence of their common origin. The interactions of the *Gullah* and the coastal groups developed a number of new staple foods based on leafy vegetables, fruit, seafoods, swine products, mainly sausages, chicken, corn and rice. As Table 12.1 shows, Gumbo, jambalaya, and various bean dishes are all prepared with rice and are common to both cultures. African-American desserts are also shared creations. Both employed local resources such as lemon, apple, pecan, sweet potato, and pumpkin. They also used corn and beans to make snacks such as hush puppies and bean cakes. In both cultures, foods are boiled and deep-fat fried. For example, greens, beans, and meats are all boiled with lots of seasoning, while chicken and fish are deep-fat fried in a seasoned batter. In America, these methods of food preparation are called *Southern* while in Liberia they are described as the *Liberian Way.*

In some instances, the cultures retained the actual name of selected staple dishes. For example, gumbo and lemon merinque pie are virtually the same in both cultures in preparation and name (Table 12.1). Smoked meats, (i.e., sausage, ham, ham hocks, fish) are important seasonings in "thick" soup-type dishes such as red beans and gumbo. Gumbo is seafood, okra, or filét based, but all gumbos are cooked with sausage, usually smoked pork, or chicken, and served over rice with corn bread. Carolina rice remains the staple crop in southeast America and gumbo is still prepared the same way by mainland African Americans and the *Gullah* on the Sea Islands. Food preference and preparation are part of a group's deep culture. They are what groups identify with and what identifies them (e.g., soul food in African-American culture).

Food Display and Consumption as Cultural Identity

The finally similarity between Liberian and African-American cultures offered in this chapter involves food display and consumption. Liberians prepare and display several major dishes at one time for consumption at lunch and dinner. Traditionally, an individual will take small portions of each dish and, as in other parts of Africa, food is usually eaten with one's hands. For example, rice is formed into a small ball, dipped into a meat, okra or other types of sauce, and eaten. The Liberian practice of eating with their hands is African in origin, but the practice of preparing and displaying several major dishes at one time is clearly an African-American tradition. This combination of elements from two different cultures to create a new but unique Liberian immigrant way of dining is a good example of cultural syncretism.

Americo-Liberians structured a new society that was a blend of selected West African traditions and their southern African-American culture. But geographical and sociocultural isolation facilitated their retention of certain elements of their African American-based culture. These cultural similarities are the potential bases for cultural convergence and ethnic solidarity. However, for reunification to occur, Liberians and African Americans in Minnesota must acknowledge their common heritage and shared culture. This becomes more difficult due to the spatial separation caused by the suburbanization of Liberian immigrants.

CONSEQUENCES OF SPATIAL SEPARATION AND ETHNIC IDENTITY

There is little doubt that the suburbanization of Liberians in the Twin Cities region is placing a greater geographic and social distance between African Americans and Liberians, making cultural convergence difficult. However, one must also recognize the strength of two different ethnic identities forged over a considerable period of time as a significant deterrent to cultural convergence of these two groups with a common heritage. Thus, geography and ethnic differences combine to present a serious barrier to the convergence of the two groups.

Ethnicity involves both shared traits and an affinity for place (home). African Americans, despite American racism, have only memories of American soil that likely splits their affinity between Africa and America, but positions their current cultural and African American ethnic identity more in the history of African American struggle and in shared traits that coalesced in the rural American south, their "home." The chapter by Frazier and Anderson discussed this Southern rural affinity of African Americans involved in the current reverse migration. Those of Liberian descent also have a strong place affinity with home. Many intend to return there one day. In the mean time this affinity for home and the Liberian way of life is replicated in many ways in their current Minnesota home. Recent Liberian immigrants are reshaping the neighborhoods and streetscapes of their new home to reflect Liberian traits learned and associated with their homeland in Africa. They also continue in the beliefs and practices they value.

Table 12.1
Liberian and African American Food Ways:
Common Heritage and Cultural Reunification

	Liberian	African American
Snacks	Bean Cake	Hush Puppies
Breads	Corn Bread	Same
	Short Bread	Same
Entrees	Rice Jallof	Jambalaya
	Chicken Dumplings	Same
	Seafood & Fish	Same
	Fried Okra	Same
Vegetables	Collards	Same
Gumbos	Seafood	Same
	Chicken	
	Filé	
	Okra	Same
Desserts	Lemon Meringue Pie	Same
	Pumpkin Pie	Same
	Butter Cake	Pound Cake
Drinks	Sweet Tea	
	Lemonade	Same

Descriptions of selected Liberian dishes are based on discussions with Ms. Manzaler Toweh, a student in my course on West Africa and a member of one of the families interviewed for this study. Also see: *Liberia's Treasured Recipes From Our Kitchens,* Preference by Eric David, Chairman of Effort Baptist Church & Friends of Effort, USA. Descriptions of African-American dishes are based on personal experience.

Cognitive Features of Special Importance: The Liberian Way

In addition to the cultural consequences of living apart in the metropolitan area as discussed above, the shared cultural heritage of African Americans and Liberians evokes a false sense of community, of oneness, of black solidarity in America. For Liberians, Brooklyn Park and adjacent communities are their spatial cognitive realities. That is, Liberians have a feel, a perception of Brooklyn Park as their "new" cultural and ethnic space, their own ethnic community with their churches, businesses, homes, and schools (i.e., their "Little Monrovia"). Liberian attachment to community objects explains why new immigrants feel comfortable in that space. Their culture and circumstance constructed a cognitive compage, a virtual homeland in America, one steeped in nationalism and ethnic attitudes and beliefs characterized as the "Liberian Way." From the perspective of all Liberians in Minnesota, the Liberian Way is the essence of their culture. It is multidimensional and constitutes the ethnic glue that binds Liberians together. The Liberian Way includes cultural awareness, respect for community and family, cultural pride and ethnic preferences, and the desire to express them, orally and through transformation of their landscapes that reflect their presence.

Liberian businesses, for example, reinforce cultural awareness. Food is one vital component of cultural maintenance. The "Pepper Charm," shown in Figure 12.3 , is a recently-established place that provides foods, spices, and condiments required to prepare most ethnic Liberian dishes preferred by members of the Liberian community. The Liberian Way also includes the preparation of a number of dishes for consumption at national, religious and family ceremonies. Liberians value and keep ceremonial practices, including weddings, religious and national holidays (e.g., Liberia's Independence Day and conformation of nationalized citizenship), as well as family celebrations.

Figure 12.3
Liberian businesses, "Pepper Charm," are located in recently established suburban shopping centers that support the "Liberian Way" by offering imported foods, spices, and condiments required to prepare most Liberian dishes.

The Liberian Way also means respect for the extended family. That is, they show great respect for elders, especially the father, as head of the household, and for other family relatives. The Liberian Way also attaches loyalty to one's vernacular region in Liberia. The home region is a special place and, along with extended family remaining in Liberia, a focus of frequent discussions at social gatherings in their new U.S. home. A significant indicator of Liberian ethnicity is the sentiment and loyalty attached to their homeland. Established or recent, young or old, all Liberians immigrants grieve for their country, the place they love and the place where many of their relatives and friends remain.

Of the many aspects of the Liberian Way brought to America, the value placed on the extended family is one of the most important. As a social unit, the extended family assembles regularly to share common interests and accommodate specific needs. For example, the extended family creates a forum and a time to rejoice and to grieve. When Liberians entertain visitors, the extended family provides a feast of traditional dishes where everyone prays and sings religious hymns in worship as they did in Liberia.

At the same time, Liberians rejoice in their new circumstance and new place in America. The Liberian Way also results in new ethnic spaces and new Liberian streetscapes in America, which become the visual evidence of their ethnic presence.

LANDSCAPE AND THE RECONSTRUCTION OF ETHNIC LIBERIAN SPACES

In cultural geography, the visible landscape is examined for insight into the society and the way of life of the people that built or altered it (Tuan, 1979, 1991; and Hart, 1995). This approach to environmental change is rooted in the belief that "geographers explore the earth less for its own sake than for what it can tell of its human residents and their character …" (Tuan, 1991, p. 100). Speaking as a cultural geographer, Hart (1995, p. 1) argued that "the inevitable starting point is the visible landscape … the form and appearance of human structures" tell us something about the technical competence, the cultural baggage and the socioeconomic status and gender of the groups who built the landscapes. Scholars extract data from landscapes for the construction of scientific hypotheses. They look for what the landscape can tell us about the socio-economic, physical and cultural well-being of a people. The total built landscape provides the ability "to see from the landscape to the values and pathos of a folk" (Tuan, 1979, p. 93).

Scholars of cultural landscapes differ over whether the purpose of the built landscape is functional or aesthetic. Geographer Yi-Fu Tuan for example argued that people everywhere construct the "ideal and humane," or aesthetic living space, often integrating the functional and aesthetic into an "all-encompassing milieu" (Tuan, 1979, p. 97). John Fraser Hart, on the other hand, argued that "most people are motivated by functional, not aesthetic consideration when they erect a structure, and most ordinary human structures must be understood in terms of their functions" (Hart, 1995, p. 13). In urban America, the functional and aesthetic typically are combined into a single landscape. Structures are erected for specific purposes and also serve the function of providing shelter and a means of expressing the occupying group's taste through embellishment. Landscapes, then, are geographical expressions of a group's functional and aesthetic values and its symbolic culture.

Liberian immigrants in Minnesota engage in the reconstruction of ethnic space within a framework of traditional African landscapes. In West Africa, the compound house is the functional expression of fundamental social and family units on the rural landscape. The compound house, or compage, a community housing development of buildings constructed from a variety of materials, consists of separate areas for families as well as shared spaces for cooking and dining. It also contains a spatial organization of units based on traditional homes (James, 1954). The compound also contains symbolic features and places, such as those that recognize the significance of ancestry, religion and family status. Liberian immigrants in Minnesota have retained this compound tradition. They also acquire material possessions that reflect the Liberian Way and place emphasis on symbolic features of space. These material and symbolic features not only represent a socially constructed space within which people are comfortable, they represent a space in which people engage in a way of life (Tuan, 1991, p. 104). They help maintain cherished values and norms in an otherwise foreign environment and preserve ethnic well-being. These dimensions of the Liberian Way will be analyzed in more detail for Liberian immigrants in Minnesota after discussion of the data acquired for the study.

Primary Data Collection

The primary data for this study were collected through observation of the Liberian business community, family or group interviews, interviews of individual business owners and information from the archives of local government and nongovernmental social service agencies. Field observation relied on the physical modifications of businesses and residences as indicators of cultural symbols and styles to determine how much the landscape has been altered by the presence of Liberian immigrants. Apart from businesses, data were collected from Liberian families displaced by war and individuals reunited with family in Minnesota. Recorded interviews consisted of open-ended questions to solicit unstructured responses rich in information detail. Capturing feelings, experiences, and expectations were deemed important for this study, due to the effects of war.

Landscapes and Social Spaces of Liberian Immigrants

The places inhabited by Liberian immigrants are undergoing landscape transformation and nowhere are they more obvious than on the streetscapes of Liberian residential neighborhoods. Ethnic businesses have become significant and visible features, often recognizable by their signage, and decorated with colors and other ethnic symbols. These streetscape changes largely occur on refurbished commercial strips and replace vacant storefronts (see Figure 12.4). They also have been opened in refurbished suburban strip malls. Business institutions, occupied and managed by Liberians, transform the inherited landscape by the use of semi-fixed ethnic cultural features, such as the Liberian flag and other items showing national colors and reflecting Liberian ethnicity. This process characterizes the behaviors of all recent immigrants who construct new living spaces to reflect their cultural identity. These transformed landscapes become culturally comfortable and result in nuanced landscapes.

African restaurants, like the Kilimanjaro shown in Figure 12.5, are examples of landscape changes in these suburban communities. They typically are located near universities and use language, colors, and other cultural symbols to attract familiar and adventurous patrons. They exist because of the concentration of Liberian homes nearby. Many recent Liberian immigrants consist of entire families whose parents are usually educated professionals. While in Liberia, the professionally trained were employed as businesses persons, bankers, and government officials. However, in the U.S. they often are not qualified for similar jobs. In many instances, such immigrant Liberians avoid years of retraining to acquire the U.S. qualifications. Instead, they engage in self-employment in small, ethnic-based businesses in suburban strip malls near their homes. Liberian businesses typically are family-owned and sometimes operated by new immigrant families working as a unit. Liberian family businesses also prefer locations near their churches and schools, integral parts of their community. Unlike Ethiopian and Somali businesses that are inner-city based and occupy the old dilapidated neighborhoods, market centers, and established shopping malls, Liberian ethnic businesses seem to be located almost exclusively in suburbs of the Twin Cities.

Liberian's preferences for suburbia are business decisions that recognize the significance of nearby Liberian residences. Location closer to the market maximizes revenue. Ethnic businesses cater to Liberian food taste, service needs, and provide opportunities that reinforce ethnic ties, including the exchange of information about relatives who live in Liberia. These "business centers" actually are more than commercial shops. They are social spaces. Thus, Liberian ethnic businesses are places that provide social, recreational and commercial functions for the Liberian community. The "T & C Barber Shop," which is located in a small strip mall, is an example of a business serving as social space for men from all over Liberia. It not only provides haircuts, but functions as a place of opportunity to reminisce about Liberian vernacular or cultural regions, and share ideas on achieving peace and prosperity in their homeland.

The size of market and competition affect ethnic businesses, making the ethnic market niche far from secure. Liberian markets are small and these ethnic-based operations have limited potential for growth, mainly due to highly ethnic commodities, especially apparels, and a reliance on the local Liberian population. As a result, products among their local stores are quite similar and competition for the small number of customers is fierce. In general, ethnic-based businesses are inward looking and culturally isolated, resulting in a high incidence of failure.

Liberian entrepreneurs may be able to expand their businesses, especially their food markets, restaurants, and bakeries, if certain conditions are met. The potential new market is African-American consumers whose tastes are similar to those of Liberians. When Liberians use local substitutes, for example, the main dishes are virtually identical. Beyond food, Liberians and African Americans have shared history and other cultural identifiers that suggest a potential for cooperation.

Figure 12.4
"Al Karama Mall" and other Somali businesses are located in refurbished commercial strips on thoroughfares near the central business district offering a wide range of retail opportunities.

Figure 12.5
African restaurants like the "Kilimanjaro" are usually located near universities and use language, colors and other cultural symbols to attract familiar and adventurous patrons.

DISCUSSION AND CONCLUSION

The strength and depth of Liberian culture unifies ethnic Liberians in Minnesota. On the other hand, when Liberians forcefully express nationalism, attitudes, and practices as the Liberian Way, their perceived community space expands and threatens others. For example, tensions flair between Liberians and African Americans when Liberians display their unique culture and African ancestry. Ethnic differences have the potential to be divisive. This is especially evident in Liberian's views on child-rearing and discipline, dependence on the extended family, and respect for elders (especially the father as head of the extended family) versus African-American preference for individual responsibly and self-expression.[2] As the Liberian community has expanded and they have become even more comfortable with their new home-space, interaction with other ethnic groups has been modest, resulting in little cultural exchange and transformation. Their Liberian self-identity and desire for ethnic distinction has strengthened. For example, when Liberians were asked how would they like to be identified in the U.S. Census, young Liberian males in particular said if they could not be called Liberian, they would rather be called "Black African" or Blacks from Africa, but not "African American." Liberians, like many other immigrant groups, wish to retain their ethnic identity. The Liberian Way is important to them as a people. This, along with their new suburban settlement geography, has meant that the "new Liberian immigrants" (post-1996) are increasingly isolated and segregated from the African-American population and, perhaps, the "established" Liberian communities in the urban core as well. Consciously or unconsciously, the Liberian community of the Twin Cities region will not assimilate into the wider African American subculture. Instead, they will be part of the pluralistic society that is growing in America, making ethnic solidarity harder to achieve. This does not mean that some cultural convergence is impossible. Rather, African Americans and Liberians must recognize their common heritage that provides a unique cultural association and, at the same time, they must realize that the two ethnic groups have also evolved different traditions and have unique attributes that provide different ethnic glue for each subculture.

Recent history indicates that the two groups can find their commonalties when interaction occurs. When Liberians and African Americans have had contact, positive outcomes follow. During the first wave of immigrants, Liberian ministries shared African-American church facilities until they were able to function on their own. During this period of adjustment, African-American and Liberian congregations participated in church dinners, funerals, marriages, and other shared ceremonies. These occasions provided opportunities for these groups to know each other, allowing for an acknowledgement of ethnic differences but also for a greater appreciation of cultural similarities. African American and Liberian self-constructed identities and perceptions of each other ignore the reality of their common heritage. Cooperation can benefit both groups, while preserving the ethnic uniqueness cherished by both.

NOTES

[1] Recent film documentaries are critical of U.S. policies toward Liberia, accusing it of abandoning Liberia during its most server humanitarian crisis (see Liberia: America's Stepchild and Liberia, An Uncivil War).

[2] Historically, the extended family was the most important social unit in the African American community, especially in the rural Southeast. However, for most African Americans today, who are highly mobile and urban, the extended family is a lost institution. On the other hand, it remains important in rural Southeast America, a factor driving the reverse migration of African American from the urban, industrial centers of the Northeast and Midwest. Again, the Sea Islands are a good example of the importance of the extended family in the rural Southeast. "The extended family is the norm in the Sea Islands. Most islands are sectioned off into family communities, where all members of one family, their close relatives, and people remotely related live or have a right to live…" (Dr. Patricia Jones-Jackson, quoted in Blockson, 1987, p. 737).

Chapter 13

The Distribution and Socioeconomic Status of West Indians Living in the United States

THOMAS D. BOSWELL AND TERRY-ANN JONES

In many ways, migration has been a way of life in the West Indies. Like all other areas in the Western Hemisphere, virtually everybody living in the non-Hispanic islands of the Caribbean can trace their origins to someplace else in the world. Even the pre-Colombian Indians, including the Ciboney, Arawaks, and Caribs, came from places outside the Caribbean (West and Augelli, 1989). Thousands of Spanish citizens immigrated to the Caribbean during the 1500s. During the 1600s and 1700s, tens of thousands of Europeans moved to the Caribbean from Spain, the United Kingdom, France, and the Netherlands, and they were joined by perhaps five million slaves who were forcibly brought from Africa. During the 1800s, the slave trade was gradually abolished and later the slaves were emancipated, although the timing of this varied among the British, French, Dutch, and Spanish colonies (Ashdown, 1979). To replace the freed slaves, the British, French, and Dutch imported indentured workers from their other colonies outside the Caribbean. The British imported workers, mostly on five-year contracts, from what was then British colonial India (now India, Pakistan, Sri Lanka, and Bangladesh). The Dutch imported several hundred thousand workers from India and the Dutch East Indies (today's Indonesia), and the French also imported workers from India mainly to work in the French islands of Guadeloupe and Martinique, but also to work in French Guiana (Henke, 2001). Until the late 1800s most migration had been **into** the Caribbean islands, but this began to change by the late 1800s as more and more West Indians left their island origins in search of better jobs elsewhere outside the Caribbean. Now, the islands of the West Indies became areas of **out-migration**. Beginning in the late 1880s and continuing to the 1920s West Indians from Jamaica, Barbados, Trinidad, and some of the smaller islands in the eastern Caribbean were recruited to work as paid laborers in building the Panama Canal, the railroads in Central America, and the banana, sugar, and pineapple plantations along the Caribbean litoral of Central America. By 1900 West Indians were beginning to make their presence felt in New York City and Miami. During the period 1900 to 1920, between 10,000 and 12,000 Bahamians had moved to Miami to work in the construction industry and an estimated 44,000 Jamaicans moved to the United States between 1900 and 1914, mainly to New York City (Henke, 2001).

There was a lull in the emigration of West Indians during the First and Second World Wars and the intervening Great Depression. After the Second World War, emigration resumed. However, most of this movement was directed toward the home countries of the former colonial islands in the West Indies, such as the United Kingdom (concentrating mainly in London and the cities of the industrial Midlands) from the former British colonies, to France (mainly Paris) from the former French Colonies, and to the Netherlands (especially Amsterdam) from the former Dutch colonies (Potter, Barker, Conway, and Klak, 2004).

During the middle 1960s the direction of emigration would dramatically change, as the United Kingdom, United States, and Canada restructured their immigration laws. The British Commonwealth Immigration Act of 1962 brought about an abrupt reduction in the number of West Indians emigrating to Great Britain. In the same year, Canada changed its immigration law to allow more West Indians to enter that country. More significantly, in 1965, the United States radically changed its immigration policy from one that enforced geographic quotas by favoring European immigration to one that was based more on family reunification and employment qualifications. This new law made it much easier for West Indians to move to the United States. As a consequence, there was a major shift in the emigration streams from the English-speaking islands away from Great Britain toward the United States and (to a lesser extent) Canada. In this chapter, we concentrate on the immigration of West Indians who have moved to the United States, especially those who moved since 1965.

By 2000 there were slightly more than two million West Indians living in the United States (U.S. Bureau of the Census, 2003). About 1.6 million of them (79%) were foreign-born. In fact, when considered collectively, they represent the second largest immigrant group living in the U.S. Only Mexico sends more immigrants to the U.S. than does the West Indies. Of course, this is a somewhat fictional statement because people from the Caribbean derive from a number of countries, rather than only one. Nevertheless, there is no doubt that the immigration of these people to the United States is significant, especially to the neighborhoods of their destinations and also to their countries of origin.

Who Are the West Indians?

We define West Indians as people who consider their ancestry to be traceable to the non-Hispanic islands in the Caribbean and to include people who came from the mainland Central American and South American countries of Belize, Guyana, and Suriname. This definition also includes Haitians, but it does not Caribbean people from Cuba, the Dominican Republic, or Puerto Rico, who are usually considered to be Hispanics. In addition to immigrants, our definition includes people born in the United States (about 21%) who consider themselves to be of West Indian ancestry. So we are including at least two generations of West Indians, the immigrants and their children, and sometimes their grandchildren.

The Census Bureau asked two questions about ancestry on the 2000 Census questionnaire, so people could indicate their first and second ancestries. In other words, a person could indicate that his/her ancestry traced to as many as two countries (U.S. Bureau of the Census, Technical Documentation, 2003). We consider people to be of West Indian ancestry if they indicated a non-Hispanic Caribbean country as their country of ancestry on either or both of these questions.

This chapter has two major components. In the first, we describe the spatial distribution of West Indians at three different scales: states, counties, and census tracts (the latter considers the West Indians' in their two primary metropolitan concentrations, New York City and Miami). In the second part of this chapter, we analyze the socioeconomic status (SES) of West Indians. First we compare the SES characteristics of West Indians to those of Hispanics, non-Hispanic whites, and non-Hispanic blacks living in the United States. Next we compare the SES characteristics of the four largest groups of West Indians to each other: Jamaicans, Haitians, Trinidadians and Tobagonians, and Guyanese. Finally, we compare the SES characteristics of West Indians living in the states of New York, New Jersey, and Florida, to determine if there are significant differences in the standards of living of West Indians in these three states, which also represent the states of their greatest geographic concentration.

The data used in this study come from three primary sources. The information for race and Hispanics derive from the Census Bureau's Summary File 1. These data are from the 2000 Census' complete count. The data for the distributions of the West Indian ancestries come from Summary File 3, which is data based on a 17 percent sample from the 2000 Census of Population and Housing. Finally, the data used to determine the socioeconomic status of West Indians come from the 2000 Public Use Microdata Sample (PUMS) for 2000. More specifically, SES data for the entire United States come from the one-percent PUMS and data for individual states come from the five percent PUMS.

Since most of our data derive from samples, it is relevant to ask how accurate these samples are. These figures have been obtained by using the Census Bureau's person weights for the sample sizes, so we can estimate the sizes of our populations. We compared these estimates with data from the 2000 Census' complete count. The results demonstrate that these samples are very accurate because the numbers in them are extremely large. For example, the one percent sample for the U.S. contains information for 2.8 million persons and its estimate for the total U.S. population is almost without error. Likewise, the samples for the states of Florida and New York each have errors of three one hundredths of a percent. The largest error (4%) is found in the West Indian file. This is because the U.S. Bureau of the Census includes a few people in its 17 percent sample of West Indians that we do not include from the PUMS file. So why do we use the 17 percent sample data? Because that sample is larger than the one or five percent samples, we can use data from it that are accurate down to the scale of census tracts. Census tracts include an average of about 4,000 people. With the five percent PUMS we can only use data down to the level of Public Use Microdata Areas (PUMAS), which are areas with an average of 100,000 people living in them.

Table 13.1
West Indian Nationalities (Ancestries) in the United States, 2000 Census

Nationalities (Ancestries)	Numbers	Percentages of U.S. West Indian Population	% of West Indian Populations in the U.S. (2000)
1. Jamaicans	736,513	36.2%	28.3%
2. Haitians	548,199	27.0%	8.6%
3. Trinidadians & Tobagonians	164,778	8.1%	12.7%
4. Guyanese	162,456	8.0%	23.2%
5. British West Indians	84,671	4.2%	NA
6. Barbadians	54,509	2.7%	18.2%
7. Belizeans	37,688	1.9%	12.6%
8. Dutch West Indians	37,681	1.9%	NA
9. Bahamians	31,984	1.6%	10.7%
10. U.S. Virgin Islanders	15,014	.7%	13.8%
11. Bermudans	6,054	.3%	NA
12. All Others in the West Indies	152,413	7.4%	NA
TOTAL	2,031,960	100.0%	14.4%

NA = Not Available
U.S. Bureau of the Census, *2000 Census of Population and Housing*, Summary File 3, American Factfinder, Table PCT 18, "Ancestry for People with One or More Ancestry Categories Reported," 2003; and Population Reference Bureau, *2000 World Population Data Sheet*, 2000, Washington, D.C.

The figures in Table 13.1 show the composition of the West Indian population by island nationalities. Jamaicans (36%) and Haitians (27%) together comprise almost two-thirds of the West Indians living in the United States. They are numerically followed somewhat distantly by Trinidadians & Tobagonians[1] (8%) and Guyanese (also 8%). Eleven groups of West Indians are able to be identified through use of the 2000 Census' ancestry table in Summary File 3. These 11 comprise almost 93 percent of all West Indians living in the United States.

Earlier in this chapter we mentioned that West Indian immigrants are important to their island origins, in addition to being important to the neighborhoods in which they concentrate in the United States. Data in Table 13.1 clearly demonstrate the importance to the home island. The West Indian population in the U.S. is equal to more than 14 percent of all the population living in the non-Hispanic West Indies. Of course, there is considerable variation among these islands. More than one-fourth of all Jamaicans and almost one-fourth of all Guyanese live in the United States. Similarly, nearly one out of every five Barbadians lives in the United States. With only a few exceptions (e.g., Belize, Guyana, Suriname, and the Bahamas), the West Indian countries in the Caribbean have population densities that range between five and 20 times that of the United States (79 people per square mile) (Population Reference Bureau, 2004). If the West Indians in the U.S. were to return to their island origins, the increase in population pressure there would be substantial. For example, Trinidad's density would increase from 664 to 748 people per square mile. For Barbados, the density would rise from 1,542 to 1,822 people per square mile. In addition to reducing population growth and pressure, the West Indians in the U.S. send substantial monetary remittances to family members living in their island origins, thereby helping significantly their local economies. In 2000, it was estimated that remittances contribute more than $600 million to Jamaica's economy (Henke, 2001). Another study found that 40 percent of the respondents along the north coast of Jamaica received remittances from Jamaicans living abroad and a similar sample in Kingston found that 30 percent of its respondents also received remittances (Chevannes and Rickettes, 1997). On the negative side, it is also true that some of the brightest young minds leave the islands in the Caribbean when they emigrate, thereby creating a "brain drain" from their island origins. However, some of this disadvantage is compensated by returning immigrants who open businesses and transfer the skills and experience they learned in the United States to their home islands.

THE DISTRIBUTION OF WEST INDIANS IN THE UNITED STATES

In this section we analyze the distribution of West Indians at three scales of inquiry: states, counties, and census tracts. Like all immigrant groups, West Indians show a strong tendency to concentrate in certain areas of the United States. If they did not do this they would hardly be noticed because they represent only about seven tenths of 1 percent of the total U.S. population.

The State Scale

There are 12 states that contain one percent or more (Figure 13.1) of the West Indian population and these states together include 92 percent of all West Indians in the U.S. (Table 13.3). The state with by far the largest concentration of West Indians is New York (39%), followed by a significant secondary concentration in Florida (25%), and a third, more minor concentration in New Jersey (6%). Slightly more than 70 percent of all West Indians reside in these three states. Because of the concentration in these three states, we have selected them for later use in an analysis of the socioeconomic status of their West Indian populations.

It turns out that there are significant differences in the distributions by states of the various West Indian nationality groups. Two-thirds of the Guyanese are concentrated in New York, with about nine percent in New Jersey, and seven percent in Florida. Bahamians are mainly concentrated in Florida (64%), with only seven percent in New York. About 57 percent of Barbadians live in New York, with nine percent in Florida. The highest concentration of Belizeans is in California (40.2%), with New York second with 20 percent. Bermudans are almost evenly split between modest concentrations in New York (15%) and Florida (13%). Sixty-one percent of the British West Indians are in New York. The Dutch West Indians are concentrated in Oklahoma (33%) and Texas (25%), presumably attracted by the petroleum industries in these two states (West and Augelli, 1989). Haitians are concentrated in Florida (43%) and New York (29%). For the first time, the 2000 Census showed that the number of Haitians living in Florida is greater than New York. New York's Haitian community is older than the one in Florida and for a long time New York City dominated the Haitian-American population. Jamaicans are distributed by state almost identically to the total West Indian population, with 37 percent in New York, 24 percent in Florida, and 6 percent in New Jersey. About half (51%) of all Trinidadians and Tobagonians in the U.S. live in New York, with about 13 percent in Florida. People from the U.S. Virgin Islands exhibit a preference for Florida (26%) and New York (22%). In summary, with the exceptions of Belizeans who show a preference for California and the Dutch West Indians who concentrate in Oklahoma and Texas, the majority of the West Indian nationalities show a preference for the states of either New York or Florida.

Figure 13.1

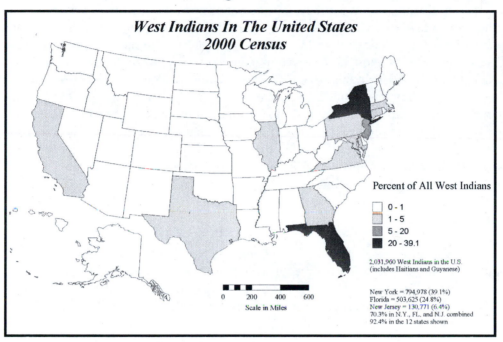

West Indians In The United States
2000 Census

Percent of All West Indians

- 0 - 1
- 1 - 5
- 5 - 20
- 20 - 39.1

2,031,960 West Indians in the U.S.
(includes Haitians and Guyanese)

New York = 794,978 (39.1%)
Florida = 503,625 (24.8%)
New Jersey = 130,771 (6.4%)
70.3% in N.Y., FL, and N.J. combined
92.4% in the 12 states shown

0   200   400   600
Scale in Miles

Figure 13.2

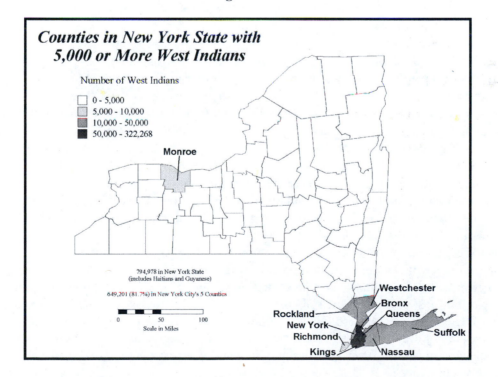

Counties in New York State with
5,000 or More West Indians

Number of West Indians

- 0 - 5,000
- 5,000 - 10,000
- 10,000 - 50,000
- 50,000 - 322,268

Monroe

794,978 in New York State
(includes Haitians and Guyanese)

649,201 (81.7%) in New York City's 5 Counties

0   50   100
Scale in Miles

Westchester
Bronx
Queens
Rockland
New York
Suffolk
Richmond
Kings
Nassau

The County Scale

We mapped the distributions of West Indians by county for each of the 12 states that contained 1 percent or more of the people living in the United States. We can summarize the patterns shown in each of these maps by saying that in all cases the West Indians were concentrated in the major urban areas of each of these states. Rather than reproducing all 12 of these maps, we restrict our attention to the three states with the largest West Indian populations, New York (Figure 13.2), Florida (Figure 13.3), and New Jersey (Figure 13.4). Almost 82 percent of New York State's West Indians live in New York City, while 64 percent of Florida's live in the Miami-Fort Lauderdale CMSA (including Miami-Dade and Broward Counties). Most of New Jersey's West Indians live in the state's northeastern counties, adjacent to New York City. New Jersey's West Indians appear to be living in suburban extensions of New York City. For this reason, when we analyze separately the socioeconomic status of West Indians living in New York and New Jersey later in this chapter, we will regard the concentration in New York City to be mainly a central city population, with the ones living in New Jersey being largely a suburban concentration. Those living in the metropolitan area of Miami-Fort Lauderdale will include both central city and suburban West Indians.

The Census Tract Scale

The especially heavy concentrations of West Indians in New York City and in the Miami-Fort Lauderdale CMSA warrant further consideration. We analyze the distributions of each of these cities at a census tract scale and begin with New York City, since it is the epicenter for West Indian residents in the United States. The place names of the neighborhoods where West Indians concentrate in New York City are shown in Figure 13.5.

NEW YORK CITY

Crowder and Tedrow have studied in considerable detail the distribution of West Indians at a census tract scale in New York City using 1980 and 1990 Census data (Crowder and Tedrow, 2001). Conway and Bigby conducted a similar study using data for 1980 collected by the former United States Immigration and Naturalization Service by zip codes in New York City (Conway and Bigby, 1992). Our intention is to update their findings with 2000 Census figures to see if the same patterns they discovered for 1980 and 1990 still prevail today. We also want to compare the residential patterns of West Indians in New York City to those in the Miami-Fort Lauderdale CMSA.

There are three major concentrations of West Indians in New York City (Figure 13.6). The largest and most diverse is in **central Brooklyn** stretching from Prospect Park in the west to Jamaica Bay in the east. It includes such neighborhoods as Flatbush, East Flatbush, Crown Heights, and Canarsie. The second is located in **southern Queens County** and includes places like Richmond Hill, Jamaica, St. Albans, Rosedale, Far Rockaway, and Cambria Heights. The third is located in **northern and eastern Bronx**, including neighborhoods like Riverdale, Wakefield, and Williamsbridge. There are several smaller concentrations in areas immediately east of Central Park and in Washington Heights in Manhattan. Noticeably few West Indians live on Staten Island with the exception of the neighborhood of Rosebank, located in the northeastern corner of the island. A small concentration also occurs in eastern Williamsburg in Brooklyn.

Because West Indians have been coming to New York City since the very early 1900s, they have been able to develop a number of mature neighborhoods in which they form a majority of the population. In 2000, there were 31 census tracts in which they represented more than 50 percent of the population. All but one of these is located in the most prominent area of concentration, central Brooklyn. The lone exception is a census tract in Cambria Heights in southeastern Queens County. The neighborhoods in southern Queens and northern and eastern Bronx are not dominated by West Indians to the same degree as many of those in central Brooklyn. For this reason the area of central Brooklyn is usually thought of by most New Yorkers as being the West Indian community of New York City.

Figure 13.3

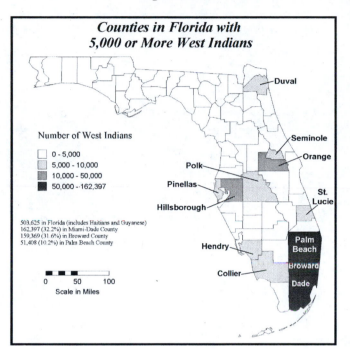

Counties in Florida with 5,000 or More West Indians

Number of West Indians

- 0 - 5,000
- 5,000 - 10,000
- 10,000 - 50,000
- 50,000 - 162,397

503,625 in Florida (includes Haitians and Guyanese)
162,397 (32.2%) in Miami-Dade County
159,369 (31.6%) in Broward County
51,408 (10.2%) in Palm Beach County

Duval
Seminole
Orange
Polk
Pinellas
St. Lucie
Hillsborough
Palm Beach
Hendry
Broward
Collier
Dade

0   50   100
Scale in Miles

Figure 13.4

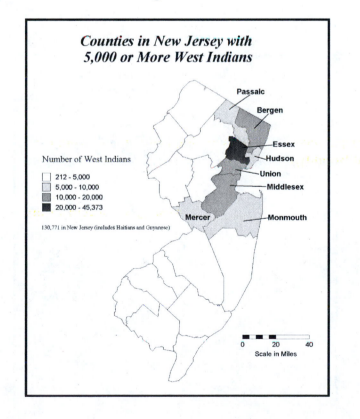

Counties in New Jersey with 5,000 or More West Indians

Number of West Indians

- 212 - 5,000
- 5,000 - 10,000
- 10,000 - 20,000
- 20,000 - 45,373

130,771 in New Jersey (includes Haitians and Guyanese)

Passaic
Bergen
Essex
Hudson
Union
Middlesex
Mercer
Monmouth

0   20   40
Scale in Miles

Figure 13.5

Place Names In New York City

Figure 13.6

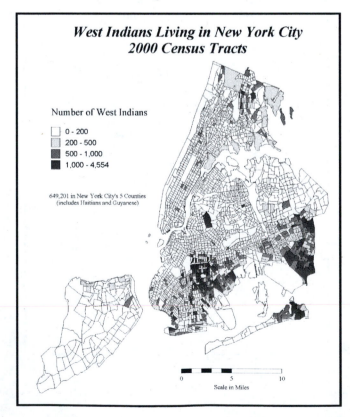

West Indians Living in New York City
2000 Census Tracts

When the distributions of West Indians are compared to those of Hispanics (Figure 13.7), non-Hispanic whites (Figure 13.8), and non-Hispanic blacks (Figure 13.9), it is clear that West Indians are primarily living in non-Hispanic black neighborhoods. In Table 13.2 we created a set of indices of dissimilarity to quantitatively measure the degree of segregation between West Indians and other groups living in New York City and the metropolitan area of Miami and Fort Lauderdale. These indices have values ranging from zero to 100. A value of zero indicates that the two populations being compared have the same percentage distribution. The value 100 means that all of one of these two populations must be redistributed for them to achieve equal distributions. Crowder and Tedrow suggest that an index of dissimilarity above 60 percent is high. A value less than 30 percent is low and one between 30 percent and 60 percent is moderate. We removed the Haitians from the West Indian category used in creating these indices because they are culturally distinct from the rest of the English-speaking West Indians and may be somewhat spatially separated from them.

Figure 13.7

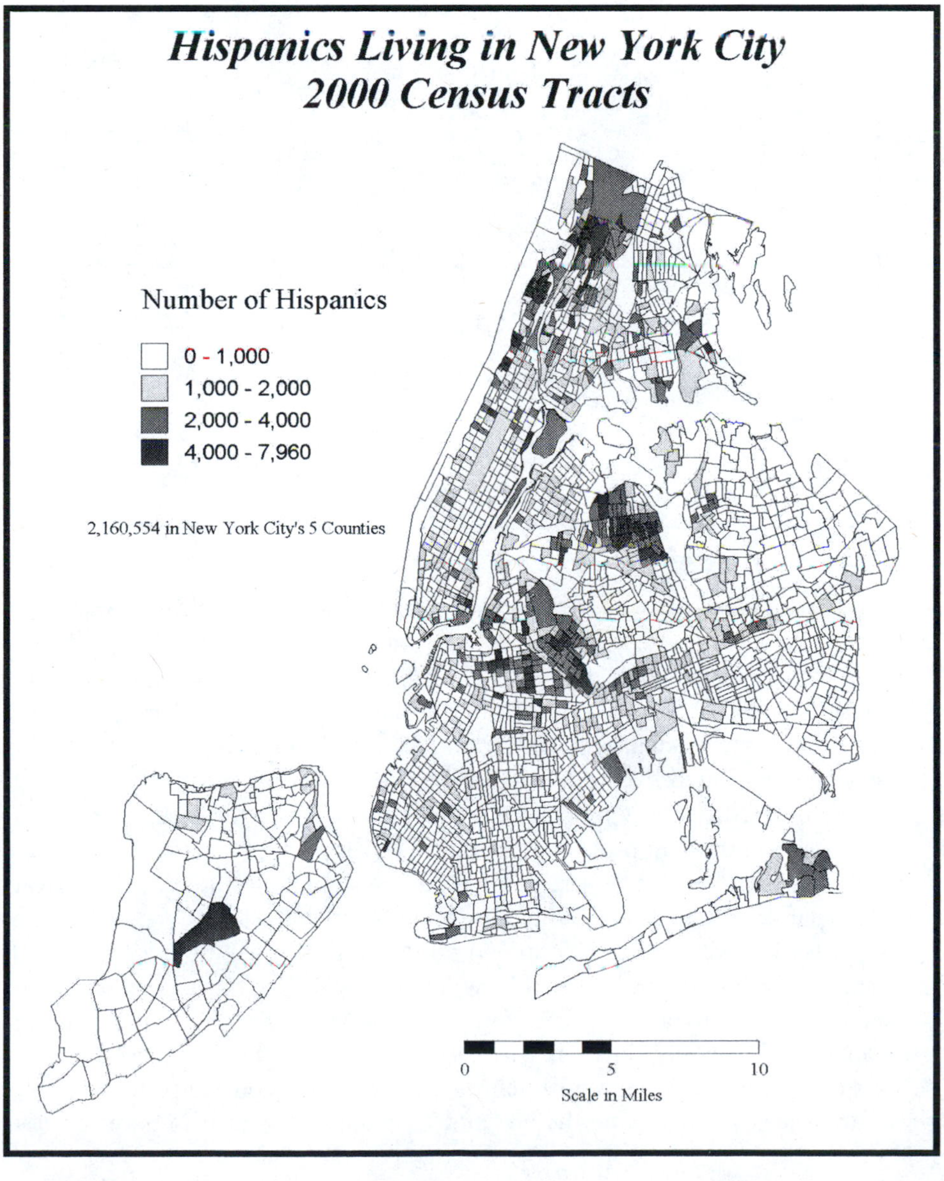

**Hispanics Living in New York City
2000 Census Tracts**

Number of Hispanics

- 0 - 1,000
- 1,000 - 2,000
- 2,000 - 4,000
- 4,000 - 7,960

2,160,554 in New York City's 5 Counties

0   5   10

Scale in Miles

Figure 13.8

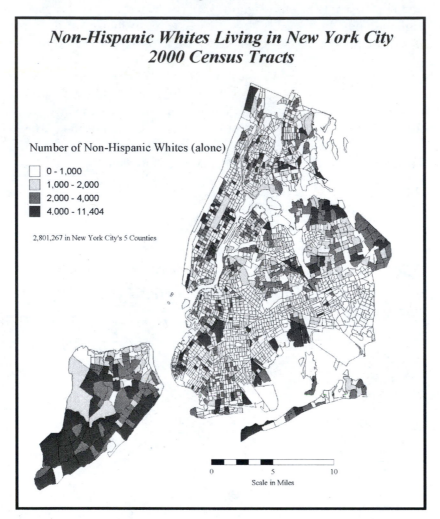

The indices of dissimilarity shown in Table 13.2 clearly show the West Indians are least segregated from non-Hispanic blacks and most segregated from non-Hispanic whites in New York City. The level of segregation of West Indians from Hispanics is between that of their segregation from non-Hispanic blacks and whites. Notice in Figures 13.7 and 13.8 how both the non-Hispanic whites and the Hispanics tend to avoid living in central Brooklyn and southern Queens, while the non-Hispanic blacks are concentrated in these two areas very similarly to the patterns exhibited by the West Indians. These findings from the maps and quantitative indices reinforce each other by clearly showing similar residential patterns for blacks and West Indians in New York City. Furthermore, they tend to support the hypothesis of segmented assimilation, whereby West Indians (90% of whom are black in the United States) are residentially assimilating to the African American population, rather than to the non-Hispanic white mainstream (Portes and Rumbaut, 1996). We will say more about this in this chapter's conclusion. By the way, the reader should notice that we have included indices in Table 13.3 that show the degree of residential segregation between New York City's Hispanics, non-Hispanic whites, and non-Hispanic blacks as standards of comparison. For example, they show that the degree of segregation between non-Hispanic whites and non-Hispanic blacks is virtually identical to that between non-Hispanic whites and West Indians. They also show that the degree of segregation between non-Hispanic blacks and non-Hispanic whites is much higher than it is non-Hispanic whites and Hispanics or than it is between non-Hispanic blacks and Hispanics.

Table 13.2
Indices of Dissimilarity (I.D.s) for West Indians* Compared to Selected West Indian Nationalities by Census Tracts in New York City and Metropolitan Miami (Miami-Dade and Broward Counties) 2000 Census Tracts

Comparisons	I.D.s for New York City**	I.D.s for Metropolitan Miami*
1. West Indians (minus Haitians) vs. Hispanics	65.2	65.0
2. West Indians (minus Haitians) vs. Non-Hispanic Whites	83.4	57.5
3. West Indians (minus Haitians) vs. Non-Hispanic Blacks	28.6	35.7
4. Non-Hispanic Whites vs. Non-Hispanic Blacks	83.4	68.9
5. Non-Hispanic Whites vs. Hispanics	67.1	56.2
6. Non-Hispanic Blacks vs. Hispanics	58.2	68.5
7. Guyanese Ancestry vs. West Indians (minus Guyanese and Haitians)	47.0	NA
8. Bahamian Ancestry vs. West Indians (minus Bahamians and Haitians)	NA	49.1
9. Haitian Ancestry vs. West Indians (minus Haitians)	58.4	51.1
10. Jamaican Ancestry vs. West Indians (minus Jamaicans and Haitians)	36.8	31.3
11. Trinidadian and Tobagonian Ancestry vs. West Indians (minus T&Bs and Haitians)	36.7	43.9

NA = not applicable because the sample is too small to be statistically significant.

*Our definition of West Indians includes the U.S. Bureau of the Census definition of "West Indian" plus persons of Guyanese ancestry.

**Values of the index of dissimilarity range between 0 (exactly the same) to 100 (100% difference).

We also have mapped (Figures 13.10 through 13.13) the residential distributions of the four largest West Indian nationalities (Jamaicans, Haitians, Guyanese, and Trinidadians and Tobagonians) in New York City and included them in this chapter.[2] These maps clearly show that the individual West Indian nationalities tend to be located within West Indian neighborhoods, mainly in one of the three concentrations of West Indian settlement mentioned earlier in this chapter. In a sense there is a triple layering effect to this pattern. They live in Black neighborhoods. However, within these Black neighborhoods, they live in West Indian areas. Finally, within these West Indian areas they live in neighborhoods that contain sizeable numbers of people who originated from the same island that they did. The small to modest indices of dissimilarity (Table 13.2) for these four nationalities confirmed this tendency. A careful look at the figures in Table 13.2 show that the indices of dissimilarity for Haitians, compared to the other four nationalities, are somewhat higher, when they are compared to West Indians. Still, the two indices for Haitians are in the moderate range, so there does appear to be considerable overlap in the Haitian neighborhoods with the ones in which West Indians predominantly live. So we continue to feel justified in including Haitians within our group of West Indians.

The following sequence appears to capture this process: most West Indians first would like to live in neighborhoods containing people from their island of origin. If they cannot find housing available in such a neighborhood, the next best thing is to move into a neighborhood that contains West Indians from other islands. These West Indian neighborhoods are almost always located either in or on the edges of African American neighborhoods. These results agree with the patterns discovered by Conway and Bigby using 1980 INS data and by Crowder and Tedrow using 1990 Census data, mentioned earlier in this chapter. Therefore, we now know that this spatial process of residential triple layering noted above has been continuing for at least three decades.

Figure 13.9

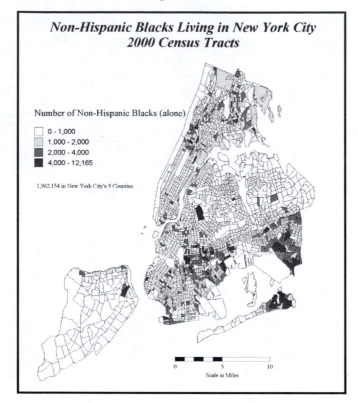

Figure 13.10

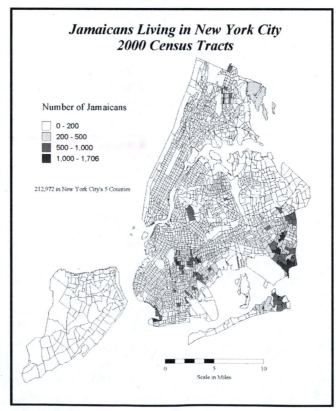

Figure 13.11

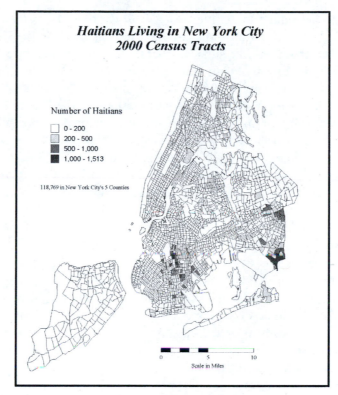

Figure 13.12

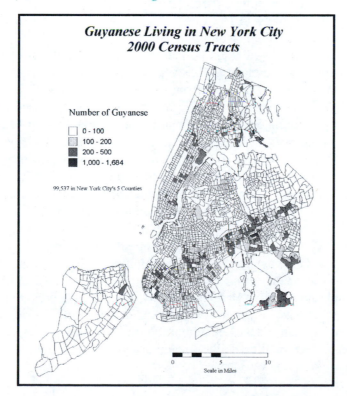

THE MIAMI-FORT LAUDERDALE CMSA

In the introduction to her edited book titled *Islands in the City: West Indian Migration to New York*, Nancy Foner notes that by far the majority of studies of West Indians living in the United States have used New York City as their place of investigation. She suggests that the migration literature can benefit especially from studies whereby New York City is compared with other cities containing West Indians and she specifically mentions metropolitan Miami in this regard (Foner, 2001). We attempt to answer that call in this part of this chapter.

The place names of the major West Indian concentrations in the Miami-Fort Lauderdale CMSA are shown in Figure 13.14. As was the case in New York City, West Indians in South Florida are concentrated in three areas (Figure 13.15). The largest is found in **northeastern Miami-Dade County**, north of Miami's CBD — including Little Haiti, North Miami, North Miami Beach, Carol City, and Miramar (just north of the Miami-Dade County line). The second largest is in **central and northern Broward County**, including Lauderdale Lakes, Oakland Park, North Lauderdale, and Margate. The third is located in **southern Miami-Dade County** in Cutler Ridge, Perrine, Homestead, and Florida City.

There are only two census tracts in the Miami-Fort Lauderdale CMSA where there are a majority of West Indians. Both are located in the northeastern area of Miami-Dade County, in Little Haiti and North Miami. These are the two oldest concentrations of Haitians in South Florida. With the exception of Bahamians who were arriving in Miami during the early 1900s, the rest of Miami's West Indian population did not begin to become significantly large until the early 1970s. As a consequence, Miami's West Indians are more recent arrivals than is the case in New York City. In addition, there are only about half as many living in South Florida as in New York City, so there are not as many West Indian neighborhoods from which to choose. As a result of there not being as many West Indians and their more recent arrival, the West Indian concentrations in South Florida tend to not be as established as those existing in New York City. In a sense they are still neighborhoods in the process of forming a West Indian identity.

Despite this distinction between West Indian neighborhoods in New York City and the Miami-Fort Lauderdale CMSA, it is remarkable how similar their residential patterns are relative to Hispanics, non-Hispanic whites, and non-Hispanic blacks (Figures 13.16 through 13.18). Again the tendency of West Indians to avoid living in Hispanic and non-Hispanic white neighborhoods in Miami-Fort Lauderdale is clear. The West Indians are much more likely to live in black neighborhoods. The indices of dissimilarity (Table 13.2) for West Indians in comparison to these other three ethnic/racial groups verified what the maps visualize. West Indians are least segregated from blacks, and most segregated from Hispanics in South Florida. This latter point is interesting because in New York City West Indians are most segregated from whites, and secondarily from Hispanics. The difference is probably at least partly related to the fact that in New York City non-Hispanic whites comprise the largest share of the population, whereas in the Miami-Fort Lauderdale CMSA Hispanics are largest component of the population. In South Florida it is easier to find a neighborhood to live in that is predominantly Hispanic than it is in New York City, especially one that contains middle- and upper-class Hispanics.

Figures 13.19–13.22 are maps showing the residential distributions of the four largest West Indian groups living in South Florida (Haitians, Jamaicans, Bahamians, and Trinidadians and Tobagonians). These maps show clearly, as do the indices of dissimilarity in Table 13.3, that each of the West Indian nationalities in the Miami-Fort Lauderdale CMSA are concentrated in the three major areas of West Indian residence, just as was the case in New York City. Once again it is clear that Haitians are somewhat more segregated from West Indians then are the other four nationality groups shown in Table 13.2. Still, it is relevant once again (as we did with the New York City sample) to note that Haitians are only moderately segregated from West Indians.

We see the same type of triple layering for West Indians in South Florida that we saw in New York City. They tend to live in predominantly Black neighborhoods, especially in those with large West Indian concentrations. And they prefer to live in West Indian neighborhoods that contain significant numbers of people who came from their island origin in the Caribbean.

Figure 13.13

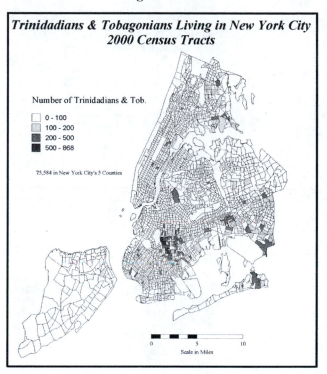

Figure 13.14

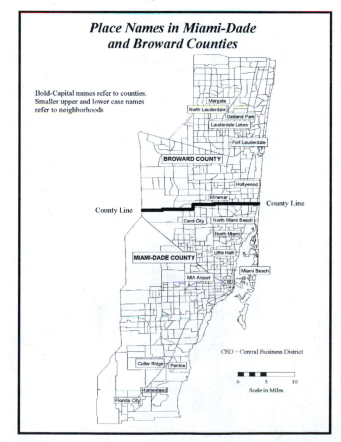

Figure 13.15

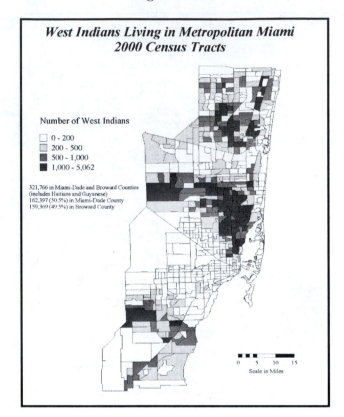

Figure 13.16

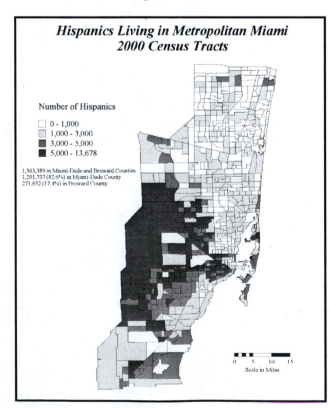

Figure 13.17

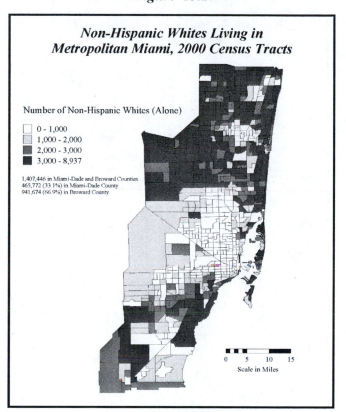

Non-Hispanic Whites Living in Metropolitan Miami, 2000 Census Tracts

Number of Non-Hispanic Whites (Alone)

- 0 - 1,000
- 1,000 - 2,000
- 2,000 - 3,000
- 3,000 - 8,937

1,407,446 in Miami-Dade and Broward Counties
465,772 (33.1%) in Miami-Dade County
941,674 (66.9%) in Broward County

0   5   10   15
Scale in Miles

Figure 13.18

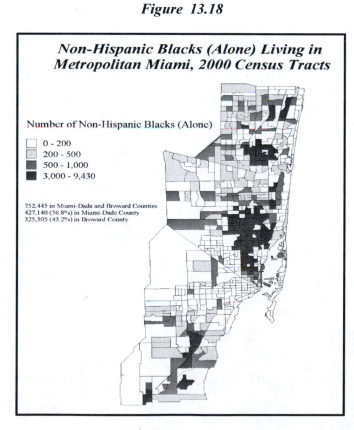

Non-Hispanic Blacks (Alone) Living in Metropolitan Miami, 2000 Census Tracts

Number of Non-Hispanic Blacks (Alone)

- 0 - 200
- 200 - 500
- 500 - 1,000
- 3,000 - 9,430

752,445 in Miami-Dade and Broward Counties
427,140 (56.8%) in Miami-Dade County
325,305 (43.2%) in Broward County

Figure 13.19

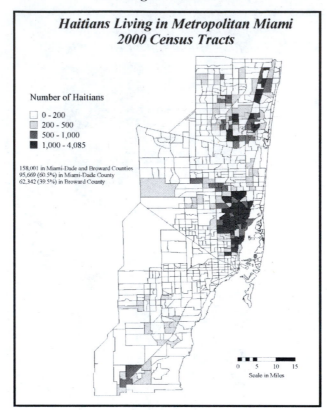

Figure 13.20

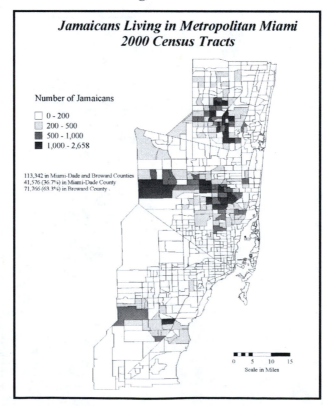

Figure 13.21

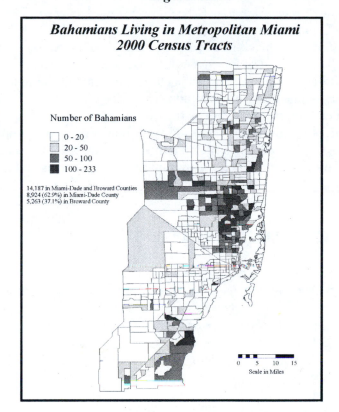

Figure 13.22

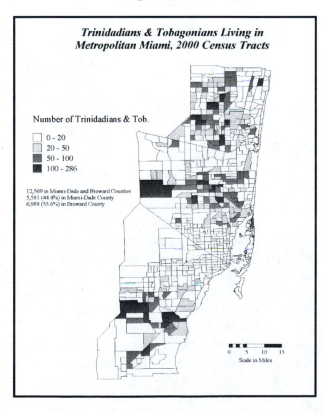

Given the fact that West Indians in both New York City and in South Florida exhibit a preference for living in black neighborhoods, it is relevant to ask the question why this is so. There are several possible explanations. One is racial prejudice in the housing market in both New York and Miami that limits their residential searches to black neighborhoods. So, black neighborhoods may seem more friendly and less prejudiced against them. A second factor may be that because they generally have higher socioeconomic status than blacks (a topic covered later in this chapter) they find it easier to compete economically in African American neighborhoods. A third reason is that the non-Hispanic black neighborhoods have large populations in New York City and Miami, which provide West Indian entrepreneurs a large market for the goods and services they produce (Foner, 1992, 1998, and 2001). In addition, a fourth reason relates to West Indian networks of information. Once a West Indian concentration is established in a particular neighborhood, it attracts additional West Indians. The new residents were alerted to housing and employment opportunities by their relatives and friends who already live there.

THE SOCIOECONOMIC STATUS (SES) OF WEST INDIANS

Now that we have established where West Indians live, it is relevant to ask: "How are they doing?" Of course, "how they are doing" is a loaded phrase because it can be defined a number of ways. We will concentrate our efforts on measuring their socioeconomic status (SES). Also, however, "how they are doing" is a relative concept. If a group of people is doing poorly or well, we have to ask, relative to whom? In this section, we compare the status of West Indians in three ways. First, we compare the SES characteristics of West Indians to that of Hispanics, non-Hispanic whites, and non-Hispanic blacks at the national scale, for all of the United States. Second, we compare the SES of the four largest groups of West Indians living in the U.S. to each other. We do this for Jamaicans, Haitians, Trinidadians & Tobagonians, and Guyanese. Finally, we compare the SES of West Indians living in the states of New York, Florida, and New Jersey.

The concept of socioeconomic status is a multiple variable concept. It is usually measured by social scientists along three dimensions using income, education, and occupation variables. This is the procedure we follow here (Tables 13.3 through 13.5). As can be seen in these three tables, we rely on five income variables, two education variables, and two occupation variables for our SES analysis.

COMPARISONS OF THE SES OF WEST INDIANS WITH HISPANICS, NON-HISPANIC WHITES, AND NON-HISPANIC BLACKS

When West Indians began moving in significant numbers to New York City during the early 1900s, they found themselves in a highly segregated society, even though segregation was not codified in law the way it was in the South. Because they were black, they were forced to live in predominantly African American neighborhoods. The neighborhoods in which they lived influenced the types of jobs they held. Because they were black, West Indians were often not welcome in white-owned establishments. So blacks (including most West Indians) had to establish their own stores, barber shops, beauty parlors, bars, real estate agencies, night clubs, and restaurants (Henke, 2001). Although some West Indians were self-employed business owners, most were not (Model, 2001). Most of them were employed as lower-paid unskilled workers. Many were porters, waiters, elevator operators, taxi drivers, clerks in stores, chauffeurs, and worked in personal services (e.g., child care, house cleaning, and care for the elderly). Over time, however, West Indians, like virtually all immigrants, gradually improved their economic position as they adjusted to living in the United States. But, so have virtually all other groups living in this country improved their status whether native or foreign born. So, how do West Indians compare to African Americans, Hispanics, and non-Hispanic whites?

There is some debate about how West Indians living in the United States compare to the nation's African-American population. The popular perception is that West Indians are an ambitious and hard-working community that has somehow achieved a standard of living that is substantially higher than that of blacks. However, Model questions whether West Indians really have higher SES than American blacks (Model, 2001). Henke notes that West Indian males earned only 88 percent what black males did in 1980. In 1990, the earnings of West-Indian and African-American males were about the same (Model, 2001). On the other hand, SES data for New York City in 1990 collected by Foner showed clearly that most West Indians have slightly higher incomes and education levels than the City's African Americans (Foner, 2001).

Our figures in Table 13.3 show that West Indians clearly have higher SES than both Hispanics and non-Hispanic blacks in the United States. On the other hand, they have lower SES than non-Hispanic whites. When compared to Hispanics and blacks, West Indians have higher average incomes (regardless of which of our income variables is used), a lower percentage living in poverty, higher educational achievement levels, and better-paying jobs. The fact that West Indians are generally better off than Hispanics makes sense for several reasons. First, there has been a recent spurt in immigration from Latin American countries. This is significant because more recent immigrants have not had as much time to adjust to living and working in the United States as immigrants who have been here longer. Second, the primary origins for the recent spurt in immigration from Latin America are some of the poorest countries (e.g., Mexico, Guatemala, El Salvador, and the Dominican Republic). Third, most immigrants from Latin America speak Spanish and have difficulties with English, something that is a disadvantage when they seek employment in higher-paying jobs.

Table 13.3
Socioeconomic Comparisons Between West Indians, Hispanics, non-Hispanic Whites, and non-Hispanic Blacks in U.S., 2000 Census

SES Characteristics	West Indians	Hispanics	non-Hispanic Whites	non-Hispanic Blacks
Income Variables for Persons 15 Years and Older				
Mean Total Income	$22,493	$17,008	$30,645	$19,289
Median Total Income	$16,600	$11,200	$20,000	$12,660
Mean Earnings for Full-Time Year Round Workers	$35,320	$29,206	$45,459	$32,522
Median Earnings	$29,000	$23,000	$34,000	$27,000
Families Living Below Poverty Level	17.2%	24.1%	11.2%	28.2%
Education Variables for Persons 25 Years and Older				
Less than High School Graduation	26.4%	47.5%	14.5%	27.6%
Percent with a B.A. Degree or Higher	19.0%	10.5%	27.0%	14.3%
Occupation Variables for Persons 16 Years and Older				
Percent in Management and Professional	25.9%	16.0%	34.0%	21.5%
Percent in Construction, Production, and Transportation	19.2%	34.3%	23.0%	26.2%

U.S. Bureau of the Census, □Public Use Micro Data Sample,□ One Percent Samples, *2000 Census of Population and Housing*, Washington, D.C., 2003.

The most interesting finding is that our data show that no matter which of our nine variables are used, West Indians are better off than blacks. These are far stronger results than what was shown by data from the 1990 and earlier censuses. Clearly, if West Indians were behind blacks in the past, that is no longer the case now. What are the possible reasons for this finding? West Indians have higher incomes and lower poverty rates than blacks because they have somewhat higher education and skill levels. They are ambitious, work hard, and they are less likely to find objectionable the fact that they are often employed in the so-called 3-D jobs (those that are physically demanding, dangerous, and dirty). Now that they have a longer history of living in the Untied States than was the case in earlier censuses, they have had time to catch up with the SES of American blacks. In addition, white employers, when questioned, almost always say they would rather hire West Indians than African Americans. They see them as more reliable, less likely to complain, and more willing to work hard than African Americans. In short, prospective white employers sense a higher work ethic among the West Indians (Model, 2001).

COMPARISONS OF THE SES OF JAMAICANS, HAITIANS, TRINIDADIANS, AND GUYANESE

When the four largest national components of the West Indians living in the United States are compared (Table 13.4), it is clear that the Trinidadians and Tobagonians (for short we will call them simply Trinidadians) have the highest SES, while Haitians have the lowest. Jamaicans generally rank second and Guyanese third. In fact, Trinidadians and Jamaicans are very similar in their SES characteristics, with a slight but consistent edge going to the Trinidadians. The Guyanese are behind the Jamaicans but not by far. Clearly, the Haitians are the poorest of the four national groups of West Indians. Still, it should be noted that Haitians have noticeably higher SES than Hispanics, and only slightly lower status than African Americans.

These relative nationality rankings are similar to what Foner found using 1990 data for New York. She found Trinidadians and Jamaicans to be virtually tied at the top, with a very slight edge going to the Jamaicans. She also found the Haitians and Guyanese virtually tied at the lower ranks. In fact, both Haitians and Guyanese in New York City had higher average earnings than both blacks and Hispanics in 1990 (Foner, 2001).

What accounts for the differences in the SES rankings of the West-Indian nationalities? We think it mainly has to do with differences in the economic well-being of their countries of origin, but this is certainly not the only answer. The rankings of these four home countries in terms of per capita purchasing power parity (PPP) are in almost the same order as their emigrants' SES ranks in the United States. The respective 2004 per capita PPPs for Trinidad, Jamaica, Guyana, and Haiti were: $9,000, $3,680, $3,940, and $1,610 (Population Reference Bureau, 2004). It is noteworthy that Jamaicans living in the United States ranked second in SES, just ahead of the Guyanese. On the other hand, Guyana has a slightly higher per capita PPP than Jamaica. So, both their ranks in terms of their SES in the U.S. and their country's per capita PPPs are very similar. For this reason, we do not want to make too much of this apparent reversal in order between SES in the U.S. and PPPs in Jamaica and Guyana.

COMPARISONS OF THE SES OF WEST INDIANS LIVING IN THE STATES OF
NEW YORK, FLORIDA, AND NEW JERSEY

Earlier in this chapter we mentioned that the three states of New York, Florida, and New Jersey were the states with the largest West Indian populations. Together they contain 70 percent of all West Indians living in the United States. We also noted that New York's West Indians are largely a central city population because 82 percent lived in New York City. In contrast, New Jersey's West Indians were mainly a suburban population because they are concentrated in the New Jersey suburbs of New York City. The Miami-Fort Lauderdale CMSA includes both central city and suburban West Indians. Its West Indian population is the newest of the three states because West Indians did not start moving in significant numbers to Miami until the 1970s, with the exception of Bahamians mentioned earlier in this chapter. Thus, most of them have had less time to establish their neighborhoods and to adjust to living in South Florida.

Table 13.4
Socioeconomic Comparisons of Selected West Indian Nationalities (Ancestries) in U.S. 2000 Census

SES Characteristics	Jamaicans	Haitians	Trinidadians & Tobagonians	Guyanese	Other West Indians
Income Variables for Persons 16 Years and Older					
Mean Total Income	$24,369	$18,393	$25,312	$22,604	$23,184
Median Total Income	$19,000	$12,200	$19,700	$17,600	$18,000
Mean Earnings for Full-Time Year Round Workers	$36,273	$31,694	$38,126	$36,025	$36,132
Median Earnings	$30,000	$24,500	$30,000	$30,000	$30,000
Families Living Below Poverty Level	15.8%	20.1%	14.1%	14.4%	17.8%
Education Variables for Persons 25 Years and Older					
Less than High School Grad	26.2%	35.2%	19.4%	28.3%	19.9%
Percent with a B.A. Degree or Higher	19.2%	15.7%	18.4%	18.3%	22.6%
Occupation Variables for Persons 16 Years and Older					
Percent in Management and Professional	25.7%	20.7%	27.5%	28.7%	29.8%
Percent in Construction, Production, and Transportation	19.0%	21.0%	17.5%	17.0%	18.9%

U.S. Bureau of the Census, ❒Public Use Micro Data Sample,❒ One Percent Samples, *2000 Census of Population and Housing*, Washington, D.C., 2003.

A comparison of the SES of West Indians living in the states of New York, Florida, and New Jersey (Table 13.5) shows that those living in New Jersey have the highest status, whereas those living in Florida have the lowest. The average incomes and education levels of the New Jersey West Indians are the highest, whereas those of the Florida West Indians are the lowest. It is somewhat surprising that the two occupation variables in Table 13.5 seem to be out of sync with the results suggested consistently by the five income and two education variables. It appears that West Indians living in New Jersey have the lowest percentage employed in the management and professional occupations (the jobs that are usually the highest paid) and highest percentage employed in the construction, production, and transportation occupations (the jobs that are normally the lowest paid). Still, it is relevant to note that these differences in percentages are very small and there is quite a bit of variation in the pay for the different types of jobs included within these two occupational classes.

SES Characteristics	New York State	Florida	New Jersey
Table 13.5 ***Socioeconomic Comparisons of West Indians Living in Selected States*** ***2000 Census***			
Income Variables for Persons 16 Years and Older			
Mean Total Income	$23,143	$18,022	$25,465
Median Total Income	$17,500	$13,000	$20,000
Mean Earnings for Full-Time Year Round Workers	$36,648	$28,329	$37,953
Median Earnings	$30,000	$23,000	$31,000
Families Living Below Poverty Level	15.1%	21.3%	10.4%
Education Variables for Persons 25 Years and Older			
Less than High School Grad	27.2%	36.0%	24.1%
Percent with a B.A. Degree or Higher	18.9%	13.3%	20.1%
Occupation Variables for Persons 16 Years and Older			
Percent in Management and Professional Occupations	26.2%	20.8%	25.9%
Percent in Construction, Production, and Transportation Occupations	18.0%	22.4%	22.1%

U.S. Bureau of the Census, ꟷPublic Use Micro Data Sample,ꟷ One Percent Samples, *2000 Census of Population and Housing*, Washington, D.C., 2003.

SUMMARY AND CONCLUSIONS

Anthropologist Nancy Foner says the following about immigration and the West Indians:

"The Caribbean has been more deeply and continuously affected by international migration than any other region in the world. Emigration has long been a way of life for many Caribbean people as they have searched for opportunities that are not available at home. Today there are large Caribbean communities in North America as well as Europe, and a significant percentage of the population of every Caribbean society lives abroad.... [The second city in population numbers for nearly every Caribbean country is now an overseas community: Miami for Cuba, for example and New York City for Haiti, Jamaica, and Barbados" (Foner, 1998).

In this chapter we have discussed some of the attributes of this migration to the United States. As we traced the historical migrations of the West Indies in general terms, we found that slightly more than 14 percent of the population of the non-Hispanic West Indies now resides in the United States. Like all immigrants living in the U.S., West Indians have concentrated in a few states, with New York, Florida, and New Jersey serving as home for about 70 percent of them. Within these states, they are further concentrated in the metropolitan areas of both

New York (including adjacent areas of New Jersey, Long Island, and Connecticut) and Miami-Fort Lauderdale. In both New York City and in the Miami-Fort Lauderdale CMSA West Indians are concentrated in three distinct areas. These areas are imbedded within large African American neighborhoods. Furthermore, individual West Indian nationalities are clustered and imbedded within the West Indian neighborhoods. So we say that West Indians are a **triple imbedded population**, being embedded within Black neighborhoods, West Indian neighborhoods, and in ethnic neighborhoods that are characterized by large numbers of the same Caribbean nationality (e.g., Jamaican, Haitian, Trinidadian, and Guyanese neighborhoods). In New York City these areas arose during the days of segregation, before passage of the United States Civil Rights Act of 1964 and the Fair Housing Act of 1968. It turns out there were some significant advantages for West Indians in living among African Americans. There was less discrimination against them in these neighborhoods because most of their neighbors were also racially Black. In addition, there was a large African American market here to be exploited by shrewd West Indian entrepreneurs. Also, West Indians found that they were able to compete on more even terms with blacks in these neighborhoods than they were with whites in predominantly white neighborhoods. As networks became established with relatives and friends in their Caribbean island origins, the streams from the islands to these neighborhoods in New York City became firmly entrenched in the landscape of this city.

As noted earlier in this text, there are two major competing theories of immigrant assimilation. The oldest is so-called **straight-line assimilation theory**. It assumes that all immigrants will eventually melt into an American majority where all people think first of themselves as Americans and eventually forget about their origins. A competing school of thought is called **segmented assimilation theory**. It suggests that when immigrants come to the United States they have several alternative streams to which they can assimilate. They can assimilate into the white American mainstream. They also can assimilate to a competing ethnic stream, like the Hispanic stream in the United States. As another alternative, they can assimilate to the African-American stream (Portes and Zhou, 1993; Portes and Rumbaut, 1996; Zhou, 1999). Our findings for West Indians clearly support the notion of segmented assimilation with West Indian choosing to live in predominantly African-American neighborhoods instead of white neighborhoods.

After investigating where West Indians live in the United States, we analyzed their socioeconomic characteristics. The truth is West Indians have made remarkable progress as immigrants or the children of immigrants in this country. They now have higher SES than either Hispanics or African Americans. They have higher incomes, higher educational achievements, and they are moving up the occupational ladder more so than either non-Hispanic blacks or Hispanics. Model found that in 1990 West-Indian men were disproportionately employed in certain industrial niches, especially in local transport (mainly as taxi cab drivers), hospitals (as janitors, aids, and nurses), working for the U.S. Postal Service, and mechanical repair (especially automobile repair). She also found that the main industrial niches occupied by West-Indian females were private households (cleaning and taking care of children), hospitals (as nurses and aids), and welfare offices (as clerks and social service workers) (Model, 2001).

When we compared the SES of the four largest West-Indian nationalities for the United States, we found that the Trinidadians and Tobagonians have the highest status, closely followed by Jamaicans and Guyanese, respectively. The Haitians have the lowest status, but they still rank in terms of their socioeconomic status ahead of Hispanics, and only slightly below African Americans. In fact, we were surprised that Haitians did not have lower status in the U.S. They come from by far the poorest country in the Caribbean, but they have made remarkable progress while living in New York and in the metropolitan areas of Miami and Fort Lauderdale. This illustrates the principle that immigration is a selective process because mainly the most ambitious people are willing to take the risks involved in moving to a new country where the language, laws, economy, and society are radically different from what they were accustomed in Haiti.

NOTES

[1] We combine the figures for Trinidadians and Tobagonians because they come from the same island country (Trinidad and Tobago) in the Caribbean.

[2] The indices of dissimilarity were calculated by using the following formula:

$$I.D. \equiv \sum \left[X_i - Y_i \right] / 2$$

Where: I.D. = the index of dissimilarity

X_i = the percent of the first population living in a particular census tract (the ith census tract)

Yi = the percent of the second population living in that same census tract (the ith census tract)

[ ] = The absolute value of the difference between the two percentages

Part III

U.S. Hispanic/Latino Geographies:
Changing Spatial Patterns and Their Implications

Section three contains six chapters that present settlement, changing patterns, landscape transformations, settlement experiences, and other issues for Hispanic/Latino populations. Chapter 14 begins with a comprehensive overview of Latino settlement and the growing Hispanic ethnic diversity. It also provides a discussion of various issues of importance to Latino Americans. The next three chapters focus on Latino settlements and particular issues in three large U.S. metropolitan areas. Chapter 15 focuses on the changing Latino settlement patterns in New York City, especially those related to ethnic diversity. It also touches upon different "settlement experiences" that immigrants have had, thus sharpening the focus of an important concept introduced in the previous chapter.

Chapter 16 focuses on Bolivian immigrants, in detail, focusing specifically on the spatial aspects of their social networks, and how their transnational status and surroundings influence their actions, in relation both to the Washington, D.C. region and their homeland.

Chapter 17 examines the issues of assimilation and cultural acclimation of Mexicans. It provides a tropical twist by examining the relationships between recent Mexican immigrants and Mexican-Americans — people who share a country, a home country, and a culture, but who suffer from class tensions.

The remaining two chapters move to small city and rural environments recently influenced by Latino inmigration. Chapter 18 is a case study of Allentown, PA, one of the Northeast's smaller cities that has become attractive to Puerto Rican and other Latino migrants from a range of Latin American cultures. It deals with the experiences of Latino migrants by examining the settlement pattern over two decades and concludes that, rather than assimilation, a case of sequent occupancies (one culture replaces another departing culture) has occurred in this city. This chapter also deals with the ways in which Latinos have changed the local landscapes architecturally, socially, and otherwise, and how their settlements have affected Allentown residents who are not Hispanic.

Chapter 19 focuses on the Hispanic and Anglo population changes in the Texas Panhandle. Like some other rural areas, this region has experienced Anglo depopulation due to declining economic opportunities. Yet, Latinos, especially direct arrivals from Mexico, perceive opportunity in the same abandoned places. Arriving Latinos do not replace the occupations once held by Anglos, but accept low-paying jobs and contribute to a new occupational structure in the regions.

Chapter 14

Latinos in America:
Historical and Contemporary Settlement Patterns

MARK E. REISINGER

INTRODUCTION

In the year 2000, 35.3 million Latinos were counted by the U.S. Census. An additional 3.8 million Latinos were enumerated in the Commonwealth of Puerto Rico. The Latino population was approximately 12.5 percent of the U.S. total. Latino-Americans now represent the largest single minority population in 21st century America. They constitute many subcultures but are bound together by language and other shared characteristics. Mexicans represented 7.3 percent, Puerto Ricans 1.2 percent, Cubans 0.4 percent, and other Latinos 3.6 percent of the total population (Guzman, 2001). The sheer numbers of Latinos make them an important and visible segment of the U.S. population. Many other factors keep them in the news and high on public policy agendas. Latinos share a common Spanish heritage, an oftentimes disadvantaged minority status, and a public image as newcomers who are welcomed by some and resented by others. Their socioeconomic and demographic characteristics are transforming America (Pinal and Singer, 1997). Geographically, Latinos are concentrated in a handful of states and cities, but also are dispersing to places unfamiliar with Latino cultures.

The settlement patterns of Latinos have significant historical dimensions and exhibit important spatial patterns. In addition, the rapidly increasing and dispersion of the Latino population in the United States has resulted in growing economic and social inequalities, increased political participation and power, and anti-immigrant movements that border on racism. This chapter has several purposes. First is an examination of the past and present spatial patterns of Latino settlement in the United States. The chapter focuses on the three main groups of Latinos in the United States: Mexicans, Puerto Ricans and Cubans. Following an examination of the settlement patterns is a look at the economic and social bifurcation between Latinos and whites, as well as between various Latino groups. The growing political power of Latinos in the United States is also investigated. Finally, this chapter tackles the issues of illegal migration and anti-immigrant sentiment in the United States.

MEXICAN-AMERICANS

The history of Latino settlement geography has been documented by Haverluk (1997), who reported the importance of the historical legacy between the U.S. and Mexico. The ancestors of Mexican-Americans were the first Europeans to settle in what is now the borderland region of the southwestern United States stretching from Texas to California. Four major areas of settlement evolved by the extension of successful colonies in northern Mexico. The initial settlement of the borderlands region was in New Mexico. Santa Fe was founded in 1610 and served as the provincial capital and principal center of the region. Albuquerque was founded in 1706 following a Pueblo Indian revolt that temporarily forced the Spanish out of the northern settlements. At the close of the Spanish period in 1821, most of the borderlands' population lived in New Mexico (Nostrand, 1979).

A second region of Spanish settlement in the borderlands region was southern Arizona. Texas was the third area of Spanish settlement in the borderlands. By the late 1700s, San Antonio had become the major provincial settlement in Spanish Texas. Other settlements followed and by 1850, some 14,000 Mexican-Americans lived in the region (Meinig, 1971). California was the last of the borderland areas to witness Spanish and Mexican settlement. The threat of Russian and British intrusion into California led to its settlement in 1769. In that year a mission/presidio complex was built at San Diego. Within twenty years, additional settlements were built. By 1850, over 9,000 Californios inhabited this part of the borderland region (Nostrand, 1979).

In the 1850s, after the Mexican-American War, there were perhaps 80,000 Mexican-Americans living in the five southwestern states that have become known as the Latino-American borderland (Nostrand, 1975). Today, the greatest numbers of the Mexican-American minority live in the borderland region. Parts of California, Arizona, New Mexico, and Texas are the major cores of this area, but a portion of southern Colorado is also part of the region. These areas represent the early nuclei of Spanish and Mexican settlement as well as expanded areas of the earliest colonizations (Nostrand, 1970). Many of the Mexican immigrants who have entered the United States since the early twentieth century also live in parts of this region.

Mexican Labor Migration

Mexican labor migration to the United States dates to the middle of the nineteenth century and Mexican immigration during the twentieth century occurred in two distinct waves (Arreola, 1985). The first took place from approximately 1900 to 1930, after which the Great Depression slowed the flow. The second was initiated by the war economy of the 1940s, and continues undiminished to the present. The mining frontiers of the western United States were the first major attraction for Mexican migrant labor. Mexican laborers from the northern states of Sonora, Chihuahua, Durango, and Zacatecas responded to the demand for workers in California, Nevada, and Arizona (McWilliams, 1968).

The major catalyst for dispersing the Mexican migrants in the United States were the railroads. Railroads integrated the Southwest into the United States industrial economy and Mexican labor became important for factory and mining employment as well as railroad construction (Garcia, 1981). When the United States passed legislation in 1902 encouraging western irrigation projects, Mexican labor again proved important to the success of citrus and cotton cultivation in California, Arizona, and the lower Rio Grande Valley of Texas. The mobility of Mexican labor also became vital to the beet sugar industry of Colorado, Kansas, and Nebraska and to the expansion of truck-farming in southern California, Arizona, and Texas (Carlson, 1973).

The Depression of the 1930s slowed the flow of Mexican migrants to the United States, and high unemployment north of the border initiated a reverse movement of Mexican migrants back to Mexico (Hoffman, 1974). In 1942, however, the United States government initiated the Bracero Program, a contract farm labor program. Under this agreement, Mexican laborers were transported to agricultural areas in the United States to bolster labor shortages brought on by World War II. The Bracero Program benefited Mexican migration in that it pointed the way north and provided a view of the economic opportunities that awaited legal and illegal immigrants in the United States (Arreola, 1985).

Regional Concentrations of the Mexican-American Population

The Mexican-American population is largely concentrated in the borderland region. However, areas outside the borderlands house significant numbers. In 1980, Mexican-Americans were located in four regional concentrations outside the borderlands: the upper Midwest, the Mountain West, the Pacific Northwest, and the South. Economic opportunity during World War I brought Mexicans to the upper Midwest states of Illinois, Indiana, Michigan, Ohio, and Wisconsin. The industries continued to draw immigrants during the Second World War as migrants established large permanent settlements in the industrial cities of the Midwest (Arreola, 1985).

Unlike the Mexican migrants who moved to the cities of the upper Midwest, Mexican-American populations in the Mountain West and Pacific Northwest had their origins in rural activities. Mexican and Mexican-

Americans began moving to these areas as mining, livestock herding, and agricultural economic activities began to demand their labor in the second half of the nineteenth century. Over time, temporary rural centers developed services that catered to Mexicans and permanent settlements became established. The Yakima River Valley and southeastern Washington, as well as the Willamette Valley of Oregon, are major agricultural areas that have developed Mexican communities far from the borderland region (Moore, 1976).

The Mexican-American population expanded considerably in the South from 1970 to 1980. The states from Virginia to Florida, west to Louisiana, and including Arkansas, Tennessee and Kentucky all experienced significant increases in their Mexican-American populations. Reasons for the dramatic growth in the Mexican-American population are unclear. Most live in places of less than 10,000 people and this suggests an agricultural orientation, although industrialization has brought on some of the area's growth (Arreola, 1985).

By 1990, the Mexican-American population in the Southwest totaled 11.2 million. Approximately 83 percent of all Mexican Americans lived in just five states: California, Texas, Arizona, New Mexico, and Colorado. California ranked the highest with 6.1 million Mexican Americans, followed by Texas with 3.8 million. Arizona, New Mexico, and Colorado each counted less than one million Mexican Americans.

Although the number of Mexican Americans increased to 15.3 million in the six Southwestern states by 2000, the region's proportion of the total U.S. Mexican-American population decreased to about 75 percent. This is an indication of the increasing dispersion of the Mexican-American population to other regions of the United States between 1990 and 2000. According to Census 2000, California continued to have the largest Mexican-American population with 8.4 million. Texas and Arizona followed with 5 million and 1 million, respectively. New Mexico and Colorado again counted less than 1 million Mexican Americans in 2000.

According to Census 2000, 11 percent of Mexican Americans lived in the Midwest, an increase from 8.5 percent in 1990. The South also saw a substantial increase in the relative number of Mexican Americans from 3.4 percent in 1990 to 7 percent in 2000. Florida's Mexican-American population more than doubled from 161,499 to 363,925 during the 1990s. The proportion of the Mexican-American population living in other regions of the country includes: the Northeast with 2 percent and the Northwest with 4.7 percent.

Mexican Americans: An Urban Population

Mexican Americans are often stereotyped as a rural population because of their connection with agricultural employment. However, Census 2000 showed that 88 percent of the Mexican American population lived in metropolitan areas. This percentage was higher than the overall proportion of 78 percent for the U.S. population. Approximately 50 percent of the Mexican-American population resided in the central cities of their metropolitan areas. While the central city areas contain large numbers of Mexican Americans, there has been dispersion to suburban locations in some cities in recent years.

By 2000 the Mexican-American population in the borderland region was nearly 90 percent urban. Fourteen SMSAs had greater than 100,000 Mexican Americans in 2000. Many of the other major cities in these regions had Mexican-American populations greater than 50,000. Mexican Americans outside of the borderland region also are largely urban. The largest concentrations of Mexican Americans in 2000 were in the cities of the upper Midwest: Chicago, Detroit, Milwaukee, East Chicago, and Aurora, OH.

In most cities, Mexican Americans are a minority population and live in distinct districts within the urban area (Camarillo, 1979). Before the second half of the nineteenth century, borderland cities were predominantly Mexican and populations concentrated around the town plaza. As Anglo populations increased, Mexican-American districts became isolated as the city expanded around or away from the old town center. The Mexican-American district became known as a barrio, by literal translation, a neighborhood (Camarillo, 1979).

Barrios, sometimes referred to as colonias (suburbs) because they were located far from the city center, were also formed in the borderlands as urban expansion engulfed agricultural settlements housing Mexican-American workers. Other rural communities, such as railroad and mining settlements, followed a similar pattern evolving into urban barrios (Camarillo, 1979).

Geographic isolation, housing restriction, and voluntary congregation perpetuated residential segregation in the borderland cities. Mexican Americans are often segregated in the central cities of their metropolitan area (Dagodag, 1974). Two general processes can explain these patterns. First, barrios became engulfed as described above. A second process involves the filtering down of housing from one group to another. As Anglos or other minority groups vacate central city locations, lower-income populations, including Mexican Americans, move into the inner city neighborhoods. Mexican Americans populated many eastside districts of Los Angeles in this way (Camarillo, 1979). Similarly, in Chicago, the Mexican-American population expanded by 84 percent between 1960 and 1970, expanding mostly into older ethnic neighborhoods (Berry, 1976).

PUERTO RICANS

Puerto Ricans represent the second largest group of persons of Latin American ancestry living in the United States. According to Census 2000, there were 3.4 million people of Puerto Rican origin living in this country, outside the Commonwealth of Puerto Rico. This number represented 9.6 percent of the United States total Latino population. An additional 3.8 million Latinos were enumerated in the Commonwealth of Puerto Rico (Guzman, 2001). Since all Puerto Ricans, whether living in Puerto Rico or on the mainland are considered U.S. citizens, the total Puerto Rican population is approximately 7.4 million, with approximately 51 percent living in Puerto Rico and 49 percent living on the U.S. mainland.

Puerto Rican Migration Patterns

Puerto Ricans have been living in New York City since the 1830s. The first year in which the U.S. Census listed Puerto Ricans as a separate group was 1910. At that time there were just over 1,500 persons who were born in Puerto Rico and living in the United States. Between 1910 and 1920 about 10,000 more were added to the U.S. population.

Emigration to the mainland increased during the 1920s when about 41,000 new Puerto Rican residents were added to the United States mainland population. The economic boom that followed WW I and the limitations placed upon European immigration through the Immigration Act of 1924 prompted this surge. The decade of the 1930s witnessed a decline in the flow of Puerto Rican migrants. During this period the Puerto Rican population increased by only about 17,000. This decline was due to a decrease in the number of job opportunities as a result of the Great Depression. In fact, between 1931 and 1934, there was a net return migration of 8,694 to Puerto Rico. By 1940, New York City had established itself as the primary residence of Puerto Ricans living on the mainland. At this time 88 percent of all Puerto Ricans born in Puerto Rico but living on the mainland were residing in New York City. Between 1940 and 1945 the flow of Puerto Ricans to the mainland saw a small increase due to the jobs created by WWII (Senior, 1965).

Immediately after World War II the flow of Puerto Ricans grew rapidly, for a number of reasons. First, there was backlog of persons that would have liked to move from the island during the early 1940s but could not because of the War. Second, many Puerto Rican men had fought in WWII and had been trained in the United States and, as a result, developed an awareness of the opportunities on the mainland. Third, by 1946 there were already over 100,000 Puerto Rican-born residents on the mainland. Many provided information to friends and relatives back home. They also helped new arrivals find jobs, and frequently offered a place to stay and food for new migrants. Fourth, the Puerto Rican government created a Migration Division within its Department of Labor that facilitated movement to the mainland and assisted new arrivals in making the necessary adjustments. Fifth, the cost and effort of traveling to New York City were greatly reduced. Sixth, heavy population growth in Puerto Rico was creating population pressure and heavy strains on the island's labor force capacity. Seventh, a shift in the island's occupational structure was beginning to take place. There was about to be a radical decline in agricultural employment. In 1948, Puerto Rican development activities were organized under a plan established in cooperation with the U.S. government. Known as "Operation Bootstrap," its objective was to attract corporations from the mainland in an effort to reduce Puerto Rican unemployment and dependence on the agricultural economy. However, much of the industrial activity that relocated there was capital intensive and required few Puerto Rican workers. Both increasing population pressure and declining agricultural employment provided strong incentives for Puerto Ricans to leave the island. Each of these seven factors encouraged emigration, especially when it is recalled that Puerto Ricans are U.S. citizens and have the freedom to move to the mainland without restriction and that there was a very big gap between the economic opportunities that existed on the mainland and those in Puerto Rico at this time (Maldonado, 1976).

Between 1946 and 1950 the number of Puerto Ricans living in the United States increased by almost 121,000 persons. It also became apparent by 1950 that the number of second generation Puerto Ricans born on the mainland was becoming significant. The decade of the 1950s represents the period of heaviest flow to the United States. The total increase (including both first and second generations) between 1950 and 1960 was almost 600,000 persons (Maldonado, 1976).

During the decades of the 1960s and 1970s the flow to the mainland began to ease progressively. Between 1960 and 1970, the net flow was 144,724, and between 1970 and 1980, the flow was down to 85,116. Three main reasons are offered for this decline: (1) there was narrowing of the income differentials between the U.S. and Puerto Rico; (2) the push factors in Puerto Rico were reduced as the standard of living began to improve, mainly due to the efforts of Operation Bootstrap; and (3) a significant amount of return migration developed that partially offset the emigration from Puerto Rico (Morales, 1986).

Emigration of Puerto Ricans to the U.S. mainland increased once again during the 1980s with a net flow of nearly half a million. Wage differentials between the island and the mainland and differing employment levels played a role in this heavy emigration. Certain groups of emigrant Puerto Rican workers, such as nurses and engineers, particularly benefited from this divergence when they moved to the United States (Rivera-Batiz, 1989).

For example, Rivera-Batiz and Santiago (1996) point out in 1980 the annual earnings of male workers in New York City were on average 2.5 times those of male workers in Puerto Rico, and the earnings of female workers in New York City were 1.9 times those of female workers in Puerto Rico. This earnings gap widened during the decade and by 1990, the average annual earnings of New York City had risen to 2.8 times those of Puerto Rican workers; earnings for New York City female workers were 2.4 times those of female workers in Puerto Rico.

In addition, a gap in unemployment rates also persisted. In 1980, the unemployment rate in Puerto Rico was twice that in New York City for both men and women. This gulf widened during the decade. In some areas of the United States in the late 1980s, especially in the Northeast, the unemployment rate dropped below 5 percent, while Puerto Rico's unemployment rate hovered around 20 percent (Santiago, 1991).

The 1990s again witnessed a slowing of the rate of emigration to the U.S. mainland. The situation during the 1990s was similar to that of the 1970s discussed above. In addition, it is possible that some of the decline can be attributed to Puerto Rican officials and the U.S. Coast Guard who worked to curtail illegal immigration from the Dominican Republic, many of whom would take on Puerto Rican identities and then move again to the United States (Boswell and Cruz-Baez, 2000). Even so, the net flow of Puerto Ricans to the mainland exceeded 250,000 during the 1990s.

Puerto Rican Settlement Patterns

Like virtually all immigrant groups before them, Puerto Ricans living on the mainland tended to concentrate in a few areas. In 1980, approximately 95 percent of all mainland persons of Puerto Rican ancestry lived in large cities (50,000 or more population). Additionally, about 75 percent of the Puerto Ricans were concentrated in the central cities of large metropolitan areas and only 20 percent lived in their suburbs. The remaining five percent lived in smaller urban centers and rural areas (Boswell, 1985b).

Collectively, the eleven states with the largest Puerto Rican populations contained 95 percent of all first and second generation Puerto Ricans living on the mainland in 1970. The largest single concentration was in the

Northeast, with New York, New Jersey, and Connecticut forming the main cluster. These three states contained three out of every four mainland Puerto Ricans in 1970. A second cluster was found in Illinois, mainly in the industrial area of metropolitan Chicago and adjacent northwest Indiana.

The New York metropolitan area has played a dominant role throughout much of the history of Puerto Rican migration to the United States. Originally the main attraction of New York was economic opportunity in the form of jobs and higher wages. It was not until WWI that the Puerto Rican element became noticeable in the City's population. The first settlement with significant numbers occurred in the area of Brooklyn Heights, next to the Brooklyn Navy Yard, in response to a demand for workers during the war years. At about the same time another cluster was developing in south Harlem, just to the north of Central Park and east of Morningside Park (Boswell, 1976).

After WWII, when immigration picked up, the Puerto Rican population overflowed from southern Harlem to East Harlem and across the Harlem River to South Bronx. From Brooklyn Heights, the growth spread northward to Williamsburg and southward to south Brooklyn. In 1940, about 70 percent of New York's 61,000 Puerto Ricans lived in Manhattan with the largest concentration living in East Harlem (Boswell, 1976).

The Puerto Rican population in New York City grew to 245,880 by 1950. By this time, however, it became apparent that a shift away from Manhattan was beginning to take place, as its share of the city's Puerto Rican population declined to about 56 percent. By 1970, Manhattan's share of the Puerto Rican population declined to only 23 percent. By then, the Bronx contained the largest share of the city's Puerto Rican population with 39 percent. Brooklyn was second with 33 percent, and the boroughs of Queens and Staten Island had a total of about 5 percent (Boswell, 1976).

A more detailed analysis of the distribution of Puerto Ricans in New York City during the 1950s and 1960s reveals three interesting characteristics. First, the primary area of concentration tended to be adjacent to the major areas of black settlement within the city. The residential proximity of blacks and Puerto Ricans is a reflection of their disadvantaged economic status and the consequent need to compete for the city's lowest quality housing. Second, Puerto Ricans did not numerically dominate the neighborhoods in which they lived to the same degree as other immigrant groups have in the past (Kantrowitz, 1973). Three factors have been cited for the low degree of neighborhood domination by Puerto Ricans: (1) a general housing shortage which made it necessary for Puerto Ricans to live wherever there was available affordable space; (2) slum clearance which caused them to leave neighborhoods which they may have dominated; and (3) the availability of public housing which was offered at relatively low rents (Glazer and Moynihan, 1970).

The third characteristic of Puerto Rican settlement in New York City was the amount of segregation within the Puerto Rican population based upon different levels of economic achievement. Wealthier Puerto Ricans tended to live in areas such as the better suburban neighborhoods of the Bronx and Queens, whereas the poor were more concentrated in the central city areas like Harlem and the Lower East Side (Kantrowitz, 1973).

While the Puerto Ricans within New York City were dispersing out of Manhattan and into the other four boroughs, they were also moving to locations outside the city. New Jersey's Puerto Rican population more than doubled between 1960 and 1970, with notable communities developing in Newark, Jersey City, Patterson, Camden, and Passaic. In New England, sizable concentrations evolved in Boston, Bridgeport, and Hartford. To the west, communities developed in Rochester and Philadelphia to provide manufacturing labor. In the Midwest, heavy industry attracted Puerto Ricans to Cleveland and Loraine (Ohio), and to Chicago. In the South, Miami developed a sizable Puerto Rican community, which has been overshadowed by the city's much larger Cuban community. In California, Los Angeles had the only noticeable Puerto Rican concentration, and here again was overshadowed by the more numerous Mexican-Americans (Hernandez-Alvarez, 1968).

The largest single concentration of Puerto Ricans remains in the Northeast, with New York and the neighboring states of New Jersey, Massachusetts, Pennsylvania, and Connecticut forming the main cluster. Together these five states accounted for approximately 60 percent of the Puerto Rican population in 2000. However, this is a decrease from 68 percent in 1990.

New York remains the leader with 31 percent of the mainland Puerto Rican population in 2000 (down from 40 percent in 1990). Between 1985 and 2000, 10 percent of New York City's Puerto Rican population, some 195,000 people, left the City (Nathan, 2004). Puerto Ricans left New York City for a number of reasons. The lack of appropriate employment opportunities, fear and safety concerns, and the high cost of housing acted as push factors from New York City (Reisinger, 2003).

During the 1990s, many New York Puerto Ricans (Nuyoricans) returned to the island. Others headed for central Florida, near Orlando. However, a large number have also flooded into several smaller cities in the Northeast's rustbelt. In New York, there are concentrations of Puerto Ricans in Buffalo and Rochester. In New Jersey, the two main clusters are in the northeast corner of the state, adjacent to New York City, and in Camden County, near Philadelphia. Massachusetts's Puerto Ricans are concentrated in the metropolitan area of Boston and Hampden County, including the industrial cities of Springfield and Holyoke. Connecticut's Puerto Ricans cluster in Hartford, Bridgeport, Waterbury, and New Haven. In Pennsylvania, they are concentrated in the Philadelphia metropolitan area and in the state's southeastern cities, such as Allentown, Harrisburg, Reading, Lancaster, and York.

A significant cluster of Puerto Ricans is forming in Florida. According to Census 2000, Florida had the second largest mainland Puerto Rican population after New York. Florida is the state that has experienced the largest growth during the 1980s and 1990s. The largest clusters of Puerto Ricans in Florida are found in three general areas: southeastern Florida (including Miami-Dade, Broward, and Palm Beach Counties), the center of the state focusing on Orange County (Orlando), and the metropolitan area of Tampa and St. Petersburg (Boswell and Cruz-Baez, 2000). Orlando is gaining Puerto Ricans faster than any other mainland U.S. city. In addition, there was a net flow of 9,420 Puerto Ricans from the island between 1995 and 2000.

The U.S. mainland Puerto Rican population is clearly an urban one. Approximately 93 percent live in large urbanized areas (metropolitan areas with a population of fifty thousand or more), and 71 percent live in the central cities of these large urban areas. Unfortunately, Puerto Ricans are highly segregated from the white populations in these urban areas.

CUBAN AMERICANS

Cuban Americans represent the third largest component of persons of Latino ancestry living in the United States. Currently, there are approximately 1.2 million Cuban Americans (Guzman, 2001). Emigrants from Cuba have not, until the 1980s, been representative of Cuba's total population. The earliest Cuban immigrants were especially selective of professionals and entrepreneurs, creating a serious brain drain in Cuba. The selectivity characteristics of the Cuban migrants have been dynamic, so that later arrivals have been significantly different than those that arrived earlier. The socioeconomic concentration of Cuban migrants has been accompanied by a spatial concentration in their American destinations (Boswell, 1985a). The two metropolitan areas of Miami, Florida and Union City-West New York in New Jersey are home to the vast majority of Cuban Americans (Boswell, 1985a).

Cubans represent the first large group of refugees who moved to the United States as their country of first asylum. As a result, they have been accepted automatically as refugees motivated by political persecution. This status has entitled them to federal government benefits that were not available to most other immigrant groups who have migrated primarily for economic reasons (Bernard, 1976). Cuban Americans have made remarkable progress in adjusting to living conditions in the United States. It is probably accurate to state that there has never been a large non-English speaking immigrant group in the United States that has exhibited more rapid upward socioeconomic mobility than the Cubans (Jaffe et al., 1980).

Migration Patterns of Cuban Americans

It seems reasonable to ask why the United States has become the home of the vast majority of Cuban emigrants, rather than one of the nearby Latin American countries that has more in common with Cuba in terms of language and culture. The answer is to be found in the cultural and economic characteristics that bound Cuba to the United States from the middle of the 1800s until 1959 (Boswell, 1985a). By the mid-1800s, there had developed a sizable exodus of Cubans in response to the political turmoil on the island. Key West, Tampa, and New York City became particularly notable as places of refuge for Cuban political exiles that were plotting to overthrow their Spanish rulers. In addition, American entrepreneurs and businessmen played a major role in reviving the Cuban economy after the Spanish-American War and Cuba's independence from Spain. Between 1898 and 1959 Cuba became as economically dependent upon the United States as it was on the Soviet Union between 1959 and 1989.

It was not surprising that, when Fidel Castro's forces overthrew the government of Fulgencio Batista in January 1959, an out-migration of backers of the ousted government occurred. It is unlikely, however, that the magnitude of the exodus was anticipated. Between 1959 and 1980, approximately 794,000 Cubans immigrated to the United States. Except for Puerto Rico, no other island in the Caribbean has experienced a comparable out-migration in such a short period (Boswell, 2000b).

More than 215,000 Cubans migrated to America between 1959 and 1962. In the beginning the majority were members of the economic and political elite openly affiliated with the Batista government. When the agrarian reform law was passed in mid-1959, with the purpose of breaking up large landholdings, members of the landholding aristocracy began to leave. In July, 1960, a law was passed authorizing the confiscation of all American-owned property. In October of the same year, and urban reform law was passed that was designed to expropriate private rental properties in the cities. By this time, middle-class entrepreneurs were feeling the widening impact of the Revolution (Gallagher, 1980).

The 1959 to 1962 era of Cuban immigration to the United States is sometimes referred to as the wave of *"Golden Exiles."* The implication is that the vast majority were former members of the elite classes in Cuba. This concept is only partly correct; the refugees were a highly diverse group. Virtually all occupations were represented among the immigrants. It is incorrect to think of all of them as having been elites in Cuba prior to their arrival in Florida. However, approximately 37 percent were from what might be considered the high-level employment categories (lawyers, judges, professionals, etc.) (Fagen et al., 1968). It is clear that these groups of refugees were over-represented relative to the Cuban population.

All legal transportation between the United States and Cuba came to a halt in 1962 with the Cuban missile crisis and the subsequent U.S. military blockade. Legal migration to the United States ended for a three-year period until September, 1965. It is estimated that close to 56,000 Cubans were able to immigrate to the U.S. during this period. Approximately 6,700 escaped in boats or planes, 6,000 prisoners from the Bay of Pigs expedition and their family members were allowed to leave in exchange for medicines and medical supplies, and another 43,300 entered the U.S. through intermediary countries (Gallagher, 1980).

Fidel Castro announced on September 28, 1965 that he would permit Cubans with relatives living in the United States to emigrate beginning on October 10. A number of tragedies occurred as people left the country on boats that were not always seaworthy. As a consequence, the United States and Cuba signed a "Memorandum of Understanding" that established airlifts of immigrants from Cuba to Miami. These flights became known as *"Freedom Flights."*

Air transportation began on December 1, 1965 and continued until April 6, 1973. It is estimated that 297,318 people arrived in the United States during the seven-year airlift. In addition, 4,993 came by boat during the two-month boatlift. Thus, a little over 302,000 Cubans migrated directly to the United States between October 10, 1965 and April 6, 1973 (Gallagher, 1980).

History repeated itself in April, 1980 when again mass emigration was allowed to the United States. The mode of transportation was by sea and the point of departure selected by Castro was the small port of Mariel, approximately 30 miles west of Havana. The Mariel Boatlift lasted for close to five months (April 21 to September 26, 1980) and included 124,779 people. Included in this number were many of Cuba's social undesirables such as people with criminal records and patients from mental institutions. Approximately 26,000 of the Mariel refugees had prison records, but many had been jailed for political reasons and minor crimes. It is estimated that fewer than 5,000 (4%) were hard-core criminals (Boswell, 2000b).

The influx of Mariel refugees was not welcomed in Florida, for a number of reasons. There was a perception that the Mariel boatlift was being used by Castro to empty his jails and mental institutions. A second reason was that the U.S. economy was undergoing a recession at the time. It is estimated that the unemployment rate in Dade County jumped from about 5 percent to 13 percent primarily due to the Mariel influx. In addition, the apartment vacancy rate was reduced to less than 1 percent, creating an acute housing shortage and resulting in high rents. Another reason for the cool reception of the Mariel refugees was that by 1980 public opinion in the U.S. was in favor of reducing immigration. A final factor was that 70 to 75 percent of the Mariel refugees settled in southern Florida, especially Dade County (Boswell, 2000b). After the heavy flow of Cuban immigrants during the five months of the Mariel boatlifts, immigration to the United States once again declined.

As the economic and social conditions deteriorated in Cuba in the late 1980s, the incidence of balseros (rafters) slowly increased. Nine thousand (9,000) Cubans came to the United States by this means between 1989 and 1993. On August 12, 1994 Castro announced that anybody who wanted leave the island would be allowed to do so. By the time 1994 ended, more than 37,000 Cubans left for the United States (Boswell, 2000b). On August 19, 1994, U.S. Attorney General Janet Reno stated that Cuban rafters would not be allowed in the United States. President Clinton confirmed that rafters would be intercepted at sea by the U.S. Coast Guard and taken to the U.S. Naval Base at Guantanamo Bay, Cuba, and would eventually be returned to Cuba.

On September 9, 1994, the United States announced it would allow 20,000 yearly visas for eligible Cubans to discourage future rafters from entering the United States. By December, 1994, the number of rafters declined to zero and this stage of Cuban immigration was over (Boswell, 2000b). The next phase is the one that has taken place since 1994 and is marked by another ebb and flow of refugees to the United States. The flow has been relatively small, but as conditions change in Cuba it will not be surprising if immigration does not increase again to approach 20,000 per year.

Settlement Patterns of Cuban Americans

Somewhat surprisingly, and unlike the Mexicans and Puerto Ricans discussed earlier, Cubans are becoming more concentrated. States with a substantial proportion of the Cuban population in 2000 included: New Jersey (6.2%), California (5.8%), New York (5.0%), and Texas (2.0%). Additionally, within Florida and these states, Cuban Americans are found almost exclusively in cities. The U.S. Census Bureau determined that 95 percent of all families of Cuban descent were living in metropolitan areas. Boswell (2000b) reported that 90 percent of the Cuban-origin population lived in 16 cities. The growth of the Cuban population in several of Florida's cities is apparent.

The emergence of the Union City-West New York metropolitan area in New Jersey as the second leading concentration of Cuban Americans is due to a small number of Cuban families that lived there prior to Castro's assumption of power in Cuba. They served as an attraction for the in-migration of other Cubans coming directly from Cuba and indirectly via a stepwise process through New York City during the 1960s and 1970s (Gallagher, 1980). Additionally, there were jobs available in blue-collar occupations such as light industry, warehousing, and transportation that provided economic opportunities for Cuban migrants. By the late 1970s, two-thirds of West New York's population was of Cuban descent (Gallagher, 1980).

The Cuban Refugee Program has had a major effect on the distribution of Cuban emigrants outside the state of Florida. When established in 1961 by President Kennedy, its purpose was to help Cuban immigrants adjust to living conditions in the United States through job placement, temporary financial assistance, and other welfare benefits. Another of its goals was to lessen the burden of concentration on South Florida by redistributing "relocatable" Cuban families to areas outside the state. Individuals with higher educational levels and skills, and those with some knowledge of English, were considered more easily resettled. If individuals were offered an opportunity to relocate outside South Florida but refused, they were denied further federal government assistance and considered to be on their own. Of the 494,804 Cubans who registered with the Cuban Refugee Program between 1961 and 1981, approximately 61 percent were resettled in this manner (Boswell, 1985a).

Cuban-American Settlement in South Florida

Prior to 1959, there were no major concentrations of Latinos living in Dade County, Florida. Although it has been estimated that there were approximately 20,000 Cubans living in metropolitan Miami at that time, they were generally a middle-class population that was scattered throughout the urban area. When Castro took power and began to severely limit the amount of money that Cuban emigrants could take out of the country, most refugees to Miami arrived virtually penniless. Most resided in an area on the southwestern edge of the city's central business district. This area had begun to deteriorate both as a residential and retail district prior to the arrival of the Cubans. Relatively inexpensive housing was available here and it was close to the transition zone that surrounded the CBD and contained the types of businesses that offered the Cubans the best employment opportunities. In a relatively short period of time Cubans were able to invade and then dominate this area that became known as Little Havana (Gallagher, 1980).

A study of Miami's Little Havana suggests that most of the Cuban residential areas expanded through the contagious diffusion process (Boswell, 1985a). The areas closest to the main Cuban concentration of settlement were the next encompassed by the expansion process. One exception was the Hialeah area, which was settled by a leap-frog or a hierarchical process. This area had many of the same advantages that Little Havana originally had for Cuban settlement and developed into a second concentration of Cuban activity. In the 1980s, Hialeah was Dade County's second largest city and contained a population that was about 78 percent Latin (Boswell, 1985a).

Two types of barriers were found to constrain the expansion of Cuban settlement. First, most Cubans avoided neighborhoods that were dominated by blacks. Second, very wealthy areas had land values beyond the reach of most Cubans and this also provided a barrier. Despite these barriers, a clear distance decay relationship existed between the distance that neighborhoods were located away from the core of Little Havana and the proportion of their population that was comprised of Cubans. Usually, the greater the distance, the lower the percentage that was Cuban (Boswell, 1985a).

A suburbanization trend in the residential patterns of Cuban Americans became apparent in the 1980 Census. It determined that only 39.5 percent of all families of Cuban descent lived in the central cities of metropolitan areas. Approximately 57.2 percent lived outside central cities but still within metropolitan areas (Portes et al., 1981). It appears likely that the core of Little Havana served as a port of entry for the new immigrants and they later moved to the middle or fringe areas of the metropolitan area (Boswell, 1985a).

ECONOMIC AND SOCIAL BIFURCATION DURING THE 1990s

This section analyzes the economic situation of Latinos at the beginning of the 21st century. An analysis of Census 2000 data (Summary File 3) reveals that although the 1990s are generally considered a period of widespread prosperity, it did not yield greater income or neighborhood equality for Latinos.

U.S. Census data show that non-Hispanic white incomes averaged just under $50,000 in 2000 — $15,000 more than Latinos. This pattern of differences is very similar to what was already in place in 1990. There were some changes, however. In absolute terms, white incomes increased over $4,500 between 1990 and 2000, an increase of approximately 10 percent. The percentage increase for Latinos was 6.6 percent from $32,677 to $34,833.

The breakdown by geographic regions shows that the Latino-white disparity was by far the greatest in the Northeast where Latino median household incomes were $18,809 less than whites. The Latino-white median household income differential was $7,977 in the Midwest, $13,350 in the South, and $11,763 in the West. The difference in the Northeast might be explained by the relatively low incomes of Puerto Ricans and Dominicans who constitute a large share of Latinos in that region (Logan, 2002). In the 50 metropolitan areas with the largest Latino populations, income disparities with whites tend to be smaller than those for blacks. However, in none of these places have Latinos achieved parity with whites in median household income. The largest income disparity is found in Newark, NJ ($27,501). Boston, New York, and Philadelphia also have income disparities between Latinos and whites that are above $25,000. The smallest disparity is found in Fort Lauderdale, a clear anomaly where Latinos' incomes were less than $2000 below whites'. In addition, Latinos earned nearly 96 percent as much as whites in Ft. Lauderdale. In no other case is the income disparity below $5000 or do Latinos have incomes more than 85 percent that of whites.

Neighborhood Gap

An analysis of the national and regional averages for the median household income of the neighborhood (census tract) where the average group member lived in 1990 and 2000 shows again that non-Hispanic whites have a considerable advantage over Latinos. The average white lived in a neighborhood with a median household income of $51,459, while the average Latino lived in a neighborhood with a median household income of $39,308 (a difference of $12,421).

Latinos have a decidedly better position in the American class structure than do blacks, and they live in better neighborhoods. At the same time, they have lower incomes and live in poorer neighborhoods than do non-Hispanic whites, even compared to whites with similar incomes. Similar to blacks, their neighborhood gap is not attributable to income differences with whites alone (Logan, 2002).

This neighborhood gap between Latinos and whites is once again greatest in the Northeast. In that region, the average white lives in a neighborhood with a median household income of $54,700 and the average Latino lives in a neighborhood with a median household income of $36,614.

The neighborhood gap increased in absolute dollar amount in 45 metro areas. In only one case (Ft. Lauderdale) do Latinos live in better neighborhoods. The average Latino in Ft. Lauderdale lives in a neighborhood with a median household income of $47,807 and the average white lives in a neighborhood with a median household income of $46,408.

The trajectory for Latinos is clearly negative. Their incomes and the quality of their neighborhoods are declining relative to whites in both absolute dollar amounts and as a proportion (Logan, 2002). There are important regional differences, however, with especially large disparities in the Northeast and a better relative position in the Midwest. Income disparities and neighborhood gaps manifest themselves in the quality of schools and school segregation between Latinos and whites (Logan et al., 2002).

Latino Socioeconomic Bifurcation

Branching out

In addition, a bifurcation in the social and economic characteristics among Latinos has become apparent at the beginning of the 21st century. The variation is most visible between Mexicans, Puerto Ricans, Central Americans and the newer immigrant groups from South America. For example, Mexicans are the least educated of the older Latino groups, with an average education of only 10.2 years (for those aged 25 and above). Puerto Ricans average 11.4 years, and Cubans 11.9 years. Other Latino groups range both below the Mexicans and above the Cubans. Salvadorans and Guatemalans have the least education (below 10 years) among the new Latino groups. But Latinos from most South American origins are better educated than Cubans, averaging 12.6 years (Logan, 2001).

Compared to Puerto Ricans and Mexicans, Cubans in the United States have always been regarded as economically quite successful. The mean earnings of employed Cubans are above $13,500, compared to about $10,000 for Puerto Ricans and $8500 for Mexicans. Only 18 percent of Cubans fall below the poverty line, compared to 26 percent of Mexicans and 30 percent of Puerto Ricans. Among the other Latino groups, Dominicans stand out for their very low incomes, with mean earnings below $8000 and more than a third in poverty (36 percent) (Logan, 2001). The major Central American groups are roughly equivalent to Puerto Ricans in average earnings, though they are less likely to fall below the poverty line. Latinos from South America do considerably better, and on average they earn more and have lower poverty rates than do Cubans.

Levels of unemployment among Latino groups are generally consistent with their average earnings. However, there are some inconsistencies. Puerto Ricans have an unemployment rate of 8.3 percent and an average income of $9,893. Meanwhile, Hondurans have an unemployment rate of 10.8 percent and average earnings of $10,244. In addition, Latinos from the Dominican Republic have higher than average unemployment and they are the group most likely to be receiving public assistance (above 8 percent — in both respects they are less successful than Puerto Ricans) (Logan, 2001). Those from South America have the lowest levels of unemployment and are even less likely to receive public assistance.

The modest educational levels of Mexicans, Puerto Ricans, and Central Americans have relegated them to the lower levels of the labor market. They have found jobs in the marginal sectors of the service and manufacturing economy. Meanwhile, Cubans and South Americans' higher levels of education have offered them better occupational opportunities. The result has been a noticeable bifurcation in social and economic characteristics between the various Latino groups.

THE GROWING POLITICAL POWER OF LATINOS

While Latino voter participation traditionally lags behind that of whites and African Americans, a growing population and extensive voter outreach efforts meant 1 million more Latinos voted in the 2004 presidential election than in the 2000 (NALEO, 2004). Latinos had the potential to significantly sway the outcome in pivotal states such as Florida (where NALEO estimated 160,000 more Latino voters in 2004 than in 2000), Arizona (a 70,000 rise), New Jersey (23,000), New Mexico (11,000) and Colorado (8,000). These projections would seem to have bolstered Sen. John Kerry given that Latinos identify themselves as Democrats more than as Republicans by a two-to-one margin.

However, according to the exit polls, Bush's share with Latinos went from 35 percent in 2000, (Gore had 62 percent of the Latino vote in 2000) to 44 percent for Bush (to Kerry's 53 percent) in 2004. And though there are some different poll numbers floating around that minimize Bush's performance among Latinos, Democrats have to acknowledge that Bush did make gains with this important group.

The Latino population is diverse in its politics. Priority issues vary regionally. Latinos in California are more likely to focus on immigration and alien residency, for example, while Latinos in New York and Chicago place more importance on the war in Iraq (NCLR, 2004). Differences can also be profound within a state. In Florida, the state's large Cuban-American population has strongly tended to be Republican (Botelho, 2004). Meanwhile, thousands of Latinos have come to the state, particularly central Florida, in recent years from other parts of Latin America. There has been greater diversification in recent years, which has made the Latino voting population very difficult to predict.

In a poll conducted by La Raza prior to the 2004 Presidential election, Latinos were asked to rank the issues of greatest importance to the their community:

- More than one-third (34%) selected education/schools.
- More than one-fifth (22%) identified the economy/jobs.
- Eight percent selected immigration, six percent identified civil rights, and five percent selected health care.
- No other issues, including national security (1%) or the war on terrorism (2%), exceeded the poll's margin of error (3.3%).

In the same survey 58 percent of Latinos said political candidates do not sufficiently address issues important to their communities (NCLR, 2004).

Alberto Gonzales, a Mexican American, who has followed President Bush from the Texas Statehouse to the White House, was Bush's choice to succeed John Ashcroft as attorney general. When confirmed, he became the first Latino attorney general. Gonzales served in Bush's administration when the president was governor of

Texas, and was named White House counsel in January, 2001. His name often has been forwarded as a likely Supreme Court nominee of the Bush' administration.

In another example of the growing importance of the Latino vote, Former Secretary of Housing and Urban Development Mel Martinez and Colorado Attorney General Ken Salazar, were the first Latinos elected to serve in the U.S. Senate in nearly thirty years (NALEO, 2004). Senator-Elect Mel Martinez became the first Cuban American elected to serve in the upper house of Congress; both are the first Latinos elected to the Senate from Florida and Colorado. The fact that a Democrat and a Republican Latino with such distinct backgrounds and experiences were both elected to the U.S. Senate demonstrates the strength and diversity of the Latino community.

After the 2004 election, the number of Latinos in Congress remained the same at 19. Seven states (California, Arizona, Texas, New York, Illinois, Florida, and New Jersey) have Latino representatives in Congress. Latino members of Congress have formed the Congressional Latino Caucus and Congressional Latino Conference (NALEO, 2004). Both organizations were formed to promote issues affecting Latino Americans through the legislative process.

Latinos seized the opportunity to continue their political progress by winning several state legislative seats according to an analysis conducted by the National Association of Latino Elected and Appointed Officials (NALEO, 2004) Educational Fund. Overall, in state legislative contests, Latinos lost one seat in State Senates, but gained eight in lower state houses. New Mexico elected the greatest number of Latinos (15) to the State Senate. California and Texas will have seven Latino members in the State Senate and New York will have four (NALEO, 2004).

ILLEGAL IMMIGRATION AND THE RISING TIDE OF ANTI-IMMIGRANT SENTIMENT

The Immigration and Naturalization Service (INS) estimated that the total unauthorized immigrant population residing in the United States in 2000 was 7 million, which constituted 2.5 percent of the total U.S population of just over 281 million (INS, 2000). According to INS estimates, the unauthorized immigrant population grew by about 350,000 people per year during the 1990s. This conclusion is derived from a draft report given to the House immigration subcommittee by the INS that estimated the illegal population was 3.5 million in 1990. The Census Bureau also developed estimates at the time of the 2000 Census that suggested that the illegal immigrant population was about eight million. For the illegal population to have reached 8 million by 2000, the net increase had to be 400,000 to 500,000 per year during the 1990s (Camarota, 2004).

The Unauthorized Latino Population — Origins

The growing unauthorized population has resulted in a rising tide of anti-immigrant feelings in many parts of the United States. In this section the origins of the unauthorized population and their destinations will be analyzed using the 2000 INS data. The increasing animosity toward illegal immigrants and, immigrants in general, and how this may translate into new policy initiatives also will be examined.

Mexico continued to be the leading source of unauthorized immigration to the United States in the 1990s. The estimated unauthorized resident population from Mexico increased from about 2.0 million in 1990 to 4.8 million in January 2000. Mexico accounted for nearly 69 percent of the total unauthorized resident population in January, 2000; the top fifteen countries of origin, including Mexico, accounted for 89 percent of the total. The estimated unauthorized immigrant population from El Salvador dropped in the 1990s because many of these unauthorized immigrants were granted temporary protected status (TPS) early in the decade. In 1997, many long-term illegal residents from Cuba, Guatemala, Nicaragua, and El Salvador were allowed to stay and work in the United States under provisions of the Nicaraguan Adjustment and Central American Relief Act (NACARA). Unauthorized residents from Central America and other countries were effectively shifted from unauthorized to lawfully resident by other legislative changes and judicial decisions in the latter part of the 1990s (INS, 2000).

Three South American countries — Colombia, Ecuador, and Brazil — had relatively large increases in estimated unauthorized residents in the United States from 1990 to 2000.

The Unauthorized Latino Population — Destinations

About 4.5 million of the estimated 7.0 million unauthorized residents in 2000 were highly geographically concentrated in the five states; California, Texas, New York, Illinois, and Florida. California and Texas had the largest numerical increases in the number of unauthorized residents in the 1990s. More than one third of the INS estimated 3.5 million total increase in the unauthorized resident population in the 1990s occurred in these two states. The INS estimated that approximately 5.5 percent of Texas's total population is unauthorized residents. In addition to California and Texas, seven States — Illinois, Arizona, Georgia, North Carolina, New York, New Jersey, and Colorado — had increases of more than 100,000 unauthorized residents between 1990 and 2000 (INS, 2000).

Many states that had relatively few unauthorized residents in 1990 experienced rapid growth of the unauthorized population in the decade. Three principal examples are Georgia, North Carolina, and Colorado. In addition, Alabama, Arkansas, Iowa, Nebraska, South Carolina, Tennessee, and Wisconsin saw significant increases in their unauthorized populations. This was a significant trend in unauthorized population change for these states in the 1990s and may provide an explanation for the growing anti-immigrant sentiment in many parts of the United States (INS, 2000).

Anti-Immigrant Sentiment

The illegal immigrant situation has received much publicity and has become highly politicized. A frequent argument against illegal immigration is that it allegedly depresses wages and increases unemployment. Undocumented or illegal immigrants often perform low-skilled tasks shunned by American workers. Areolla (2000) argues that the illegal Mexican immigrants have little difficulty finding these jobs in the United States and that they do not displace American labor to a great extent.

A second charge against illegal immigrants is that they "freeload" on social services. This practice has not been well documented, and the evidence suggests the opposite. Undocumented workers pay state and local taxes and must have federal and social security deducted from their earnings. Studies suggest that illegal Mexican immigrants make very little use of social services beyond public schools for their children, who are entitled to a public education. In California and Texas, undocumented Mexicans have used public assistance services. However, they have contributed many times the amount annually to the support of such services (Arreola, 2000).

Immigration has been a source of controversy in American politics since the first part of the nineteenth century. Throughout, critics of immigration have argued that mass immigration would flood the country with people who were culturally alien and would fail to contribute economically. Hence, the Irish, Southern and Eastern European, Jews, East Asians (Chinese and Japanese) and, most recently, South East Asians and, in particular, Latinos from Central and South America, have successively been the target of anti-immigrant sentiment.

Originally, opposition came from nativist Americans, or those who believed that the purity of the Northern European Protestant stock would be corrupted by the new arrivals. The 1924 Immigration Act was specifically designed to favor Northern and Western Europeans. Today, a racist-nativist sentiment persists in some places. There are three main dimensions to the current debate. First, opponents of immigration argue that many Latinos, and especially immigrants of Mexican origin, hold a greater allegiance to the mother country than to the U.S. Unlike earlier waves of immigrants, they maintain their linguistic and cultural identity across generations. Second, illegal immigration is widespread across poorly policed borders. Third, they argue that during difficult economic times, the new immigrants, especially their children, constitute a strain on hard-pressed welfare and social services (AFSC, 2003).

For the past 150 years, attitudes towards immigrants have changed cyclically, often undergoing rapid shifts in response to economic or political conditions. In periods of social and economic turmoil, such as the years following WWI or the post-WWII McCarthy Era, anti-immigrant sentiments tend to flare up as people look for someone to blame. During times of economic growth and social stability, nativism tends to die down. As always, it is difficult to tell to what extent media and political figures reflect public attitudes, and to what extent they create them (AFSC, 2003).

Politicians have often turned waves of nativist feeling to political advantage, voting for policies that penalize immigrants. Two particularly clear examples are the 1882 Chinese Exclusion Act, which banned Chinese-born laborers from entering the country, and "Operation Wetback," in which more than 500,000 people of Mexican descent (including numerous U.S. citizens) were rounded up and deported to Mexico.

Anti-immigrant feeling ran high in the early 1990s, partly because the country faced a prolonged recession, and partly because of the marked growth of immigration, particularly in California. Some observers believe that the growth of anti-immigrant sentiment in that period was also a reflection of racial anxieties among the white population, as it became increasingly obvious that white Americans would eventually cease to be the majority, a shift that has already occurred in California and is projected to occur after 2050 for the country as a whole (AFSC, 2003).

In addition, a series of economic changes related to globalization were becoming increasingly apparent to most U.S. working people. Such changes included steadily declining real wages, shrinking benefits and protections, the marked growth of temporary and contingent jobs, declining rates of unionization, increasing privatization, and cutbacks in health care and education. Although most of these changes may be traced back to the early 1970s, it was not until the 1990s that they became more widely recognized and discussed.

In 1994, California voters passed an anti-immigrant measure known as Proposition 187, a law that excluded undocumented immigrants from public schools, medical assistance, and other government services. That year, a New York Times/CBS News survey found that 61 percent of U.S. residents thought that immigration levels should be reduced, up from 49 percent in 1986. Although Proposition 187 was ultimately ruled unconstitutional, many of the same measures were incorporated in federal legislation passed in 1996 (AFSC, 2003).

The end of the 1990s brought a period of economic expansion and rising wage levels, and anti-immigrant sentiment grew more muted in many parts of the country. The tide turned once again, however, following the World Trade Center attacks of Sept. 11, 2001. Rather than being stigmatized as an economic drain, immigrants became demonized by some as dangerous terrorists, as the violent acts of a few extremists are blamed on all immigrants, regardless of who they are or why they are here.

Anti-immigrant politics also have given rise to an increase in vigilante activity, particularly in the U.S.-Mexico border region. Vigilantes have vowed to stop "illegal" immigration by patrolling the border with binoculars and guns, "arresting" at gunpoint anyone they presume to be an undocumented immigrant. Despite the threat of bloodshed, several political figures have defended such vigilante activity, including former INS Commissioner Doris Meissner, who has said that ranchers near the border "have legitimate concerns about the trespassers on their property." In one 17-month period in 1999 and 2000, at least 30 incidents of vigilante violence were reported in a single section of the Arizona-Mexico border. Other ranchers, by contrast, have installed humanitarian aid stations on their land to assist border crossers who might otherwise face sickness or death due to dehydration (AFSC, 2003).

Roots of Anti-Immigrant Activism

European Americans have held a dominant position in the United States, both culturally and politically, for the country's entire history. Among some non-Hispanics whites, racial anxieties over losing their majority status have lead to a backlash, combining with resistance to multiculturalism and other movements that seek to include communities of color as equal partners in all aspects of U.S. society (SPLC, 2001).

While illegal immigration is a serious problem, although hardly a new one, the criticisms have little foundation in fact. It is difficult to know how the Mexican American and other Latino communities will develop over time. The same criticisms were directed at Italian, Jewish and Polish communities at the beginning of the twentieth century. As for constituting an economic burden on social services, in the longer run the opposite is likely, for immigrants play a large part in bringing down the average age of the American population. As such they or their children may be the very people who will pay the taxes to finance the pensions and medical care of older, longer established Americans.

Chapter 15

Latinos in New York City:
Ethnic Diversity, Changing Settlement Patterns, and Settlement Experiences

KEITH D. GALLIGANO AND JOHN W. FRAZIER

INTRODUCTION

Founded in the 1600s by Dutch colonists due to its coastal location, New York City is the "metropolis of the world" and an area of opportunity. As a result, diverse migrants come to this area seeking economic and political stability, and the "American Dream." Before the 1960s, European ancestries dominated New York City's foreign-born population, primarily a result of the 1924 National Origins Act, which favored European migrants by restricting non-Europeans through the use of national quotas. However, after 1965, the number of non-European migrants increased dramatically because changes in U.S. policy extended immigration opportunities to non-Europeans by favoring family reunification (1965 Hart-Celler Act) and political circumstances (1980 Refugee Act) over country of origin. This produced large increases in Hispanic[1] and Asian populations. Also, increased economic disparities between developing and developed countries resulting from globalization have "pushed" many immigrants from developing countries into urban areas of developed countries in search of economic stability. As a result of these external factors, "white flight," and black reverse migration to the South, New York City's population has continued to diversify racially and ethnically. Latino immigration provides an excellent example of this diversity.

The Latino population of New York City has diversified greatly, resulting in the historically dominant Puerto Ricans representing less than a majority of the total Hispanic population for the first time in 1990 (Alba, 1995). This is a product of large increases in Mexican, Dominican and "Other Hispanic" ancestries after 1965. Due to the increasing diversity in origin within the Latino population of New York City, interethnic discontinuities may exist in socioeconomic status, settlement, and migration patterns. This chapter examines the socioeconomic status, settlement and migration patterns of Dominicans, Mexicans, and South Americans in New York City. These ethnic groups exhibit the largest percentage increases in population between 1990 and 2000 in New York City, compared to other Latino subgroups. It should be noted that the South American ancestry group consists of an aggregate of ancestries originating in South America because they are not listed separately in the 2000 U.S. Census.

CHANGING RACIAL AND ETHNIC PATTERNS IN NEW YORK CITY

Puerto Rican Settlement

As a result of forced shifts in Puerto Rico's primary agricultural export — from coffee to sugar and then back to coffee — and mechanization of farming techniques, unemployment rates soared in Puerto Rico in the late 19th and early 20th centuries. Many of the unemployed became involved in family based part-time businesses, like sewing, in order to survive. Others took advantage of favorable U.S. immigration policy as well as the prospects of economic prosperity and moved to the mainland U.S., primarily to New York City. Migrants were "pulled" into this city for economic opportunity, a result of the labor shortage produced by World War I and the booming economy of the 1920s. Two acts that helped Puerto Ricans take advantage of favorable economic opportunity in America were the Jones Act of 1917, which gave citizenship to Puerto Ricans, and the Johnson Act of 1921, which severely limited the flow of foreign immigrants into America (Sanchez, 1994). Migration of Puerto Ricans to New York City continued to increase marginally in the 1920s, until the beginning of the Great Depression. It rose once again during the labor shortages of WWII. Sanchez states that the efficient decrease in migration from Puerto Rico to New York during economic lapses can be somewhat contributed to family networks, which communicated the lack of job opportunities to Puerto Rico (Sanchez, 1994).

In addition to social networking, migration rates increased and decreased due to recruitment. Through the use of U.S. federal funding, migrants were frequently given free transportation to the United States, in order to encourage migration in times of labor shortages. Furthermore, foreign recruitment agencies, like the Migration Division of Puerto Rico's Department of Labor in New York City, were created to help educate potential migrants on job opportunities. Although the jobs that were available to Puerto Ricans were low-skilled, blue-collar jobs, migrants continued to come to the mainland due to more favorable employment conditions (Sanchez, 1994).

With the increased migration of Puerto Ricans into New York City in the mid 20th century, ethnic enclaves, or colonias, that were geographically isolated, helped foster and perpetuate social and cultural unity of "traditional" Puerto Rican society. Within New York City, the main colonias included: East and South Central Harlem, and northern Kings County (Brooklyn) (Sanchez, 1994). In these colonias, many Latino-specific commercial, professional, and retail amenities developed, which did not exist elsewhere in New York City, making colonias a prime destination for Puerto Rican migrants.

Early colonias depended heavily on employment opportunities. The Brooklyn colonia was created due to the American Manufacturing Company, which employed and recruited Puerto Ricans (sometimes directly from Puerto Rico) to make rope from hemp, provided free transportation to and from work for its workers, and allowed use of company-owned buses for recreation (for a minimal fee). Sanchez argues that this service allowed "Puerto Rican workers to familiarize themselves with the city neighborhoods, transmitting this information in letters to friends and family in Puerto Rico" (Sanchez, 1994, p. 54).

The second major colonia area, the Harlem community (or el barrio), unlike the Brooklyn colonia, grew due to the existence of Latino-based services, rather than a specific industry. The largest Puerto Rican commercial market in New York City, as well as the offices of many Puerto Rican professionals and entertainment venues, developed in el barrio. As a result, many Puerto Ricans would travel from Brooklyn to Manhattan for goods and services. Other differences between the two colonias existed in housing quality and availability, which favored the Manhattan community. Consequently, a rift between Puerto Rican establishments developed.

As the size and population of New York City Puerto Rican colonias increased, many Puerto Rican-owned commercial businesses were established. The owners of these businesses became the "backbone" of the definition of the Puerto Rican community in New York City, due to their involvement within the community. Latino businessmen helped create Puerto Rican organizations and clubs, and gave advice to new migrants. In spite of the perceived friendly nature of merchants and professionals, competition between similar establishments was significant. Professionals and merchants helped protect cultural solidarity in the colonias, as did the common language and traditions. While English was the primary language of business, Spanish was the community language and provided an invisible bond. Also, community functions, like La Prensas (or balls) and sporting events also played a pivotal role in Puerto Rican solidarity, while Puerto Rican music helped cure "homesickness" and provided a common interest (Sanchez, 1994).

After WWII, the Puerto Rican community in New York City was unique, due to the interconnection between the island and mainland, which transplanted native Puerto Rican beliefs, attitudes and customs to New York City neighborhoods. Although most migrants who entered New York City planned to return to Puerto

Rico, many stayed, creating new family networks. Sanchez separates the post-Great Migration movement of Puerto Ricans into three stages. The first migration was dominated by low-skilled, blue collar workers, who moved from Puerto Rico to primarily New York City between the end of WWII and 1960. During this migration wave, the Puerto Rican population of New York City increased nearly tenfold — from 61,463 to 612,574 — the majority of which were under the age of 30. While many of these new immigrants moved into the traditional colonias of Spanish Harlem and Brooklyn, a new concentration in the South Bronx emerged. The majority of these new migrants were able to obtain low-level, blue-collar jobs in urban industries.

Unlike the first-stage migrants, second-stage migrants (1960–1970) faced economic hardships and discrimination, due to fluctuations in the U.S. economy. As a result, many Puerto Ricans moved into non-New York City urban areas of the northeast in search of blue-collar jobs. The last migration (1970 to the present) "has been marked with high levels of return migration," as a result of fewer low-skilled occupational opportunities and low wages (Sanchez, 1994, p. 215). Return migrants to Puerto Rico were lured by the new economic opportunities established by Operation Bootstrap, an American based plan to industrialize Puerto Rico by relocating American corporations to the island. The early years of Operation Bootstrap were very successful, as seen in the doubling of the per capita income of Puerto Ricans between 1954 and 1964, but by the 1970s, the agrarian sector was destroyed, as farming was replaced by capital-intensive industries. As a result, unemployment and dependence on America for food supplies increased.

Although the Puerto Rican population originally was easily able to assimilate occupationally into the U.S. economy, by 1980, the New York City Puerto Rican workforce was "undermined" by four indirect effects of capitalism. First, the restructuring of New York City's economy away from manufacturing occupations to low-skilled service jobs lowered wages. Second, industrial technological innovations increased unemployment. Third, many corporations relocated to Sunbelt and other regions to take advantage of cheap labor. Fourth, increased competition for low-skilled service jobs resulting from an increase in undereducated non-European immigrants to New York City contributed to unemployment. As a result of these four reasons, the Puerto Rican population is considered "impoverished" in comparison to other Latino ethnicities in New York City. Many Puerto Ricans departed New York City in the 1980s and 1990s for perceived opportunities in smaller cities, such as those in southeastern Pennsylvania.

LATINO SETTLEMENTS IN NYC: THE UNANSWERED QUESTIONS AND METHODS

The changing U.S. immigration laws, the deaths of people of European ancestry, and the political and economic instability in many developing countries, have contributed to the growth and diversity of the U.S. Latino population. By 2000, Latinos in America differed by place of origin and socioeconomic status, and it is likely that these differences changed settlement patterns and experiences in the U.S. (Clark, 2002). New York City is no exception to this trend.

We employed three analytical stages to examine these patterns. The first stage examined population trends and geographies of Hispanics, Asians, blacks and whites in New York City by studying predefined areas of racial concentration (AORCs), 1970 and 2000, at the census tract level to illustrate the diversification of New York City's population. The second stage evaluated the differences in socioeconomic status and migration flows of Latino in-migrants from predefined regions to New York City using SF4 and U.S. Census Migration Data (CMD) for the selected Latino ethnic groups: Mexicans, Dominicans, and South Americans. These ethnic groups exhibited the largest percent change in population between 1990 and 2000. The final step of the analysis presents the settlement patterns and socioeconomic status, inferred by housing, nativity and poverty characteristics of Dominicans, Mexicans, and South Americans, to determine differences in location and social status, or the "settlement experience."[2]

THE STUDY AREA

Two clusters of Latino concentrations exist on the Eastcoast of the U.S. — the New York City and the Washington, D.C. regions. The Washington, D.C. region includes the District of Columbia, as well as suburban counties in Maryland (Montgomery and Prince Georges) and Virginia (Fairfax and Arlington), and Virginia cities (Fairfax, Falls Church and Alexandria). The 5 counties (boroughs) of New York City — Bronx, Kings, New York, Richmond, and Queens — define the New York City region.

The study area was determined by establishing a population threshold for inclusion for each ethnic group. Each ethnic group had to have a minimum population of 10,000. Only New York City met that requirement; Washington, D.C. had an insufficient number of Dominicans. Thus the New York City area was selected as the study area.

"Tract" level analysis is the most suitable: tracts are theoretically homogenous neighborhoods and inferences can be made from spatial analysis. While New York City consists of five counties (or boroughs), for administrative purposes, it also is reduced to fifty-nine different community districts. This research uses community districts, counties, and tracts to describe phenomena spatially.

LATINO DIVERSITY, MIGRATION AND SETTLEMENT PATTERNS IN NEW YORK CITY

Population Trends and the Distribution of Areas of Racial Concentration in New York City: 1970–2000

Many factors contribute to the racial/ethnic structure of New York City, including U.S. immigration policy and the negative economic effects of globalization in developing countries. Many of the new racial/ethnic groups in New York City have settled in highly concentrated areas, due to political, social and economic constraints (Lobo, 2002; Alba, 1995). As new immigrants settled, whites departed to suburban areas, away from areas of minority settlement. So that by 2000, a population that was once dominated by black and white racial groups diversified dramatically, and included large Asian and Hispanic populations.

The most significant contributor to the diversification of New York City's neighborhoods between 1970 and 2000 was the decrease in white population (due to white flight), rather than the population increase of any one minority group. However, Asians, blacks, and Hispanics experienced significant increases in population during this time period. Asians had the most significant increase in population at the tract level, followed by Hispanics and blacks, respectively. Hispanics will likely become the largest minority group in New York City in the near future.

The significant increase in the population of non-white groups and white flight resulted in not only the diversification of New York City's neighborhoods, but also the change in number and location of areas of racial/ethnic concentration. In 1970, New York City's neighborhoods were dominated by black and white populations, which were highly isolated from one another. After 1970, as the population of non-white racial/ethnic groups increased and whites continued to depart from areas with increasing minority populations, many racially diverse "mixed" neighborhoods developed. These areas gradually changed into minority concentration areas, as white residential succession completed.

Compared to the other minority groups examined, areas of black concentration presented the least dramatic change in number and location. Black settlement in New York City predated other minority settlements, thus black residential patterns were established early, isolating black settlement in various parts of the City (Alba, 1995). As a result, by 1970, areas of black concentration clustered in: northern New York (Central Harlem), central Kings (Crown Heights North, Bedford/Stuyvesant and Crown Heights South/Windgate) and central Queens (Jamaica/St. Albans/Hollis). The size of these clusters grew substantially between 1970 and 2000, as areas of white concentration that were located on the fringes of the black clusters gradually changed into areas of black concentration. In 2000, areas of black concentration comprised nearly 22 percent of the City's census tracts.

Very few areas of Hispanic concentration existed in the five-county area in 1970. Hispanics primarily settled in traditional Puerto Rican enclaves of southern Bronx/northern New York Counties and northern Kings County, in white-Hispanic neighborhoods. However, by 1980, these neighborhoods quickly changed from combined white-Hispanic neighborhoods to areas of Hispanic concentration, due to "white flight." Also, by 2000, Hispanic settlement had dispersed into northern Queens County, into the Jackson Heights/North Corona and Elm Hurst/South Corona community districts, a result of the diversification of the Hispanic population from primarily Puerto Rican to a multitude of ancestry groups that tend to locate away from one another (Massey, 1981). By 2000, over 17 percent of New York City's neighborhoods were areas of Hispanic concentration.

Similar to Hispanic settlement trends, small numbers of areas of Asian concentration existed in 1970, which were clustered in Chinatown in southern New York County. By 1990, the size of the Chinatown cluster increased dramatically, and Asian settlement diffused into northern Queens County in the Flushing/Bay Terrance community district. Between 1990 and 2000, Asian settlement dispersed from Flushing/Bay Terrance cluster into surrounding neighborhoods, and areas of Asian concentration developed in the Fresh Meadows/Briarwood and Bayside/Douglaston/Little Neck community districts of Queens County. Also, large numbers of white-Asian neighborhoods developed by 2000, located on the fringes of areas of Asian concentrations and will likely develop into areas of Asian concentration, if white residential out-migration continues.

Latino Migration Patterns into New York City

Since 1970 New York City became increasingly diverse racially and ethnically, partially as a result of an increase in Hispanic populations. What are the Hispanic origins and the socioeconomic and demographic characteristics of Hispanic in-migrants? Hispanics were highly mobile between 1995 and 2000 within New York City, with almost 42 percent of the Hispanic population moving at least once. Of the three Hispanic ethnic groups analyzed, Mexicans (58%) had the highest tendency to live in a different residence between 1995 and 2000, followed by South Americans (49%) and then Dominicans (43%). However, the majority of movement was intra-urban; 72 percent of Hispanics resided in a different house in 1995 but in the same city.

However, large regional differences existed in the origins of out-of-state migrants among these three Hispanic groups. The largest proportion of Mexican non-New York State domestic migrants originated from the West, while the largest proportion of non-New York State domestic migrants of Dominicans and South Americans originated in the Northeast and South, respectively, reflecting regional concentrations of each group. For example, the majority of Mexicans still reside in the West region. Regarding the sources of foreign immigrants, 36 percent of Mexicans, 29 percent of South Americans, and 18 percent of Dominicans who lived in a different residence in 2000, originated from a foreign country after 1995. This trend reflects the liberalization of U.S. immigration law and the attraction of New York City as a gateway for many Latinos. Mexican immigration to New York City, for example, is a fairly new phenomenon compared to the other ethnic groups. However, under immigration law, immediate family members are able to reunite with family, which many Mexicans, as well as others, are opting to do. New York City is likely perceived as an internationally friendly city with economic opportunities for immigrants who also have a support network of family and friends in place in the City.

Figure 15.1 illustrates the regional origins of New York City in-migrants from U.S. Census regions, between 1995 and 2000. Hispanic in-migrants moved to New York City from primarily northeastern states, yet large flows also existed from California and Florida, both traditional "gateway states." At the county level (not shown on the map), Hispanics moved to New York City from both urban and rural counties of the northeast region that are in close proximity to New York City. Hispanics from non-northeastern regions migrated primarily from urban counties that contain a "gateway city" (for example Los Angeles and Miami-Dade counties). These patterns illustrate the continued importance of New York City as a destination of domestic Hispanic migrants.

Significant, yet modest differences (p < .01) between the six migratory regions were found to exist for the four socioeconomic variables (median household income, nativity, education and age) analyzed. Hispanic migrants originating in the Northeast and New York City regions were younger, more likely to be foreign-born, and of lower socioeconomic status compared to the migrants from the other regions. Latino migrants originating from the West region tended to have the highest education levels, and Latino migrants originating from the Midwest region had the highest income levels, suggesting that migrant selectivity could be influenced by socio-economic status.

Figure 15.1

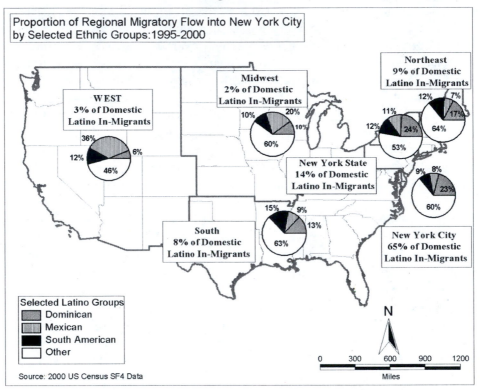

Settlement Patterns and Well-Being: Latino Ethnic Groups in New York City

The migratory flows of the selected Latino ethnic groups (Dominicans, Mexicans and South Americans) into New York City varies by domestic and foreign origin. The socioeconomic and demographic attributes of Latino migrants that move to New York City differ substantially by region. Because past research illustrates that these differences in origin and socioeconomic status result in different settlement patterns, one can infer that location and the social status, or the "settlement experience," of these ethnic groups may differ in the settlement areas within New York City (Massey, 1981; Haverluk, 1997).

Between 1990 and 2000, New York City became less segregated, primarily the result of "white flight." Thus, New York City is an increasingly multicultural city. However, inter-ethnic differences in spatial segregation exist between the selected Latino populations and the major racial/ethnic categories reported by the U.S. Census (Asians, blacks and whites). Dominicans, for example, are highly segregated from whites in 1990 and 2000, while Mexicans and South Americans are only moderately segregated from the white non-Hispanic population. Furthermore, Dominicans were significantly more segregated from these whites than from blacks. The Mexican and South American populations showed the reverse trend.

South Americans and Asians locate in the same neighborhoods in New York City. Mexicans and South Americans were significantly less segregated from each other, compared to Dominicans and South Americans and Dominicans and Mexicans, suggesting that Dominicans may be unusually isolated from Mexicans and South Americans.

Figure 15.2

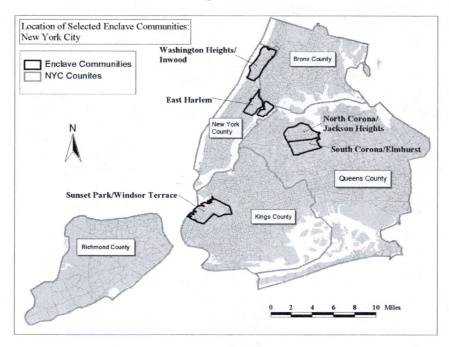

Figure 15.2 shows the locations of selected important Latino enclaves. Figure 15.3a and Figure 15.3b display the multiethnic enclaves and those that were dominated by a single Latino ethnic group. Figure 15.3a reveals several multiethnic enclaves. The majority of the multi-ethnic enclaves existed in the Jackson Heights/ North Corona and South Corona/Elmhurst community districts, suggesting large levels of ethnic diversity in these areas in both 1990 and 2000. Between 1990 and 2000, the number of Mexican/South American multi-ethnic enclaves increased dramatically, while the number of Mexican/Dominican and South American/ Dominican remained relatively small, implying the isolation of Dominicans in the study area.

In 1990 and 2000, small numbers of Dominican enclaves met the population criteria of any AORC type (Asian, black and white), indicating that Dominican enclaves are either dominated by the Dominican population, or, have large proportions of other Latino populations. Conversely, the number of Mexican and South American enclaves that were found to meet AOAC (Area of Asian concentration) and AOWC (Area of white concentration) population thresholds increased dramatically between 1990 and 2000, indicating increased racial/ethnic mixing among the groups.

Between 1990 and 2000, the location of Dominican enclaves, or concentration areas, has remained highly clustered in northwestern New York County in the Washington Heights/Inwood community district. However, small amounts of dispersion are evident, as Dominican enclaves developed in the Riverdale/ Kingsbridge/Marble Hill and Bedford Park/Norwood/Fordham community districts of southern Bronx County by 2000. Very few Mexican enclaves existed in 1990; those that did were located in four of the five New York City counties. The number of Mexican enclaves increased 508 percent between 1990 and 2000, and became mildly clustered in the following community districts: Sunset Park/Windsor Terrace in western Kings County, in East Harlem in northeastern New York County, and North and South Corona in northern Queens County in 2000. In comparison with the other ethnic groups, Mexican enclaves are the least clustered in 1990 and 2000. Like the number of Mexican enclaves, the number of South American enclaves were fairly small in 1990, but were moderately clustered in the Jackson Heights/North Corona and Elmhurst/South Corona community districts in northern Queens County. By 2000, the majority of the tracts in these community districts developed into South American enclaves. Accordingly, the levels of spatial dependency of South American enclaves increased dramatically between 1990 and 2000, and were the highest clustered type of ethnic enclave in 2000.

Figure 15.3a

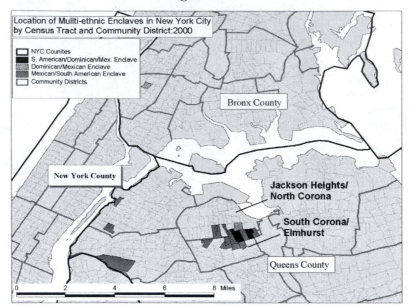

Figure 15.3b

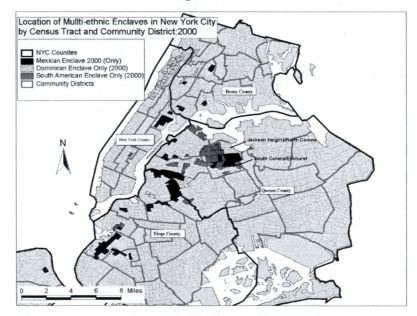

Interethnic differences in the social status of these Latino populations residing within enclaves prevailed in 2000. South Americans displayed the lowest percentage of individuals in poverty within enclaves (19.54%), followed by Dominicans (32.54%), and Mexicans (37.95%). Furthermore, the percentage of South Americans in poverty within enclaves was less than the citywide average for the total population (21.25%), suggesting that South Americans who settle in enclaves may not be economically disadvantaged. Surprisingly, 47 percent of South American households within enclaves were overcrowded in 2000, the second largest proportion in comparison to the other evaluated Latino populations, suggesting that some South Americans are sharing living space while getting a foothold in the U.S. in general and New York City in particular.

Mexican households living within these enclaves, on the other hand, by far live within the most over-crowded units, with over 75 percent of households reporting more than one person per room. Finally, poverty levels of "new immigrants," (entered the United States 1990–2000), living within the "new immigrant areas," varied greatly. Recent Mexican immigrants had the highest percentage of individuals living in poverty within "new immigrant areas" (35%), followed by Dominicans (33%) and South Americans (26%).

NEW YORK LATINOS: FUTURE PROSPECT

New York City, like other geographic regions, is subject to changes. Diverse ethnic groups have long created their unique cultural landscapes and fashioned parts of this city as places of their own. Increased Hispanic settlement has significantly altered the urban landscape of New York City. However, since Hispanics migrate to New York City from a large number of domestic and foreign origins, distinct demographic, socioeconomic, and cultural differences exist between Hispanic populations. As a result, Latino ethnic subgroups settle in many notable neighborhoods and the settlement experience of different Latino ethnicities varies greatly. Some Latino ethnic groups tend to reside in multiethnic/racial neighborhoods, while others are highly isolated in specific areas of the City. Furthermore, significant differences exist in the social status among different Latino populations, putting into question issues of social equity. These issues must be addressed nationwide as Hispanics numbers increase for Latinos are a growing economic and political force that is not likely to be a silent minority in the 21st century. The dispersion of Latinos across America will strengthen their clout in particular places, and their growing presence within regions like New York City will likely make their voices increasingly louder in local political arenas.

NOTES

[1] The terms Hispanic and Latino are used interchangeably in the research.

[2] Locations of AORCs are based upon previous research conducted by Frazier and others (2003). They used population percentages at the tract level as thresholds to designate areas of minority concentration (AOMCs). A shortcoming of this procedure is that it could fail to account for an area with a high population density of a specific group. On the other hand, density measures also have limitations, including large areas with non-residential land use that yield low racial/ethnic densities.

Chapter 16

Placing Transnational Migration:
The Sociospatial Networks of Bolivians in the United States

MARIE D. PRICE

IMMIGRATION, GLOBALIZATION, AND PLACE

One of the less appreciated consequences of globalization has been the increase in economic migrants, especially the movements of international laborers. As global capitalism recreates economic space, it inevitably triggers labor movements (both domestic and international). The United Nations Population Division estimated that 185 million people lived outside their country of birth for at least 12 months in 2000, or roughly 2 percent of the world's population. One in six of these people are found in the United States, the county that in absolute terms attracts more immigrants than any other. The 2000 U.S. Census counted 31 million foreign-born individuals, which equaled 11 percent of the U.S. population. Immigrants, both legal and undocumented, continue to settle in the United States. The most recent Census Bureau figures in 2004 estimated that 36 million foreign-born resided in the U.S., representing over 12 percent of the total population.

The narrative of the immigrant nation is a well-developed theme in United States, and interest in immigration seems to grow with the intensity of the immigrant flows themselves. The booming economy of the 1990s witnessed a parallel surge in immigration to the U.S, comparable to the great wave of immigration at the turn of the 20th century. The major difference between these two great immigrant waves is the composition of the foreign-born by region of birth. In 2000, over half of the foreign-born (52%) were from Latin America; one-quarter of the foreign-born (26%) were from Asia. By contrast, Europeans accounted for just 16 percent of the foreign-born population in Census 2000.

Given the large number of recent immigrants, and their racial and ethnic diversity, it is nearly impossible to discuss race and ethnicity in the U.S. without addressing the impact of immigrants. Perhaps the most dramatic demographic shift is the increase of Hispanics, now the largest minority group in the United States. A recent U.S. Census Bureau report estimated that there were over 41 million Hispanics (both native-born and foreign-born) in 2004, which is approximately 14 percent of the total U.S. population. Well over half of all Hispanics are of Mexican ancestry but there are significant numbers of Hispanics with ancestry in the Caribbean (Cuba and the Dominican Republic), Central America and South America.

This chapter will focus on a small and relatively new group of Hispanic immigrants from the Andean country of Bolivia. By studying a small group that is concentrated in a few cities, it is possible to document how a new immigrant community gains a foothold in the United States, and how it maintains connections with its place of origin. This case study is based on an analysis of census data, government documents, newspaper accounts, and interviews with Bolivians in both the United States and Bolivia. Through the Bolivian experience, the importance of transnational linkages between sending and receiving communities is revealed, even when actual travel between countries can be limited (commonly due to the expense of travel or problems with legal status). The case study also demonstrates the importance of place, both real and remembered, in the everyday practices and experiences of Bolivian immigrants.

Before turning to the Bolivian example, I want to highlight two biases perpetuated in the migration literature that undervalue both place and scale. First is the tendency to focus on <u>immigration</u> (and receiving countries)
rather than emigration (and sending countries). One's perception of migration changes sharply when viewed from
the economic periphery in countries such as Bolivia. Today, emigration is often a response to social and economic
crises brought about by structural adjustment policies and neo-liberalism, political upheaval, demographic growth,
and the accelerated integration of developing economies into global markets. Throughout Latin America, individuals, households and communities are responding to these changes by considering themselves part of an international (if not global) workforce. As one former Bolivian migrant told me "we send workers everywhere, not just to
the U.S. and Argentina. In this village there are pioneers who have moved to Israel, Japan, Spain and Germany to
find work. If they find it, others follow." Thus, it is vital to understand migration as a dynamic system that impacts
sending and receiving communities in different ways.

Secondly, immigration scholars rely on the nation-state as the container of convenience when analyzing
immigration flows. Most migrants move, not to countries per se, but to particular cities that are significant in the
global economy (Benton-Short et al., in press). Thus the impact of immigration looks extremely different when
one shifts scale from nation-level data to urban-level data. Nationally, immigrants made up 12 percent of the
total U.S. population in 2004. In classic immigrant destinations such as metropolitan New York or Los Angeles,
the foreign-born make up one-third of the total population (Singer, 2004). In metropolitan Washington, the leading destination for Bolivian immigrants, one-in-six residents are foreign-born (U.S. Census, 2000). Metropolitan
areas in the U.S. host the majority of the foreign-born. From that scale, the intensity of the immigrant question
becomes much more important when examining labor markets and the supply of basic services (most notably
education, housing, public transportation and healthcare). This case study seeks to correct these imbalances in
the immigration literature by documenting the impact of immigration on sending and receiving localities and
focusing on the urban scale. But before developing the Bolivian example, it is important to consider the concept
of the transnational migrant.

THE RISE OF THE TRANSNATIONAL MIGRANT

The concept of transnationalism as applied to migration began to surface in late 1980s, largely through
the work of anthropologists studying the social and economic impacts of migration on households and sending
communities (Thomas-Hope, 1988; Georges, 1990; Grasmuck and Pessar, 1991; Basch et al., 1994). Transnationalism is an attempt to theorize the complex linkages and dual identities that a globalized economy is bound
to generate. In the book *Nations Unbound* (1994), the authors offer a working definition of transnational migration as "the process by which immigrants forge and sustain multi-stranded relations that link together their
societies of origin and settlement" and in the process "immigrants today build social fields that cross geographic, cultural and political borders" (Basch et al., 1994, p. 7).

Whether or not transnational migration is anything new is a subject of considerable debate. Nancy Foner's
detailed work comparing New York City's immigrants over 100 years is a clear reminder that the processes we call
transnational today have a long history (Foner, 2000, p. 169). She offers the compelling example of Italian immigrants at the turn of the 20th century who maintained social, political and economic links with their communities
of origin while at the same time building social networks among themselves in their new home. Italian immigrants
did this for many of the same reasons that today's "transnational migrants" maintain linkages: there were relatives
left behind, and many others who either returned or intended to return to Italy. Further, lack of full acceptance in
America stimulated migrants' continued involvement with home (Foner, 2000, p. 171). Similarly, Italian government officials over a century ago recognized that members of the diaspora were an important resource that should
not be lost. Similar efforts occur today when politicians court and respond to the needs of emigrants abroad.

Foner is correct in observing that there is a tendency to overuse the concept and ascribe transnational
qualities to all international migrations (1997). Migration scholars Castles and Miller suggest that the defining
aspect of the transnational migrant is that "transnational activities are a central part of a person's life" (2003, p.
30). In this Bolivian case study, I contend that the transnational migrants are those who actively maintain link-

ages with their sending countries, and in the process create an identity that is someplace in-between being Bolivian and being American. Not all Bolivians are transnational migrants. Yet transnationalism is fostered within the Bolivian community by the continuous flows of immigrants form particular localities, the availability of employment in the U.S., improvements in communication and money transfer technologies, and uncertain legal status that makes it important to maintain linkages with one's home country. Together, these factors increase the likelihood for transnational connections to be maintained for both the good of the individual migrant and the sending community. The decision to emigrate is still a difficult one, yet as transnational livelihoods become more common, sociospatial networks are created that cater to a transnational existence where individual migrants live someplace in-between being a settler and a sojourner.

An outgrowth of transnationalism is the idea of a transnational community (Levitt, 2001). Alejandro Portes (1997) argues that transnational communities are fueled by the dynamics of globalization itself and have become a popular means for places on the economic periphery to respond to the pernicious and transformative reach of global capital. The formation of such communities is an unanticipated and a relatively understudied outcome of globalization. To quote Portes:

> "What common people have done in response to the process of globalization is to create communities that sit astride political borders and that, in a very real sense, are 'neither here nor there' but in both places simultaneously. The economic activities that sustain these communities are grounded precisely on the differentials of advantage created by state boundaries. In this respect, they are no different from the large global corporations, except that these enterprises emerge at the grassroots level and its (*sic*) activities are often informal" (1997, pp. 2–3).

Transnational communities are a response to structural economic forces but human agency, cultural practices, and cumulative-causation models are equally important in explaining their existence (Massey et al., 1994). Transnational communities need to be understood as fluid spatial fields rather than concrete and discrete spaces, which poses a challenge to conventional notions of ethnic space. Whether transnational communities can be maintained into the second or third generation remains to be seen.

In many immigrant gateways such as Washington, D.C., transnational communities are not ethnic enclaves, like a Chinatown, which can be clearly identified by outsiders. Today's transnational communities are more likely to be heterolocal in nature; that is, communities without propinquity (Zelinksy and Lee, 1998). Folded into the suburban fabric of the major metropolitan areas in the United States, for example, transnational communities exist through weekend religious, sporting, and other cultural events. Through such activities a sense of community is maintained and real ties between sending and receiving communities are nurtured.

In order to place the workings of a transnational community, I turn to the case of Bolivian migration to metropolitan Washington, D.C. There are four aspects of this immigrant group that will be addressed: 1) these are economic migrants who decided to leave their country based on poor economic conditions there and greater economic opportunities in the United States; 2) the study area in Bolivia, the Valle Alto of Cochabamba, has an established history of emigration, especially to Argentina and the United States, so that strategies to cope with long-distance livelihoods exist; 3) once in metropolitan Washington, immigrants have developed extensive social networks, this facilitates the difficult transition into a new country, reinforces the likelihood of future migrations, and maintains a transnational flow of goods, people and information; and 4) transnational linkages between Valle Alto villages and Bolivian residents abroad materially sustain these Bolivian localities, while providing a valuable emotional space for Bolivians in Washington, even if they are unable to visit that place for many years.

BOLIVIANS IN METROPOLITAN WASHINGTON

At the national level, Bolivians are a tiny immigrant group representing 0.2 percent of the foreign-born in 2000. Yet, if we shift to individual states, the picture is different. In the state of Virginia, which has the largest number of Bolivians, they represent nearly three percent of the state's foreign-born. In metropolitan Washington, individuals born in Bolivia total some 20,000, which makes them about 2.5 percent of Washington's foreign-born. Yet, the most striking statistic is that 37 percent of Bolivians recorded in the 2000 Census reside in metropolitan Washington, making it the top destination for this immigrant group (Table 16.1). This percentage is four times greater than the second most popular destination, metropolitan New York.

Table 16.1: Top Metropolitan Areas for Bolivian Immigrants

Top Metropolitan Areas for Bolivian Immigrants	Total Number of Foreign-Born Bolivians	Percent of all Bolivians in U.S.
Washington, DC — MD — VA — WV, PMSA	19,558	37
New York, NY, PMSA	4,384	8
Los Angeles — Long Beach PMSA	3,245	6
Miami, FL, PMSA	2,981	6
Orange County, CA, PMSA	1,665	3
Houston, TX, PMSA	1,191	2
United States	**53,278**	**100**

Source: U.S. Bureau of the Census, Census 2000, Summary File 3

Figure 16.1

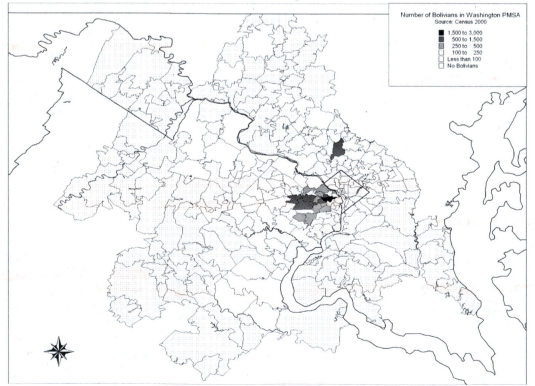

Bolivians in the Washington D.C. PMSA

Bolivian emigration to Washington has its roots in the late 1960s, but the numbers of migrants were very small and mostly of European ancestry. The vast majority of Bolivians today have settled here in the past 20 years and are more representative of Bolivia's mixed ancestry of Indian and European. From 1980 to 1990, the Bolivian community in Washington tripled in size. It then doubled in size from 1990 to 2000, nearing 20,000.[1] Bolivians initially came to Washington in the 1980s because there were plenty of jobs and relatively little competition from other Latino immigrants. The community grew via chain migration, family unification policies, and an ethnic economy in which small Bolivian businesses based on home services (especially house cleaning and child care) and construction grew by employing other co-ethnics or sponsoring immigrants.

As Figure 16.1 illustrates, Bolivians reside throughout the metropolitan area but they are more likely to live in the suburban counties than in the District of Columbia proper. Arlington, Annandale, and Springfield, Virginia, as well as Wheaton, Maryland, are important areas of concentration for Bolivian immigrants. In these localities one is likely to find restaurants that serve Bolivian specialties such as peanut soup or *salteñas*. There are also likely to be social organizations such as soccer leagues and folkloric dance groups. Yet it is not possible to find a "Little Bolivia," that is, an ethnic enclave of only Bolivians. The localities in which Bolivians are concentrated tend to be the same areas popular with many other immigrants in the region, and this reality precludes the formation of a distinct ethnic enclave (Price et al., 2005).

Rather than a discrete neighborhood, it is a vibrant network of immigrant-created organizations that maintain social networks and supply a sense of belonging and familiarity that support Bolivian immigrants and a transnational livelihood. One young woman who came from Bolivia as a child and now works for a state government, described her upbringing in Arlington as part of a rich and protective Bolivian social world in which weekends were filled with Bolivian activities, family and friends. "As a child in the U.S., I lived Bolivian and ate Bolivian. I had never been to a Bennigan's (a chain restaurant) until I was a college student. In Arlington this is possible." Such an ethnic cocoon can facilitate immigrant economic integration into the American mainstream but it may impede social integration.

Bolivian migrants have a different socio-economic profile than the average Hispanic migrant (who typically is Mexican). The considerable distance traveled and the expense of travel from South America tends to screen out poorer and less educated potential migrants. In general, those who come to the U.S. have a level of education comparable to U.S. averages, and in some cases higher. Based on U.S. Census data regarding people who reported Bolivian ancestry, 96 percent had high school diplomas, 36 percent had bachelor's degrees or higher, and 11 percent had Master's degrees or higher; each of these levels exceeded U.S. averages for educational attainment. Of those reporting Bolivian ancestry, only one in four was born in the United States, underscoring the relative youth of this immigrant flow. This group also had a median household income of $47,000, which was $5,000 more than the U.S. median household income (U.S. Census, 2000). While these data do not capture all Bolivian immigrants, they do suggest that those who come to the U.S. arrive with more social capital, which tends to place them in a privileged position relative to other Hispanic immigrants.

Bolivian educational attainment does not automatically translate into professional recognition in the United States. Many Bolivians who settle in the U.S. do not have their professional credentials recognized and find employment in jobs for which they are over qualified. It is not uncommon for medical doctors to work as lab technicians or as home healthcare aides. Bolivian-trained engineers and architects may get jobs in construction. For these people, migration to the U.S. almost always results in earning more money than one could in Bolivia but also experiencing a loss in social status, either temporarily or permanently.

Perhaps most surprising to new Bolivian immigrants, is that migration to the U.S. often results in a new racial identity. Many Bolivians who consider themselves white in Bolivia are surprised to learn they are not viewed as "white" in the U.S. but as non-white Hispanic and part of an ethnic minority. Bolivia has its own national hierarchy regarding race that carefully distinguishes white, mestizos (mixed-race peoples) and Indians (Klein, 1992). Fitting into U.S. racial categories is not easy, and many Bolivians immigrants who sit atop the racial hierarchy in their own country experience racism for the first time as a minority in the United States.

For some immigrants the difficult transition to an American lifestyle, coupled with the experience of discrimination and lower social status, drives them to return. Bolivian immigrant Israel Canelas wrote a small paperback book, *The Dishwashers of the North* (1994), describing his experiences in Northern Virginia in the 1980s. The dishwashers he refers to are recent immigrants in low-status jobs. The book testifies to the tough circumstances facing recent immigrants such as over-crowding, distance from family, language problems, legal status, alcoholism, racial discrimination, and exploitation by Americans and other Bolivians. The fact that such a book exists and is sold in the bookstores in Cochabamba indicates that there is public interest in the topic of emigration. Canelas' stated intent is to debunk the myth of Bolivian immigrant success. He implores readers not to journey north but to do their best to remain in Bolivia.

Bolivians arrive as legal migrants and as undocumented ones. Immigration and Naturalization Services (INS)[2] data from 1990–98 recorded 5,644 Bolivians intending to reside in the Washington metropolitan area (Singer et al., 2001). There are also many undocumented arrivals, with Bolivians crossing the border illegally (using Mexican coyotes and paying up to $8,000 to enter) or legally entering on a tourist visa and then overstaying their visa and thus becoming an illegal migrant. For example, from July 1998 to July 1999, over 18,000 non-immigrant tourist visas where issued by the U.S. Embassy in La Paz, Bolivia (a typical figure for much of the 1990s). Embassy staff interviewed also acknowledged that visa seekers from Cochabamba were disproportionately greater (both in visas granted and denied).

The costs and benefits associated with straddling such vast distances intensify when an immigrant enters the U.S. illegally or overstays a visa. In the summer of 2003, Catalina Morrales sat in front of the newly constructed church and plaza in the small village of La Loma in the Department of Cochabamba. The handsome additions were built with money sent form villagers working in Washington, and they are so recognized by a bronze plague placed in the plaza. All six of Catalina's adult children live in metropolitan Washington; the boys work in construction and the girls clean houses. The first two entered in 1999, another two followed in 2000, and the last two left in 2002. All entered without papers. "They left" she says, "because there is no work here." Her children left with their spouses and have had their own children in the U.S. whom Catalina knows only through photos. "When my children get their *residencia* (green card) they will come every year to see me, but now they can't." Given their undocumented status in the U.S., a trip home without legal residence would result in their deportation and the imposition of a ten-year ban from legal entry to the U.S. as tourists or immigrants. Yet those who cannot physically return to their homelands use money and social networks to maintain contact with far away homes.

The Importance of Place: The Bolivian Context

As geographers Rachel Silvey and Vicky Lawson (1999) observe, migration studies in geography in the 1960s through the 1980s often took a developmentalist perspective in which the "origins and destinations (of migrants) were the unproblematic stages upon which migration was played out" (1999, p. 122). We now know that these stages matter greatly, providing the sociospatial setting in which identities are shaped, decisions to move or not to move are made, and for those places that send labor abroad, sometimes transnational connections are fostered.

Bolivia is a poor country, one of the poorest in the Western Hemisphere. Labor mobility has been a time-honored strategy in Bolivia for dealing with limited resources and the country has experienced significant demographic shifts in the past century from the highlands to lowland frontiers, from rural areas to cities, and increasingly to labor markets abroad. Much of the scholarly work on Bolivian emigration has focused on an older and far greater stream of migrants to Argentina (Whiteford, 1981; Benencia and Karasik, 1994; Dandler and Medeiros, 1988), where 1.5 million ethnic Bolivians live, many of them of mestizo and Indian ancestry.

Within this context of internal mobility, certain areas of Bolivia are known for producing emigrants, especially the Department of Cochabamba. Considered in colonial times through the 19th century as the breadbasket of Bolivia, this department is known now as a region that expels labor (Larson and Harris, 1995). Part of the problem is limited land resources and the division of land between more and more people reduces the amount of land available to any one person. Climatic change has found the valley drier throughout the 20th century, which has limited its agricultural productivity. Furthermore, as free trade has opened up new markets, cheaper grains from elsewhere in South America has made grain production in Cochabamba less financially viable.

Opportunities elsewhere within Bolivia also contributed to the tendency for people to leave rural Cochabamba, especially the region known as the Valle Alto. In the 1950s and 1960s peasant farmers were attracted to the tropical plains around Santa Cruz where both large-scale mechanized farming and land colonization schemes turned the plains into Bolivia's most dynamic and productive agricultural region (Stearman, 1985). Like other developing countries, rural people moved to urban areas and the city of Cochabamba grew disproportionately faster than its surrounding municipalities. In the 1970s and 1980s, Cochabamba peasants also took advantage of the coca boom (the plant used to produce cocaine), moving into the forests of the Chapare to plant coca (Sanabria, 1993). This particular flow of settlers slowed in the 1990s with international and internal pressure to reduce coca production.

International labor flows from Cochabamba were evident by the 1960s as seasonal migration to wealthier Argentina began with sugarcane harvests in northern Argentina and evolved into more permanent settlement of Bolivian immigrants in the city of Buenos Aires (Repado, 1981). By the 1980s, employment opportunities in the United States became widely known and the trickle of economic migrants to cities such as Washington, New York, Miami, and Los Angeles began. As Argentina's economic situation worsened in the 1990s, the search for foreign employment destinations became more targeted to the U.S. (Figure 16.2).

Figure 16.2
***Teenagers in the Valle Alto share their plans to emigrate to the United States where most
already had extended family living and working in Washington. (Photo by author).***

When driving the dirt roads of the Valle Alto, the villages that have migrants working in Washington are easily spotted. These are the settings where new and large homes rise above the one-story whitewashed adobe structures that dominate small villages. New cars, bicycles, and satellite dishes dot the landscape. Renovated plazas and schools, new churches, basketball courts, and soccer fields are found. Yet there is often a strange quiet about these places, which tend to be disproportionately populated by the young and the old, with working-age people scarce. The rhythms of village life are punctuated by long lines of people at the end of the month looking for remittances sent via wire transfer services. Also common are lines of women and children waiting for international calls outside the village telephone service. There are the festive days, especially around Christmas, Carnival, and August when triumphant migrants return with gifts and lavish parties are thrown. However, the long days of waiting for news, money or a telephone call from a loved one far away are not uncommon.

Data obtained from the Department of Migration in Cochabamba show the importance of the United States as a destination. In the year 2001 alone, over 7,000 of the 20,000 Cochabambinos who moved abroad, indicated the United States was their intended destination (35%).[3] From this same government registry data for the years 1994–2003 (although incomplete for some years), show that over 24,000 people from the Department of Cochabamba reported travel to the United States with the intent to reside there. It should also be noted that these patterns can suddenly shift given political changes both in the U.S. and elsewhere. During the first five months of 2003, the number of Cochabambinos leaving remained the same but the destination shifted to Spain (40% of the flow), while the U.S. received just 16 percent of the flow. Tourist and immigrant visas became more difficult for Bolivians to get after the terrorist attacks in September, 2001. In contrast, Spain had opened its doors to immigrants from its former colonies.

Within the Department of Cochabamba, most emigrants seem to come from the city of Cochabamba and its environs, and the villages south of the city in an agricultural area referred to as the Valle Alto. When asked why them came to Washington, nearly every immigrant mentions jobs. The Washington metropolitan area is affluent, with one of the highest median household incomes in the country; and it is growing. Thus, there is a sizeable population demanding cleaning services, nannies, home improvements, new housing, and ready-made meals. Up until the mid-1980s, there were relatively few Hispanics in the metropolitan area. This meant that there was less competition for domestic, service, and low-skilled jobs that immigrants often fill, especially when compared to the larger Hispanic immigrant destinations such as Los Angeles, New York City, and Miami. But most importantly, the social networks Bolivians rely upon to emigrate, lead them to the suburbs of Washington.

BOLIVIAN SOCIAL NETWORKS

Although Washington is the principal destination for Bolivians, their imprint on the region is surprisingly limited as no discrete ethnic enclave exists. Socially, however, a remarkable network of soccer clubs, cultural and village-based associations, travel services, and media exist that support the Bolivian community and build upon their transnational identity. Thus there is a contradiction between the limited physical expression of their community and the complex social networks that have evolved that support Bolivian immigrants abroad and maintain important transnational linkages with their communities of origin.

Adult recreational soccer leagues are an essential component of Bolivian immigrant life. What is more interesting, is that they are often organized along Bolivian regional/provincial lines so they provide an opportunity for laborers to get together with other people from their home villages once or twice a week and play a game that they love. On Sundays, wives, sisters, sons, and daughters come to watch the games and socialize. In metropolitan Washington there are at least four exclusively Bolivian soccer leagues, each with a dozen teams or more. One Bolivian league, INCOPEA, has organized its teams to represent various villages in the Valle Alto. The league uses soccer events to raise money for building basketball courts, schools, churches, and new soccer fields in the villages represented by the teams (Price and Whitworth, 2004). Thus team Tiataco supplied money to build a social hall in the center of their village, while team Achamoco raised funds to build a new Catholic church and improve the village school. For many immigrant men, soccer leagues are the first and often only Bolivian organization they join while living in the U.S. Yet through soccer they maintain contact with people from their village or province, learn of job opportunities, socialize, and play a game they love with people who know them. In many ways soccer leagues epitomize the real yet ephemeral social spaces that Bolivian immigrants carve for themselves in Washington. Yet such networks are vital for the transnational linkages that sustain Bolivians in the U.S. and communities in Bolivia.

Like soccer, folkloric dance groups are also important for fostering transnational ties, especially for the children of immigrants. Through dance, children and teenagers learn to take pride in Bolivian culture and perform at numerous festivals in the U.S. and Bolivia. As one young woman described to me, "I didn't feel very Bolivian until I joined a dance group. At first my mom made me go, but now I do it because I love it." There are nearly two dozen Bolivian dance groups in greater Washington. Most of the groups purchase their costumes directly from sources in Bolivia. For over a decade, most major Washington, D.C. parades include a Bolivian dance troop marching down the street in their brightly colored costumes complete with layered mini-skirts and boots. Such groups are a public face of Bolivian culture present at such events as the Cherry Blossom Festival, the Latino Festival, and Independence Day parades on the Mall. Yet, dance groups are also networked among metropolitan areas. Groups travel to compete in regional competitions, such as the one held in Alexandria, Virginia in 2004 that included 15 groups from Washington, New York and Florida. The best funded groups even travel to Cochabamba to participate in the Virgin de Urkupiña festival in August where thousands of people dance in the streets.

Village-based associations are another expression of transnationalism used by many immigrant communities. Such groups are formed to channel resources, provide social outlets and to organize charity work for the communities of origin. One group, the Comité Pro-Tarata, represents over 300 people from the small town of Tarata in the Valle Alto. Their various activities have included reconstructing a historic tower in their town plaza and sponsoring artists from Tarata to perform at annual events in Washington. Another group, representing the village of Mizque, sent money and goods to the village after a major earthquake in 1998. Another group Comité Pro-Boliviana organizes yearly charitable contributions of clothes, toys and medicines for Cochabamba.

In addition to cultural organizations, print and broadcast journalism are vital tools for information exchange among Bolivians. Bolivian-produced Spanish language newspapers and radio shows draw an audience in Washington and Cochabamba. Free weekly/monthly newspapers such as *Bolivia Today* or *El Bolivariano* have existed for nearly a decade. In 2004, the largest newspaper in Cochabamba, *Los Tiempos*, began a weekly U.S. edition of its paper just for the Washington community. A radio show (Radio Barinquen) has a weekly simulcast show (*Viva mi Patria Bolivia*) between Washington and Cochabamba where callers from either continent can all in and communicate with each other and the rest of the Bolivian community. And, like many other immigrant communities, Bolivians use their independence day (August 6) to organize a massive outside gathering of Bolivians to celebrate their national culture, and cuisine. Figure 16.3 is an independence celebration in the late 1990s that brought over 10,000 Bolivians together at an Arlington, Virginia high school.

Finally, the Bolivian School (*Escuela Bolivia*) was established in 1998 through cooperation with the Bolivian Embassy and the Arlington County School District; the school runs on Saturdays in an Arlington elementary school. Most of the instructors are volunteers and the curriculum is taught in Spanish. Using Bolivian textbooks, children learn music, culture, government, geography, and history of Bolivia. The cost is minimal (only $60 a semester) and typically 100–200 students enroll. Although anyone can enroll, most of the students are either Bolivian by birth or their parents are Bolivian. One of the school's founders, Emma Violand-Sanchez, is Bolivian-born and works for the Arlington County School District. The purpose of this school is to make sure that the children of immigrants maintain their identity with and understanding of Bolivia. In a transnational world, such an education is valued not just by individuals but by the state, as the Bolivian Embassy contributes to this program.

TRANSNATIONAL MIGRANTS/TRANSNATIONAL SPACES

The aim of this case study is to ground transnational migration by selecting two points (Washington and Cochabamba) and articulating the social fields created by migrants that link these localities. In so doing, it suggests that transnational flows, rather than being amorphous, are tied to specific points on the map. Transnational lives become ones in which identity can be uncoupled from place (like the U.S.-born child raised in a Bolivian social world). Yet real places, be they the villages of the Valle Alto or the suburbs of Washington, are also changed by these transnational labor flows.

Figure 16.3
An independence celebration in the late 1990s that brought over
10,000 Bolivians together at an Arlington, Virginia high school.

From the Bolivian perspective this transnational experience is driven by economic need. Structural, political and environmental forces have conspired time and again to drive Bolivians out. Consequently, systems of reciprocity and labor migration have been modified and adapted through time to accommodate basic survival. Today in Latin America's neo-liberal climate, dollars freely circulate in the country and most shops will take them as willingly as they take their national currency. People leave and yet they return (perhaps with a hybrid identity). A recent Bolivian President, Sanchez de Lozada, who was forced out of office in 2004, was referred to as the "Falso Gringo" because of his heavily accented Spanish after years of living and working in the United States.

Perhaps the maintenance of linkages to one's country of birth is instilled in Bolivians from an imbedded sense of reciprocity that is nurtured through time and experience. A pattern of exporting labor to sustain rural places and livelihoods is well established, especially in the Valle Alto. Moreover, one cannot underestimate the value of staying connected to far away places as an emotional safety net when the lives of immigrants in Washington can be extremely challenging economically, socially and culturally.

Immigration is the human face of economic globalization: the flows may shift, but there is little room for doubt that the number of people who leave their country of birth for employment elsewhere will continue to grow. Given that, it is important that we as scholars develop multiple field sites and make linkages between real places. In conducting this work, sensitivity to scale results in understanding different kinds of flows of people and different levels in which places are impacted. In addition to awareness of scale, there is also the need to be sensitive to the differentiation of place — the different meanings migrants ascribe to the places they leave and where they settle, but also the different ways these same people are perceived in places. Lastly, the socio-spatial challenge of transnationalism is to understand how place, space, and identity are reconceptualized by the experiences of immigrants resulting in new social spaces that are neither here nor there but some place in between.

NOTES

[1] This figure is only the foreign-born counted in the U.S. Census in 2000, the children of Bolivians would not be counted thus the ethnic community is certainly larger.

[2] INS became CIS (Citizenship and Immigration Services) in 2003 and was transferred from the Department of Justice to the Department of Homeland Security. CIS no longer makes the intended zip code of residence data available for legal permanent residents entering the U.S.

[3] The next most popular destination was Chile (19%) and then Argentina (17%). This is a significant departure from earlier patterns, in 1994 one-third of all people leaving Cochabamba for abroad were headed to Argentina.

Chapter 17

Immigrant Accommodation and Intra-Ethnic Friction:
The Case of Mexicans and Mexican Americans in San Antonio

RICHARD C. JONES

INTRODUCTION

"The Changing Heartland," the "Hispanic Disapora," "Tragedy in a Place of Quiet Serenity" are bylines of popular articles that have captured the attention of Americans in the past few years and placed on the map towns such as Morganton and Siler City, North Carolina; Rogers, Arkansas; Dalton, Georgia; Denison, Iowa; and Garden City, Kansas (Foust et al., 2002; Yeoman, 2000; Campo-Flores, 2001; Fountain, 2002; Stull and Broadway, 2004). Latino immigrants, especially Mexicans, have arrived in homogenous rural communities of the Midwest and traditionally bi-racial communities of the South, in such numbers that the only way to express it is demographic metamorphosis. At the same time, communities with long histories of immigration continue to receive immigrants and are finding challenges as they reshape urban landscapes. Such is the case of San Antonio, Texas. Located in a border state, San Antonio has a Mexican-American population that traces back generations. It also has experienced substantial Mexican immigration in recent decades. One might suspect that given its legacy with Mexico and having a large Mexican-American population in place, this community would provide a relatively friendly environment that would readily accommodate the newer Mexican immigrants. As we shall see, this is not the case for a number of reasons.

This chapter investigates the **spatial patterns** and the **accommodation** (social and cultural adjustment to the larger society) of Mexican immigrants in relation to Anglos and Mexican Americans in Bexar County (San Antonio), Texas — a metropolitan county with 1.4 million persons in 2000. Census tract data from the 1990 and 2000 U.S. Census; photographs; and household interviews are employed to describe and visualize these patterns. This chapter spotlights first-generation immigrants — not the second and later generations that are the focus of most assimilation studies. Obviously, changes in the attitudes and behaviors of the immigrants themselves cannot be used to form final opinions on accommodation. However, in the U.S. (as in San Antonio) a 60 percent increase in Latino immigration over the 1990s suggests that first-generation assimilation (or lack of it) is an important issue that researchers and policy makers would be wise to address now, rather than defer to future generations.

ACCOMMODATION OF MEXICAN IMMIGRANTS IN THE SOUTHWEST

The literature reveals two separate processes involved in immigrant accommodation: (1) **integration**, defined as social interaction with the host society at various levels, and (2) **acculturation**, defined as adoption of host society cultural traits. These are, in fact, two distinct dimensions of accommodation, suggesting a typology (Figure 17.1). A situation of low acculturation and high integration is exemplified by many Chinese, Asian Indian, and Arab communities in the United States. These groups provide a good example of **selective acculturation** (Portes and Rumbaut, 1996) — the adoption or exercising of cultural traits that benefit their integration (such as education, hard work, and honesty), while rejecting others that impede it (such as aberrant religious or marriage practices).

Conversely, an ethnic group may lose or be forced to abandon its culture, and at the same time lack any significant societal contacts. The situation of high acculturation and low integration would apply to an urban immigrant underclass such as "Cholos" (chicanos) or black Caribbean and African migrants, who acculturate into dysfunctional inner-city subcultures, and thus remain isolated and marginalized, a process termed ***dissonant acculturation*** (Portes and Rumbaut, 1996; Berry, 1990; Hintzen, 2001; Smith, 2001; Stoller, 2001). Integration accompanied by acculturation is exemplified by Western European groups that have been in the U.S. for generations and are ethnically and culturally indistinguishable from the White Anglo-Saxon Protestant (WASP) mainstream. Finally, the joint absence of both acculturation and integration is exemplified by Hmong and Mexicans. These groups are separated by low socio-economic status and discrimination from the traditional mainstream, but they are not socialized into an urban underclass.

Figure 17.1

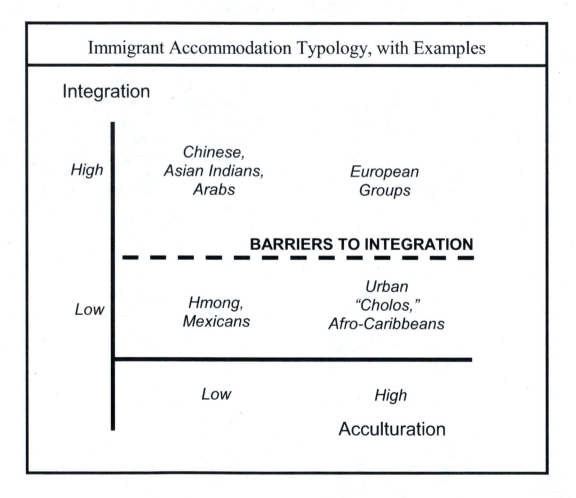

The literature recognizes several *barriers to integration* that tend to separate different immigrant groups on the integration dimension of the above typology. These include: (1) discrimination toward that group by the host society, (2) the pressure to conform to dissonant norms, (3) lack of incentives to interact with the larger society, (4) low levels of community and family resources, and (5) immigration status. These barriers are represented by the horizontal dashed line in Figure 17.1. Where, as in the case of Mexican immigrants, the group faces discrimination on the job (in part owing to undocumented status), temporariness, and low socioeconomic status, the level of integration with the larger society is lower than in the cases of "model minorities" such as those indicated at the top of the figure.

The popular articles initially cited reflect nativism and discrimination towards Mexican migrants in Southern and Midwestern communities. These migrants practice their culture under the microscope of community disapproval, which coupled with their legal status causes many of them to "navigate under the radar" and keep a low profile. In the Southwest, Mexican immigrants often face this same covert and overt disapproval on the part of "Anglo" residents (Ortiz, 1996; Ramos, 2002, p. 29). This is not really surprising, given the upper southern and midwestern roots of most Anglo-Texans (Meinig, 1969; Jordan et al., 1984).

However, in the Southwest, Mexican immigrants would seem to have the benefit of a mediating culture — that of Mexican Americans — to represent their interests and concerns. As two immigration scholars noted:

> "(American) mainstream culture, which is highly variegated in any event — by social class and region, among other factors — changes as elements of the cultures of the newer groups are incorporated into it. The composite culture that we identify with the mainstream is made up of multiple interpenetrating layers and allows individuals and sub-populations to forge identities out of its materials to distinguish themselves from others in the mainstream" (Alba and Nee, 2003, p. 13).

Based on this notion of the reconstituted cultural mainstream, some would argue that a single "composite culture" of Mexicans and Mexican Americans exists in the Southwest, and that this culture is slowly merging with Anglo culture. In support of this notion one might cite the increasingly conservative political leanings of upwardly mobile Hispanics (Michelson, 2001), or recent reports suggesting that Hispanic residential segregation is declining in the Southwest, even as it increases elsewhere in the country (Fields and Herndon, 2001).

Few, however, have examined the social and spatial relationships between Mexicans and Mexican Americans in the Southwest. It is often assumed that Mexican Americans constitute a step in the process of transforming Mexicans to Americans. However, Dan Arreola's book *Tejano South Texas* (2002) dispels that notion, by documenting a new culture and cultural province defined by foods, music, fiestas, language and political organizations, which are resilient and quite separate from core (interior) Mexican culture. Other research suggests that an adversarial relationship exists between Mexicans and Mexican Americans. The immigration literature, for example, expounds on reciprocal stereotypes — by Mexicans of the "cholo" or "pachuco" (Mexican American) who has abandoned his roots and country (López-Castro, 1986), and by Mexican Americans of the poor, uneducated immigrant fleeing Mexican poverty, corruption, and crime (Shain, 1999; 2000). Mexican Americans may attempt to distance themselves from their Mexican roots by criticizing Mexico in various ways to others, avoiding travel there, and de-emphasizing Spanish in the home — part of a process that has been referred to as *disidentification* with one's own ancestry group (Kibria, 2002, p. 88). Interestingly, the majority culture of both countries looks down on Mexican Americans, identifying them with the vices of the other country. Arguably, this mutual estrangement has contributed to the emergence of the Tejano cultural region. As Mexican Americans move more into the mainstream owing to economic and political success — i.e., as they move closer to Anglo majority norms — they may become less concerned about discrimination against immigrants of their own ethnic group. Hispanic support of immigrants in the middle 1990s (Rosales et al., 2001) hinged upon issues such as Proposition 187 in California and IRIRA (The Immigration Reform and Immigrant Responsibility Act of 1996); this support declined as Hispanics advanced economically in the late 1990s. The Hispanic political agenda shifted to emphasize crime, gangs, and drugs, rather than immigration (Lee et al., 2001; Michelson, 2001; Michelson and Pallares, 2001; Ono, 2002).

For this research on San Antonio, the following questions were asked: (1) Has the segregation of Latino immigrants (from both Anglos and Mexican Americans) increased or decreased since 1990? (2) Are Mexican homes clustered together, and do they stand out on the urban landscape? (3) Do Mexican immigrants exhibit low or high levels of accommodation with Mexican Americans, and how does this compare to their accommodation with Anglos? Before discussing findings of this research, a brief geographical and historical sketch of San Antonio is offered to provide context for the analysis.

SAN ANTONIO: GEOGRAPHICAL AND HISTORICAL BACKGROUND

The Spanish found San Antonio an ideal site and situation for establishment of their five missions and civil settlement in the early 1700s. The city provided spring water and agricultural land on the San Antonio River, limestone and timber along the Balcones escarpment, a healthful climate, and a position midway between their provincial capital in Coahuila and their strategic East Texas missions. During the Spanish (1720–1821) and Mexican (1821–36) periods, the city was the administrative capital of south Texas and the effective boundary between Mexico and Anglo-Texas — a place quite different from either Austin, the administrative core, or Nacogdoches, the frontier outpost for upper southern Anglos (Meinig, 1969).

After Texas independence (1836–45) and statehood (1846+), the demographic and industrial growth of the state was concentrated in the latter areas, particularly Dallas, Houston, and (later) the High Plains. The border region — mostly hot, dry ranching country — grew slowly, largely due to natural increase, even after railroad connections were forged to the south and west. Until the 1960s, San Antonio exemplified the familiar south Texas pattern of an Anglo elite and a "Mexican" working class. The city's business elite was overwhelmingly European (German, English, Irish, Polish, Belgian) and its service and manufacturing workers were Mexican (Jones, 2005). Hispanics had limited opportunities in politics, higher education, and business.

This changed after 1960. The American Civil Rights Movement, political activism on the part of South Texas Hispanics (beginning in Crystal City in 1963), and rapid demographic growth stimulated by migration from Mexico reversed these trends and led to the emergence of Mexican Americans as a political and economic force in San Antonio and South Texas. In 1973, COPS (the Communities Organized for Public Service) was founded to campaign for flood control in Hispanic neighborhoods (Rosales, 2000). It evolved into a broad social movement dedicated to bringing better jobs and social services to Hispanics in the inner city. In the 1970s and 1980s San Antonio-based organizations such as MALDEF (the Mexican American Legal Defense and Education Fund), LULAC (the League of United Latin American Citizens), SVRP (the Southwest Voters' Registration Project), WVRI (the Willie Velasquez Research Institute), and HACU (the Hispanic Association of Colleges and Universities) became forces for change in San Antonio and the entire Southwest. San Antonio's Hispanic "minority" has since grown to a majority, aided by the strong representation and mobility of Hispanics in the military, health care, tourism, and trade sectors — mainstays of the city's economic base. With their newfound economic and social mobility, San Antonio's Hispanic community is today on equal political footing with Anglos in city government as well as in the schools, the community college district, and the hospital district. Furthermore, they enjoy a much more equitable access to social services and infrastructure than in the recent past.

Onto this picture of an emerging Tejano political-economic force, another pattern has been superimposed in recent years — rapid immigration from Mexico. Over the 1990s the population of Bexar County grew 18 percent while the Mexican American population grew 28 percent, and the Latino immigrant population, 58 percent. These new Mexican immigrants are more urbanized and educated than past waves; still, they are typically of much lower socio-economic status than their hosts, and they are politically powerless given their (often) undocumented status. They present a series of dilemmas to their hosts. For Mexican Americans specifically, the question is this: How can these new Mexican immigrants be embraced as equals when they compete for lower-echelon jobs currently filled by Mexican Americans, and when their allegiances, culture, and needs are so different from those of mainstream Mexican Americans?

RESULTS: SPATIAL PATTERNS AND ACCOMODATION PROCESSES

Spatial Patterns and Segregation in San Antonio: 1990–2000

A reference map of San Antonio, including the neighborhoods interviewed and photographed for this chapter, is provided as Figure 17.2. The location of San Antonio's Latino immigrants (foreign-born) are shown in

Figure 17.3, which illustrates the concept of *locational inertia*: turn-of-the-century jobs in food and garment manufacturing on the near southwest side that attracted Mexican migrants initially but have since disappeared, coupled with the existence of extended family in this area, keep families from moving en masse to the suburbs (Jones, 2005). The Mexican immigrant pattern (Figure 17.3) is quite close to the Mexican American pattern (not shown), implying correctly that immigrants seek out areas of their own ethnicity and language, in addition to areas of less-expensive housing. The somewhat greater downtown and near north side presence of immigrants reflects ties to jobs in the downtown tourist industry, and in construction and warehousing in the booming northern half of the city, respectively.

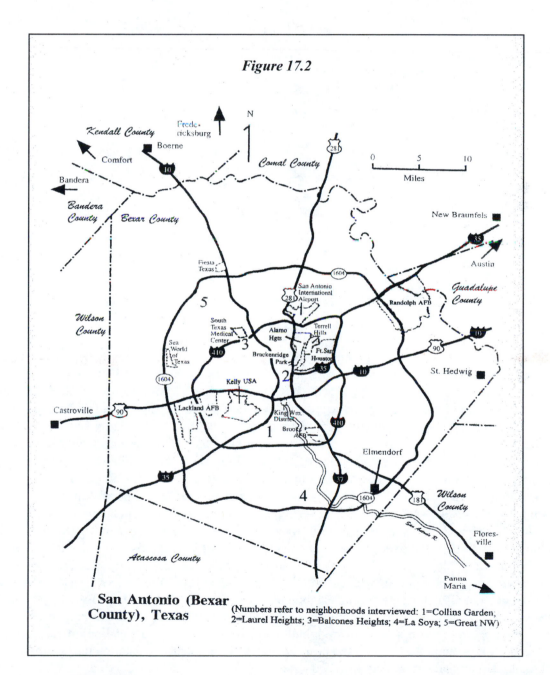

Figure 17.2

San Antonio (Bexar County), Texas

(Numbers refer to neighborhoods interviewed: 1=Collins Garden; 2=Laurel Heights; 3=Balcones Heights; 4=La Soya; 5=Great NW)

Figure 17.3

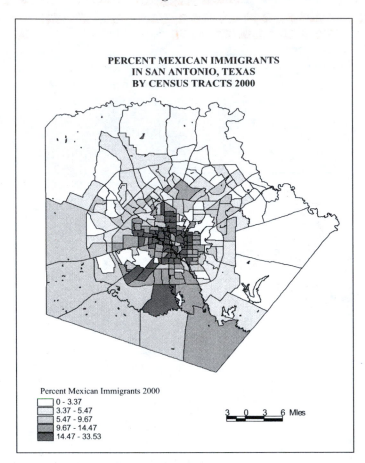

PERCENT MEXICAN IMMIGRANTS
IN SAN ANTONIO, TEXAS
BY CENSUS TRACTS 2000

Percent Mexican Immigrants 2000

- 0 - 3.37
- 3.37 - 5.47
- 5.47 - 9.67
- 9.67 - 14.47
- 14.47 - 33.53

3 0 3 6 Miles

Residential segregation is conceptually related to a group's social acceptance by the mainstream society. It was the basis for the question raised by two sociologists, Park and Bogardus, "Would you accept [a particular outgroup member] as your neighbor?" It became the basis for the original *social distance* scale developed to measure the acceptance of immigrants in U.S. society during a period of ethnocentrism and isolationism (Park, 1924; Bogardus, 1925). More recently, segregation is measured by the standard Dissimilarity Index (DI), based on the absolute difference between a census tract's percentage of a particular ethnic or ancestry group in a city (here, Mexican immigrants), and that tract's percentage of another group (here, either Mexican Americans or Anglos). The summed differences for all tracts (standardized to a 1–100 scale) is a good indicator of how separated a particular group is from other groups in the city. The higher the index, the more the groups are separated.

To illustrate, consider several groups' segregation from the rest of the population in San Antonio in 2000 (see Table 17.1), based on 226 Bexar County census tracts and the SF3 and SF4 sample files from the U.S. Census. The city's German ancestry population, owing to its nineteenth century rural presence to the northwest, northeast, and southeast and to its cultural assimilation, was broadly distributed across the city, and DI = 29.8. Its Filipino population, tracing to the early 1900s and currently holding military and professional occupations, was spread across the north side but also clustered around the military bases: DI = 42.8. The city's Hispanic population, with a long history but experiencing rapid recent influxes of lower-status migrants, was concentrated on the south and west sides inside Loop 410, with a DI of 47.5. Finally, San Antonio's Arab population, of recent vintage, were clustered around professional job opportunities near the South Texas Medical Center on the near northwest side of the city: DI = 54.2 (Jones and Crum, 2004).

Table 17.1
Dissimilarity Index for Selected Ancestry Groups in Bexar County (San Antonio), 2000[*]

Group	Population	Dissimilarity Index
German	142,172	29.8
English	82,130	34.7
Filipino	5,236	42.8
Black	100,025	45.6
Chinese	3,779	47.5
Hispanic	757,033	47.5
Asian Indian	3,858	50.3
Arab	9,636	54.2
County total	1,392,931	—

* based on the difference between a census tract's percentage of the given ancestry group, and the tract's percentage of **all other groups**. See text.

Regarding segregation of Mexicans and Mexican Americans from other groups in San Antonio, the results are informative. Mexican immigrants and Anglos (non-Hispanic whites) were relatively segregated from each other in 2000: the DI was 56.5. This was somewhat higher than Mexican American-Anglo segregation in the same year: 50.8. Both figures represented declines from 1990, in keeping with patterns found across the Southwestern U.S. The segregation of Mexican immigrants from Mexican Americans stands in stark contrast to the above figures: it was only 15.0 in 2000 (also a decline from 1990), emphasizing that Mexican immigrants and Mexican Americans live in the same areas of the city. To place the DI of 50.8 (above) in context, consider recent figures on "Hispanic-White" segregation in 2000: Houston (55.7), Dallas (54.1), Phoenix (52.5), San Diego (51.0), and Denver (50.2). Similarly, Los Angeles' Hispanic/white DI in 2000 was 63.2, while New York's was 66.7 and Chicago's, 62.1 (Logan et al., 2004). Apparently, the larger the city, the more powerful the forces of segregation. The reasons for this have not been systematically addressed in the literature, but appear related to the lower socioeconomic status of Mexicans, the competitive multi-ethnic nature of large cities, and the relatively low value of Mexican ethnic identity capital (Kibria, 2002) in such settings.

It is important to note that, unfortunately, the DI is an overarching statistic that sometimes obscures processes at work in different parts of a city (such as the inner city and the suburbs). In San Antonio, one of these processes is *spatial substitution* between Mexicans and Mexican Americans in the inner city — defined here as inside Loop 410 (the inner ring in Figure 17.2). Over the past decade, Mexican American and Mexican immigrant populations have increased in the inner city. However, the growth of the Mexican immigrants was proportionately higher and resulted in an increased concentration of Mexican immigrants who replaced many Mexican Americans who moved in substantial numbers to the suburbs. Thus, a spatial substitution process, in which Mexican immigrants are replacing Mexican Americans, has taken place.

Inner City Mexican Cultural Landscapes: Field Research

Another shortcoming of the DI is a scale issue. Mapped at the census tract level, it can obscure what is happening at the more micro level, street by street. The demographic maps presented in Figures 17.2 and 17.3 indicate that Mexican immigrants and Mexican Americans tend to occupy the same census tracts. However, this provides no insight as to what occurs in small neighborhoods or city blocks. Are Mexican residences clustered together along the street, and do they stand out on the urban landscape?

Field research conducted in San Antonio neighborhoods, which are numbered in Figure 17.2, revealed that there is a loose clustering of Mexican immigrant homes, often adjacent to unattractive (or disamenity) features such as creek beds, railroad tracks, or manufacturing and warehousing. This is illustrated by the photograph that appears as Figure 17.4. However, freestanding homes are not the only structures occupied by Mexicans. Many reside in apartment complexes, trailers, and homes converted to apartments, including those in old mansions near the city center. Sometimes garages are transformed into living quarters for Mexican migrants. In the inner city, rental apartments and home conversions prevail, whereas in the suburbs an even mix of rental and owned homes is prevalent. Over 70 percent of the Latino foreign-born in San Antonio reside in the inner city in these varied housing types. As noted earlier, their residences are located within a few miles of jobs in the inner city or on the city's near north side.

It is often impossible to determine whether a home is occupied by a Mexican immigrant or by a Mexican American family without interviewing the family or asking the neighbors. However, as depicted in Figure 17.5, some first-generation Mexican homes do exhibit certain features, as noted by Arreola (1988): colorful wood trim, yard statuary, small shrines, potted plants, and prickly pear cactus (*nopales*). While some clustering may occur, it is often the case that a Mexican immigrant family's home is not adjacent to another Mexican immigrant household. In Figure 17.5, an Anglo family lives in an old Victorian home to the left, while a Mexican American family lives in a less-adorned wood home to the right. Neighborhoods with large numbers of Mexican immigrants are also identifiable by their high levels of yard and street activity. Examples include fiestas (with music and piñatas) in yards, families sitting on porches or under trees, men fixing cars on the street or in driveways, boys playing basketball or soccer on the street, musical ice cream trucks plying their goods, and in general a much more lively street atmosphere than in Anglo or Mexican American neighborhoods. However, there is not a single type of Mexican immigrant neighborhood landscape. Rather, diverse conditions exist within an area generally dominated by those of Mexican ancestry.

Figure 17.4.
Mexican Immigrant Home Adjacent to Industrial District

Figure 17.5.
Mexican Immigrant Home Identifiable by Yard Activity

Social Accommodation Processes: 2004 Survey Results

The research results presented in this section were derived from a survey conducted by the author in 2004 in five different neighborhoods that experienced high growth rates of the Latino foreign-born between 1990 and 2000. These neighborhoods are labeled in Figure 17.2 and were selected non-randomly to represent different locations (inner city vs. suburbs), different socio-economic levels, different job opportunities, and different ethnic compositions. A questionnaire was administered to one of the heads (male or female) of household. Forty composition questions on family demography, contacts, acculturation, discrimination, and self-esteem were part of the survey. These questions were administered in a format that required choices from a list of responses. These close-ended questions were supplemented by two open questions inviting commentary on personal experiences of acculturation and discrimination. The sampling was designed to represent the characteristics noted above and to secure in-depth qualitative data. Seventeen in-depth interviews were completed on a face-to-face basis. The results are discussed using a narrative approach, rather than employing tabular statistics.

Demographically, the sample is cosmopolitan in its Mexican context. Unlike some previous samples of San Antonio immigrants (Jones, 1995 and 1996), two-thirds of the present sample were born in metropolitan areas of Mexico, and about half came from interior as opposed to border states in Mexico. This origin profile reflects the economic crisis in Mexico between 1982 and 1994 and that country's oscillation between depression and recovery ever since. This crisis was not exclusively lodged in rural areas, as in the past, but was equally severe in large urban areas. Although cosmopolitan, our sample is socioeconomically marginal by U.S. standards, less than a quarter having completed high school (vs. more than 4/5 in the U.S.); their median family income of $15,000 is less than one-third the U.S. median. The average interviewee had been in the U.S. for 13 years, was 37 years old, and was as likely to be male as female. Our inner-city respondents (12 of the 17) are spatially perched on the fringes of the booming downtown tourist district where the men work as cooks, waiters, construction workers, and craftsmen, while the women toil as cleaners, shop-tenders, craftspersons, and the like.

Regarding integration, no measure indicated that members of our sample are deeply involved with either Mexican Americans or Anglos, on a social basis or otherwise. To the contrary, between half and two-thirds have principally Mexican friends and neighbors. These findings are somewhat surprising given that Mexican immigrants and Mexican Americans tend to live in the same neighborhoods. In addition, a substantial proportion of our sample worked under a Mexican-American boss or supervisor. These findings suggest that there is a certain social distancing occurring between the two groups of Mexican ancestry. This contention is supported by responses to the question, "Do you think that the Mexican community of San Antonio is more in contact with the (Anglo-Mexican American) community than some years ago?" All respondents answered positively in reference to Anglos, but several answered negatively in reference to Mexican Americans. Overall, however, it must be stressed that Mexican immigrants' contacts with neither group are particularly strong. Our Mexican immigrant sample appears to lead a somewhat isolated and estranged existence. The following statements from three respondents support the observation that Mexican immigrants feel distant from their new neighbors:

> "Here, neighbors are very isolated and families don't visit like in Mexico. I can't send my kids into the street to play."

> "(Even after 20 years), I feel one hundred percent Mexican, and my friends are totally Mexican."

> "Here, the Mexican has constructed buildings, has constructed houses, has done many things, but the American does not see them; he zips about here and there, and when he doesn't need us any longer, he has *la migra* [U.S. immigration authorities] cast us back into Mexico."

As can be surmised from these comments, our Mexican immigrant sample is not acculturating, either. All but one respondent were functionally monolingual, and although some language shift was evident (one-half had used the Tex-Mex expressions "*jonke*" [junk] and "*te llamo para atras*" [I'll call you later], this is hardly indicative of socialization into Tejano culture. Almost exclusively, our respondents preferred Mexican food and Mexican music; and interestingly, American food and music were preferred over Tejano. Our interviewees identified themselves as "Mexican" in two out of three cases. The other preferred terms were "Hispanic" and "Latino"; interestingly, none preferred the terms "Mexican American" or "Chicano."

Perceived discrimination against Mexicans in the schools, on the job, and in public agencies is apparently an important barrier to Mexican integration and acculturation in San Antonio. In response to the question "Do teachers here give less attention to Mexican than to other students?" a fifth of the respondents agreed. Mexican American teachers (owing to their bilingualism) were believed to be less discriminatory towards Mexican students than Anglo teachers. In contrast, job supervisors and public servants of Mexican ancestry were viewed by Mexican immigrants as treating them in a more discriminatory fashion than Anglos in the same positions. In response to the questions "Do bosses here mistreat workers because they are Mexican?" and "Do public servants here help Mexicans less than they help other persons?" one-half of our sample agreed, but indicated that those of Mexican ancestry treated them with more discriminatory behavior than did Anglos. The statements below were typical among our respondents:

> "At work, they haven't given me a raise for two years. The (Mexican-American) manager says: 'I will check on this, but the boss may say to get rid of you.' Thus, your request is ignored, or the boss never replies."

> "Personally, I feel that Mexican (-American) bosses mistreat Mexicans more than American bosses. They abuse us more, they pay us less."

> "Once I was driving a car that emitted a lot of smoke. An American policeman stopped me and said 'Send a Mexican-American agent, I can't understand him.' The American said to the Mexican-American official 'I'm going to give him a warning, but he has to get this problem fixed.' The Mexican American said to me 'OK, go ahead.' But before leaving he said: 'He's [the American cop] a good guy. He's giving you a chance. But if it were me, I would put you in jail and impound your car.' And there are many experiences such as this by people I know."

It is also interesting that earlier (pre-1990) arrivals are not better-adapted to U.S. life than later arrivals. Their contacts and acculturation are basically the same, except that earlier arrivals identify themselves as "Hispanic" almost as frequently as "Mexicano," whereas later arrivals see themselves almost exclusively as Mexicans. This suggests some level of acculturation — but not into Mexican American culture. When it comes to perception of discrimination on the job and in public agencies, however, earlier arrivals actually perceive more such discrimination than later arrivals, particularly from Mexican American bosses and public servants. Just what this means is open to question. Our sample exhibits low socioeconomic attainment on all three criteria — education, income, and occupation. Although earlier arrivals earn more than later arrivals, their median income is still only $22,500 — not even half the U.S. average, despite averaging twenty years in the United States. Recent arrivals may discount their low incomes, believing the American dream is still attainable. Earlier arrivals, perhaps feeling they have worked hard and deserve more compensation, conclude that there is discrimination against Mexicans in U.S. society.

CONCLUSIONS

The United States has entered an era of accelerated immigration from Latin America and Asia that brings challenges for immigrant accommodation to the American "heartland" as well as to metropolitan gateway cities. The challenges are taking on many forms as expressed in this text. Racial conflict, ethnic diversity, and class distinctions are among the factors complicating racial/ethnic geographies and leading to societal challenges. It is true that the American mainstream is in a state of flux due to the accommodation of new groups. However, this process will take generations to play out, especially given the rapidity of the current influx that shows no indication of slowing. Meanwhile, regional complexities are resulting in new multicultural geographies and unique adjustment challenges on a local and regional basis. Resurgent waves of Mexican immigration in the U.S. are revealing a new rigidity in Anglo acceptance of Mexicans, evident in stricter welfare policies, backlash against bilingual programs, incidents of violence at the border, a new Border Patrol policy that has proven deadly for undocumented border crossers, and the rise of a new anti-Hispanic ethnocentrism as evidenced in the writings of scholars such as Samuel Huntington and Peter Brimelow.

In the Southwest, the existence of a mediating culture, that of Mexican Americans, might be expected to lessen these problems, but an emerging literature, as well as the findings of this chapter, suggest otherwise. In fact, a somewhat adversarial relationship appears to exist, which the recent literature is only beginning to explain in terms of the economic success and changing political priorities of Mexican Americans, who now distance themselves from newcomers of common ancestry. In other words, *intra-ethnic friction* inhibits the accommodation of Mexicans into established Mexican American society. In San Antonio, despite the fact that Mexican Americans and Mexican immigrants tend to live in the same neighborhoods, friendships and neighboring are quite limited and the perception of discrimination against Mexicans by Mexican American job supervisors and public servants (e.g., police) is widespread among immigrant families. Consequently, first generation Mexicans have not acculturated to Mexican American norms, nor have they acculturated to Anglo norms.

The barriers to Mexican accommodation and well-being, which were discussed in this chapter, include discrimination, the lack of incentives for integration due to their temporariness and undocumented status, and their low levels of community and family resources. Related to this last point, Kibria's notion of *ethnic identity capital* (politico-economic power and adjustment potential possessed by groups whose cultural traits are revered by the host society) is relevant (Kibria, 2002). Whereas first-generation Europeans, Asian Indians, and Cubans have such capital, groups like the Indochinese and Mexicans do not. The latter often lack the socio-economic status to lend credibility (in American eyes) to, and finances for, the formal promotion of their cultures. Finally, where there is a continuing antagonistic relationship between the origin and host countries, as between the U.S. and Mexico, there will be a carryover or halo effect resulting in stereotyping and disrespect of immigrants (although not refugees) from that country. This chapter has presented evidence for a negative image of Mexican immigrants by both alienated Americans and Mexican Americans who wish to maintain their status (and status quo) by distancing themselves from immigrants and thus controversy.

Other research indicates that Mexican accommodation is more rapid for the second generation. English skills are better, cultural baggage is less, legal status is not a problem, and even though family resources are still modest, this generation is part of the Mexican American majority in San Antonio, with all the advantages that entails. Nevertheless, in San Antonio, the economic and social elite are still Anglo, so there is a second strong barrier to accommodation, because discrimination against Mexican Americans by Anglos is persistent. In a sense, the Tejano subculture is defined and fueled by these two types of discrimination, one which separates it from Mexico, and the other which separates it from mainstream Anglo culture. Only time will tell whether Mexican American culture redefines the American mainstream, dissolving the Tejano-American boundary, or whether it will endure indefinitely.

Chapter 18

Patterns and Issues in the Latinization of Allentown, Pennsylvania

MARK E. REISINGER, JOHN W. FRAZIER, AND EUGENE L. TETTEY-FIO

INTRODUCTION

The Latinization of the United States has become pervasive, affecting nearly all major regions and communities of various sizes. Puerto Ricans, once highly concentrated in New York City neighborhoods, have decentralized within the northeastern U.S. in particular, and have begun to migrate to other regions as well. Because of changes in U.S. immigration policy, these American citizens have been joined by other highly diverse Latino cultural groups in recent decades, including those from the Dominican Republic, Central America, and South America. This chapter explores certain dimensions of the Latinization of Allentown (located in Lehigh County), Pennsylvania, although a similar process is unfolding in at least three other small cities in southeastern Pennsylvania. We use census data and interviews to explore the nature of Latino settlement in Allentown and certain Latino experiences and perceptions since arriving. We also provide photographs that illustrate the Latino imprints on this post-industrial city, once exclusively controlled by European Americans, particularly the Pennsylvania Dutch.

Despite numerous issues regarding the Latinization of Allentown, we framed this chapter around five specific sets of questions.

1. Questions surrounding migration and population change. How many Latinos live in Allentown? Why have they selected Allentown?
2. Questions of geographic settlement patterns. We asked where Latinos live in Allentown and how this settlement structure relates to other ethnic settlement patterns described in social science literature.
3. Questions related to Anglo and Latino perceptions. We are interested in early cultural conflicts and whether or not Latinos feel they are treated fairly by their Anglo neighbors (Hispanics with whom we spoke did not differentiate European-American identities, rather they termed non-Latino whites as Anglos).
4. Questions about employment and fair treatment in the regional labor market. We asked whether or not Latinos were over represented in particular job categories and whether or not they felt fairly treated in the labor market.
5. Questions related to the cultural landscape of Allentown. We asked what types of Latino imprints are visible on the streetscapes of Allentown.

Where possible, we used the reports of *New York Times* reporter Laurence Stains, who visited Allentown and wrote of Latinization as he observed it through interviews and direct observations in 1994 (Stains, 1994). His work is helpful in providing a baseline for Latino landscapes, perceptions and cultural conflicts a decade earlier than our observations.

WHY ALLENTOWN? MIGRATION THEORIES AND
LATINO MIGRATION TO ALLENTOWN

Geography is only one among many disciplines that share interest in understanding and explaining migration patterns. For example, economists tend to focus on the role of labor and labor markets; sociologists, on institutional changes.

The most frequently-heard explanation for migration is the push-pull theory, which states that some people move because they are pushed out of their former location, whereas others move because they are pulled or attracted to someplace else. This idea was first put forward by Ravenstein (1889), who concluded that pull factors were more important than push factors. Ravenstein posited that the desire to get ahead (economically) is more responsible for the voluntary migration of people than the desire to escape.

Lee (1966) expanded upon some of Ravenstein's ideas. He began by classifying the elements that influence migration into the following groups:

1. factors associated with the migrant's origin;
2. factors associated with a the migrant's destination;
3. obstacles between the two that the migrants must overcome (intervening obstacles); and
4. personal factors.

Using Census migration data from 1985 to 1990, Reisinger (2003) showed that the greatest number of Latino migrants to the Allentown area came from the New York City metropolitan area. A similar pattern is apparent in the Census migration data from 1995 to 2000. That data indicates that approximately 2700 Latino migrants came to Lehigh County from New York City. In addition, there is a substantial flow of migrants to Lehigh County from adjacent Pennsylvania counties and directly from Puerto Rico.

Reisinger (2003) argues that it is difficult to use any one theory to explain migration patterns. The authors' field research in Allentown in 2004 included four focus groups of Latinos, who were asked to explain their reasons for moving to Allentown. Their responses support Reisinger's position. While many Latinos stated that their reason for moving to Allentown was for job and employment (see Inés's comments), many others had different reasons.

"When I arrived here the goal was to obtain a better quality of life, a good job and I am in the process; I am working in the area that I am graduated from in my country, that is, accounting." Inés

Marriage and family reasons, tranquility and safety, housing costs, and the ability to purchase a home were all ranked very high as reasons for relocating to Allentown (see Miriam's comments below). Unlike the simple economic theories and views documented above, many Latinos reported that fear was the main reason for leaving New York City and coming to Allentown (Reisinger, 2003). In addition, Allentown's social and physical structure is changing and is attractive to Latino migrants. Results from the same research indicate that only a small majority of Latino migrants know English very well. With its many Spanish speaking residents, Allentown is highly attractive for this demographic.

"Look, I came from New York; I lived most of my life there. And somebody said to me that here was very tranquil and safe for children, but in reality it is not as safe as they made me believe (several laugh). When I moved here, we bought a house and that is the reason that we live here." Miriam

What Reisinger (2003) was trying to illustrate is the fact that, though there are many accurate and interesting theories concerning migration, it is clear that there is more to the migration puzzle. One has to take into account all factors when explaining migration patterns, including the fact that different places may provide certain individuals and groups with greater utility than their current location. Simmons (1968) defined place utility as "… a measure of attractiveness or unattractiveness of an area, relative to other locations, as perceived by the individual decision maker" (also, see Wolport, 1965).

A utility function to summarize the relationships between variables describing the migrant household, its current location, and potential alternative locations would be difficult to devise because a migrant's judgment of utility is often subjective. In any case, a migrant's relocation decision can be very complex and include economic and non-economic considerations.

LATINO-WHITE SEGREGATION IN THE ALLENTOWN REGION

Since Latinization is occurring throughout the U.S. in large and small communities, it is important to place the Allentown region in a broader context of segregated communities. By 1990 the local Latino population had reached 12, 274, up from about 4,000 in 1980. Between 1980 and 2000 the local Latino population quadrupled to 26, 058 and Latinos were now about 25 percent of the entire Allentown population. How segregated is this population in the metropolitan region? How does it compare with other communities with large and growing Latino populations? One way to examine such questions is through the use of the dissimilarity index, which is a measure of segregation, or spatial unevenness of groups in a community. It is derived by comparing the sum of the differences in the proportion of the two groups — in this case Latinos and white non-Latinos — in a geographic area. The index values range from zero (no segregation) to 100 (complete segregation). Table 18.1 reports these indices for the twenty metropolitan regions with the highest values in the U.S.

Table 18.1

	DISSIMILARITY INDEXES 2000	
Rank	**Area Name**	**White/Latinos Index**
1	Lawrence, MA-NH PMSA	75
2	Reading, PA MSA	72
3	Providence-Fall River-Warwick, RI-MA MSA	68
4	Bridgeport, CT PMSA	67
5	New York, NY PMSA	67
6	Newark, NJ PMSA	65
7	Hartford, CT MSA	64
8	Los Angeles-Long Beach, CA PMSA	63
9	Springfield, MA MSA	63
10	Allentown-Bethlehem-Easton, PA MSA	62
11	Chicago, IL PMSA	62
12	Lancaster, PA MSA	62
13	Waterbury, CT PMSA	61
14	Lowell, MA-NH PMSA	61
15	Tyler, TX MSA	60
16	Philadelphia, PA-NJ PMSA	60
17	Worcester, MA-CT PMSA	60
18	Milwaukee-Waukesha, WI PMSA	60
19	New Haven-Meriden, CT PMSA	60
20	Salinas, CA MSA	59
21	Boston, MA-NH PMSA	59
22	York, PA MSA	58

Four of southeastern Pennsylvania's small metro regions appear in this list. Reading has the second highest index in the nation, indicating that only the Lawrence, Massachusetts-New Hampshire metro area has a higher level of Latino-white segregation. Allentown is number ten in this ranking and, while being less segregated than metro regions like New York, Newark, and Los Angeles, it has a higher degree of segregation than Chicago, Philadelphia, Boston and other metropolitan areas with significant Latino populations.

How is this relatively high level of Latino-white segregation reflected on a local level? This question is addressed in the next section below.

Assimilation or Sequent Occupance?

Before visualizing the settlement evolution of Latinos in Allentown, it is important to have an understanding of the theory of immigrant ethnic settlements in the U.S. Many years ago, geographers coined the phrase "sequent occupance." This phrase described a process in which one cultural group replaced another due to the host culture's abandonment of the area, or from forces that pushed it out. In either case, the new culture brought its ways of life to the region and imprinted them on the visible cultural landscape. Certainly, remnants of the old culture remained visible, but the new arrivals eventually transformed the appearance of the place to reflect their ways. A more popular view of ethnic settlement in the 20th century involved the notion of an "invasion" of a new ethnic group into the host community, typically in center city of industrializing societies, and gradually the new group became assimilated, or absorbed, into the host culture. This classic one-way assimilation model was what Stains had in mind when he suggested that the newly-arriving New York City Puerto Ricans would easily assimilate in Allentown:

> "Is there anything about the Puerto Rican experience or culture that would keep it from doing what virtually every other immigrant group has done — intermarry, and melt into the main stream?" (Stains, 1994, p. 62).

Accepting this historical explanation of spatial and social assimilation, Stains suggested that educational and employment opportunities would hasten the assimilation of Puerto Ricans, who also tended to have a weak ethnic identity.

Puerto Ricans have migrated to Allentown for decades and it has been slightly more than a decade since Stains' observations. While a generation may be an insufficient period to gauge the validity of Stains' claim for rapid assimilation, we should expect some strong signs if his assumptions are valid. Specifically, we should expect the spatial integration of Latinos into neighborhoods in the outer city and into suburban Allentown, as opposed to continued high concentration in the inner city, where these Latinos first settled more than two decades ago. In addition, less segregation and more Latino-Anglo social relationships, especially neighbors and those sharing social institutions, would develop and be visible. We explore the questions of settlement structure and social assimilation through the use of census data and focus groups conducted in 2004. First, we briefly explore the literature on recent ethnic settlement geography.

Immigrant Ethnic Settlement Patterns of the Late Twentieth Century

Immigrant ethnic settlement patterns have become much more complex than the one-way assimilation model mentioned above. Social scientists have studied the settlement structure associated with various ethnic groups and have discovered multiple settlement forms. Among these, geographers Skop and Li (2003) noted that, while "chain migration" still links some new migrants to traditional inner city ghettos such as Cubans in Little Havana, newer forms also mark metropolitan regions, including those described as multiethnic ghettos (no single ethnic group majority) and more novel forms such as Wei Li's "ethnoburb" (Li, 1998). Li's ethnoburb contains ethnic business concentrations and distinct residential clusters, as identified in Los Angeles' Chinatown, Monterey Park, and the San Gabriel Valley (Li, 2006). Some of these newer ethnic forms also involve enclaves and clusters in both urban and suburban settings. Geographer Christopher Smith and sociologist John Logan also reported the evolving, complex ethnic settlement patterns, and the growing influence of Asians in Flushing, New York, including clustering in nearby suburbs (Smith and Logan, 2006). Latino settlement patterns also have been discussed in the literature, including in suburban California (Clark, 1998).

Given the increasingly complex and varied patterns of ethnic settlements, what should we expect for Latinos in the Allentown region after more than two decades of in-migration? Have Latinos moved in significant proportions to the suburbs and created new enclaves there? Or, have they remained in inner city Allentown? Some hints are in the literature on New York City Puerto Rican settlements. Sociologist Nathan Kantrowitz found that New York City Puerto Ricans, while tending not to dominate their neighborhoods, did reside in close proximity to poor blacks due to their low socioeconomic status (Kantrowitz, 1973). The persistent pattern of poverty and low incomes among most Puerto Ricans led to their classification as the other "underclass," and linked them to African Americans socially and spatially. Economic bifurcation of New York's Puerto Rican population over time, however, also led to distinct classes and settlement patterns; the poorer lived on the Lower East Side and in Harlem, while those with more resources resided in suburban Bronx and Queens (Kantrowitz, 1973; Boswell, 1976).

Puerto Rican settlements also evolved outside of New York City. As the Puerto Rican *colonias* (communities) continued to mature and second-generation, U.S. mainland-born Puerto Ricans moved to employment-age, many left the *colonias* because they were more upwardly mobile than their parents. These Puerto Ricans became integrated into the broader Anglo society of the metropolitan area (Hernandez-Alvarez, 1968).

Where are Puerto Ricans and other Latinos residing in the Allentown region? Stains, speaking of a Puerto Rican family, explained their early attraction to center city:

> "Buying a $67,000 row house in Allentown will save them money: the payment of $650 on their Federal Housing Authority mortgage will be $100 less than the rent on their three-bedroom apartment in Bay Ridge" (Stains, 1994, p. 67).

In a broader context, Stains suggested that the migration decision was "beyond economics," that Puerto Ricans as a culture suffered from "urban discomfort," which pushed them out of the threatening and unpleasant streetscapes of the City and attracted them to the tranquil environs of southeastern Pennsylvania. However, the affordable home ownership of row houses abandoned by Anglos and the opportunity for a better education have placed them in the inner city of Allentown. The initial settlement, then, revolved around those opportunities between Linden and Second Streets in the "older neighborhoods, from the Lehigh River to 10th Street, in the dilapidated brick row houses the native Allentonians don't want to live in any more" (p. 58).

The continued influx of Latinos, Puerto Ricans, and other Hispanic groups created a growing need for housing. At the same time, many families had entered the labor force and were accumulating capital that could move renters to ownership and allow others to leave starter homes for better neighborhoods. Where would newcomers reside? Where would mobile Latinos relocate? What sort of geographic distribution would result?

One way to understand the relatively high level of Latino-white segregation in the metro region is to examine Allentown in relation to Lehigh County. In 2000, approximately 82 percent of Lehigh County Latinos resided within the city of Allentown. In the same year, approximately 73 percent of all Latinos resided within 1.5 miles of its original settlement area, the intersection of Second and Linden Streets. While a modest number of Latinos moved outside the city limits by 2000, clearly Latinos remained highly concentrated in the central city and this explains the relatively high rate of Latino-white segregation in the region. Figure 18.1 provides a time series of boundaries of Latino concentration within the city, beginning in 1980, when Latinos were in the inner city cluster described by Stains. As the map illustrates, Latinos spread within Allentown in a largely contagious fashion. The map portrays concentrations of Latinos of 20 percent or more at the city block level, a threshold that was more than triple their national percentage in 1980. This threshold was applied to successive time periods for consistency. Also, while space does not permit details, it can be noted that scores of these inner city blocks are 50 percent or more Latino. It seems logical that as whites fled Allentown (the white population of Allentown declined 22.3% between 1990 and 2000), Latinos replaced them in readily available, very affordable housing. This leads us to conclude that rather than social assimilation by 2000 Latinos were merely replacing white, non-Hispanics in a more sequent occupance mode.

Figure 18.1

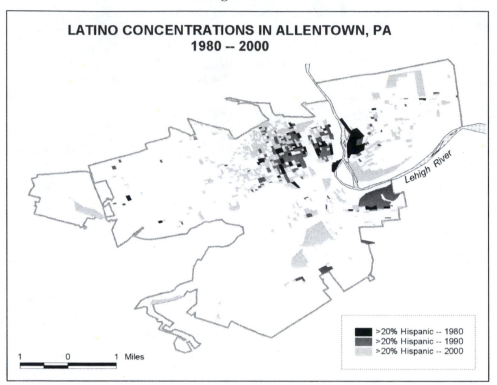

SOCIALIZATION: PERCEPTIONS OF ANGLO TREATMENT AND SOCIAL DISTANCE

It is difficult to address socialization directly. Are the cultural issues reported by Stains in the early 1990s still present? He reported cultural conflicts of various kinds and suggested that such clashes tend to be "more intense" in small cities undergoing rapid ethnic changes. His observation of some local Anglos included perceptions of Latinos brandishing a "Big Apple attitude" and being indiscrete, boisterous, and loitering, as well as having an association with crime, gangs and drugs. There was a fear among some natives that the Latino influence was a threat to women and children. On the other hand, Stains suggested that Latinos saw themselves as practicing their culture, including their "island impulse" to be outdoors, sharing conversation and listening to music. They also are quick to express affection through an embrace (*abrazo*) and to kiss one another, something far less common among Anglos. Stains quoted a Latino who captured the cultural difference in social interaction:

"Picture a Latino and an Anglo talking: the Latino is moving forward, and the Dutchman is moving backward" (Stains, p. 59).

Despite such cultural differences, which sometimes translated into clashes and discrimination, the Latino population has continued to grow through migration into the new century.

One way to address the existence of cultural issues is to ask Latinos: How fairly are you treated by native Anglos today? We pursued that broad question by asking our interviewees to respond to a questionnaire and then, through focus groups, elaborate their feelings and experiences with Anglo Allentonians. We asked them to respond to a series of short questions about fair treatment using one of three responses: "treated fairly," "not treated fairly," "no opinion." Seven topical questions were asked, including perceptions of fair treatment by neighbors, police, retail sales clerks, educational institutions, and in the workplace, among others (see Table 18.2). The majority of our interviewees felt fairly treated by Anglos in all seven areas. However, the responses can be divided into two types of majority positive responses. In the first class of responses, at least two-thirds of our respondents reported fair treatment. The second involved only a slim majority, who reported being fairly treated by Anglos in local government agencies and at the workplace. We will focus only on neighbors and treatment in the workplace in the remainder of this chapter.

Table 18.2

Issues of Fair Treatment in Various Contexts	
Retail shopping places	86%
Neighbors	70%
Police	72%
Healthcare providers	67%
Schools	64%
Local government support and recreation facilities	55%
Workplace	53%

Regarding treatment by Anglo neighbors, 70 percent indicated that they received fair treatment. A few reported very positive feelings about their neighbor's treatment. One, Maritza, had a very positive reception in a recent move into her new northern Allentown neighborhood:

" My neighbors gave me a warm welcome and I include both Anglos and Hispanics. In the area where I am, Americans gave me better treatment than Hispanics" (Maritza, 2004).

However, there are the different experiences as well. One Latino man, who moved to Allentown in 1966, felt that many Anglos simply do not like Hispanic people and unfairly associate all Hispanics with crime and the drug culture of Allentown:

"When we first arrived here, we were very suspected by our neighbors. We bought a house the first year. My mother and my brothers worked and saved. In the second year, we bought another house on the same street. Neighbors said 'No way can they have that much money without dealing drugs.' We were under investigation for the next year" (Felix, 2004).

Felix also explained that today things are not nearly as bad as Anglos perceive them and he finds it upsetting that some Anglos negatively classify Latinos and their neighborhoods:

"They now refer to our Hispanic neighborhoods as the ghetto" (Felix, 2004).

Perhaps the most common perception of Anglo treatment, which expresses the cultural difference that still drives a wedge between some Latinos and their Anglo neighbors, is related to social distance. It was expressed multiple times. A Latino woman, who has lived in Allentown with her family for nearly eight years, told us:

"My neighbors are nice. They are fair to my family. They wave and say 'hi' ... But, I don't know, they just won't let you get close to them.

In my culture, we cook for our neighbors. It is more the warmth of a family. Here, they won't let you get close" (Ruth, 2004).

Thus, some elements of the social distance unveiled by Stains remain evident a decade later. Another indicator of ethnic separation lies in the sharing of institutions. While social interaction is inevitable in some venues, language and culture differences still seem to keep people apart in Allentown. One such institution is the church. Many storefront churches appeal strictly to Latinos, while others, including Roman Catholic, Lutheran and other denominations, provide separate services for Spanish and English-speaking audiences. We observed a Latino ethnic festival to celebrate the diverse Latino cultures in the city's largest Catholic Church. It was held after mass on a Sunday and the event was highly publicized within the Church by posters and on placards in the parking lot. We attended the event and witnessed very few Anglo visitors from the Church in attendance.

Perceptions of Crime and Its Local Geography

Stains also mentioned the concern of the spreading of Latino influence away from city center. That too remains an issue where crime is considered. Latinos are quick to point out that crime is an issue but that it also has a geographic dimension, rather than being associated with Latino neighborhoods. In this vein, a Latino woman told us of her experience and the geography of crime:

> "... Allentown has good and bad parts.... But, let me tell you, when I arrived I was not in a very good area and I saw the boys doing disorder, drinking beers and leaving bottles in front of houses. I began to listen that in the downtown things are not going so well ... people are arriving from outside and are a bad influence in the town" (Maritza, 2004).

Another Latino woman, who moved away from the downtown area added:

> "The place where I am is good.... Yes, I listened about the shootings but we are distant and they do not affect us ... the problem (crime) in Allentown is by places, by sectors" (Norma, 2004).

Thus, perhaps like other cities that have low-income and problem inner cities, Allentown seems to evolve in the model of an ethnic ghetto, where in many cities this has meant African Americans have replaced fleeing whites and are associated by public perception with rising crimes in particular declining inner city neighborhoods. The problem is that some Latinos perceive white attitudes as "blaming" Latinos generally for the rise in crime.

The Latinization of Allentown appears to be a classic case of a poor ethnic group being attracted to the affordability of inner city neighborhoods. Once established, they push out into other neighborhoods, replacing natives that have fled. This appears to represent the classic ghetto expansion process, wherein the sequence involves a new ethnic group replacing the host culture. In such a case, the ethnic newcomers may have some social interaction with the hosts but rather than assimilate, they remain imbedded within their culture. Some Latinos are interacting with whites, especially those who are moving to neighborhoods further away from the problems of the urban downtown core. It may be too early to fully assess social and racial integration in Allentown. Yet, the strengths of culture and cultural differences, whether perceived or real, remain. Participation and experiences in the labor force help us better understand the depth of some of these cultural differences. Cultural landscapes also can reveal the reflection of these significant new ethnic groups in a region once dominated by industrial and European influence. We now turn to these subjects.

LATINOS' EXPERIENCES IN THE ALLENTOWN LABOR MARKET

This section of the chapter analyzes the situation of Latinos' in the Allentown labor market. If you recall from the above discussion, the workplace is where Latinos felt the least fairly treated. This may be due to a language barrier and discrimination. These issues are examined from the responses generated during the focus group discussion. In addition, structural issues, such as spatial mismatch between residence and employment, the existence of a dual labor market, and unemployment, are examined.

Language Barriers and Discrimination in the Workplace

The inability to speak English well may have a significant impact on a person's labor market outcome. From our focus group discussions, this became apparent for the Latinos living in Allentown. The following quote from Inés (2004) is indicative of this:

> "When we arrive here we need to speak English and if you don't know English you begin at the bottom. I began in the factory at the bottom, but now the same factory promoted me to administration."

Feelings of discrimination in the workplace also became apparent during the focus group discussions. Several of the people that participated in the discussions felt that discrimination was responsible for not being promoted at their workplace or for the dismissal of Latinos from their jobs. The two comments below by Julian (2004) and Felix (2004) are indicative of such feelings:

> "For example, I have worked for Kraft for 24 years and I was fighting for the position of industrial mechanic for seven years and they denied me, no matter how qualified I was" (Julian, 2004).

> "They dismissed a Latino because of racism and it continues. In the biggest companies and the scholarly district of the city, prejudice exists for simply being Hispanic. You can have all the education and be bilingual but simply being Latino is a mark against you in finding a job" (Felix, 2004).

Structural Issues in the Allentown Labor Market

The spatial mismatch hypothesis argues that low-skilled minorities living in U.S. inner cities incur poor labor market outcomes because they are disconnected from suburban job opportunities. Over the second half of the twentieth century, dramatic changes have occurred in U.S. metropolitan areas. In particular, the concentration of jobs has continuously decreased in central cities and increased in the suburbs. Over the same period, many minority households have remained or located in central cities while whites have continuously decentralized to suburban residential areas. The combination of these two trends is said to have created a situation of spatial mismatch to the extent that minorities are now located far away from suitable suburban employment opportunities (Gobillon et al., 2003).

A spatial mismatch between residences and employment opportunities may also affect the unemployment rates for minorities. There are several different underlying mechanisms that explain how distance to job opportunities could be harmful:

- Workers' job search efficiency may decrease with distance to jobs (they get little information about distant jobs).
- Workers residing far away from jobs may have few incentives to search intensively.
- Workers may incur high search costs that cause them to restrict their spatial search horizon to the vicinity of their local neighborhood.
- Workers may refuse jobs that involve commutes that are two long because commuting to that job would be too costly in view of the proposed wage.
- Employers may refuse to hire or prefer to pay lower wages to distant workers because commuting long distances make them less productive.
- Employers may discriminate against residentially segregated workers because of the stigma or prejudice associated with their residential location.
- Employers may think that their white local customers are unwilling to have contacts with minority workers.

Thus, there are several consequences that are thought to be a result of the spatial mismatch between jobs and residences for minorities. First, minorities incur greater costs of time and travel to suburban employment opportunities. Second, minorities may have higher unemployment rates than other workers. These issues were examined using 2000 U.S. Census data.

Eight percent of the Latino labor force in Allentown travels 90 minutes or more to work while only two percent of Allentown's Anglo population has that travel time to work. In addition, 25 percent of Allentown's Latino population has a travel time of 30 to 60 minutes to work. The corresponding value for the Anglo population is 18 percent. It appears evident that there is a spatial mismatch between Latino residences and employment opportunities in the Allentown labor market. The mismatch not only affects the cost in time of travel but also impacts the mode of travel to work.

Another indication of the cost of traveling these distances to work can be illustrated by the means of travel-to-work data. Fifty-six percent of the Latinos living in Allentown either used public transportation (29%) or carpooled (27%) to work. By contrast, only 15 percent of the Anglo population used these two means of travel to work (12% carpooled and 3% used public transportation).

As noted, it is suspected that the spatial mismatch between residence and employment opportunities affects the unemployment rate of minorities. The 2000 Census data indicates that this is the case for Latinos in the Allentown labor market. The Latino male unemployment rate for 2000 was 11.8 percent and the female rate was 16 percent. This compares to Anglo rates of 5.6 percent for males and 6 percent for females. The fact that Latinos live relatively farther from employment opportunities than Anglos and are segregated in specific parts of the city, may provide an explanation for their higher unemployment rates.

Allentown's Dual Labor Market

The dual labor market approach to analyzing local labor markets revolves around three basic hypotheses. First, the labor market is permanently dichotomized into a primary and secondary sector of labor opportunities. The primary sector includes jobs that are characterized by a high degree of job security, good working conditions, high earnings, career and promotional opportunities, and adequate fringe benefits. The secondary sector is different. It offers little on-the-job training, poor promotion prospects, low-paid jobs, repetitive work, and no security. The sector generally refers to the lowest level of the hierarchy of business activity (Peck, 1996).

Second, well-defined procedures and norms govern job security, pay increases, and promotions in the primary labor market. The operation of secondary labor markets comes closest to the assumptions of the competitive market of the neoclassical approach; employment and wage rates are contingent on the demand and supply for labor. Third, mobility between the two markets is strongly limited and controlled. In particular, certain groups in the secondary market, such as older workers, women, and immigrants, have the least chance to move up (Peck, 1996). Workers with modest levels of education, skills, or ability to speak English would most likely find opportunities in the secondary labor market.

To determine if there is a dual labor market operating in the Allentown area, we analyzed 2000 U.S. Census occupational data. Latino males were found to be over-represented in jobs such as production, transportation, material moving and laboring, food preparation and serving, building and grounds cleaning, personal care and service, and healthcare support. These are occupations usually considered to be part of the secondary labor market. Latino males in the Allentown labor market were under-represented in primary labor market jobs such as professional and related occupations, management, business and financial services, and sales and related occupations.

Female Latinos in the Allentown labor market were as over-represented in certain occupations as the Latino males. The highest proportion, 28 percent, of Latino females were employed in production jobs. Not surprisingly, Latino females also were under-represented in the primary sector of the labor market. Apparently, a dual labor market is operating in Allentown with Latino males and females filling many of the jobs in the secondary sector of that market, while Anglos are filling the majority of the jobs in the primary sector.

CULTURAL LANDSCAPES

A Latino ethnoscape — "the landscape of group identity" (Appadurai, 1990 and 1996) is becoming increasingly apparent in the City of Allentown. Religious institutions are a major cultural identifier. Figures 18.2 through 18.5 illustrate a varied Latino religious landscape in Allentown. Traditionally associated with Roman Catholicism, the Allentown Latino religious landscape shows that a number of Protestant denominations also are represented in the community. Figure 18.2 is a photograph at St. Paul's Lutheran Church. The signage reflects both an English- and Spanish-speaking congregation. This is not unusual in Allentown. Many of the inner city churches offer both English and Spanish services. In many cases the Spanish-speaking members of the congregation now outnumber the English-speaking members. In some cases the church congregations have become entirely Latino (see Figure 18.3).

Figure 18.2
St. Paul's Lutheran Church — notice service times announced in both English and Spanish.

Figure 18.3
A former Anglo Methodist Church that now has an all Latino congregation.

Figure 18.4
One of the many "storefront" Latino churches that have recently appeared in Allentown.

Figure 18.5
A "storefront" Pentecostal Church.

Figures 18.4 and 18.5 show examples of the many "storefront" churches that recently have begun to appear in Allentown. Often the established place of worship for these denominations is located far away from the Latino community. Latinos of those faiths therefore have established their own places of worship locally. Because of the small number of worshippers, the first floor of a residential building is used to hold services.

Food constitutes another major cultural identifier. The area between American Parkway and North 12th Street is developing as an ethnic business enclave and provides evidence of the critical mass of Latino consumers concentrated in this area of Allentown. This becomes apparent in at least two important ways: the types and ownership of food outlets and the types of food offered for sale. Elvis Diaz, from the Dominican Republic by way of New York, opened a C-Town that is now Allentown's biggest Latino-oriented grocery store (see Figure 18.6). Neighborhood bodegas are thriving in Allentown as well. Dominguez Grocery (Figure 18.7) is also operated by a transplanted Dominican. The store is bulging with an enormous variety of foods that cater to Latino tastes. Figure 18.8 shows a sidewalk tropical fruit and vegetable market with produce trucked in from the Hunt's Point market in the Bronx.

The sidewalk market and the types of items sold there are indicative of the growing demand for Latino ethnic foods. This demand is not only being met by Latino-owned stores, but is also being met by long established chain food stores in the city. For example, Little Apple Grocery, an IGA chain store, sells numerous food items that cater to Latino tastes, including tropical fruits and root crops (see Figure 18.9). Interestingly, the Latino produce is displayed prominently close to the entrance of the store and the fruits and vegetables that are usually in demand by Anglos are relegated to a less prominent positions. The religious and food cultural markets provide evidence that a Latino ethnoscape has emerged in Allentown.

Figure 18.6
C-Town is a Dominican owned grocery chain.

Figure 18.7
A Dominican owned bodega.

Figure 18.8
Sidewalk fruit and vegetable market.

Figure 18.9
Little Apple, an Anglo owned grocery chain sells foods that cater to its Latino customers.

SUMMARY

This chapter has addressed several issues related to the Latinization of Allentown, PA. The research was framed around five general sets of questions, to which we now return in this summary.

The first issue was concerned with migration to (and population change in) Allentown. We illustrated that Allentown experienced a dramatic demographic shift between 1980 and 2000, and that the population of the city is now about 25 percent Latino (of which 67 percent is Puerto Rican). The growth of the Latino population is largely due to in-migration of Latinos from the New York City area and from other origins in the Northeast and overseas. Many Latinos stated that their reason for moving to Allentown was for job opportunities. Others had different reasons, such as marriage and family reasons, tranquility and safety, housing costs, and the ability to purchase a home.

Second, we were concerned with questions of Latino settlement patterns in Allentown. We showed that Latinos are highly segregated from Anglos in the Allentown area. One way to understand the relatively high level of Latino-white segregation in the metro region is to examine Allentown in relation to Lehigh County. In 2000, approximately 82 percent of Lehigh County Latinos resided within the city of Allentown. In the same year, approximately 73 percent of all Latinos resided within 1.5 miles of its original settlement area, the intersection of Second and Linden Streets. We concluded that rather than social assimilation tied to spatial assimilation, by 2000 Latinos were merely replacing white, non-Hispanics in a more sequent occupance mode.

The third issue that we explored in the Latinization of Allentown had to do with Anglo and Latino perceptions. Drawing on Stains (1994) work we demonstrated that Anglos were concerned with Latinos brandishing a "Big Apple attitude" and being indiscrete, boisterous, and loitering, as well as having an association with crime, gangs and drugs. There was a fear among some Anglos that the Latino influence was a threat to women and children.

To gain some sense of Latino perceptions of Allentown, we conducted interviews and asked how fairly treated they felt in a number of different circumstances. The majority of our interviewees felt fairly treated by Anglos in the areas about which they were questioned. For example, 70 percent indicated that they received fair treatment by their Anglo neighbors. There are different experiences however, and some Latinos felt that many Anglos simply do not like Hispanic people and unfairly associate all Hispanics with crime and the drug culture of Allentown. The most common perception of Anglo treatment was related to social distance.

Another area of concern in this chapter had to do with employment and fair treatment in the regional labor market. We found, from our interviews, that the place of employment was where Latinos felt the least fairly treated. Structural issues, such as spatial mismatch between residence and employment, the existence of a dual labor market, and unemployment, were also examined. U.S. Census data illustrated a spatial mismatch between Latinos' residential location and places of employment. The mismatch might be at least partly responsible for higher unemployment rates among Latinos. In addition, we found that a dual labor market exists in Allentown with Latinos (especially males) concentrated in secondary occupations.

Finally, we illustrated with photographs that a Latino ethnoscape is becoming increasingly apparent in the city of Allentown. We concentrated on two major cultural identifiers, religion and food, to show how the cultural landscape of the city is changing. The religious landscape is being modified through the establishment of "storefront" churches and the language change from English to Spanish in formerly all-Anglo congregations.

The grocery industry has changed in a variety of ways in Allentown. First, was the appearance of the Latino (Dominican) owned bodega. Second, Anglo-owned chain grocery stores began to offer produce and other items to cater to Latino tastes. The most recent change has been the opening of C-Town, a Latino (Dominican)-owned chain store based in New York City. In both cases, religion and food, Latinos have brought their culture with them to Allentown and it is becoming clearly imprinted on the landscape.

Between 1980 and 2000, the Latino population of Allentown has quadrupled. Although the Puerto Rican population is the largest Latino group in the city, the Latino population is very diverse; there are substantial numbers of Mexicans and Dominicans living in Allentown. The rapid pace of the Latino influx would have strained the social fabric anywhere, but the strain has the potential to be particularly acute where it upsets the Germanic (Pennsylvania Dutch) sense of order in small cities like Allentown.

Many questions arise concerning the link between these population shifts and what it means for the future of small cities. As cities continue to search for methods to deal with dwindling budgets and increased competition in attracting highly selective and mobile capital, the probability of growing urban isolation and inequality by racial and ethnic groups should undoubtedly be viewed as a social problem on the rise.

Chapter 19

Population Change in the Texas Panhandle and Resultant Latino Occupational Structures:
1980–2004

LAWRENCE E. ESTAVILLE, EDRIS J. MONTALVO, AND BROCK J. BROWN

INTRODUCTION

The Great Plains of North America was the topic of the cover article in the May 2004 issue of the *National Geographic Magazine*. It devoted 52 pages to portraying journalistically the environmental consequences of human settlement and the subsequent depopulation of the huge region once called "the Great American Dessert" and later "the Breadbasket of the Continent." The *National Geographic Magazine* report builds on these conflicting perceptions to highlight the environmental and economic challenges facing an increasingly concerned region.

These anxieties about the environmental stresses and depopulation of the Great Plains are well documented in a considerable scholarly literature (e.g., Blouet and Luebke, 1979; Lawson and Baker, 1979; Luebke, 1980; Caldwell, Schultz, and Stout, 1983; Nickles and Day, 1997). We wish to add to this body of research in a different way, by underscoring the in-migration that is counterbalancing the depopulation of one part of the Great Plains. As Latinos replace some departing Anglos in the Texas Panhandle Plains, significant restructuring of the labor market is occurring. Differential perceptions of place utility of this region by Anglos and Latinos have led to changes in the labor force tied to ethnicity. A distinctive Latino occupational structure has resulted.

THE TEXAS PANHANDLE PLAINS

The vastness of the Great Plains reaches deep into Texas and terminates at the Rio Grande (Figure 19.1). As defined by the Center for Great Plains Studies at the University of Nebraska, most of West Texas and much of Central Texas, including the Edwards Plateau, are parts of the Great Plains. Although broken by such picturesque landscapes as the Texas Hill Country and Palo Duro Canyon, so flat is this immense Texas territory that the Spanish termed much of it as the "llano estacado" (staked plains) because during their explorations they had to plant stakes every so often to ensure they could find their return routes. Figure 19.2 illustrates the region's flat topography and the existence of oil.

The Great Plains in the "Panhandle" of Texas are called the Texas Panhandle Plains. The Texas Panhandle Plains region covers some 52,200 square miles, about the size of the state of Arkansas, and is a drought-prone land that receives less than 20 inches of annual precipitation. It lies over a large portion of the Ogallala Aquifer, a principal source of water for agriculture and communities that has been seriously depleted by years of "water mining." First attracted by the opportunities of cattle ranching and the farming of such crops as wheat, cotton, and sorghum, and later by oil and natural gas discoveries, much of the region now suffers from economic decline, having been devastated in the 1980s by the "oil bust" and serious droughts in recent years (Kraenzel,

1955; Blouet and Luebke, 1979; White, 1994; Nickles and Day, 1997). Nevertheless, perceptions of economic opportunities vary in the Texas Panhandle.

Through most of the 20th century, the Texas Panhandle was the home of Anglos who were the predominant ethnic group and who became prosperous in ranching, farming, and working in the oil and gas fields. Significant numbers of Latinos, mainly of Mexican heritage, did not arrive in the region until the beginning of the federal Bracero Program in 1942. In 1970, the first census after the 1964 close of the Bracero Program, the Latino resident population in the Texas Panhandle had grown to 113,200 people (Blouet and Luebke, 1979; Frugitt, Brown, and Beale, 1989; The Farmworkers Website, 2004; U.S. Census, 1970). Today, most of the region's people are either Anglos or Latinos, who differ somewhat in their perceptions of the region's economic opportunities.

Figure 19.1.
The 54 Study Counties and 12 Focus Counties in the Texas Panhandle Plains.

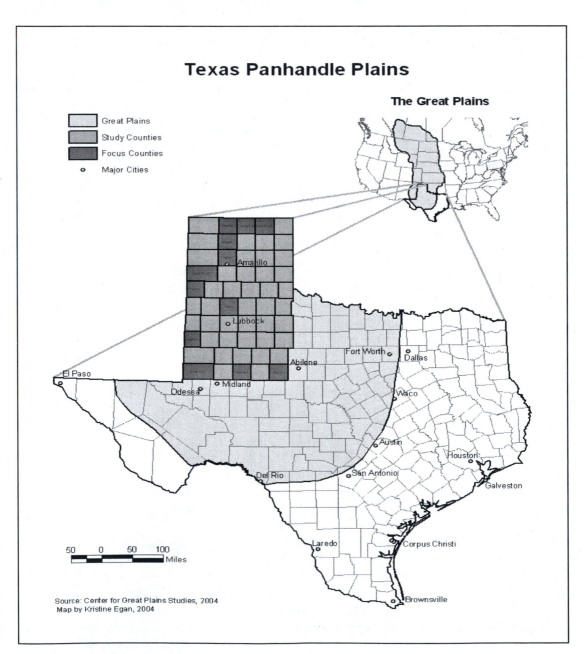

Figure 19.2.
The Flat Topography and Oil in the Texas Panhandle Plains.

PLACE UTILITY THEORY

Place utility theory provides insight into how voluntary migration occurs when individuals or families perceive that other places may offer superior benefits or utilities — economic, social, political, or environmental — in comparison to their current home. Potential migrants assess the utilities of their present location with other potential destinations to determine if they should migrate (Wolpert, 1965; Root, 2003). Because economic reasons have traditionally been the most important factors in the migration decision-making process, we focused our research efforts on population change and the Latino occupational structure that resulted within this theoretical context. However, we did include some social factors in our fieldwork in order to explore whether or not they played a role in the push or pull of Anglos out of and Latinos into the region.

DATA

We used all 54 counties of the Texas Panhandle in our population change analysis. For our analysis of the Latino occupational structure in 2000 and our fieldwork, we selected 35 counties of the Texas Panhandle from the original 54 that had populations of at least 25 percent Latino in the 2000 Census, thus allowing for substantial numbers of Latinos for sampling in our fieldwork. From these 35 Texas Panhandle counties, we then selected the ten counties that had the largest increases in Latino populations from 1980 to 2000 (Table 19.1). Because we wanted both Metropolitan Statistical Areas, Amarillo and Lubbock, represented in our sample, we also added Hale County. Finally, to ensure adequate spatial coverage throughout the region, we divided the Texas Panhandle study area into four quadrants to determine that at least one county was present in each quadrant. The results required the addition of one more county, Nolan County. From this four-step selection process, twelve counties became the focus counties for the analysis of the 2000 Latino occupational structure and our fieldwork (Figure 19.1).

Table 19.1.
Ten Largest Population Percentage Increases of Latinos in
the Texas Panhandle Counties, 1980–2000.

County	Percent Increase in Latino Population, 1980–2000
Moore	27.88%
Ochiltree	22.43%
Hansford	19.85%
Andrews	18.22%
Yoakum	18.14%
Deaf Smith	16.74%
Parmer	16.52%
Howard	16.44%
Potter	16.41%
Sherman	15.96%

The timeframe of our population change study includes three decennial censuses — 1980, 1990, and 2000. However, because the greatest increase in Latino population in the Texas Panhandle occurred in the 1990s, we concentrated our Latino occupational analysis on the 2000 census data for the twelve focus counties. We extracted the data for the Latino occupational analysis from the 2000 Summary File 4 (SF 4), which is a robust yet confidential sample of the original census data (see the 2000 U.S. Census for the specific parameters of this sample).

We also conducted in 2004 all of our survey interviews in the twelve focus counties. Our fieldwork in the twelve focus counties centered on interviewing residents in an effort to better understand the results of our population and occupational analyses and to discover any trends that were not readily discernable in these census data investigations. We used two very similar survey instruments, one of 11 questions for Anglos and the other consisting of 13 questions for Latinos. Both of the surveys highlighted each group's perceptions of out-migration in general from each county and specifically Anglo out-migration as well as Latino in-migration. We further probed the reasons for Anglo out-migration and Latino in-migration and the locations of their respective destinations and places of origin, thereby attempting to seek answers regarding their assessments of place utility prior to moving. Questions about the recency of the migrations and possible chain migrations were useful. During each of the 94 conversations, we followed up with questions in impromptu ways to understand the responses more fully and to uncover other relevant or unanticipated information.

STUDY FINDINGS

Population Change Analysis

In 1980 the total population of the 54 counties of the Texas Panhandle was 881,000, which decreased to 868,000 in 1990, but, unlike the declining trend across the entire Great Plains, then rebounded to 913,000 in 2000 (Table 19.2). The Anglo population in the Texas Panhandle did indeed mirror that of the entire Great Plains by decreasing from 662,000 (75 percent of the total population) in 1980 to 609,000 (70 percent) in 1990 and to 577,000 (63 percent) in 2000. Conversely, the Latino population increased from 169,000 (19 percent) in 1980 to 188,000 (22 percent) in 1990 and to 267,000 (29 percent) in 2000. Thus, over the two decades, Anglo population declined by 85,000 (13 percent), while Latino population increased by 98,000 (58 percent), thereby more than offsetting the Anglo decrease. The strong Latino population growth in the 1990s (79,000 people or 43 percent) was the main contributor to the increase in the total population of the Texas Panhandle in 2000 (U.S. Census, 1980, 1990, 2000).

Table 19.2.
Population Trends in the Texas Panhandle, 1980–2000.

	1980	1990	2000
Anglo Population	662,000	609,000	577,000
	75.14%	70.16%	63.20%
Latino Population	169,000	188,000	267,000
	19.18%	21.66%	29.24%
Total Population (includes other ethnic groups)	881,000	868,000	913,000

At the county level, from 1980 to 1990, except for one county, each of the 54 counties of the Texas Panhandle lost Anglo population (Figures 19.3 and 19.4). Twelve counties had more than 7 percent Anglo losses in the 1980s. In the 1990s, only four counties had gains in their Anglo populations, all of which were less than 3.5 percent. In the same decade, 23 counties lost more than 7 percent of their Anglo populations. For the entire study period, 1980–2000, only three counties experienced increases in Anglo population — all less than 2.5 percent. In contrast, 41 counties lost more than 7 percent of their Anglo populations, 16 of which lost more than 14 percent. The total decrease in Anglo population in all of the 54 counties between 1980 and 2000 was 85,000 people, a 13 percent decrease, which caused for the first time in the 20th century, Anglos to become minorities in ten counties of the Texas Panhandle (U.S. Census, 1980, 1990, 2000).

Figure 19.3.
Population Percents of Anglos and Latinos in the Texas Panhandle.

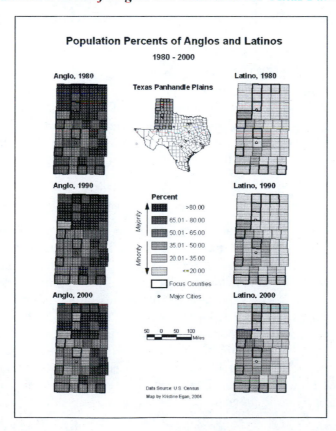

Figure 19.4.
Percent Change in Populations of Anglos and Latinos in the Texas Panhandle.

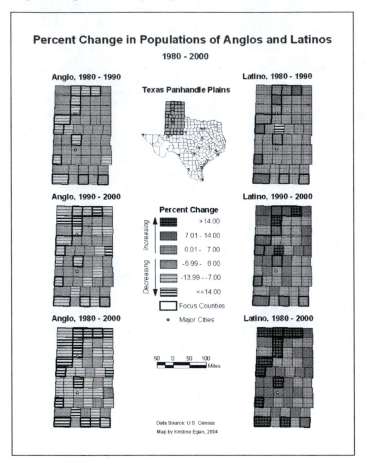

On the other hand, from 1980 to 1990, all but four counties in the study area showed increases in Latinos. In the 1990s, Latino increases were even more vigorous. All but three of the 54 counties had increases in Latino population, with 26 counties experiencing Latino gains of 7 percent or more. Over the twenty-year period, 53 of the 54 counties had Latino increases, 25 of which were more than 10 percent. The total increase in Latino population in all of the 54 counties between 1980 and 2000 was 98,000 people, showing an extraordinary growth of 58 percent (U.S. Census, 1980, 1990, 2000).

Latino Occupational Analysis

The results of these significant population changes in the Texas Panhandle — Anglo out-migration and Latino in-migration — from 1980 to 2000 produced a distinctive Latino occupational structure at the end of the 20th century. To examine this 2000 Latino occupational structure, we relied on U.S. Census data for the twelve focus counties. Overall, the twelve focus counties in 2000 showed that Latinos comprised one-third of the total Texas Panhandle workforce of 115,320 workers and that half of the Latino labor force worked primarily in two occupational sectors — Production/Transport/Material Moving (29%) and Service (21%). Latinos made up 51 percent of the workers in Production/Transport/Material Moving sector in the twelve counties. Twenty-nine percent of the Latino workforce, 10,537 Latinos, worked in this sector, mostly in meatpacking plants and as general laborers and truck drivers. More than 43 percent of Service sector workers in the twelve counties were Latinos, and 7,656 Latinos, or 21 percent, of the Latino labor force worked in this employment sector, largely in food preparation and serving, and building and grounds maintenance.

Latinos comprised nearly a quarter of the Sales and Office jobs, mainly retail cashiers and sales, and more than a third of the Construction/Extraction/Maintenance jobs, especially construction (Figure 19.5) and extraction (oil and gas) labor and vehicle and electrical maintenance. However, only 15 percent of the Latino workforce and 13.5 percent of all Latinos worked in these jobs, respectively. Interestingly, although Latinos comprised 56 percent of the Farming/Fishing/Forestry employment sector (almost all agricultural in the Texas Panhandle), less than 10 percent of the Latino workforce, or 3,430 laborers, worked on farms and ranches in the twelve focus counties, which emphasizes the increasingly high degree of mechanization of these huge agricultural operations. Also noteworthy is that the proportion of Latinos in the Management/Professional sector, 14 percent, corresponds to their 11 percent representation in the workforce. This indicates some upward occupational mobility by the turn of the 21st century in the Texas Panhandle.

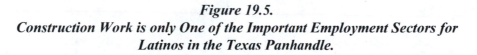

Figure 19.5.
***Construction Work is only One of the Important Employment Sectors for
Latinos in the Texas Panhandle.***

Tables 19.3a, b, c divide the twelve focus counties into three groups (see Figure 19.1): a) four counties — Deaf Smith, Moore, Parmer, and Yoakum — mostly located in the western part of the Texas Panhandle and that have large numbers of livestock feedlots and associated meatpacking plants; b) three counties — Hansford, Ochiltree, and Sherman — located on the northern edge of the Texas Panhandle and that possess more diversified economies split among oil and gas production, ranching, and feedlot operations; and c) five counties — Andrews, Hale, Howard, Nolan, and Potter — that are within the Amarillo and Lubbock Metropolitan Statistical Areas or near other cities in the Texas Panhandle and are thus influenced by urban occupations (University of Texas at Austin, 2005).

In the four counties of the first group (Table 19.3a), Production/Transport/Material Moving averaged 37 percent of the Latino workforce, and the meatpacking industry primarily employed these workers. Because of the several small towns in these counties, particularly Hereford, Dumas, Farwell, and Denver City, the proportion of the Latino workforce in the Service sector averaged almost 20 percent, mainly in food preparation and serving, and building and grounds maintenance. Yoakum County stands out in this group because Denver City is the traditional center of the county's oil and gas industry within the southern fields of the Texas Panhandle. In Yoakum County, the oil and gas industry employed nearly 20 percent of the Latino workforce.

Table 19.3a.
Latino Occupations in the Twelve Focus Counties of the Texas Panhandle in 2000.

		Total for Twelve Counties	Deaf Smith	Moore	Parmer	Yoakum
Total Workforce		115,329	7,122	8,599	3,855	2,861
Latino Workforce		36,147	3,560	3,456	1,680	1,112
% Latino of Work-force		33.12	49.99	40.19	43.58	38.87
Management/ Professional	% Latino of Total Workforce	13.86	24.84	14.22	14.43	14.32
	% of Latino Workforce	11.34	13.15	6.94	9.40	9.53
Service	% Latino of Total Workforce	43.14	65.15	46.93	57.00	51.79
	% of Latino Workforce	21.18	21.69	20.54	16.49	18.17
Sales/Office	% Latino of Total Workforce	24.49	39.49	23.37	35.17	27.57
	% of Latino Workforce	15.37	15.79	10.24	16.31	14.93
Farming/Fishing/ Forestry	% Latino of Total Workforce	55.74	57.92	60.41	54.91	66.67
	% of Latino Workforce	9.49	6.26	5.12	10.65	10.79
Construction/ Extraction/ Maintenance	% Latino of Total Workforce	37.01	54.46	30.29	44.57	47.74
	% of Latino Workforce	13.48	10.39	9.20	7.08	18.97
Production/ Transport/ Material Moving	% Latino of Total Workforce	50.96	76.34	65.24	74.61	60.55
	% of Latino Workforce	29.15	32.72	47.95	40.06	27.61

The three counties in the second group (Table 19.3b) had the highest average, 22 percent, of the three county groups for agricultural occupations, mostly ranching and feedlot operations, in the Latino workforce. At the same time, these three counties had a substantial proportion of the Latino workforce, 41 percent, employed as general laborers, maintenance workers, and truck drivers in the oil and gas industry in the northern fields of the Texas Panhandle. Because total population of these three counties was less than 8,000 people, the percent of the Latino workforce in Service jobs, 16 percent, was the smallest of the three county groups.

Table 19.3b.
Latino Occupations in the Twelve Focus Counties of the Texas Panhandle in 2000.

		Hansford	Ochiltree	Sherman
Total Workforce		2,419	4,146	1,373
Latino Workforce		615	1,110	278
% Latino of Workforce		25.42	26.77	20.25
Management/ Professional	% Latino of Total Workforce	7.89	11.01	6.83
	% of Latino Workforce	9.27	10.00	12.23
Service	% Latino of Total Workforce	33.13	35.16	23.08
	% of Latino Workforce	17.40	16.76	14.03
Sales/Office	% Latino of Total Workforce	14.35	11.81	9.20
	% of Latino Workforce	11.22	10.45	8.63
Farming/Fishing/ Forestry	% Latino of Total Workforce	50.49	82.80	52.10
	% of Latino Workforce	16.75	18.65	31.29
Construction/ Extraction/ Maintenance	% Latino of Total Workforce	35.14	35.97	19.64
	% of Latino Workforce	16.91	21.71	7.91
Production/ Transport/ Material Moving	% Latino of Total Workforce	44.53	35.22	43.37
	% of Latino Workforce	28.46	22.43	25.90

Urban centers influenced the Latino occupational structure of the third group of five counties (Table 19.3c). Only 2.9 percent of the Latino workforce consisted of agricultural workers in the third group of counties. The Latino workforce in the five counties still had substantial proportions of jobs in the Production/Transport/Material Moving sector (particularly meatpacking, laborers, and truck drivers) at 25 percent, as well as in the Construction/Extraction/Maintenance sector (largely construction and building and grounds maintenance) at 14 percent. However, the Latino workforce in this third group was the highest of the three groups in the Service sector (26%), in Sales/Office employment (19%), and in Management/Professional positions (13%), all emphasizing urban occupations.

In sum, Latino workers in the Texas Panhandle varied geographically in their occupations but generally were workers in meatpacking and feedlot operations, the oil and gas industry, and restaurants, as well as in general labor and truck driving. In 2000, most Latinos worked in low-paying jobs that were mainly at the bottom of the occupational ladder — jobs that many Anglos refused to continue to do. Anglos, therefore, moved in the decade of the 1990s, especially from the rural areas of the Texas Panhandle in search of more rewarding occupations in nearby cities or in large metropolitan areas elsewhere in Texas, while Latinos moved into the region in search of better jobs in comparison with those they had in South Texas or Mexico, if they had jobs at all. Our fieldwork corroborated this generalization.

Table 19.3c.
Latino Occupations in the Twelve Focus Counties of the Texas Panhandle in 2000.

		Andrews	Hale	Howard	Nolan	Potter
Total Workforce		5,064	14,646	12,092	6,430	46,722
Latino Workforce		1,641	6,362	3,277	1,598	11,458
% Latino of Workforce		32.41	43.44	27.10	24.85	24.52
Management/ Professional	% Latino of Total Workforce	15.16	20.74	14.42	11.69	10.77
	% of Latino Workforce	11.94	13.36	16.42	13.95	9.83
Service	% Latino of Total Workforce	44.42	53.27	41.95	54.08	31.69
	% of Latino Workforce	22.55	20.23	33.08	25.84	27.33
Sales/Office	% Latino of Total Workforce	28.49	38.86	22.33	22.74	20.47
	% of Latino Workforce	18.40	20.75	16.84	19.52	21.31
Farming/Fishing/ Forestry	% Latino of Total Workforce	39.06	68.26	50.98	51.55	33.73
	% of Latino Workforce	1.52	5.85	3.17	3.13	0.74
Construction/ Extraction/ Maintenance	% Latino of Total Workforce	42.02	46.18	29.78	30.00	28.34
	% of Latino Workforce	21.02	9.31	12.69	12.02	14.55
Production/ Transport/ Material Moving	% Latino of Total Workforce	40.58	66.77	34.19	33.94	36.13
	% of Latino Workforce	24.56	30.51	17.79	25.53	26.23

Fieldwork Outcomes

We interviewed 94 people in the twelve focus counties in a non-random, "by convenience" sample. We attempted to interview as many people as possible when we visited each county seat. To gain a better understanding of the socioeconomic conditions and Latino occupational structure of each of the twelve focus counties and the perceptions of economic opportunities of the region, we interviewed Anglos and Latinos in a variety of occupations, ranging from government officials, college administrators and hotel employees to shop owners, restaurant waitresses, students, and construction workers. Of the 94 individuals, 50 were Anglo (18 males, 32 females), who had a mean age of 48 years and who all possessed a high school education, with several having college degrees. The 44 Latinos (19 males, 25 females), had a younger mean age of 35 years and a significantly lower educational attainment than the 50 Anglos; about 20 percent of the Latinos had not completed high school. We found that many Latino males, mainly laborers did not wish to be interviewed, perhaps fearing we were U.S. Immigration and Naturalization Service (INS) agents. Several Anglo governmental officials told us that they were too busy with their work to talk with us. Nevertheless, we believe that our face-to-face survey sample of 94 people is a solid one that produced information from almost all sectors of the region's socioeconomic structure and confirmed the major findings of our analyses of population change and Latino occupational structure in the Texas Panhandle. It also gave us fresh insights and confirmed our place utility theoretical framework for the study.

In the interviews, 58 percent of Anglos and 49 percent of Latinos thought that people were leaving their counties and that the declining economy was the major reason for this out-migration. Seventy percent of the Anglos surveyed said they knew of another Anglo individual or family member who moved out of their county to search for better economic opportunities in mostly urban areas. When asked the same question, 64 percent of Latinos declared that they, too, knew Anglos who had left their county. A 45-year-old Latina restaurant worker contended that the primary reason for Anglos leaving is that they do not want the types of jobs that most Latinos have. She cautioned:

> " It's hard to land a good job. If you find a job here, you'd better keep it."

When asked about the increasing numbers of Latinos in their home counties, 82 percent of Anglos felt that the numbers of Latinos were increasing as they searched for better jobs and economic prosperity. Sixty-seven percent of Latinos confirmed that they were searching for places with more economic utility. After finding successful economic circumstances in their counties, 18 percent of Latinos had encouraged other Latinos from other places to move into their county to live, thereby substantiating that some Latinos did indeed engage in chain migration into the region.

The question, "Do increasing numbers of Latinos cause Anglos in any way to move from the county," resulted in some passionate responses by both Anglos and Latinos as they agreed that the dynamic does, in fact, take place. Yet, most Anglos and Latinos were unsure if more Latinos really caused Anglos to move.

While most Anglos viewed Latinos in positive ways as valuable members of their communities, some Anglos had negative comments about their Latino neighbors. For instance, a middle-aged female manager of one town's Chamber of Commerce emphasized:

> "Oh, you're talking about the wetbacks.... I think that they should learn English so we don't have to use our tax money to print things out in English and in Spanish."

Another Anglo woman, a 35-year-old part-time hotel clerk, expressed concerns about not being able to find a job because of the increasing need for bilingual workers:

> " I can't find a job and it's hard to find a job because I don't speak Latino ... so I'm moving to Dallas."

This latent bigotry seemed to be the exception rather than the rule in our twelve focus counties.

Some Latinos felt a degree of discontent toward Anglos. A migrant from Mexico at an early age and now a 35-year-old male owner of a Mexican food restaurant expressed his thoughts about Anglo out-migration and Anglo behavior toward Latinos:

> "The Anglos leave because they don't like to do the jobs we do, but they don't want to pay us enough to work either or for the food they like to eat."

Another migrant from Mexico who is a 44-year-old woman with only a sixth-grade education disagreed:

> "I came for the American dream, and opportunities are here for anyone who wants to work hard."

Most Anglos and Latinos have learned to work together, but, interestingly, Anglos and Latinos both complained of inadequate Latino representation in county and municipal government. However, neither group articulated reasons for this lack of Latino community leadership.

CONCLUSION AND FURTHER RESEARCH

Like most of the Great Plains, the 54 counties of the Texas Panhandle Plains have experienced Anglo depopulation since 1980, yet this out-migration has not been the only salient population development. As place utility theory predicts, Anglos, in fact, do perceive declining economic opportunities in their longtime home in the Texas Panhandle and are pulled to better jobs mostly in urban places in Texas. However, Latinos, especially those who come directly from Mexico, evaluate the economic opportunities positively in relationship to other possible places and decide to move into a new homeland to create a better life for themselves and their children. By 2000, the out-migration of Anglos and in-migration of Latinos had caused significant occupational restructuring in which Latinos had taken most of the low-paying agricultural, meat processing, service, and laborer jobs. When Anglos find better jobs in large urban areas, Latinos do not replace the Anglos in higher-paying occupations because those types of jobs are generally lost, but, instead, Latinos provide mainly low-cost labor for a Texas Panhandle economy that continues to struggle with profit margins.

Three important questions remain to be answered: 1) Will Latinos become the majority population in the Texas Panhandle? 2) When will Latinos begin to capture political control in the counties they currently comprise the majority population? and 3) How will the continued Anglo out-migration and Latino in-migration, along with economic restructuring more dependent on a labor-intensive workforce, affect future environmental degradation in a very sensitive ecosystem?

Part IV

Asian and Pacific-Islander Geographies: Cultural Persistence and Changing Patterns

Section four continues the themes of changing geographic settlement patterns, racial discrimination against minorities, and the infusion of cultural and ethnic meaning into particular places. It illustrates how America's early Asian immigrants carved their respective niches in spite of racial discrimination. The historical settlement patterns, experiences, and adjustments of the three largest Asian groups in the early 20th century are reviewed in Chapter 20, which also provides contemporary geographies of more recent immigrant Chinese, Koreans, and Vietnamese. Three additional chapters explore other contemporary issues and patterns. Chapter 21 examines the role of place-people connections in current native Hawaiian identity, the factors that challenge its maintenance, and the place-based educational strategies that seek to ensure its preservation.

Chapter 22 examines ethnic identity for Japanese-Americans. After tracing the early geographies of Japanese-American migration, it explores the early ethnic life of Los Angeles' Little Tokyo, a traditional urban ethnic enclave with distinctive landscape characteristics. It explains the etching of cultural features onto the landscape, and how racism and nativism led to its decline. It reveals the ethnic persistence that reshapes ethnic identity and adjusts to political and economic pressures of the host society. This chapter provides an example of how agencies (social institutions) create landscapes that "reflect and impact" contemporary ethnic identities and are a part of place-making.

One of America's fastest growing Asian ethnic groups in recent times is Asian Indians. Chapter 23 examines the settlement patterns and ethnic identities of this controversial "racial classification." As in the case of other immigrants, commercial spaces have become important symbolic and landscape markers for this otherwise "invisible" immigrant group. This chapter examines the methods of "identity re-formation" used by Asian Indians, who tend to be geographically dispersed in metropolitan regions but remain connected by various forms of interaction that reinforce their ethnic identities.

Chapter 20

Asians in the United States:
Historical and Contemporary Settlement Patterns

JOHN W. FRAZIER

INTRODUCTION

The term "Asian" describes a substantial range of cultures spread over thousands of miles of the globe. Even descriptive Asian sub-phrases can be deceiving. For example, "East Asian," meant to refer to people in one geographic region, actually describes distinctly different cultures separated by the great distance from Pakistan to southern India. Grouping dissimilar cultures into a single class has obvious drawbacks. However, it facilitates addressing three greatly different cultures as Asians in pre-1965 America: the Chinese (who initially brought to the U.S. numerous dialects that were not understandable to one another), the Japanese, and the Filipinos. Although from very different cultures, these immigrants to America were viewed monolithically as "Orientals" whose presence was termed an "Asiatic Coolies Invasion" by the early 20th century (Organized Labor, 1906). These Asians shared more than locations in the Pacific. Each found resentment rooted in fear and racism, related to the contexts that existed at the time of their arrival in the U.S. The result was prejudice, discrimination, and hardship, as well as actions that halted the future entry of their people. Geographic settlement patterns of these early arrivals were governed by social institutions.

Prior to the Great Depression, thousands of Asians had entered America. However, by the beginning of World War II, Asian immigration had been reduced to a trickle, and would remain so until major changes in U.S. immigration law in the 1960s. The purpose of this chapter is to examine the historical and contemporary patterns of Asian immigration to the U.S., especially Asian immigration and settlements from the mid-19th century through the Great Depression, which is the topic of the first part of this chapter. The historical contexts for early Asian immigration and their eventual exclusion are provided.

In a contemporary context, the term "Asians" also facilitates the discussion of numerous Asian ethnic groups that are contributing to changing America and its human geography. The second section of the chapter examines the massive influx of Asians to the U.S. commencing in the mid-1960s and continuing into the early 21st century. The emergence of new geographic patterns, specific Asian ethnic places, and Asian-American landscapes are presented.

ASIANS IN AMERICA PRIOR TO 1965

In 1845, American journalist John Louis O'Sullivan set forth the concept of Manifest Destiny as a defense for U.S. expansionist behavior. By the time gold was discovered in Sutter's Creek, attracting prospectors of all ethnic backgrounds (white Easterners as well as foreigners) to California, politicians and business leaders endorsed the concept of Manifest Destiny as a God-given right for the expansion of American democracy across North America. The public of a young and expanding nation was easily convinced of their nation's moral and economic superiority. They, too, endorsed the mission of westward expansion as right, or perhaps even as an obligation, which would result in so much European progress. Constantly improving technology and advancements on the frontier strengthened these convictions.

Prior to 1965 and, in fact, before World War II, three groups from the Pacific entered the United States in distinctive waves. These were the Chinese, Japanese, and Filipinos. Each group provided cheap labor vital to the expanding U.S. economy.

The Chinese

The Chinese were the first Asian ethnic group to enter the U.S. in large numbers. By 1850, although Hispanic California was already "whitening" from U.S. eastern migrants, the Gold Rush greatly increased that flow and also attracted to California for the first time a large influx of Chinese. Chronic poverty and strife had pushed the Cantonese of China towards "Gold Mountain" in an effort to become rich and return home. Initially, the numbers were moderate: only 50 Chinese resided in California in the 1840s. That changed quickly as more Chinese sought riches and others were recruited as laborers. By 1852, the Chinese population of San Francisco had reached 25,000 and continued to grow for decades. The former Chief of Police, writing in 1931, recalled "the Chinese were coming in from the Orient at about 1,400 on every steamer" (Cook, 1931, p. 1). By 1876, more than 150,000 Chinese had entered the U.S. and 116,000 resided in California (McClain, 1994).

Given the initial labor shortages, especially for the difficult and hard work associated with field labor and construction, it is no surprise that the Chinese were welcomed, as noted by Norton:

> "Here were men who would do the drudgery of life at a reasonable wage, when every other man had but one idea — to work at the mines for gold.... The result was that the Chinaman was welcomed; he was considered quite indispensable. He was in demand as a laborer, as a carpenter, as a cook; the restaurants which he established were well-patronized; his agricultural efforts in draining and tilling the rich lands were praised. Governor McDougal referred to him as, 'One of the most worthy of our newly adopted citizens.' In public functions he was given a place of honor ... their cleanliness, unobtrusiveness, and industry were everywhere praised" (H. K. Norton, 1924, p. 1).

Nowhere was their labor more necessary or desired than in the building of western railroads. Railroad companies recruited them. In 1863, the Pacific Railroad employed only a few (about 50) Chinese workers, but by 1867, the Chinese accounted for 80 percent of their labor force and totaled approximately 20,000 laborers.

Only a few short years later, the Panic of 1873 resulted in depressed prices and vast surpluses of agricultural goods, including those of California. However, in 1877, the western economy hit bottom and unemployment became an enormous issue. Labor now had two enemies, greedy capitalists and the Chinese who benefited California development. By 1880, fifty thousand Chinese lived in San Francisco, which by that time had become the focus of anti-Chinese activities.

In 1877, Irish-born Denis Kearney became one of the leading labor voices of California, speaking against capitalism and the Chinese. His ability to attract listeners to his orations against big business and Chinese immigrants, who together caused white workers to suffer low wages and unemployment, led to the formation of the Workingmen's Party in 1877. He quickly rose to the leadership and unions rallied across the state for support of striking railroad men, an eight-hour day, taxes on the wealthy, and for immigration restrictions. California's 1877 Depression was a short-term context for racial oppression. Kearney's slogan "bullets will replace ballots" marked the threat of violence that exploded in a three-day riot against the Chinese. Hostility was directed towards places that symbolized Chinese existence, the laundries they operated profitably, and the Pacific steamship wharves to which Chinese arrived. Several Chinese were killed in this riot, and major property damage occurred. Violence against the Chinese occurred at various places along the West Coast, and was supported by others, including those in the South. Norton expressed this in 1924, when describing the earlier Los Angeles riot:

"Their (labor radicals') method of procedure was in most cases to sack and burn the Chinese laundries and other commercial establishments operated by the Orientals. It was left for Los Angeles to furnish the most terrible example of all. Here nineteen Chinamen were hanged and shot in one evening. The massacre was accompanied by theft of over $40,000 worth of their goods....

It was in the South, in fact, that the violent opposition to the Chinese had first found strong supporters. Here were many who were accustomed to assert the superiority of their race and to attach the idea of servitude to all inferior races" (H. K. Norton, 1924, pp. 283–96).

Kearney's Party extended its threats to those who would employ Chinese labor and its influence to the 1878 California Constitution Convention, pressing for new laws against the Chinese, and later to the passage of national legislation. The state would virtually exclude Chinese residents from their civil rights and employment. Federal law would restrict further Chinese immigration.

Much has been written about the legal barriers established to Chinese citizenship and civil rights. One example of legal exclusion helps clarify the position of the California courts, including the state Supreme Court. In the *People* vs. *Jones* (1869), a White appellant convicted of robbery of a Chinese man was released because:

"Under the laws of this State, Chinamen are disqualified from being witnesses or giving testimony in any case in which a white man is party ..." (Grant, 1994, p. 88).

As Grant noted, the Supreme Court not only supported Chinese exclusion under California law, it degraded the Chinese in its findings, describing them as:

"... a degraded, brutal, and vicious race, peculiarly addicted to crime and vice, and demanding more stringent regulations for their government than are required for the general mass of citizens ..." (findings quoted by Grant, 1994, p. 90).

The politics of Chinese exclusion, which officially occurred with passage of the U.S. *1882 Chinese Exclusion Act*, must be viewed in broader-than-regional context. Racism was prevalent throughout American regions by 1882. Also, the U.S. had engaged Chinese and Japanese in treaties to stimulate American foreign trade in the Pacific. A treaty with Japan in 1858 had followed Commodore Perry's "opening" of Japanese ports five years earlier. In 1868, the Burlingame Treaty between the U.S. and China confirmed U.S. trading privileges and appealed to American expansionist interest in the Pacific; it also contained articles requiring the protection of Chinese immigrants that were so desperately desired for the provision of cheap labor. This agreement eventually led to a conflict between federal executives (presidents) and Congress, as well as to discontent among Californians toward the federal government.

Hune's analysis of this controversy revealed that Presidents Hayes and Garfield opposed legislation that would restrict Chinese immigration due to its potentially negative implications for global trade (Hune, 1994). However, she also clarified the influence of prevailing racial attitudes on these two presidents and the fact that few politicians considered the victims of the proposed policy:

"... At first glance, it would appear that Chinese restriction was a matter of congressional policy to which the executive office eventually acquiesced. However, a closer examination of the attitudes and actions of the presidents of this period suggest that Chinese restriction was also a matter of executive policy and that the legislature and the executive office were not in basic conflict. George Sinkler has noted that the racial attitudes of presidents have tended to mirror the times and the general populace. Thus in their private and public papers, Hayes, Garfield, and Arthur expressed their own misgivings about the presence of the Chinese, whom they viewed as unassimilable and a potential danger to American civilization....

... Thus, although the vetoes of Presidents Hayes and Arthur forestalled the adoption of Chinese restriction, their other activities also prepared the way for the passage of a restriction bill while ensuring a more important concern for many Americans — maintaining an open door policy in China. Therefore, the division within Congress and especially the conflict that took place between the legislative and executive branches over the Chinese issue centered largely over the *means* and not upon the goal of restriction itself. A minority voice in Congress spoke in favor of the value of an open pluralistic American society" (Hune, 1994, pp. 110–11).

The passage of the 1882 law was the only U.S. immigration law ever directed at a single racial/ethnic group. It reduced Chinese immigration to a trickle (although "*paper sons*" continued to enter in small numbers for decades). The decline in the Chinese population was precipitous, falling from 105,000 in 1880 to 85,000 in 1920. The contexts described earlier resulted in the victimization of the Chinese and, as shown in the next section, Chinatown, as a place, became a social construct created by European cultures for self-serving purposes.

Chinatown as Social Construct

As noted earlier, the Chinese sought refuge from white violence and discrimination by congregating in what would be termed Chinatowns, which became fixtures in San Francisco, Oakland, and later in other cities. The eastward migration of Chinese fleeing prejudice and discrimination resulted in the growth of eastern Chinatowns, including those in Chicago, New York City and Boston. The physical appearance of late 19th and early 20th century Chinatowns differed significantly from America's contemporary image of bright and colorful landscapes that attract tourists and diners. They consisted of small, crowded unattractive structures that gained the criticism of local whites.

Despite this fact, over time, Chinatowns became popularized as unique landscapes expressing social organization and cultural pride. Some social scientists have suggested that these communities function as "points of contact" for other immigrants seeking cultural assimilation, while others see Chinatown as a reaction to white prejudice and discrimination. Kay J. Anderson has taken issue with these positions by suggesting "Chinatown is a social construction with a cultural history and a tradition of imagery and institutional practice that has given it a cognitive and material reality in and for the West" (Anderson, 1987, p. 581). She argued that, rather than prejudice, the key explanatory variable in the Western creation of Chinatowns was racial ideology, which combines race (Chinese) and place (Chinatown) in the creation of a racial classification that was meant to benefit Western white societies. The creation of a negative racial class was linked to a place of unnecessary and unacceptable "evils," which justified the use of powerful white institutions to define the boundaries and contents of the place and to support actions to drive away the vile race occupying it.

Anderson used Vancouver to illustrate the use of this social construct. By 1886, the Chinese, largely a bachelor society, were already under the control of the government and were geographically concentrated in a small neighborhood of Vancouver. Admittedly, the Chinese contributed to their self-definition and local cultural landscape. However, the local white European culture created the essence of "Chineseness" and the regional image of Chinatown "on capricious grounds" (p. 583). According to Anderson, the stereotyping of Chinese was rooted in 18th century western interpretations of China. Traders, visitors, and other Western opinion leaders, including Protestant missionaries, offered highly unfavorable characterizations of the culture. Not only were Chinese backward and "peculiar," they also were treacherous, immoral, "conscious agents of Satan" (Anderson, p. 591).

In Vancouver, as in San Francisco and other American communities, the Chinese were described as undesirable outsiders and their living quarters as a despicable, repulsive, and threatening local geography. This social construction allowed the white majority to create a racial classification that not only affirmed white identity and privileged status, but also provided a basis for ridding local society of its problems. Racial classification used place (Chinatown), to create a "social fact" and imbedded racial ideology (Anderson, 1987).

Anderson explained the creation of the social construct by equating notions, like the "Chinaman seems to be the same everywhere," with the Chinese as "dirty and undesirable" and their Chinatowns as "unsanitary sink[s]" and "morally aberrant communit[ies]" (Anderson, p. 586). Local government institutions then designated "official definitions of Chinatown" as essential to monitor questionable activities and, then, to limit their locations, such as by controlling Chinese laundries (p. 587). Much of this was offered in the name of "sanitary reform," to eliminate "fear of contamination from the Orient" (p. 586).

Although gambling and prostitution were widespread in the city, Chinatown became the location of choice to stop vice. Local political and police actions were necessary to rid white society of these drug lords, prostitution houses, and gambling operations. The "disgrace" of their existence was attributed to the Chinese "menace," and white participation in vice was simply a verification of the problems of the undesirable Chinese race. Chinatown, a den of inequity wedged into white society, was the place that magnified the shortcomings of this race. Despite the protests of Chinese merchants and leaders and their efforts to correct these false race-based images, the strength of social construct created by whites prevailed and resulted in prejudicial and discriminatory behavior by the white population and its institutions towards the Chinese people.

Anderson's powerful explanation of the social construction and "evaluative classification" of Chinatown can be compared to Wilson's description of the 20th century black ghetto "underclass." It is striking that in both constructs, racial classification results in the demonization of a particular group in a way that permits depersonalization. The human geography of both places is perceived as crowded, filthy, and dangerous. Both groups also participate in "aberrant behaviors" that threaten the social order cherished by the ruling class (Wilson, 1987). Even this brief comparison suggests the validity and power of Anderson's explanation.

For American Chinatowns, historical experiences of violence and institutional controls were strikingly similar to those of Vancouver. We noted particularly their experiences in San Francisco, but those of other communities, such as Oakland, have also been documented (Frazier, Margai, and Tettey-Fio, 2003). We also noted the roles of California State and local institutions, especially the courts, and of the federal government in actions that led to the only U.S. immigration law ever to target a specific racial/ethnic group. With the creation of the quota system in the 1920s, the fate of Chinese immigration became fixed for decades. The additional insult came with the treatment of Chinese who sought entry as "paper sons," those permitted entry due to "proven" family relationships with former Chinese immigrants. Angel Island, the Western port of entry, became synonymous with questionable treatment of entering Chinese. Millions of Europeans entering through Ellis Island faced few questions and a simple physical exam, while Chinese often were detained at the Angel Island facility for months in unpleasant conditions. The Chinese developed a sense of bitterness for this very unfortunate period and worked to preserve Angel Island as a landmark and symbol of what was involved in becoming a Chinese American.

The Japanese

Although a few Japanese entered the U.S. prior to the Civil War, their total population in the U.S. in 1880 was about 150 (Buell, 1994, p. 26). In 1885, the Japanese government legalized emigration, although with the stipulation that Japanese emigrants owed allegiance to their home nation. Shortly thereafter, Japanese emigration companies worked with American labor contractors, for great profit, to provide cheap Japanese labor that was in demand on the American Pacific Coast. Pushed away by poor Japanese agricultural conditions and pervasive poverty, and attracted to the prospect of employment, the Japanese increasingly answered the call of labor contractors. By 1891, more than one thousand annually entered the U.S.; 12,000 entered in the single year of 1900. The trend continued and soon the Japanese replaced the Chinese as a problem:

> "In the five years between 1898 and 1903, the number of emigrants (Japanese) going to foreign countries, excluding Korea and China, were 84,576. Eighty percent went to the United States. In the year 1900, four times as many Japanese entered America as in the previous year. Naturally, this irritated the sensibilities of California — easily aroused after a riotous twenty-year struggle with the Chinese immigrants" (Buell, 1994, p. 608).

A series of labor-related and civil actions followed. When word of a potential health plague emerged in San Francisco in 1900, arguably forwarded for political reasons, city officials quarantined Japanese and Chinese districts, and nowhere else (Buell, 1994). Increasingly, public health fears and labor concerns led to public meetings led by labor and the agitation for inclusion of Japanese in a modified Chinese Exclusion Law (Buell, 1994). The Japanese response, sometimes termed the "First Gentlemen's Agreement," was to tighten emigration. This was not enough to quiet growing concern among labor leaders. California's economy had returned to prosperity by the time of the Spanish-American War, particularly in San Francisco. This prosperity had favorable impacts on labor. Despite the demise of the Workingman's Party only a few years earlier, a new political party, the Union Labor Party, emerged and became very influential.

Although the government of Japan promised emigration concessions, its immigrants kept coming. Japanese labor continued to supply Hawaiian sugar plantations. Many of the same Japanese laborers made it to America's Pacific Coast, attracted by its higher wages. Incoming annually from Hawaii to the U.S. mainland, their numbers increased from slightly more than 1,000 in 1902 to nearly 14,000 in 1904 (Buell, 1994). The labor movement of California feared the same from Japanese as it did from Chinese "Coolie labor," as reported in *Organized Labor*:

> "Thousands of fair-minded and well-meaning people who were biased and ignorant on the question of Japanese immigration have, during the last year, entirely changed their views on the subject. They have learned the truth, that the Japanese coolie is even greater a menace to the existence of the white race, to the progress and prosperity of our country than is the Chinese coolie....
>
> The great calamity which befell San Francisco will furnish the Orient with lurid tales of opportunity for employment and profit. California, the land of fabulous wealth, revenue, and mountains of gold, and San Francisco with its wonderful wages, will be exploited before the ignorant coolies until they will come in shiploads like an endless swarm of rats....
>
> Great as the recent catastrophe has been, let us take care, lest we encounter a greater one.
>
> We can withstand the earthquake.
> We can survive the fire.
>
> As long as California is white man's country, it will remain one of the grandest and best states in the union, but the moment the Golden State is subjected to an unlimited Asiatic coolie invasion, there will be no more California" (Organized Labor, 1906, pp. 1–2).

In the previous year, the *San Francisco Chronicle* had published a large piece suggesting that the increasing Japanese "menace" held serious consequences for California and the nation. The paper "greatly exaggerated" the Japanese population in the U.S. at 100,000 (Buell, 1994). The agitation provided by the media and labor was constant. An earthquake, fire, and the position of President T. Roosevelt prevented immediate exclusionary policy. However, anti-Japanese sentiment continued and was fueled by racist convictions, as well as economic fears associated with continued Japanese immigration and the relocation of Japanese after the San Francisco fire:

> "But the reconstruction of the city again resurrected anti-Japanese sentiment. Ten thousand Japanese had been affected by the fire. In an effort to find new homes and business locations, many invaded the Western districts of San Francisco which hitherto had been 'white man's land.'
>
> Meanwhile, other sources of irritation manifested themselves. Immigration by no means had ceased. For the first six months of 1906, the excess of Japanese arrivals over departures in San Francisco alone was 5,772, a figure which led the *Chronicle* to declare, 'If the next Congress does not act in this matter, it will assume very grave responsibilities'" (Buell, 1994, p. 41).

Labor publications chided whites for patronizing Japanese businesses and requested cooperation. A wave of violence, including burglary, arson, of property destruction, and murder, followed.

A single event in 1906, however, brought international attention to San Francisco. The city's School Board, controlled by the Mayor and directed by the Exclusion League, issued a decree that mandated all Asian children attend segregated schools. This would require Japanese children, 93 of a total enrollment of 25,000, to attend school in Chinatown. The absurdity of the expressed purpose, which was dealing with overcrowding, was quickly recognized. The racial overtones were obvious. An international incident unfolded. The Japanese were offended and said so. President Roosevelt immediately criticized the action and argued it violated a U.S. treaty with Japan. After posturing on both sides, the *1907 Gentlemen's Agreement* was reached. President Roosevelt got the School Board to discard the segregationist plan, and the Japanese government agreed to voluntarily restrict emigration to the U.S. and Hawaii. The Agreement also banned further Korean immigration as laborers. This opened up opportunities for Filipinos in Hawaiian, and later U.S., agriculture.

Another outcome of the Agreement was a change in the location of Japanese in the U.S. Prior to the Agreement, the Japanese resided in urban centers and were the targets of labor unions. After the Agreement, the Japanese migrated to the California countryside and competed with white farmers. Not surprisingly, institutional efforts to drive out the Japanese turned to land law. McClain noted that states could discriminate against Japanese due to constitutional law:

> "... the Supreme Court affirmed that states, in the absence of overriding treaty provisions, could deny aliens the right to own real property within their borders. Farming, as noted above, was the preponderant occupation of the Japanese immigrants. The treaties between the United States and Japan, while guaranteeing certain rights to Japanese immigrants, said nothing about agricultural land. Here, then, was an opening for the western states to accomplish their objectives, and California led the way" (McClain, 1994, p. x).

In 1913 and 1923, the state passed "*Alien Land Laws*." The first law restricted land ownership by "aliens ineligible for citizenship," but allowed "three-year leaseholds" (McClain, p. x). The 1923 law, although avoiding racist language, was designed to eliminate Japanese landholdings in the state. It closed loopholes in the 1913 law that was successfully exploited by the Japanese, including ownership through their children and the use of corporations to hold agricultural lands. The new law also added criminal penalties for those attempting to circumvent the laws. Other western states followed with similar laws modeled after California's (McClain, 1994). The Japanese and others challenged these laws. However, except for the success in striking down that portion that prohibited aliens from being guardians of their minor children's land, the Supreme Court upheld the challenges. Hardship, of course, resulted for the Japanese residents.

However, the biggest blows to Japanese immigration and Japanese-American civil rights were yet to come. In 1924, a provision of the Federal Immigration Act barred Japanese immigration. The ultimate insult came with the outbreak of WWII, when Japanese Americans were taken from their homes and businesses and placed in internment camps. This was, and continues to be, one of the most embarrassing events in American history.

The Filipinos

U.S. political involvement in the Philippines came at the conclusion of the Spanish-American War with the 1899 Treaty of Paris, which transferred the Philippines (and Puerto Rico) to the U.S. Increased migration followed. Ethnically diverse, rural Filipino populations were "pushed" away from the countryside by the economic hardships of their homeland and were "pulled" toward the potential of employment and education in America. According to Melendy, Filipinos entered America in two distinct waves, one between 1903 and 1942, entailing young Filipino men seeking advanced education, and another between 1907 and 1935, including a stepwise movement to Hawaii and then to the U.S. (Melendy, 1977). He explained the early acceptance of thousands of Filipinos as a perceived American "obligation" tied to the "White Man's Burden" that likely would result in young Filipino leaders returning home as advocates teaching American values (Melendy, 1977).

The Hawaiian plantations and mills became employment opportunities for young Filipino males, who replaced restricted Japanese and Chinese workers. Recruiters actively sought Filipino workers and the president of the Hawaiian Immigration Board informed the U.S. government "that the Philippine Islands had become the only available source of plantation labor" (Melendy, p. 34). Thus, thousands of Filipino laborers were allowed entry to Hawaii on an annual basis. The result was a burgeoning Filipino population that reached 21,031 in 1920 and 63,052 by 1930. The Great Depression dramatically stopped this growth trend by 1932 and in 1940 there were fewer Filipinos residing in Hawaii than in 1930, due to return migration to the Philippines.

The relative location of the American West Coast to Hawaii and the Philippines was a significant geographic factor in Filipino entry into the U.S. Its economic growth and employment opportunities made California attractive to both Filipinos traveling directly from Manila and for those relocating from Hawaii to the U.S. In 1910, approximately 400 Filipinos lived in the U.S. (Hawaii excluded). This population was widely scattered among California, Alaska, and Louisiana (New Orleans had the greatest concentration), as well as other locations. However, by 1920, the U.S. Filipino population exceeded 5,000 with approximately 50 percent of that total residing in California. Other settlements were scattered among the Northeastern U.S., Alaska, and Washington (Melendy, 1977).

Filipino population increases of the 1920s were even more dramatic, and included not only California and other West Coast states, but eastern urban centers due to immigration from the Philippines and relocations from Hawaii:

> "During these years, some 45,000 Filipinos arrived on the Pacific Coast; about 16,000 ... from the Hawaiian Islands. While most immigrants remained on the West Coast, many moved to Chicago, Detroit, New York, and Philadelphia. California's Filipino population increased about 91% in the 1920s. In 1930, California (reported) ... for the ten-year period, 1920–1929, just over 31,000 disembarked at the ports of San Francisco and Los Angeles ... In 1923 ... one-third came from Hawaii, where a major sugar strike was in progress ... 35 percent of the total arrived from Manila, 56 percent moved from the Hawaiian Islands, and the remaining nine percent came from Asian seaports ..." (Melendy, pp. 41–42).

Like their Asian predecessors, these young Filipino men (one-half in the age group 22–29) generally did not speak English and were of darker skins than the white society that received them. Not surprisingly, these low-paid, low-skilled young "foreigners" employed in agriculture fisheries, and services, became the targets and scapegoats when the Great Depression hit California and other states. Young Filipino men were characterized as criminals, gamblers, and sexual predators. Of course, the white majority's concern for racial segregation and separation had been well established with the Chinese. This led to the passage of miscegenation laws in California and other states (Foster, 1932) that forbade whites from marrying blacks, mulattoes, or those of the Malay race. These laws effectively kept many from marriage and resulted in economic and social hardships for Filipinos and others. Among the financial penalties were denials of monetary allowances, health care and insurance, all of which required that military couples be legally married.

One of the unique curses faced by Filipinos was related to their legal status. The 1916 Jones Act conferred the status "*American national*." However, the 1917 U.S. Immigration Law made Filipinos ineligible for citizenship. As "nationals" they could migrate freely to the U.S. mainland, but once here, they were denied the privileges associated with citizenship status. They faced economic discrimination and employment restrictions. Of particular importance were the Depression years, when Filipino legal status made them eligible for federal public works projects, but denied them the employment preference provided citizens for project employment. Other legalities also negatively influenced their employability. The Merchant Marine Law, for example, required that sailing crews be "75 percent American," causing Filipinos to compete with aliens and face fewer prospects for employment. Filipino professionals also faced employment difficulties. For example, Filipinos could sit for federal qualifying examinations for professional employment, but faced exclusion at the state level, due to variable licensing laws. Finally, Filipinos faced discrimination in efforts to lease agricultural lands (Nomura, 1994).

During the same period, Filipinos, like the Chinese who preceded them, saw their stock as "steady, ideal workers" shift dramatically to "shiftless deadbeats" who gambled away their wages, chased white women, and mixed "with near-moron white girls" (Melendy, 1977, p. 61). As a result, discrimination against them intensified. In addition to the hardships already described, they also experienced difficulty with credit and were restricted from property ownership in the 1940s.

In 1929, California sought federal restrictions against future Filipino entry into the U.S. on moral and racial grounds. By 1934, a single act made that unnecessary. The 1916 Jones Act had granted legislative power to the Philippines under the direction of a governor-general appointed by the U.S. president. The 1932 Gare-Hawes-Cutting Act, after a 10-year transition period, granted full independence to the Philippines. In 1934, the *Tydings-McDuffie Act* solved "the Filipino problem." It not only confirmed independence for the Philippines, it brought Filipino entry into the U.S. to a virtual halt by reclassifying their status. In short, as a foreign Asian nation, the Philippines now faced a 50-persons-per-year immigration quota. This was accepted by both governments. Later exceptions were tied to labor shortages defined by the U.S. Commerce Department. Of particular note in this regard was the effort of the state of California, which sought Filipino labor in place of the Mexican guest workers of the Bracero Program. As a result, the Filipino population of the U.S. continued to grow, but modestly, through 1960. This would change in 1965.

BACKGROUND: THE TRANSITION FROM PRE- TO POST-WWII AND THE 1965 IMMIGRATION ACT

Previous sections of this chapter demonstrated that successive waves of Asian immigrants, after initially being welcomed as hard-working laborers, faced discrimination, violence, segregation, and exclusion. Their pay was low, their accommodations poor, and eventually they became geographically segregated due to limited mobility, residential decision-making, and discrimination. Each of the Asian immigrant groups experienced occupational as well as geographic segregation and were excluded from advanced sectors of the economy.

The Chinese were overrepresented in mining and service occupations at the beginning of the 20th century. For example, they were the majority of laundry workers in 1910 (Bonacich, 1984). The Japanese were narrowly concentrated in a set of occupations, including farm labor, services, and manufacturing. Filipinos were overrepresented in agricultural labor and, by the 1930s, in lower levels of the service sector (Bonacich, 1984).

Second-generation Asians in 20th century America thus saw little improvement. Segregated Asian-American communities and their employment problems were subjects studied by sociologists and geographers of the Chicago School and others in the 1920s, including Park, Mears, and Smith (Woo, 1994). Issues of underemployment, unemployment, wage inequities, and lack of promotions were the patterns of the day among the Chinese and other second-generation Asian Americans due to discrimination by the dominant white society. All of this occurred despite good English language skills. Geographer Mears suggested that Asian Americans were trapped in the occupations of their parents and had little chance of success outside their segregated neighborhoods unless they were willing to work for less, or had exceptional educational qualifications compared to white competitors (Mears, 1928). This meant remaining in the pursuits of their parents, such as agriculture, or seeking opportunities in specific areas of the service sector. These were permitted because Asian Americans in such positions as accounting required little interaction with whites, who generally wished to minimize professional and social contacts with Asians (Woo, 1994).

Woo, in her 1994 report to the U.S. Department of Labor, spoke of the barriers faced by this second generation:

"Even as they began to professionalize, they also encountered barriers to entering more remunerative and satisfying work. Despite being college-educated, they found it hard, if not impossible, to find jobs outside the racial-ethnic enclaves encased by formal and informal discriminatory practices. Whatever their professional training, they often could not find jobs commensurate with their education. Their situation would not radically improve until the onset of World War II, which made it necessary for the nation to utilize a wider band of its human resources, including this untapped supply of technical reserve labor" (Woo, 1994, p. 12).

It took a global war and major labor shortage to open up the domestic labor market, skilled and unskilled, to Asian immigrants (Japanese excluded). Wartime industries required factory workers, technicians, engineers, clerical workers, and other positions. The fact that China was fighting a common enemy, Japan, helped the status of Chinese Americans, who also raised war funds and worked hard. The status of Filipinos also rose slowly. Frazier, Margai, and Tettey-Fio (2003) noted the remarkable emergence of the Chinese Americans in Oakland during WWII, after years of discrimination and exclusion. This became the case in other American cities and states and represented a transition in Asian-American status in American life.

After WWII, a number of factors led to the liberalization of U.S. immigration laws. The U.S. became one of the world's two superpowers and entered a Cold War that would last for nearly a generation. The spread of communism resulted in the "Red Scare" and the desire of America to protect those negatively affected by communist regimes. This led to immigration preference for refugees. In spite of periodic recession, the U.S. economy expanded, and then experienced a structural shift as it moved from emphasis on manufacturing employment to increasing reliance on service sector employment. Many of the new service employment opportunities were unskilled and low-paying, but these were supported by the higher-paying jobs for doctors and other health care professionals, engineers, technicians, and later computer scientists. This expansion occurred at rates unmatched by the production of educational credentials necessary to fill professional positions. By the 1960s, America had a shortage of physicians, for example, that resulted in a maldistribution among city and suburb and urban and rural regions of the nation. The same was true for nurses, pharmacists, and dentists. The labor shortage extended to other professions, as well.

Finally, the 1960s can be characterized not only by the expanding economy, but also by racial conflict, the Civil Rights era, and a more liberal view in Washington. All of these factors contributed to the rethinking of U.S. immigration policy that culminated in passage of the *1965 Hart-Celler Act*. This act abolished the quota system and established hemispheric limitations that sought redress of the discrimination of previous immigration laws. The new law applied the numerical limits to the multiple category preference system established by the *1952 McCarran-Walter Act*. The provisions of the law permitted preference for trained professionals that would benefit the labor needs of the U.S. economy, which greatly facilitated the entry of health care professionals, engineers, technicians, computer scientists, and others, especially those from the Eastern Hemisphere. Another key feature of this law was its exemption from the numerical limits those with immediate family ties in the U.S., including spouses, offspring, and parents. Although debated in Congress, few thought that this liberalization of immigration policy would have a dramatic impact on diversification of the U.S. population. They were wrong. The influx of Asians and Latinos set immigration records in the 1990s and resulted in a new racial-ethnic mix and changing geographic patterns around the nation, both at regional and local scales. A number of other pieces of federal legislation have contributed to increased immigration. These fall into two classes. One provides asylum for political refugees and the other expands employment-based immigration law. Among the latter class is the *1990 U.S. Immigration Act*, which allocated 140,000 immigrant visas to the "employment" category. Also, U.S. high-tech corporations successfully lobbied Congress to pass legislation that increased the number of annual *H-1B visas* meant to bring immigrants with special skills to fill unfilled but increasing numbers of high tech jobs. The H-1B visas now stand at 195,000 annually and those holding these visas can apply for permanent residency while in this status.

In the remainder of this chapter, three issues are examined. First, the growth and increase in Asian ethnic diversity since 1960 is explored. Second, the economic bifurcation of the Asian-American population is examined, especially within the context of continuing discrimination, the model minority myth, and the metropolitan locations of this ethnically diverse group. Finally, we report the contemporary geography of the Asian population with an emphasis on concentration in American "gateways," dispersion from these entry points, and new urban/metropolitan settlement patterns that have required new theories of assimilation.

SELECTED ASIAN-AMERICAN TRENDS SINCE 1960

Growth and Diversification

The growth of the Asian-American population since the 1965 Immigration Law has been dramatic. In 1960, the U.S. Census reported nearly one million Asian/Pacific Islanders. This represented about 1 percent of the total U.S. population. By 1970, the Asian total was just over 1.5 million. This population continued to increase, reaching approximately 3.7 million by 1980 (more than doubling the 1970 figure), 7.2 million in 1990, and reaching nearly 12.3 million in 2000, which accounted for about 4.4 percent of the U.S. population. In 2003, the U.S. Census Bureau reported that Asian population growth between 2000 and 2002 increased 9 percent and reached approximately 13 million (Armas, 2003). The same report credited immigration with about two-thirds of that growth.

In addition to this rapid growth, the Asian-American population has greatly diversified. By 1980, the U.S. Census Bureau reported twenty different Asian ethnic groups in the U.S. Among the newcomers of this post-1965 era were Koreans, Vietnamese, Cambodians, Laotians, and the Hmong people. All of the better-established Asian ethnic groups increased their proportional representations between 1960 and 2000, except the Japanese, who lost their ranking as the third largest Asian-American group to Asian Indians in the 2000 Census. The Chinese and Filipinos retained their number one and two population rankings among Asian Americans.

The increasing diversity among Asian Americans due to the 1965 immigration law perhaps can best be appreciated by examining the increases among several of their most rapidly growing ethnic groups between 1960 and 1970. Table 20.1 reports those data and the percent change by group, for the years 1960 and 1970. The data illustrate that the one-year entries of these four ethnic groups together increased approximately sixfold for the two years in question. The most dramatic increase occurred within the Asian Indian population, which built strongly on a very low base. The increase of Filipino entries was extremely dramatic, increasing from nearly three thousand in 1960 to 31,203 in 1970. This was not an aberration. The U.S. Census reported that between 1965 and 1974, the U.S. Filipino population increased 950 percent to 210,269 in 1974. Only Mexicans accounted for a larger number in that period. Table 20.1 also illustrates the significant gains for Chinese/Taiwanese and Koreans.

By 2000, Asian ethnic diversity in the U.S. was clear (Armas, 2001). Table 20.2 reports Asian ethnicity as a percent of the total U.S. Asian population. Three groups, the Chinese, Filipinos, and Indians, account for just over one-half (57%) of the total U.S. Asian population. The next three, Koreans, Vietnamese, and Japanese, constitute an additional nearly 30 percent. Approximately 13.5 percent are spread among other Asian ethnic groups, such as the Hmong, Cambodians, and Laotians. Thus, numerous Asian ethnic groups, speaking different languages and representing very different cultures, are represented among the Asian-American population at the beginning of the 21st century.

Economic Bifurcation: The Model Minority Myth and the Persistence of Discrimination

Whenever aggregate statistics are employed to profile the U.S. Asian/Pacific Islander population, a strikingly positive picture emerges. Such was the case in the U.S. Census 2000 profile in the "U.S. Department of Commerce News" that reported that married couples accounted for 80 percent of their households and that 42 percent earned annual incomes of $75,000 or more (McKinnon and Grieco, 2001). The report went on to summarize other important dimensions of this positive profile:

- Forty-four percent of Asian and Pacific Islanders age 25 and over had a bachelor's degree or higher and 86 percent had at least a high school diploma in 2000.
- In 1999, Asian and Pacific Islanders had a record-low poverty rate of 10.7 percent.
- There were 2.5 million Asian and Pacific Islander families; 13 percent were maintained by women with no spouse present and 7 percent by men with no spouse present.
- Asian and Pacific Islander families tended to be relatively large. For example, 23 percent of Asian and Pacific Islander married-couple families had five or more members.

- Fifty-three percent of Asian and Pacific Islander households owned their home.
  (McKinnon and Grieco, 2001)

There is no doubt that many Asian families are doing very well economically and that family values and a strong work ethic are vital parts of Asian cultures. However, this aggregate depiction hides a number of serious equity issues according to Asian-American social scientists. It also supports the *Asian model minority myth* in America. Deborah Woo introduced her executive summary of a report written for the U.S. Labor Department:

"For Americans who are not of Asian ancestry, meaningful, empirically-based discussion of the realities of a glass ceiling for Asian Americans, runs up against a powerful counter-image: a media-saturated view of Asian Pacific Americans as highly educated and occupationally successful. Complementing this picture of upward mobility is that part of a generally non-violent and law-abiding citizenry, relatively passive politically, and overall culturally resourceful. However, is it the comparative educational and occupational success of Asian Americans — over and against that of African Americans, Latino-Americans, and Native Americans — that has generated the idea of Asian Americans as a 'model' for other minorities. Insofar as this understanding has come to occupy the status of conventional wisdom in the contemporary United States, it has eroded our collective capacity to confront an alternative reality" (Woo, 1994, p. 1).

Table 20.1
Number of One-Year Entries to U.S. by Asian Ethnic Group Immigrants,
1960 and 1970

Number of 1-Year Entries: Year and Percent Changes

Asian Ethnic Group	1960	1970	% Change from 1960–1970
Filipinos	2,954	31,203	956%
Chinese/Taiwanese	3,681	14,093	283%
Asian Indians	391	10,114	2,487%
Koreans	1,507	9,314	518%
Totals	8,523	64,724	659%

Table 20.2
Asian Ethnic Groups as a Percent of the Total 2000 U.S. Asian Population

Asian Ethnic Group	Percent of U.S. Asian Population, 2000*
Chinese	22.3%
Filipinos	19.3%
Indians	15.5%
Koreans	10.0%
Vietnamese	10.0%
Japanese	9.4%
Other	13.5%
Total	100.00%

* calculated by author from U.S. Census, 2000.

Woo makes several points about the reported aggregate incomes. First, she noted that the geographic concentration of the majority of Asians in the American West, especially California, meant relatively higher earnings in a region of high standard of living. Put simply, higher average incomes in California are necessary due to much higher living costs (e.g., housing). When Western incomes are put into national averages, they artificially inflate the purchasing power of Asian Americans.

Also, the existence of a "glass ceiling" and income disparities are issues not conveyed by positive, aggregate national profiles. Woo found that inferences related to mobility based solely on educational data were misleading. Both occupational segregation (such as Asian college-educated women concentrated in low-level clerical positions) and lower returns on educational accomplishments compared to whites, challenge the upwardly mobile, financially successful stereotype associated with the model minority (Woo, 1994). Barriers to promotion and equal pay for comparable work and education suggested the existence of a "glass ceiling," blocking promotion and its associated status, as well as the existence of "race-typed jobs" guided by prejudice and carrying lower salary schedules (Woo, 1994).

The Asian professionals' glass ceiling and Asian-white income disparities were considered as early as the 1970s. Jobu, for example, argued that Chinese suffered socioeconomic disparities with whites due to a low return of education (Jobu, 1976). In the 1980s, Fong and Cabezas suggested that professional Asian women of the three largest ethnic groups suffered job segregation and associated poor wages (Fong and Cabezas, 1980). In 1987, Martinelli and Nagasawa (1987), in rejecting the model minority concept, reported that white men were twice as likely to hold managerial positions as Japanese-American men because the Asian men received less return from their education than their white counterparts. In 1988, Lau argued that separate tracking for Asian employees resulted in the glass ceilings experienced by Asian professionals (Lau, 1988). Similarly, Cabezas and Kawagnchi (1988) reported that Asian Americans commonly earn less than whites due to their marginalization into unimportant jobs with little security and low pay. Similar findings continued into the 1990s (such as Duleep and Sanders, 1992) and support Woo's contentions that a number of visible and invisible barriers, often rooted in prejudice, have created an Asian glass ceiling and related income disparities. There is a strong perception among Asian-American professionals that they are invisible at promotion time, face unfair subjective criteria, or are directed to specific employment that holds little hope for advancement (Woo, 1994; Cabezas, Tse, Lowe, Wong, and Turner, 1989).

The lower end of the income distribution occupied by Asians who are unskilled workers and the unemployed, also has received attention. For example, Ong (1993) noted the significant proportion of Asian Americans living in poverty. The Hmong, Cambodian, and other refugee immigrant groups experienced double-digit poverty rates in the 1980s and, in 1989, Asian Americans overall experienced a 14 percent poverty rate, compared to the 13 percent national rate. Sections of Chinatowns in Chicago and Boston and ethnic enclaves elsewhere experienced relatively high poverty rates as recent Asian immigrants became entrapped in local ethnic economies with little mobility due to no skills and poor education.

Some research on the economic differentiation of Asian Americans reveals that their economic status is somewhat related to their time of arrival in the United States. A number of social scientists recognized two distinct waves of Asian immigration to the U.S. after 1965. Waldinger and Bozorgmehr (1996), for example, noted that the highly educated Chinese, Asian Indians, and Koreans characterized the first wave, whereas uneducated and unskilled refugees from Southeast Asia led the second wave. The latter settled in inner cities, such as Los Angeles and Oakland, where they swelled poverty rolls and found economic survival a challenge (Waldinger and Borzorgmehr, 1996; Allen and Turner, 1997). A host of other authors have pointed out the fallacies of the model minority hypothesis that was first presented during the Civil Rights era to combat the complaints of the black minority against the white-dominated economic system. This hypothesis, as noted by Woo, suggested that Asians are good, hardworking people, who, despite facing the barriers of an unjust and discriminating system, found ways to overcome them through peaceful means. This is due, the hypothesis argues, to Asian perseverance, pride, patience, and, above all, the emphasis they place on family values, education, and the work ethic. These are the keys to success that permit all minorities to overcome systemic obstacles. Cheng and Yang (1996), among others, have offered empirical evidence to debunk this *model minority myth*. Their findings support the works reviewed above. They supplied data from labor, household income, and wage statistics to illustrate that Asian success varies by ethnicity and is related to the entry of Asian minority groups of differing education and skill levels (two waves above). Their data also illustrated that Asian Americans earn less than whites in terms of equal financial rewards for similar skills and work. They conclude that, "Asian ethnic groups do not seem to be progressing at comparable rates (compared to whites), no matter how hard they try" (p. 324). Asian Americans invest time learning the skills of the job, typically at a lower than standard wage, and then face a glass ceiling and lower pay scales compared to whites in certain occupations (Cheng and Yang, 1996). David Wong's research has also indicated that substantial economic differentiation among Asians, coupled with ethnicity, has resulted in Asian class distinction and residential segregation (Wong, 1999 and 2000).

ASIAN-AMERICAN GEOGRAPHIES AT THE BEGINNING OF THE 21ST CENTURY

A complex Asian-American geography is evolving at the beginning of this century. The historical importance of "Chinatown" has already been noted. Recently, American Chinatowns are experiencing a number of problems, despite the public perception that they are booming tourist areas. As noted earlier, some low-skilled immigrants became entrapped in these inner-city ethnic enclaves. Part of Boston's Chinatown was included in its federal economic development zone proposal, due to the substantial poverty levels there in the 1990s. Similarly, Oakland's inner-city neighborhoods contain poor Asians, as well as Latinos and African Americans. Housing problems and poverty suffered by Oakland's poor are obvious from the city's Consolidated Plan, 2000, which noted examples of combined Asian and African-American concentrations, such as those in the formerly all-black San Antonio neighborhood (City of Oakland, 2000).

Chinatowns like those in New York and Chicago provide a neighborhood support system for new Asian immigrants. This has resulted in substantial crowding and inadequate affordable housing. New York's Chinatown is expanding into other formerly ethnic neighborhoods on Manhattan's Lower East Side. In most cases, the local ethnic economies of Chinatowns do not supply adequate employment opportunities for newcomers. Some actually are based on restaurant or other service employment in the suburbs. Others may provide jobs but many of them may be in areas that result in under-employment or trap immigrants in sweatshops or other low-end jobs. In Chicago, which by 1970 boasted the fourth largest Chinatown in the U.S., Asians faced a variety of inner-city problems when immigration law changed. Just before the rapid increase in immigrants occurred, nearly one-half of the city's Chinatown had recently been eliminated from city projects, which exacerbated other problems presented by the Chinese American Service League (CASL) in 1997:

> "The large influx of Chinese to Chicago in the 1960s aggravated an existing housing problem … (and) some banks had no confidence in lending money to Chinese due to racial discrimination … (also) available housing was outside of the Chinese community at a time when Chinese buyers were not always welcome …" (p. 2).

This article also explained the support functions provided by Chicago's Chinatown, including the provision of protection, teaching English, busing Chinese to employment, and providing temporary housing. These problems still persist. The League argued that new immigrants and the elderly, many of whom are classified as "economically disadvantaged," must fight for scarce affordable housing. They also suggested a need to attract foreign investments to move Chinatown out of its dependence on a single form of employment for immigrants (restaurants). Their desire is to upgrade the quality of life so that it is "no longer at the survival level" (CASL, 1997, p. 5). Similar concerns were echoed in a cry for revitalization of Los Angeles' Chinatown. *Times* staff writer Connie Kang reported that Chinatown had "for years suffered from poor retail sales, stagnant property values and image problems," and quoted Patrick Lee, president of the Los Angeles Chinatown Business Council as saying, "If we don't do something now, Chinatown will become a dead town" (Kang, 2000, p. 1). Part of the problem, of course, is more wealthy Asian Americans have abandoned Chinatowns for the suburbs and, like other old commercial districts, Chinatown has had little success in drawing them back (Kang and Gee, 2000).

This clearly indicates the economic bifurcation among the Asian American population. It also underscores the fact that Asian Americans, like all Americans, have two locations, inner city and outer city, which reflect their place in the American economic hierarchy. The suburbanization of Asian Americans therefore deserves closer scrutiny.

Numerous examples of Asian-American suburbanization exist. The expansion of the American economy in the 1970s demanded scientific and technical expertise that outpaced U.S. educational production in their areas. Growth in the 1990s also required an increasingly educated workforce in various types of technological fields, such as bioengineering, microelectronics, and computer programming. All of these labor needs fueled Asian immigration to the U.S. As Ong and Blumenberg noted, "no other minority group contributed more" to this need than Asians (1994). Thus, despite the glass ceiling discussed earlier, thousands of Asians continued to enter professionally paying jobs in the 1990s and had the resources to seek housing in suburbia. These immigrants experience a very different America than those entering via the city center; they face less overt forms of discrimination and very different living environments. Their experiences, unlike their inner city counterparts, were not at all analogous to those historically persecuted laborers of the 19th and early 20th century U.S. As noted by O'Hare, Frey, and Fost (1994), some Asians are segregating by choice and are preserving their cultures. These authors provided numerous examples of suburban clusters around the nation where Asians have become significant proportions of suburbia and have chosen to cluster with countrymen: Koreans make up 21 percent of suburban Washington, D.C., the Chinese are one-third of Los Angeles suburbanites, and Japanese are one-third of Honolulu's suburbs (1994). They also describe the existence of a large Filipino middle-class that relocated from Manila to Daly City, CA. In describing Monterrey Park, CA, where the Chinese/Taiwanese increased from three percent in 1960 to the majority by 1990 and the title, "Chinese Beverly Hills," they noted Fong's characterization of residents: "They are men and women generally much better educated and more affluent than either their Chinese predecessors or their white counterparts" (p. 35).

These authors suggested that suburban Asians are typically well-assimilated, but economically work to preserve the customs of their homelands. There are other points to be made about Asian American experiences: both in their urban and suburban locations in the U.S. Wealth and class divide American people. So does race. While contemporary Asian Americans may seek separate enclaves in suburbia, historical experiences of rejection set the tone for separation both prior to and after WWII. Chang, for example, related the case of the Chinese in post-war Reading, PA. Already educated, working as researchers, engineers, and in other professions, the Chinese moved into the white suburbs of Reading and interacted with whites at work. However, as Chang related: "But in the Reading region, that mingling ended with the workday" (Chang, 1999, pp. 109–10).

Chang also related the experiences of her mother in Hartford, Connecticut, where the choice for outsiders was to "live apart and be ignored, or ape [sic, slang term for mimicry] those around you, and be grudgingly tolerated" (p. 121). She also spoke of the distinct and socially distant communities of Los Angeles, including some that are closed by gates or guarded. She argued that race matters there, too. Quoting a friend, she continued:

> "Wealth presents one divide; race, another. The worlds don't mix. The white community belongs to the country clubs. Then, all these Chinese — they're completely separate. They never intersect" (Chang, 1999).

Then Chang described the growing isolation of the Chinese Palos Verdes community:

> "The Chinese in Palos Verdes represent a community within a community. They may live next door to white neighbors and send their children to the same schools, but in their own way they are as isolated from the mainstream as any Chinatown on the East Coast. These days, they might even conduct their business — import-export, clothing manufacturing, real-estate development — only with other Chinese, in Hong Kong, Taipei, Shanghai, or nearby Monterey Park. Their isolation differs in one important way from the ghettos in Boston and New York. The Chinese of Palos Verdes have achieved all the trappings of the American dream" (Chang, 1999, p. 140).

One of the ironies in contemporary Asian-American settlement patterns is that both isolation and assimilation are occurring. Within the span of about a half-century, white Americans forced Asian segregation; then, post-1965, some Asian immigrants have chosen segregation. Both processes create isolation. However, speaking to the complexity of Asian-American settlement patterns noted earlier in this chapter, it is also true that many Asian Americans have quietly assimilated into American suburbia. These complex patterns support the concepts of segmented and racialized assimilation presented by Wei Li in a previous chapter of this text.

The final point to be made about Asian-American geography is that of its rapid dispersion away from its two major centers and other "gateways" of entry. The forces that drew Asians in great numbers to California and the West Coast were discussed earlier in the chapter. It was also noted that many Chinese migrated eastward due to the violence toward them in the late 1800s. These migrants fueled the growth of Chinatowns in Eastern cities, especially New York. Despite this migration, the West remained the population center of Asian Americans for more than a century. The 2000 Census, however, noted that just less than one-half (49%) of all Asians in the U.S. resided in the West. This was the first time a majority of Asian Americans lived elsewhere. The Census reported that 75 percent of all Asians were living in just ten states, largely those with "Gateway cities" (New York, California, New Jersey, Florida, Washington, Massachusetts, Illinois, Virginia, Texas, and Hawaii). California had the largest number of Asians in 2000. Asian Americans are the most urbanized (93%) and New York City had the largest number (873,000), followed by Los Angeles (407,000). Honolulu was two-thirds Asian, which was the largest proportion of any American city (Tolbert, 2002).

Despite these existing concentrations, Asian Americans are rapidly spreading geographically across the national urban landscape. In the process, new urban Asian ethnic patterns are being created. In the next section, several examples of recently emerging Asian places and landscapes are provided to illustrate the range and complexity of contemporary Asian settlements.

Asian American Places and Landscapes

As noted earlier, Asian Americans are the most urbanized, minority group in the U.S. Given the influx of a wide variety of ethnic groups since 1965, it should come as no surprise that there is a substantial variation in the representation of particular Asian ethnic groups within metropolitan regions. Historical and contemporary immigration patterns have led to large numbers of a specific ethnic group settling in a community. In some cases, this group represents the dominant share of the local Asian population. In other instances, recent entries mix with other Asian ethnic groups. All of these processes contribute to complex and evolving Asian ethnic patterns in 21st century.

A few examples help clarify this complexity and diversity within the American urban system. The New York and Los Angeles PMSAs contained highly diversified Asian populations in 2000. Although the actual proportions of Asian ethnic groups differ in these two metropolitan regions, both contain significant Chinese populations mixed with other Asian groups. Three examples of diverse cities with a different Asian mix are Dallas, Atlanta, and Washington, D.C., where the Chinese also are an important ethnic group, there is a greater presence of Asian Indians and Vietnamese than in the previous examples.

In other cases, a single Asian ethnic group appears influential due to its proportion of the total local Asian population. For example, the Vietnamese are more than one-third of the Asian population in New Orleans and constitute at least one-fifth of the Asian total in Houston, Fort Worth-Arlington, and San Jose. Similarly, Asian Indians account for about 25 percent of Detroit's Asian population, Koreans are more than 25 percent of the Bergen-Passaic metropolitan region, and nearly 50 percent of the Asian population of Vallejo-Fairfield-Napa metropolitan region is Filipino.

It was previously noted that the Asian-American population increased 9 percent between 2000 and 2002 and that nearly two-thirds of this growth was credited to immigration. It has been projected that by 2025, the U.S. Asian population will be nearly 22 million. This type of growth ensures an evolving set of Asian-American geographies. The ones described below are places where Asians have created places of their own and transformed landscapes in those places. Each place, however, illustrates the unique combination of culture and space in that transformation and a process quite different from that proposed long ago by the Chicago School's spatial assimilation model.

An Ethnoburb in Los Angeles' San Gabriel Valley

Wei Li's ethnoburb concept was defined in a previous chapter. Recently, she provided an analysis of the transformation of the Los Angeles Chinese community, from the downtown Chinatown, to the San Gabriel Valley ethnoburb (Li, 2006). Using a variety of data sources, she traced the historic change in Chinese settlement and assessed the function and nature of this ethnoburb, covering the issues of assimilation, ethnic identity, and global economics.

According to Li, the downtown Chinatown in Los Angeles dominated Chinese residential and business patterns until the 1960s when the Chinese began to suburbanize. Chinese immigrants had settled in Los Angeles in the mid-19th century and by 1890 had reached 4.4 percent of the county's population. More than two-thirds of all Chinese there resided in Chinatown and worked largely as laborers, vendors, merchants and in railroad construction. Despite early 20th century decentralization of the Chinese to areas such as West Adams ("the first Chinese suburb"), Chinatown was the main business core and cultural center of the Chinese community. The large influx of immigrant Chinese in the 1960s, however, brought change. Many Chinese immigrants by-passed the downtown area and settled directly in the suburbs. This immigrant stream contained both wealthy and poor people, skilled and unskilled workers, who went directly to the suburbs. By 1980, the San Gabriel Valley Chinese ethnoburb had formed. This unusual process did not entail complete assimilation, rather it involved the spatial transformation of the Chinese community into something unique. It also ran contrary to the traditional straight-line assimilation described by the Chicago School's spatial assimilation process, which required that the immigrant ethnic group move downtown and reside in enclaves or ghettos of the poor, uneducated and spatially concentrated inner city. This contemporary mixed-class migrant stream moved directly to the suburbs and behaved differently. This requires a different perspective of the assimilation process (Li, 2006). In particular, within an ethnoburb, the population is concentrated near ethnic residential and business clusters, while being polarized in terms of socioeconomic status. In this process, immigrant ethnic groups are better able to maintain their native culture while adapting only to parts of the host's mainstream society, as argued by Li in chapter 5 of this text.

Li also suggested that several factors facilitated the establishment of this ethnoburb. Chinese investors and realtors acquired properties sold by empty nesters for the purpose of establishing businesses and multi-family units (conversion) for Chinese immigrant families. The Chinese people and the Chinese financial institutions established important interactions that contributed to the formation of this ethnoburb. The region had a strong ethnic financial community consisting of 27 local Chinese-American and 20 foreign-Chinese bank offices, which worked together with the Chinese immigrant population to create new residential growth and other economic activity. As a result, by 2000, each of nine cities of the San Gabriel Valley reached a population of 10,000 Chinese that constituted at least one-quarter of each city's total population. Each also contained other foreign-born groups, such as Pacific Islanders. As a result, Li claimed that the Valley had surpassed Chinatown in importance. The ethnoburb also transformed the landscape in important ways, including architecture and buildings, signage and other characteristics that resulted in a resemblance of Asian cities. Music and language added to this perception. In fact, Li maintained that the ethnoburb, besides being a concentration of Chinese businesses, also came to function as a global economic outpost. Its labor force was characterized as having both skilled, high-wage and low-skilled, low-wage immigrant workers, indicating its position in the global economy (Li, 2006).

Finally, despite the importance of the ethnoburb to the Chinese population, the San Gabriel Valley is a multi-ethnic community, consisting of more than one-third white non-Hispanics, nearly one-third Hispanic, less than five percent African American and about one-fifth Asian and Pacific Islander populations, and others. Li also noted that on occasion the influx of large numbers of Chinese immigrants has resulted in competition for resources and employment, as well as conflict over political and cultural issues. Thus, ethnoburbs, while transforming American landscapes, are not exempt from racial, ethnic and social clashes.

Korean Places in Metropolitan Los Angeles

The Los Angeles region is one of the most ethnically diverse areas in the world. Yet, there still exists some segregation among ethnic groups. A recent analysis by Hans Dieter Laux and Gunter Thieme focused on the Los Angeles Korean population, in terms of its locations, residential mobility, ethnic identity, and assimilation (Laux and Thieme, 2006). In particular, they assessed the spatial decentralization of Koreans on the cohesion of their ethnic community. As has been mentioned several times in this text, the Chicago model of spatial assimilation would predict that Koreans would disperse eventually along the same lines as the general population. However, in this case, new multi-ethnic communities in suburbia have given rise to the notion of permanent ethnic enclaves. Laux and Thieme suggested that this immigrant population has achieved integration through the combination of economic success and deliberate preservation of traditional cultural values, illustrating that assimilation is a complex, multidimensional process that does not necessitate loss of ethnic identity. They argued that through an economic niche of small business ownership, upward mobility and integration are achieved by relocating to the suburban periphery, away from the urban core. Despite these changes, Koreans have maintained a strong sense of ethnic attachment.

These authors use human and social capital approaches to discuss the factors that influence assimilation. Assimilation is often influenced by the cultural characteristics of ethnic origin and by the sociopolitical conditions of the host country, in this case the U.S. Human capital refers to the capabilities and skills of the immigrant group, while social capital involves the nature of interactions within the immigrant group, which have been shown to be important to first- and second-generation assimilation. For Korean immigrants, ethnic attachment, as demonstrated by the preservation of cultural traditions and the existence of strong social networks, is stronger than for other Asian ethnic groups (Laux and Thieme, 2006). This is due to Koreans being a relatively small and culturally homogeneous group, Korean ethnic churches, and the numerous small Korean-owned businesses.

It is clear that social institutions play important roles in Korean ethnic identity. The social functions and services offered by ethnic churches are pivotal in the maintenance of Korean social networks. Similarly, Korean-owned small businesses reinforce ethnic identity through the provision of Korean staples and atmosphere that stimulates interaction. This results in retail independence from the U.S. market and reinforces linguistic isolation.

Koreans in the Los Angeles region, in addition to settling in inner and outer city residential patterns often associated with other ethnic groups, exhibited an interesting residential mobility pattern. Laux and Thieme were able empirically to demonstrate that the classic pattern of outward mobility, from core to periphery, is still significant. However, the Korean movements among and within communities in the outer suburbs of Los Angeles were even stronger, indicating that the traditional "Koreantown" enclave is of less importance in Korean community building and mobility than suburban locations. They studied the potential relationship between the Los Angles Koreans spatial dispersion and tendency to choose suburban locations with Korean ethnic identity. They found social networks are influenced by tight associations with ethnic churches, friendship ties within their ethnic group, and "linguistic isolation" (Laux and Thieme, 2006). They concluded that the ethnic attitudes of Koreans located in the core tend to be polarized, while those of suburban Koreans reflect a population that is integrated with its ethnic group.

The Vietnamese in Northern Virginia

The Vietnamese population in the Washington, D.C. metropolitan region, approximately 75,000, is the fourth largest in the U.S. and largest on the entire Atlantic Coast. This location is related to a historical connection with the Pentagon. The Vietnamese first came as refugees and chain migration followed. Perhaps somewhat surprisingly, this ethnic population is highly dispersed. A recent study by Joseph S. Wood reported that no census tract in this region had more than nine percent of this population. Wood used Zelinsky's concept of "hetero-localism" to argue that decentralized ethnic communities have a dependency on cultural concentrations, held together by institutions such as social clubs, churches, business associations, and retail functions, to maintain culture and ethnicity (Wood, 2006). Like others in this text, Wood argued that the traditional ethnic assimilation model no longer applies to the American immigrant experience. Rather, "cultural amalgamation" occurs, wherein immigrants retain certain of their own cultural traits and adopt characteristics of the host. In the U.S., this process involves the reinvention of places and landscapes, as was the case for the Vietnamese immigrants in the Northern Virginia area.

Wood maintains that the most visible marker for many ethnic communities is clustered ethnic retail activity. Thus, he focuses on the unique cultural retail landscapes created by the Vietnamese in this region. He illustrates how retail shopping centers have evolved into vital community centers with distinctly Asian decorative appearance. The Vietnamese revived older shopping areas of the 1950s in some of the region's older suburbs. There are two primary Vietnamese retail centers located in primary highway corridors but in decline due to the creation of new modern centers in the area. The attractions to these for redevelopment lie in large available spaces at relatively low rents. They survived because Vietnamese see them as community-sanctioned places where capital investment created a distinct Vietnamese symbol in the U.S. Wood suggested that the design of these centers resemble Vietnamese market towns, where buildings are situated close to the road, are low in profile, and have large ground-openings and covered sidewalks. These centers are called "Little Saigons."

The first location ("Little Saigon") for establishing a Vietnamese retail cluster was in Clarendon, Virginia in the 1970s. However, by 1980, this no longer was singularly Vietnamese. In 1984, Vietnamese Americans purchased and converted part (20,000 square feet) of the Plaza Seven Shopping Center into a mini-mall arcade. They named it the "*Eden Center*," after a 1960s arcade in Saigon called the "*Khu Eden*." The arcade was combined with the Rex Mini-mall and collectively they became the "Eden Center." It attempts to recreate the Saigon atmosphere in America. Signage and music are Vietnamese, and so are the majority of customers. The developer continued expansion, adding a third arcade and creating a tower and pagoda to resemble Saigon's Ben Thanh Public Market. These latter additions sparked some controversy because of increased rent and some vacancies in retail space. According to Wood, only time will tell if these were wise and economically feasible additions to the Eden Center. Nonetheless, there is no doubt that the Eden Center created a sense of place for the Vietnamese in Northern Virginia. It functions as far more than a retail center. It has become a social as well as economic center that maintains ethnic familiarity. The Vietnamese appear more concentrated and unified, despite being geographically dispersed in the region. It sometimes suggests a uniformity that may be lacking, such as political unity. The Center, for example, has been the site of ceremonies of war veterans and for protests of the Hanoi government, perpetuating the effects of a war fought a generation ago. The flag of the former republic of Vietnam has been displayed there as well.

Finally, Wood noted the roles of America's Chinatowns as gateways with social institutions that perpetuated cultural heritage, and affirmed ethnic identity and cultural norms, while assisting the transition to a new society. He compared the Eden Center functions to these notorious gateways and concluded that similarities exist. The Eden Center creates a refuge for Vietnamese in America. It represents a mixture of commercialization promoting consumption, a variety of experiences, and provides a sense of place while immigrants blend their old culture with their new (Wood, 2006).

Asians in Flushing, New York

Just as places on the U.S. West Coast have experienced changes due to the influx of immigrant groups since the 1960s, so too have many East Coast communities. Global transformations are influencing local demographic, economics, and cultural relationships in a variety of communities. Flushing, New York is the example provided in this section. This community, like so many others, has experienced economic restructuring and a major influx of immigrants. Smith and Logan studied this area using U.S. Census data, fieldwork, and survey research (Smith and Logan, 2006). Before discussing Flushing in detail, they reported several racial/ethnic changes in the composition of the overall New York City population: non-Hispanic whites declined as a significant presence, from 76 percent to 35 percent, between 1970 and 2000; between 1990 and 2000, the black population increased by about 6 percent. Hispanics increased by 21 percent, and Asians by nearly 60 percent. These led to a number of important observations about Flushing, including increased racial/ethnic diversity, "the growth of all-minority (Black and Hispanic) neighborhoods, and the decline in predominately white neighborhoods." An anticipated fourth trend did not come to pass. These researchers anticipated the emergence of Asian ethnic enclaves. Having said this, however, they pointed out that several small areas of Asian concentration did appear, including those in Flushing. Interestingly, Smith and Logan found that many Asians were either unable or unwilling to reside in suburban neighborhoods, but chose neighborhoods that were ethnically diverse and likely to evolve into increasingly Asian areas. New York City also experienced a decentralization of Asians away from Chinatown and into the outer boroughs, especially Brooklyn and Queens. The result was smaller "little Chinatowns" of urban rather than suburban flavor. These researchers also noted that significant numbers of new immigrants are middle-class and professional households that have human capital that enables them to bypass the traditional ethnic enclaves and instead select other options, resulting in the rise of multi-cultural neighborhoods.

Flushing has increased its population since 1970 because of the influx of immigrants, including those from South and Central America, but especially due to increases in three large Asian ethnic groups: the Chinese, Koreans, and South Asians. These groups more than counterbalanced a decline in the African-American population and a relatively high level of "white flight" during the period. According to the research of Smith and Logan, Asians moved into the Flushing area for several reasons, including job opportunities, easy access to other parts of the City (subway to Manhattan), affordable and available housing, and perceived safety of the local environment. Also, Asians with human and financial capital moved directly to Flushing and were able to minimize the urban decay typically associated with white flight. Asian investment, including foreign investment from Hong Kong, South Korea, and Taiwan, stimulated the economy and contributed to the continued growth of the economy.

Growth and change did not occur without conflict, which resulted from two cultures competing for contested space. Opponents tended to be long-time white European residents who were located in the periphery of Flushing. They felt "locked out" of their own community, which was changing before their eyes; they were competing for limited housing, witnessing new businesses and new social institutions that catered to new immigrants, and signage was increasingly in non-English languages. This undermined their sense of place associated with an older version of Flushing. They sought to protect "old Flushing" from the interests of the business-oriented "new Flushing." As Smith and Logan noted, the socioeconomic status, professional stature, and contributions to the local economy, did not make the Asians in Flushing "immune from local criticism" or cultural conflict (Smith and Logan, 2006).

By 2000, the Hispanic population seemed to have stabilized at about 20 percent of Flushing, while the Asian population increased and constituted nearly 52 percent; Flushing had become the second most concentrated Asian population in the New York area. Asians had replaced the white flight, especially in the core of the city. As a result, the core area in which Chinese had increased most rapidly (followed by South Asians, and Koreans) was termed "Asian Flushing." One impact of this changing landscape was political in nature. A long-term city council member, who had been perceived as anti-immigration and possibly anti-Asian, had been challenged in the 1996 election but managed to hold off that challenge. By 2000, the same council person could not run again due to term limits. As a result a four-way race ensued for that council seat. In the end, John Liu, a Chinese businessman, won the seat, which illustrated for the first time the increasing economic and political power of Asian Americans in Flushing, New York.

SUMMARY AND CONCLUSIONS

The term "Asians" is a short hand that represents a wide variety of cultures scattered across thousands of miles. Among these many groups, three stand out as early 19th and 20th century U.S. immigrants: the Chinese, Japanese and Filipinos. These three cultures, after fleeing harsh conditions in their homelands, came to the U.S. to find work or to secure an education. Most planned to return to their homelands, but did not. Each contributed cheap labor and provided important contributions to the early economic development of America's West Coast. Each also was treated poorly due to changing economic conditions and suffered a variety of indignities and forms of discrimination that rendered them second-class citizens or worse. In fact, American institutions restricted the flow of additional members of all three cultures through various actions. As a result of these various forces, each group saw little increase in their population until American immigration laws were modified after WWII. All three Asian ethnic groups, through perseverance, gradually stabilized their positions in America. These groups developed definable geographic settlement patterns, sometimes representing racial rather than ethnic geography. These patterns changed over time but often included visible cultural landscapes.

U.S. immigration laws changed dramatically after WWII, culminating in the 1965 law that resulted in unpredicted large volumes of immigrants, particularly from Latin America and Asia. Asian Indians replaced the Japanese as the third largest Asian population living in the U.S., but a very wide range of additional Asian ethnic groups greatly diversified the Asian-American population. Part of this was due to legislation that permitted even more foreigners to enter the U.S. for employment reasons or as refugees. However, the family preference provision of the former law continued to have the most significant impact on migration increases. The new Asian immigrant streams, though diverse, contained a significant number of Asians that had social and human capital. As a result, there is an economic bifurcation within the Asian population and within Asian ethnic groups. This has influenced Asian settlement geography in the U.S. because, while some immigrants still initially settle in American inner cities, including ethnic enclaves, many are also able to settle directly in suburbs. This reality has forced a reconsideration of the classic spatial assimilation model to explain immigrant settlement patterns and processes in America. Conventional theory now recognizes the role of heterolocalism, or the ability of immigrant ethnic groups to disperse geographically but maintain their ethnic identities. There also is the notion that multiple assimilation (and non-assimilation) paths are open to immigrants and result in complex settlement geographies, including racialized assimilation. Cultural clashes still occur between various groups, but in some places Asian ethnic groups are gaining increased political representation in local politics. Several examples of Asian ethnic settlements and their corresponding cultural landscapes have been provided to demonstrate the uniqueness of place, as well as the human ethnic tendency to reshape landscapes as reflections of the ethnic values of the occupying culture. Thus, as with other cultures and ethnic groups, we now speak of contemporary Asian places in America.

Chapter 21

This Land is My Land:
The Role of Place in Native Hawaiian Identity

SHAWN MALIA KANA'IAUPUNI AND NOLAN MALONE

Some critiques of contemporary geographic growth patterns point out the rise of placelessness across U.S. landscapes. Relph (1976), in a provocative analysis of this phenomenon, argues that place has been a critical foundation of human cognition and identity throughout history. He reviews how contemporary urban and suburban (and most recently, exurban) growth patterns have diminished the unique, historical, and cultural meanings of place to human society today. This point may bring no argument from most Americans, who may not feel any overwhelming ties to a particular place, who are quite mobile in today's global society, and who, in fact, may be quite accustomed to the increasing standardization of places, such as strip malls, retail, food, and service chains. Add to this the relative homogeneity of most suburban architectures and the constantly shifting topography of metropolitan landscapes. The objective of this essay is to expand our understanding of the significance of place to racial and ethnic diversity and to demonstrate how place continues to be an unequivocal focal point in the identity processes of some social groups and individuals today. Specifically, we examine these processes in the context of Native Hawaiians, the aboriginal people of the Hawaiian Islands.[1]

Our study builds on prior studies indicating that place — the consciousness of land, sea, and all that place entails — is fundamental to indigenous identity processes (Battiste, 2000; Kame'eleihiwa, 1992; Kamakau, 1992; Mihesuah, 2003; Allen, 1992; Meyer, 2003; Kana'iaupuni and Liebler, 2005; Memmott and Long, 2002). Although this analysis of the relationship between place and identity centers on Hawaiians, it offers important insights that may extend to other indigenous groups or cultures whose members are highly intermarried and mobile, whose language is endangered, and whose culture is known more in its commercial tourist, rather than authentic, form. Under these conditions, place is critical to the cultural survival and identity of a people, as we illustrate in the case of Native Hawaiians.

Place is intertwined with identity and self-determination of today's Native Hawaiians in complex and intimate ways. At once the binding glue that holds Native Hawaiians together and links them to a shared past, place is also a primary agent that has been used against them to fragment and alienate. Yet, place, in all of its multiple levels of meaning, is one light that all Hawaiians share in their spiritual way finding to a Hawaiian identity; one that is greatly significant to their existence as a people and culture, both past and present. And so begins our exploration into the various meanings of place to Hawaiian identity today.

In addition to indigenous theories of place, this study is informed by other perspectives on the role of place in racial identity and ethnicity. For example, certain geographers view place as the context within which racial partnering, residential choices, and family identification processes are differentially distributed across spatial categories (e.g., neighborhoods, cities, metropolises) (Wong, 1999; Peach, 1980). By "spatializing" household patterns of family formation, mobility, and other behavioral characteristics, we can understand where (and why) they survive and flourish. Research shows that Hawai'i, for instance, is one of those places in North America that is spatially significant for its flourishing intermarriage rates (Lee and Fernandez, 1998; Root, 2001).

Perspectives in anthropology add to our understanding of the concept of identity as it relates to place. Saltman (2002) defines the relationship between land and identity as the dynamic arena within which social realities are acted out in individual cognition and perception. For example, identity may be the shared understandings between persons of the same culture that enable them to rally together for a political cause. In relation to place, Saltman argues, "identity achieves its strongest expression within the political context of conflicting rights over land and territory" (2002, p. 6); evidence of the latter is certainly found in the story we tell here.

Our study draws on indigenous perspectives of place and identity that interweave the spiritual and the physical with sociocultural traditions and practices. As Memmott and Long (2002) explain, whereas Western explanations view places purely in terms of their geomorphology (with little human influence), indigenous models view people and the environment as overlapping and interacting. For example, unlike the way "Western thought classifies people and their technology apart from nature," indigenous knowledge and beliefs may include ancestral heroes with special powers who helped to shape land and marine systems (Memmott and Long, 2002, p. 43). Likewise, both weather and agricultural or other natural events may be influenced through human rituals, song, dance, or other actions performed in specific places. And, between places and people occurs a sharing of being — places carry the energies of people, history, and cultural significance; in turn, people carry the energy of places as some part of their being (Memmott and Long, 2002).

The concept of place in Hawaiian perspective reflects understandings found throughout Pacific voyaging societies and shares certain similarities with other Native American and aboriginal cultures (Memmott and Long, 2002; Lindstrom, 1999; Martin, 2001; Schnell, 2000). Place, in this case Hawaiʻi, the homeland of the *kānaka maoli* or indigenous people of Hawaiʻi, transcends physical realities of land (Kanaʻiaupuni and Liebler, 2005). It is their *honua* (*whenua, henua, fonua, fanua, fenua* — the words meaning "earth" in Māori, Marshallese, Tongan, Samoan, and Tahitian languages, respectively); it signifies relationships, spanning spiritual and kinship bonds between people, nature, and the supernatural world (Kanahele, 1986). The understanding conveyed by indigenous writings spanning the Pacific is that place breathes life, people, culture, and spirit (Tusitala Marsh, 1999).

Place is, we argue, a key force in the interplay of internal and external influences on contemporary Hawaiian identity processes. In the discussion that follows, we demonstrate how the strength of ties to the land influences Native Hawaiian identity processes through physical, spiritual, genealogical, and historical forces. We examine some of the challenges to identity stemming from displacement, separation from the land, and migration away from Hawaiʻi. We conclude with a discussion of the implications of place to identity processes for Hawaiian children and describe ongoing efforts in education that draw upon the relationships to places as a tool for cultural survival.

SETTING THE HISTORICAL CONTEXT OF PLACE

Native Hawaiians were the first discoverers of the 1,500 mile-long Hawaiian archipelago in the Pacific Ocean. They migrated to Hawaiʻi by sea using advanced navigation skills where they survived and flourished for hundreds of years prior to Western contact. Native Hawaiians evolved a complex system of resource management, developing sophisticated knowledge bases and skills to survive on these remote islands with limited resources.

Cosmogonic and religious beliefs of Native Hawaiians tie the Hawaiian Islands to kānaka maoli beginning with creation, or *pō* (darkness, obscurity). The islands were born from *Papahānaumoku*, earth mother, and *Wākea*, sky father, who also gave birth to *kalo*, the taro plant and main staple crop of traditional Hawaiians, and, ultimately, to people. As such, "the genealogy of the Land, the Gods, Chiefs, and people intertwine with one another, and with all the myriad aspects of the universe" (Kameʻeleihiwa, 1992, p. 2). In these beginnings, the Hawaiian archipelago is intimately connected to *kānaka maoli* through genealogy, culture, history, and spirituality. The natural elements (land, wind, rain) and creatures of the islands are considered primordial ancestors; they are the older relatives of living *kānaka maoli*. Both share an interdependent, familial relationship that requires *mālama* (care) and *kiaʻi* (guardianship) for the older siblings who, in turn, provide for the well-being of the younger siblings (Kanahele, 1986; Kameʻeleihiwa, 1992).

Historically, the Hawaiian Islands were divided into four chiefdoms until the late 18th century, when King Kamehameha I consolidated them through conquest. United under single rule, the archipelago then modernized rapidly through economic commerce in sugar, pineapple, shipping and related industries. By the late 19th century, Hawaiʻi was a fully recognized nation-state with multiple international treaties, including one with the United States (Daws, 1968; Perkins, 2005).

During the same century, however, two things were occurring that devastated Native Hawaiian ties to the land. First, Native Hawaiians were progressively becoming a minority in their own homeland (see Figure 21.1). Estimates suggest that the native population, afflicted by Western disease and to a much lesser extent, warfare, dropped by at least 90 percent in the 100 years following Captain Cook's arrival. By the end of the century only about 40,000 aboriginal Hawaiians remained alive. Meanwhile the immigrant population gained steadily in number, including whites who outnumbered Hawaiians by the early 1900s (Nordyke, 1989). Today, Native Hawaiians comprise about one-fifth of the state population.

Figure 21.1
The Hawaiian Population in Hawaiʻi.

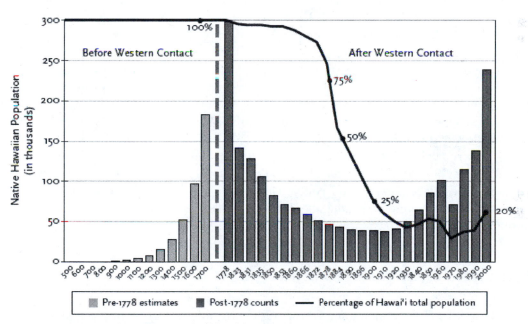

Source: Kanaʻiaupuni, Malone, and Ishibashi (2005)

Second was the gradual and systematic erosion of indigenous control over the land primarily through the insertion of Western legal tactics, government, and religion. John Weeks described "while we looked to the heavens for their gods, they stole the land beneath our feet." Gradually, foreigners took more and more control, exploiting fully Hawaiian cultural beliefs in land as collective property (Kameʻeleihiwa, 1992; Osorio, 2001). The eventual privatization of land played an important role in the displacement of Native Hawaiians. In *kānaka maoli* perspective, it was unfathomable that someone else could deny their rights to place, a precious ancestor, the same land that a family had worked and lived for generations and generations. As Kanahele describes, Hawaiians "belonged to the land. How could you ever own a place, let alone sell it as a commodity, if its true value is found in the sum of the lives, memories, achievements, and *mana* (spiritual power) of the generations who once dwelled upon it?" (1986, p. 208). In the failure of most aboriginals to recognize that they had to formally claim the private ownership of their land, white foreigners, mostly missionaries and businessmen, rapidly bought up the property where Native Hawaiians lived and worked, forcing them to move elsewhere in most cases.

These displacing events culminated in 1893, when a small oligopoly of American businessmen and missionary descendents staged a coup d'état, capturing the Hawaiian Queen Lili'uokalani and imprisoning her in the royal palace with the help of U.S. Marines (Coffman, 1998). Although the overthrow violated existing treaties and established procedures for annexation, Hawai'i was proclaimed a U.S. territory by Congress via the Newlands Resolution in 1898 (Trask, 2002).

What many do not know is that annexation occurred despite a petition signed by nearly every living Native Hawaiian at the time (an estimated 38,000 of 40,000) in protest of losing their sovereign nation (Coffman, 1998; Silva, 2004). In recognition and formal apology by the U.S. government for these actions, U.S. Public Law 103–150, signed in 1993, cites that indigenous Hawaiians never relinquished claims to their inherent sovereignty as a people or over their lands to the United States. Hawai'i became a state in 1959.

Fast forward to the present where land struggles still occupy center focus. In September of 2004, thousands of Native and non-Native supporters marched for *Kū i ka Pono* (Justice for Hawaiians) through the heart of Waikīkī. Their purpose: to support three cases, all directly or indirectly concerning land issues. The first was to protest a Hawai'i state law that has been used to systematically take leased land holdings from the Hawaiian monarchy (*ali'i*) trusts, among others, to sell off to individuals.[2] The second and third cases were to support Hawaiian rights in two cases heard by the 9th Circuit U.S. Court of Appeals in early 2005. The second case challenged Kamehameha Schools, which is a private trust holding the legacy land assets of the Kamehameha monarchy in endowment explicitly to fund the education of Hawaiian children (see www.ksbe.edu). It is responsible for the education of nearly 24,000 Native Hawaiian children since opening its doors in 1887. Ironically, Kamehameha Schools is being sued for providing educational services to Native Hawaiians under constitutional amendments that were designed to protect the rights of disenfranchised minorities.

The third case challenged the Department of Hawaiian Home Lands (DHHL) which holds for Native Hawaiian homesteaders a small fraction of the original lands belonging to the Hawaiian Kingdom that were taken by the U.S. government after the overthrow. In a state troubled by inadequate housing, especially for Native Hawaiians, the wait for DHHL lands can take decades — sometimes even occurring postmortem. All three cases concern land, aboriginal rights, and the Native Hawaiian quest for self-determination. For many, they are evidence of the continued struggle over land and continued attempts of colonizing entities to displace Native Hawaiians from their homeland and rightful place in the world (see Figure 21.2).

CULTURE, IDENTITY, AND PLACE OF NATIVE HAWAIIANS

Recent research by Kana'iaupuni and Liebler (2005) examines the role of place in identity processes of Native Hawaiians. As they point out

"... the diverse ethnic mix that comprises the state of Hawai'i, and the resulting multiracial mix of today's Hawaiians in the state and on the U.S. Continent, complicate questions of identity for Hawai'i's host culture. For people of any racial or ethnic group, the characteristics of place — its location, social and ethnic composition, physical features, and historical significance to a people — can have profound symbolic and practical effects on identity and identification processes.... Living or growing up in Hawai'i is certainly a notable experience that affects the identity processes of all its diverse residents.... But one unique characteristic that Hawaiians will always have is their genealogical connection to Hawai'i as the ancestral homeland. No other group holds this claim" (p. 691).

Figure 21.2
A Nation in Distress: Kū i ka Pono supporters marching with the Hawaiian flag upside down.

In questions of identity, they argue, place plays a critical role through Hawaiian traditions and customs that weave together: 1) physical and spiritual, 2) genealogical, and 3) sociopolitical ties to the land and sea.

Physical and Spiritual Ties to Place

Physically, a deep source of Hawaiian identity is found in ties to the land and sea, expressed in the proverb "*ka mauli o ka 'āina a he mauli kānaka, the life of the land is the life of the people*" (Oneha, 2001). As a subsistence society, living off the natural resources of the land was fundamental to the social identities of Native Hawaiians, specific to the island or region where they lived (Kanahele, 1986). The interconnections of place and people were influenced by traditional practices of collective ownership, where, unlike Western land tenure systems, rights to land/sea access were negotiated by generation and family lineage as well as personal, family and community need (Rapaport, 1999). '*Āina*, the Hawaiian word for land most commonly used today, also means "to eat," signifying the physical relationship between people and the earth that they tended. Important to identity processes, Hawaiians to this day see a dynamic, intimate relationship in the reciprocal nature of caring for the land (*mālama 'āina*) as it cares for the people, much like a family bond (Kame'eleihiwa, 1992).

These symbolic connections of places to the ancestry and cultural values of people are made explicit through various cultural customs; one example is found in the extensive naming practices of places associated with land, sea, and heavens. No place with any significance went without a name in Hawaiian tradition (Kanahele, 1986), and today, considerable scholarship goes into documenting thousands of place, wind, and rain names in Hawai'i to preserve the rich legendary and historical significance of places to Hawaiian cultural identity (e.g., Pūku'i, Elbert and Mo'okini, 1974; Nakuina, 1990). Place names span past and present, and through their meanings, the significance of place is transmitted socially and across generations. These types of practices underscore the inseparability of physical and spiritual interconnections between place and people in the Hawaiian worldview.

Genealogical Ties to Place

Another example of this inseparability is found in genealogical traditions. Across the Pacific, identity is borne of establishing one's genealogical ties to ancestral beginnings. Ancestral ties include not only people, but also the spiritual and natural worlds, since all things were birthed by the same beginnings. Kame'eleihiwa argues that genealogical chants "reveal the Hawaiian orientation to the world about us, in particular, to Land and control of the Land" (1992, p. 3).

In Hawaiian tradition, genealogical chants identify the lines of trust and social connection in addition to telling family histories. These traditions are still important to many in contemporary Hawai'i. Formal introductions at public events commonly include reciting a lineage of people and places, including connections to a specific mountain, valley, wind, rain, ocean, and water. Culture-based leadership training, schools, and education programs continue to instill these practices in today's young Hawaiians (see Figure 21.3). Central to identity processes, articulating these connections in social interactions provides important context for social relationships and negotiations between individuals and groups.

Sociopolitical Ties to Place

The third set of place-people identity relationships that Kana'iaupuni and Liebler (2005) discuss is very critical to many Native Hawaiians today as it accompanies the struggle for self-determination. They state:

> "The importance of place to Hawaiian identity is powered not only by ancestral genealogy, but also by the collective memory of a shared history. Hawai'i, the place, connects the Hawaiian diaspora through 'social relations and a historical memory of cultural beginnings, meanings and practices, as well as crises, upheavals and unjust subjections as a dispossessed and (mis)recognized people'" (Halualani, 2002, p. 693).

As a catalyst for strengthened identity, Spickard and Fong point out in agreement that:

> "It is as invigorating to ethnicity when a Pacific Islander American politician recites the history of abuse that her people have suffered, as when an island spiritual leader chants a genealogy.... It is true history, but it is more than that: it is the act of rhetorically, publicly remembering, and thus it serves to strengthen the ethnic bond" (1995, p. 1375).

In this fashion, the history of colonization and cultural oppression creates a context for shared cognitive understandings that relate identity to place (Kana'iaupuni and Liebler, 2005; Halualani, 2002). For example, calling on this understanding, Kame'eleihiwa writes, "Hawaiians have been in Hawai'i for at least two thousand years. As harsh as the past two hundred years have been, there is yet hope; we still exist on this earth. After all the horror that has rained down upon us, we are alive. We are a nation of survivors!" (1992, p. 321). Thus, these images of history and place fuel Hawaiian identity in the growing context of political self-determination.

Figure 21.3
Students offer a traditional Hawaiian chant.

Together, these cultural practices and social relations illustrate how place serves as a key connection linking Native Hawaiian families and children to their indigenous heritage, despite the extensive and long-standing multicultural and multiethnic mixing in the state of Hawai'i and beyond.

THE HAWAIIAN DIASPORA: MIGRATION, INTERMARRIAGE, AND IDENTITY

Although values about place and culture reach Hawaiians living outside of Hawai'i as well as those in Hawai'i (Oneha, 2001; Kauanui, 1998), questions about identity, and even culture and ethnicity, all may be affected by the context of place. For example, studies show that multiracial Hawaiians living in Hawai'i are especially likely to racially identify as Hawaiian (and not as another race), compared with their counterparts in the continental United States (e.g., Kana'iaupuni and Liebler, 2005). What this means is that the relationship between place and identity is fluid. In the context of shifting cultural and geographic landscapes, population diversity, and the effects of colonization, place serves a pivotal role in Native Hawaiian identity processes today.

Hawaiʻi — the cultural home — becomes a beacon, vital to the survival and vibrancy of the Hawaiian culture, language, and native people today.

Through the economic and racial transformation of the islands, Native Hawaiian migration and inter-marriage have created the Hawaiian diaspora, spread across the nation and into others since the 1700s (Kauanui, 1999; Halualani, 2002). The diaspora presents a modern challenge to Native Hawaiian identity and culture, bringing separation of people from each other, from the land, and the ancestral home. U.S. Census 2000 statis-tics show that fewer Native Hawaiian people moved *to* Hawaiʻi between 1995 and 2000 than those who moved *away*. About 40 percent of self-reported Native Hawaiians live in the continental United States, while 60 percent continue to reside in Hawaiʻi. Some Hawaiian scholars argue that the mobility of Hawaiians, the diaspora, un-dermines native identity. Yet, others describe how place is the powerful mobilizing force to off-island Hawai-ians urging them to "come home" to struggle (see Kauanui, 1998). The voices call to the spirit, to the body, to the memory of cells and DNA — for the undeniable link is genealogical: "our mother is our land, *Papahānau-moku*, she who birth the islands" (Trask, 1993, p. 122).

Recent migrations of Native Hawaiians respond to "push" and "pull" factors described by migration and economic theories (Massey et al., 1993). These theories find support in the modern Hawaiian experience of low wages, high rents, and limited educational opportunities that drive Native Hawaiians to various destinations in the continental United States. The cost of living in Hawaiʻi continues to average about 30 percent higher than the rest of the nation; with some of the highest home prices in the country, the median price of a single-family home was $550,000 in 2005. For the indigenous population, which tends to have lower education and higher poverty rates (even when fully employed) than other groups in the state, it has become increasingly difficult to survive (Kanaʻiaupuni, Malone, and Ishibashi, 2005). Thus, the promise of education, jobs, and lower home prices attract many Hawaiians northeast to the 48 states, and once there, they are often held by new social and familial ties.

Population diversity is another threat to Native Hawaiian identity (Kanaʻiaupuni and Malone, 2004). Like other Native American groups in the United States, Native Hawaiians are predominantly multiracial. They claim the highest rates of multiracial status, next to Alaska Natives: about two-thirds of Native Hawaiians are of mixed-race.[3] Census 2000 data show that among *all* married Native Hawaiians, only 19 percent were married to other Hawaiians. Yet, the effects of increasing geographic diversity are immediately apparent in the intermar-riage rates of those living in the 48 continental states compared with those still in Hawaiʻi. The data in Figure 21.4 show that whereas 34 percent of married Native Hawaiians in their homeland are married to other Hawai-ians, the percentage drops to only 7 percent among those residing elsewhere. Because the vast majority involves white partners, this marriage trend has been described by some scholars as a "whitening of the Hawaiian race."

For all groups, interracial mixing complicates questions of identity (see Root, 2001; Liebler, 2001; Xie and Goyette, 1997). The real question for the perpetuation of ethnic or cultural groups is what happens to the children? What we find is that the chances of identifying children as Hawaiian in Hawaiian couple families are quite high, as might be expected. But, for Hawaiians that marry out, the likelihood that children are identified as Hawaiian diminishes. Thus, rather than creating greater potential for Hawaiian population growth through in-termarriage, the data show diminishing returns to Hawaiian identification in mixed-race households.

Geography affects not only who people marry, but also their identity choices. In some cases, multi-racial identity may permit greater ethnic options for Native Hawaiians on the continent, depending on where they live. For instance, a Native Hawaiian, Chinese, Puerto Rican individual in Northern California may opt to adopt a Chinese ethnic affiliation, while the same individual may find greater expression in her/his Puerto Rican ethnicity in New York. In other cases, individuals may adopt different situational identities, depending on the circumstances. Certainly not unique to Native Hawaiians, these individual decisions are complicated by both geographic and racial/ethnic diversity, and, for many, can be difficult to resolve (see Spickard and Fong, 1995; Franklin, 2003).

Figure 21.4
Intermarriage of Native Hawaiians, Census 2000.

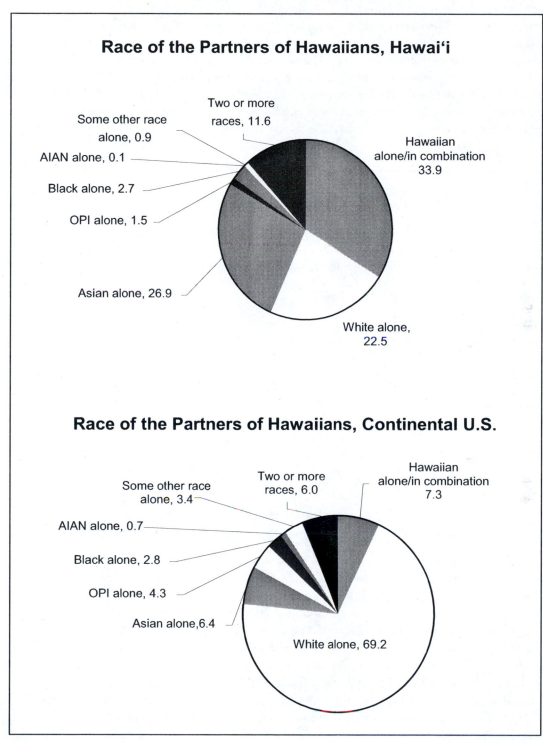

Race of the Partners of Hawaiians, Hawai'i

Two or more races, 11.6

Some other race alone, 0.9

AIAN alone, 0.1

Black alone, 2.7

OPI alone, 1.5

Hawaiian alone/in combination 33.9

Asian alone, 26.9

White alone, 22.5

Race of the Partners of Hawaiians, Continental U.S.

Some other race alone, 3.4

Two or more races, 6.0

Hawaiian alone/in combination 7.3

AIAN alone, 0.7

Black alone, 2.8

OPI alone, 4.3

Asian alone, 6.4

White alone, 69.2

Kana'iaupuni and Liebler (2005) found that, compared with those in the continental United States, mixed-race families are much more likely to report their children as Native Hawaiian if the children were born in Hawai'i, if the family resides in Hawai'i, or if the Hawaiian parent was born in Hawai'i, in the absence of other explanatory factors. Moreover, suggesting that returning home is a profound event, the highest odds ratio of reporting Native Hawaiian occurred in mixed-race families that had lived outside Hawai'i and returned home, compared with other families. Recent data from Census 2000 are consistent, confirming the deep significance of place to racial identification. As shown in Figure 21.5, Kana'iaupuni and Malone (2004) found that mixed-race children with birth or residence ties to Hawai'i were significantly more likely to be identified as Native Hawaiian than were other children. Still, only about half of children in interracial families with one Native Hawaiian parent were identified as Hawaiian in Census 2000 (Kana'iaupuni and Malone, 2004).

Figure 21.5

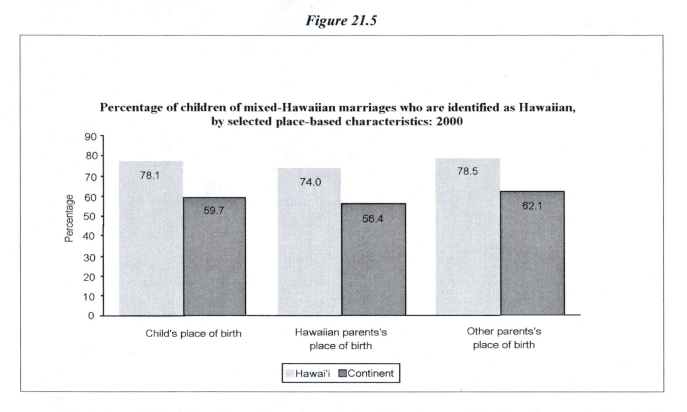

For displaced Native Hawaiians who seek to sustain their culture and identity, other mechanisms in foreign locations help perpetuate cultural identity through the continuation of traditional practices or the reinforcement of cultural values and ideals. In many of the 48 states, Native Hawaiians regularly come together for cultural gatherings involving music, art, language, and recreation. They have formed Hawaiian-based organizations and groups to assist continental Hawaiians with life away from their ancestral home. A number of Hawaiian civic clubs exist throughout the United States, especially in regions in which large numbers of Hawaiians reside (e.g., on the West Coast). Alumni associations, such as that of the Kamehameha Schools, also maintain regional districts to help keep the network of families and friends informed and connected. Smaller groups that practice traditional Hawaiian arts, such as hula and canoe paddling, exist across the continent, thereby offering practical outlets for Hawaiians living far from home. Kauanui (1999) notes a few: Hui Hawai'i of San Diego, E ola Mau Ka 'Ōlelo Makuahine in Huntington Beach, Na Kolea (aptly named after the golden plover birds that fly between Hawai'i and Alaska) of San Jose, and others.

BUILDING THE FUTURE OF PLACE

It is difficult for many 21st century Native Hawaiians to share the same degree of involvement and connection with ancestral lands as Native Hawaiians could in former times. But recognition of the pivotal role that place plays in their identity processes has begun to transform the service and delivery of many educational and social programs for Native Hawaiians. The reforms integrate the rich history, stories, and knowledge about the land and sea, and at the same time reinforce the integral link between the *'āina* and identity.

Primarily fueled by the concern and passion of Hawaiian community members, parents, and advocates, these efforts are an organic solution to the chilling negative statistics that plague Native Hawaiian children: high rates of poverty, substance abuse, juvenile deviance and criminal activity, teenage pregnancies, poor educational outcomes, domestic abuse, depression, and suicide. For example, place-based learning is a pillar of educational reform through the Hawaiian charter school movement. Typical of this approach, schools (e.g., *Kanu o ka 'Āina* New Century Public Charter School) boast a project-based and place-based curriculum for children that integrates community and the natural environment. Students engage in authentic experiences at particular *wahi pana* (sacred places) that serve as outdoor learning laboratories. They conduct science experiments to assess the relative successes of various methods to revive endangered endemic species. Their curriculum includes learning about lifestyles, knowledge, and values of Native Hawaiians. In this way, connections to the land create the space for Native Hawaiians to maintain traditional practices that nourish spiritual, physical, and educational well-being.

From a sense of place grows a sense of *kuleana* (responsibility). Various programs in schools and other organizations encourage responsibility toward the land and sea as part of a broader educational strategy. These range from post-high leadership (e.g., Na Ala Hele i ke Ao at Chaminade University), to agricultural, resource management, substance abuse rehabilitation (e.g., Ho'omau ke Ola offering adult outpatient and residential services), and many other programs. Programs teaching stewardship of the oceans stress Native Hawaiian thought that the sea works in partnership with the land, providing sustenance and serving as a pathway and communication link with other lands and peoples (Amona, 2004). As such, maritime programs, fishpond restoration, and voyaging and ocean learning (e.g., Polynesian Voyaging Society) are all examples of promising directions in Native Hawaiian communities today (see Figure 21.6).

The results indicate progress. Studies show that best practices among successful teachers of Native Hawaiian students include experience-based, authentic activities (e.g., Kawakami and Aton, 2001). Data from Hawaiian charter schools provide evidence of higher attendance and achievement scores than exhibited by Native Hawaiian students in conventional public schools (Kana'iaupuni and Ishibashi, 2005). Evaluation research finds higher levels of engagement (attendance, timely completion, postsecondary aspirations) among Native Hawaiian students enrolled in public school-within-school models that offer hands-on experiences at significant places within students' communities such as streams, freshwater ecosystems, and ancient burial grounds, (Yamauchi, 2003). The findings are consistent with research on other indigenous groups. For example, studies have found that Native American students exhibit greater preference for tactile and concrete learning experiences than do their peers (Rhodes, 1990). Many studies indicate the positive effects of place-based forms of education in a wide variety of settings (Gruenewald, 2003; Becket, 2003; Kawakami, 1999; Smith, 2002).

DISCUSSION

This essay has traced some of the place-people connections that influence identity. We have documented the spatial linkages between the place of indigenous Hawaiians today and their identity by locating the present in the historical locations and subjugations of place, by tracing the genealogical, cultural, and ancestral relations of Native Hawaiians and place, and by mapping how place serves a pivotal purpose for the progress of Native Hawaiians.

In some ways, Hawaiian identity has been "conceived, manufactured, and fabricated" by external forces that do not share the interests of the indigenous peoples that they mold and shape to fit their own reality (Halualani, 2002). Identity is not simply a subjective cognitive process, but one subjected to external biases, intentional misrepresentation, and political tactics. Countless examples exist where Western powers convince the world of their right to colonize indigenous peoples by recreating them as *other* (than Western), from the distorted hula girl images of the Hawaiians to the purposeful portrayal of American Indians as primitive savages. Indigenous theory focuses on returning the gaze to expose the ulterior motives behind such tactics, which careful documentation reveals are influenced by Western imperialism, power, and capitalism. Even defining indigenous peoples by blood quantum, as is the case for Hawaiians and many American Indian people, is an explicit legal maneuver to ensure that they eventually disappear into oblivion.

Figure 21.6
Students learn ancient and modern lessons at Kahuwai Villiage on Hawaiʻi Island.

In the Hawaiian case, the purpose — perhaps not explicit, but definitely systematic — was to dismember *lāhui*, the Hawaiian nation, to de-historicize place from its people, and to justify taking the land from its indigenous people (Osorio, 2002). In the end, the place itself may have been the motivating factor, a precious land that still captures the hearts of many visitors. As Mark Twain fondly recalled — in the same speech where he betrayed the indigenous Hawaiians, calling them stupid, dishonest, immoral cowards:

> "no alien land in all the world has any deep strong charm for me but that one, no other land could so longingly and so beseechingly haunt me, sleeping and walking, through half a lifetime, as that one has done" (Sandwich Island Speeches cf. Wood, 1999, p. 94).

It is crucial to understand that these forces did not occur without consistent resistance. Although never with violence, Native Hawaiians successfully fought to have the island of Kahoʻolawe, however sick or devastated by bombing, returned to them by the military. We have regained place-based knowledge systems that had lapsed into disuse, including renewing traditional navigation systems via ocean and constellations; restoring ancient agricultural and aquacultural technologies that once sustained hundreds of thousands of islanders in environmentally healthy ways; reviving Hawaiian martial arts, ancient chant and hula forms; and reclaiming traditional healing practices and medicinal plant knowledge. We have struggled to revitalize the Hawaiian language from just a few thousand speakers twenty years ago to many more today. In fact, Census 2000 estimates possibly as many as 25,000 Hawaiian language speakers, making Hawaiian one of the only indigenous languages to have grown between 1990 and 2000 (Steton, 2005). The vast majority reside in the cultural home of Hawaiʻi. We fight hard for self-determination, exploring multiple models of a potential future as a sovereign people. We are national leaders in the battle against environmental degradation and protection of endangered species. The most powerful driving force in these efforts is the intensity of feeling for place. The mobilizing energy comes from the land itself, from the sea, from the children (see Figure 21.7) and the compelling vision of a future where indigenous Hawaiians are in their rightful place as a vibrant, thriving people.

Figure 21.7
A young marcher.

NOTES

[1] We use Native Hawaiian, Hawaiian, and kānaka maoli to refer to those descended from the aboriginal people that inhabited the Hawaiian archipelago prior to 1778, when Captain James Cook arrived to Hawaiʻi.

[2] The law was repealed successfully in the following spring, 2005.

[3] According to Census 2000, 64.9 percent of Native Hawaiians report more than one race. Alaska Natives most often reported multiple races (92%), followed by Native Hawaiians, and then American Indians (53%).

Chapter 22

Little Tokyo:
Historical and Contemporary Japanese American Identities

JAMES M. SMITH

INTRODUCTION

This chapter considers processes that have provided a classic framework of constraints and opportunities for Japanese Americans in Los Angeles. These processes include market capitalism and technological change, racism, and cultural practices. In particular, geographers are interested in how these kinds of economic, social, and cultural processes produce landscapes in various kinds of places. In this case study, we consider Little Tokyo, in Los Angeles, California. This district is a traditional urban ethnic enclave, an area that has many landscape and cultural features of Japanese-American life, ranging from Japanese signage to architectural features. We are especially interested in how the social practices and cultural forms have been etched onto the landscape of this special place, how the enclave has reinforced a sense of being Japanese American, and how Little Tokyo has changed over the last one-hundred years.

Although no longer the largest concentration of Japanese-American residences, Little Tokyo has been revived as a center for voluntary cultural, religious, and political practices that have reinforced Japanese-American identities in the post WWII-postwar era. Like other ethnic groups, Japanese Americans build and use places to maintain businesses, create ethnic residences such as senior homes, and reinforce their identities through a sense of place. Although these places are no longer the enclave ghettos of old, and no longer spatially constrained, the residential pattern of a racially-defined people, the three remaining California *Nihonmachi* (Japantowns), are still socially significant as places of ethnic boundary maintenance (Barth, 1998) and survival in the face of structural and cultural assimilation.

EARLY GEOGRAPHIES OF JAPANESE-AMERICAN MIGRATION

Push Factors for Japanese Migrants

The onset of the Meiji Era in Japan (1868–1912), with its nationalist projects of industrialization, militarization and empire-building, provided the context for Japanese emigration to the Americas and Hawai'i. The Japanese elites were determined to transform a mostly feudal society into a modern powerful nation-state with an effective military, overseas colonies and a strong urban-industrial economy. This proved to be a difficult shift for certain groups. For example, a combination of legislative inducements and coercion effectively removed possible threats to the Meiji regime from the samurai or warrior class, many of whom were unhappy with Western influence over their country and a loss of social status due to the reforms of the new government. Even more troublesome was the issue of the peasantry, and how they would be brought into the new order.

Despite promises to the contrary, the Meiji regime had no intention of large-scale land redistribution or relief of heavy tax burdens on farmers. To the Meiji leadership, industrialization meant squeezing the agricultural sector. This was done through the initiation of cash economies in the rural areas, and the establishment of a land tax, to be paid in cash (Halliday, 1975; Hane, 1990).

The result for rural families was even greater hardship than they had known before, as the peasants now depended on the sale of rice to pay the tax. Fluctuations in agricultural commodities prices were determined largely by financial policies set in Tokyo, which generally favored deflation and high interest rates, particularly in periods of crisis. When crops failed and debts came due, hunger and occasional famine resulted, and peasants migrated to the cities and overseas, most of the latter group to Hawai'i and the west coast of the U.S. and Canada (Halliday, 1975; Hane, 1990, 1982; Takahashi, 1997). These changing conditions in the Japanese countryside were the key push factors in the migration of the *Nikkei*, a term that refers to the overseas Japanese.

Approximately 275,000 Japanese entered the United States between 1861 and 1924, with 245,000 of them migrating from 1900 to 1924. Most were young and male, fitting the profile of long-distance migration that is typical for this specific historical period. Given the nature of the work that labor contractors sought to fill, and conditions in peasant villages, most were rural farmers. The predominant source region for intra-Japanese rural to urban movement, as well as international migration, was southern Japan, particularly productive rice-producing areas such as Yamaguchi, Hiroshima and Okayama prefectures in southwestern Honshu, where the peasants bore a harsh burden of land taxes (Takahashi, 1997; Hane, 1990, 1982; Takaki, 1989).

Most of the *Issei* (those who came and stayed) had clear economic motives to leave Japan, but many did not anticipate staying in the United States. Earning money to build a home, to acquire an education, and to establish businesses were prominent reasons for emigration.

The Japanese and California's Emerging Market Economy

In California, the production of winter fruits and vegetables in the Mediterranean climatic setting, combined with transcontinental freight rail and refrigeration, established economic complementarities with the demand for fresh produce in Midwestern and Eastern seaboard markets. Because of the skills of Japanese farmers in intensive wet-rice agriculture and vegetable gardening, both of which demanded heavy labor and attention to detail, trans-Pacific labor contracts were lucrative for white-owned agricultural operations (Takahashi, 1997).

The use of Japanese laborers as a strategy to increase the profits of agribusiness reflects a pattern in the creation of economic geographies in the Americas from the Columbian expansion to the present day strategies of capitalist enterprises in California (Walker, 1997; Ong, Bonacich, and Cheng, 1994). Exploitation of culturally isolated workers, whether through slavery or contract, was a feature of plantation and food crop agriculture in global and regional peripheries. Characteristically, in the California context, the first-generation Japanese immigrants, the *Issei*, were forbidden to own land. Nevertheless, the nativist-inspired Alien Land Laws and other measures in the racialization of land tenure did not succeed in preventing the establishment of productive small farms run by Japanese immigrants, who devised creative strategies to circumvent the restrictions (Ichioka, 1988; Iwata, 1990).

Initially, local elites in California and other states welcomed male Japanese migrants as temporary reservoirs of labor, cheap and politically compliant. This situation leads us to the question of why anti-Japanese racism was eventually supported by political leaders and local businesses after their initial acquiescence to, or tolerance of, the *Issei*. The attitude of the local state shifted dramatically with the large-scale movement of Issei into various forms of self-employment in horticulture and truck farming. The Issei were able to accomplish this major shift in status despite the strong social pressure on white landowners not to rent land to Japanese tenants, let alone sell it. By 1913, the first of the Alien Land Laws were designed to provide the coercive instrument to terminate the movement of the California Japanese into agricultural self-employment that required at least the use of land, if not its ownership (Chuman, 1976).

The Issei were often disliked by the local white farmers and business leaders because they could not be effectively controlled as they moved into self-proprietorship, which enabled them to escape the role of unskilled workers. As successful farmers in the production of specialty truck-farming produce such as lettuce, onions, garlic, strawberries and flowers, the Issei were able to form agricultural cooperatives that established self-sufficiency by creating chains of businesses at different stages of the production, distribution, and marketing processes. Japanese immigrants ran large regional vegetable and flower markets, as well as smaller mom-and-pop operations. All of this was achieved despite the relegation of the Japanese immigrant farmers to leased lands with marginal soils, and the lack of startup capital from outside of the community (Iwata, 1990).

ETHNIC LIFE IN EARLY LITTLE TOKYO

With the arrival of increasing numbers of "picture brides," women who migrated from Japan through trans-Pacific arranged marriages without meeting their prospective husbands, the overwhelmingly male character of the *Nikkei* communities began to change. The Issei experience and that of their second-generation children, the *Nisei*, defined the early Japanese-American experience in southern California's Nihonmachi, and in rural clusters of the ethnic group, who engaged in farming.

A visitor from outside of the community in the 1920s or 1930s would have seen that Little Tokyo was built as a vibrant center of business activity, worship, and social life. For farmers who needed supplies such as seeds and tools, wholesale markets provided these necessities with business transactions conducted in Japanese, as most of the early immigrants had little or no command of English. Children would help out in the retail green groceries by washing vegetables such as carrots and *daikon*, a Japanese radish. They prepared flower displays and worked the cash register. Tofu, a paste made of soybeans and cut into blocks, was a key source of protein and was at that time hard to find outside of the community. Fresh fish was the other principal source of protein in the Japanese diet, and the "fish man" merchants were a common sight. They sold *maguro* (red tuna), *ebi* (shrimp) and other favored species caught in the cold waters off the California coast. At night, neon lights with mixed Japanese and English script created an exotic atmosphere of the "Orient" designed to give tourists or native Los Angelenos the impression that they were traveling to a distant locale to dine and shop, even if Little Tokyo was just a few miles from home.

Religious institutions were a crucial force in the life of the community, with several dozen Buddhist temples and Christian churches providing weekly worship, marriage, and funeral service. The scent of incense and the chanting of sutras, Buddhist sacred scripts, would have reminded the visitor of the uniqueness of Little Tokyo as a place. Most services were conducted exclusively in Japanese, although English services became more common as the Nisei came of age. Most children attended Japanese school for one or two hours every weeknight and on Saturdays, with classes often held in temples and churches. Strict discipline prevailed, and Japanese values such as *giri* (contractual obligation), *on* (profound debt to parents), and respect for traditional learning and authority were emphasized.

Temples and churches were also the center for social life, as they help to organize appropriate functions for young people to meet, arranged marriages, and were the focus of sports leagues in baseball, basketball, volleyball, and martial arts. These were typically exclusively comprised of Japanese Americans, for this allowed for competition in safe social spaces, in which the ethnic group members could feel more comfortable and avoid potential tensions with the majority community.

Other centers of social activity included special bars that catered exclusively to men, typically serving *sake*, Japanese rice wine, and specialty foods. Gambling and *shogi* (Japanese chess) were favorite pastimes, and news and information vital to the community was available in the *Rafu Shimpo*, the largest of several newspapers published in Little Tokyo, which was an exclusively Japanese-language paper until 1926.

PROBLEMS FOR THE EARLY JAPANESE AMERICAN COMMUNITY IN LITTLE TOKYO: RACISM, NATIVISM, AND THE GHETTO

The Japanese-American experience in the region, like other minorities, was shaped by racism and the needs of a growing market economy. The Japanese came to California to make a living, but were confronted over competition for jobs and resources. As in the case of their Chinese predecessors, racism also was a major problem for early Japanese-American communities.

A number of "nativist" social movements and political organizations emerged from the dominant ethnic group in California in the early 20th century. As with the earlier agitation against Chinese migrants, the anti-Japanese movement's advocates were found among labor groups who feared the presence of Japanese workers would lower wages. These fears were fanned by those who feared and hated the Japanese due to their different cultural practices and physical appearance. The Japanese were labeled as aliens and nativist movements claimed that they could never be successfully assimilated into American life. The racial tenor of the nativism grew increasingly shrill with the periodic rise in geopolitical tensions between the United States and Japan (Penrose, 1973; Daniels, 1977).

The nativists used what is sometimes referred to as Yellow Peril. They tried to portray the Japanese-American population as a fast-breeding and treasonous group preparing for a future Japanese invasion of California, which the nativists claimed to be inevitable. The nativists played on various fears and emotions. For example, Japanese men were said to want to abduct and rape white women. These images were similar to stereotypes applied to African-American males during the Antebellum and Jim Crow periods. The idea of an economic "threat" posed by the Japanese-American population was now transformed into a political threat through the prism of race. All Japanese were claimed to be a fifth column of aliens attempting to capture California for Japanese companies, as a prelude to eventual military conquest (Takaki, 1989; Dower, 1986; Daniels, 1962).

The Yellow Peril idea was far more effective in mobilizing a broad base of Californians because of the multiple stereotypes it expressed. One or more of these stereotypes appealed to all classes and political persuasions within white society, while other stereotypes appealed to specific class and political constituencies.

The same Yellow Peril idea that had been applied to Chinese migrants (Anderson, 1987; Chang, 2003) were used as weapons against all Japanese Americans, immigrant or native-born. Geographically, the Alien Land Laws of 1913 and 1920 prohibited the Issei from owning land, and placed spatial restrictions on Japanese Americans by limiting the areas where they could live and work. Other discriminatory practices included segregated education, which actually provoked a political crisis between the U.S. and Japanese governments in the first decade of the twentieth century. Likewise, housing segregation was imposed through informal discriminatory practices. The latter were usually accompanied by verbal and physical intimidation, not only against Japanese migrants, but also toward those whites in the local communities who were sympathetic and willing to lease land and housing to the Nikkei. Thus, the Issei and their children were confined to specific housing in both rural and urban areas. In California alone, urban segregation led to the creation of forty *Nihonmachi*, or Japantowns, including Little Tokyo, Los Angeles.

As with the early development of Chinatowns, Japanese enclaves were originally ghettos built as a consequence of, and a response to the racism in the larger society. Anderson (1987) provides insights into the specific case of Asians in North America, and the manner in which discourses of the "Oriental" Other were applied as tools to create racialized ghettos (Said, 1978). Thus, ideology of the dominant ethnic group imposed the ghetto and reinforced outside perceptions and stereotypes of it by creating conditions of crowding and lack of hygiene through poor access to water, sanitation, and adequate living space. This was discriminatory public policy, and it imposed conditions that were then used to reinforce stereotypes of the group, such as claims that the Japanese always stick together, and therefore cannot be trusted. This combination of public policy, racism, and spatial isolation created a feedback loop of place making based on discriminatory treatment. Chinatowns and Japantowns were evidence of the racial fears and obsessions of the dominant ethnic and class groups in the host society. They were products of a specific regional type of racism in California (Omi and Winant, 1986), which shaped everyday attitudes, laws, and politics at all scales.

However, rather than forcing Japanese immigrants to return to Japan or migrate elsewhere, the effect of this intense discrimination was to motivate the Issei to build an integrated ethnic economy that proved to be remarkably resilient (Takahashi, 1997; Bonacich and Modell, 1980).

Little Tokyo, which is the most famous of the Japanese urban enclaves, does not have a single founding date, but the term was coined by white "native" Californians in the early twentieth century, and soon used by the Japanese Americans themselves. Because the Japanese were labeled "unassimilable aliens," and denied the right to seek citizenship, they were effectively excluded from the political system, even if they were English-speaking second-generation Nisei. This meant that the Japanese community could not seek redress for grievances or crimes committed against them, let alone have any effect on the outcome of elections. Likewise, they were forced into a marginal niche economy, socially and geographically isolated and politically disempowered. These conditions worsened for Japanese Americans during the 1930s and 1940s, when increasing tensions and eventual war between the U.S. and Japan led to their incarceration in camps from the spring of 1942 until 1945.

After the war, due to continued discrimination in housing practices, Japanese Americans moved to specific neighborhoods that were characterized by more tolerance and job opportunities in landscaping and small business, work in which the Japanese Americans had thrived before the incarceration. By the late 1950s and especially the 1960s, as legal barriers to assimilation began to crumble under the pressure of the Civil Rights movement, the *Nikkei* began to disperse to outlying suburbs such as Gardena and Torrance in the South Bay region of Los Angeles, as well as the San Gabriel Valley. These changes put pressure on Little Tokyo and the enclave began a period of demographic and economic decline, resulting in the deterioration of its built environment.

In the 1970s, significant investment from Japanese corporations resulted in a process of gentrified businesses. These are institutions that charge higher prices and cater to upscale tourists, in this case from Japan. Older buildings that had been used as senior residences were torn down to make way for hotels and shopping malls. This led to considerable resistance from community activists, and the decade was marked by frequent negotiations and conflicts among the activists who wished to preserve what they termed "Lil Tokio for workin folks," the City of Los Angeles, and Japanese companies that hoped to develop the area. By the 1980s, it was clear that redevelopment was winning out, and the decade marked the high point of Japanese corporate investment in the enclave. However, a severe recession in Japan during 1990 eventually led to a sharp decrease in foreign direct investment in Los Angeles. This forced Little Tokyo businesses and institutions to shift their attention to greater cooperation with City Hall, and an emphasis on local resources.

ETHNIC IDENTITIES, INSTITUTIONS, AND PLACE IN LITTLE TOKYO

What is an Ethnic Group?

An ethnic group is a form of social organization, whose members identify themselves as part of the community. From this perspective, processes of social *boundary maintenance* that accompany self-ascription and *out-group recognition* play out in daily life by providing rules of what is allowed and disallowed for ethnic group members when interacting with those from another ethnic group. This emphasis on boundary maintenance explains *ethnic persistence* better than a definition of ethnicity based on traits, some of which change over time with shifts in historical and social conditions (Barth, 1998). In addition, ethnic identities are expressed differently depending on the situation of different class, gender and political groups within the ethnic label. This means that the "definition" of who belongs and how one can tell who belongs is contested (Marston, 2002). This fact tells us that ethnic identities are a crucial form of human bonding, perhaps even more crucial to human societies in our own time, because the forces of globalization bring rapid and disorienting changes to places and peoples all over the world (Castells, 1997, 1996; Harvey, 2000).

Japanese-American experiences play out in specific social forms such as religious practice, historical representation, and cultural consumption. These are social processes of identity construction and boundary maintenance, and lead to the constant creation and re-creation of ethnic landscapes that help Japanese Americans to maintain a reassuring sense of identity and meaning within the context of rapidly changing places such as Little Tokyo. According to geographers Kate Berry and Martha Henderson (2002), the resulting landscapes are like an "etched glass vase," which reveals the social and cultural impact of a particular group of people on a specific place.

A brief discussion of two institutions will illustrate this point, as they have historical and long-standing practical and symbolic importance: religious sites and the annual Nisei Week Festival.

Religious Institutions and Japanese Americans in Little Tokyo

Interviews conducted during fieldwork confirmed the importance of houses of worship to the endurance of ethnic identities. In the prewar era, these sites were the socio-spatial nexus of ethnic life. However, after the outbreak of war between the United States and Japan, over 120,000 Japanese Americans were imprisoned in camps throughout the western United States from 1942 to 1945. Little Tokyo became a predominantly African-American enclave of migrant workers from the South who settled in Los Angeles in hopes of finding work in the armaments industries that thrived during the war.

Through this process of incarceration, most Japanese Americans lost almost everything they materially owned, and when internees were allowed to leave the camps in early 1945, Buddhist temples and Christian churches played a key role as temporary housing sites for families with no money who wanted to resettle in their home region. As a result, temples and churches serving as temporary hostels were crucial in reclaiming the enclave as a Japanese-American place (Yokota, 1996; Interview with Buddhist priest).[1]

In the Japanese-American context, Buddhist temples and (mostly Protestant) Christian churches were key institutions in the trans-generational reproduction of ethnic differences and cultural forms (Barth, 1998). Furthermore, religious institutions were the social epicenter for singles, even after the relaxation of racially discriminatory miscegenation laws, thus reinforcing patterns of endogamous marriage, or marriage within the Japanese-American community. This pattern of a complete set of institutions is crucial for maintaining ethnic identities (Breton, 1964), and the Japanese-American community has always been characterized by its richness and depth of ethnic institutions (Fugita and O'Brien, 1991).

Social research has shown that persons who attend ethnic religious institutions will also participate in voluntary activity within the group. The historical and current importance in the Japanese-American community of ethnic in-group sports leagues for example, is very closely tied to the direct involvement of churches and temples (Interviews with Buddhist priest and Community Social Worker).[2]

The Nisei Week Festival

Since the 1930s the Nisei Week Festival has been a cultural event of singular importance in Japanese-American life in Los Angeles. In the prewar era, businesses thrived as the ethnic economy, by necessity, provided the jobs and social setting for those who did not work directly in agriculture. Cultural institutions emerged as an effort to help Little Tokyo businesses increase sales during the Great Depression, and reach out to the larger community (Kurashige, 2002). This event provides a case study of how a particular site of ethnic reproduction changes form and content with shifting social, economic, and political conditions inside and outside of the ethnic community. For example, in the 1930s, as relations between the United States and Japan deteriorated due to the latter's invasion of China, the organizers of the Nisei Week Festival began to de-emphasize the ties of the Japanese-American community to Japan, and adopted a posture of "Americanism" and loyalty to community and country. This posture was reflected in the "commodification" of Japanese-American ethnicity that took place during this period, in which white tourists were brought to the enclave to enjoy exotic culinary and visual pleasures, while also experiencing Little Tokyo as an ethnic place that was politically loyal to the American system (Kurashige, 2002). This was an example of the "economics and politics of racial accommodation" (Modell, 1977). But it is also typical of how the stuff of ethnic identities can change, though the overall purpose of ethnic persistence is retained.

In the postwar era, the annual beauty pageant associated with the Festival changed its rules of participation with shifting community identities, as multi-ethnic contestants with only partial Japanese ethnicity have forced a redefinition of the meanings of *Nikkei* experiences in Los Angeles. Today, the Nisei Week Festival reflects the much more flexible definition captured by the term Nikkei. For example, the annual beauty pageant associated with the Festival allows women of partial Japanese ancestry to participate, and several of these contestants have won the contest, the first in 1980. This showcase of ethnicity enables its participants to pleasurably express identities through artistic performance in the most symbolic setting for Japanese Americans in southern California (Figure 22.1).

Figure 22.1
Japanese-American women in parade during the Nisei Week Festival in Little Toyko.

LITTLE TOKYO IN RECENT TIMES: A SENSE OF PLACE AND IDENTITY

To a tremendous degree, the landscape of Little Tokyo has changed with politico-economic shifts at various scales, from early 20th century southern California agriculture to geopolitical turbulence and war, and in a global economy characterized by Foreign Direct Investment (FDI) from transnational corporations. Large Japanese companies such as Mitsui and Mitsubishi have acquired properties throughout southern California, and Little Tokyo is an excellent example of this process. However, after the Japanese economy went into a deep recession in the 1990s, the capital flows from Japan began to diminish, as did the flows of Japanese tourists visiting the area. This had an adverse effect on ethnic businesses. As if this were not enough, the Northridge earthquake of January 17, 1994 damaged some of the historic district on First Street and Los Angeles' huge distinctive City Hall building had to be retrofitted to withstand future earthquakes. The resulting relocation of city workers meant less lunchtime business for Little Tokyo's popular eateries. The mid-1990s were therefore probably the most trying period for the ethnic economy in the district.

As a consequence, the ethnic businesses were forced to adapt to changing conditions. Like many former residential enclaves, Little Tokyo became a place of consumption geography not only for local office workers and senior residents, but for tourists from other places in California and all over the world. This trend towards commodification of the uniqueness of places has been given terms such as *"postmodern" geographies* and *"the urban spaces of late capitalism"* (Castells, 1997, 1996; Harvey, 1989).

Ethnic institutions are key mechanisms in the making and consumption of place, which is integral to ethnic identity reinforcement as a social process (Barth, 1998; Brass, 1991). Likewise, the commodification of culture in urban settings (Harvey, 2001) is especially apparent in regions that have seen capital flight and uneven development processes intensify, particularly since the 1960s. The interplay of these processes at various scales shapes the built environment of ethnic places (Peet, 1997).

Through an understanding of global and regional changes in society and economy, and the strength of ethnic groups to create their own etchings in the cultural landscape, geographers emphasize the persistence of an ethnic sense of place. Even though Japanese Americans are no longer forced to settle in urban and rural enclaves, few would contest that Little Tokyo is a distinctive urban landscape with layers of *Nikkei* cultural and architectural imprint. Even with social and cultural assimilation, Japanese-American ethnic identities and economies, and those of numerous socio-cultural groups, have proven to be remarkably resilient, as manifested in the ethnic geographies of Los Angeles.

Perhaps the best example of how Little Tokyo has had a trans-generational effect is captured by a community center worker who has a deep local knowledge of the enclave through a lifetime of work and service. In Brian Ishii's case, his experiences working in Little Tokyo had an unexpected effect on his daughter's sense of ethnicity. He states that he used to bring his daughter to work with him when she was young, and she would have a chance to explore Little Tokyo. His daughter does not speak Japanese, but accompanied Ishii on a visit to Japan in 2000, where they spent a couple of weeks. He was surprised at her comfort level as they traveled:

> "But you know when we went to Japan, she was like twenty-one I think then, and I'm a little *hazukashii* [embarrassed] I guess to let other Japanese in Japan know that I'm not Japanese. But my daughter was just totally free. I was surprised — we'd be in a crowded train, you know, and she'd say, 'Hey Dad, look at that over there!'… And then people were looking around, 'Who said that,' you know. But she felt totally free … I said, 'How do you feel? How do you feel being over here in Japan?' She said, 'You know, I think because you brought me to Little Tokyo, I feel fairly comfortable here.' I said, 'You're kidding, Little Tokyo is nothing like Japan.' She goes, 'Oh no, it's not true, I mean Little Tokyo is a little bit like Japan.' But she said that little bit helped her to feel like it's not that far. And I thought that's quite an interesting thing. I never even thought that" (Brian Ishii, personal interview conducted 24 March, 2005).

By having the opportunity to interact with the ethnic institutions and symbolic landscapes of Little Tokyo, Ishii's daughter offers confirmation that place matters in the experiences and processes that shape ethnic identities.

Finally, we can see in Little Tokyo material witness to Berry and Henderson's observation (2002) that the agency of ethnic actors creates landscapes that reflect and impact the identities of those who live and work in such landscapes. Ethnic economic patterns of labor, cultural preference (e.g., Zen landscape gardening and religious architecture), and socio-cultural performance are mediated and articulated into localized landscape outcomes. These landscape elements of Little Tokyo express a constant theme in the stories of Japanese Americans and of ethnic groups generally: that ethnicity is about the "social organization of culture difference" (Barth, 1998), and the making of place which reinforces in a spatial way, the boundaries and consciousness that maintains those differences.

NOTES

[1] Interview with Rev. Noriaki Ito, Higashi Honganji Buddhist Temple, Los Angeles, California. March 26, 2004. Transcript and audiotape in author's possession.

[2] As Above. Interview with Bill Watanabe, Director, Little Tokyo Service Center, Los Angeles, California. March 25, 2004. Transcript and audiotape in author's possession.

Chapter 23

The Invisible Immigrants:
Asian Indian Settlement Patterns and Racial/Ethnic Identities

EMILY H. SKOP AND CLAIRE E. ALTMAN

INTRODUCTION

Often in vernacular language, all people from the Asian continent are labeled as "Asian." This taxonomy is a gross overgeneralization of the variation of countries and ethnicities within the vast continent. The Census Bureau defines an Asian as "a person having origins in any of the original peoples of the Far East, Southeast Asia, or the Indian subcontinent" (American Fact Finder, 2004). Yet the Asian population living in the United States is a remarkable collection of individuals in terms of their immigration history, settlement patterns, and human and social capital. Even so, at varying times in American statistics and academics, Asians have been amalgamated into general "Asian," "white," or "other" categories. These vague and extensive racial or ethnic labels have been used despite distinct geographic origin, languages, social, and cultural traits.

With the emergence of social and racial/ethnic consciousness in the late 1960s and 1970s, subgroups of Asians desired a more specific and representative categorization than the pan-umbrella term "Asian." As a result, the Census Bureau created a variety of new classifications for the Asian population, including the Japanese, Korean, Chinese, and Vietnamese. The new grouping "Asian Indian" also appeared in the 1980 census and defined Asian Indians as "including people who indicated their race as 'Asian Indian' or identified themselves as Bengalese, Bharat, Dravidian, East Indian, or Goanese" (Xenos, Barringer, and Levin, 1989, p. 5). The 2000 Census was the first time in the history of the Census that respondents could choose more than one racial category. Even with this monumental alteration in racial self-identification, the Census Bureau reports that in 2000 only 2.4 percent of all Americans reported more than one race (U.S. Bureau of the Census, 2001). On the other hand, 11.6 percent of the Asian Indian population chose the category "Asian Indian in combination with one or more other races and/or detailed Asian categories" (U.S. Bureau of the Census, 2002). Many of these individuals are second-generation Indians who are biracial, while others are individuals who chose "in combination" as a form of protest against the whole process of racial classification in the U.S. (Sailer, 2002). As one immigrant put it:

> "The impulse to call us all 'Asians,' using such a broad label to encompass everyone from Koreans to Pakistanis, seems both meaningless and demeaning to me. There's no utility in lumping together an entire continent of peoples with such different cultures and religions, and refusing to allow for these differences is, I think, unfair and fundamentally colonialist" (Sailer, 2002, p. 2).

The many controversies surrounding the racial classification of Asian Indians have a good deal of influence on the immigrant groups' settlement patterns and racial/ethnic identities. In this chapter, we focus on Asian Indians (and use the "in combination" category). We answer four key questions: What is the history of Asian-Indian immigration to the United States? Where do the 1.9 million Asian Indians settle and reside in the United States? How do the immigrants negotiate their racial/ethnic identities? And finally, why do the immigrants remain largely invisible as a racial/ethnic group? Our goal is to understand why racial/ethnic identities and settlement patterns matter, and how these characteristics influence the immigrant adaptation process.

ASIAN-INDIAN IMMIGRATION TO THE UNITED STATES

Like many other racial/ethnic groups in the U.S., Asian-Indian immigrants have been subject to America's xenophobia, immigration quotas, partisan politics, and/or economic and technical needs. There were few Asian-Indian residents in the U.S. very early (1700s–1800s), but more continuous and steady flows of migration have occurred for the last one hundred years at varying speeds and intensities (Lal, 1999). In 1907, in Bellingham, Washington, a group of Asian Indians were the target of racial riots. During this time the Asiatic Exclusion League tried to inhibit Indian immigration to the States. By 1913, supporters of India's struggle for independence, primarily Indian students, came into view in the Western United States, especially California, where we still see large populations of Asians today, particularly Asian Indians. Then, the Immigration Act of 1917 disallowed any and all Asians from entering the United States. The court battle *US* vs. *Bhagat Singh Thind* in 1923, established a further deterrent to Asian-Indian immigration, stating that Asian Indians were not "white" and could not be naturalized citizens.

The historical experience of Asian-Indian immigrants in the U.S. demonstrates the power of the racialization process in creating and sustaining racial categories and racial hierarchies. When they first arrived on American shores in the mid-19th century, Asian Indian labor migrants encountered both *de facto* and *de jure* racial discrimination. The combination of social tensions and economic competition provoked much hatred toward this group. Exclusionary national immigration and naturalization laws and restrictive state legislation on marriage, landholding, and voting reflected this prejudice (Juergensmeyer, 1982; Jensen, 1988). These discriminatory regulations, along with prohibitive social practices, determined that Asian Indians would be cast as racialized minorities in American society well into the 20th century. Classified as non-whites, the group was barred from becoming naturalized U.S. citizens and they experienced continuous socioeconomic inequity. The exclusionary era resulted in declining Asian-Indian immigration and population, extreme sex ratio imbalances, limited occupation choices, and forced spatial segregation in isolated communities (Leonard, 1992; Lee, 2003). Indeed, the 1940 Census saw a dramatic decrease in the number of Asian Indians living in America because of the government's exclusionary laws. It was only during World War II, with the implementation of the Luce-Celler Bill (when India became a war ally of the U.S.) that Asian-Indian residents were granted the right for naturalized citizenship (Takaki, 1998). Between 1946 and 1965 just over 9,000 Asian Indians received citizenship (Jensen, 1988).

The Immigration and Naturalization Act of 1965 opened the way for immigration to the United States by allowing the yearly entry of 20,000 migrants from each country (Frazier, Margai, and Tettey-Fio, 2003). This prompted new emigration from India to the United States. During the last twenty years Asian-Indian immigration to the United States has increased at dramatic rates.

Bouvier and Agresta (1993) are noted for their population projections for Asian and Pacific Islanders. In 1980, the estimated population for all Asian-American categories was 3,466,000. Of that 3.5 million, only 387,223 or 11.2 percent were Asian Indian. By 1990, the Asian-Indian population had nearly doubled in size to a population of 684,339. They projected that the 2000 Indian population would be around 1 million. However, the 2000 Census provides evidence that the population of Asian Indians in the U.S. far exceeded Bouvier and Agresta's previous projections. According to *The Asian Population: 2000: Census 2000 Brief*, **1,899,599** respondents reported Asian Indian alone or in any combination on the 2000 Census race question. Thus, Asian Indians represent a significant racial/ethnic group within the United States that continues to grow. Indeed, as a result of liberal U.S. immigration policy, India is now the second largest source country of U.S. immigrants, just after Mexico. Nearly two-thirds (more than 65%) of Asian-Indian immigrants in the U.S. arrived between 1990 and 2000 (U.S. Immigration and Naturalization Service, 2000a).

SETTLEMENT PATTERNS OF ASIAN-INDIAN IMMIGRANTS

Settlement patterns continually need to be readdressed because of newly arriving immigrants, people's mobility, changing social capital, and time-sensitive motivations for changing residences. To explore the issue of Asian-Indian settlement patterns in the United States in 2000, it is necessary to describe Asian Indians and their spatial arrangements on a variety of scales with several different indicators. Here, we provide a snapshot of Asian-Indian settlement patterns utilizing the *2000 Census of Population*.

Several telling facts emerge in the results of Asian-Indian settlement. First, the largest percentage of the Asian-Indian population lives in the Middle Atlantic States that encompass New York, New Jersey, and Pennsylvania. Such a large percentage in this region is not unexpected; the area is a large gateway to the U.S., and a haven for immigrants. Indeed, the area absorbed a large number of Indian immigrant medical professionals in the late 1960s and early 1970s, resulting in a high concentration of Asian-Indian immigrants in this region (Sheth, 1995). Particularly, the urban portions of New York and New Jersey continue to be primary magnets for Asian-Indian settlement, because these areas provide a variety of opportunities for incoming migrants employed in health, educational, and service occupations (Kalita, 2003).

With the expansion of the information technology industry in the U.S. economy, new areas emerge as the latest destinations for Indian immigrants. The Pacific region, which includes Washington, Oregon, California, Alaska, and Hawaii, has experienced intense growth. California, especially, led all states in 1990 and 2000, where the population now numbers more than 350,000. U.S. Immigration and Naturalization Service data on immigrants' state of intended residence for 1991–1998 indicates that over 20 percent of Asian-Indian immigrants reported that they intended to stay in California, suggesting that California has replaced New York and New Jersey as the principal area for new immigrant settlement (U.S. Immigration and Naturalization Service, 2000a). It appears that employment opportunities play an important role in determining settlement patterns for this immigrant group (Kanjanapan, 1990).

In addition to the relative dispersion at the regional level, the state level analysis reveals an even more obvious pattern of dispersal. Figure 23.1 displays key states of Asian-Indian settlement. This visualization illustrates the bi-coastal nature of Asian Indian settlement, with the majority of the population either living in New York or California. Smaller numbers of Asian Indians live in Texas, Illinois, and Michigan.

Figure 23.1
Asian Indians in the United States, 2000.

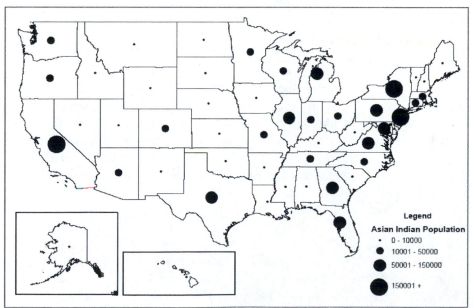

Legend
Asian Indian Population
· 0 - 10000
● 10001 - 50000
● 50001 - 150000
● 150001 +

Table 23.1

Metropolitan Areas with More than 10,000 Asian Indians in 2000			
Metropolitan Area	Population Size	Metropolitan Area	Population Size
New York	453,896	Sacramento	21,366
San Francisco	158,396	Minneapolis / St. Paul	17,187
Chicago	125,208	Orlando	15,138
Los Angeles	121,745	Cleveland	14,026
Washington DC	98,179	Phoenix	13,136
Houston	57,158	Tampa	12,446
Philadelphia	57,124	San Diego	12,145
Dallas / Fort Worth	53,975	Raleigh / Durham / Chapel Hill	11,849
Detroit	49,879	Austin	11,837
Boston	48,188	Columbus	10,571
Atlanta	40,381	Portland	10,391
Miami	29,247	Denver	10,376
Seattle	24,010	Fresno	10,111
Total of Cities Above		1,487,965	

Source: US Bureau of the Census. 2000. *2000 Census of Population*. Summary Tape File 2-C. Washington, D.C.: US Government Printing Office.

When we move the scale downward to the metropolitan level, we discover that Asian Indians tend to primarily live in very populous metropolitan areas. All of the top 26 metro areas for Asian Indians have over 10,000 Indians. These 26 metropolitan areas contain more than 78 percent of the entire Asian-Indian population residing in the United States. Table 23.1 illustrates some important emerging and expanding metro areas that may not commonly be thought of as immigrant destinations, particularly for Asian Indians. For example, ten years ago Tampa, Raleigh/Durham/Chapel Hill, Austin, Columbus, Portland, and Denver were not significant metropolitan areas in terms of their Indian populations. But today, each of these cities is home to more than 10,000 Asian Indians. Indeed, places like Austin, Texas and Phoenix, Arizona have experienced dramatic increases in their Asian-Indian population since 1980; while Asian Indians numbered less than 1500 in both cities in 1980, today Austin and Phoenix are home to over 11,000 Asian Indians (Skop and Li, 2006).

Finally, it is a fact that Asian Indians do not settle in patterns of extensive clusterings within various metropolitan areas, except for the notable examples of residential enclaves in New York City, Northern New Jersey, and Chicago, as well as around universities with large Asian-Indian populations (Skop, 2002). Indeed, empirical studies have increasingly documented the suburban-bound trend of contemporary Asian-Indian immigrants in the United States (Allen and Turner, 1996; Zelinsky and Lee, 1998; Alba et al., 1999; Singer, Friedman, and Price, 2001; Clark, 2003; Skop and Li, 2003). This pattern of suburban settlement has been especially recognized since the release of 2000 census data (Logan, 2001; Allen and Turner, 2002; Barnes and Bennett, 2002; Logan, Alba, and Zhang, 2002; Tolbert, 2002; Fan, 2003). Results illustrate that newly-arrived immigrants do not consider the often crowded and run down neighborhoods in central cities as places to reside. Many have the financial resources to afford the newer houses, nicer neighborhoods, and better schools that suburbs typically offer. Consequently, increasing numbers of Asian-Indian newcomers settle directly in the suburbs without ever having experienced living in a centralized ethnic enclave.

ASIAN-INDIAN RACIAL/ETHNIC IDENTITY FORMATION

Despite the absence of recognizable, visible racial/ethnic communities, many Asian-Indian newcomers celebrate their emerging and (re)emerging racial/ethnic identities through social and religious gatherings. Here we discuss two ways in which Asian Indians (re) create and maintain a sense of cohesion and solidarity, without being spatially near other Asian Indians. Some of the immigrants sell cultural products or goods that are reminiscent of home, while others use the Internet to keep in touch with their community (both abroad and at home).

Commercial spaces are significant symbolic and material markers of race/ethnicity in urban landscapes. As Lee (1992) suggests in her research on Korean small businesses in the Los Angeles area, there are many immigrants who "appropriate ethnicity as an element to sell for economic survival" (Lee, 1992, p. 264). The "ethnic-ness" offered to clients is often staged and packaged for their consumption (Helzer, 2001). Indeed, restaurants, grocery stores, and specialty stores are often intentionally contrived with the bottom-line in mind. In this manner, a process of commodification occurs — whereby racial/ethnic identities come to be treated as a product (Anderson, 1991; Lin, 1998; Walton-Roberts, 1998; and Chang, 2000).

This commodification of race/ethnicity, which Figure 23.2 illustrates, encourages the racial/ethnic business community to reproduce racial/ethnic identities in profitable ways to attract clientele. That "Indian-ness" is a product that possesses a quality that consumers' desire is the result of a variety of complex factors. In one way, racial/ethnic businesses cater specifically to Asian-Indian clientele. They provide a venue in which immigrants can gather together, buy ethnically distinctive products they cannot find elsewhere, and at the same time, simulate "home." In another way, many Asian-Indian commercial spaces offer a kind of "ethnic tourism" for individuals looking for a diversion from the homogeneity of franchise restaurants and grocery stores (Hoelscher, 1998, p. 185). For that reason, some business owners keep non-Indian customers in mind as they (re)construct particular visions of "Indian" ethnicity. This process of commodification has become an increasingly recognized trend in which "people's actions and experiences as consumers have an increasingly formative role to play in maintaining social life" (Miles and Paddison, 1998, p. 815).

Figure 23.2
One of the many stores in Phoenix that sells cultural goods from India. Photo by first author.

Another method of identity re-formation is through the creation of Internet spaces for Asian Indians. In cyberspace, the immigrants can gather together and affirm their racial/ethnic identities (Adams and Ghose, 2003; Adams and Skop, n.d.). As Figure 23.3 demonstrates, the Internet, web and news groups, and regular communication through e-mail, help immigrants in the U.S. to create virtual spaces of interaction with their home communities.

Interestingly, the Internet is creating alternative communication linkages in the 21st century that supplement print journalism, television, radio, and other media. These Internet linkages allow virtually instantaneous interaction across great distances, the archiving and sharing of images and text, and up-to-date coordination of activities, all of which have been put to use by Asian-Indian immigrants in the United States. Indeed, many immigrants from India, whose affluence and technological skills have favored computer use and networking, are perhaps the most prolific group of immigrants to use cyberspace to recreate a sense of community. Many immigrants (and their children) utilize the Internet for a variety of purposes, including organizing religious and social events, acquiring specialty goods and services, obtaining news and information from India, and developing a base of political and economic support for local and at-home events. Users are split across various social divides: age, gender, place of origin within India, and attitudinal disposition (traditional versus nontraditional). Migration-specific variables, like time of arrival in the United States, also affect Internet use.

Even as the Indian community becomes spatially distributed throughout many parts of the United States, its members are dependent to greater or lesser degrees on their local social environments for interaction. The Internet provides a means of building local community, on the one hand, and an alternative to local community, on the other. The Internet also becomes a tool for maintaining ties with homeland communities and for forging ethnically- and culturally-defined social ties and personal identities in the United States (Adams and Skop, n.d.).

Figure 23.3
A popular website that links members of the Indian Diaspora across the globe.
Source: Screen capture by first author.

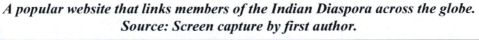

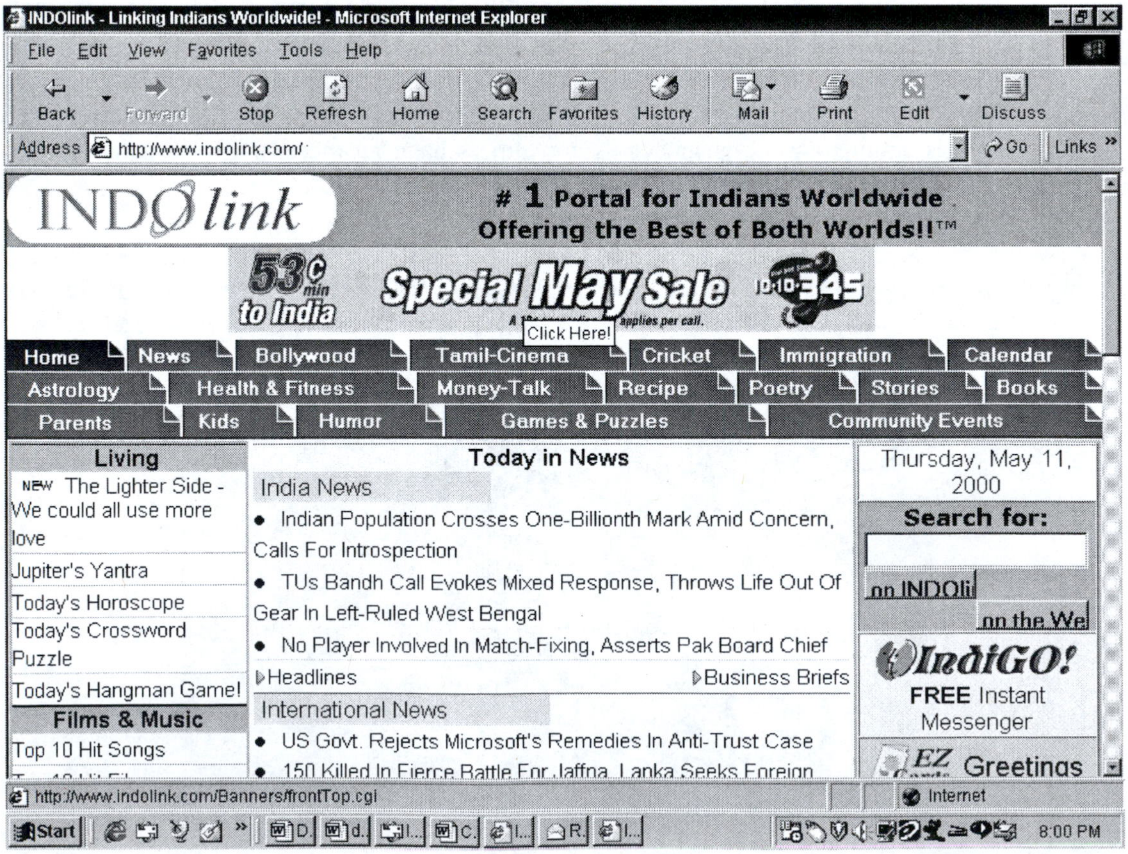

CONCLUSION: THE IMPLICATIONS OF INVISIBILITY FOR ASIAN INDIANS

As the population of Asian Indians begins to burgeon in the U.S. at the end of the 20th and the beginning of the 21st century, so too has academic interest in Asian-Indian history, culture, migration, social capital, and settlement patterns. Interestingly, the overwhelming theme in the literature on Asian Indians is their "invisibility" (Xenos, Barringer, and Levin, 1989; Skop, 2002). The imperceptibility of Indians takes place at all levels from the international to the neighborhood scale. Dubey (2003) was the first to point out that despite the magnitude of the global Indian diaspora, Indians are not highly visible. He reports that by the early 21st century, approximately 20 million People of Indian Origin (PIO) were living outside the political boundaries of India, but that this is a little known fact. And Kotkin (1993) also notes how "oblivious" most individuals are to the enormity of the global Indian Diaspora. Kim (2001), too, points out that, despite the fact that nearly two million Asian Indians live in the United States, there is a notable lack of coverage of the group in the national press. As a result, Asian Indians are often characterized as the "unnoticed minority" (Tinker, 1977, p. 195) and the "Invisible Americans" (Kar, 1995/1996). While a variety of explanations has been proposed, four arguments stand out to account for this "invisibility": the immigrants' passivity, their heterogeneity, their calculating maneuvering, and their geography of settlement.

In part, "invisibility" results from the passivity and apathy of the individual Asian-Indian immigrant. In "Invisible Americans," Kar (1995/1996) claims that by being "politically rather inactive … they became lost within the vast expanse of the American mass society; they became functionally invisible as a separate ethnic group" (Kar, 1995/1996, p. 29). Asian-Indian leaders worry about the impact of their community in broader U.S. society. Manoranjan Dutta articulates this concern as a key leader in the movement to make "Asian Indian" a category in the 1980 U.S. Census: "Asian Indian Americans have yet to make their presence known in American public life" (Dutta, 1982, p. 79). Other leaders of pan-Indian organizations argue that "a strong and broad-based politically active 'Asian Indian' association is necessary if Indians are ever to become an ethnic group with any power in this country" (Fisher, 1980, p. 191).

But without political urgency or economic need for empowerment, Asian Indians tend to maintain the status quo and remain "invisible" (Shankar, 1998a). The overall success of Asian-Indian immigrants discourages visibility — and their continued climb up the socioeconomic ladder indicates that this apathy is unlikely to disappear. For most immigrants, economic security is their highest priority, augmented by the strong sense of responsibility that Asian Indians feel towards their families. This leads to another rationalization for why Asian Indians are detached from social, civic, and political activity in the U.S. — the immigrant's general distaste for politics and volunteerism (Agarwal, 1991, p. 73). "The middle passage for desis (those of South Asian cultures) is comfortable and even profitable" (Prashad, 2000, p. 82). The impetus to get involved and get noticed by the American political system just is not sufficiently compelling for many Asian-Indian immigrants.

Diversity has also been proposed as a second potential cause for the "invisibility" of Asian-Indian immigrants (Lowe, 1996; Mitra, 1996; Shankar, 1998b; and Davé et al., 2000) "To understand anything about India, one must come to terms with its defining, and some say dooming characteristic: diversity. This diversity analogously impedes the formation of a South Asian American panethnic identity" (Davé et al., 2000, p. 73). Most Asian Indians identify with their region first and nation second. Lacking cultural homogeneity discourages solidarity, and thus visibility in the U.S. polity. Class diversity also creates friction and distrust among Asian Indians, with lower-class participants feeling shortchanged and excluded by upper-class constructions of "Indian-ness." Moreover, generational differences ensure a fundamental divide within the community — the types of issues concerning first-generation adults typically disengage their second-generation children. Clashing sets of regional, linguistic, religious, class, and generational interests deepen cleavages among Asian-Indian immigrants, lessening the ability of Pan-Asian Indian identities to work, and thus, Asian-Indian "visibility" to emerge.

Thirdly, there are those that argue that "invisibility" is a racial strategy — to avoid self-identification by skin color or race (Varma, 1980; Kibria, 1998; George, 1997; and Morning, 2001). This calculated maneuvering of individuals is an attempt to avoid becoming racialized by the mainstream, native-born, non-Hispanic white majority. In other words, a favorable impression of the community as the "model minority" triggers the Asian-Indian immigrant's wish to remain "invisible" in the eyes of the native-born, non-Hispanic white American mainstream. At the same time, Varma (1980) suggests that a significant proportion of Asian Indians "fear a backlash" if they become involved in racial politics (Varma, 1980, p. 35). Nationwide campaigns seeking to discredit race-oriented social programs and affirmative action agendas have secured a prominent place in today's political milieu. By staying "invisible," Asian-Indian immigrants become racially undefined — and more importantly, not labeled Black, "Oriental," or Latino (Morning, 2001, p. 65). "The desire to hold onto whiteness if only in ambiguous denial" (George, 1997, p. 42) allows Asian Indians to remain simultaneously privileged and unmarked.

There is a fourth reason for the invisibility of Asian Indians in the U.S. (Skop, 2002). We argue that the immigrants' geography plays a critical role in the racialization process. In other words, we contend that the general absence of racial/ethnic clustering by Asian-Indian immigrants in particular neighborhoods and communities discourages the immigrants (and their leaders) from articulating their interests in a collective voice. The lack of spatial propinquity and proximity reinforces Asian-Indian invisibility. Whereas many other Asian, European, and Latin American/Caribbean immigrant groups establish commercial and residential ethnic enclaves like "Chinatown," "Little Italy," or "Little Havana," Asian Indians rarely construct "Little Indias" in American cities (Skop and Li, 2003). Because racial/ethnic landscapes reinforce social categories (i.e., racial/ethnic identities), when the visible markers are taken away, the social category becomes less readily constructed.

Suburban America was once the citadel of native-born, non-Hispanic whites (Marcuse, 1997), but we now see many Asian Indians living in the suburbs (especially when we compare those living in the suburbs versus those residing in the central city). Zelinsky (2001) describes this phenomenon very well:

> "... there is the possibility that an ethnic community can exist without any significant clustering, that is, when the members of a particular group are scattered throughout a city, metropolitan area, or some larger spatial domain. Thus extreme and instant dispersion characterizes recently arrived Asian Indians. Their homes are scattered throughout the suburban reaches of the metropolitan area with only moderate tendencies toward a loose sort of clustering" (Zelinsky, 2001, p. 134).

Thus, as a result of living, working, and socializing in the suburban spaces and suburban places associated with "whiteness," Asian-Indian immigrants have reinforced their invisible status within the larger sociopolitical community (Skop, n.d.).

In many ways, this research reinforces the theme of invisibility experienced by Asian Indians living in the United States. While it is easy to capture their broad settlement patterns, either at the regional, state, or metropolitan scale, it proves more difficult to identify the ways in which the immigrants (re) create their racial/ethnic identities, and thus, how they adjust to living in the U.S. One thing is certain, as the newcomers have become settled within American mass society, they have simultaneously become largely invisible as a separate racial/ethnic group. What remains to be seen are the implications of this invisibility for both the immigrants and their children, especially given the resilience of the U.S. racial/ethnic hierarchy.

Part V

Diversity, Culture, and Place

Previous chapters provided examples of increasing ethnic diversity among U.S. minority populations, expressions of culture and the issues they create, and the creation and re-creation of geographic spaces and places. This final section pursues the interrelationships between these topics.

Chapter 24 examines the relationship of land to American-Indian identity. It reports efforts by tribes to reclaim ancestral lands as a symbol of group identity but also considers the interrelation between land and sovereignty, and between economic development and cultural sustainability.

The next two chapters remind us of the continued importance of Europeans to American ethnic diversity. Chapter 25 explores "whiteness" in a unique way, by examining its spatial and socioeconomic basis in Portland, Oregon. It illustrates how white identities have been re-created among Russian and Ukranian immigrant refugees for a unique purpose, to share in the resources provided needy minority populations. In the process, the chapter explores relationships between social institutions, shifting ethnic identities, and the geographic patterns of these recent immigrants.

Greek-Americans came to the U.S. in substantial numbers during different immigration waves and settled in "Greek Towns" of some large inner cities. These visible ethnic enclaves were evidence of a Greek-American presence that centered on the cultural triad of language, family and church. American suburbanization contributed to the decline of Greek Towns, as the younger, educated, and affluent Greek-Americans became part of white flight. Chapter 26 examines challenges to Greek-American ethnic traditions posed by suburbanization. In doing so, it reveals the persistence of particular cultural traits that continue to define Greek-American ethnicity for multiple-age cohorts at the beginning of the 21st century.

As the number of foreign-born increased after the 1965 Hart-Celler Act, particular gateway states and their cities gained a disproportionate number of immigrants. New Jersey is one example, and Chapter 27 explains the disparities of economic status among native-born and foreign-born in a case study of Paterson. It illustrates that factors other than educational attainment explain economic disparities in this increasingly ethnically diverse city.

Ethnic diversity also has reached the American Heartland, both in rural and urban areas. Chapter 28 uses Louisville, Kentucky to illustrate this process. It focuses on the characteristics of that city's highly diverse foreign-born population, including the diversity within major groups, such as Asian Americans. It also stresses landscape changes and immigrant trajectories toward middle-class status.

This text closes by examining one of America's greatest dilemmas, racial and ethnic disparities in U.S. health and health care. Chapter 29 describes health inequalities within a geographic framework for the major U.S. ethnic groups and illustrates the unique health problems of each group. It also briefly examines health intervention strategies.

Chapter 24

Cultural and Economic Change in Indian Country

EDMUND J. ZOLNIK

INTRODUCTION

Signs of American Indian culture have never been more evident than in the first half of the first decade of the 21st century. The grand opening of the Smithsonian Institution National Museum of the American Indian (NMAI) on September 21st, 2004 in Washington, D.C. reflects the greater national visibility of American Indian culture (Figure 24.1). As the first exclusively Native-American museum in the world, the NMAI showcases the history and culture of more than a thousand tribal and indigenous groups from North, Middle and South America (National Museum of the American Indian, 2005a). Approximately 25,000 Native Americans from more than 500 tribes from Alaska to Chile — one of the largest Native American celebrations in modern history — were participants in the Native Nations Procession to kick off the First Americans Festival. In the first week of operation, patronage at the NMAI was more than 100,000 and the two museum stores set a Smithsonian record of more than $1 million in sales. The NMAI rests on the last open space on the National Mall between the Smithsonian Institution National Air and Space Museum and the United States Capitol (National Museum of the American Indian, 2005b). Native American symbols were integral to the design of the NMAI especially the eastward orientation of the entrance to capture rays of the sun at dawn as well as via a prism window and an atrium. The NMAI features three permanent exhibitions and one temporary art gallery as well as demonstrations, films, music and dance. The three permanent exhibitions known as "Our Universes," "Our Peoples," and "Our Lives" reflect three main exhibit themes — philosophy, history and identity — to facilitate the rotation of exhibitions from other tribes and indigenous groups into the NMAI.

The permanent exhibition of "Our Lives," also known as "Our Lives: Contemporary Life and Identities," examines the question of Native-American identity in the 21st century. One common theme in the academic literature on American-Indian identity is that of land. As per Deloria, "certain lands are given to certain peoples. It is these peoples only who can flourish, thrive, and survive on the land" (1988, p. 177). Deloria continues to assert the culture of a people is a function of their homeland. But to sustain a culture, a people must retain or reclaim the land so as to create a viable "economic reality" (p. 179). The Meriam Report, a publication from the Brookings Institute on the condition of Indian Country in 1928, articulates the synergy between the cultural and the economic reality for American Indians: "The economic basis of the primitive culture of the Indians has been largely destroyed by the encroachment of white civilization. The Indians can no longer make a living as they did in the past.... This advancing tide of white civilization has as a rule largely destroyed the economic foundation upon which the Indian culture rested" (Meriam, 1928, pp. 6, 87). In sum, cultural sustainability is a function of economic viability, the basis of which is the land. To understand the changes in Indian Country since the last decade of the 20th century, one must examine the past cultural and economic reality of American Indians who continue to struggle to retain and reclaim their ancestral lands.

The thesis of this chapter is the role of the land in the cultural identity of American Indians. Present efforts by tribes across the United States to retain and reclaim ancestral lands are a sign of the significance of the land to group identity. Furthermore, development on tribal lands is a symbol of the advancement of the economic reality of American Indians. Three themes are most relevant to the examination of the synergy between the cultural and the economic reality of American Indians. First, retention and reclamation of ancestral lands is the foundation of American-Indian sovereignty. The movement towards greater independence of tribal governments across the United States is the catalyst for the economic development in Indian Country. Second, economic development is the crux of the cultural sustainability of tribes. And third, Indian gaming (gambling operations) is not the only economic development strategy in Indian Country; just as Indian culture is not homogeneous, neither is the economy.

Figure 24.1
National Museum of the American Indian Opening on the Mall.
Smithsonian Institution Photo No. 2004-53063.

HISTORY OF THE INDIAN PROBLEM

Among all of the ethnic groups in the United States, American Indians are unique in their relationship to their ancestral lands, perhaps with the exception of native Hawaiian culture. While the study of other minority groups requires a discussion of immigration and/or settlement patterns, American Indians are the only group for whom a discussion of dispossession and relocation are more appropriate. The history of displacement in Indian Country reflects the past and present struggles of tribes and indigenous groups to reclaim and retain homelands, the possession of which no treaty could guarantee (Deloria, 1974). Beyond the struggle for their ancestral lands, American-Indian cultural renewal is all the more impressive given the legacy of ignorance of past and present occupants of the Americas. The very label Indian was and is a misnomer. Europeans did not discover a new route to India. Another European misjudgment occurred in New England, a region of first contact and the region where the European influence has had the greatest effect on the cultural and economic reality of American Indians. In this case, Europeans misinterpreted the American Indians' relationship with the land (Attaquin, 1990; Cronon, 1983). As subsistence agriculturalists, as well as hunters and gatherers, Indian settlements were often impermanent so as to minimize the ecological demands on any one site per season. Property was not the land, but whatever the land could offer the Indians to sustain life. To that end, Indian place names were often references to the best usage of the land so as to create a literal map of life-sustainable information. For example, with regard to Connecticut ("at the long tidal estuary") place names, Mashantucket means "place of big trees," Nipmuck means "fresh water fishing place," and Podunk means "where you sink in mire, a boggy place, at the miry place, at the place where the foot sinks" (Masthay, 1990, pp. 13–14, 16). But colonists saw Indian mobility as a means to deny American-Indian claims to the land. To rationalize the consequent dispossession of the Indians from their ancestral lands, the colonists put forth a Eurocentric ideology of land tenure. To the colonists the only lands to which the Indians held title as property were those brought into agricultural cultivation, which the colonists considered improvements to the land; all other lands were thought vacant and therefore free for expropriation. To further dispossess American Indians from their ancestral lands, the colonists were able to purchase land from American Indians without respect for the sovereignty of their governments, but rather only the sovereignty of the English Crown. The differences in land use philosophy and in assumptions of sovereignty led to the colonial ideology of conquest of both the land and the people in the New World.

The legacy of ignorance toward American-Indian sovereignty born in the initial decades of contact helps us to understand the cultural and economic struggles of American Indians. From the American Revolution, federal and state governments were unable to effectively address the Indian Problem: "the 'proper,' i.e., ethical or moralistic, policies and methods of treating a people who occupy lands that a nation claims for its own" (Goodman and Heffington, 2000, p. 52). The magnitude of the Indian Problem only grew with the perpetuation of the dominant European-American relationship to the lands of the New World known as Manifest Destiny (Public Broadcasting System, 2005). The term did not enter the American nationalistic vernacular until 1845 when John L. O'Sullivan wrote:

> "… the right of our manifest destiny to over spread and to possess the whole of the continent which Providence has given us for the development of the great experiment of liberty and federaltive development of self government entrusted to us. It is right such as that of the tree to the space of air and the earth suitable for the full expansion of its principle and destiny of growth" (Brinkley, 1995, p. 352).

However, the philosophy is illustrative of two important aspects of the differences between Indians and European-Americans with regard to rights and sovereignty. First, the allusion to "Providence" invokes a natural right to possess the land. Second, O'Sullivan articulates the rights of American self-government, but not the rights of Indian self-government. Therefore, the philosophy of Manifest Destiny was to supersede the references in the Constitution of the United States to the recognition of Indian sovereignty with regard to commerce. Specifically, it states: "Congress shall have the power to regulate Commerce with foreign nations, among the several states, and with the Indian tribes" (U.S. Constitution, Art. I, Sec. VIII, Cl. 3). Further, Manifest Destiny was accepted to the point of overshadowing Indian rights to land and property in the Northwest Ordinance of 1787:

"The utmost good faith shall always be observed towards the Indians; their lands and property shall never be taken from them without their consent; and, in their property, rights, and liberty, they shall never be invaded or disturbed, unless in just and lawful wars authorized by Congress; but laws founded in justice and humanity, shall from time to time be made for preventing wrongs being done to them, and for preserving peace and friendship with them" (U.S. Congress, Northwest Ordinance of 1787, Art. 3).

To summarize, the impetus for American expansion west of the Ohio River and the Mississippi River was economic (Public Broadcasting System, 2005). Depressions in 1818 and 1839 as well as population pressures from birth rates and immigration were all push factors for westward expansion. Furthermore, the frontier of the West was rich in inexpensive or free land whose ownership was a font of economic and political wealth for Americans, but denoted displacement for Indians.

So great was the demand for land, the Indian Removal Act of 1830 lead to the displacement of tribes to lands in the Louisiana Purchase (Wikipedia, 2005). Ultimately, the race across the Great Plains and Rocky Mountains was to create a new Indian Problem of peaceful displacement in lieu of war. The solution fell to President Ulysses S. Grant to create a "Peace Policy" to relocate Indians from ancestral lands to reservations. Not only were reservations to solve the new Indian Problem, but because religious, rather than government, representatives were to administer Indian services, reservations were to Christianize and ultimately then civilize Indians to prepare for assimilation and citizenship. Also, reservations were to preclude hunting and so force permanence and an agricultural economic reality upon Indians. Unfortunately, for those Indians who did accept relocation, reservation lands were often beyond cultivation and starvation was the grim reality. For those who did not accept relocation, the results were bloody wars between Indians and the United States such as the Sioux War with the Battle of Little Big Horn and the Nez Perce War. The bloodshed led President Rutherford B. Hayes to phase out the "Peace Policy" and withdraw religious representatives from Indian service. In 1887, symptomatic of a new reservation policy to civilize Indians, the Dawes, or General Allotment, Act also sought to appease the demand for Indian lands. Rather than grant a block of land to tribes, the Dawes Act was to grant parcels of land, or allotments, to the heads of Indian households so as to create "silent and peaceful" farmers (Deloria, 1974, p. 5). Because the total area of allotments was less than the area of the original reservations, the surplus was sold to non-Indians, the proceeds of which went to Indians. The failure of allotments to solve the Indian Problem was set out in the Meriam Report of 1928. In 1934, the Indian Reorganization Act led to the elimination of allotments as well as the recognition of the right for Indian self-government. Unfortunately, the allotment policy had had a disastrous effect on total Indian lands. Between 1887 and 1932, total Indian lands went from 140 million acres to 52 million acres: a decrease of 140 percent (Goodman and Heffington, 2000).

The Employment Assistance Program of 1952 was the next generation of Indian policy to force assimilation via the termination of reservations. If reservations as places were not economically prosperous, it was considered that perhaps relocation of Indians to places such as urban areas with greater opportunity for employment would improve the Indian condition. But the passage of the Indian Self-Determination and Education Assistance Act of 1975 was another sign of the perpetual shifts in policy toward the intransigent Indian Problem. Rather than force assimilation via termination of reservations, recognition of Indians as stakeholders in the cultural and economic reality of Indian Country was the new policy. The cases of *Seminole Tribe of Florida* v. *Butterworth*, 658 F.2d 310 (1981), cert. denied, 455 U.S. 1020 (1983) and *California* v. *Cabazon Band of Mission Indians*, 480 U.S. 202 (1987) further clarified the parameters of economic self-determination in Indian Country. In both cases, the courts recognized the rights of Indian tribes to establish and operate gaming venues on their reservations in states where gaming was legal.

INDIAN COUNTRY

In 2000, the total number of American Indians and Alaska Natives was 2,475,956 — only 0.9 percent of the total population of the United States (Ogunwole, 2002). In fact, since 1890, the first census year to attempt a total enumeration of American Indians, the American-Indian percentage of the total United States population has never been more than 1.0 percent (Gibson and Jung, 2002). As a departure from previous census years, the Census 2000 questionnaire was the first to allow respondents to report one or more races for themselves and other household members. The race in combination population for American Indians of 4,119,301, or 1.5 percent of the total United States population, is further indication of the trend for Americans to embrace their Indian ancestry. Furthermore, the percentage increase between 1990 and 2000 was a minimum of 26.4 percent for the American Indian and Alaska-Native (alone) population — more than twice the percentage increase for the total United States population of 13.2 percent — or a maximum of 110.3 percent for the American Indian and Alaska Native in combination population. Given that the percentage increases in American-Indian and Alaska-Native populations are not due to the rate of natural increase — birth rates minus death rates for American Indians and Alaska Natives — the data highlight greater American-Indian self-identification (Hayden, 2004).

As for the geographic distribution of the American-Indian and Alaska-Native alone or in combination population in 2000, that is, respondents who self-identify as American Indian, the majority (43.0 percent) resides in the West region, while the minority (9.1 percent) resides in the Northeast region. California is the state with the largest number of American-Indian and Alaska-Native alone or in combination population at 627,562, but the state with the largest percentage of American-Indian and Alaska-Native (AIAN) alone or in combination population is Alaska at 19.0 percent (Figure 24.2). Fully 41.6 percent of the American-Indian and Alaska-Native alone or in combination population in the United States resides in five states in the West region: California (15.2 percent); Oklahoma (9.5 percent); Arizona (7.1 percent); Texas (5.2 percent); and New Mexico (4.6 percent) — consistent with the 1990 state distribution (Goodman and Heffington, 2000). Like the general United States population, the American-Indian and Alaska-Native alone or in combination population is more urban than rural. Seventy-nine percent of the general United States population resides in urban areas, while 68.5 percent of the American-Indian and Alaska-Native alone or in combination population resides in urban areas (United States Bureau of the Census, 2005a; United States Bureau of the Census, 2005b). But while the balance of the state distribution is to the west, among urban places in the United States with 100,000 or more population, New York City and Chicago rank first (87,241) and eighth (20,898) as homes to the largest American-Indian and Alaska-Native alone or in combination populations.

Presently, Indian Country consists of 562 tribes with federal recognition (Bureau of Indian Affairs, 2005). The Census 2000 geography divides Indian Country via legal and statistical definitions (United States Bureau of the Census, 2005c). The legal definitions include American Indian Reservations and American Indian Off-Reservation Trust Lands, as well as tribal subdivisions of reservations and off-reservation lands known as state American Indian Reservations, Alaska Native Regional Corporations (ANRC) and Hawaiian Home Lands (HHL). The statistical divisions include Alaska Native Village Statistical Areas (ANVSA), Oklahoma Tribal Statistical Areas (OTSA), Tribal Designated Statistical Areas (TDSA) and State Designated American Indian Statistical Areas (SDAISA). Census 2000 indicates the most populous Reservation and Off-Reservation Trust Land is the Navajo Nation in Arizona, New Mexico, and Utah at 175,228. In addition to data on respondents who identify more than one race besides American Indian and Alaska Native, Census 2000 also asks respondents to provide the name of their tribal enrollment or principal tribe. The largest tribal group alone or in combination is the Cherokee at 729,533, while the largest tribal group alone is the Navajo at 298,197.

ECONOMIC CHANGE IN INDIAN COUNTRY

Data on the economic reality of Indian Country from Census 2000 indicates the employment status and the income of the American Indian and Alaska Native (alone) population is lower than for all races in the United States. The unemployment rate for American Indians is twice that for all races, while the median household and per capita incomes for all races are 37.2 percent and 67.4 percent greater than for American Indians (Table 24.1). Further, the family and individual below the poverty level percentages were more than twice as great for American Indians in 1999. Also, the mean public assistance income was $206 greater for American Indians than for all races in 1999. The sectoral distributions of American Indian employment as well as the classes of the American Indian worker help to understand the present economic gap in Indian Country. American Indian occupations tend toward primary (farming, fishing and forestry), secondary (production, transportation and material

Figure 24.2
States with the Largest AIAN Alone or In Combination Population and Percentage: 2000.

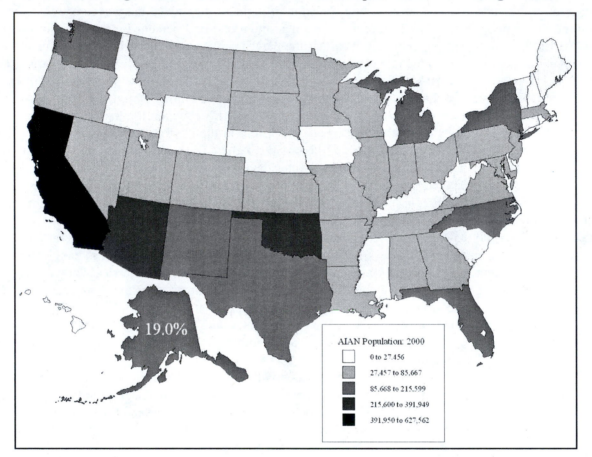

moving), and tertiary (service) sectors of employment that require fewer skills and lower educational attainment, and thus are not as lucrative or secure as quaternary (management, professional and related) sector employment. Further, as a legacy of the economic dependence of American Indians on government for employment, the percentage of government employment for American Indians is 7.5 points greater than for all races and the percentage of self-employed workers amongst American Indians is 1.1 points less than for all races.

But while the overall economic reality in Indian Country is one of low-employment status and low income in comparison to all races, the trend in the data from the 1997 Economic Census on economic self-sufficiency is positive. An indication of the greater entrepreneurship in Indian Country is the growth in the number of American Indian- and Alaska Native-owned businesses (United States Bureau of the Census, 2001). Between 1992 and 1997, the number of American Indian- and Alaska Native-owned businesses grew by 83.7 percent; 12.3 times the percentage increase for all United States businesses of 6.8 percent, while receipts rose by 178.5 percent; 4.4 times the percentage increase for all United States businesses of 40.2 percent. California was home to the largest number of American Indian- and Alaska Native-owned businesses, while Alaska was home to the largest proportion of American Indian- and Alaska Native-owned businesses. Furthermore, the geographic distribution of American Indian- and Alaska Native-owned businesses by state and metropolitan area indicates that the greatest proportion are in states west of the Mississippi River and in nonmetropolitan areas. Average receipts for American Indian- and Alaska Native-owned businesses were $174,100 in 1997 and the largest numbers were in the service and construction industry. Part of the explanation for the greater entrepreneurship of Native Americans and Alaska Natives has been the increase in access to small business loans from the Small Business Administration (SBA) since 1990 (United States Bureau of the Census, 2005d). The percentage increase in the number of SBA minority loans was 16.0 percent between 1990 and 2003. Over the same time period, the number of SBA minority loans to American Indians was 9.3 times greater; more than for any other minority group and the aggregate amount of SBA minority loans to American Indians was 8.4 times greater; second only to the Asian-American minority group at 8.7 times greater. But business capital is not universally accessible in Indian Country. The Pine Ridge Chamber of Commerce — the only Chamber of Commerce in the United States on an Indian reservation — recently set a goal to establish a $10 million pool known as the Lakota Fund to help present and future entrepreneurs on the Pine Ridge Reservation in South Dakota where unemployment estimates are 80 percent (Melmer, 2005). Entrepreneurship is especially important to battle the pernicious triad of unemployment, school dropouts, and "brain drain" (those of high intellect leave) in Indian Country (Smith, 2000). Chronic unemployment due to a shortage of employment opportunity on Indian lands decreases the incentive to attain a high school or equivalency diploma education, while those who attain a postsecondary education often must migrate from their homelands to areas with greater employment opportunity — particularly urban areas. The barriers encountered by American-Indian and Alaska-Native entrepreneurs, such as access to capital, infrastructure and labor to start and operate new businesses, can be mitigated by Indian strategies. Further, "unlearning the supposed fact that Indians cannot be entrepreneurial because of the communal nature of Indian societies creates the potential for growth" in Indian Country (Smith, 2000, p. 141).

Table 24.1

Economic Profile of the AIAN Alone Population: 2000		
Subject		Race
Category	All (%)	AIAN (%)
Employment Status (Population 16 Years and Over)		
Employed	59.7	53.0
Unemployed	3.7	7.5
Occupation		
Management, Professional and Related	33.6	24.3
Service	14.9	20.6
Sales and Office	26.7	24.0
Farming, Fishing and Forestry	0.7	1.3
Construction, Extraction and Maintenance	9.4	12.9
Production, Transportation and Material Moving	14.6	16.8
Class of Worker		
Private Wage and Salary	78.5	72.0
Government	14.6	22.1
Self-Employed in Own Not Incorporated Business	6.6	5.5
Unpaid Family	0.3	0.3
Income: 1999 (Dollars)		
Median Household Income	41,994	30,599
Mean Public Assistance Income	3,032	3,238
Per Capita Income	21,587	12,893
Poverty Status: 1999 (Below Poverty Level)		
Family	9.2	21.8
Individual	12.4	25.7

But while entrepreneurship in Indian Country is on the rise, by far the most successful economic enterprise in Indian Country is tribal government gaming (National Indian Gaming Association, 2005). Following the recognition of tribal rights to operate gaming venues in *Cabazon*, the enactment of the Indian Gaming Regulatory Act (IGRA) of 1988 set the parameters for the use of tribal government gaming revenues "to promote [t]ribal economic development, [t]ribal self-sufficiency and strong [t]ribal government" (National Indian Gaming Association, 2005, p. 6). According to the National Indian Gaming Association (2005), 223 tribes in 28 states presently operate 411 Indian gaming venues. In 2004, Indian gaming brought in $18.5 billion in gross tribal government revenues to Indian Country — 10.8 percent more than in 2003 — with an additional $2.5 billion in gross revenues from ancillary businesses. An analysis of how the 168 member tribes of the National Indian Gaming Association spent the revenues from Indian gaming in 2003 reveals the majority went towards education, child/elder care, cultural preservation, and charity, (20%), as well as economic development (19%). As an example of the cultural and philanthropic uses of Indian gaming revenues, tribes were able to donate more than $35 million to the construction of the NMAI.

Contrary to common perceptions, gaming is but one of the reasons for the economic development in Indian Country. Taylor and Kalt (2005) report improvements in the economic status of gaming and non-gaming reservations between 1990 and 2000. For example, real per capita income was up 36 percent on gaming reservations and 21 percent on non-gaming reservations, while real per capita income was up only 11 percent overall in the United States. Likewise, family poverty was down 11.8 points on gaming reservations and 8.1 points on non-gaming reservations, while family poverty was only down 0.8 points overall in the United States. Taylor and Kalt (2005) attribute such economic progress, especially among non-gaming tribes, to the policy of Indian self-government. To return to the main thesis of the chapter, Indian self-government is only possible for tribes with a land base. To that end, the reclamation and retention of a land base is the key to tribal economic viability and cultural sustainability. To further explore the relationship between land and tribal viability, the next section presents a case study regarding the past and present struggles of the Mashantucket Pequot Tribal Nation of Connecticut to reclaim and retain a land base.

MASHANTUCKET PEQUOT TRIBAL NATION

The success of the Foxwoods gaming and tourism venues which the Mashantucket Pequot Tribal Nation operates is well-known (Carstensen et al., 2000; d'Hauteserre, 1998; d'Hauteserre, 2000; Eisler, 2001; Pasquaretta, 2003). But what is less well-known is the cultural renewal of Pequots as well as for Indians throughout North America due to the Mashantucket Pequot Tribal Nation gaming and tourism revenues. The Mashantucket Pequot Ethnohistory Project to reconstruct Pequot history and culture, as well as the Mashantucket Pequot Museum and Research Center (a resource for scholars of American and Canadian Native history and culture as well as for an annual average of 250,000 patrons), are signs of greater regional visibility of American Indian culture (McBride, 1987; Mashantucket Pequot Museum and Research Center, 2005a). Furthermore, the Mashantucket Pequot Tribal Nation hosts the Feast of Green Corn and Dance, known as Schemitzun (Mashantucket Pequot Tribal Nation, 2005). The annual powwow includes: the World Championship of Dance and Song with over 3,000 participants from North America, the Schemitzun Indian Marketplace with over 100 Native American artists, and a rodeo. Clearly, the Mashantucket Pequot American Indian Reservation and Off-Reservation Trust Lands are, and will continue to be, a regional, national, and international hub of American-Indian culture. But the cultural and economic success of the Mashantucket Pequot Tribal Nation would not be a reality without past and present struggles to reclaim and retain the ancestral lands of the Pequots. In 1666, a land grant from the Connecticut colony left the Pequots with a land base of 3,000 acres (Mashantucket Pequot Museum and Research Center, 2005b). But by 1855, the land base was only 989 acres. The State of Connecticut then sold all but 214 acres to help the tribe survive financially. Questions as to the right of the State of Connecticut to sell Pequot land, albeit for economic benefit (in conflict with the Indian Trade and Intercourse Act of 1790, which was to preclude the sale of Indian lands without prior approval from the federal government), would create the legal and political leverage for the Pequots to reclaim their ancestral lands. The act of the Connecticut state government was in conflict with the federal government. The enactment of the 1983 Mashantucket Pequot Land Claims Settlement Act granted the Pequots federal recognition, a land claims settlement, and an economic development trust fund. Critics of Pequot federal recognition called for Congress to revoke that status; Senator Joseph Lieberman of Connecticut introduced a bill to limit the ability of tribes to acquire land in trust for commercial or gaming uses in response to the efforts of the Pequots to reclaim more of their ancestral lands (Benedict, 2000; Blakemore, 2005). Clearly, "American Indian wars are no longer fought on the [P]lains, they're fought in ... courts" as well as in Congress (Nagel, 1996, p. 53).

DISCUSSION AND CONCLUSIONS

Presently, the Bureau of Indian Affairs administers and manages 55.7 million acres of land for American Indians and Alaska Natives, or 7.1 percent more land than in 1932 (Bureau of Indian Affairs, 2005). But further reclamation of ancestral lands beyond the borders of American Indian Reservations is a controversial issue in the United States. For example, the Oneida Indian Nation of New York recently lost a Supreme Court land claim case to purchase former lands via the real estate market (Stout, 2005). The point of contention is the recognition of Oneida sovereignty over lands set out in the Treaty of Canandiagua in 1794 and the right to place said lands after purchase into tax-exempt, trust status. From an original land base of 300,000 acres the Oneida Indian Nation retains only 32 acres in New York. Even so, due to the success of the Turning Stone Casino Resort and 15 other economic enterprises, the Oneida Indian Nation is the largest employer in both Oneida County and Madison County, New York (Oneida Indian Nation, 2005). The economic clout of the Oneida Indian Nation notwithstanding, an 8 to 1 majority of the Supreme Court wrote: "[t]he Oneidas long ago relinquished governmental reins and cannot regain them through open-market purchases from current titleholders ... [t]oday we decline to project redress for the tribe in the present and future, thereby disrupting the governance of central New York's counties and towns" (Stout, 2005).

The legal relationship between Indians and the United States is "unlike that of any other two people in existence" (National Gambling Impact Study Commission, 1997, p. 6-3). In exchange for land successions, the federal government was to hold Indian lands in trust; protect the sovereignty status; and promote the economic well-being of tribes. Unfortunately, the record of the federal government with regard to the "trust relationship" with American Indians is poor. Except for the Indian Health Service, the trend in per capita federal funds for American Indians has declined since 1985 (National Indian Gaming Association, 2005). The decrease in federal funds to address the triad of unemployment, school drop outs, and brain drain is all the more serious given the empirical evidence from the spatial analysis of American Indian poverty. That is, areas with high shares of American-Indian population have significantly lower levels of income than areas with low shares of American-Indian population (Leichenko, 2003). Further, while the impact of Indian gaming on American-Indian income has been very positive in some cases, overall results are mixed. Indian gaming has a positive effect on income in Oklahoma Tribal Statistical Areas (OTSAs) and Tribal Designated Statistical Areas (TDSAs), but a negative effect on income in areas with a high share of American Indians. While more research on the effects of gaming on the economic reality of Indian Country is necessary, the present research indicates gaming is not a panacea for the plight of Indians and the opportunity for high-profit gaming in the United States is finite (National Gambling Impact Study Commission, 1997; d'Hauteserre, 1998).

The evolution of Indian policy from termination to self-determination meant economic development on Indian lands was necessary to decrease the dependence of tribes on federal funds. As per President Ronald Reagan in the Statement of Indian Policy from 1983: "[i]t is important to the concept of self-government that tribes reduce their dependence on federal funds by providing a greater percentage of the cost of self-government" (National Gambling Impact Study Commission, 1997, pp. 6–7). Self-determination means tribes enjoy the right to pursue an economic development strategy which retains the cultural integrity of the tribe (Smith, 2000). But regardless of the economic development strategy of the tribe, self-sufficiency is vital to cultural preservation.

ACKNOWLEDGMENTS

The author thanks the following for background information to help in the preparation of this chapter: Jon Ault, Head, Archives and Special Collections, Mashantucket Pequot Museum and Research Center; Arthur Henick, Director of Media Relations, Mashantucket Pequot Tribal Nation; David Holahan, Manager of Public Relations, Mashantucket Pequot Museum and Research Center; Kevin McBride, Director of Research, Mashantucket Pequot Museum and Research Center; Wesley Johnson, Mayor (1995–2003), Ledyard, Connecticut; Cedric Woods, Deputy Chief Operating Officer, Mashantucket Pequot Tribal Nation. Special thanks to Matthew Craigie for research assistance in the preparation of this chapter.

Chapter 25

The Geography of Whiteness:
Russian and Ukrainian "Coalitions of Color" in the Pacific Northwest

SUSAN W. HARDWICK

INTRODUCTION

"Whiteness never has to speak its name, never has to acknowledge its role as an organizing principle in social and cultural relations" (G. Lipsitz, 1998, p. 1).

"Denying white as a racial category, neglecting to see that whiteness has a history and a geography — as Americans have done — allows whiteness to stand as the norm" (S. Hoelscher, 2003, p. 662).

Whiteness is both a historical construction and a spatial phenomenon. According to Steven Hoelscher, unmasking the processes by which whiteness is enacted and identifying the material consequences of such a construction is the first step toward formulating workable antiracist politics (2003, p. 662). In this chapter, I examine whiteness in the context of the shifting identities and related spatial expressions of a large group of white refugees in a metropolitan area long dominated by a majority white culture.[1] Portland, Oregon is located in a region variously known as Cascadia, Ecotopia, and "the last Caucasian bastion in the United States" (Kaplan, 1998). Since my focus in this chapter is on the economic, social, cultural, and political implications of whiteness, I prefer to label it *Caucasia*.

This chapter reports on the findings of a longterm multi-method project that is documenting and analyzing the post-1980s refugee diaspora in the Canadian and American Pacific Northwest. I limit my focus to the relationships between the religious networks, shifting identities, and spatial patterns of refugees in a state that surprisingly now ranks eleventh in the nation in the total numbers of migrants arriving with refugee or asylum-seeker status. The largest — ethnic Russians and Ukrainians — rarely refer directly to their whiteness, although expressions of their feelings, perceptions, and use of racial categories have emerged throughout the project that can only be understood within a whiteness problematic. Their large numbers, relative economic stability, activist religious and social networks, and political savvy — along with the color of their skin — make this group an appropriate point of analysis.

I focus attention on this large group of recent migrants to Portland and environs in response to Peter Jackson's call for studies of the constructions of whiteness at a variety of scales from the nation to the neighborhood (1998, p. 100), and the earlier pioneering work of Frankenberg (1993), Jackson and Penrose (1993), Bonnett (1997), Fine et al. (1997), and Dyer (1997). Incidentally, it was Bonnett's disturbing comment: "it is extraordinary to note that the only sustained debate about white identity ever conducted within geography took place between 1890–1930 and concerned the possibility of white acclimatization to the 'wet tropics'" (Bonnett, 1997, p. 193 from Trewartha, 1926), that was the nudge that most encouraged me to write this chapter for a book on race, ethnicity, and place.

SPACE, PLACE, AND REFUGEE RESETTLEMENT IN PORTLAND

The popular perception of Portland as a white person's city is deeply entrenched and has been shaped by the city's larger historical context of settlement primarily by western and northern Europeans. The dominant culture, especially in the earliest years of settlement of the city, created a homogeneous place that actively worked against incorporation of the "other" — from the earliest territorial laws prohibiting African Americans to the KKK in the 1920s to restrictions against Chinese land-ownership to anti-Japanese sentiment in the 1940s to skinhead violence in the 1980s and 1990s. These long-seated attitudes and perceptions linger among many residents of today's new, more diverse Portland.

The region's earliest migration flows were dominated by Germans, people from the British Isles, and Scandinavians, along with Euro-American settlers from the mid-Atlantic, New England, and Midwestern states. For the past twenty-five years, new migrants from Montana, Idaho, California, and Colorado have joined other (primarily white) migrants from the northern Rockies and Great Plains. Since the mid-1980s, (primarily white) "equity immigrants" from California, in particular, have continued to flow into Portland to escape congested urban places and the high cost of living south of the state border.

In the years during and after WWII, African Americans moved to Portland to work in the shipbuilding industries. Soon thereafter in the early 1950s, the city's entire African-American community was displaced by a devastating flood that demolished the African-American settlement of Vanport, a high risk, high density housing development located on an island in the Willamette River. African Americans displaced by this flood were strongly encouraged by social service workers and city politicians to relocate in a low-income, north Portland neighborhood called the Albina district. Except for some scattered attempts at gentrification by young white urban professionals looking for affordable housing near the city's downtown located just across the river, the Albina district remains primarily African-American today. Redlining by real estate agents and brokers in the 1950s and 1960s, along with the location of low-income housing projects funded by local and federal housing authorities in the Albina District that attracted first white, then primarily African-American workers, are the primary reasons for a lingering residential black-white spatial dichotomy in Portland.

During the last decade and a half, formerly white-dominated residential districts located farther east of the Willamette River have become more diverse as new immigrants and refugees find affordable and available housing in the city's original "streetcar suburbs" (Abbott, 1987, p. 75). The northeast and southeast quadrants of the city, in fact, are now home to native-born white, Latino, and Asian working-class families, along with refugees from Bosnia, Southeast Asia, Afghanistan, Russia, and Ukraine.

While Portland's population has become more diverse in recent years due to the influx of large numbers of immigrants and refugees, its demographic profile is still dominated by white/European-origin peoples. In 2000, almost 80 percent of the metropolitan area's population was reported as white (single-race). The minority races included 7 percent black/African American, 6 percent Asian, 1 percent American Indian and Alaska Native, and 0.4 percent Native Hawaiian and Other Pacific Islander. Over 4 percent reported more than one race, which is higher than the national figure of 2.4 percent. In addition, almost 7 percent of Portland's population in 2000 was counted as Hispanic.

SITUATING RUSSIAN AND UKRAINIAN MIGRATION AND SETTLEMENT

New migrants from the former Soviet Union have relocated in large numbers to the Portland metropolitan area since the early 1990s (see Figure 25.1). As I have discussed elsewhere (see Hardwick, 1993, 2002, 2003), most of these approximately 60,000 new residents are Russian and Ukrainian fundamentalist Christians who are categorized by the U.S. government as refugees. This status provides them with eight months of support for housing, employment assistance, and language training. The vast majority reside in the northeast and southeast parts of the city and in rural towns and small cities in the northern Willamette Valley, a region long known for its homogeneous Anglo-dominated population. The dramatic increase in Oregon of migrants born in the former USSR outnumbers increases in Vietnamese, Chinese, Asian Indians, and other Asian groups (U.S. Census of Population, 2000). The reasons for this unexpected migration stream to the Pacific Northwest are centered primarily in the religious networks that link migrants still residing in Russia or Ukraine with sponsors and church congregations in host communities in the Pacific Northwest.

Figure 25.1
Young Russian Pentecostal Refugees in the Pacific Northwest, 2004

Most of the Russians and Ukrainians who relocated to the U.S. in the past decade arrived as a response to the easing of emigration laws in the former USSR during the late Cold War years, and the subsequent passage of the Lautenberg Amendment to the 1980 Refugee Act by the U.S. Congress in 1989.[2] Chief among the groups who were able to prove they fit the definition of *refugees* were Jews and evangelical Christians such as Pentecostals, Baptists, and Seventh Day Adventists who were persecuted for their religious beliefs under the Soviet system. Following the breakup of the USSR in 1991, out-migration began in earnest. Jewish migrants from the former Soviet Union most often relocated to New York, Chicago, the San Francisco Bay Area, and Los Angeles, while the Oregon, Washington, and California Central Valley migration stream was dominated by Russian and Ukrainian evangelical groups.[3] Most decided to seek a new life in communities located along the I-5 corridor linking Fresno with Bellingham, Washington after listening to Sacramento's "Word to Russia" evangelical radio programming that encouraged them to come to the western U.S., Russian language articles in religious newsletters, and/or talking with friends and relatives who extolled the virtues of life in the American West (via phone calls, letters, and videotapes) also encouraged large numbers to leave their homeland and relocate to towns and cities along the I-5 corridor in northern California, Oregon, and Washington.

The results of structured and unstructured interviews and responses to survey questionnaires documented that almost all Ukrainian and Russian migrants in the region relocated to the Portland metropolitan area, (which includes Vancouver, WA located directly north of the Columbia River), and its hinterland in the Willamette Valley because of their connections with evangelical religious networks. According to Irina who moved to Portland in 1997:

> "My sister gave me the idea really. She said we should go to Oregon to be with others who already left our city. Then the minister here sent us a letter urging us all to try to come to his church. He assured us that my father and my mother could come too."

Religious networks, the housing location decisions of refugee resettlement agencies, and the availability of affordable housing in eastside neighborhoods are some of the factors that explain the patterns shown on the map in Figure 25.2. In addition, most newcomers prefer to live in the same neighborhoods as others who share their language, religious beliefs, and place of origin. According to an interview with the State Refugee Coordinator, more than 90 percent of newly arriving Russians choose to stay in the Portland area after their initial arrival because of the support provided by neighbors and family members from home and from outsider political, religious, and social networks.

Based on counts in the *Slavic Yellow Pages*, there are more than 400 businesses in Portland that are owned by Russian-speaking entrepreneurs. Many are in the construction industry. Russians and Ukrainians also own beauty salons, chiropractic practices, and taxi services. They also work in restaurants, homes for the elderly, and small businesses. "A person can get medical and dental care, open a checking account, attend church, build or buy a house and die without learning English here" is a sentiment commonly expressed by newcomers. Services and support from one business to another are often exchanged or traded as needs arise. These economic networks, along with the religious networks discussed above, tighten the internal connections within and between Russian-speaking business owners and help maintain ethnic economic and cultural cohesion in the Portland metropolitan area.

The location patterns of Russian and Ukrainian businesses in the urban area are somewhat surprising since most are located outside residential districts. In contrast, Russian and Ukrainian churches are embedded within or located very close to Slavic neighborhoods in eastside Portland and in Vancouver (Washington) Russian and Ukrainian neighborhoods.

THE SLAVIC COALITION AS A "COMMUNITY OF COLOR" IN OREGON

This overlying narrative, analyzing why Russians and Ukrainians reside in eastside Portland and across the river in Vancouver bears further examination. An analysis only listing affordable housing, refugee resettlement agency decision-making, and religious networks leaves out other critically important and less visible confounding factors such as race, whiteness, and historical precedents. While the availability of affordable housing in northeast and southeast Portland, and refugee preferences to live near others who share their language, values, and culture help explain why Russian and Ukrainian spatial patterns look the way they do in the study area, there is much more to the story. Uncovering the racialized subtext now hidden behind the patterns shown on the map (Figure 25.2) will help shed light on some of the more complex reasons for the distribution of Russian and Ukrainian space and place in Portland.

I frame this more nuanced argument by: (1) commenting in more depth on the powerful role of social service agencies in determining refugee settlement, (2) discussing the formation of the Slavic Coalition and its successful effort to urge the Portland Community of Color Coalition to allow a white group to become a participating member and thus be able to share in the funding pot, and (3) reporting on the findings of our survey questionnaires on Russian and Ukrainian identity and adjustment to their new lives in the U.S.

First, it is essential to note that the refugee resettlement process in Portland is a tightly organized system dictated by rules of the federal and state governments (who control funding for individual refugee support and resettlement agency staff), and local agencies such as county governments (who control funding for programmatic support). In Portland, the large and very successful Immigrant and Refugee Community Organization (IRCO) was formed from two agencies founded in the mid-1970s to assist refugees from Southeast Asia. It now employs more than 140 multi-lingual staff who help find housing, teach English, and network for employment opportunities for newly arriving refugees. As such, IRCO assists voluntary organizations such as the Lutheran Social Services in placing all new refugees in appropriate housing when they first arrive in the city.

Figure 25.2
Refugee Households from the former Soviet Union in the Portland Metro area, 1989–2001

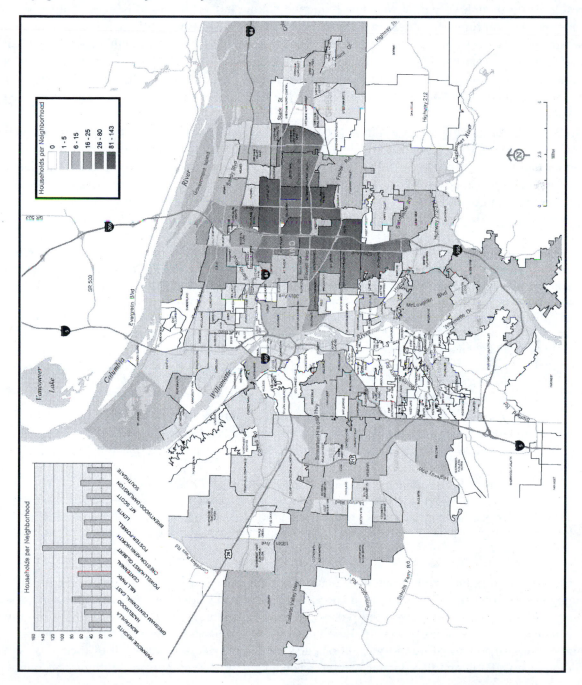

My interviews between 2002–2005, with the staff of several of the city's voluntary organizations revealed new information about exactly how appropriate housing is selected for new refugee arrivals. When queried about their choice of apartments and houses in eastside Portland instead of in other affordable parts of the city like the Albina district, I was told that usually a decision is made to keep as many of the white groups of refugees as possible in neighborhoods where white low and middle income families traditionally have resided. "This will make it easier for them to adjust in school classrooms and with their other neighbors," I was told without hesitation. This "back-door racial steering" has resulted in communities of whiteness in east Portland made up of primarily native-born Oregonians and refugees from Russia, Ukraine, and Bosnia. This is in direct contrast to African refugees from Somalia, Ethiopia, Eritrea and elsewhere, who are steered to housing in the Albina district — or to outlying suburbs such as Beaverton where small pockets of other African Americans currently reside. Even though very little social or economic mixing has yet occurred between native-born African Americans and African refugees in these neighborhoods (Hardwick and Hume, 2005), it is important to note that social service agency decision-makers continue to steer white refugees to white neighborhoods and black refugees to African-American districts believing that this is the "most logical way" to handle the resettlement process. It is therefore no coincidence that Russians and Ukrainians reside in a nodal heterolocal pattern limited to neighborhoods located in eastside Portland and across the river in Vancouver and not in north Portland in the Albina District.

A second contributing factor to the well-bounded black-white residential divide in Portland is the work of insider social and political "networks of ethnicity" (Mitchell, 2000). Urged by the support of a civic empowerment grant that funded an initiative called the Interwoven Tapestry Project, Russians and Ukrainians recently formed an organization called the Slavic Coalition. This group met for the first time in January, 2004 at a retreat where goals were laid out and funding possibilities were discussed for providing support for this self-identified ethnic community. According to the official description of the work of the Coalition that grew out of this retreat:

> "There are a lot of problems that Slavic people face in the U.S.A. It's a lack of a bridge between Russian-speaking community and authorities (court, police); important forms and announcements — information is not available in Russian; lack of legal interpretation; poor understanding of American laws and their consequences; lack of information about social and legal systems and structures and knowing one's rights and privileges under American Law (innocent until proven guilty, etc.); not understanding economic system (collection agencies, Better Business Bureau, etc.); no recognition of the benefits associated with citizenship and voting rights; not enough culturally specific, appropriate, or relevant activities; nor enough representation in mainstream media; lack of information about population demographics and so on" (Golovan, 2002, p. 1).

These needs are very real, especially for recent arrivals from Russia and Ukraine. But to find ways to fund programs that will help address these problems, the Slavic Coalition had to come up with some creative racializing. According to secretary Golovan's report of the outcomes of this first organizational meeting (2002, p. 1):

> "It is not easy for a Slavic community to be recognized by officials as a minority group (we do not look like a minority group based on our skin color) … but we already made steps to succeed in this field. Coalition of Color finally recognized us as a minority group" (it's an organization that unites coalitions of different minority groups like Latino Network, Asian-Pacific Islanders, African Americans, African Immigrants, Native Americans).

Key to declaring this group's status as a community of color is an understanding of the new county and city funding system in Portland. Beginning in late 2001, Multnomah County and other government jurisdictions in the metropolitan region reorganized the process of grant distribution for services to minority groups. The county declared that it would no longer fund individual groups or agencies for programs, but rather wanted to limit funding to partnerships of minority coalitions and service providers. As a result of their successful coalition building effort, IRCO and the Slavic Coalition received a $340,000 grant from Multnomah County in early

2004 to provide culturally-specific school-based and school-linked programming for the Slavic community. Gaining this funding would have been impossible without membership in the city's Community of Color Coalition. Not coincidentally, these funds address the overarching goal of the Slavic Coalition: "to advocate for the Slavic community" (Retreat Agenda, 2004).

Clearly the Slavic Coalition's status as a member of the Portland Community of Color Coalition carries important messages about the changing meanings and definitions of race in local and national politics. As constructed whiteness is expressed and exposed in differing ways among and between refugee and immigrant communities in the U.S. and native-born people of color, implications for the impact of these evolving definitions for funding minority programs in Portland and elsewhere are immense.

An unexpected finding of my research from survey questionnaire responses further complicated the effort to lay out a simple list of reasons to explain refugee residential patterns in the study area of the project. One hundred questionnaires were distributed to Russians and Ukrainians using our network of contacts in the metro area. These Russian language "Acculturation and Identity" surveys were developed and tested and then taken or mailed to church leaders and distributed in language and employment training classes at IRCO.

To learn more about the adjustment experiences and attitudes of post-Soviet Russians and Ukrainians in the Pacific Northwest, I distributed another 250 surveys to Portland's Slavic Coalition members and to other Russians and Ukrainians who reside in Seattle, Bellingham (WA) and Vancouver (B.C.) During this widescale distribution effort, a total of 47 surveys were completed and returned to me (even though all past efforts to use this methodology with Russians and Ukrainians failed completely, with a consistent zero return rate!). Respondents ranged in age from 18–68; 12 were male and 35 female; and 10 had lived in Oregon for less than one year, 21 for 1–5 years, and 16 for more than five years. All were born in cities and towns in either Russia or Ukraine.

Survey responses seem to contradict the argument put forth by the Slavic Coalition insisting that Russians and Ukrainians need additional funding to adjust to life in the U.S. Despite strong cultural and ethnic characteristics, (all respondents claiming that Russian was the language spoken at home; and all reported still eating mostly all Russian or Ukrainian foods; being married to another person from their homeland; and belonging to a Russian or Ukrainian church and primarily participating only in Russian-speaking social circles), their responses indicated a high comfort level with life in a foreign culture and foreign place. The following sample responses to questions about the challenges of adapting to life in Portland provide evidence of the unexpectedly positive answers provided on the surveys:

1) *I feel unsure of myself and foreign in the U.S.:*

Total agreement:	*1*
Agree to a certain extent:	*4*
Do not agree:	*8*
Absolutely do not agree:	*34*

2) *It is difficult for me to understand American life:*

Total agreement	*3*
Agree to a certain degree:	*2*
Do not agree:	*22*
Absolutely do not agree:	*20*

3) *I feel alone in America:*

Total agreement:	*2*
Agree to a certain degree:	*2*
Do not agree:	*7*
Absolutely do not agree:	*36*

In other questions, such as the ease of finding friends among Americans; feelings of belonging in American society; and comfort in understanding American life, responses were equally positive. Although comparative survey questionnaires have not yet been collected and analyzed for non-white refugee groups in the study area, it can be assumed that despite language barriers and lack of employment skills, the whiteness of Russians and Ukrainians, along with their intact and active pre- and post-migration religious networks, greatly eases their adjustment to life in the Pacific Northwest.

CONSTRUCTING, DE-CONSTRUCTING, AND RE-CONSTRUCTING WHITENESS

In this chapter, I used the Portland case study to respond to Bonnett's call for geographers to expose the invisible traditions of geographical research on race by examining the multiple ways that "white" identities are currently being (re)constituted (1997, p. 197). Understanding whiteness as a social construct not only contributes new ways of thinking to critical race theory, it also will help other scholars sort out the interrelated and quite complex set of cultural, social, economic, and political factors that explain the spatial patterns of refugees and immigrants.

For the members of Portland's Slavic Coalition, whiteness is only seen as a quality worth redefining when it is confronted with some form of the "other" (Said, 1995). Russian and Ukrainian "othering" includes both setting themselves apart as distinct from other refugees and local residents of the city who are people of color, while at the same time, insisting that their Slavic community is a distinct minority group who possesses the same urgent social service needs as other members of the Community of Color Coalition.

Thus, in the case study examined here, it appears that the benefits of constructing an identity related to whiteness can work both ways. As survey questionnaires and interviews established, adjusting to life in Portland has proceeded smoothly for many Russian and Ukrainian respondents. Most were quickly able to gain an understanding of American life, perhaps partly because their lives at home in Russia or Ukraine revolved around active membership in a church congregation that was closely linked to related congregations of believers in the U.S. American refugee sponsors were usually members of the same religious group. This made the migration and settlement of migrants from Russia and Ukraine proceed more smoothly than for other refugees from other places. In addition, and perhaps most importantly, the invisibility of this group caused by their white skin color, is another key reason why Slavic refugees are able to blend in and adapt to their new life, particularly in this white homogeneous region of the western U.S.

Accustomed to living and working within a frustrating system of restrictions and scarcity in their homeland, this group of new refugees is especially adept at using whatever skills and resources they have available to them to gain a larger share of the pie. The formation of the Slavic Coalition and its successful effort to become part of Portland's Community of Color Coalition provides evidence of the group's resourcefulness and years of Soviet and post-Soviet era training in using the system to their own benefit. In this era of increasingly challenging economic problems in the U.S., especially in Oregon (a state with one of the highest unemployment rates in the nation), the ethics and efficacy of re-defining and re-constructing race are particularly worthy of attention.

Regardless of the unusual nature of "race by choice," this case study has been presented in this chapter to make a contribution to the debate now underway by human geographers and other scholars centered in viewing race, ethnicity, gender, and identity as social constructions (see, for example, Anderson, 1987, 1991; Jackson, 1987; Kobayashi and Peake, 1994; Bonnett, 1997; Hoelscher, 2003; and Hume, 2005). Recognizing that race is socially constructed is no longer enough. It is essential for human geographers interested in critical race theory to re-examine the impact of shifting racial identities, meanings, and definitions on the politics of people and place to begin to understand the broader implications of certain groups who have choices about their own definitions of race — while other groups do not.

Race is not fictional, it has serious material and spatial effects. Further studies of racialized exclusion, constructions of whiteness by so called invisible groups, and the process of making and marking groups outside the whiteness paradigm as the "other," are not only long overdue in our disciple, they are also essential for the evolving notion of what it means to be an American.

NOTES

[1] This article could not have been written without the generous support of Victoria Libov of the Portland Immigrant and Refugee Community Organization. The research was funded by NSF Grant Number BCS – 0214467) and undertaken in collaboration with James E. Meacham, Director of the InfoGraphics Laboratory, University of Oregon. Research assistance from Ginger Mansfield, Susan Hume, and Rebecca Marcus was also invaluable to completion of the project. Likewise, cartographic support from Erin Aigner and Will Jensen made a major contribution to the spatial analysis central to my argument.

[2] Refugee status is defined by the U.S. Refugee Act as "persons living outside their homeland who are unwilling or unable to return home because of persecution or a well-founded fear of persecution."

[3] Because all but approximately 500 new post-Soviet residents of Portland are Jewish, and Christian fundamentalists have a common ethno-religious identity in their homeland, Jewish refugees are not discussed in this paper. In addition, upon arrival in Portland, because of their higher education levels, Jewish migrants have a different professional status and live in different parts of the metropolitan area than do most Russian and Ukrainian Baptists, Pentecostals, and Seventh Day Adventists.

Chapter 26

The Persistence of Greek American Ethnicity among Age Cohorts Under Changing Conditions

STAVROS T. CONSTANTINOU AND MILTON E. HARVEY

The purpose of this chapter is to present the major themes of Greek American ethnicity and to examine their change across generations. Historically, the Greek nation was burdened by a long and tumultuous history, which resulted in a synthesis of the classical Hellenic tradition and Byzantine Orthodoxy. Greek immigrants brought this complex cultural identity to America. Although Greek immigrants made some adjustments and changes within the pluralistic American society, they maintained certain core aspects of the Hellenic cultural triad: language, the family, and the Orthodox church. Language is central to the Greek Diaspora as asserted by Moskos:

> "one's cultural roots and political sensitivities must be nourished by a responsiveness to contemporary Greek realities — even at a distance" (Moskos, 1990, pp. 145–146).

The Greek language links Greeks across the globe, who

> "… share a destiny somehow connected with other people who call themselves Hellenes" (Moskos, p. 146).

The family, by encouraging the use of the Greek language at home, acts as the transmitter of the Hellenic culture. The church and its affiliated organizations sponsor a great variety of religious services and sociocultural activities, which are well attended by all Greek generations. Regional and local organizations also reinforced the role of the church in transmitting ethnic values across generations. The process of maintenance and transmission of Greek-American ethnicity is best understood from the historical context in which Greek migration to the United States occurred.

GREEK EMIGRATION IN A HISTORICAL CONTEXT

At any geographic location, such as a place of residence, an individual is exposed to stressors from the external environment. When stress occurs, the individual invokes stress-coping mechanisms that may reduce the stress to tolerable levels. In a migration context, when such strategies fail, however, the individual considers relocation and initiates a search process that may lead to either migration or adjustments that result in coping at the same location. Greek emigration is an example of the migration decisions made by many individual Greeks who were willing to travel thousands of miles for a new beginning in places that were culturally and linguistically very different from their homeland.

Emigration is a phenomenon that has characterized the Greek nation throughout its long history. Given the geographical limitations of the country and its insular character, the Greeks turned to the sea as a means of improving their economy. A rich seafaring tradition has been an integral part of Hellenic life from ancient times to the present. In ancient times, Greek communities existed mostly along the Mediterranean littoral, but in modern times they migrated and established settlements in distant countries, including the United States, Canada, Australia, South Africa, and Russia (Clogg, 1999).

United States as Destination

The first documented Greek to arrive upon American shores was Don Teodoro (Theodoros), who served on the Narvaez expedition of 1528 (Moskos, 1980). The first serious effort to establish a Greek presence in America was undertaken in 1768 by Andrew Turnbull, a Scottish physician (Panagopoulos, 1966), who sponsored an estimated 500 Greek laborers from the region of Mani in the Peloponnesus to set up the ill-fated colony of New Smyrna, about 75 miles south of St. Augustine, Florida. During the years following the New Smyrna expedition, immigration from Greece was sporadic and small until the latter part of the nineteenth century, when a large number of Greeks arrived on American shores. In a historical perspective, we analyze immigration from Mediterranean Greece to the United States from the perspectives of the receiving and the sending country.

Conceptually, immigration to the United States is an example of the push-pull forces that initiate and maintain a migration process. Certain political events and the role of institutions in Greece and the U.S. slowed or accelerated the influx of Greek immigrants and the rate of emigration from Greece. Greek immigration to the U.S. has been characterized by an uneven pattern (Constantinou and Diamantides, 1985), resulting from developments on both sides of the Atlantic. The high point of immigration from Greece, part of a larger flow of immigrants from Southern and Eastern Europe, was reached during the period 1901 to 1920. As noted in earlier chapters, the U.S. passed a new immigration law that created the quota system in 1921. This law limited annual Greek entries to a total of 3,294. Three years later, in 1924, the restrictive Johnson-Reed Act limited the total immigration from Europe to 150,000 per year and further reduced each country's quota to two percent of their total population that was residing in the U.S. during the 1890 Census. Because fewer Greeks resided in the U.S. in 1890 than in 1910, the number of immigrants from Greece was reduced to a meager 100. The McCarran-Walter Act of 1952, previously discussed in this text, maintained the highly discriminatory restrictive quota and limited Greek immigration to a total of 308. The changes in U.S. immigration law in 1965 included elimination of the quota system and creation of a limit of 20,000 immigrants from any single nation. As a result of these changes, the numbers of Greek immigrants increased.

Examination of particular phases of Greek immigration to the U.S. helps clarify the impacts of the changing laws and the evolution of Greek-American settlements. A total of 735,059 immigrants arrived from Greece during the period 1820 to 2003, an annual average of 3,995. This 184-year period, when divided into eight distinct immigration phases (Table 26.1), reveals peak-immigration periods. These have been classified as shown in Table 26.1. The Great Wave and New Wave phases of Greek immigration accounted for approximately one-half of the total number of Greek immigrants to the United States. The bulk of Greek immigrants arrived during the Great Wave Phase, when a total of 341,214 entered, an annual average of 18,956. During the New Wave, a total of 157,304 Greeks arrived in the United States because of changes in the law that allowed relatives of persons already in the country to immigrate. During the remaining phases, immigration was at very low levels due to restrictive legislation and other factors.

Push Factors: Conditions in Greece

Wars, crop failures, political upheaval, poverty, and harsh environmental conditions in Greece were the most important determinants (or push factors) of emigration, which drained the population of Greece in a serious way during the 20th century. The 1907 immigration figures of the Great Wave indicate that 1.39 percent of the population of 2.6 million emigrated to the United States in a single year. Although the percentage may seem small, the spatial impact was felt most seriously in the rural areas of Greece. Also, most early immigrants were young males.

Other periods of Greek emigration, although not of the same magnitude, were related to economic problems. Many were forced to seek employment opportunities in the U.S. Poor economic conditions during the modern history of Greece pushed impoverished Greeks to emigrate to various other nations as well, including Canada, Europe, South Africa, and Australia. Emigration from Greece continued until the 1980s, when economic improvements reduced annual migratory flows. In fact, during recent years, Greece, in a dramatic role reversal, has become a receiving country of immigrants.

Table 26.1

Immigration from Greece to the United States			
Phase	Duration	Immigrants	Annual Average
Sporadic Migration	1824–1872	217	5
Early Migration	1873–1899	14,915	204
Great Wave	1900–1917	341,214	18,956
Last Exodus	1918–1924	54,440	7,777
Closed Door	1925–1945	21,376	1,018
Postwar Migration	1946–1965	75,867	3,793
New Wave	1966–1979	157,304	11,236
Declining Migration	1980–2003	60,682	2,528
		725,798	4,101

Source: Adopted and modified from Charles Moskos "The Greeks in the United States," In The Greek Diaspora in the Twentieth Century, edited by Richard Clogg, 103–119. New York: St. Martin's Press, 1999.

THE SPATIAL DISTRIBUTION OF GREEK AMERICANS, 1970–2000

Generally, the spatial distribution of Greek Americans was stable over a long period of time. Greek Americans have persisted in some patterns established in their early settlement history. Some changes, however, have occurred and are noteworthy.

U.S. Regional and State Trends

Geographically, early Greek immigrants preferred the Eastern Seaboard, the Great Lakes, and the Pacific Coast, especially California. Also, during the 19th and early 20th centuries, Greeks were lured to the Mountain States by employment prospects, including the belief that Leonidas G. Skliris, a Salt Lake City-based labor agent, would find jobs for them. Many Greeks worked on the railroads and in the mines in that region. This regional population, however, was unstable and, by 1930, began to leave the Mountain States, returning mainly to the Northeast and the Great Lakes regions. Since WWI, the number of Greeks settling in the Midwest increased gradually.

The continuing decline of the Greek-American population in the Mountain States coincided with another trend, the increased growth of the Greek-American population in the American South. The Sunbelt effect, which influenced the relocation decisions of the general population, also had an impact on the regional patterns of Greek Americans. In 1910, the South contained 5.6 percent of the total Greek American population, but, by 1990, it accounted for more than 21 percent. The most impressive increase in population growth in the South occurred from 1970 to 1990. Presently, the South has the third largest concentration of Greek Americans, after the Northeast and the Midwest. Should the present attraction persist, the South will rival the other two regions for being the home of the greatest proportion of Greek Americans. This regional shift may be due to a number of factors, including job opportunities and retirement living.

By the 2000 Census, Greek Americans resided in every state. In descending order, the largest number resided in New York, followed by California, Illinois, Massachusetts, Florida, New Jersey, Pennsylvania, Ohio, Michigan, and Texas. This ranking has varied from census period to census period. For example, in the 1990 Census, California displaced Illinois from second place and Florida surpassed the traditional clusters of New Jersey, Pennsylvania, Ohio, and Michigan. The states with the smallest numbers of Greek Americans (fewer than 3,000) are rural: North Dakota, South Dakota, Alaska, Hawaii, Wyoming, Montana, Vermont, Arkansas, Mississippi, and Idaho.

The relative importance of the Greek-American population to the total population, which can be expressed as a ratio or percentage, varied somewhat over time at the state level. Between 1980 and 2000, however, the five states with the largest percentages of Greek-American populations, remained the same, while varying their rank within the top five (see Table 26.2). Those with the smallest ratios of Greek Americans are mostly southern or rural states. Mississippi has the lowest number of Greeks in relation to the total state population, followed by North Dakota, Kentucky, Arkansas, South Dakota, and Louisiana.

In summary, the bulk of the Greek-American population continues to reside in the Northeast and the Great Lakes regions, notwithstanding important shifts to the South. California also remains an important state in terms of total Greek-American population.

Table 26.2

Relative concentration of Greek Americans in top 18 states.			
Rank	**1980 Census**	**1990 Census**	**2000 Census**
1	Massachusetts	New Hampshire	New Hampshire
2	New Hampshire	Massachusetts	Massachusetts
3	New York	New York	New York
4	Illinois	Illinois	Connecticut
5	Connecticut	Connecticut	Illinois
6	New Jersey	New Jersey	New Jersey
7	Utah	Maryland	Rhode Island
8	Maryland	Rhode Island	Maryland
9	Nevada	Utah	Utah
10	Rhode Island	Nevada	Florida
11	California	Florida	Nevada
12	Delaware	Delaware	Pennsylvania
13	Pennsylvania	Pennsylvania	Ohio
14	Ohio	Michigan	Michigan
15	Michigan	Ohio	Delaware
16	Florida	Maine	Maine
17	Wyoming	California	Vermont
18	Maine	Virginia	California

U.S. County-Level Patterns

An examination of the distribution of Greek Americans at the county level reveals some interesting patterns. In terms of total population, the largest concentrations of Greek Americans in 2000, were in Cook (Illinois), Queens (New York), and Los Angeles (California) counties. The number of Greek Americans in these counties was 56,579, 45,257, and 27,715, respectively. These three are among the most populated counties in the U.S. Consequently, the large Greek populations in these counties are not too surprising. A different pattern emerges from an analysis of relative distribution of Greeks. Three counties have more than two percent of their total populations being Greek Americans in 2000, Carbon (Utah), Essex (Massachusetts), and Queens (New York). Thus, only Queens leads in both measures; it has one of the largest total Greek populations in the country and has a relatively larger proportion of Greeks than any other U.S. county.

Underlying the Greek-American spatial distributions are the basic processes that influence the spread of ethnic groups in a dominant population over time. Immigrants historically created initial settlement patterns based on gateways and employment opportunities. Eventually, other regional patterns evolved. An example is the early settlement of Irish Americans in New York. Later, the Irish migrated westward for canal building in the Midwest, particularly in Chicago. Also, an immigrant population grows through the influx of additional migrants and by natural increase. This may result in two situations: (a) the growth of temporary clusters in areas of economic opportunity (Greeks in the Mountain states), and (b) the emergence of new sustaining clusters in response to national population shifts (e.g., as in response to the Sunbelt factor).

U.S. Metropolitan Patterns: Urbanization and Suburbanization Trends

The initial waves of Greek immigrants, largely young males, avoided rural America because it invoked images of their impoverished rural homeland. They settled in ethnic enclaves in central cities within walking distance of the factories and other business establishments where they worked. When the number of immigrants reached a critical mass, Greeks organized local institutions, including a dues-paying community centered on the church. The importance of financially supporting the church was a new lesson that the early immigrants had to learn quickly. Unlike the situation in Greece, where as part of a state church they did not pay dues, Greek-American immigrants were required to support the church due to the separation of church and state. This formation of a dues-paying institution was a grassroots activity, rather than a structure imposed by church authorities in Athens or Constantinople.

Initially, early Greek immigrants rented a neighborhood building that functioned as a place of worship until sufficient funds could be raised to build a church. The church provided a point of reference for the community and became the leading social institution in Greek-American life. In many cases, early Greek immigrants described their residential locations relative to the location of their church. Thus, for early Greek immigrants, the parish church was an essential part of their ecological milieu. The Greek-American community consisted of an action space, where daily activities occurred, and a functional region focused on the centrality of the parish church. Their functional region included other cultural and ethnic markers too, including grocery stores, local social clubs, and coffeehouses (*kafeneia*). The coffeehouses were a particularly useful institution for the maintenance of Greek culture and ethnicity because immigrants, mostly bachelors, gathered there to socialize with one another and discuss Greek and Greek-American issues. In addition, and at a time when news about their ancestral home was scarce, the coffeehouses provided a forum for exchanging information about the motherland and their particular village homes. These are typical social spaces that were and continue to be created by ethnic groups across the U.S., as indicated in other chapters of this text. Like other immigrants, Greek Americans marked their communities with Greek language, signage, and other features that gave their living space a unique cultural appearance. Eventually, due to visually apparent Greek-American ethnic markers, the term Greek Town became the common language used by non-Greeks to describe these urban ethnic landscapes. Greek Towns were located in Chicago, Detroit, and Astoria, in New York City.

After WWII, the interaction of many factors led to the relocation of the Greek population and the decline of their inner-city Greek Towns. First, Greek emphasis on education meant that subsequent Greek-American generations secured better jobs and enjoyed higher disposable incomes, which led to their consideration of better neighborhoods. Second, the large influx of low-income blacks and other minority groups into American central cities accelerated white flight to the suburbs and the dispersal of the middle-class, including Greek-Americans, from the central city. Suburbanization contributed further to the decline of Greek Towns. It created new opportunities and more attractive environments that pulled many Greek Americans away from their traditional ethnic enclaves. This dispersal of a large part of the Greek-American population away from its church-coffeehouse-residential nexus in the old city centers presented new challenges to the preservation of Greek-American culture and ethnicity.

The survival of any ethnic group requires homeland ties, national linkages, and the local initiatives of social institutions to maintain group identity from generation to generation. When locational changes occur, an ethnic group must find ways to emphasize certain aspects of culture to maintain its ethnic cohesion. This makes the geographic study of ethnicity an important undertaking, especially at the local, or place level. This chapter restricts study to the Northeastern Ohio region, specifically to the Akron-Cleveland area, where the local dynamics of the Greek-American population remain strong.

GREEK AMERICANS IN THE NORTHEASTERN OHIO REGION

The suburbanization process covered in the previous section occurred in the urban areas of Akron and Cleveland, Ohio. In the case of Akron (Summit County), where our work has been more focused, Greek immigrants settled in its central city in the early 20th century. Proximity to work in the booming rubber factories was an important determinant. As Akron prospered as an industrial city, it attracted migrants from other parts of the country, including a black minority that settled in the central city. The development of the local and state highway system and the addition of a set of interstate highways (I-77, I-76), induced suburban growth and white flight from Akron city proper. Like other ethnic whites, Greek-American families relocated to particular suburbs, such as the communities of Hudson, Stow, Fairlawn, Bath, Copley, and, later, to more distant communities in Medina County, including Medina and Macedonia. Census data for the period 1970 to 2000 support these observations about Greek-American suburbanization. In 1970, the number of Greeks in the city of Akron was 1,080 (394 foreign-born and 686 natives of foreign or mixed parentage). The Census did not report ethnicity information by county, where suburbs were growing by 1970. By 1980, the Census reported 1,089 Greek persons of single ancestry in Akron and 2,003 in Summit County. The 1990 Census reported 1,318 Greek persons of single ancestry as residing in Akron, while 2,546 were living in Summit County. By 2000, the U.S. Census data indicated that persons claiming Greek as first ancestry had fallen to only 1,803 in the city of Akron, while 2,974 of the same ancestry resided in suburban Summit County. Thus, by 2000, nearly three of every four persons of Greek ancestry were living in the Akron suburbs.

With this dispersal of the Greek population, Greek-American parishioners were faced with the choice of either relocating the parish church to the more affluent suburbs, where most of them lived, or upgrading the existing church. Communities such as Chicago decided to relocate whereas Akron and the four parishes in Cuyahoga County (Cleveland area) chose to renovate. This decision to renovate rather than relocate caused some spatial behavioral adjustments by many Greek Americans in these five parishes. The increasing spatial discordance between the church and the distribution of Greeks in Summit County, which is essentially conterminous with the Akron parish, was evident from a series of maps generated by Constantinou and Harvey (1981) from data from six church directories for each of the decades between 1930 and 1980. Specifically, these maps showed the gradual dispersal of the Greek population away from the downtown, along the major arteries and out to the emerging suburbs, especially to the northwestern part of the city of Akron.

An inter-generational perspective of the patterns discussed in the last paragraph is also reported in this chapter from the mapping of a sample of Greek Americans by generations (Figure 26.1). These maps show that members of first, second, and third generation still form a cluster close to their church. Most of the first generation still reside close to the church along a northwest-southeast axis around the University of Akron. The patterns for the second and third generations are dispersed into the surrounding suburbs. It remains to be seen whether younger members of the third generation also will relocate to the suburbs as they accumulate wealth and position. In addition to Akron, Constantinou (1982) surveyed four Greek parishes in the Greater Cleveland Area and the parish of Saint George in Massillon, Ohio. The patterns in these four were similar to those of Akron. Survey information suggested that a small number of New Wave immigrants to the area, mostly professionals, did not follow the dispersal pattern of the Great Wave immigrants. Instead, they settled directly in the suburbs.

Changes in the residential patterns of some Greek Americans in Northeastern Ohio have led to functional changes in their behavior. Greek Americans still place an important emphasis on the Greek church but value their suburban locations. The result has been larger religious functional regions that require longer travel distances for participation in the liturgy. It is also important for some Greek Americans to provide a cultural education for their children. In some instances, parents in our sample population travel a distance of at least 30 miles, twice a week, to take their children to a different parish where afternoon classes are taught in Greek. These parents believe that their children should be fluent in the Greek language and retain important aspects of their culture. For example, six families that reside in Akron, Ohio, traveled an average distance of 30 miles per trip to the Mother church in downtown Cleveland, where classes are offered in Greek. In an extreme case, one family traveled an average distance of 60 miles per trip to permit their child to attend Greek-American classes.

The challenges presented by changing residential geography highlight one of the difficulties faced by Greek Americans, who seek to perpetrate the core elements of their culture by passing them on to their offspring. In the next section, we examine some of the core elements of Greek-American self-identity, using results from survey research.

Figure 26.1

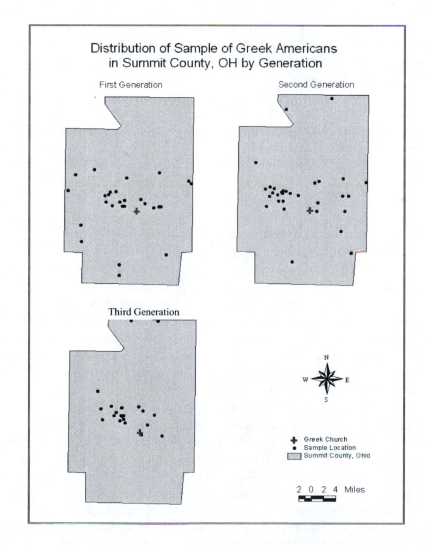

DEFINING GREEK-AMERICAN ETHNICITY IN THE AKRON-CLEVELAND REGION

Earlier in this chapter, we alluded to issues faced by Greek immigrants seeking entry into Anglo-American culture. The corollary issue is the erosion of aspects of Greek culture (Greek identity). The former is studied in the framework of acculturation theories, the latter in the context of maintenance of ethnic identity. As Berry (2001) asserted, acculturation consists of two uncorrelated dimensions: identification with a person's heritage, and identification with the dominant society. After more than four generations of presence in the United States, identification with the customs and norms of the United States increased and certain Greek traditions and cultural practices were either dropped or modified. One of the characteristics of early Greek immigrants was the formation of *topika somateia,* or local societies whose membership included immigrants from a particular village, region, or island of Greece. Although this place-based spirit of localism was very strong among first-generation immigrants, it declined sharply among American-born members of the second and subsequent generations. With a few exceptions, most of the local societies ceased to exist with the passage of the first generation. The cultural attributes that are maintained constitute the core of the Greek-American ethnicity. This core provides the basis of Greek-American identity and serves as the glue that binds Greek Americans together. Defining this core in its entirety is no easy matter.

Despite the decline of several other Greek traditions and practices, a number of ethnic elements remain as the glue of Greek-American ethnicity (Constantinou and Harvey, 1981; Constantinou, 1982; Constantinou and Harvey, 1985; Constantinou, 1989). A survey conducted among Greek Americans in the Akron-Cleveland region established a number of key dimensions of Greek-American ethnicity. The study focused on those who were actively or nominally participating in the life of the Greek-American church. The sample was drawn from church populations because studies of ethnic identity have demonstrated that ethnic group self-identification is prerequisite to being included in such studies. The inclusion of only Greek Church members in our study was a purposeful design to establish membership in the Greek community. More than 80 percent of all Greek Americans are known to be dues-paying members of the Greek Orthodox Church. Thus, a sample drawn from church records is representative of the Greek community at large. Our survey covered the six Greek Orthodox parishes in the Cleveland Standard Consolidated Statistical Area. We begin our discussion of Greek-American identity using these data from the 1980s. Although the information is dated, they are unique because they provide information on three generations of Greek Americans. After a discussion of these data, we use the results of a recent focus group to test the perseverance of these traits of Greek-American ethnicity.

The questionnaire used in the survey considered many aspects of Greek-American life, established by other scholars of Greek-American ethnicity (e.g., Buxbaum, 1980). In addition to the usual questions about personal attributes, such as education, age, income, and residence, the questionnaire included more than 70 questions covering numerous aspects of Greek-American ethnicity. The questionnaire, printed in both English and Greek, was pretested on a sample of volunteers from the parish of the Annunciation in Akron, Ohio. It was then revised and distributed to adults in the six parishes. There were 446 usable responses. The sample included a few more males (53%) than females, more married families than singles (about 70% vs. 30%), and was an educated and economically well-off population (more than 58% had at least a year of post secondary education and earned more than $50,000.00 per year). Also, there was an obvious tie to Greece because slightly more than 70 percent of all respondents had visited Greece at least once. Of the total sample (446), 165 were first-generation Greek immigrants, while 167 were second-generation, and 114 reported that they were third-generation members born in the United States. Despite the sample being drawn from Church records, about 5 percent did not regard themselves as members of the Greek Orthodox Church.

We used 17 measures from the survey questions that repeatedly appeared in the ethnic literature as the basis for ethnic self-identification. These included such items as the use of the Greek language at home and in correspondence, participation in ethnic institutional life, interests in Greek and Cyprus politics, and ethnic shopping, food preparation and cooking. These became the basis for our analysis of Greek-American ethnicity, which we discuss next within the context of ethnic persistence and change. Having data from three generations made the survey particularly useful for examining cross-generational patterns involving the first generation, immigrants born in Greece, the second generation, the children of immigrants, and the third generation, the grandchildren of immigrants.

Discussion of the results illustrates how changing circumstances may require adaptation to retain a degree of ethnicity as cultural and ethnic norms are challenged by subsequent generations. Despite such challenges, certain core elements of Greek-American ethnicity are being perpetuated at the local level in this Northeastern Ohio region. We focus on the key elements that bound these Greek Americans together as a distinct community within the 1980s. This will be followed by a brief update that examines their contemporary importance.

GREEK-AMERICAN ETHNICITY: PERSISTENCE AND CHANGE

The average responses to the 17 measures of ethnic self-identification are summarized by generation in Table 26.3. It is clear from the table that each of the three generations views the importance of these variables differently and that the overall importance of each declines with successive generations. In the first-generation responses, only three variables had a score of less than 3, while for the third generation only six variables had a score of 3 or higher. Those associated with use of the Greek language were among the most striking differences in the averages for the first- and third-generations. Specifically, third-generation Greek Americans were much less likely than Greek natives to rate knowledge of Greek and use of the Greek language in family communications as important dimensions of Greek ethnicity. Display of the flag of Greece was also less important to U.S.-born Greek Americans.

It is interesting to note, however, that certain variables retained relatively high scores across generations. These included an emotional orientation toward the homeland (a key component of ethnicity), frequent attendance at church, and socialization with other Greek Americans. The preparation of Greek food (cooking) also maintained a relatively high rating among all three generations of Greek Americans. These examples of intergenerational cultural invariance are particularly impressive given the changing settlement geography of Greek Americans in the region. Because these measures are indicators of the trinity that is at the core of Greek American ethnicity (the Church, the Greek language, and the family) (Buxbaum, 1980, pp. 11–12), we discuss them in some detail below.

Greek Language and Ethnicity

The preservation of language is an extremely important component of culture and often is a dimension of ethnicity. In the case of Greek language use in America, great effort and sacrifice led to its common use in Greek homes in the early 20th century. This was the result of the concerted efforts and hard work of the family, the church, and the Greek school. Language strengthened family, preserved tradition, and served as a bond between Greek-American families. Among early immigrants, maintaining the language was an article of faith and the church organized parochial afternoon and Saturday schools to teach Greek language and culture to the Greek American youth.

Despite these efforts, however, fluency in the Greek language declined in the U.S. Proportionately, as the numbers of first-generation members declined and numbers of subsequent generations increased, the use of the Greek language in the U.S. became less important. In addition, increasing numbers of Greek Americans have intermarried with other groups and converted to other religions (Constantinou, 1989). Not surprisingly, then, the importance of the Greek language in the home, as a component of Greek-American identity, declined in the Akron region (Table 26.3). This declining fluency in language beyond the first generation created a problem for understanding the church liturgy, which traditionally was chanted in Greek. Thus, a generational issue within the Greek-American population occurred, as younger people felt less of a need to speak the Greek language in their ethnic church.

The language issue became even more complicated and divisive in the 1960s due to the infusion of large numbers of Greek immigrants. The language needs of the recent immigrants sparked considerable debate regarding the use of Greek language in the liturgy. This issue was formally addressed by the Clergy Laity Congress of 1970. The Congress decided, depending on the needs of the individual parish, to permit the use of either English or a combination of Greek and English, in church services after consultation with the bishop of each diocese. In cities where there are large numbers of Greeks and more than one church, a church's membership size was largely determined by how much Greek was used in the liturgy. In communities with only one church, the dual language option creates tension that may be resolved by using both languages. In some parishes, the priest addresses this issue by labeling specific liturgies as Greek, English, or both. Thus, in addition to the normal pressures of assimilation within the host society, differences in a generational outlook and the needs of recent immigrants further complicate the retention of language as a cultural component, a dimension of Greek-American society.

While use of the Greek language among Greek Americans declined significantly among the three generations (Table 26.3), the Greek Church, serving as a social institution, attempted to accommodate the third generation with English-based services, while meeting the needs of older and immigrant Greeks in the society. These efforts made the Church important and respected by all three generations.

Table 26.3

Mean Responses by a Sample of Greek-Americans in the Cleveland-Akron Area			
	GENERATIONS		
VARIABLES	First	Second	Third
Age	4.21	3.69	1.83
Correspondence with Greece	4.17	2.78	1.99
Frequency of attendance at Church Liturgy	4.24	4.01	3.28
Knowledge of Greek Language	4.32	3.39	2.65
Emotional orientation toward Greece	4.38	3.83	3.45
Frequency of display of Greek flag	1.39	0.81	0.66
Frequency of listen to Greek radio at home	4.14	3.14	2.39
Frequency of Greek cooking at home	4.52	4.01	3.53
Frequency of shopping at Greek grocery stores	4.08	3.32	2.77
Frequency of exchange visits with Greek Americans	4.53	4.53	3.99
Frequency of invite Greek Americans to home	4.58	4.58	4.28
Frequency at Greek dances	4.35	4.26	4.12
Frequency of close watch on Greek politics	3.76	2.59	2.11
Protest messages to Congressmen	3.94	2.96	2.27
Use Greek in family communication	2.27	0.44	0.16
Vote for Greek American candidates irrespective of political affiliation	3.58	2.17	1.86
Office in Greek-American organizations including the Church	2.62	2.83	2.14
Committee membership	2.67	3.16	2.38

The Greek Orthodox Church

The issue of language notwithstanding, the Greek Orthodox Church remains the central Greek-American institution, as it had been during the four centuries of Ottoman rule in Greece. Greek-American ethnicity and Orthodoxy are tightly interwoven and, for the first generation immigrant, synonymous. Early immigrants knew that the church was an institution through which they could maintain their language, faith, family, and cultural traditions. Although the immigrants were not socially or geographically homogeneous, they rallied around a single purpose: maintenance and transmission of the Hellenic ethos to future generations. Thus, ethnic life revolved around the parish church and its various programs. Church programs involved religious teaching, language, and other social activities that united Greek-American families and preserved ethnicity.

In the early decades of the 20th century, the organizational structure of the church went through turbulent changes. The formation of new church parishes was a phenomenon that correlated with the waves of immigration from Greece. Immigrants organized the largest number of parishes during the years from 1911 to 1930, mirroring the peak years of immigration. The Greek Orthodox Church is organized both functionally and spatially into a hierarchy. Functionally, the top of the hierarchy is the Greek Orthodox Archdiocese of America which is headquartered in New York City and headed by an archbishop. Subsumed under this Archdiocese are eight metropolises (formerly dioceses), and the Archdiocesan District in New York. While the archbishop is the presiding head of the Direct Archdiocesan

District, a metropolitan (formerly bishop) presides over each of the eight metropolises which are composed of parishes in several states. In 2005, there were approximately 500 Greek Orthodox parishes in the United States organized into nine administrative units (Greek Orthodox Archdiocese of America, 2005).

Greek Orthodox parishes exhibit a great degree of variability in terms of the extent to which they adhere to orthodox practices. Some parishes are more traditional, but others are more diluted and acculturated to American society. A critical development in the process of the Americanization of the church is the growing number of non-Greeks who have joined through marriage. As these converts assume an active role in parish affairs, the Americanization of the church will proceed at a faster pace.

At the generational level, frequent church attendance was less important for third-generation Greek Americans than those of the other two generations. Despite this difference, the Greek Church remains the focal point of Greek-American identity for all three generations.

In summary, there is no other Greek-American institution that rivals the Greek Orthodox Church in terms of membership, organizational structure, national visibility, or its influence on the preservation and transmission of ethnicity. Tied closely with the church is the Greek-American family unit.

Social Organizations and Ethnic Networks

Social institutions are the basis for a great deal of ethnic interactions. Ethnic networks develop and generate interactions between individuals at various geographic scales. Spatially, Greek-American organizations operate at three levels: national, regional and local. Networks have both a spatial and a functional dimension. National Greek-American organizations are of national scope and their memberships cut across local and regional origins. The American Hellenic Educational Progressive Association (AHEPA) is an example of such a national organization. Naturally, they bring ethnic unity to Greek Americans by providing important formal means of connecting those separated by distance and busy schedules. They are connected by an interest in broad Greek and Greek-American issues, including the Church and activities in their ancestral home.

Regional organizations are those that appeal to immigrants from a certain province of Greece. Examples are organizations representing immigrants from the provinces of Epirus, Macedonia, Peloponnesus, and Sterea Hellas. The attachment of immigrants to their region and place of birth forms the underlying criterion for the formation and existence of one such network. To clarify attachment to place, one must consider that the physical geography of Greece promoted the isolation of many communities, such as the ancient city-states. Steep mountains divide the country into small valleys and plains that have little connection to surrounding areas. Such isolation promoted attachment to one's native place. This attachment to place was transferred to the expatriates' communities in the form of societies and organizations. Once a number of emigrants had established themselves in a certain area, they formed a society that was limited to people from the same region. A psychological need to socialize with people from similar surroundings was met through the creation of regional societies that were tied to the homeland.

Local societies are those organized by immigrants from a specific village. Historically, Greeks have shown a passion for the formation of local societies, *topika somateia*. The criterion for the formation of a large number of such organizations was place of origin — small villages, islands, and the Hellenic Diaspora (Asia Minor, Cyprus, etc.). In 1907, there were about 100 such societies in the United States, with New York alone having thirty (Saloutos, 1964). This pattern continued, and by 1994 there was a total of 493 Greek societies (Greek Orthodox Archdiocese of North and South America, 1994). Immigrants from Macedonia had 172 societies; those from the Peloponnesus had 123 societies. Research has shown that several attributes of ethnicity relate to the activities of these societies (Constantinou, 1996). Although members of different ethnic organizations, even local societies, often rise above narrower group interests and support broader ethnic causes and concerns, the local organization performs important networking functions. The Kalavasos Fraternity is an example of a local society. It represents immigrants from the village of Kalavasos on the island of Cyprus. In 2001, the village of Kalavasos had a population of 638 inhabitants (Statistical Service, 2002).

As noted earlier, social networks thrive through local institutions and the Greek-American Church is one of the most vital institutions that provides important functions that unite the local church population. Members of local place-based organizations also participate in the various parish programs and activities, connecting one social institution with another. Together, these organizations (church and place-based) play an integral role in total community life.

These are the bases for keeping many Greek Americans united through ethnic interactions, including festivals, food preparation and consumption, church discussions, and other issues important to ethnic identity.

In summary, ethnic networks developed from social institutions and spatial and functional dimensions that reinforce Greek-American ethnicity. National, regional, and local institutions have created overlapping networks. In an effort to remain connected and assist the villages and towns left behind, Greek-Americans formed social institutions. These institutional networks link Greek-Americans in important ways, reinforcing Greek-American ethnic identity through fraternity, work, socialization, and worship. Social institutions indeed are the glue for maintaining ethnicity.

Our survey results for 1980–81 revealed some sharp differences between the first and third generation respondents on some factors, perhaps indicating some precipitous decline in the importance of some items that historically supported Greek-American ethnicity. At the same time, the results of that survey substantiated the vital roles of the Greek-American church, family, and ethnic networks among the sample population in establishing the key dimensions of Greek-American self-identification across three generations. Attending church frequently, Greek food preparation and cooking, affinities to homeland, and socialization remained important dimensions of Greek self-identity by 1981. Social networks were key linkages in the maintenance of ethnicity. The importance of exchanging visits with other Greek-Americans, inviting Greek-Americans to one's home, and frequently attending Greek dances as ethnic social functions, were strong factors for all three generational groups. Social networks remain a strong component of Greek-American identity.

DIMENSIONS OF CONTEMPORARY GREEK-AMERICAN ETHINICITY: A PRELIMINARY REPORT FROM A 2005 FOCUS GROUP

Given the new suburban patterns, the aging of the Greek-American population, and the generational differences reported from our previous survey, we decided to update the information in 2005 via focus group analysis. Space limitations here prohibit a lengthy discussion of the results. Our major goal for this chapter is to examine the persistence of the key dimensions of Greek-American ethnicity that were self-defined among the three generations in the previous study of Northeastern Ohio Greek Americans. An initial focus group conducted by the first author in 2005 at the Annunciation Church in Akron, Ohio, was completed in time to furnish preliminary results for this chapter. A total of ten parishioners participated in an hour-long session with the author serving as the facilitator. The generational status of participants was as follows: two were first generation, three were second generation, two were third, one was fourth, and two were converts to the Greek-American Church. The same ethnic identity categories that appeared in Table 26.3 were provided as a hand-out to the participants. They were asked to select and rank the top five attributes of Greek-American ethnicity, or, alternatively, they could create their own. After the selections were completed, participants were asked to comment on their selections. The entire focus group session was taped and transcribed.

The following ranking emerged from the combined ratings of the participants: frequency of attendance at the liturgy, emotional orientation toward Greece, knowledge of Greek language, Greek cooking at home, holding office in Greek-American organizations, including the church, and frequency of exchange of visits with Greek Americans. It is clear from these preliminary findings that most of the key dimensions of Greek-American ethnic identity reported in our previous study remain important as we begin the 21st century. Church, socialization with other Greeks, preparing and cooking Greek foods in the home, and an emotional attachment to Greece remain important to Greek-American identity in this Northeastern Ohio region. Only knowledge of the Greek language seems to change. Perhaps additional results from our other focus groups will clarify the role of the language factor in the current period.

Table 26.4 reports the typical comments of the participants of the focus group. Although a wide range of opinions was expressed during the one-hour session, the comments seemed inevitably to return to the importance of place, socialization, family, and the Church. As aptly expressed by one participant: "I was attracted to the family and the religion ... it all comes back to the Church, the center point of keeping the Greek thing going."

SUMMARY AND DISCUSSION

According to the official records, 735,059 immigrants from Greece arrived in the United States during the period 1824 to 2003. The number of Greek immigrants peaked during the first two decades of the 20th century. A record of 184,201 immigrants arrived between 1911 and 1920. Smaller flows occurred since then and, after 1980, the flow of Greek immigrants declined.

Table 26.4

Summary of Comments of a Focus Group Session		
Comment	Generation	Gender
Our faith has to be preserved: the Greek Orthodox faith saved our tradition, and should be maintained	First	M
Church is the number one. If you don't belong to the Church, you are lost	First	F
Back in the 1930s, you said what part of Greece you were from, Arcadian, Cretan	First	M
Being Greek means being Greek Orthodox. Exceedingly difficult to separate	Second	F
Greek dances was the only contact and diversion we had. I felt I belonged somewhere	Second	F
Marrying someone who was Greek was very important. Dances: an extension of my whole life	Second	F
My Greek American identity goes hand in hand with the church and attending the liturgy. I am so proud of our Greek heritage, we have such a rich and deep heritage, it is what has kept us strong, in addition to our Orthodoxy	Third	F
Greek cooking at home enforces traditions and enlightens the holidays Nowadays, everybody loves the fact that I am ethnic; they see a sense of belonging heritage, things Americans don't have anymore. My great grandparents were the complete opposite, they shortened their name	Fourth	F
As a convert, I married a Greek and there was no question that I would become Greek Orthodox ... that is where we are centered	Convert	F
I was attracted to the family and the religion ... it all comes back to the church, the center point of keeping the Greek thing going	Convert	M

The Hellenic identity is considered the synthesis of the classical Hellenic tradition and the influence of Byzantine Orthodoxy. This is the cultural identity that Greek immigrants brought to the United States. Although Greek immigrants made some adjustments and changes within the pluralistic American society, they maintained certain core aspects of the Hellenic ethos, namely the pivotal social institutions of language, church, and family. The church and its affiliated organizations have sponsored religious services and sociocultural activities, which continue to focus on family and attract all Greek-American generations. These institutions, therefore, contribute to Greek-American ethnicity. Regional and local societies also reinforced the role of the church in transmitting Greek-American ethnic values across generations and provided social networks that nurture ethnicity.

In broad terms, early Greek communities formed functional regions centered on the parish church, which often was located in the center of a major U.S. city. Since WWII, a gradual but constant movement of the Greek-

American middle class to the suburbs occurred. This resulted in a larger geographic activity space for Greek Americans, who traveled longer distances to participate in ethnic activities at central city parish churches in the Akron-Cleveland region. Consequently, Greek-American ethnic space has been redefined and expanded.

The Greek immigrant tendency to form organizations and societies is largely a manifestation of the localism and provincialism that characterized Greek society since ancient times. While many of these organizations were short-lived, some have survived to the present. As Greek immigrant numbers declined, some organizations were unable to make the transition from an immigrant to an American-born membership. The smaller societies, for the most part, could not survive. Even those that remain face obstacles in maintaining their membership rosters and in getting the youth involved. Changes in American society, such as employed parents and suburbanization, likely make participation in social activities more difficult. Based on these changes, the future may not be bright for traditional local societies. Yet, some continue to play a basic role in the social exchanges that occur through networks that these organizations foster.

The story of Greek-American ethnicity is one of persistence and change in the face of changing national, regional, and local milieus. Despite important social changes, survey results have demonstrated the continuing importance of family, affinity to homeland, church, and social interactions to the maintenance of Greek-American ethnicity.

As the American society and the Greek-American ethnic group evolve, there will be other factors to challenge and support the maintenance of Greek-American ethnicity. While social interactions based on church likely remain the glue of Greek-American ethnic identity, changes in technology may offer some different opportunities for ethnic maintenance. Although unstudied at present, the availability of relatively inexpensive television programming from Greece via satellite technology and the Internet may provide critical new ways to overcome the friction of geographic distance and busy schedules that prohibit third generation members from securing information about their ancestral home and culture. The Internet also may provide new opportunities for learning the Greek language and therefore supporting its use in the home. The maintenance of the language also would dramatically increase the level of awareness of changes in the ancestral land.

Chapter 27

Disparities in Economic Status among Native-Born and Foreign-Born Populations in Paterson, New Jersey

THOMAS Y. OWUSU

INTRODUCTION

Immigration continues to contribute significantly to the growth of the U.S. population. In the last two decades, about one million immigrants have been admitted every year. Although the number of immigrants has remained high, the source regions have changed. Since the 1960s, the numbers and share of immigrants coming from Latin America, Asia, Eastern Europe, and Africa have increased, while the proportion of immigrants coming from traditional sources in Europe has declined. Like earlier groups, however, recent immigrants are redefining the economic, demographic, social, and cultural character of American cities, which are often their preferred destinations (Cross, 1998; Castles and Miller, 1993). Given the continuing high levels of immigration and the impact of immigrants on American society, the level of academic attention given to the issue is high (Camarato, 2001; Kraly and Miyares, 2001; 1999; Borjas; Portes and Rumbaut, 1990).

The economic impacts of American immigration policy, and the economic difficulties experienced by immigrants in particular, have been the subject of considerable research effort and public debate. Some studies have concluded that immigration has become a major factor in the size and growth of poverty. According to Camarato (2001), despite a strong economy over much of the last two decades, the poverty rate for persons in immigrant-headed households not only has remained high, but actually has increased significantly. While the above assertion may be generally valid, it is of course recognized that immigrants in the U.S. are not a homogeneous group; they differ in terms of their demographic, economic, and social attributes, including educational background and skills, period of immigration, age, race, language proficiency, and so forth. Thus it is expected that their economic experiences will also differ considerably. It is known, for example, that poverty rates among immigrants in the U.S. varies significantly by region of origin. In general, immigrants from Latin America and the Caribbean have the highest poverty rates, while those from Europe and Asia tend to have the lowest rates (Camarato, 2001). These findings are consistent with those from similar studies in Canada (Lo et al., 2001).

Furthermore, relatively little research has focused on the experiences of immigrants groups in different urban settings. The paucity of research in this area is striking, given that the economic experiences of immigrants depends in part on the local labor market. Indeed income disparities may reflect unequal opportunities available to immigrants and native-born Americans in different urban markets. Research also shows that immigrants who work in urban areas with large immigrant concentrations can benefit from the presence of enclave businesses, although the precise effects of the immigrant enclave economy on the earning capacity of immigrants remains contentious. Urban locations also differ in unemployment rates, which adversely affect opportunities of job seekers, especially recent immigrants. The preceding observations suggest that generalizations about the economic experiences of immigrants may be misleading. What is required, therefore, are case studies that seek to analyze variations in the economic conditions of immigrant groups in different cities. These observations provide a rationale for this study. This chapter will examine differences in the economic status (measured by income) of native-born Americans and the foreign-born in Paterson, New

Jersey, and then explain the disparity in terms of a variety of human capital and personal factors including education, occupation, period of immigration, race, and English language proficiency.

The City of Paterson is located within the New York-New Jersey Metropolitan Area (see Figure 27.1), and it is the third largest city in New Jersey, with a population of approximately 170,000. The city provides a suitable urban setting for exploring various propositions in the literature regarding the economic experiences of immigrants in U.S. cities. First, immigration has not only contributed to the growth of the city's population, but it has shaped its economic and social character. Second, in accordance with a broader national trend, the origins of immigrants coming to Paterson has changed significantly in the past three decades. The majority of immigrants coming to Paterson since the 1970s have come from Latin America, Asia, and Eastern and Central Europe. Third, the poverty rate in Paterson has varied considerably since 1970, but has remained consistently higher than the rate for most cities in Passaic County and New Jersey as a whole. The development and growth of Paterson and the dynamics of economic and demographic transition in the city are further discussed in the following sections

ESTABLISHMENT AND GROWTH OF THE CITY OF PATERSON

Founded in 1792, Paterson is recognized as the first planned industrial city in America. After the Revolutionary War of 1765, Alexander Hamilton (Washington's first secretary of state) and his associates concluded that while the war had established the political independence of the U.S., there was the need to establish its independence from a commercial and manufacturing viewpoint. With this in mind they set out to lay the foundation of a system of domestic manufacturers. After examining several localities, Paterson was selected because it offered more locational advantages than any of the other sites examined. In 1791, therefore, Hamilton and his associates formed the Society for Useful Manufacturers (SUM). A year later, the directors of SUM bought 700 acres of land above and below the Passaic Falls, and proposed to build a mill and a dam to divert the Passaic River onto their property and return it to the river below the Falls. Two days later, a six-square mile area surrounding the Falls was created as a town and called Paterson, in honor of William Paterson, the Governor of New Jersey and one of the framers of the U.S. Constitution (Carpenter, 1947).

Paterson's site offered unique physical advantages for manufacturing including the availability of water power source, abundant natural resources, and a natural river way. The Great Falls of the Passaic afforded water power not equaled in any of the states in the eastern portion of the U.S. The lack of accessible waterways was adequately compensated by good land transportation facilities, including access to many interstate roads. Its proximity to major markets in the Northeast, particularly its position between New York and Philadelphia, with their mercantile interests, and proximity to raw materials, also contributed to Paterson's growth. Massive immigration to Paterson provided labor of all types, both skilled and unskilled. Most of the immigrants who came were an overflow of those who had originally planned to settle in New York City.

From the time of its founding to the first-half of the twentieth century, Paterson experienced a period of economic growth. By 1900 Paterson was among the top five purely industrial cities in the nation. Its principal industries were cotton, locomotives, and silk. Paterson dominated the silk industry in the U.S. and became known as the "Silk City of the World." By the turn of the century, however, Paterson was experiencing economic difficulties, including the great silk strike of 1913. Paterson also failed to keep pace with developments in the textile field. In the process, the advantages of Paterson passed to other regions. The 1929 Depression marked the final demise of the silk and locomotive industries. Economic decline in Paterson continued in post-WWII era. A wide variety of manufacturing establishments in Paterson left for suburban locations. The development of shopping malls in surrounding suburbs also forced the closure or relocation of many downtown retailing operations. The economic and social impacts of economic decentralization in Paterson were significant. Among other things, it resulted in a high rate of unemployment, poverty, and urban decay. In 1970, Paterson ranked 47th among the nation's poorest cities, but by 1980 it was fourth among the nation's cities with populations of 100,000 or more. The poverty rate for Paterson (25.2%) was more than double the estimated national average of 12.5 percent.

Despite this economic history, Paterson's population has been relatively stable since the turn of the century. The relative population stability stands in stark contrast to trends in many other older central cities in New Jersey in particular and in the Northeast in general. Although the city's population has remained stable, the ethnic and racial characteristics of its residents have changed. Up until 1950, the white population represented 95 percent of the total population, but by 1990, this proportion had declined to 41 percent. Massive immigration from non-traditional sources, Latin America, Asia, and Africa contributed to this ethnic diversity. In 1990, fifty-six different ethnic groups were represented in Paterson. Figure 27.2 shows the spatial distribution of the foreign-born and native-American populations in Paterson. There is a heavy concentration of the foreign-born population in the inner city, with relatively small proportions in the fringe areas. The economic and social history of Paterson makes it an ideal urban setting for exploring issues regarding immigration and the economic status of immigrants. This is especially relevant given the view that increased immigration has contributed to a high rate of poverty in U.S. cities (Camarato, 2001).

FACTORS INFLUENCING THE ECONOMIC PERFORMANCE OF IMMIGRANTS

The economic performance of immigrants in the labor market has been well researched. In these studies, the economic difficulties experienced by many recent immigrants have been attributed to several factors including lack of qualifications and education, restructuring and the changing economic opportunities (Hicks and Nivin, 1996), and discrimination in the labor market (Reitz and Bretton, 1995).

Figure 27.1

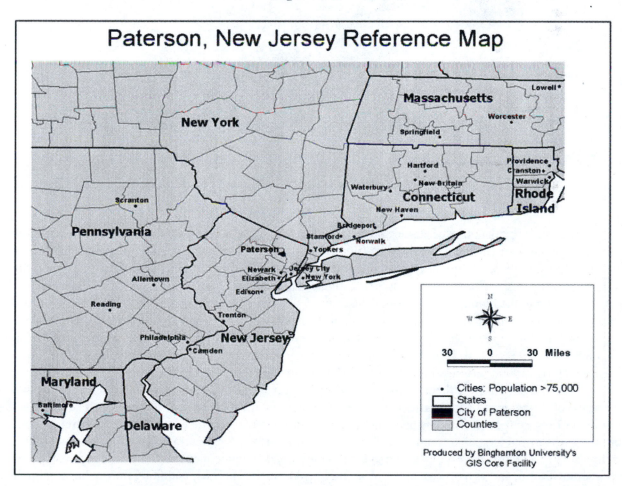

Figure 27.2

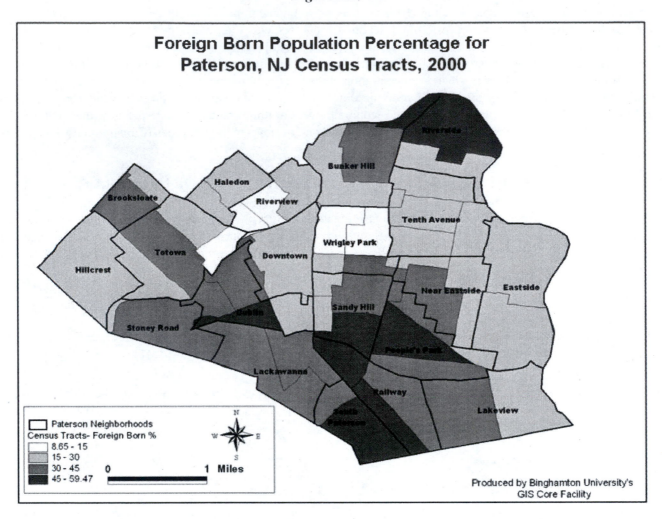

The primary explanation of ethnic and racial differences in economic status stems from theories of ethnic assimilation. In general, investigators using the assimilationist framework have tended to examine ethnic income and occupational inequality following the theory of human capital and status attainment. Scholars in this tradition view labor market outcomes as a function of individual human capital characteristics and resources (Singh and Kposowa, 1996). According to the human capital model, the primary determinants of a person's earnings are his or her investments in schooling, on-the-job training, and labor market experience (Singh and Kpsowa, 1996). The model tends to downplay ascribed individual characteristics such as race, color, sex, or national origin. In immigration research, frequently other variables such as duration of residence in the receiving country, English proficiency, and region of residence are included in the earnings models as controls (Borjas, 1994).

Tests of human capital theory, however, have generally found that human capital differences do not account for all of the observed income inequality between immigrants and the native-born population. Consequently, the interpretation of residual difference has been the subject of much debate. Some investigators interpret the residual as labor market discrimination, that is, unequal rates of income returns among individuals with equivalent backgrounds (Hirchman, 1978). Others have suggested that the remaining racial/ethnic inequality is due to differences in human capital, sociocultural, and psychological variables excluded from the analysis, including the quality of schooling, job performance, motivations, aspirations, ambition, hard work, and frugality (Sowell, 1981). The empirical support for this is however rather weak. In the following sections, the literature on some of the determinants of income is reviewed.

DETERMINANTS OF EMPLOYMENT INCOME

Educational Attainment

Immigrants are extremely diverse in terms of their education and skill levels; they include highly skilled persons as well as large numbers of poorly educated, low-skilled persons. Research shows that immigrants are more likely than natives to lack a high school diploma, and are also more likely than natives to have a college degree. As a result of the disparities in education, significant concentrations of immigrants are found in occupations that require both relatively high and relatively low levels of education. Also, some are recruited directly for well-paid professional and managerial positions.

Immigrant women often face additional burdens because of their gender (Boyd, 1992). Largely responsible for domestic work, immigrant women find that competing demands of home and paid work often restrict their job search to the local neighborhood. Marked by gender relations in their countries of origin, many immigrant women enter the American job market at a serious disadvantage because of limited education and training and restricted access to paid employment in their countries of origin (Gabaccia, 1992). Immigrant women also confront the same barriers to employment as native-born American women, including labor market segmentation that concentrates women in poorly paid secondary occupations.

English Language Proficiency

Language skills — the set of skills required to communicate with others in printed, written and verbal form — are among the most basic factors affecting performance in the labor market. Thus English language proficiency is a major determinant of economic progress for immigrants in the U.S. Indeed schooling and pre-immigration labor market experience may be of little, if any, value to an immigrant with no knowledge of the language of the destination country. Previous research has shown for several immigrant receiving countries that greater proficiency in the destination language enhances labor market earnings and that this investment provides a high rate of return (Chiswick and Miller, 1995). Greater proficiency in the destination language can enhance earnings by enabling immigrants to find a better labor market match between their skills and the requirement of employers. English language deficiency acts to depress the wages of immigrants substantially below what their other human capital endowments — education, and on the job experience — suggest they should earn in the American labor market.

Studies in Canada also show that immigrants who cannot conduct conversation in an official language and those who usually speak a non-official language at home, have earnings around 10 to 12 percent lower than immigrants who usually speak an official language at home, when other variables are the same (Chiswick and Miller, 2003). Although other studies have found significant effects of English proficiency on the economic condition of immigrants in the U.S. and Canada, the matter remains clouded in ambiguity. Surprisingly, some studies have not found a significant connection between English proficiency and economic performance among immigrants. One explanation is that some surveys, like the U.S. Census of Population, do ask individuals to specify qualitatively how well they speak/understand English, with responses such as very well, well, and not well. However, they ignore the importance of reading and writing. They are also based on subjective, self-reported assessments that can be subject to personal bias and are difficult to quantify. The lack of a clear relationship between language proficiency and income is also evident in the fact that Asian immigrants have the highest wages among all groups but their English proficiency levels are just slightly above the average for all immigrants. This can be partly explained by higher levels of education.

Occupational Concentration

Besides education and language, income disparity may also be explained in terms of the concentration of immigrants in certain occupations. It is known that immigrants, especially those in central cities, frequently live and work in communities dominated by co-ethnics, and may be isolated from the mainstream economy. Thus they may be concentrated in secondary and tertiary labor markets in which rewards for human capital tend to be relatively low. Waldinger argues that immigrant enclaves serve as economic launching pads for immigrant workers, creating opportunities for entrepreneurship and upward economic mobility. In addition, immigrant enclaves could reduce or elimi-nate the need for mastery of English (Waldinger, 1996). Basic economic theory, however, suggests that a system of enclaves could also restrict opportunities for immigrants. Excess supplies of immigrants in enclaves could produce "crowding" effects that drive down wages for immigrants (LaLonde and Topel, 1991). Evidence compiled by Wald-inger strongly suggests adverse effects of immigrant crowding on immigrant earnings within New York City enclaves. His analysis of earnings of workers shows that average earnings of immigrants working in ethnic enclaves are signifi-cantly lower than those of immigrants of the same group outside the enclave (Waldinger, 1996). Thus, it is possible that enclaves could simultaneously facilitate the integration of immigrants into the economy, and, as a result of crowd-ing, reduce immigrant earnings. That is, low earnings and rapid integration may co-exist in enclaves.

DATA SOURCES AND METHODOLOGY

Data for this study were drawn primarily from the U.S. Census Bureau's 1990 Public Use Micro Data Sam-ples (PUMS, 1 percent sample, New Jersey). PUMS 1 percent data contain records for a sample of housing units (in metropolitan areas in the U.S. with a population of at least 100,000), with information on the characteristics of each of the housing units and the persons within it, including educational attainment, ethnic origin, hours worked, type of in-come, and other relevant information. The Statistical Package for the Social Sciences (SPSS) is employed to analyze the data, using both univariate and multivariate statistics.

Given that the number of weeks worked in a year and whether the employment was part-time or full time have an obvious effect on the level of employment income reported, the analysis was limited to those who reported working mainly full-time and for 40 weeks or more in 1990. This approach has the advantage of eliminating immi-grants who had lived and worked in Paterson for only a short time in 1990, who may have experienced prolonged un-employment during the first year in the country. It also excluded all those who, whether on a voluntary or involuntary basis, were not employed for a large part of the year, together with those who were employed mainly part-time. In this way a better understanding could be gained concerning the determinants of employment income for most labor force participants and a fairer comparison made between groups.

ANALYSIS AND FINDINGS

Results of an independent-samples test indicate that there is a statistically significant difference ($p<0.01$) in the mean employment income of native-born Americans and the foreign-born population. The income of native-born Americans ($23,678) was 13 percent more than that of the foreign-born population ($20,493). The causes of this dis-parity are examined in the following sections.

Educational Attainment

Employment income is influenced by educational attainment. In general, those with a college degree earn sig-nificantly more than those with lower educational attainment. The proportion of the foreign-born without a high school diploma was higher (44%) than that of the native-born population (36%). At the same time, a higher propor-tion of native-born Americans had a high school diploma or some college education (51.3%) compared to (44.3%) of the foreign-born population. Furthermore, 12.4 percent of native-born Americans had completed a college education or more compared to 11.4 percent of the foreign-born population. However, these differences in educational attain-ment were not statistically significant ($p>0.05$). This means that the disparity in income between the native-born and the foreign-born is not caused by differences in educational attainment between the two groups. Disparities in income remain even after controlling for educational attainment (Table 27.1). For example, among those with college degree or higher, native-born Americans earned 15 percent more than their foreign-born counterparts. Obviously, the rewards for education are higher for native-born than for the foreign-born.

English Language Proficiency

The economic performance of immigrants in the U.S. depends in part on their English language proficiency. As expected, a high proportion of immigrants (40%) have no or limited proficiency in the English language, compared with 5 percent of the native-born. As Tables 27.2 and 27.3 show, immigrants with lower proficiency in English language, as well as those who speak a language other than English at home, have lower earnings than those who are more proficient in English and those who speak only English at home. Thus, while the educational attainment of immigrants is comparable to that of the native-born, their low English language proficiency may have served to limit the employment opportunities otherwise available to them, and led to their concentration in specific occupations, often low-skilled and low-paying.

Table 27.1

Educational attainment * Income * Birthplace				
Education	Place of Birth	Mean	N	Mean Difference
Less than High School Diploma				
	Born in the U.S.	$20,472	230	
	Foreign-Born	$17,478	140	$2994 (15% more)
	Total	$19,339	370	
High School Graduate / Some College				
	Born in the U.S.	$23,400	326	
	Foreign-Born	$21,366	140	$2034 (10% more)
	Total	$22,789	466	
College Graduate or more				
	Born in the U.S.	$34,157	79	
	Foreign-Born	$28,823	36	$5334 (16% more)
	Total	$32,487	115	
Total				
	Born in the U.S.	$23,678	635	
	Foreign-Born	$20,493	316	$3185 (13% more)
	Total	$22,619	951	
Total population		***$22,619***		
Native-born Americans		$23,678		
Foreign-born		$20,493		
Less than High School		$17,478		
High School / Some College		$21,366		
College Graduate or more		$28,823		

Source: Author's calculation

Industrial and Occupational Segregation

Given the variation in wages by industry and occupation, the incomes of immigrants may be explained in terms of their concentration in particular industries and occupations. In general, immigrants are over-represented in specific industries compared to the native-born, especially in manufacturing (41% vs. 29%), wholesale and retail (23% vs.16.4%), and construction (7% vs. 4.4%). In contrast, they are underrepresented in transportation and communications (4.7%), finance, insurance, and real estate (1.9%), and professional services (11.1%). Given comparable educational attainment, this occupational segregation may be attributed to their weak language skills, recency of their migration and, perhaps, the reliance on ethnic networks in the job search process. Immigrants are concentrated not only in specific industries but also in specific occupations (Table 27.4). Specifically, immigrants are heavily concentrated in low-skilled jobs, especially precision production and craft repair occupations (19.3%), operators, laborers, fabricators (25.6%), and also in service and transportation occupations compared to 13 percent, 17.7 percent and six percent of the native-born population, respectively. In contrast, they are under-represented in professional, managerial, and administrative support and clerical jobs.

Table 27.2

English Language Proficiency * Income			
Ability to speak English	Place of Birth	Mean	N
Speaks only English			
	Born in the U.S.	$24,691	452
	Foreign-Born	$22,012	38
	Total	$24,691	490
Very Well			
	Born in the U.S.	$23,007	87
	Foreign-Born	$21,217	75
	Total	$22,178	162
Well			
	Born in the U.S.	$20,295	60
	Foreign-Born	$21,823	96
	Total	$21,236	156
Not well			
	Born in the U.S.	$16,605	32
	Foreign-Born	$18,111	76
	Total	$17,665	108
Not at all			
	Born in the U.S.	$31,125	4
	Foreign-Born	$18,598	31
	Total	$20,003	35
Total			
	Born in the U.S.	$23,678	635
	Foreign-Born	$20,493	316
	Total	$22,619	951

Source: Author's calculation

Table 27.3

Language Other than English at Home * Income			
	Place of Birth	Mean	N
Yes, Speaks another Language at home			
	Born in the U.S.	$21,176	183
	Foreign-Born	$20,285	278
	Total	$20,639	461
No, Speaks only English at home			
	Born in the U.S.	$24,691	452
	Foreign-Born	$22,012	38
	Total	$24,483	490
Total			
	Born in the U.S.	$23,678	635
	Foreign-Born	$20,493	316
	Total	$22,619	951
Source: Author's calculation			

Table 27.4

Occupation * Birth Place				
Occupation	US-Born		Foreign-Born	
	Number	Percent	Number	Percent
Managerial/Professional	108	17.0	28	8.9
Technical/Admin Support	21	3.3	2	6.0
Sales Occupation	38	6.0	26	8.2
Admin Support/Clerical	130	20.5	25	7.9
Service Occupations	89	14.0	50	15.8
Farming/Forestry	5	0.8	1	0.3
Precision production, Craft Repair Occu	83	13.1	61	19.3
Operators, Fabricators, Laborers	74	17.7	81	25.6
Transportation/ Material Moving Occupations	87	13.7	42	13.3
Chi square=69.988; p<0.001; Phi=0.271				
Source: Author's calculation				

Table 27.5

Birthplace * Occupation * Income				
Occupation	Place of Birth	Mean	N	A-B
Managerial/Professional				
	Born in the U.S.	$29,274	108	$925 (3% more)
	Foreign-Born	$28,349	28	
	Total	$29,084	136	
Technical/Admin Support				
	Born in the U.S.	$24,128	21	$775 (3% more)
	Foreign-Born	$23,353	1	
	Total	$24,060	23	
Sales Occupation				
	Born in the U.S.	$30,688	38	$13625 (44% more)
	Foreign-Born	$17,063	26	
	Total	$25,153	64	
Admin Support/Clerical				
	Born in the U.S.	$21,377	130	$4468 (21% more)
	Foreign-Born	$16,909	25	
	Total	$20,657	155	
Service Occupations				
	Born in the U.S.	$16,892	89	-$2324 (12% less)
	Foreign-Born	$19,216	50	
	Total	$17,728	139	
Farming/Forestry				
	Born in the U.S.	$19,860	5	-$140 (1% less)
	Foreign-Born	$20,000	1	
	Total	$19,883	6	
Precision production, Craft Repair Occupations				
	Born in the U.S.	$28,048	83	$4481 (16% more)
	Foreign-Born	$23,567	61	
	Total	$26,148	144	
Operators, Fabricators, Laborers				
	Born in the U.S.	$20,622	74	-$174 (1% less)
	Foreign-Born	$20,796	81	
	Total	$20,713	155	
Transportation/Material Moving Occupations				
	Born in the U.S.	$22,592	87	$6734 (30% more)
	Foreign-Born	$15,858	42	
	Total	$20,399	129	
Total				
	Born in the U.S.	$23,678	635	$3185 (13% more)
	Foreign-Born	$20,493	316	
	Total	$22,619	951	

Source: Author's calculation

The income disparity remains even after controlling for occupation (Table 27.5). For every occupational category, except services and farming and forestry, the native-born population earned more than the foreign-born population.

Analysis also shows that a lower proportion of the foreign-born population (4%) is employed in the public sector compared to the native-born population (18%). This difference, which is statistically significant, has implications for the economic status of the two groups because public sector employees earned significantly more than those employed in the private sector. The employment income for a private company employee was $22,493 compared to $27,600 for a public sector employee. This under-representation of immigrants in the public sector may be due partly to the recency of immigration and weak language skills. It may also be due to the fact that American citizenship or permanent residence status are required for public sector employment. Thus, while many immigrants may possess the required education and training for these jobs, their immigration status would have prevented them from applying for these jobs.

Immigrants, however, are more likely to operate their own businesses compared to the native-born population (7.5% vs. 4.5%). This finding is consistent with those of previous studies regarding immigrant entrepreneurship. It has been suggested that language barriers and the desire to establish themselves in their new society may motivate immigrants to establish their own businesses. Interestingly, employment income is higher for those who are self-employed, suggesting that immigrants may significantly improve their economic situation through self-employment.

Duration of Residence

The income of immigrants often depends on their length of residence in the host country. In general, according to assimilation theory, as the length of residence increases, immigrants may improve their English, gain more work experience, and acquire additional education. These factors, acting individually or in combination, may increase the incomes of immigrants. A one-way between — groups analysis of variance was conducted to explore the relationship between period of immigration and income (Table 27.6a & 27.6b). At the > 0.05 level, the groups that are statistically different in terms of their mean incomes are the native-born Americans (M=$24, 522) and the most recent immigrant group (M=$18,297). Although the actual difference in mean score between the groups was quite small, the data provides support for the assimilation theory.

Table 27.6a

Period of Immigration * Income		
Period of Immigration	N	Income
Born in the U.S.	494	$24,522
1980–1990	156	$18,297
1970–1979	144	$22,251
1960–1969	114	$21,288
1950–1959	38	$20,760
Before 1950	5	$24,598
All Immigrants	316	$20,493
Total	951	$22,619

Source: Author's data

Table 27.6b

Year of Entry (I)	Year of Entry (J)	Mean Difference (I-J)	Sig
Born in the U.S.	1980–1990	6224.8539 *	.000
1970–1979		2271.2198	.513
1960–1969		3234.5418	.218
1950–1959		3761.7348	.592
Before 1950		-75.3704	1.000
*The mean difference is significant at the .05 level			
Source: Author's calculation			

Gender and Income

Employment income is also influenced by gender. For the population as a whole, males earned more than females ($24,695 vs. $18,990). Foreign-born males earned more ($21,738) than their female counterparts ($15,867). Indeed disparity in income was wider between foreign-born females and the U.S.-born population ($23,678) or the total population ($22,619). These findings suggest that foreign-born females face several constraints. They tend to have lower levels of schooling and lower English proficiency. Their domestic duties may also serve to limit the employment opportunities available to them.

Race and Income

Racial differences in income are shown in Table 27.7. Employment income was higher for whites ($25,031) than for blacks ($21,889) and "other race" ($19,641). Even among the foreign-born population, whites earned higher income ($22,053) than blacks ($19,175), and other race ($19,297). These differences may reflect racial differences in educational attainment. For example, 33 percent of whites had less than a high school diploma compared to 36 percent of blacks and 56 percent of other race. At the same time, 18 percent of whites had college degree or higher compared to seven percent of blacks and 10 percent of other race. The lower incomes of the foreign-born population may be related to their marital status. Specifically, immigrants who were divorced or separated earned considerably less ($15,694) than their married ($21,250) or single ($21,384) counterparts.

To determine the combined effect of several variables on income disparity, a logistic regression analyses was performed. The goal was to correctly predict the category of outcome (or group membership) for the individual cases, based on several predictor (independent) variables, namely education, occupation, English language proficiency, place of birth, occupation, race, gender, and marital status. Cases were classified into two groups, namely a low-income group and a high-income group, based on the median income: those who earned below the median income were classified as low income and those who earned above the median income were classified as high income. Each individual variable was able to correctly predict from 48 to 60 percent of group membership. Education, gender, race, marital status, and English language ability were all found to be statistically related to income (p<0.00). The model was able to correctly classify 67 percent of those in the low-income group and 64 percent of those in the high-income group, for an overall success rate of 65.5 percent. Clearly, these variables are not sufficient to completely account for the income disparity between the native-born and the foreign-born. This suggests that factors other than those discussed in this chapter, especially discrimination based on race, national origin, immigration status, and language ability, may have contributed to this disparity.

Table 27.7

Birthplace * Race * Income				
Race	Place of Birth	Mean	N	Difference
White				
	Born in the U.S.	$26,648	256	$4595 (17% more)
	Foreign-Born	$22,053	139	
	Total	$25,031	395	
Black				
	Born in the U.S.	$22,321	270	$3146 (14% more)
	Foreign-Born	$19,175	43	
	Total	$21,889	313	
Other Race				
	Born in the U.S.	$20,063	109	$766 (4% more)
	Foreign-Born	$19,297	134	
	Total	$19,641	243	
Total				
	Born in the U.S.	$23,678	635	$3185 (13% more)
	Foreign-Born	$20,493	316	
	Total	$22,619	951	
Total Foreign-Born				
	Foreign-Born White	$19,157		
	Foreign-Born Black	$22,053		
	Foreign-Born Other	$19,927		
Source: Author's calculation				

CONCLUSION

This chapter has examined income disparity between native-born Americans and the foreign-born population in the City of Paterson, and accounted for the observed disparity in terms of both human capital factors and personal characteristics. Analysis showed that native-born Americans have considerably higher incomes than the foreign-born population. Contrary to expectation, this income disparity is not due to differences in educational attainment. Analysis shows that the foreign-born and native-born populations have comparable educational attainment. At the very least, this suggests that the educational credentials of immigrants are not fully recognized. Thus the income disparity reflects differences in how human capital and its holders are differentially evaluated.

Income disparity is also related to English language proficiency. Many immigrants have low English language proficiency. This may have lowered the premium placed on their level of education, contributed to discrimination against them in the labor market, and to their concentration in specific occupations and ethnic enclaves where wages are relatively low. Also, relatively few immigrants are employed in the public sector, where incomes are relatively higher. While this may be due to low language skills, it may also reflect the fact that American permanent residency or citizenship is required for eligibility for such jobs. The analysis also revealed that race, gender, marital status, and duration of residence partly explain the income disparity between native-born Americans and the foreign-born population. Among the foreign-born population, blacks, females, divorcees, and new arrivals have lower incomes than whites, males, married, and long-term residents respectively.

The analysis of income disparity presented here has implications for immigration and immigrant integration policies. It may be argued that an immigration policy that screens immigrants by their official language skills would result in higher earnings among the foreign-born. Also, a policy that promotes investments in official language skills after migration and how these skills can be used in the labor market can enhance the value of the skills immigrants bring with them and hence their economic well-being (Chiswick and Miller, 2003). At the same time, the findings suggest that a high educational attainment and training do not necessarily translate into higher incomes for immigrants. Thus, it is equally important to make and implement policies that will remove various barriers in the labor market including discrimination based on place of origin, race, immigrant status, and gender.

While this study provides insights into the performance of immigrants in the labor market, the findings reported here cannot be generalized to the economic situation of all immigrants. Urban areas tend to differ in terms of the human capital and personal characteristics of their foreign-born populations. Comparative case studies of the economic performance of immigrants in different places will help contribute to our understanding of the diversity of the immigrant experience in the U.S. labor market.

Chapter 28

Changes in the Heartland:
Emerging Ethnic Patterns in Louisville, KY

WILLIAM DAKAN

INTRODUCTION — THE TRANSFORMATION OF LOUISVILLE

One of the pervasive characteristics of contemporary American society is the remarkable increase in international migration to large metropolitan areas. In general, the focus of current research is on these Gateway Cities. The extremely large size of immigrant streams to these cities, along with a few others, justifies these numerous studies. We are able to see the dynamics of immigration written on a large scale: high levels of segregation, contrasting levels of assimilation, the suburbanization of new communities, secondary settlements, the rise of an immigrant entrepreneur class and increasing political influence (Alba et al., 1999).

The emphasis on larger cities needs to be augmented by studies of smaller places including middle-sized and small-sized metropolitan areas, micropolitan areas, and selected rural sites where immigrants have had a significant impact. Louisville is one of those cities that is undergoing visible transformation, due to international migration. Migrants in Louisville are making their presence known in numerous ways.

The impact of immigrants in Louisville has profoundly affected the social and commercial life of that city. Louisville recently merged with its county to form a consolidated metro government and is now 16th in size among American cities. With the merger, there has been an increase in public discourse as to what "big city" status means in the way the local government operates and the issues that need to be addressed. Within this context, there is a heightened interest in the role the city plays in international affairs and the international economy. Some of the interest has been symbolic. The airport name was changed from Standiford Field to Louisville International Airport to acknowledge the presence of United Parcel System's major hub. The sense of a greater internationalization of the city was illustrated to me through an encounter at a local restaurant when I hosted a visitor from Montreal at a breakfast buffet. She piled a yellow substance on her plate and asked me what it was. I said that it was "grits" (a Southern dish consisting of boiled ground corn). The waitress, who overheard the exchange, replied "We're international now, they ain't grits, they's polenta." Polenta is an *Italian* dish consisting of boiled ground corn.

On a more serious note, the number of Sister Cities has tripled, there is an active international Visitor's Center and the metro mayor's office has a department dedicated to immigrant and refugee affairs. In addition, there are several religious and non-profit organizations devoted to the well-being of refugees. The school district has directed considerable resources toward the education of immigrant students. TARC, the local bus system, prints schedules in English, Russian, Spanish, Serbo-Croatian, Chinese, and Vietnamese.

This official welcome mat is of recent vintage. As a border-line Southern city, Louisville has had a mixed record in its attitude toward immigrant populations. In the 1800s, the Scot-Irish majority had established roots in the community. In the 1900 Census, Louisville had a higher percentage (approximately 4%) of foreign-born than all other Southern cities but that value was lower than all other Northern cities. In this context, the current immigrant community has had to create a presence without linkages to older, more established, communities of foreign-born. In larger cities, established second-generation immigrant communities provide new immigrants with a guide to residential choices, access to essential social services, and employment opportunities.

Many of the first new migrants were refugees, ranging from Bosnians to Somalian. More recently, free migrants from Mexico, Cuba, and Vietnam have enriched the area. Both private social service agencies and local government have responded to the influx by providing a broad range of social and acculturation services to an increasingly diverse population. In some areas of the county, there has been a significant change in the cultural landscape with new restaurants, churches (and foreign-language services in traditional settings) and a diverse range of goods in groceries in immigrant-intensive areas. This chapter will focus on the characteristics of the increasing international diversity within the broader community, but also on the marked diversity *within* the immigrant community. In particular, the differences in migration history, education, occupation, and economic impact on the community across the major foreign born groups will be stressed. Of special importance are the different trajectories each of the major groups takes as they strive to take their places within the middle class. In that respect, immigrants are similar to long-standing residents in their aspirations, locational choices and, ultimately, their contribution to the economic and social life of the community.

THE SCOPE OF IMMIGRANT SETTLEMENT

The PUMS Data Sources for Immigrant Analysis

For this study, the data from the Public Use Micro Samples (PUMS) is used to select and analyze immigration in Louisville. The PUMS data is collected on an individual and household basis with a 5 percent sample of all households. Each household in the sample is given a unique serial number and each individual in the household is assigned the same serial number as well as a sequence number (heads of households are assigned a 1). An additional code identifies the relationship of each individual to the householder. One of the characteristics of the PUMS files is that the data are not aggregated but are masked by their availability only at large spatial aggregations. Allen and Turner (1996) used the 1990 version of the PUMS files to effectively examine the patterns of immigration. Louisville is divided into five PUMS areas and the scale of spatial variation is relatively coarse. However, the choice of PUMS data, even with limited spatial specificity, permits a much more detailed comparison of the immigrant groups in the overall community.

General Immigrant Numbers, Distribution, and Arrival Dates

The numbers of immigrants, using the generally broad definition of foreign-born arrivals to the United States, is not always a clear-cut and simple enumeration. For example, the following tabulation (Table 28.1) is constructed by identifying the place of birth of foreign-born heads of households as well as the place of birth of all family members for a selected number of immigrant groups representing a strong majority of immigrants. As shown, there is a wide range of source regions (combined from smaller countries of origin) and countries. Important to the immigrant community in establishing roots in Louisville are the large number of second-generation family members as noted by the number born in the United States. The only serious anomaly in the table is the large number of "immigrants" from Western Europe. Due to the proximity of Fort Knox, immediately to the South of Louisville, a large number of West Europeans are dependent spouses of returned military personnel who were, themselves, born in the United States. Roseman (2002) has noted that the dispersal of some groups into scattered locations is due to the locations of universities (for Chinese, Koreans, and Asian Indians) and military bases (for Filipinos and Koreans). To that point, I would add the distribution of Germans is due to the deployment of a number of Fort Knox personnel to Germany. Louisville is also the home of the second largest university in Kentucky.

All of Jefferson County is divided into five PUMS sub-areas composed of census tracts. The West End (names have been supplied for identification purposes) is adjacent to the Central Business District and extends to the Ohio River on the West and North. It is comprised largely of tracts that were in the former City of Louisville and is the largest concentration of African-Americans. The East End is a moderate- to upper-middle class area that is also comprised of former city tracts. The East Suburbs sector, in its Northern part, is the most affluent part of the city and the area is the most rapidly growing. It is, for the most part, comprised of former county tracts. The Southside is a group of tracts of moderate and working class neighborhoods. The Southwest is quite similar to the Southside PUMS area and contains the Americana Apartments, which has evolved as a gateway community for new immigrants, especially Vietnamese and Hispanic. A common misconception locally is that, because there is a concentration of immigrants in the Southside, that it is the only place in which they are found in large numbers.

Table 28.1

Place of Birth		
Country or Region	Number	Percent
Mexico/Latin America	2590	5.99
India	2018	4.66
Cuba	1981	4.58
China	1519	3.51
Vietnam	1470	3.40
Bosnia	988	2.28
Korea	1269	2.93
Philippines	754	1.74
Japan	522	1.21
East Europe	1231	2.84
Mideast	1547	3.57
West Europe	4562	10.54
Other Foreign	4871	11.26
United States	17951	41.48
Total	43273	

Table 28.2

Year Entered the United States						
Country or Region	Born in US	1920–1969	1970–1989	1990–1993	1994–1995	1996–1998	1999–2000
Mexico/Latin America	35.5 %	0.5 %	3.8 %	8.6 %	7.5 %	26.7 %	17.4 %
India	17.5 %	9.4 %	11.5 %	8.8 %	10.5 %	24.0 %	18.3 %
Cuba	25.6 %	8.2 %	0.0 %	4.1 %	1.2 %	33.1 %	27.8 %
China	31.1 %	1.9 %	10.9 %	17.9 %	16.9 %	16.0 %	5.2 %
Vietnam	22.9 %	0.0 %	2.8 %	22.8 %	32.1 %	18.2 %	1.2 %
Bosnia	7.2 %	0.0 %	0.0 %	0.0 %	0.0 %	80.1 %	12.7 %
Korea	39.9 %	2.8 %	9.6 %	21.1 %	7.3 %	13.5 %	5.9 %
Philippines	34.6 %	18.0 %	11.6 %	4.6 %	2.3 %	15.0 %	13.9 %
Japan	52.4 %	15.2 %	11.6 %	2.0 %	1.3 %	13.1 %	4.3 %
East Europe	19.7 %	4.0 %	2.7 %	3.7 %	14.1 %	47.5 %	8.3 %
Mideast	39.5 %	3.1 %	16.8 %	0.0 %	3.1 %	27.9 %	9.7 %
West Europe	54.6 %	23.9 %	13.0 %	1.3 %	3.2 %	3.4 %	0.6 %

Figure 28.1 shows the relative distribution of the leading immigrant groups in Louisville by PUMS areas. Immigrants in Louisville, like their counterparts in many large gateway cities, have initially settled or found secondary locations in the suburbs. Each of the two largely "city" PUMS areas have approximately 12 percent of the total immigrant population. There are some significant exceptions such as Chinese and Mexicans in the West End as well as Koreans and Asian Indians in the East End. The largest concentrations of the majority of the twelve identified groups reside in the East Suburbs. Ample social service contact data and visible transition services exist at the Americana Apartments for Hispanics and Vietnamese to support a concentration in a small area in the Southwest. Similarly, Jewish Vocational Services support several resettlement programs in the East Suburbs.

Figure 28.1

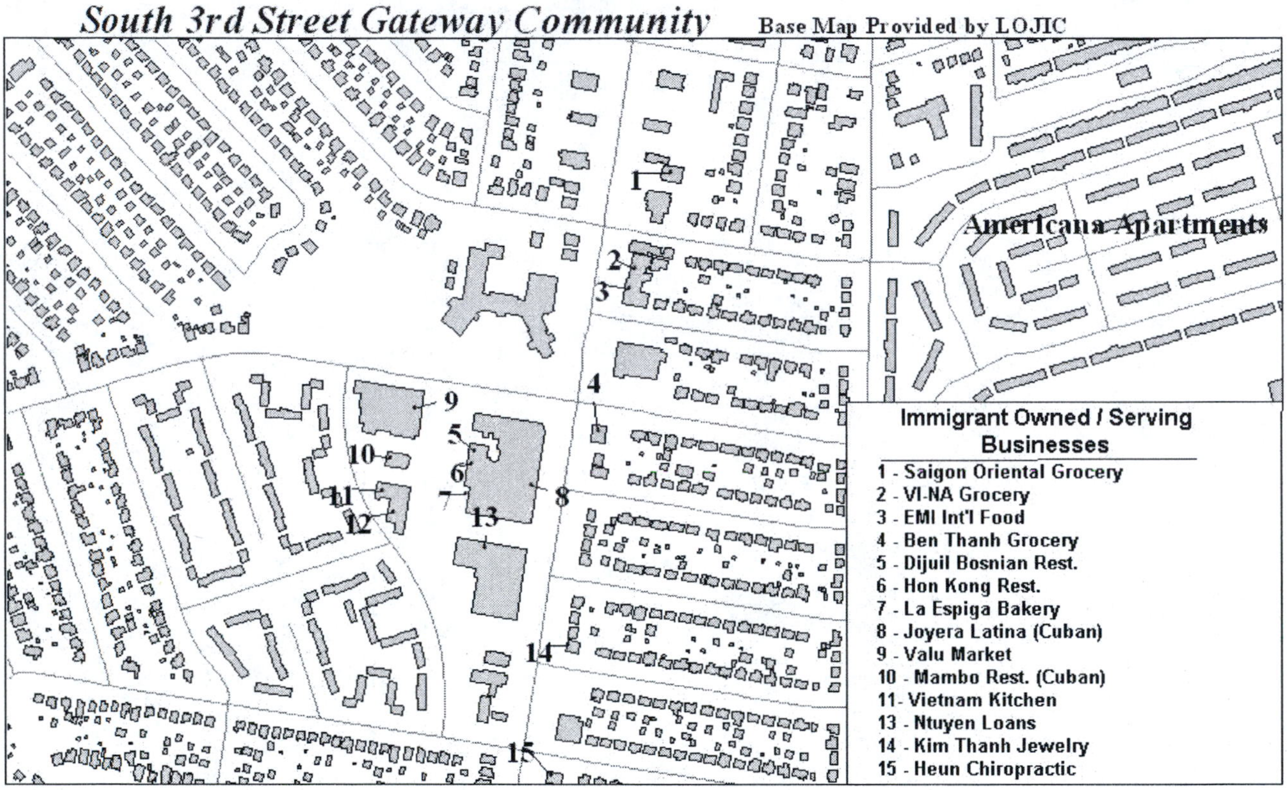

South 3rd Street Gateway Community   Base Map Provided by LOJIC

Immigrant Owned / Serving Businesses
1 - Saigon Oriental Grocery
2 - VI-NA Grocery
3 - EMI Int'l Food
4 - Ben Thanh Grocery
5 - Dijuil Bosnian Rest.
6 - Hon Kong Rest.
7 - La Espiga Bakery
8 - Joyera Latina (Cuban)
9 - Valu Market
10 - Mambo Rest. (Cuban)
11 - Vietnam Kitchen
13 - Ntuyen Loans
14 - Kim Thanh Jewelry
15 - Heun Chiropractic

Impact on the Visible Landscape

Although the area around the Americana Apartments, locally identified as South 3rd Street Corridor or Iroquois neighborhood, is not a gateway community for the majority of the immigrant population, it has a special significance as the most visible concentration of immigrants in the city. There is a serendipitous relationship in time and space as the Americana Apartments (Figure 28.2) evolved as a very low market rate and Section eight subsidized living area of considerable size just as the near by Iroquois Shopping Center went into decline. The introduction of an immigrant population into the area through the Americana Apartments and other complexes rejuvenated the shopping center and the strip of commercial buildings. In particular, Valumarket has opened up a broad line of foreign foods to satisfy the dietary needs of Asian Indians, Cubans, Mexicans, Vietnamese, and Chinese found in high numbers in the surrounding residences. Those who are not in the apartments occupy small-frame Cape Cod houses. The immigrant population has spurred the establishment of numerous ethnic-oriented and -owned businesses as shown in Figure 28.2. Other than signage, there is no visible alteration of the buildings from their prior uses.

Other than these and a few other concentrations in selected apartment clusters, there is scant evidence of developing sizable enclaves of individual immigrant groups.

Figure 28.2

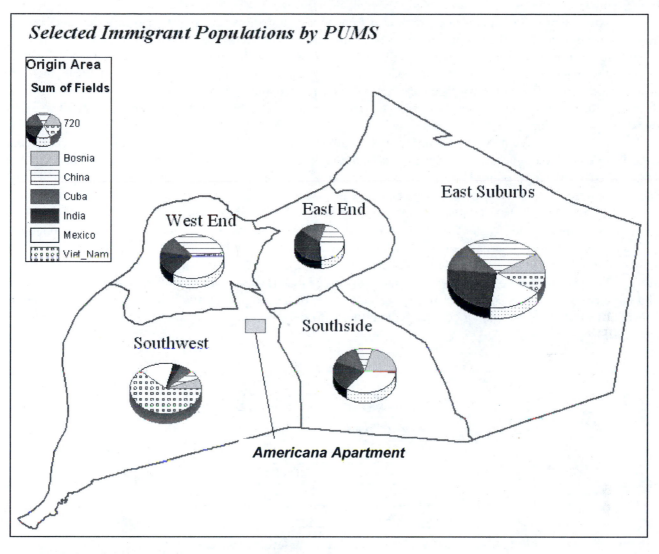

Diversity Within the Immigrant Community

Other that the obvious point that they come from different places, the immigrant groups are widely divergent in terms of time of entry, length of stay, educational levels, employment, and language isolation. These characteristics are interrelated and will be shown to have an influence on how groups strive toward middle-class status.

Table 28.2 depicts the number and percent of each group by the date each individual (weighted) entered the United States. PUMS data provide each year for date entered. The year categories are skewed to emphasize the dominance of recent years for most of the groups. For the most part, the "Born in the U.S." category consists of dependent children of immigrants. A small portion of migrants are born outside the U.S. but not in the country of origin of the householder or in other states, suggesting step-wise migration for the family unit.

The periods of concentration for the groups reflect national events in international migration and local conditions in Louisville. Several examples should be noted. A small percentage of Bosnians were born in the United States. This low number reflects the fact that most of the Bosnians arrived during and after the regime of ethnic cleansing in the former Yugoslavia. The Bosnians are recent arrivals and none entered the U.S. before

1996. A large number of Bosnians are young and have not yet begun to start families, so the number born in the U.S. is small.

The Japanese have the longest tenure in Louisville and their family structure shows that over half the household members have been born in the U.S. In the 1980s, Toyota opened a major auto assembly plant approximately sixty miles away from Louisville and the subsequent decade saw the introduction of suppliers, many with Japanese managers located in Louisville. In general, the Asian groups of Chinese, Korean, and Japanese have modal periods of entry in the early 1990s and prior periods. For all of the remaining groups, except for the Vietnamese, the modal period is 1996 to 1998. (1999 to 2000 is not a full two-year period). The overall impact of period of arrival is a little clearer in Table 28.3.

Table 28.3 presents the average age and length of time in the United States (duration) of each respondent. With some exceptions, the average ages are not too dissimilar. The critical variable in this table is duration. There are two distinct groups. The first consist of relatively long-time residents (duration > 18 years). The impact of the military as discussed by Roseman is evident in the relatively long duration of immigrants from places where the United States has stationed troops since the end of WWII. Theses places of origin include the Philippines, Korea, Japan, and Western Europe. Note that East Europeans have the highest average age, relative to their average duration. A large number of older Russian and Ukrainian Jewish settlers were reunited with their adult children living in the United States, particularly after the break-up of the former Soviet Union.

The youthfulness of the Mexican immigrants is due to a large number of single, young men who are part of a large labor pool in selected industries. A large number of them did not arrive from the gateways of Los Angeles but from local surrounding counties where most of the employment was in the agricultural industry (Dakan, 2005).

Table 28.3

Mean Age and Duration in the US		
Country or Region	Age	Duration
Mexico/Latin America	32.8	10.6
India	40.3	13.6
Cuba	42.2	8.6
China	42.3	14.3
Vietnam	38.6	11
Bosnia	35.7	2.9
Korea	44.3	16.4
Philippines	45.9	20.4
Japan	47.3	23.4
East Europe	51.1	18.3
Mideast	38.7	18.3
West Europe	56.4	30.8

SOCIAL AND ECONOMIC CHARACTERISTICS: MIDDLE CLASS STATUS

Language Ability

In addition to arriving in different periods and with differing motivations for settlement in Louisville, the immigrant population is very diverse in occupation, education, and English language ability. These social factors play an important role in what W. A. V. Clark has identified as a milestone in the assimilation of immigrants into American society, the arrival into the middle class (Clark, 2003). The method used to weigh the factors that affect entrance into the middle class in this chapter draw heavily from the seminal work by Clark.

One of the key elements in at least economic assimilation, if not cultural assimilation, is the ability of household to use English (Carliner, 2000). The PUMS data indicate that, in general, more than half of the immigrant households have some language ability. The Census categories report persons in households that speak English "very well," "well," or "some" (the lowest ability in the PUMS data is "not at all"). These definitions are somewhat broad, but the Census descriptions would place the minimum use of "some spoken English" as approximately the fluency of what most Americans would have in a foreign language after a year of freshman language instruction.

The language of instruction in most Asian-Indian schools is English, so it is not surprising that their skills are substantial in this area. Similarly, many European educational systems teach English as a second language. It is likely that there is a generational gap in language ability. Language ability is not presented by age groups, but it is clear that in a large number of households that, particularly among recent Asian immigrants, children are the principal interpreters for the household. Although I did not produce the table of school attendance, almost all of the immigrant children of school age are enrolled in local schools. Many are in college or community college.

Educational Attainment and Professional Employment

The greatest internal diversity among immigrant heads of households (Table 28.4 and subsequent tables were tabulated strictly for the approximately 10,000 immigrants identified as head of household as the household is the principal economic unit and the economic status of that unit is dependent on the major earner) lies in the highest educational level attained. This table tells a story of highly divergent trajectories as each group prepares for and participates in the economy. It is clear that within group diversity of educational attainment is high, but not nearly as high as the diversity across groups.

The Mexican and Latin American populations are faced with a plurality in the lowest level of educational attainment and decline in proportion with successively higher levels of education. There are no Hispanics in the PUMS sample with post-baccalaureate degrees. Vietnamese and Bosnians have similar low levels in the graduate school ranks, yet Bosnians recorded no immigrants with less than some high school and most had a high school diploma. The Vietnamese (23.04%) were second to the Hispanics (35.58%) in inability to rise above the 8th grade, followed by the Japanese (15.25%). However, over a quarter of the Japanese graduated from college.

The Asian Indians, Chinese, and Koreans had the overall highest levels of education. Fully one-third of the Chinese heads of households held professional degrees or doctorates. The Ph.D. was also common among the Asian Indians and the Koreans. The rates of higher educational attainment for these groups far surpass that of the resident population, native or immigrant, in Metro Louisville. These levels of attainment and professional accomplishment identify the individuals with such achievement as "globalized professionals" (Poulson, 2002), who would be comfortable in a number of cities linked to the global economy (see Table 28.5).

The preceding table confirms the wide range of personal attainment within the immigrant community. These occupational categories include those that require credentials generally beyond that which can be earned by a bachelor's degree only. The type of professional occupation differs across the various groups but includes accountants, clergy, lawyers, medical doctors, scientists, dentists and college professors. Immigrants from India and China clearly have relatively high concentrations in the professions which exceed the rates for the general population. East Asian Indians are more likely to be physicians than those from China, who, in turn, are more likely to be college professors. If managers were added to the list, we would see an increase in both Hispanics and Koreans, but in different types of establishments. Because of the very high concentrations in the groups noted above, immigrants overall exceed professional employment by a substantial margin over the native-born population.

Table 28.4

Highest Grade Attained (percent)									
Country	8th Grade	12th No Grad	HS graduate	Some college	BA/BS	Masters	Professional	PhD	Total
Mexico/LA	35.58	31.32	15.25	13.74	4.12	0.00	0.00	0.00	100
India	2.39	5.05	7.80	2.39	37.41	21.81	5.59	17.55	100
Cuba	8.84	30.87	16.38	12.17	14.64	0.43	15.65	1.01	100
China	2.08	5.65	15.45	6.84	17.68	18.57	15.30	18.42	100
Vietnam	23.04	22.30	32.84	4.17	15.20	2.45	0.00	0.00	100
Bosnia	0.00	6.89	71.68	0.00	17.09	4.34	0.00	0.00	100
Korea	0.00	24.35	39.64	6.99	11.14	4.15	0.78	12.95	100
Phillipines	0.00	4.20	23.10	28.08	37.01	2.62	4.99	0.00	100
Japan	15.25	0.00	0.00	53.11	24.29	7.34	0.00	0.00	100
East Europe	0.00	0.00	16.00	35.22	13.46	18.24	7.22	9.85	100
Mideast	2.39	9.42	17.17	34.64	17.25	12.75	5.22	1.16	100
West Europe	7.23	11.32	21.56	20.48	15.97	10.94	7.37	5.12	100
Total	7.21	12.11	21.39	18.47	18.69	10.16	5.97	5.99	100

Table 28.5

Percent Professional Employment	
Mexico/Latin America	7.42
India	76.60
Cuba	6.38
China	61.07
Vietnam	19.36
Bosnia	7.65
Korea	27.20
Philippines	35.43
Japan	41.81
East Europe	39.80
Mideast	23.04
West Europe	34.43
Total	33.25

Table 28.6
Regression Results Related to Middle-Class Status

Odds Ratios							
Variable	Total	Mexico/LA	India	Cuba	China	Vietnam	Bosnia
Professional	1.00	5.44	0.22	7.23	2.90	2.96	4.11
Duration	2.07	0.74	7.86	1.15	18.05	1.80	4.05
Workers	0.31	3.42	0.24	4.50	0.25	0.25	2.64
Education	1.08	2.45	0.74	2.39	0.75	0.75	1.06
Language Access	1.52	29.21	2.13	1.80	9.79	1.91	1.71
Age	1.04	1.19	0.98	5.50	0.97	0.97	1.79
Variable	Korea	Philippines	Japan	East Europe	Mid East	West Europe	
Professional	3.25	14.37	3.75	4.63	0.50	1.04	
Duration	3.30	0.66	8.50	7.02	1.32	1.17	
Workers	0.23	11.07	0.89	0.01	0.40	0.21	
Education	0.91	0.27	0.78	1.77	1.40	1.00	
Language Access	9.77	0.23	1.97	2.88	0.33	2.26	
Age	5.47	1.48	1.66	1.47	1.08	1.03	

The Emergence of a Middle Class

Setting aside the issue of cultural assimilation, Clark notes that the hallmark of economic assimilation is the arrival of immigrants into the middle class. Using the same techniques as Clark, but with slightly altered variables (Dakan, 2004a), the impacts of the social characteristics noted above on entry into the middle class are measured. The middle class is defined as those households earning at least twice the poverty level but less than four times the poverty level and also own a home. The following variables were used to calculate the odds ratios for each of the groups presented in this chapter.

Variable Selection

Middle Class — binomial dependent variable based on income *and* home ownership
Professional employment — binomial value for head of household (1 = professional)
Two-worker household — binomial (1 = more than one working)
Language isolation — binomial (1 = not isolated)
Educational attainment — multinomial with 8 categories
Age — interval — chronological age
Duration — length of time living in U.S.

Table 28.6 shows the results of a logistic regression of these variables on middle-class status. The odds ratio has a relatively simple interpretation and it should be noted that the ratios are calculated holding all other variables constant for each group. An odd ratio of 2.00 for a variable for a particular immigrant group indicates that a high value in the independent variable doubles the chances of a member of that group achieving middle-class status. Similarly, and odds ratio of 3.00 triples the chances of attaining middle class status.

As with every other characteristic, there is diversity across all of the groups in the trajectories that impel or block their entry into the middle class. One of the relative constants across all groups is the positive impact of duration, suggesting that middle class status is, in many cases, just a matter of time. For all migrants combined, duration is twice as predictive of middle-class status as most of the other variables and language access is also extremely important. Language is a major barrier for Mexicans, Chinese, and Koreans. Surprisingly, educational levels are not quite as important for some groups when holding the other factors constant. Like many middle-class Americans, having two (or more) workers in the household was particularly important for the later arriving groups such as Mexicans, Cubans, and Bosnians. Filipinos were especially affected by the presence of an additional worker in the household. More recent arrivals from the Philippines do not appear to be in large households or connected to the military. As one-person households, they seem to be unable to acquire the assets for moving into the middle class.

ECONOMIC ACTIVITY AND THE CULTURAL LANDSCAPE

In spite of the diversity across occupations and the broader community, the relative small and growing number of immigrants is spread so thinly throughout the community that the impact on the cultural landscape is marginal as yet. The major exception is found in the increasing number of immigrant-owned or -operated businesses throughout the community. Most striking of these, because of their broad appeal to native residents and immigrants alike, is the very impressive increase in ethnic restaurants. Since 1995, over 100 new eating places with ethnic origins have been established. The cuisine includes Mexican (most regions in Mexico are represented), Vietnamese, Cuban, Chinese, Thai, Uzbek, Armenian, Bosnian, Middle Eastern of various sorts, Greek, African, and Latino.

The commercial impact of immigrants is heightened by the concentration of certain groups in niche economies where there is often a near monopoly in commonly found business types. Without going into the details of acquiring the data (Dakan, 2004b), the last names of selected ethnic groups (www.pedom.com, 2004) were identified and matched against a roster of business owners' or managers' last names. Table 28.7 identifies the results in terms of the concentration of selected groups in certain niche business clusters.

The identification of broad ethnic background (immigrants and native-born cannot be separated) indicates the diversity of niche development among the groups identified here. Hispanics manage almost half of the construction businesses, most of which are roofing contractors. Motels are the purview of the Asian-Indian population, as is common across the United States. Nail care is dominated by the Vietnamese and most of the owner-managers are women. Dry cleaners and alterations are done by Koreans. This sort of specialization can even break down into sub-categories. Asian Indians own eleven restaurants, eight of which are all of the Subway sandwich shops in the city.

CONCLUSIONS

Immigrants to Louisville are anything but a monolithic group. They are as diverse in origin as they are in residential location, educational levels, occupations, and contributions to the cultural and commercial vitality of the community. They are an essential part of the growth of the community, accounting for half of the population increase in Louisville for the past decade. Because of local leadership in metro government, the schools, the University of Louisville and other local colleges, and social service agencies, the community is undergoing a palatable change from aversion to tolerance to increasing support for immigrants within the community.

Table 28.7
Business Type and Ethnic Origin

Business Type		Korean	Chinese	Hispanic	Asian Indian	Vietnamese	Arabic
		Origin Group					
Construction	Count	3	2	7	0	1	2
	%	20.00	13.33	46.67	0.00	6.67	13.33
Wholesale-Retail	Count	21	6	12	2	7	7
	%	38.18	10.91	21.82	3.64	12.73	12.73
Grocery	Count	1	0	3	0	3	3
	%	10.00	0.00	30.00	0.00	30.00	30.00
Convenient	Count	1	1	1	3	0	3
	%	11.11	11.11	11.11	33.33	0.00	33.33
Professional	Count	4	2	8	4	4	20
	%	9.52	4.76	19.05	9.52	9.52	47.62
MD/Dentist	Count	4	3	7	14	2	24
	%	7.41	5.56	12.96	25.93	3.70	44.44
Motel	Count	0	1	0	8	0	1
	%	0.00	10.00	0.00	80.00	0.00	10.00
Restaurant/Fast Food	Count	6	33	12	11	10	2
	%	8.11	44.59	16.22	14.86	13.51	2.70
Beauty/Nails	Count	0	7	1	0	67	1
	%	0.00	9.21	1.32	0.00	88.16	1.32
Dry Cleaning/Alterations	Count	10	2	0	0	2	0
	%	71.43	14.29	0.00	0.00	14.29	0.00
Total	Count	50	57	51	42	96	63
	%	13.93	15.88	14.21	11.70	26.74	17.55

Chapter 29

Racial/Ethnic Disparities in Health and Health Care in the U.S.:
A Geographic Overview

FLORENCE M. MARGAI

INTRODUCTION

Recent research efforts to document the nature and scope of health disparities have focused on various segments of the U.S. population by race/ethnicity, gender, socio-economic status, language proficiency and geography (Geronimus, 2000; Liao et al., 2004; Kawachi et al., 2005; Moy et al., 2005; and Frist, 2005). By far, the most persistent inequities with potentially ominous consequences for the health of the nation as a whole are those based on the racial/ethnic profile of the population (Carter-Pokras and Woo, 1999; Kingston and Nickens, 2000). Minority groups, who, as we know, already face major economic and social disadvantages, encounter even greater challenges when it comes to their health status. When compared to the white majority, these groups, especially blacks, Latinos and Native Americans, face more chronic health conditions, greater risk factors, inequitable access to health care resources, and limited utilization of these services. Previous attempts to explain these disparities have focused on traditional biomedical factors such as genetic susceptibility and the personal responsibility of individuals including their behavioral, nutritional and occupational characteristics. However, it is increasingly apparent that the evaluation of these individual characteristics alone cannot fully explain the observed trends in racial and ethnic disparities (Kingston and Nickens, 2000). Rather, attempts to address these complex disparities must take place within a broader context to include the settlement geography of these groups, their immigration and generation histories, levels of acculturation and assimilation into the U.S. society, the institutional policies that impact their communities, including land use and zoning regulations, housing discrimination and neighborhood segregation patterns, and the negative impacts of environmental exposures to pollution.

The purpose of this chapter is to describe the patterns of health inequalities among the major racial and ethnic minorities in the United States: African Americans, Latinos, Native Americans, and Asian Americans. These issues are addressed within a geographical context to illustrate the sociospatial experiences and health outcomes that are unique to each of these groups. An effort will also be made to document the key determinants, pathways, and mechanisms that account for these disparities, and outline some of the intervention strategies that are now being pursued by governmental agencies to promote health parity.

HEALTH DISPARITIES AND INEQUITIES BY RACE, CLASS AND PLACE

Central to the analysis of race-based differences in health are two keywords, health disparities and health inequities, which are used interchangeably in the literature yet have different implications for health policy. From a broad perspective, the term **health disparities** can be defined as the disproportionate burden of disease and disability between specific population groups and the rest of the population in the United States. But various agencies and researchers have portrayed it differently in the literature, some focusing on the disparate outcomes and others highlighting the underlying causes. For example, the U.S. Health Resources and Services Administration (HRSA, 2000) described health disparities as population-specific differences in the presence of disease, health outcomes or access to health care. The Institute of Medicine characterized disparities as differences that remain after accounting for patient's needs, preferences, and availability of health care (Smedley et al., 2002). Others have described disparities as adverse health outcomes that result from personal responsibility, provider prejudices, and a complex mixture of systemic quality and access problems coupled with historical injuries (Frist, 2005; Moy et al., 2005). Throughout this chapter, we will adopt a three-pronged approach that blends these multiple perspectives through the description of differential health *outcomes*, the underlying *causes* and systemic factors that account for these patterns, and the *responses* that are currently being implemented to redress the problems. Hence our discussion will place more emphasis on the term **health inequities** to enable us to focus on all three areas. Specifically, the use of the term, health inequities will remind us that the differential outcomes in health are not only inequitable and morally unacceptable, they also require immediate governmental response. The root causes of these disparities must be acknowledged including the contrasts between the majority and minority groups and the socioeconomic advantage that one group continues to have over the others. We follow the path of Gatrell (2002), who argues that greater emphasis be placed on health inequities since health disparities are inevitable in any population whether they are spatially-based, temporal in nature, or based on some other dimension. He contends, and rightly so, that:

> "... what really matters and what 'inequity' implies is the fact that these differentials may be avoidable, and should be capable of being narrowed; their existence is, in a sense, unethical" (Gatrell, 2002, p. 91).

Racial health inequities are not only unethical they are indeed complex, pervasive, and persistent. The disparities cut across *all health domains* including morbidity and mortality rates, major risk factors, health access and utilization, and overall health status. There are significant racial and ethnic differences among *all forms of disease* including emerging and re-emerging infectious diseases such as tuberculosis and HIV/AIDs, environmental diseases such as lead poisoning and pesticide exposures, developmental diseases such as learning disabilities and birth defects, neoplastic diseases such as liver and prostrate cancer, and nutritional conditions such as hypertension and obesity. These disparities also cut across *all age groups*, literally, from cradle to grave. For example, black infants are two to three times more likely to die before their first birthday than white infants. Likewise, Hispanic children especially from migrant farm households face higher rates of morbidity and mortality as a result of increased exposure to farming and industrial pollutants than non-Hispanic children. These differences in survival rates extend well beyond infancy and childhood to all stages of life, the most glaring patterns evident among adults with chronic degenerative diseases.

Health inequities among the different racial and ethnic groups also have an element of *place*. Specifically, the health status of each group is largely a function of their settlement geography (metropolitan vs. non-metropolitan; segregated vs. non-segregated), the institutional and zoning practices, housing quality and neighborhood environmental conditions. These negative spatial dimensions of health are perhaps best witnessed in the urbanized areas where blacks, for example, face serious risks of disease and mortality. In the words of Galea and others (2004):

> "... the urban environment influences every aspect of health and well-being; what people eat, the air they breathe, and the water they drink, where (or if) they work, the housing that shelters them, their sex partners and family arrangements, where they go for health care, the dangers they encounter on the street, and who (if any) is available for emotional and financial support" (p. 1018).

Characterizing these impacts as the *urban health penalty* many studies have shown that minority groups in these areas have excessively high rates of adverse health outcomes such as tuberculosis, sexually transmitted diseases, HIV/AIDS, asthma, homicides, and infant mortality. These health risks are heightened further by zoning laws and policies that fail to protect the disadvantaged groups. In examining the relationships between urban land use policies, equity and public health, Mantaay (2001), for example, concluded that zoning in New York City was clearly not a benign or neutral process. Rather, the decisions regarding the location of industrial land uses and noxious facilities often had racial and class implications that resulted in a significantly greater percentage of poor and minority people in high-risk neighborhoods. Acknowledging these locational disadvantages and the need to mitigate the negative influences on minority health, Geronimus (2000) concluded therefore that all

> "… attempts to understand and to reverse the growing health inequalities will be partial without considerations of the socioeconomic factors and even more critical, the historical and structural factors that have produced modern ghettoes in central cities with predominantly minority populations. About 80 percent of the residents in high-poverty urban areas in the U.S. are minority and this figure is over 90 percent in the largest metropolitan areas" (p. 867).

Yet, the analyses and interpretation of these varied historical contexts and structural determinants of health have been problematic and in some instances suppressed by ideological and political interpretations that blame these disparities on biological differences in group susceptibility to disease. Kawachi et al. (2005), in their discussion of the obstacles hindering such analyses, identified three major causal interpretations of racial disparities in health:

i)   *Race as a Biology*;
ii) *Race as a proxy for Class*; and
iii) *Race and Class as Separate Constructs*.

Using *race as biology* for explaining health disparities has been based, historically, on the misconception that some groups are innately inferior to whites and therefore more susceptible to disease and disability. For example, historically, physicians purported that blacks had unique physiological features such as small brains that made them intellectually inferior, or had thick skins that resulted in a high tolerance for the sun, heat and pain. These formulations of biological determinism not only rationalized the continued use of blacks as slaves but also justified their use as subjects in federally sponsored research projects such as the Tuskegee syphilis study.

Even though the biological construction of race has been refuted many times over, there are still traces of evidence pointing toward the ongoing mistreatment of blacks and other minorities in the health care system based on the false pretenses of "genetics." As recently reported, "the genetic explanation for ethnic differentials in social position and health persists despite a considerable lack of evidence, and more than 100 years of research evidence exposing the limitations of such assumptions" (Karlsen and Nazroo, 2002, p. 624).

Examples of research efforts to identify race-based genetic susceptibility to diseases are rampant and so too are reports of discrimination in health care settings. For example, in a survey of roughly 3,900 residents in Kings County, Washington, investigators found that one in six blacks had experienced discrimination in the health care facilities. In a follow-up survey that involved more detailed interviews of 51 educated and insured African Americans, many confirmed episodes of discrimination. Their experiences ranged from reports of rude behavior and racial slurs by health care workers, to instances of personnel reluctance to distribute pain medication based on the notion that the patients' generational history of slavery increased their tolerance for pain. As a result of these experiences, many minority patients reported changing their health seeking behaviors such as delaying medical treatment or avoiding these institutions altogether. Similar conclusions were drawn in another study that reported negative health consequences as a result of experiences of interpersonal racism and perceptions of racism in the wider society (Karlsen and Nazroo, 2002).

In examining the second causal interpretation of racial disparities in health, *Race as a proxy for Class*, Kawachi et al. (2005), characterized this perspective as one in which race is often used as a substitute construct for class. This perspective, they contend, is driven by the strong empirical correlation between minority status and low socio-economic status (SES) of residents in the United States. Specifically, minority groups are over-represented among low income and disadvantaged groups, and in the absence of data on income, researchers are likely to use race as a proxy in evaluating and explaining health disparities. Kawachi et al. (2005), argue, and correctly so, that this perspective is not only misguided, it is at best a very rough proxy, and from a statistical viewpoint, could lead to the over-controlling of the causal effect of race on health. Other researchers have arrived at similar conclusions noting that race and SES are two separate constructs, and that race remains a significant determinant of health even after controlling for the SES of individuals (Carter-Pokras and Woo, 1999; Williams, 1997).

The consensus among many researchers is to use the third causal perspective which involves the use of *race and class as separate constructs* for explaining racial disparities in health. One of the strongest advocates of this approach is David Williams, who argues for a more deliberate and thoughtful examination of the role of race. In 1997, he proposed a causal framework for studying racial/ethnic differences in health. Figure 29.1 shows a modified version of this framework that includes the basic causes of health (culture, biology, geography, economic, political and legal structures), which impact social and occupational status of individuals. These in turn produce surface causes such as the evolution of disadvantaged neighborhoods, stressful conditions, and poor health practices in those areas. Eventually, these preceding factors take a toll on the human biological processes (such as the endocrine, neurological, immune systems), resulting in poor health outcomes. The original model has been modified further in this chapter to elucidate the importance of geography, beyond the nativity and origin of individuals, to include housing, settlement patterns, and poor environmental conditions that impact the health of residents in minority neighborhoods.

Figure 29.1

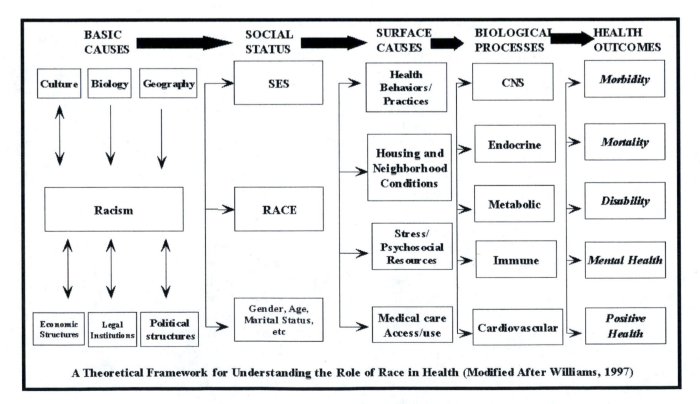

A Theoretical Framework for Understanding the Role of Race in Health (Modified After Williams, 1997)

Acknowledging these factors as the fundamental causes of racial health disparities, the next section will discuss the major health concerns facing each of the minority groups in their communities across the United States. We will examine the health outcomes and key indicators of disparity between each group and the dominant white majority. This will be followed by a discussion of the policy implications for the U.S. population as a whole. Given the wide-ranging scope of this topic, and the need to target the material to the undergraduate audience, the discussion will be descriptive for the most part, but supplemented with data from federal and state health agencies. Case studies, including detailed accounts of specific health outcomes are found in the articles that are cited throughout the chapter.

OVERVIEW OF HEALTH CONCERNS IN MINORITY COMMUNITIES

Health Concerns in Black Communities

As of the 2000 census, Black Americans constitute 13 percent of the U.S. population (roughly 34.5 million people). Several articles, including those documented in this book, have articulated the settlement history and emerging patterns of blacks in the 21st century (Jargowsky, 1997; Geronimus, 2000; and Tettey-Fio, 2003). It is important to note, however, that despite high rates of migration to northern states in the early 1900s and the sequential development of black enclaves in urban settlements across the country, roughly 55 percent of all blacks continue to reside in the South and recent trends in reverse migration point toward even greater numbers in the future. Settlement patterns also continue to point toward highly urbanized characteristics of the group. Nearly 52 percent of all blacks live in the central city of metropolitan areas (U.S. Census Bureau, 2000). Further, based on the five notable dimensions of segregation (clustering, dissimilarity, isolation, centralization, and concentration), blacks are the only group to have experienced the full impact of hypersegregation in the U.S. as well as more endemic levels of discrimination (Acevedo-Garcia et al., 2003; Polednak, 1996).

The spatial attributes of blacks, being urban and hypersegregated in environmentally and socioeconomically stressed neighborhoods, exact a heavy toll on their health status, resulting in a stiff urban health penalty. The long term impacts are best captured in the *weathering hypothesis,* in which Geronimus (1992) proposed to show that early and continued exposure of blacks to systemic and structural disadvantages such as segregation, material hardship, psycho-social conditions of acute and chronic stress, overburdened or disrupted social supports, and toxic environmental exposures often result in cumulative health outcomes.

An examination of the aggregate measures of mortality (Table 29.1) shows that the top three leading causes of death among blacks are chronic health conditions: heart disease, cancer, and cerebrovascular diseases. The diseases account for almost 60 percent of all deaths among blacks. Even though these three conditions are similar to those found among whites (Table 29.1), further evaluation using age-adjusted, cause-specific statistics shows that far more blacks die of these diseases than whites. For example, the death rate from coronary heart disease among blacks is 186.6 per 100,000, as compared to only 125.6 per 100,000 for whites. The incidence rate for cancer, the second leading cause of death, is 10 percent higher, and the death rate 35 percent higher among blacks than whites. There are also specific cancers that afflict blacks more than any of the other groups. Of particular concern is lung cancer, which is the leading cause of cancer deaths among black men and women. The risk of developing lung cancer is 50 percent higher among black men and they are more likely to die of the disease than do white men. Prostrate cancer also remains a major health concern among black men who are twice more likely to be diagnosed than white men. Among African-American women, breast cancer is the common cancer risk, as with women in other racial/ethnic groups. However, even though the incidence rate of breast cancer is slightly lower for African-American women, they are more likely to die of the disease than white women. In general, the survival rates of most of these cancers among black men and women are poor. Five years after diagnosis of cancer, the survival rates are significantly lower for blacks (44%) than for whites (60%).

Table 29.1

Leading Causes of Deaths Among the U.S. Racial and Ethnic Groups (Both Sexes, All Ages)				
Rank	**Whites** (Non Hispanic)	**Blacks** (Non Hispanic)	**Latinos**	**Asian Americans and Pacific Islanders (AAPIs)**	**American Indians/ Alaskan Natives (AI/ANs)**
1	Heart Disease(29.2)	Heart Disease (26.8)	Heart Disease (23.8)	Cancer (26.1)	Heart Disease (19.9)
2	Cancer (23.1)	Cancer (21.6)	Cancer (19.8)	Heart Disease (26.0)	Cancer (17.5)
3	Cerebrovascular Disease/ Stroke (6.7)	Cerebrovascular Disease/ Stroke (6.5)	Accidents (8.6%)	Cerebrovascular Disease/ Stroke (9.2)	Accidents (12.0)
4	Respiratory Disease(5.7)	Diabetes (4.4)	Cerebrovascular Disease/ Stroke (5.5)	Accidents (4.9)	Diabetes (6.0)
5	Accidents (4.1)	Accidents (4.3)	Diabetes (5.0)	Diabetes (3.5)	Cerebrovascular Disease/ Stroke (4.6)
6	Influenza and Pneumonia (2.8)	Homicides (2.8)	Chronic Liver Disease (2.9)	Pneumonia and Influenza (3.1)	Chronic Liver Disease (4.4)
7	Alzheimer's Disease (2.7)	Respiratory Disease(2.7)	Homicides (2.7)	Respiratory Disease (3.0)	Respiratory Disease(3.6)
8	Diabetes (2.6)	HIV/AIDS (2.7)	Respiratory Disease (2.6)	Suicide (1.7)	Suicide (2.6)
9	Nephritis, Nephrotic syndrome (1.5)	Nephritis, Nephrotic syndrome (2.6)	Pneumonia and Influenza (2.4)	Nephritis, Nephrotic syndrome (1.7)	Pneumonia and Influenza (2.4)
10	Suicide (1.3)	Septicemia (2.1)	Birth Defects (2.1)	Septicemia (1.1)	Homicides (2.2)
	All other causes/ Residual (20.2)	All other causes/ Residual (23.5)	All other causes/ Residual (24.6)	All other causes/ Residual (19.7)	All other causes/ Residual (24.9)

Numbers in parentheses denote percentage of total deaths.
Source: Anderson, R.N and B.L. Smith (2005) Leading Causes of death for 2002. National Vital Statistics Reports; Vol 53(17). Hyattville, MD: National Center for Health Statistics.

The risks of diabetes, HIV/AIDS, infant mortality, and homicides are also of concern in African-American communities. The trends in HIV/AIDS have been particularly disturbing in recent years. Blacks now account for half of all new HIV cases that are diagnosed, of which 72 percent are black women, and the disease is now the leading cause of deaths among young black women between ages 25 and 34 (Dyer, 2000). Blacks also now account for a significant amount (98%) of all cumulative AIDS cases among the incarcerated. Within the context of the urban health penalty alluded to earlier, the scourge of the AIDS pandemic is most evident in the nation's metropolitan areas such as Washington, D.C. where case rates are ten times higher than the national rate.

The other health concern, Infant Mortality Rate (IMR), has been historically a key indicator of health disparities between blacks and whites. This black/white gap has persisted despite the dramatic reduction in national IMR rates over the last several decades. The rate among African Americans (14.1%) continues to be more than twice the rate of whites (5.7%). The consensus among many researchers is that Low Birth Weights (LBW), or babies born weighing less than 2500 grams, account for nearly two-thirds of the observed black/white disparity in IMR. The racial differential in LBW is equally large, with prevalence rates of 13 percent among blacks compared to only 6.5 percent among whites. Such babies are known to face greater health risks including cognitive and developmental problems, congenital anomalies, respiratory ailments, higher rates of hospitalization, and possibly death from health complications prior to their first birthday (McCormick, 1995).

Attempts to explain the black-white gap in LBW have yielded complex interactions between risk factors that go beyond personal characteristics of the mother such as age, income, substance abuse or high risk behaviors. Instead, researchers are now examining neighborhood and contextual factors such as access to prenatal care, occupational hazards, neighborhood segregation, and exposure to toxic substances. Grady (2003) for example investigated the risks of LBW among mothers in segregated and non-segregated tracts in Kings county,

New York. She concluded that the risks were higher for black mothers regardless of where they lived. Another study reported on environmental quality and the likelihood of poor reproductive outcomes due to exposure to contaminants such as pesticides, industrial solvents, metals, and endocrine disrupting chemicals that lead to adverse reproductive outcomes (Margai, 2003).

Overall the health status of blacks appears to be worsening in many respects. The gap persists in preexisting health disparities such as heart disease, cancers, and IMR, but even more disconcerting is the increasing evidence of the disproportionate number of case rates in emerging diseases such as HIV/AIDS. The reasons for these disparities are complex but linked primarily to poverty, access to health services, utilization of the services, the late diagnoses of the diseases, and disparities in treatment and participation in clinical trials (Howell, 2004). These problems of health access and utilization, and long-term consequences, are addressed later in the chapter.

Health Concerns in Latino-American Communities

Latinos are now the largest minority group, comprising 13 percent of the U.S. population in 2004. Demographic patterns suggest a 58 percent increase in this population between 1990 and 2000, the largest among all racial/ethnic groups in the country. These increases are due both to the arrival of recent immigrants as well as the high birth rates among the Latino population. Not surprisingly, a key attribute of this population is its relative youthfulness: the median age is 26 years and 35 percent of the population is less than 18 years, compared to the rest of the U.S. population (with a median age of 35 years with only 26 percent of the population below 18 years of age). These demographic differences are even more dramatic in certain states such as California, where by the year 2010, some experts predict that half of all children will be Latinos (Flores et al., 2002).

Given the rapidly changing demographic profile of this group, several studies are now beginning to examine the detailed health statistics of the population including those of the children. Previous studies commonly used the term *epidemiological paradox*, or the Latino paradox, to describe the fact that even though Latinos face the same demographic/economic risk factors and sociospatial barriers as blacks, their overall health status is more favorable than blacks and better yet, comparable to those of the dominant white majority (Amaro and Dela Torre, 2002; Grady, 2003; Margai, 2003). However, closer scrutiny of health measures reveals that there are certain conditions that disproportionately impact the group. As will be shown here, these problems are linked to wider systemic problems including their immigration status, occupation, linguistic barriers, and the environmental quality of their neighborhoods.

Comparing the leading causes of deaths among Latinos and whites, one finds that a major concern has to do with unintentional injuries (accidents), which account for the third leading cause of death for Latinos (see Table 29.1). The employment of Latinos in menial jobs, such as meat packing, crop-picking/farming, and construction, places them at high risk of occupational injuries and long-term health problems due to cumulative exposures to pesticides and other toxins. For example, between 1995 and 2000, Mexican foreign-born workers accounted for more than two-thirds of fatal injuries among foreign-born workers. Further, employers are likely to take advantage of the undocumented status of some of these workers by offering them low pay with no benefits. As a result, 34 percent of Latinos are uninsured, nearly three times the rate for non-Hispanic whites.

Latino children, especially those from migrant families also face poorer health outcomes. Of the one million children in the United States whose parents are migrant and seasonal workers, about 94 percent of them are Latinos (Flores et al., 2002). As shown in Table 29.1, birth defects are among the ten leading causes of death among Latinos, and these health events have been linked to migrant exposure to pesticides and other hazardous substances (Cooper et al., 2001a and 2001b). Other studies have documented additional health problems among these children, including inadequate preventive care, high rates of infectious diseases, farm injuries, greater risk of nutritional disorders, and low educational attainment, as well as endocrine, neurological and behavioral disorders that also have potential links to exposure to hazardous substances (Flores et al., 2002; Schenker, 1995).

Other health concerns in the Latino community include increasing rates of HIV/AIDS, obesity/diabetes, homicide, teenage pregnancy, and tuberculosis. However, the severity of these outcomes varies among the different subgroups. Comparing the three major Latino subgroups, Puerto Ricans face more disparate health outcomes than Mexican Americans and Cubans. For example, the age-adjusted death rate for HIV among Puerto Ricans living on mainland is 32.7 per 100,000, more than 13 times the rate for non-Hispanic whites. The diabetes rate is 172 per 100,000, compared to 122 per 100,000 for Mexican Americans, and 47 per 100,000 for Cuban Americans.

The severity of health outcomes among Latinos also depends on nativity and the varying levels of Latino *acculturation* into the U.S. society. Acculturation has been evaluated using variables such as place of birth, year of residency in the U.S., and language use. Most studies have demonstrated negative effects of acculturation on the health of subsequent generations. The foreign born and less acculturated Latinos have been found to experience fewer health problems, but this relative advantage declines with increasing stay in the U.S. Second-generation Latinos or those who are more acculturated have been shown to face greater health problems such as obesity, illicit drug use, adverse birth outcomes, and high rates of teenage pregnancy. Examining the differentials in overweight conditions in the Latino community, Gordon-Larsen et al. (2003) noted that there are certain patterns of acculturation and structural factors that placed Latino youths at risk. Specifically, immigrant adolescents were likely to be influenced by what the researchers referred to as an obesegenic environment characterized by "sedentary lifestyles, large-portion sizes, heavy advertising of fatty and energy-dense foods and mass media" (p. 2030). These conditions along with the existing socioeconomic disadvantages result in greater risk factors and adverse health conditions that are worrisome for this rapidly growing population.

Health Concerns in Asian-American Communities

During the 2000 U.S. Census, 4.4 percent of the U.S. population identified themselves as Asian Americans and Pacific Islanders (AAPI). Like Latinos, this group has undergone explosive growth in recent decades, from just one million in the 1960s to 12 million in 2000, and is expected to reach 36.7 million by 2050. Among the factors contributing to this contemporary growth pattern are the relaxation of U.S. immigration laws, the previous involvement of the U.S. military in Southeast Asia, and associated resettlement of refugees, globalization, and the increasing interconnection of U.S. and Asian economies, and the well established migration networks (Zhou and Gatewood, 2000).

Asian Americans in the U.S. today represent a diverse mix of ethnic groups that differ by language, religion, immigration into the U.S., and length of stay, as well as the degree to which they have acculturated or assimilated into society. Japanese and Chinese Americans for example have a longer generational history, whereas other groups such as Indians, Koreans, Vietnamese, Cambodians, Laotians, and the Hmong people are fairly recent immigrants with more limited levels of assimilation. Despite these notable differences, the public's perception of Asian Americans is still misguided with long-term implications for their health. Asian Americans are often seen as foreigners, mostly medical doctors, computer programmers, accountants, nerds, high achievers and compliant workers who rarely encounter problems of racism or institutional discrimination. Further, they are misperceived as people who because of their high earning potential have no major social, economic or health needs, and are all physically and mentally healthy. This erroneous characterization, which is associated with the *model minority myth,* fails to acknowledge the real health concerns or disparities that exist in the Asian-American community. Researchers who have investigated the SES and health characteristics of this group have identified a line of bifurcation that separates Asian Americans into categories of varying demographic, socioeconomic and health status instead of a single homogenous population (Frazier, 2003; Zhou and Greenwood, 2000). For example, when examining the demographic profile of the group by nativity and age, the Asian-American population has a disproportionately large foreign-born component and a disproportionately young native-born component (Zhou and Greenwood, 2000). It also has diverse occupational backgrounds that relate to the unique migration patterns of each subgroup, their national origin and their basis of admission into the U.S. (family-sponsored, employer-sponsored, or refugee resettlement). Their occupations range from physicians and nurses, computer programmers, small business entrepreneurs, middle-class professionals to low skilled workers on farms, sweat shops and other economic entities. These differential skills translate into varying levels of SES and income by national origin. Immigrants from India, the Philippines, and Taiwan reportedly have higher income levels than those from Vietnam, Cambodia or Laos. Similarly, the poverty rates range from seven percent for Filipinos, Indians and Japanese-Americans to 42 percent for Cambodians and more than 60 percent for Laotians (Zhou and Greenwood, 2000).

Examining the health indicators of Asian Americans, one finds that the patterns are equally mixed. While the group as a whole experiences a good health status with the lowest recorded death rates from the top three leading causes of death, the detailed statistical data provide clear indications of high incidence and death rates from certain types of cancers. Unlike the other groups, cancers (not heart disease) account for the leading cause of death among AAPIs (Table 29.1). Examining the cause-specific cancer rates, one finds that this group experiences the highest incidence of liver cancer (13.8 per 100,000) and stomach cancer (17.3 per 100,000), compared to those of whites (4.8 per 100,000 for liver cancers and 7.7 per 100,000 for stomach cancers).

Other major risk factors for Asian-American health are smoking, exposure to tuberculosis, and hepatitis but these vary significantly by population subgroup. For example, a study by Ma et al. (2002) concluded that tobacco use was a serious public health problem among Asian Americans but the rates were significantly higher among Southeast-Asian men. The authors indicated that smoking rates varied from 33 percent among Koreans, 55 percent among Chinese, 35 percent to 56 percent among Vietnamese, to 71 percent among Laotians and Cambodians. Noting that current smokers were more likely to be foreign-born, these authors revealed that the subgroup differences were related to country of birth, immigration status, and length of stay in the U.S. Similar findings have also been noted for tuberculosis levels among Asian Americans. Even though the overall risk of tuberculosis among Asians (33 per 100,000) in the U.S. is fifteen times the rate of whites, the rates have been shown to vary among the different subgroups, highest during the first few years of immigration and then decline gradually to less than 5 percent after 10 years or more of residency.

Asian Americans have also been disproportionately affected by hepatitis B (HPV), a virus that attacks the liver and results in chronic infection, scarring, cirrhosis, and possibly liver cancer and death. Even though the rates of HPV have been decreasing (due to the increasing availability of the vaccine), the reported rate among Asians is still high (2.95 per 100,000) and twice more than the white population. Yu et al. (2004), in their study of health disparities among AAPI children, contend that overall, the health issues facing this community are largely related to issues of citizenship/nativity status and the presence of cultural and linguistic barriers. These factors limit their use of health resources regardless of eligibility. They recommend the use of outreach and promotional programs to educate the Asian immigrant populations on how to access and navigate the health care system.

Health Concerns in Native-American Communities

U.S. citizens who are descendants of the original peoples of the Americas and still maintain tribal affiliation in their communities are classified as American Indians/Alaskan Natives (AI/AN). In 2000, there were approximately 560 federally recognized tribes residing in about 35 states (U.S. Census, 2000). Together these groups comprised roughly 4.1 million or 1.5 percent of the total U.S. population. Contrary to public perceptions of negative growth and decimation of the group by disease and/or absorption into the larger U.S. population, the trend over the last four decades shows a steady upward increase at an average annual rate of about 4 percent. Noting that this demographic trend is nearly impossible without immigration, some authors have credited the positive growth to the increasing number of self-identifying people with partial or distant Native-American ancestry (Cunningham, 1996). The increase in fertility levels has also played a part. For example, roughly 45 percent of Native American women have their first child as teenagers, as compared to 21 percent of white women. Another contributory factor has been the improvement in mortality levels that has accompanied the epidemiological transition in the U.S. as a whole, benefiting all groups. Infectious diseases that once afflicted more than 90 percent of the Native American population, killing many and weakening others, have been mostly eradicated. Despite these developments, the AI/AN population continues to be disproportionately affected by health conditions that result in significantly higher morbidity and mortality levels. A report in 2004 concluded that

Native Americans still bear a greater burden of health risk factors and chronic diseases than any other minority population (Liao et al., 2004). This group has been previously described as the poorest of the poor in the U.S. with poverty rates of 26 percent, compared to 13 percent for the total population and only eight percent for white Americans. Further, nearly 40 percent of the Native-American adults are likely to be unemployed throughout the year and more than two-thirds have family incomes below the poverty line compared to only a third for the general population (Cunningham, 1996). As with the other minority groups, the root causes of these disparities are linked to racial stereotypes, discrimination, geographic isolation, and limited access to health services. Native Americans have been caricatured and stereotyped as lazy, alcoholic savages, wearing feathers and living in teepees. Until recently, minimal reference was made to the diversity of this group as separate nations with different names, languages, cultures, adaptive behaviors, and preferences.

Also important is the settlement geography of Native Americans, which unlike the other groups, is the result of a number of signed treaties and the unique relationship between the various tribal nations and the federal government. Native Americans are allowed to exist as sovereign entities but also entitled to health and educational services provided by the federal government. Specifically, the Indian Health Service (IHS) was set up in 1955 as the primary agency responsible for providing health care to the Native-American population that resides on or near the reservations. Despite these benefits, the Indian reservations remain as relatively isolated pockets of extreme poverty, unemployment, and poor health conditions. Access to health care is still very limited due to the sparse distribution of those that are eligible for IHS services. Using a survey of AI/AN population, a study concluded that almost two-thirds of the population resides in non-metropolitan areas and 31 percent reside in non-metro areas with very low density (less than 10 per square mile). This distribution is in stark contrast to the rest of the U.S. population with 75 percent in urban areas and only 3 percent in areas with very low density (Cunningham, 1996).

Examining the profile of the leading causes of death, heart disease and cancer account for the leading causes of deaths among the AI/AN population. The good news about cancer among the group is that the aggregate mortality rates are generally lower (161 per 100,000) than the overall national rate (206 per 100,000). However, in 2003, Paisano and others documented some regional variability in these levels with some AI/AN communities reporting higher levels such as in Alaska (248 per 100,000) and the Northern Plains (292 per 100,000). Among the cause-specific cancers, the most serious risks are for lung cancer, colorectal cancer, stomach, and liver cancer. The incidence rates for stomach and liver cancer among the AI/AN population is higher than the overall U.S. rates and reportedly related to the high levels of alcohol consumption.

Another area of health concerns among Native Americans is the large number of deaths from unintentional injuries (accidents). This is the leading cause of death for Native Americans ages 1–44 years and the third leading cause of death for the group as a whole (Table 29.1). A study by Wallace and others (2003) showed that injury-related deaths among Native Americans was twice the rate for the U.S. as a whole and accounted for 75 percent of all deaths among children and youth. Unlike Latinos, where accidental deaths are caused by occupational hazards, Native Americans' deaths are caused by unintentional motor vehicle accidents. Native Americans have the highest deaths from motor vehicle accidents, pedestrian events, and suicides. These crashes are caused primarily by impaired driving, often caused by alcohol abuse, which is estimated to be as high as 70 percent in some areas, compared to prevalence rates of 11–32 percent among whites and blacks. Further, some authors contend that these accidents occur due to the traffic safety and regulatory codes that are less restrictive in these sovereign nations when compared to the rest of the country (Wallace et al., 2003).

Other health problems facing Native Americans include chronic health conditions such as diabetes and psychiatric problems. In a sample of blacks, Hispanics, Asians and Native Americans, the highest prevalence of obesity, current smoking, cardiovascular disease, and diabetes were found among Native Americans. Approximately 80 percent of the AI/ANs had one or more adverse risk factors or chronic conditions and one-third had three or more of these conditions (Liao et al., 2004). Mental health conditions are also problematic in these AI/AN communities. Researchers have blamed these conditions on the depressive state of life on the reservations, due to the poverty and alienation of these communities.

EMERGING THEMES IN RACE-BASED GEOGRAPHIES OF HEALTH

The preceding section of this chapter has focused on the unique experiences and health concerns facing racial and ethnic minorities in the U.S. In describing their health status, a number of geographic patterns and processes emerged, all of which underscore the complexities of the race-based dimensions of health but also suggest certain commonalities among the groups. These include: the urban health penalty, the relationships between segregation, zoning and health, the weathering hypothesis, the epidemiological paradox, acculturation, and the link between geographic isolation, alienation, and health. Even though these patterns were discussed with reference to specific minority groups, they are by no means unique to those groups. Rather, these characteristics are shared by the other minority groups, and they further illustrate the wide-ranging scope of the problems in the health care system. For example, the negative effects of acculturation, as described among Latinos, have also been demonstrated for Asian Americans and are now being explored for immigrants from the African Diaspora (Margai, forthcoming). Similarly, the epidemiological paradox, a positive dimension of Latino health, also has been noted when comparing U.S.-born blacks versus foreign-born blacks, as well as comparing Asian Americans by nativity.

Comparing blacks in urbanized communities to Native Americans in the rural areas, one finds that both groups have different settlement geographies, yet face similar problems of relative isolation and alienation from the rest of society. In effect, the weathering hypothesis, as noted earlier to explain the cumulative health outcome among blacks, also applies to Native Americans and possibly other minority groups residing in segregated ethnic enclaves.

Finally, access to health care is an issue of critical importance to all racial/ethnic groups. Health care access is defined here as an individual's ability to obtain health and medical service on a timely, geographical, and financially acceptable basis. From a geographic perspective, it is a multidimensional construct that is measurable using indicators such as the availability of health services, geographic accessibility, accommodation, cultural acceptability, and affordability (Cromley and McClafferty, 2002). Studies focusing on these various dimensions have identified group disparities in all five areas.

The most troubling aspect of access has been health care affordability, which reflects the prices of health services and the people's ability to pay. This disparity has been documented using income levels and group differences in health insurance coverage. At the national level, the number of people lacking health insurance has increased significantly over the last ten years to approximately 41 million, with some estimates as high as 60 million. The differences between the groups are best seen using the age-adjusted rates of all persons under 62 years of age without health care insurance (Table 29.2). Also included in this table is the index of disparity for each group, which can be computed by taking the average of the absolute difference between the rates observed for the specific group (r) and the reference population group (R), divided by the rate of the reference group (R) (Pearcy and Keppel, 2002). The index is expressed as a percentage.[1] The computed information confirms that Native Americans indeed face the greatest disparity in health care access with an index of disparity that is 207 percent different from the white population. Hispanics have an index of 168 percent. The index for blacks is lower (at 52%), yet statistically significant when compared to their white counterparts.

As expected, there are serious consequences for those without health insurance (American Medical Association, 2003). These people are less likely to get routine medical check-ups or get preventive care. They are likely to face major financial problems in the event of a chronic or catastrophic health event. They are also more likely to visit the emergency hospital rooms with longer waiting times, poorer health outcomes, and greater charges for care, which ultimately are subsidized by public tax dollars. So from a societal viewpoint, disparities in health access not only result in poor health outcomes, they are expensive and have negative financial implications for the nation as a whole.

Table 29.2
Persons under 65 years with No Health Insurance Coverage, 2002

Race/Hispanic Origin	Age-Adjusted Percent	Absolute Difference from "best"	Percent Difference from "best"
American Indian/Alaskan Native	38.8	26.1*	207.1
Asian Only	17.2	4.6*	36.5
Native Hawaiian or Pacific Islander	24.0	11.4*	90.5
Hispanic	33.8	21.2*	168.3
Black, Non-Hispanic	19.2	6.6*	52.4
White, Non Hispanic ("best" group)	12.6	Reference group	Reference Group
*The difference between the rate for this group and the "best" groups rate is significant at p<0.05			
Index of Disparity: The average percent difference of the all group rates from the best groups rate is 101.2			

Source: National Health Interview Survey, NCHS, CDC.

CONCLUSIONS AND IMPLICATIONS FOR HEALTH POLICY

This chapter has outlined the major health concerns among the racial and ethnic groups in the United States including an overview of the underlying causes and processes that account for these patterns. Using the race and class perspective as the basis for causal interpretation, we have documented the pervasiveness of health disparities that cut across all domains in the health care system with possibly long-term consequences for the nation as a whole. The disparities exist in access, treatment, outcomes, and the overall health status of the minority populations. The immigration and generational histories of the different groups, their spatial distribution and settlement patterns, occupational environments, poverty, discrimination, alienation and access were all noted as relevant factors in explaining the differential risks and prevalence of certain ailments and conditions among the various groups. Federal acknowledgment of these inequalities has recently led to the establishment of the Healthy People 2010 initiative, a set of objectives designed to eliminate health disparities by the year 2010. The reports issued by the various federal agencies associated with this program have identified six areas that require immediate attention: infant mortality, cancer screening and mortality, diabetes, cardiovascular disease, HIV infection and AIDS, and child/adult immunizations. A series of interceptive strategies have been put in place and are now being monitored to identify the practices that produce the most meaningful results. So far, the changes have been very slow, and in some instances, unproductive with health disparities reportedly increasing instead of decreasing between the groups (Moy et al., 2005). Many, however, are optimistic that these improvements are possible, though such changes are more likely to occur at the local level rather the national level. Further, since the geographical variability in race/ethnicity is more apparent at less aggregate spatial scales, it may be worthwhile to implement and track these reforms at the local community level, such as the program established by Calman (2005) and others in the Bronx, New York City. Based on a coalition of local health care providers, faith-based institutions and other community organizations, this group has implemented a seven-point health advocacy agenda that includes: i) efforts to eliminate residential and neighborhood segregation and related impacts on residents, ii) working to create a more representative and diverse health care workforce, iii) making it possible for everyone to get culturally competent health care, iv) providing universal health care coverage, v) ensuring accountability for state uncompensated care funds, vi) expanding public health education, and vii) recognizing and ending environmental racism and the toll it takes on communities of color. We believe that these strategies are universally applicable to other communities, and certainly worthy of further exploration as the nation struggles to develop an equitable health care system.

NOTE

[1] To express the index as a percentage, the computed value is multiplied by 100:

$$\text{Index of disparity} = \left(\sum |r_{(1-n)}) - R| \; /n \right) /R * 100$$

Works Cited

Abbot, C. 1987. *The New Urban America: Growth and Politics in Sunbelt Cities.* 2nd rev. ed. Chapel Hill, NC: University of North Carolina Press.

Abrahamson, M. 1996. "Chinatown in San Francisco and Little Taipei in Suburban Los Angeles." In *Urban Enclaves: Identity and Place in America,* 67–84. New York: St. Martin's Press.

Acevedo-Garcia, D., K. Lochner, T. Osypuk, and S. V. Subramanian. 2003. "Future Directions in Residential Segregation and Health Research: A Multilevel Approach." *American Journal of Public Health* 93(1): 215–221.

ACORN. 2003. The Great Divide: Home Purchase Mortgage Lending Nationally and in 115 Metropolitan Areas. http://www.acorn.org/>www.acorn.org.

Adams, A. 2000. *Hidden from History: The Latino Community of Allentown, PA.* Lehigh County Historical Society.

Adams, P. and R. Ghosh. 2003. "India.com: The Construction of a Space Between." *Progress in Human Geography* 27(4): 414–437.

Adams P. and E. Skop. "Indian Immigrants in Cyberspace." Unpublished Manuscript.

Africa: Global Studies, "Liberia." Guilford, Connecticut: The Dushkin Publishing Group, Inc., 1987, p. 37.

Africa Survey, 1973. "Liberia: Disappointing 'Rally' Results," No. 23, July, p. 37.

AFSC. 2003. "Understanding Anti-Immigrant Movements." American Friends Service Committee website: http://www.afsc.org/immigrants-rights/learn/anti-immigrant.htm.

Agarwal, P. 1991. *Passage from India: Post-1965 Indian Immigrants and Their Children: Conflicts, Concerns, and Solutions.* Palos Verdes, CA: Yuvati Publications.

Agócs, C. 1981. "Ethnic Settlement in a Metropolitan Area: A Typology of Communities." *Ethnicity* 8(2): 127–148.

Alba, R. 1990. *Ethnic Identity: The Transformation of White America.* New Haven: Yale University Press.

Alba, R. and J. R. Logan. 1991. "Variation on Two Themes: Racial and Ethnic Patterns in the Attainment of Suburban Residence." *Demography* 28(3): 431–454.

Alba, R. D., J. R. Logan, W. Zhang, and B. Stults. 1999a. "Strangers Next Door: Immigrant Groups and Suburbs in Los Angeles and New York," pp. 108–132 in P. Moen, H. Walker, and D. Dempster-McClain (eds.), *A Nation Divided: Diversity, Inequality, and Community in American Society.* Ithaca: Cornell University Press.

Alba, R. D., J. R. Logan, B. Stults, G. Marzan, and W. Zhang. 1999b. "Immigrant Groups in the Suburbs: A Reexamination of Suburbanization and Spatial Assimilation," *American Sociological Review* 64(3): 446–460.

Alba, R. et al. 1999. "Immigrant Groups in the Suburbs: A Reexamination of Suburbanization and Spatial Assimilation." *American Sociological Review* 64: 446–460.

Alba, R. and V. Nee. 2003. *Remaking the American Mainstream.* Cambridge: Harvard University Press.

Aldrich, H. 1975. "Ecological Succession in Racially Changing Neighborhoods: A Review of the Literature." *Urban Affairs Quarterly* 10: 327–348.

Aldrich, H. and R. Waldinger. 1990. "Ethnicity and Entrepreneurship." *Annual Review of Sociology* 16: 111–135.

Allen, J. 1999. "Spatial Assemblages of Power: From Domination to Empowerment." In *Human Geography Today,* D. Massey, J. Allen, and P. Sarre (eds.). Cambridge, United Kingdom: Policy Press, pp. 194–218.

Allen, J. A. and E. Turner. 1988. *We the People: An Atlas of America's Ethnic Diversity.* New York: Macmillan.

Allen, J. A. and E. Turner. 1992. *An Atlas of Population Patterns in Metropolitan Los Angeles County 1990.* Northridge, CA: California State University, Northridge.

Allen, J. P. and E. Turner. 1996. "Ethnic Diversity and Segregation in the New Los Angeles." In *EthniCity,* C. C. Roseman, H. D. Laux, and G. Thieme (eds.). London: Rowman and Littlefield Publishers, Inc., pp. 31–50.

Allen, J. P. and E. Turner. 1996. "Spatial Patterns of Immigrant Assimilation." *Professional Geographer* 48(2): 140–155.

Allen, J. P. and E. Turner. 1997. *The Ethnic Quilt: Population Diversity in Southern California.* Northridge, CA: California State University Center for Geographical Studies.

Allen, J. P. and E. Turner. 2002. *Changing Faces, Changing Places: Mapping Southern Californians.* Northridge, CA: Center for Geographical Studies, Northridge.

Allport, G. W. 1954. "The Nature of Prejudice." In *Urban Racial Violence in the Twentieth Century*, J. Boskin (ed.). London: Collier Macmillan Publishers, 1776.

Almaguer, T. 1994. *Racial Fault Lines the Historical Origins of White Supremacy in California.* Berkeley, CA: University of California Press.

Amaro, H. and A. De La Torre. 2002. "Public Health Needs and Scientific Oppurtunities in Research on Latinas." *American Journal of Public Health* 92(4): 525–529.

American Medical Association (AMA). 2003. "Health Insurance Costs and Coverage." *Health Care Financial Trends.* August 2003. www.ama.assn.org/go/healthpolicy. (Last accessed June 23, 2005.)

Amona, K. 2004. "Native Hawaiian Wellness and the Sea." Paper presented at the Kamehameha Schools 2004 Conference on Native Hawaiian Well-Being, Kea'au, HI. http://www.ksbe.edu/pase/pdf/KSResearchConference/2004 presentations/Amona.pdf.

Anderson, K. J. 1987. "The Idea of Chinatown: The Power of Place and Institutional Practice in the Making of a Racial Category." *Annals of the Association of American Geographers* 77(4): 580–598.

Anderson, K. J. 1988. "Cultural Hegemony and the Race-Definition Process in Chinatown." *Environment and Planning D: Society and Space* 6: 127–149.

Anderson, K. J. 1991. *Vancouver's Chinatown: Racial Discourse in Canada, 1875–1980.* Montreal, ON: McGill-Queen's University Press.

Anderson, R. N. and B. L. Smith. 2005. "Leading Causes of Death for 2002." *National Vital Statistics Reports* 53(17). Hyattville, MD: National Center for Health Statistics.

Anonymous. 2000. "African Immigrants in the United States are the Nation's Most Highly Educated Group." *Journal of Blacks in Higher Education,* No. 26.

Appadurai, A. 1990. "Disjunction and Difference in the Global Cultural Economy." *Theory, Culture, and Society* 7(2/3): 295–310.

Appadurai, A. 1996. *Modernity at Large: Cultural Dimensions of Globalization.* Minneapolis, MN: University of Minnesota Press.

Armas, G. C. 2001. "Census Data Revealing U.S.'s Growing Diversity." Associated Press.

Arreola, D. D. 1985. "Mexican-Americans." In J. O. McKee (ed.), *Ethnicity in Contemporary America: A Geographical Appraisal.* Dubuque, IA: Kendall/Hunt.

Arreola, D. D. 1988. "Mexican American Housescapes." *Geographical Review* 78: 299–315.

Arreola, D. D. 2000. "Mexican-Americans." In J. O. McKee (ed.), *Ethnicity in Contemporary America: A Geographical Appraisal,* pp. 111–138.

Arreola, D. D. 2002. *Tejano South Texas: A Mexican American Cultural Province.* Austin: University of Texas Press.

Arreola, D. D. (ed.). 2004. *Hispanic Spaces, Latino Places: Community and Cultural Diversity in Contemporary America.* Austin: University of Texas Press.

Arthur, J. 2000. *Invisible Sojourners: African Immigrant Diaspora in the United States.* Westport, CT: Praeger Press.

Ashabranner, B. 1999. *The New African Americans.* North Haven, CT: Linnet.

Ashdown, P. 1979. *Caribbean History in Maps.* London: Longman Caribbean.

Attaquin, H. 1990. "There are Differences." In *Rooted Like the Ash Trees: New England Indians and the Land.* 2nd ed. Edited by R. Carlson. Naugatuck, CT: Eagle Wing Press.

Bakal, V. and K. Job. 1992. *Paterson by the Numbers.* Paterson: Paterson 2000 History Committee.

Ballard, R. 2002. "Race, Ethnicity, and Culture." In *New Directions in Sociology,* M. Holburn (ed.). Ormskirk: Causeway.

Bamshad, M. J. and S. E. Olson. 2003. "Does Race Exist?" *Scientific America* 289(6): 78–85.

Barnes, J. S. and C. E. Bennett. 2002. *The Asian Population, 2000.* Washington, D.C.: U.S. Bureau of the Census.

Barone, M. 2005. "Cultures Aren't Equal." *U.S. News and World Report.* August 15–22, p. 26.

Barth, F. 1998. Introduction. *Ethnic Groups and Boundaries: The Social Organization of Culture Difference.* F. Barth (ed.). Prospect Heights Illinois: Waveland Press, 9–38.

Barthes, R. 1983. *Empire of Signs.* New York: Hill and Wang.

Barrera, M. 1979. *Race and Class in the Southwest: A Theory of Racial Inequality,* Notre Dame, IN: University of Notre Dame Press.

Barringer, H. R., R. W. Gardner, and M. J. Levin. 1993. *Asians and Pacific Islanders in the United States.* New York: Russell Sage Foundation.

Basch, L., N. Glick Schiller and C. Szanton Blanc. 1994. *Nations Unbound: Transnational Projects, Postcolonial Predicaments and Deterritorialized Nation-States.* Langhorne, PA: Gordon and Breach Publishers.

Battiste, M. (ed.). 2000. *Reclaiming Indigenous Voice and Vision.* Vancouver, BC: University of British Columbia Press.

Becket, J. 2003. "Land and Literature: Teaching about the Hawaiian Forest." In *Wao Akua*: *Sacred Source of Life.* Division of Forestry and Wildlife, Department of Land and Natural Resources, State of Hawai'i, 43–49. Honolulu, HI: Hawai'i Department of Land and Natural Resources.

Benedict, J. 2000. *Without Reservation: The Making of America's Most Powerful Indian Tribe and Foxwoods, The World's Largest Casino.* New York: HarperCollins.

Benencia, R. and G. Karasik. 1994. "Bolivianos en Buenos Aires: Aspectos de su integración laboral y cultural." *Estudios Migratorios Latinoamericanos* 9(27): 261–299.

Benton-Short, L. M., M. Price and S. Freidman. In press. "Globalization from Below: The Ranking of Global Immigrant Cities." *International Journal of Urban and Regional Research.*

Bernard, W. S. 1976. "Immigrants and Refugees: Their Similarities, Differences, and Needs." *International Migration* 14(3): 267–280.

Berry, B. J. L. 1976. *Chicago: Transformation of an Urban System.* Cambridge, MA: Ballinger.

Berry, J. W. 1990. "Acculturation and Adaptation: A General Framework," in *Mental Health of Immigrants and Refugees,* W. H. Holtzman and T. H. Bornermann (eds.). Austin: Hogg Foundation for Mental Health, 90–102.

Berry, K. A. and M. L Henderson. 2002. "Envisioning the Nexus between Geography and Ethnic and Racial Identity." In *Geographical Identities of Ethnic America: Race, Space, and Place.* K. A. Berry and M. L. Henderson (eds.). Reno and Las Vegas, Nevada: University of Nevada Press, 1–14.

Bigman, L. 1995. "Contemporary Migration from Africa to the USA." In *The Cambridge Survey of World Migration,* R. Cohen (ed.). New York: Cambridge University Press, 260–262.

Blakemore, E. 2005. "Lieberman Introduces Bill to Limit Native American Annexation." Retrieved on April 24, 2005 from http://academic.udayton.edu/race/02rights/s98blak2.htm#Lieberman.

Blockson, C. L. "Sea Change in the Sea Islands: 'Nowhere to Lay Down Weary Head,'" *National Geographic,* Vol. 172, No. 6, Dec. 1987: 735–763.

Blouet, B. W. and F. C. Luebke (eds.). 1979. *The Great Plains: Environment and Culture.* Lincoln, NE: University of Nebraska Press.

Bobo, L., M. Oliver, J. Johnson, Jr. and A. Alenzuela. 2000. *Prismatic Metropolis: Inequality in Los Angeles.* New York: Russell Sage Foundation.

Bogardus, E. S. 1925. "Social Distance and Its Origins." *Journal of Applied Sociology* 9: 216–226.

Bonaicich, E. and J. Modell. 1980. *The Economic Basis of Ethnic Solidarity: Small Business in the Japanese American Community.* Berkeley and Los Angeles: University of California Press.

Bonaicich, E. 1984. "Some Basic Facts: Patterns of Asian Immigration and Exclusion." L. Chen and E. Bonaicich (eds.). *Labor Immigration under Capitalism: Asian Workers in U.S.* Berkley: University of California, 60–77.

Bonnett, A. 1997. "Geography, 'Race' and Whiteness: Invisible Traditions and Current Challenges." *Area* 29(3): 193–199.

Booker, M. K. 1994. *Dystopian Literature.* Westport, CT: Greenwood Press.

Borjas, G. 1994. "The Economics of Immigration." *Journal of Economic Literature* 32: 1667–1717.

Borough, D. 2001. "A New Strategy for Mapping Multiple Ethnic Concentrations and for the Study of Neighborhood Transition and Spatial Assimilation." Paper presented at The Association of American Geographers Annual Meeting, New York.

Boskin, J. 1976. *Urban Racial Violence in the Twentieth Century.* London: Glencoe Press. 1994.

Boswell, T. D. 1976. "Residential Patterns of Puerto Ricans in New York City." *Geographical Review* 66(1): 92–94.

Boswell, T. D. 1985a. "The Cuban-Americans." In J. O. McKee (ed.). *Ethnicity in Contemporary America: A Geographical Appraisal.* Dubuque, IA: Kendall/Hunt.

Boswell, T. D. 1985b. "Puerto Ricans Living in the United States." In J. O. McKee (ed.). *Ethnicity in Contemporary America: A Geographical Appraisal.* Dubuque, IA: Kendall/Hunt.

Boswell, T. 1993. *The Cubanization and Hispanicization of Miami.* Miami: Cuban American Policy Center, Cuban American National Council.

Boswell, T. D. and A. D. Cruz-Báez. 1997. "Residential Segregation by Socioeconomic Class in Metropolitan Miami." *Urban Geography* 18(5): 474–496.

Boswell, T. D. and A. D. Cruz-Baez. 2000a. "Puerto Ricans Living in the United States." In J. O. McKee (ed.). *Ethnicity in Contemporary America: A Geographical Appraisal,* 2nd ed. Boston: Rowman Littlefield.

Boswell, T. D. 2000b. "Cuban-Americans." In J. O. McKee (ed.). *Ethnicity in Contemporary America: A Geographical Appraisal,* 2nd ed. Boston: Rowman Littlefield.

Botelho, G. 2004. "Latinos Could Hold Key to Win." CNN, Monday, October 18, 2004. Posted: 9:13 PM EDT http://www.cnn.com/2004/ALLPOLITICS/10/18/latino.vote/index.html.

Bouvier, L. F. and A. J. Agresta. 1993. "The Future Asian Population of the United States." In *Asians and Pacific Islanders in the United States,* H. R. Barringer, R. W. Gardner, and M. J. Levin (eds.). New York: Russell Sage Foundation.

Boyd, M. 1992. "Gender, Visible Minority and Immigrant Earnings Inequality: Reassessing an Employment Equity Premise" in V. Satzewich (ed.). *Deconstructing a Nation: Immigration, Multiculturalism, and Racism in the 1990s Canada,* pp. 279–322. Toronto: Fernwood.

Bradford, C. 2002. "Risk or Race?" *Racial Disparities and the Subprime Refinance Market.* Washington D.C.: A Report of the Center for Community Change.

Brass, P. 1991. *Ethnicity and Nationalism.* London: Sage Publications.

Breitman, G. 1968. *The Last Year of Malcolm X: The Evolution of a Revolutionary.* New York: Schocken Books.

Breton, R. 1964. "Institutional Completeness of Ethnic Communities and the Personal Relations of Immigrants." *The American Journal of Sociology* 1(1): 193–205.

Brinkley, A. 1995. *American History: A Survey.* 9th ed. New York: McGraw-Hill.

Brown, L. A. and D. B. Longbrake. 1970. "Migration Flows in Intraurban Space: Place Utility Considerations." *Annals of the Association of American Geographers* 60(2): 368–384.

Buchanan, S. 2005. "The Rift." *Intelligence Report* 118: 8–15.

Buell, R. L. "Some Legal Aspects of the Japanese Question." C. McLain (ed.). *Japanese Immigrants and American Law.* Garland Publishing, Inc., 2–23.

Buist, H., I. Megbolugbe, and T. Trent. 1994. "Racial Homeownership Patterns, the Mortgage Market, and Public Policy." *Journal of Housing Research* 5: 91–116.

Bureau of Indian Affairs. 2005. "Bureau of Indian Affairs." Retrieved on April 26, 2005 from http://www.doi.gov/bureau-indian-affairs.html.

Burgess, E. 1925. "The Growth of the City: An Introduction to a Research Project." In *The City,* R. Park, E. Burgess, and R. McKenzie (eds.). Chicago: University of Chicago Press, pp. 47–62.

Cabezas, A. and G. Kawaguchi. 1988. "Empirical Evidence for Continuing Asian American Income Inequality: The Human Capital Model and Labor Market Segmentation." G. Y. Orihiro, S. Hune, A. H. Hansen, and J. M. Liu (eds.). *Reflections on Shattered Windows: Promises and Prospects for Asian American Studies.* Pullman: Washington State University Press, 144–164.

Cabezas, A., T. M. Tam, B. M. Lowe, A. Wong, and K. O. Turner. 1989. "Empirical Study of Barriers to Upward Mobility of Asian Americans in the San Francisco Bay Area." In G. M. Nomura, R. Endo, S. H. Sumida, and R. C. Leong (eds.). *Frontiers of Asian American Studies.* Pullman: Washington State University Press, 85–97.

Caldwell, W. W., C. B. Schultz, and T. M. Stout (eds.). 1983. *Man and the Changing Environments in the Great Plains.* Lincoln, NE: Transactions of the Nebraska Academy of Science and the Center for Great Plains Studies.

California v. Cabazon Band of Mission Indians, 480 U.S. 2002 (1987).

Calman, N. 2005. "Making Health Equality a Reality: The Bronx Takes Action." *Health Affairs* 24(2): 491–499.

Camarillo, A. 1979. *Chicanos in a Changing Society: From Mexican Pueblos to American Barrios in Santa Barbara and Southern California, 1848–1930.* Cambridge, MA: Harvard University Press.

Camarota, S. 2001. *Immigrants in the United States — 2000: A Snapshot of America's Foreign-Born Population.* Center for Immigration Studies: Washington, D.C.

Camarota, S. A. 2004. "Economy Slowed but Immigration Didn't: The Foreign Born Population, 2000–2004." Washington, D.C.: Center for Immigration Studies. http://www.cis.org/articles/2004/back1204.html.

Campo-Flores, A. 2001. "A Town's Two Faces," *Newsweek* 137(23): 34–35. June 4.

Canelas, I. V. 1994. *Los Lavaplatos del Norte.* Cochabamba, Bolivia: Veloz.

Canner, G. 1991. "Home Mortgage Disclosure Act: Expanded Data on Residential Lending." *Federal Reserve Bulletin* 77: 859–81. http://www//responsiblelending.org/CoaltionStudies/PL%20Issue%20-%20Case%20(full).htm.

Carliner, G. 2000. "The Language Ability of U.S. Immigrants: Assimilation and Cohort Effects." *International Migration Reviev* 34(1): 158–182.

Carlson, A. W. 1973. "Seasonal Farm Labor in the San Luis Valley." *Annals of the Association of American Geographers* 63(2): 97–108.

Carney, J. A. 2001. *Black Rice: The African Origins of Rice Cultivation in the Americas.* Cambridge, Massachusetts: Harvard University Press, pp. 174–177.

Carpenter, J. A. 1947. *The Industrial Development of Paterson: 1792–1913.* New York: Columbia University.

Carr, J. H. and L. Kolluri. 2001. Predatory Lending: An Overview. *A Report of the Fannie Mae Foundation.* Washington D.C.

Carstensen, F. et al. 2000. *The Economic Impact of the Mashantucket Pequot Tribal Nation Operations on Connecticut.* Storrs, CT: Connecticut Center for Economic Analysis, University of Connecticut.

Carter-Pokras, O. and V. Woo. 1999. "Health Profile of Racial and Ethnic Minorities in the United States." *Ethnicity and Health* 4(3): 117–120.

Cary, F. C. (ed.). 1996. *Urban Odyssey: A Multicultural History of Washington, D.C.* Washington, D.C.: Smithsonian Institution.

Castells, M. 1996. "The Rise of the Network Society." *The Information Age: Economy, Society, and Culture,* Volume I. Oxford: Blackwell.

Castells, M. 1997. "The Power of Identity." *The Information Age: Economy, Society, and Culture,* Volume II. Oxford: Blackwell.

Castles, S. and M. Miller. 1993. *The Age of Migration.* New York: Guilford Press.

Castles, S. and M. J. Miller. 2003. *The Age of Migration,* 3rd Edition. New York and London: Guilford Press.

Center for Great Plains Studies. 2004. Available at http://www.unl.edu/plains. Accessed May 10, 2004.

Chacko, E. 2003. "Ethiopian Ethos and the Making of Ethnic Places in the Washington Metropolitan Area." *Journal of Cultural Geography* 20(2): 21–42.

Chacko, E. 2003. "Identity and Assimilation Among Young Ethiopian Immigrants in Metropolitan Washington." *Geographical Review* 93(4): 491–506.

Chang, I. 2003. *The Chinese in America.* New York: Penguin.

Chang, L. 1999. *Beyond the Narrow Gate.* New York: Penguin Putnam, Inc.

Chang, T. C. 2000. "Singapore's Little India: A Tourist Attraction as a Contested Landscape." *Urban Studies* 37(2): 343–366.

Chant, S. and S. Radcliffe. 1992. "Migration and Development: The Importance of Gender." In *Gender and Migration in Developing Countires,* edited by S. Chante. London: Bellhaven Press.

Cheng, L. and P. Q. Yang. 1996. "Asians: The Model Minority Deconstructed." In R. Waldinger and M. Bozorgmehr (eds.). *Ethnic Los Angeles.* New York: Russell Sage Foundation, pp. 305–44.

Chevannes, B. and H. Ricketts. 1997. "Return Migration and Small Business Development in Jamaica," in P. R. Pessar (ed.), *Caribbean Circuits*: *New Directions in the Study of Caribbean Migration.* New York: Center for Migration Studies. pp. 161–195.

Chinese American Service League (CASL). 1997. "Chicago's Chinatown." www.CASL.org. (Accessed March 15, 2003.)

Chiswick, B. R. and P. Miller. 1995. "The Endogeneity between Language and Earnings: International Analyses." *Journal of Labor Economics* 13(2): 246–288.

Chiswick, B. R. and W. P. Miller. 2003. "The Complimentary of Languale and other Human Capital: Immigrant Earnings in Canada." *Economics of Education Review* 22: 469–480.

Chuman, F. 1976. *The Bamboo People: The Law and Japanese-Americans.* Del Mar, California: Publisher's Inc.

City News Service, Inc. 2002. *Little Ethiopia.* August 8, 2002.

City of New York Department of Planning Report. 2004. The Newest New Yorkers, 2000: Immigrant New York in the New Millennium. October.

City of Oakland. 2000. "Consolidated Plan, 2000–2005."

Clark, T. A. 1979. *Blacks in Suburbs. A Natural Perspective.* New Brunswick: Rutgers University.

Clark, W. A. V. and P. Morrison. 1995. "Demographic Foundations of Political Empowerment in Multi-Minority Cities," *Demography* 32(2): 183–201.

Clark, W. A. V. 1998. *The California Cauldron: Immigration and the Fortunes of Local Communities.* New York: Guilford Press.

Clark, W. A. V. 2002. "Ethnic Preferences and Ethnic Perceptions in Multi-Ethnic Settings." *Urban Geography* 23(3): 237–256.

Clark, W. A. V. 2003. *Immigrants and the American Dream: Remaking the Middle Class.* New York: The Guilford Press.

Clark, W. A. V. 2003. "Voicing Allegiance." In *Immigrants and the American Dream: Remaking the Middle Class.* New York: Guilford Press, 163–193.

Clark, W. A. V. and S. A. Blue. 2004. "Race, Class, and Segregation Patterns in U.S. Immigrant Gateway Cities. *Urban Affairs Review* 39(6): 667–688.

Clemetson, L. 2004. "Coalition Seeks Action on Shared Data on Arab-Americans." *New York Times,* August 1, 2004. http://www.nytimes.com/2004/08/13/politics/13census.html. Last accessed 8/13/04.

Clogg, R. (ed.). 1999. "The Greek Diaspora in the Twentieth Century." New York: St. Martin's Press.

Clotfelter, C. T. 1999. "Public School Segregation in Metropolitan Areas." *Land Economics* 75: 487–504.

CNN, 2004. "Immigrant Nation, Divided Country." Aired October 17, 2004, Hosted by Maria Hinojosa. Transcript available at http://www.transcripts.cnn.com/TRANSCRIPTS/0410/17/cp.01.html.

Coalition for Responsible Lending. 2001. "The Case against Predatory Lending." http://www.responsiblelending.org/CoaltionStudies/PL%20Issue%20-%20Case%20(full).htm.

Coffman, T. 1998. *Nation Within: The Story of America's Annexation of the Nation of Hawaii.* Chicago, IL: Epicenter.

Coleman, J. S., S. D. Kelly, and J. Moore. 1975. *Trends in School Segregation, 1968–1973.* Washington, D.C.: The Urban Institute.

Collins, R. P. and A. P. Bailey. 1998. *Seventh Child: A Family Memoir of Malcolm X.* New York: Kensington Publishing.

Cone, James H. 1991. *Martin & Malcolm & America: A Dream or a Nightmare.* Maryknoll, NY: Orbis Books.

Conference of State Bank Supervisors. 2000. "States Act to Curb Predatory Lending while Ensuring Viable Subprime Market." www.cbs.org/news_PR.

Conquergood, D. 1992. "Life in Big Red: Struggles and Accommodations in a Chicago Polyethnic Tenement." In *Structuring Diversity: Ethnographic Perspectives on the New Immigration,* L. Lamphere (ed.). Chicago: University of Chicago Press, 95–114.

Constantinou, S. T. and M. E. Harvey. 1981. "A Spatio-Dynamic Model of Greek Residential Shifts in Akron, Ohio." Paper presented at the 77th annual meeting of the Association of American Geographers, Los Angeles, California.

Constantinou, S. T. 1982. "A Geographic Systems Approach to Ethnicity: The Greek Americans in Northeastern Ohio." Ph.D. dissertation, Kent State University.

Constantinou, S. T. and N. D. Diamantides. 1985. "Modeling International Migration: Determinants of Emigration from Greece to the United States, 1820–1980." *Annals of the Association of American Geographers* 75: 352–369.

Constantinou, S. T. and M. E. Harvey. 1985. "Dimensional Structure and Intergenerational Differences."

Constantinou, S. T. 1989. "Dominant Themes and Intergenerational Differences in Ethnicity: The Greek Americans." *Sociological Focus* 22 (May): 99–118.

Constantinou, S. T. 1996. "Greek American Networks." In *Les Réseaux des Diasporas The Networks of Daisporas,* edited by G. Prévélakis, pp. 305–322. Nicosia, Cyprus; Paris: KYKEM (Cyprus Research Center); L'Harmattan.

Conway, D. and U. Bigby. 1992. "Where Caribbean Peoples Live in New York City," in C. R. Sutton and E. N. Chaney (eds.). *Caribbean Life in New York City: Sociocultural Dimensions.* Staten Island, NY: Center for Migration Studies, pp. 70–78.

Cook, J. B. 1931. "San Francisco's Old Chinatown." *San Francisco Police and Peace Officers' Journal.* Reprinted at website www.sfmuseum.org. (Accessed April 30, 2003.)

Cooke, T. J. and J. M. Shumway. 1991. "Developing the Spatial Mismatch Hypothesis: Problems of Accessibility to Employment for Low Wage Central City Labor." *Urban Geography* 12: 310–323.

Cooper, S., K. Burau, A. Sweeney, T. Robison, M. A. Smith, E. Symanski, J. S. Colt, J. Laseter, and S. H. Zehm. 2001a. "Parental Exposures to Pesticides: A Feasibility Study among Migrant and Seasonal Farmworkers." *American Journal of Industrial Medicine* 40(5): 578–585.

Cooper, S., K. Burau, A. Sweeney, T. Robison, M. A. Smith, E. Symanski, J. S. Colt, J. Laseter, and S. H. Zehm. 2001b. "Ascertainment of Pesticide Exposures of Migrant and Seasonal Farmworker Children. Findings from Focus Groups." *American Journal of Industrial Medicine* 40(5): 531–537.

Cose, E. 1993. *The Rage of a Priviledged Middle Class.* New York: Harper Collins.

Cressey, P. F. 1938. "Population Succession in Chicago, 1898–1930." *American Journal of Sociology* 64: 364–74.

Cromartie, J. and C. B. Stack. 1989. "Reinterpretation of Black Return and Non-return Migration to the South 1975–80." *Geographical Review* 79(3): 297–310.

Cromley, E. K. and S. McClafferty. 2002. *GIS and Public Health.* New York: The Guilford Press.

Cronon, W. 1983. *Changes in the Land: Indians, Colonists, and the Ecology of New England.* New York: Hill and Wang.

Cross, M. 1998. *Ethnic Minorities and Industrial Change in Europe and North America.* London: Cambridge University Press.

Crowder, K. D. and L. M. Tedrow. 2001. "West Indians and then Residential Landscape on New York," in N. Foner (ed.). *Island in the City: West Indian Migration to New York.* Berkeley, CA: University of California Press, pp. 81–114.

Cunningham, P. 1996. "Changing Numbers, Changing Needs: American Indian Demography and Public Health." *Commission on Behavioral and Social Sciences and Education*. National Academies Press.

Dagodag, W. T. 1974. "Spatial Control and Public Policies: The Example of Mexican-American Housing." *Professional Geographer* 26(3): 262–269.

Dakan, W. 2000a. "Becoming Middle Class in Louisville: The Place-Time Trajectories of Recent Imigrants." Presented at the Conference on Race, Ethnicity, and Place, Howard University.

Dakan, W. 2000b. "Entrepreneurs and the American Dream: Immigrant and Ethnic Businesses in Louisville, KY." Presented at the Applied Geography Conference, St. Louis.

Dakan, W. 2005. "Gateway Migration to Interior Cities: Country to County Mobility of Immigrants." Presented to Association of American Geographers, Denver.

Dandler, J. and C. Medeiros. 1988. "Temporary Migration from Cochabamba, Bolivia to Argentina: Patterns and Impact in Sending Areas" in *When Borders Don't Divide*, P. Pessar (ed.). New York: Center for Migration Studies.

Daniels, R. 1977. *The Politics of Prejudice: The Anti-Japanese Movement in California and the Struggle for Japanese Exclusion*. 2nd ed. Berkeley: University of California Press.

Darden, J. T. 1990. "Differential Access to Housing in the Suburbs." *Journal of Black Studies* 21: 15–22.

Darden, J. T. 2003. "The Plight of African Americans in Michigan: Residential Segregation and Predictable Outcomes in Mortgage Lending and Educational Achievement." In J. W. Frazier and F. M. Margai (eds.) *Multicultural Geographies*. Binghamton, NY: Global Academic Publishing, pp. 41–54.

Dasgupta, P. and I. Serageldin (eds.). 2000. *Social Capital: A Multifaceted Perspective*. Washington, D.C.: World Bank.

Davé, S. et al. 2000. "De-Privileging Positions: Indian Americans, South Asian Americans, and the Politics of Asian American Studies." *Journal of Asian American Studies* 3(1): 67–100.

Davis, M. 1999. "Magical Urbanism: Latinos Reinvent the U.S. Big City." *New Left Review*, March–April: 3–43.

Daws, G. 1968. *Shoal of Time: A History of the Hawaiian Islands*. Honolulu: University of Hawaii Press.

DeAre, D. 1990. "Longitudinal Migration Data from the Survey of Income and Program Participation." *Current Population Reports, Series P20–166*.

DeCaro Jr., L. A. 1996. *On the Side of My People: A Religious Lie of Malcolm X*. New York: New York University Press.

DeCaro Jr., L. A. 1998. *Malcolm and the Cross: The Nation of Islam, Malcolm X, and Christianity*. New York: New York University Press.

Delany, D. 1998. *Race, Place, and the Law*, 1836–1948. Austin: University of Texas Press.

Deloria, V. 1974. *Behind the Trail of Broken Treaties*. New York: Delacorte Press.

Deloria, V. 1988. *Custer Died for Your Sins*. Norman, OK: University of Oklahoma Press.

Demissie, Y. 2002. "In the Beginning was Fairfax Avenue." *Branna* 1(2): 6–7.

Denton, N. A. and D. S. Massey. 1989. "Residential Segregation of Blacks, Hispanics, and Asians by Socioeconomic Status and Generation." *Social Science Quarterly* 69: 797–808.

Denton, N. A. 1994. "Are African Americans Still Hypersegregated?" In *Residential Apartheid: The American Legacy*, R. D. Bullard, J. E. Grigsby III, and C. Lee (eds.). Los Angeles: Center for Afro-American Studies, University of California, pp. 49–81.

Department of Housing and Urban Development. 2000. "Unequal Burden: Income and Racial Disparities in Subprime Lending in America." www.hud.gov/library/bookshelf 18.

d'Hautesserre, A. 1998. "Foxwoods Casino Resort: An Unusual Experiment in Economic Development," *Economic Geography*, pp. 112–121.

d'Hautesserre, A. 2000. "Lessons in Managed Destination Competitiveness: The Case of Foxwoods Casino Resort," *Tourism Management* 21: 23–32.

Dingemans, D. and R. Datel. 1995. "Urban Multiethnicity." *The Geographical Review* 85(4): 458–477.

Dower, J. W. 1986. *War Without Mercy: Race and Power in the Pacific War*. New York: Pantheon.

Dubey, A. (ed.). 2003. *Indian Diaspora: Global Identity*. Mayur Vihar, Delhi: Kalinga Publications.

DuBois, W. E. B. 1901. "The Black North: A Social Study. New York City." *New York Times*. November 17 and 24. In J. P. Shenton and G. Brown (eds.). 1978. "Ethnic Groups in American Life." New York: *The New York Times*, Arno Press.

Dutta, M. 1982. "Asian Indian Americans: Search for an Economic Profile." In *From India to America: A Brief History of Immigration, Problems of Discrimination, Admission, and Assimilation*, S. Chandrasekhar (ed.). La Jolla, CA: Population Review Publications, pp. 76–86.

Dyer, R. 1997. *White: Essays on Race and Culture*. London: Routledge.

Dyer, E. 2004. The New Face of AIDS: Young, Black and Female. *The Crisis*. November/December 2004: pp. 29–32.

Dyson, M. E. 1995. *Making Malcolm: The Myth and Meaning of Malcolm X*. New York: Oxford Press.

Eisler, K. 2001. *Revenge of the Pequots: How a Small Native American Tribe Created the World's Most Profitable Casino*. New York: Simon and Shuster.

Ellwood, D. T. 1986. "The Spatial Mismatch Hypothesis: Are there Teen Age Jobs Missing in the Ghetto?" In R. B. Freeman and H. J. Holzer (eds.). *The Black Youth Employment Crisis*. Chicago: University of Chicago Press, pp. 147–187.

Ellis, M. and R. Wright. 1998. "The Balkanization Metaphor in the Analysis of U.S. Immigration." *Annals of the Association of American Geographers* 88(4): 686–698.

Engel, K. and P. McCoy. 2001. "The Law and Economics of Remedied for Predatory Lending." DRAFT copy.

Engesaeter, P. 1995. "A Geographical Approach to the Study of Well-being," In R. Bivand and K. Stokke (eds.). *Investigating the Local: Structure, Place and Agency*. Bergen, Serie B: Monografier fra Institutt for Geografi, Nr. 1.

Espiritu, Y. L. and I. Light. 1991. "The Changing Ethnic Shape of Contemporary Urban America." In *Urban Life in Transition,* M. Gottdiener and C. G. Pickvance (eds.). Newbury Park, CA: Sage Publications, pp. 35–54.

Estaville, L. and C. Rosen (eds.). 1997. *Teaching American Ethnic Geography*. Indiana, PA: National Council for Geographic Education.

Ethiopian Yellow Pages. 2002–2003. Accessed from http://www.ethiopianyellowpage.com/on August 3, 2003.

Fagan, R. R., R. A. Brody, and T. J. O'Leary. 1968. "Cubans in Exile: Disaffection and the Revolution." Stanford, CA: Stanford University Press.

Fan, C. 2003. "Chinese Americans: Immigration, Settlement, and Social Geography." In *Chinese Diaspora: Space, Place, Mobility, and Identity,* L. J. C. Ma and C. L. Cartier (eds.). Lanham, MD: Rowman and Littlefield Publishers, Inc., pp. 27–42.

Fanon, F. 1967. *Black Skin, White Masks*. New York: Grove Press.

Farley, R. and W. Allen. 1987. *The Color Line and the Quality of Life in America*. New York: Russell Sage Foundation.

The Farmworkers Website. 2004. The Bracero Program. Available at http://www.farmworkers.org/bracerop.html. Accessed on 1 August 2004.

Fellers, L. 2003. "Artesia Split on Little India Proposal." *Los Angeles Times*. June 10, Metro Section, Part 2, page 3.

Fernandez, R. M. 1994. "Race, Space, and Job Accessibility: Evidence from a Plant Relocation." *Economic Geography* 70(4): 390–416.

Fields, R. and R. Herndon. 2001. "Segregation of a New Sort Takes Shape: Census: In a Majority of Cities, Asians and Latinos have Become More Isolated from Other Racial Groups." *Los Angeles Times*. July, 5.

Fine, M., M. Wong, I. Weis, and L. Powell (eds.). 1997. *Off-White: Readings on Society, Race, and Culture*. London: Routledge.

Fishbein, A. and H. Bunce. 2000. "Subprime Market Growth and Predatory Lending." www.huduser.org/publications.

Fisher, M. P. 1980. *The Indians of New York City: A Study of Immigrants from India*. Columbia, MO: South Asia Books.

Fitzpatrick, J. P. 1995. "Puerto Rican New Yorkers." *Migration World Magazine* 23(1): 16–19.

Flores, G., E. Fuentes-Afflick, O. Barbot, and O. Carter-Pokras et al. 2002. "The Health of Latino Children: Urgent Priorities, Unanswered Questions, and a Research Agenda." *Journal of the American Medical Association* 288(10): 82–91.

Foner, N. 1992. "West Indians in London and New York City: A Comparative Analysis," in C. R. Sutton and E. M. Chaney (eds.). *Caribbean Life in New York City: Sociocultural Dimensions*. Staten Island, NY: Center for Migration Studies, pp. 108–120.

Foner, N. 1997. "What's New About Transnationalism?: New York Immigrants Today and at the Turn of the Century." *Diapora* 3: 355–76.

Foner, N. 1998. "Towards a Comparative Perspective on Caribbean Migration," in M. Chamberlain (ed.). *Caribbean Migration: Globalised Identities*. New York: Routledge, pp. 47–60.

Foner, N. 2000. *From Ellis Island to J.F.K.: New York's Two Great Waves of Immigration*. New Haven and New York: Yale University Press and the Russell Sage Foundation.

Foner, N. 2001. "West Indian Migration to New York: An Overview," in N. Foner (ed.). *Islands in the City: West Indian Migration to New York*. Berkeley, CA: University of California Press, pp. 1–22.

Fong, P. and A. Cabezas. 1980. "Economic and Employment Status of Asian American Women." In *Conference on the Educational and Occupational Needs of Asian-Pacific-American Women*. Washington, D.C.-U.S. Department of Education.

Foster, N. 1932. "Legal Status of Filipino Intermarriages in California." In C. McClain (ed.). *Asian Indians, Filipinos, Other Asian Communities and the Law*. New York: Garland Publishing, Inc., pp. 5–19.

Fountain, J. W. 2002. "Trajedy Chose a Place of Quiet Serenity," *New York Times.* October 17.

Foust, D., B. Grow, and A. Pascual. 2002. "The Changing Heartland: An Influx of Newcomers Both Buoys and Burden Small-town America," *Business Week.* September 9.

Frankenberg, E., C. Lee, and G. Orfield. 2003. "A Multiracial Society with Segregated Schools: Are We Losing the Dream?" Cambridge, MA: The Civil Rights Project, Harvard University, January. http://www.civilrightsproject.harvard.edu/research/reseg03/reseg03_full.php. [Accessed April 5, 2005.]

Frankenberg, R. 1993. *White Women, Race Matters: The Social Construction of Whiteness.* Minneapolis: University of Minnesota Press.

Franklin, M. 2003. "I Define My Own Identity: Pacific Articulations of 'Race' and 'Culture' on the Internet." *Ethnicities* 3(4): 465–490.

Frazier, E. F. 1932. *The Negro Family in Chicago.* Chicago: University of Chicago Press.

Frazier, J. W. 2003. "Asians in America: Some Historical and Contemporary Patterns." In *MultiCultural Geographies: The Changing Racial and Ethnic Patterns of the United States.* J. W. Frazier and F. M. Margai (eds.). Binghamton, NY: Global Academic Publishing.

Frazier, J. W. and F. L. Margai, eds. 2003. *Multi-Cultural Geographies: Persistence and Change in U.S. Racial/Ethnic Geography.* Binghamton, NY: Global Academic Publishing.

Frazier, J. W., F. M. Margai, and E. Tettey-Fio. 2003. *Race and Place: Equity Issues in Urban America.* Boulder, CO: Westview Press.

Frey, W. H. 2001a. "Migration to the South Brings U.S. Blacks Full Circle." www.prb.org/template.cfm (accessed June 6, 2003).

Frey, W. H. 2001b. "Foreign-Born Make Up Growing Segment of U.S. Black Population." www.prb.org/template.cfm (accessed June 6, 2003).

Frey, W. H. 2004. "The New Great Migration: Black Americans' Return to the South, 1965–2001." Washington, D.C.: The Brookings Institution.

Frist, W. 2005. "Overcoming Disparities in U.S. Health Care." *Health Affairs* 24(2): 445–452.

Fugita, S. S. and D. J. O'Brien. 1991. *Japanese American Ethnicity: The Persistence of Community.* Seattle: University of Washington Press.

Frugitt, G., D. L. Brown, and C. L. Beale. 1989. *Rural and Small Town America.* New York: Russell Sage Foundation.

Funkhouser, E. 2000. "Changes in the Geographic Concentration and Location of Residence of Immigrants." *International Migration Review* 34(2): 489–510.

Gabaccia, D. 1992. *Seeking Common Ground: Multidisciplinary Studies of Immigrant Women in the United States.* Westport, CT: Praeger.

Galea, S., N. Freudenberg, and D. Vlahov. 2004. "Cities and Population Health." *Social Science and Medicine* 60 (2005): 1017–1033.

Gallagher, P. L. 1980. *The Cuban Exile: A Socio-Political Analysis.* New York: Arno Press.

Gann, L. H. and P. J. Duignan. 1986. "The Hispanics." In L. H. Gann and P. J. Duignan (eds.). *The Latinos in the United States: A History.* Boulder, CO: Westview Press, pp. 69–93.

Gann, L. H. and P. J. Duignan. 1986. "The Puerto Ricans." In L. H. Gann and P. J. Duignan (eds.). *The Hispanics in the United States: A History.* Boulder, CO: Westview Press, pp. 69–93.

Garcia, M. C. 1996. *Havana USA.* Berkeley: University of California Press.

Garcia, M. T. 1981. *Desert Immigrants: The Mexicans of El Paso, 1880–1920.* New Haven: Yale University Press.

Gatrell, A. C. 2002. *Geographies of Health.* Oxford, UK: Blackwell Publishers.

George, R. M. 1997. "From Expatriate Aristocrat to Immigrant Nobody: South Asian Racial Strategies in the Southern Californian Context." *Diaspora* 6(1): 31–60.

Georges, E. 1990. *The Making of a Transnational Community: Migration, Development and Cultural Change in the Dominican Republic.* New York: Columbia University Press.

Geronimus, A. T. 1992. "The Weathering Hypothesis and the Health of the African American Women and Infants: Evidence and Speculations." *Ethnicity and Disease* 2: 207–221.

Geronimus, A. T. 2000. "To Mitigate, Resist, or Undo: Addressing Structural Influences on the Health of Urban Populations." *American Journal of Public Health* 90(6): 867–872.

Gibson, C. and K. Jung. 2002. *Historical Census Statistics on Population Totals by Race, 1790 to 1990, and by Hispanic Origin, 1970 to 1990, for the United States, Regions, Divisions, and States.* Washington, D.C.: United States Bureau of the Census.

Gilmore, R. W. 2002. "Fatal Couplings of Power and Difference: Notes on Racism and Geography." *The Professional Geographer* 54(1): 15–24.

Glazer, N. and D. P. Moynihan. 1970. *Beyond the Melting Pot.* Cambridge, MA: MIT Press.

Gobillon, L., H. Selod, and Y. Zenou. 2003. "Spatial Mismatch in U.S. Cities: Facts and Theories." Institute for the Study of Labor (IZA) Discussion Paper 693. http://www.iza.org/ (accessed June 9, 2005).

Godfrey, B. 1988. *Neighborhoods in Transition: The Making of San Francisco's Ethnic and Nonconformist Communities.* Berkeley: University of California Press.

Goldman, P. 1979. *The Death and Life of Malcolm X.* New York: Harpur and Row, 2nd ed.

Golovan, V. 2004. *Slavic Coalition of Oregon: Past, Present, Future.* Portland: Slavic Coalition.

Golovan, V. 2004. *Slavic Coalition of Oregon Retreat Minutes.* Portland: Slavic Coalition.

Gomez, M. A., *Exchanging Our Country Marks: The Transformation of African Identities on the Colonial and Antebellum South.* Chapel Hill: The University of North Carolina Press, 1998, pp. 27, 155.

Goodman, J. and D. Heffington. 2000. "Native Americans." In *Ethnicity in Contemporary America: A Geographical Appraisal.* 2nd ed. Edited by J. McKee. New York: Rowman and Littlefield Publishers.

Gordon-Larsen, P., K. M. Harris, D. S. Ward, and B. M. Popkin. 2003. "Acculturation and Overweight Related Behaviors among Hispanic Immigrants to the U.S.: The National Longitudinal Study of Adolescent Health." *Social Science and Medicine* 57: 2023–2034.

Gordon, M. M. 1964. *Assimilation in American Life: The Role of Race, Religion, and National Origins.* New York: Oxford University Press.

Gordon, P., A. Kumar, and H. W. Richardson. 1989. "Gender Differences in Metropolitan Travel Behavior." *Regional Studies* 23: 499–510.

Gottdiener, M. and C. Pickvance. 1991. "Introduction." In *Urban Life in Transition,* M. Gottdiener and C. D. Pickvance (eds.). Newbury Park, CA: Sage Productions, pp. 1–11.

Gottlieb, E. 1992. *The Orwell Conundrum: A Cry of Despair or Faith in the Spirit of Man?* Ottowa: Carleton University Press.

Gottlieb, E. 2001. *Dystopian Fiction East and West: A Universe of Terror and Trial.* Montreal and Kingston: McGill-Queen's University Press.

Grady, S. 2003. "Low Birth Weight and the Contribution of Residential Segregation. New York City, 2000." In *Multicultural Geographies: The Changing Racial and Ethnic Patterns of the United States.* J. W. Frazier and F. M. Margai (eds.). Binghamton, NY: Global Academic Publishing.

Grant, J. A. C. 1994. "Historical Note: Testimonial Exclusion Because of Race: A Chapter in the History of Intolerance in California." C. McClain (ed.), *Chinese Immigrants and American Law.* New York: Garland Publishing, Inc., pp. 82–91.

Grasmuck, S. and P. R. Pessar. 1991. *Between Two Islands: Dominican International Migration.* Berkley: University of California.

Graves, J. L., Jr. 2004. *The Race Myth, Why We Pretend Race Exists in America.* New York: Dutton.

Gray, J. 2000. *Two Faces of Liberalism.* Cambridge: Cambridge University Press.

Greek Orthodox Archdiocese of North and South America. 1994. *1994 Yearbook.* New York: Greek Orthodox Archdiocese of North and South America.

Greytak, D. 1974. "The Journey to Work: Racial Differences and City Size." *Traffic Quarterly* 28(2): 241–256.

Groth, P. 1997. "Frameworks of Cultural Landscape Study." In *Understanding Ordinary Landscapes.* P. Groth and T. W. Bressi (eds). New Haven: Yale University Press.

Gruenewald, D. 2003. "Foundations of Place: A Multidisciplinary Framework for Place-conscious Education." *American Educational Research Journal* 40(3): 619–54.

Guest, A. M. 1978. "The Radical Composition of Suburbs, 1950–1970." *Urban Affairs Quarterly* 14: 195–206.

Guzman, B. 2001. Census 2000 Paints Statistical Portrait of the Latino Population. Department of Commerce News, Press Release CB01-81, U.S. Census Bureau, Washington, D.C.

Hacker, A. 1992. *Two Nations: Black and White, Separate, Hostile, Unequal.* New York: Charles Scribner & Sons.

Halliday, J. 1975. *A Political History of Japanese Capitalism.* New York: Pantheon.

Halualani, R. T. 2002. *In the Name of Hawaiians: Native Identities and Cultural Politics.* MN: University of Minnesota Press.

Handlin, O. 1951. *The Uprooted.* New York: Grosset & Dunlap.

Handy, E. S. C. and E. G. Handy. 1972. *Native Planters in Old Hawaii: Their Life, Lore, and Environment.* Honolulu: Bishop Museum Press.

Handy, E. S. C. and M. K. Pukui. 1998. *The Polynesian Family System in Kau, Hawaii*. Honolulu: Mutual Publishing.

Hane, M. 1982. *Peasants, Rebels, and Outcastes: The Underside of Modern Japan*. New York: Pantheon Books.

Hane, M. 1990. *Modern Japan: A Historical Survey*. Boulder, CO and London: Westview Press.

Hanson, S. and G. Pratt. 1995. *Gender, Work, and Space*. New York: Routledge.

Hanson, S. and I. Johnston. 1995. "Gender Differences in Work-Trip Length: Explanations and Implications." *Urban Geography* 6: 193–219.

Hardwick, S. W. 1993. *Russian Refuge: Religion, Migration, and Settlement on the North American Pacific Rim*. Chicago: University of Chicago Press.

Hardwick, S. W. 2002. "California's Emerging Russian Homeland." In *Homelands: A Geography of Culture and Place Across America*, R. Nostrand and L. Estaville (eds.). Baltimore: The Johns Hopkins University Press, pp. 210–24.

Hardwick, S. W. 2003. "Migration, Embedded Networks and Social Capital: Toward Theorizing North American Ethnic Geography." *International Journal of Population Geography* 9(1): 163–79.

Hardwick, S. W. and S. E. Hume. (Forthcoming). "Migration, Culture, Place: The Impacts of Refugee Resettlement on the Portland Urban Area." *Geographical Review*.

Harner, J. "Place Identity and Cooper Mining in Sonora, Mexico." 2001. *Annals of the AAG* 91(4): 660–680.

Harris, R. 1990. "Working-Call Home Ownership in the American Metropolis." *Journal of Urban History* 17(4): 46–69.

Harris, R. 1991. "Self-Building in the Urban Housing Market." *Economic Geography* 67(1): 1–21.

Harris, R. 1992. "The Unplanned Blue-Collar Suburb in Its Hey-Day." In D. G. Janelle (ed.). *Geographical Snapshots of North America*. New York: Guilford Press.

Harris, R. 1996. *Unplanned Suburbs: Toronto's American Trgedy*. Baltimore: Johns Hopkins Press.

Hart, J. F. 1960. "The Changing Distribution of Negro Population in the United States." *Annals of the Association of American Geographers* 50: 242–266.

Hart, J. F. 1995. "Reading the Landscape." *Landscape in America*. G. F. Thompson (ed.). Austin: University of Texas Press, pp. 23–42.

Hartshorn, T. A. and P. O. Muller. 1986. *Suburban Business Centers: Employment Expectations*. Washington, D.C.: Final Report for the U.S. Department of Commerce, EDA.

Harvey, D. 1989. *The Condition of Postmodernity*. Cambridge, MA and Oxford, UK: Blackwell.

Harvey, D. 2000. "The Body as an Accumulation Strategy." In *Spaces of Hope*. Berkeley, CA: University of California Press, pp. 97–116.

Harvey, D. 2001. "The Art of Rent: Globalization and the Commodification of Culture." In *Spaces of Capital: Towards a Critical Geography*. New York: Routledge, pp. 394–411.

Haverluk, T. 1997. "The Changing Geography of U.S. Latinos, 1850–1990." *Journal of Geography,* May/June 1997, pp. 134–145.

Hayden, D. 1995. *The Power of Place: Urban Landscapes as Public History*. Cambridge, MA: MIT Press.

Hayden, T. 2004. "Tribes and Tribulations," *U.S. News and World Report* 137(11): 44–50.

Head, B. 1986. *Serowe: Villiage of the Rain Wind*. London: Heineman Educational Books Ltd.

Health Resources and Services Administration (HRSA). 2000. *Eliminating Health Disparities in the United States*. Report prepared by HRSA Workgroup for the Elimination of Health Disparities.

Hellerich, M. H. 1987. *Allentown, 1762–1987. A 225 Year History*. Vol. 2. Lehigh County Historical Society.

Helzer, J. J. 2001. "Old Traditions, New Lifestyles: The Emergence of a Cal-Ital Landscape." *Yearbook of the Association of Pacific Coast Geographers* 63: 49–62.

Henke, H. 2001. *The West Indian Americans*. Westport, CT: Greenwood Press.

Hernandez-Alvarez, J. 1968. "The Movement and Settlement of Puerto Rican Migrants Within the United States, 1950–1960." *International Migration Review* 2 (Spring): 40–51.

Hicks, D. A. and S. R. Nivin. 1996. "Global Credentials, Immigration, and Metro-Regional Economic Performance." *Urban Geography* 16: 230–243.

Hill, G. W. 1941. "The Use of the Culture-Area Concept in Social Research." *American Journal of Sociology* 47(1): 39–47.

Hintzen, P. 2001. *West Indian in the West: Self-Representations in an Immigrant Community*. New York: New York University Press.

Hirchman, C. 1978. "Prior Residence in the United States among the Mexican Immigrants." *Social Forces* 56: 1179–1202.

Hirchman, C. 2001. "The Educational Enrollment of Immigrant Youth: A Test of the Segmented-Assimilation Hypothesis." *Demography* 38(3): 317–336.

Hodge, D. C. 1996. "And in Conclusion: It Depends." *Professional Geographer* 48: 417–419.

Hoelscher, S. D. 1998. *Heritage on Stage: The Invention of Ethnic Place in America's Little Switzerland.* Madison, Wisconsin: The University of Wisconsin Press.

Hoelscher, S. 2003. "Making Place, Making Race: Performances of Whiteness in the Jim Crow South." *Annals of the Association of American Geographers* 93(3): 657–686.

Hoffman, A. 1974. *Unwanted Mexican-Americans in the Great Depression: Repatriation Pressures, 1929–1939.* Tucson: University of Arizona Press.

Hofstadter, R. and S. M. Lipset. 1968. *Turner and the Sociology of the Frontier.* New York: Basic Books.

Holli, M. G. and P. Jones (eds.). 1995. *Ethnic Chicago: A Multicultural Portrait.* Grand Rapids, MI: William B. Eerdmans Publishing Company.

Holzer, H. J. 1991. "The Spatial Mismatch Hypothesis: What Has the Evidence Shown?" *Urban Studies* 28(1): 105–22.

Holzer, H. J., K. Ihlanfeldt, and D. L. Sjoquist. 1994. "Work, Search, and Travel among White and Black Youth." *Journal of Urban Economies* 35: 320–345.

Hong, Y.-H. and G. Sommers. 2000. "Predatory Lending and its Impact on Inner City Neighborhoods." Proposal to the Ohio Urban University Program.

Howard-Pitney, D. 1990. *The Afro-American Jeremiad: Appeals for Justice in America.* Philadelphia: Temple University Press.

Huffman, A. 2004. *Mississippi in Africa: The Saga of Slaves of Prospect Hill Plantation and Their Legacy in Liberia Today.* New York, New York: Gotham Books, p. 159.

Hume, S. E. 2005. *The Ethnic, Panethnic, and Racial Identities of African University Students in Their Home Countries and in the United States.* Ph.D. Diss. University of Oregon, Department of Geography.

Hune, S. 1994. "Politics of Chinese Exclusion: Legislative-Executive Conflict." C. McClain (ed.). *Chinese Immigrants and American Law,* pp. 93–116.

Iceland, J., D. Weinberg, and E. Steinmetz. 2002. *Racial and Ethnic Residential Segregation in the United States: 1980–2000.* U.S. Bureau of the Census, Census Special Report, CENSR-3. Washington, D.C.: Government Printing Office.

Ichioka, Y. 1988. *The Issei: The World of the First Generation Japanese Immigrants, 1885–1924.* New York: The Free Press.

Ignatiev, N. 1995. *How the Irish Became White.* New York: Routlege.

Ihlanfeldt, K. and D. L. Sjoquist. 1989. "The Impact of Job Decentralization on the Economic Welfare of Central City Blacks." *Journal of Urban Economies* 26: 110–130.

Ihlanfeldt, K. R. 1992. "Intraurban Wage Gradients: Evidence by Race, Gender, Occupational Class, and Sector." *Journal of Urban Economies* 32: 70–91.

Ihlanfeldt, K. R. and M. V. Young. 1994. "Housing Segregation and the Wages and Commutes of Urban Blacks: The Case of Atlanta Fast-Food Restaurant Workers." *Review of Economics and Statistics* 76: 425–33.

Ihlanfeldt, K. R. and D. L. Sjoquist. 1998. "The Spatial Mismatch Hypothesis: A Review of Recent Studies and Their Implications for Welfare Reform." *Housing Policy Debate* 9: 849–892.

Immergluck, D. and M. Wiles. 1999. *Two Steps Back: The Dual Mortgage Market, Predatory Lending, and the Undoing of Community Development.* Chicago: The Woodstock Institute.

INS, 2000. "Estimates of the Unauthorized Immigrant Population Residing in the United States: 1990–2000." Office of Policy and Planning, U.S. Immigration and Naturalization Service, http://www.uscis.gov/graphics/shared/aboutus/statistics/Ill_Report_1211.pdf.

Iwata, M. 1990. *Planted in Good Soil: A History of the Issei in the United States Agriculture.* 2 vols. New York: P. Lang.

Jackson, K. T. 1985. *Crabgrass Frontier: The Suburbanization of the United States.* New York: Oxford University Press.

Jackson, P. (ed.). 1987. *Race and Racism: Essays in Social Geography.* London: Allen and Unwin.

Jackson, P. and J. Penrose. 1993. *Constructions of Race, Place, and Nation.* London: UCL Press.

Jackson, P. 1998. "Constructions of 'Whiteness' in the Geographical Imagination," *Area* 30(2): 99–106.

Jaffe, A. J., R. M. Cullen, and T. D. Boswell. 1980. *The Changing Demography of Spanish Americans.* New York: Academic Press.

James, P. and C. Jones (eds.). 1954. *American Geography Inventory and Prospect.* Syracuse, NY: Syracuse University Press.

Jargowsky, P. A. 1997. *Poverty and Place: Ghettos, Barrios, and the American City.* New York, NY: Russell Sage Foundation.

Jargowsky, P. 2003. "Stunning Progress, Hidden Problems: The Dramatic Decline in Concentrated Poverty in the 1990s." Washington D.C. Center of Urban and Metropolitan Policy. The Brookings Institute.

Jefferson, M. 1976. "Black Rebels," *Newsweek,* July 4.

Jencks, C. S. and S. E. Mayer. 1990. "Residential Segregation, Job Proximity, and Black Job Opportunities." In *Inner-City Poverty in the United States.* L. E. Lynn, Jr. and M. G. H. McGeary (eds.). Washington, DC: National Academy Press: 197–222.

Jensen, J. M. 1988. *Passage From India: Asian Indian Immigrants in North America.* New Haven, CT: Yale University Press.

Jobu, R. M. 1976. "Earnings Differential between Whites and Ethnic Minorities: The Cases of Asian Americans, Blacks, and Chicanos." *Sociology and Social Research* 61(10): 24–38.

Johnston, R., M. Poulsen, and J. Forrest. 2002. "Rethinking the Analysis of Ethnic Residential Patterns: Segregation, Isolation, or Concentration Thresholds in Auckland, New Zealand." *Geographical Analysis* 34(3): 245–261.

Johnston-Anumonwo, I. 1995. "Racial Differences in the Commuting Behavior of Women in Buffalo, NY, 1980–1990." *Urban Geography* 16: 23–45.

Johnston-Anumonwo, I. 1997. "Race, Gender, and Constrained Work Trips in Buffalo, NY, 1990." *Professional Geographer* 49: 306–317.

Johnston-Anumonwo, I. 2000. "Community Constraints of Black Women: Evidence from Detroit, Michigan." *The Great Lakes Geographer* 7(2): 66–75.

Johnston-Anumonwo, I., S. McLafferty and V. Preston. 1995. "Gender, Race, and the Spatial Context of Women's Employment." In *Gender in Urban Research,* J. A. Garber and R. S. Turner (eds.). Thousand Oaks, CA: Sage Publications, pp. 236–255.

Jones, L. 1979. *From Brown to Boston: Desegregation in Education, 1954–1974,* Volume II. Metuchen, NJ: The Scarecrow Press, Inc.

Jones, R. C. 1995. "Immigration Forms and Migrant Flows: Compositional and Spatial Changes in Mexican Migration after the Immigration Reform Act of 1986," *Annals of the Association of American Geographers* 85(4): 715–730.

Jones, R. C. 1996. "Spatial Origins of San Antonio's Mexican-Born Population," *Rio Bravo* 5(1): 1–26.

Jones, R. C. and Shannon Crum. 2004. "Changing Spatial Patterns of Ethnic and Immigrant Groups in San Antonio, 1990–2000." Paper presented at the 2004 Conference on Race, Ethnicity, and Place. Washington, DC: Howard University, September 16–18.

Jones, R. C. 2005. "Cultural Diversity in a 'Bi-Cultural' City: Factors in the Location of Ancestry Groups in San Antonio." *Cultural Geography,* forthcoming.

Jordan, T. G., J. L. Bean, and W. M. Holmes. 1984. *Texas: A Geography.* Boulder: Westview Press.

Juergensmeyer, J. 1982. "The Gadar Syndrome: Ethnic Anger and Nationalistic Pride." In *From India to America: A Brief History of Immigration, Problems of Discrimination, Admission, and Assimilation,* S. Chandrasekhar (ed.). La Jolla, CA: Population Review Publications, pp. 48–58.

Kain, J. 1968. "Housing Segregation, Negro Employment, and Metropolitan Decentralization." *Quarterly Journal of Economics* 82(2): 175–197.

Kain, J. 1992. "The Spatial Mismatch Hypothesis: Three Decades Later." *Housing Policy Debate* 2: 371–460.

Kalita, S. M. 2003. *Suburban Sahibs: Three Immigrant Families and Their Passage from India to America.* New Brunswick, NJ: Rutgers University Press.

Kamakau, S. M. 1992. *Ruling Chiefs of Hawaii.* Honolulu, HI: Kamehameha Schools Press.

Kameʻeleihiwa, L. 1992. *Native Land and Foreign Desires.* Honolulu, HI: Bishop Museum.

Kanahele, G. 1986. *Kū kanaka Stand Tall: A Search for Hawaiian Values.* Honolulu: University of Hawaii Press.

Kanaʻiaupuni, S. Malia, and K. Ishibashi. 2005. "Hawaiʻi Charter Schools: Initial Trends and Select Outcomes for Native Hawaiian Students." Honolulu, HI: Kamehameha Schools–Policy Analysis & System Evaluation, 04–05:22.

Kanaʻiaupuni, S. Malia, and C. A. Liebler. 2005. "Pondering Poi Dog: Place and Racial Identification of Multiracial Native Hawaiians." *Ethnic and Racial Studies* 28(4): 687–721.

Kanaʻiaupuni, S. Malia, N. Malone, and K. Ishibashi. 2005. *Ka Huakaʻi: 2005 Native Hawaiian Educational Assessment.* Honolulu, HI: Kamehameha Schools, Pauahi Publications.

Kanaʻiaupuni, S. Malia and N. Malone. 2004. "Got Koko? Hawaiian Racial Identity in Multiracial Families." Paper presentation to the Population Association of America, Boston, MA.

Kang, C. 2000. "Chinatown Leaders Push Revitalization Plan, Local Levy for Beautification." www.latimes.com/news (accessed April 11, 2003).

Kang, C. and E. Gee. 2000. "Reinventing Chinatown." www.latimes.com/news (accessed April 11, 2003).

Kanjanapan, W. 1990. "The Immigration of Asian Professionals to the United States: 1988–1990." *International Migration Review* 24(1): 7–32.

Kantrowitz, N. 1973. *Ethnic and Racial Segregation in the New York Metropolis: Residential Patterns among White Ethnic Groups, Blacks, and Puerto Ricans.* New York: Praeger.

Kaplan, D. H. 1997. "What is Measured in Measuring the Mortgage Market." *The Professional Geographer* 48(4) (November 1996): 356–367.

Kaplan, D. 1998. "The Spatial Structure of Urban Ethnic Economies." *Urban Geography* 19(6): 489–501.

Kaplan, R. D. 1998. "Travels into America's Future: Southern California and the Pacific Northwest." *The Atlantic Monthly* 282(1): 37–61.

Kalpan, D. and S. Holloway. 2001. "Scaling Ethnic Segregation: Casual Processes and Contingent Outcomes in Chinese Residential Patterns." *GeoJournal* 53(1): 59–70.

Kaplan, D. H. 2004. "Predatory Lending and Race: A Case Study of a Washington, D.C. Lender." *Multi-Cultural Geographies: Persistence and Change in U.S. Racial/Ethnic Geography,* J. Frazier and F. Margai (eds.).

Kaplan, D. H., G. Sommers, and B. Sommers. 2004. Report to the Ford Foundation.

Kar, S. B. 1995/1996. "Invisible Americans: An Exploration of Indo-American Quality of Life." *Amerasia Journal* 21(3): 25–52.

Karlsen, S. and J. Y. Nazroo. 2002. "Relation Between Racial Discrimination, Social Class and Health among Ethnic Minority Groups." *American Journal of Public Health* 92(4): 624–631.

Kauanui, J. K. 1998. "Off-island Hawaiians 'Making' Ourselves at 'Home': A [Gendered] Contradiction in Terms?" *Women's Studies International Forum* 21(6): 681–693.

Kauanui, J. K. 2002. "The Politics of Blood and Sovereignity in *Rice* v. *Cayetano.*" *PoLAR* 25(1): 110–128.

Kauanui, J. K. (in press). "A Diasporic Deracination and 'Off-island' Hawaiians." In J. Kamakahi, I. K. Maoli, *Navigating Hawaiian Identity.* Honolulu: University of Hawai'i Press.

Kaufman, C. J. and S. A. Hernandez. 1991. "The Role of the Bodega in a U.S.-Puerto Rican Community." *Journal of Retailing* 67(4): 375–96.

Kawakami, A. J. 1999. "Sense of Place, Community, and Identity: Bridging the Gap Between Home and School for Hawaiian Students." *Education and Urban Society* 32(1): 18–40.

Kawakami, A. J., and K. K. Aton. 2001. "Ke a'o Hawai'i (Critical Element of Hawaiian Learning): Perceptions of Successful Hawaiian Educators." *Pacific Educational Research Journal* 11(1): 53–66.

Kawachi, I., N. Daniels, and D. E. Robinson. 2005. "Health Disparities by Race and Class: Why Both Matter." *Health Affairs* 24(2): 343–352.

Kearns, K. C. 1977. "Irish Tinkers: An Itinerant Population in Transition." *Annals of the Association of American Geographers* 67(4): 538–548.

Keil, R. 1998. *Los Angeles: Globalization, Urbanization, and Social Struggles.* New York: John Wiley.

Kellog, J. 1997. "Negro Urban Clusters in the Post-Bellum South." *Geographical Review* 67: 310–321.

Kevels, D. J. 1985. *In the Nature of Eugenics and the Use of Human Heredity.* New York: Alfred A. Knopf.

Khandelwal, M. S. 1995. "Indian Immigrants in Queens, New York City: Patterns of Spatial Concentration and Distribution." In *Nation and Migration: The Politics of Space in the South Asian Diaspora.* P. van der Veer (ed.). Philadelphia: University of Pennsylvania Press, pp. 178–196.

Kibria, N. 1998. "The Racial Gap: South Asian American Racial Identity and the Asian American Movement." In *A Part, Yet Apart.* L. D. Shankar and R. Sikanth (eds.). Philadelphia: Temple University Press, pp. 69–78.

Kibria, N. 2002. *Becoming Asian American: Second-Generation Chinese and Korean American Identities.* Baltimore: Johns Hopkins University Press.

Kingston, R. S. and H. W. Nickens. 2000. "Racial and Ethnic Difference in Health: Recent Trends, Current Patterns, Future Directions." In *America Becoming*: *Racial trends and Their Consequences,* Volume 2. The National Academy of Sciences. www.nap.edu/openbook/0309068401/html/253.html (accessed April 15, 2003).

Kizilbash, A. H. and E. T. Garman. 1975. "Grocery Retailing in Spanish Neighborhoods." *Journal of Retailing* 51(4): 15–29.

Klein, H. S. 1992. *Bolivia: The Evolution of a Multi-Ethnic Society,* 2nd Edition. New York: Oxford University Press.

Kobayashi, A. and L. Peake. 1994. "Unnatural Discourse: 'Race' and Gender in Geography." *Gender, Place, and Culture* 1(3): 225–43.

Kotkin J. 1993. *Tribes: How Race, Religion , and Identity Determine Success in the New Global Economy.* New York: Random House.

Kposowa, A. (2002) "Human Capital and the Performance of African Immigrants in the U.S. Labor Market." *The Western Journal of Black Studies* 26(3): 175–183.

Kraenzel, C. F. 1955. *The Great Plains in Transition.* Norman, OK: University of Oklahoma Press.

Kraly, E. P. and I. Miyares. 2001. *Immigration to New York City: Policy, Population, and Patterns in From the Hudson to the Hamptons: Snapshots of the New York Metropolitan Area.* I. Miyares, M. Psvlovskaya, and G. Pope (eds.). Washington, D.C.: Association of American Geographers.

Krieger, N. 2000. "Refiguring 'Race': Epidemiology, Racialized Biology, and Biological Expressions of Race Relations." *Int J Health Services* 30: 211–216.

Kumar, A. 2000. *Passport Photos.* Berkeley: University of California Press.

Kurashige, L. 2002. *Japanese American Celebration and Conflict: A History of Ethnic Identity and Festival, 1934–1990.* Berkeley: University of California Press.

Kwong, P. 1996. *The New Chinatown*, revised edition. New York: Hill and Wang.

Lal, V. 1999. "Establishing Roots, Engendering Awareness: A Political History of Asian Indians in the United States." Philadelphia, PA: Balch Institute for Ethnic Studies. Accesses September 30, 2004. http://www.sscnet.ucla.edu/southasia/Diaspora/roots.html.

Lalonde, R. J. and R. H. Topel. 1992. "The Assimilation of Immigrants in the U.S. Labor Market" in G. Borjas and R. B. Freeman (eds.). *Immigration and Workforce: Economic Consequences for the United States and Source Areas.* Chicago: The University of Chicago Press.

Langley, Ph. 1976. "Changes in the Production of the Built Environment in Rural Areas." *African Environment* 2(1–2): 37–51.

Langley, Ph. 1975. "Housing the Rural Communities: A Study of House Building Techniques and Housing Standards in Rural Areas of Ghana (Atakpane House)," book review. In *African Environment: Rural Habitat in Africa.* G. Brasseur (ed.), pp. 180–181.

Larson, B. and O. Harris (eds.). 1995. *Ethnicity, Markets and Migration in the Andes.* Durham, NC: Duke University Press.

Lau, Y. M. 1988. *Alternative Career Strategies Among Asian American Professionals: The Second Rice Bowl.* Evanston: Unpublished doctoral dissertation.

Laux, H. D. and G. Thieme. 2006 (forthcoming). "Koreans in Greater Los Angeles: Socioeconomic Polarization, Ethnic Attachment, and Residential Patterns." In W. Li (ed). *From Urban Enclave to the Ethnic Suburb: New Asian Communities in Pacific Rim Countries.* Honolulu: University of Hawaii Press.

Lawson, M. P. and M. E. Baker (eds.). 1979. *The Great Plains: Perspectives and Prospects.* Lincoln, NE: University of Nebraska Press.

Lee, D. O. 1992. "Commodification of Ethnicity: The Sociospatial Reproduction of Immigrant Entrepreneurs." *Urban Affairs Quarterly* 28(2): 258–275.

Lee, E. S. 1966. "A Theory of Migration." *Demography* 3: 47–57.

Lee, E. 2003. *At America's Gates: Chinese Immigration During the Exclusion Era 1882–1943.* Charlotte, NC: University of North Carolina Press.

Lee, S. and M. Fernandez. 1998. "Trends in Asian American Racial/Ethnic Intermarriage: A Comparison of 1980 and 1990 Census Data." *Sociological Perspectives* 4(2): 323–342.

Lee, Y.-T., V. Ottati, and I. Hussain. 2001. "Attitudes Toward 'Illegal' Immigration into the United States: California Proposition 187." *Hispanic Journal of Behavioral Sciences* 23(4): 430–443.

Leichenko, R. 2003. "Does Place Still Matter? Accounting for Income Variation Across American Indian Tribal Areas." *Economic Geography* 79(4): 365–386.

Leonard, K. I. 1992. *Making Ethnic Choices: California's Punjabi Mexican Americans.* Philadelphia: Temple University Press.

Levinson, D. and M. Ember (eds.). 1997. "Ethiopians and Eritreans." In *American Immigrant Cultures: Builders of a Nation* I: 263–269. New York: Simon and Schuster Macmillan.

Levitt, P. 2001. *The Transnational Villagers.* Berkeley: University of California Press.

Li, W. 1998. "Anatomy of a New Ethnic Settlement: The Chinese *Ethnoburb* in Los Angeles." *Urban Studies* 35(3): 497–501.

Li, W. 1998. "Los Angeles's Chinese Ethnoburb: From Ethnic Service Center to Global Economy Outpost." *Urban Geography* 19(6): 502–517.

Li, W. (ed.). 2006. *From Urban Enclave to Ethnic Suburb: New Asian Communities in Pacific Rim Countries.* Honolulu: University of Hawaii Press.

Li, W., Y. Zhou, G. Dymski, and M. Chee. 2001. "Banking on Social Capital in the Era of Globalization—Chinese Ethnobanks in Los Angeles." *Environment and Planning A* 33(4): 1923–1948.

Li, W., G. Dymski, Y. Zhou, C. Aldana, and M. Chee. 2002. "Chinese American Banking and Community Development in Los Angeles County." *Annals of the Association of American Geographers* 92(4): 777–796.

Li, W. 2006 (forthcoming). "Spatial Transformation of an Urban Ethnic Community: From Chinatown to Ethnoburb in Los Angeles." In W. Li (ed). *From Urban Enclave to Ethnic Suburb: New Asian Communities in Pacific Rim Countries.* Honolulu: University of Hawaii Press.

Lewis, G. M. 1969. "The Distribution of the Negro in the Conterminous United States." *Geography* 54: 410–418.

Lewis, P. 1979. "Axioms for Reading the Landscape: Some Guides to the American Scene." In *The Interpretation of Ordinary Landscapes: Geographical Essays.* D. W. Meinig (ed.). New York: Oxford University Press, pp. 11–32.

Liao, Y., P. Tucker, C. A. Okoro, W. H. Giles, A. H. Mokdad, and V. B. Harris. 2004. REACH 2010. "Surveillance for Health Status in Minority Communities—United States, 2001–2002." *MMWR Surveillance Summaries* August 27, 2004/53 (SS06): 1–36.

Liberia Map. 1968. *Official Standard Names Gazetteer No. 106 United States Board of Geographic Names Prepared by the Geographic Names Division, Army Map Service*, Washington, D.C., 20315 (Map DT 623. U48).

Liebler, C. A. 2001. *The Fringes of American Indian Identity*, Ph.D. dissertation, Department of Sociology, University of Wisconsin–Madison, WI.

Lieberson, S. 1981. "An Asymmetrical Approach to Segregation." In *Ethnic Segregation in Cities.* C. Peach, V. Robinson, and S. Smith (eds.). London: Croom Helm, pp. 61–82.

Light, I. 1984. "Immigrant and Ethnic Enterprise in North America." *Ethnic and Racial Studies* 7: 195–216.

Light, I. 2002. "Immigrant Place Entrepreneurs in Los Angeles 1970–1999." *International Journal of Urban and Regional Research* 26(2): 215–228.

Lin, J. 1998. "Globalization and the Revalorizing of Ethnic Places in Immigration Gateway Cities." *Urban Affairs Review* 34(2): 313–339.

Lindstrom, L. 1999 "Social Relations" in M. Rapaport (ed.). *The Pacific Islands: Environment and Society.* Honolulu, HI: Bess Press.

Lipsitz, G. 1998. *The Possessive Investment of Whiteness: How White People Profit from Identity Politics.* Philadelphia: Temple University Press.

Listokin, D. and C. Casey. 1980. "Mortgage Lending and Race: Conceptual and Analytical Perspectives of the Urban Financing Problem." New Brunswick, NJ: Center for Urban Policy Research.

Loewen, J. W. 1995. *Lies My Teacher Told Me.* New York: Simon & Schuster.

Lo, L. et al. 2001. *Immigrants Economic Status in Toronto: Rethinking Settlement and Integration Strategies.* Unpublished Paper.

Logan, J. R. 2001a. *The New Ethnic Enclaves in America's Suburbs.* Albany, NY: Lewis Mumford Center for Comparative Urban and Regional Research.

Logan, J. R. 2001b. *Immigrant Enclaves in the American Metropolis, 1990–2000.* Albany, NY: Lewis Mumford Center for Comparative Urban and Regional Research.

Logan, J. R. 2001. "The New Latinos: Who They Are, Where They Are." Lewis Mumford Center for Comparative Urban and Regional Research, University at Albany, NY. http://mumford1.dyndns.org/cen2000/LatinoPop/Hsp Report/HspReportPage1.html.

Logan, J. R. 2002. "Separate and Unequal: The Neighborhood Gap for Blacks and Latinos in Metropolitan America." University at Albany: Lewis Mumford Center for Comparative Urban and Regional Research. http://mumford1.dyndns.org/cen2000/SepUneq/SUReport/SURepPage1.htm.

Logan, J. R., J. Stowell, and D. Oakley. 2002. "Choosing Segregation: Racial Imbalance in Public Schools, 1990–2000." University at Albany: Lewis Mumford Center for Comparative Urban and Regional Research. http://mumford1.dyndns.org/cen2000/SchoolPop/SPReport/page1.html.

Logan, J. R. and M. Schneider. 1984. "Racial Segregation and Racial Change in American Suburbs, 1970–1980." *American Journal of Sociology* 89(4): 874–888.

Logan, J. R., R. Alba, and T. McNulty. 1994. "Ethnic Economies in Metropolitan Regions: Miami and Beyond." *Social Forces* 72(3): 691–724.

Logan, J. R., R. Alba, T. McNulty, and B. Fisher. 1996. "Making a Place in the Metropolis: Locational Attainment in Cities and Suburbs." *Demography* 33(4): 443–453.

Logan, J. R., R. D. Alba, and W. Zhang. 2002. "Immigrant Enclaves and Ethnic Communities in New York and Los Angeles." *American Sociological Review* 67: 299–322.

Logan, J. R. and D. Oakley. 2004. "The Continuing Legacy of the Brown Decision: Court Action and School Segregation, 1960–2000." Lewis Mumford Center for Comparative Urban and Regional Research, University at Albany.

Logan, J. R., B. J. Stults, and R. Farley. 2004. "Segregation of Minorities in the Metropolis: Two Decades of Change." *Demography* 41: 1–22.

Lomax, L. E. 1968. *To Kill a Black Man: The Shocking Parallel in the Lives of Malcolm X and Martin Luther King, Jr.* Los Angeles: Holloway House.

Long, L. 1988. *Migration and Residential Modility in the United States.* New York: Russell Sage Foundation.

López-Castro, G. 1986. *La Casa Dividida: Un Estadio de Caso Sobre la Migración a Estados Unidos en un Pueblo Michoacano.* Zamora, MI: El Colegio de Michoacán.

Lopez, D. E., E. E. Popkin and E. Telles. 1996. "Central America: At the Bottom Struggling to Get Ahead." In R. Waldinger and M. Bozorgmehr, *Ethnic Los Angeles.* New York: Russell Sage Foundation, pp. 279–304.

Lowe, L. 1996. *Immigrant Acts.* Durham and London: Duke University Press.

Luebke, F. C. (ed.). 1980. *Ethnicity on the Great Plains.* Lincoln, NE: Center for Great Plains Studies.

Madden, J. F. 1981. "Why Women Work Closer to Home." *Urban Studies* 18: 181–94.

Malcolm X. 1965a. *The Autobiography of Malcolm X,* as told to Alex Haley. New York: Balentine Books.

Malcolm X. 1965b. *Malcolm X Speaks,* edited with prefatory notes by George Breitman. New York: Grove Weidenfeld.

Malcolm X. 1970. *By Any Means Necessary.* New York: Pathfinder Books.

Malcolm X. 1991. *Malcolm X Talks to Young People: Speeches in the U.S., Britain, and Africa.* New York: Pathfinder Books.

Malcolm X. 2001. *The End of White World Supremacy: Four Speeches of Malcolm X.* New York: Pathfinder Books.

Maldonado, R. M. 1976. "Why Puerto Ricans Migrated to the United States in 1947–73." *Monthly Labor Review* 99(9): 7–18.

Mantaay, J. 2001. "Zoning, Equity and Public Health." *American Journal of Public Health* 91(7): 1037–1041.

Marcuse, P. 1997. "The Enclave, the Citadel, and the Ghetto: What has Changed in the Post-Fordist U.S. City." *Urban Affairs Review* 33(2): 228–264.

Margai, F. M. 2003. "Using Geodata Techniques to Analyze Environmental Health Inequities in Minority Neighborhoods: The Case of Toxic Exposures and Low Birth Weights. In *MultiCultural Geographies: The Changing Racial and Ethnic Patterns of the United States.* J. W. Frazier and F. M. Margai, (eds.). Binghamton, NY: Global Academic Publishing.

Margai, F. M. 2006. "Acculturation, Assimilation and the Health of Black Immigrant Families in the United States." In *The New African Diaspora: Assessing the Pains and Gains of Exile.* Symposium held at the Department of Africana Studies. Binghamton University.

Marston, S. A. 2002. "Making Difference: Conflict over Irish Identity in the New York City St. Patrick's Day Parade." *Political Geography* 21(3): 373–392.

Martin, R. 2001. "Native Connection to Place: Policies and Play." *American Indian Quarterly* 25(1): 35–41.

Martin, R. W. 2004. "Can Black Workers Escape Spatial Mismatch? Employment Shifts, Population Shifts, and Black Unemployment in American Cities." *Journal of Urban Economics* 49: 179–194.

Martinelli, P. C. and R. Nagasawa. 1987. "A Further Test of the Model Minority Thesis: Japanese Americans in the Sunbelt State." *Sociological Perspectives* 30(3) July: 666–788.

Mashantucket Pequot Museum and Research Center. 2005a. About the Museum. Retrieved on March 25, 2005 from http://www.pequotmuseum.org/Home/GeneralInformation/AbouttheMuseum.htm.

Mashantucket Pequot Museum and Research Center. 2005b. The Mashantucket Land Grant. Retrieved on March 25, 2005 from http://www.pequotmuseum.org/SocietyCulture/MashantucketLandGrant/.

Mashantucket Pequot Tribal Nation. 2005. SCHEMITZUN 2005. Retrieved on April 28, 2005 from http://www.schemitzun.com/index.html.

Massey, D. S., A. B. Gross, and K. Shibuya. 1994. "Migration, Segregation, and Geographic Concentration of Poverty." *American Sociological Review* 59: 425–445.

Massey, D. and B. P. Mullan. 1984. "Processes of Hispanic and Black Spatial Assimilation." *American Journal of Sociology* 89: 836–71.

Massey, D. S. 1985. "Ethnic Residential Segregation: A Theoretical Synthesis and Empirical Review." *Sociology and Social Research* 69(3): 315–330.

Massey, D. S. and B. Bitterman. 1985. "Explaining the Paradox of Puerto Rican Segregation." *Social Forces* 6: 306–331.

Massey, D. and N. Denton. 1988. "The Dimensions of Residential Segregation." *Social Forces* 67: 281–315.

Massey, D. S. and N. A. Denton. 1993. *American Apartheid: Segregation and the Making of the Underclass.* Cambridge, Massachusetts: Harvard University Press.

Massey, D. S. et al. 1993. "Theories of International Migration: A Review and Appraisal." *Population and Development Review* 19(3): 431–466.

Massey, D. S., J. Aranjo, G. Hugo, A. Kouaouci, A. Pellegrino, and J. E. Taylor. 1994. "International Migration Theory: The North American Case." *Population and Development Review* 20(4): 699–751.

Massey, D. S. and Z. L. Hajnal. 1995. "The Changing Geographic Structure of Black-White Segregation in the United States." *Social Science Quarterly* 76(3): 527–542.

Masthay, C. 1990. "New England Indian Place Names." In *Rooted Like the Ash Trees: New England Indians and the Land.* R. Carlson (ed.). 2nd ed. Naugatuck, CT: Eagle Wing Press.

McBride, K. 1990. "The Mashantucket Pequot Ethnohistory Project." In *Rooted Like the Ash Trees: New England Indians and the Land.* R. Carlson (ed). 2nd ed. Naugatuck, CT: Eagle Wing Press.

McClain, C. (ed.). 1994. "Introduction." *Asian Americans and the Law.* Garland Publishing Inc., pp. ix–xiv.

McCormick, M. 1995. "The Contribution of Low Birth Weight to Infant Mortality and Childhood Morbidity." *The New England Journal of Medicine* 3, 12(2): 82–89.

McKee, J. O. (ed.). 2000. *Ethnicity in Contemporary America.* 2nd Edition. Lanham, MD: Rowman and Littlefield.

McKinnon, J. and E. Grieco. 2001. "Nation's Asian and Pacific Islander Population Profiled by Census Bureau." www.census.gov/. Press Release, June 28, 2001.

McLafferty, S. and V. Preston. 1991. "Gender, Race and Commuting among Service Sector Workers." *Professional Geographer* 43: 1–15.

McLafferty, S. and V. Preston. 1992. "Spatial Mismatch and Labor Market Segmentation for African American and Latina Women." *Economic Geography* 68: 406–431.

McLafferty, S. and V. Preston. 1996. "Spatial Mismatch and Employment in a Decade of Restructuring." *Professional Geographer* 48: 420–31.

McLafferty, S. and V. Preston. 1997. "Gender, Race, and the Determinants of Commuting: New York in 1990." *Urban Geography* 18: 192–212.

McWilliams, C. 1968. *North From Mexico: The Spanish-Speaking People of the United States.* New York: Greenwood Press.

Mears, E. G. 1928. *Resident Orientals on the American Pacific Coast: Their Legal and Economic Status.* Chicago: University of Chicago Press.

Meinig, D. 1969. *Imperial Texas: An Interpretive Essay in Cultural Geography.* Austin: University of Texas Press.

Meinig, D. W. 1971. *Southwest: Three Peoples in Geographical Change, 1600–1970.* New York: Oxford University Press.

Melendy, H. B. 1977. *Asians in America: Filipinos, Koreans and East Indians.* Boston: G. K. Hall and Co.

Melmer, D. 2005. "Pine Ridge Chamber Message is Growth." *Indian Country Today.* April 12, 2005. Retrieved on April 20, 2005 from http://www.indiancountry.com/content/cfm?id=1096410732&print=yes.

Memmott, P. and S. Long. 2002. "Place Theory and Place Maintenance in Indigenous Australia." *Urban Policy and Research* 20(1): 39–56.

Meriam, L. 1928. *The Problem of Indian Administration.* Baltimore, MD: Johns Hopkins Press.

Meyer, M. 2003. *Ho'oulu Our Time of Becoming: Hawaiian Epistemology and Early Writings.* Honolulu, Hawai'i: Native Books.

Michelson, M. R. 2001. "The Effect of National Mood on Mexican American Political Opinion," *Hispanic Journal of Behavioral Sciences* 23(1): 57–70.

Michelson, M. R. and A. Pallares. 2001. "The Politicization of Chicago Mexican Americans: Naturalization, the Vote, and Perceptions of Discrimination." *Aztlan* 26(2): 63–85.

Mihesuah, D. A. 2003. *Indigenous American Women: Decolonization, Empowerment, Activism.* Lincoln, NE: University of Nebraska Press.

Miles, S. and R. Paddison. 1998. "Urban Consumption: An Historiographical Note." *Urban Studies* 35(5–6): 815–823.

Mitchell, K. 2000. "Networks of Ethnicity." In E. Sheppard and T. J. Barnes (eds.). *Companion to Economic Geography.* Blackwell Publishers, pp. 392–407.

Mitra, A. M. 1996. "Romantic Stereotypes: The Myth of the Asian American Khichri-Pot." In *Contours of the Heart: South Asians Map North America.* S. Maira and R. Srikanth (eds.). New York: The Asian American Writers' Workshop, pp. 421–431.

Miyares, I. M. 1997. "Changing Perceptions of Space and Place as Measures of Hmong Acculturation." *The Professional Geographer* 49(2): 214–224.

Miyares, I. M. 1998. "'Little Odessa'—Brighton Beach, Brooklyn: An Examination of the Former Soviet Refugee Economy in New York City." *Urban Geography* 19(6): 518–530.

Model, S. 1991. "Caribbean Immigrants: A Black Success Story?" *International Migration Review* 25: 248–276.

Model, S. 1995. "West Indian Prosperity: Fact or Fiction?" *Social Problems* 42: 535–553.

Model, S. 2001. "Where West Indians Work," in N. Foner (ed.). *Island in the City: West Indian Migration to New York.* Berkeley, CA: University of California Press, pp. 52–80

Modell, J. 1977. *The Economics and Politics of Racial Accommodation: The Japanese of Los Angeles 1900–1942.* Chicago: University of Illinois Press.

Mogelonsky, M. 1995. "Asian Indian Americans." *American Demographics* 17 (August): 32–39.

Moore, J. W. 1976. *Mexican-Americans* (2nd edition). Englewood Cliffs, NJ: Prentice Hall.

Morales, J. 1986. *Puerto Rican Poverty and Migration: We Just Had To Try Elsewhere.* New York: Praeger.

Morning, A. 2001. "The Racial Self-Identification of South Asians in the U.S." *Journal of Ethnic and Migration Studies* 27(1): 61–79.

Moskos, C. 1980. *Greek-Americans: Struggle and Success.* Englewood Cliffs, New Jersey: Prentice-Hall.

Moskos, C. 1999. "The Greeks in the United States." In *The Greek Diaspora in the Twentieth Century.* R. Clogg (ed.). New York: St. Martin's Press, pp. 103–119.

Mouw, T. 2000. "Job Relocation and the Racial Gap in Unemployment in Detroit and Chicago 1980–1990." *American Sociological Review* 65: 730–753.

Moy, E., E. Dayton, and C. M. Clancy. 2005. "Compiling Evidence: The National Healthcare Disparities Reports." *Health Affairs* 24(2): 376–388.

Muller, P. 1981. *Contemporary Suburban America.* Englewood Cliffs: Prentice Hall.

Muller, P. 1997. "The Suburban Transformation of the Globalizing American City." *Annals of the American Academy of Political and Social Sciences* 551: 44–58.

Murphy, A. D., C. Blanchard, and J. Hill. 2001. *Latino Workers in the Contemporary South.* Athens: The University of Georgia Press.

Nagel, J. 1996. *American Indian Ethnic Renewal: Red Power and the Resurgence of Identity and Culture.* New York: Oxford University Press.

Nakunia, M. 1990. *The Wind Gourd of La'amaomao.* Translated by E. Mo'okini and S. Nākoa. Honolulu, HI: Kalamaku Press.

NALEO (National Association of Latino Elected and Appointed Officials Education Fund). 2004. LATINOS WIN BIG ON ELECTION NIGHT News Release, November 3, 2004. http://www.naleo.org/press_releases/PR_NALEO_Eday_Win_110304.pdf.

NALEO (National Association of Latino Elected and Appointed Officials Education Fund). 2004. LATINOS GRAB SEATS IN STATE HOUSES NATIONWIDE News Release, November 9, 2004. http://www.naleo.org/press_releases/latinosgrab.htm.

NALEO (National Association of Latino Elected and Appointed Officials Education Fund). 2004. Mobilizing the Latino Vote, NALEO 04 Annual Conference. http://www.1chc.org/documents/Mobilizing theLatinoVotebyJ.Carrillo.pdf.

Natambu, K. 2002. *The Life and Work of Malcolm X.* Indianapolis, IN: Alpha Books.

National Community Reinvestment Coalition. 2002. Anti Predatory Lending Tool Kit. Washington. NCRC.org.

National Council of La Raza (NCLR). 2004. Latinos Optimistic About Future, Feel Candidates Ignore Their Issues, and Have a Shared Policy Agenda, Poll Finds. http://www.nclr.org/content/news/detail/25333/.

National Gambling Impact Study Commission. 1997. *National Gambling Impact Study Commission Report.* Chapter 6. Native American Tribal Gaming. Retrieved on April 25, 2005 from http://govinfo.library.unt.edu/ngisc/reports/6.pdf.

National Geographic Society. 2004. "Change of Heartland: America's Great Plains." *National Geographic,* May: 2–53.

National Indian Gaming Association. 2005. *An Analysis of the Economic Impact of Indian Gaming in 2004.* Retrieved on April 20, 2005 from http://www.indiangaming.org/NIGA_econ_impact_2004.pdf.

National Institute of Education. 1977. *School Desegregation: A Report of State and Federal Judicial and Administrative Activity.* Washington, D.C.: U.S. Department of Health, Education and Welfare.

National Institute of Education. 1978. *Supplement to School Desegregation: A Report of State and Federal Judicial and Administrative Activity 1978.* Washington, D.C.: U.S. Department of Health, Education and Welfare.

National Museum of the American Indian. 2005a. Facts and Figures from the Grand Opening of the Smithsonian's National Museum of the American Indian. Retrieved on March 27, 2005 from http://www.nmai.si.edu/press/releases/10-29-04_facts_and_figures_opening.pdf.

National Museum of the American Indian. 2005b. National Museum of the American Indian Now Open at the Smithsonian. Retrieved on March 27, 2005 from http://www.nmai.si.edu/press/releases/10-29-04_now_open.pdf.

Newbold, K. B. 2004. "Chinese Assimilation Across America: Spatial and Cohort Variations." *Growth and Change* 35(2): 198–219.

Nickels, C. R. and F. A. Day. 1997. "Depopulation of the Rural Great Plains Counties of Texas." *Great Plains Research* 7: 225–250.

NIH 2000 Strategic Plan to Reduce and Ultimately Eliminate Health Disparities. October 6, 2000.

Nomura, G. 1994. "Within the Law: The Establishment of Filipino Leasing Rights on the Yakima Indian Reservation." C. McClain (ed.). *Asian Indians, Filipinos, Other Asian Communities, and the Law,* pp. 49–68.

Nordyke, E. 1989. *The Peopling of Hawaii.* Second edition, Honolulu, HI: University of Hawai'i Press.

Norman, J. 2000. "A Modest Gain for the Black Middle Class: African American Workforce in Milwaukee Saw Limited Growth in the 1990's." *Milwaukee Journal Sentinel,* February, 2000.

Norton, H. K. 1924. *The Story of California From the Earliest Days to the Present.* Chapter xxiv reprinted at www.sf museum.org/hist6 (accessed April 30, 2003).

Norwood, C. 1974. *About Paterson: The Making and Unmaking of An American City.* New York: Saturday Review Press.

Nostrand, R. L. 1970. "The Latino-American Borderland: Delimitation of An American Cultural Region." *Annals of the Association of American Geographers* 60(4): 638–661.

Nostrand, R. L. 1975. "Mexican-Americans Circa 1850." *Annals of the Association of American Geographers* 60(4): 378–390.

Nostrand, R. L. 1979. "Spanish Roots in the Borderlands." *Geographical Magazine* 51 (December): 203–209.

Numrich, P. D. 1997. "Recent Immigrant Religions in a Restructuring Metropolis: New Religious Landscapes in Chicago." *Journal of Cultural Geography* 17(1): 55–76.

Ogunwole, S. 2002. *The American Indian and Alaska Native Population: 2000.* Washington, DC: United States Department of Commerce.

O'Hare, W. P., W. H. Frey, and D. Fost. 1994. "Asians in the Suburbs." *American Demographics* 16 (May): 32–38.

O'Kasick, J. 2004. "Minnesota's Liberians Pray Peace Will Hold," *Minnesota Spokesman-Recorder* 70(1), August 5–11: pp. 1 and 15.

O'Kasick, J. 2004. "It Takes Two Wings to Fly: African Americans and Liberians Discover They have a Lot in Common," *Minnesota Spokesman-Recorder* 70(2), August 12–18: pp. 1 and 11.

Olsen, L. 2001. "Public Education, Immigrants, and Racialization: The Contemporary Americanization." In G. Gerstle and J. Mollenkopf, (eds.). *Project e pluribus umun: Contemporary and Historical Perspectives on Immigrant Political Incorporation.* New York: Russell Sage Foundation, pp. 371–401.

Omi, M. and H. Winant. 1986. *Racial Formation in the United States: From 1960's to the 1980's.* New York: Routledge and Kegan Paul.

Omi, M. and H. Winant. 1994. *Racial Formation in the United States: From 1960's to the 1990's,* 2nd ed. New York: Routlege.

Oneha, M. 2001. "Ka Mauli o Ka 'Āina a He Mauli Kānaka: An Ethnographic Study from an Hawaiian Sense of Place," *Pacific Health Dialog* 8(2): 299–311.

Oneida Indian Nation. 2005. A Brief History of the Oneida Indian Nation. Retrieved on April 25, 2005 from http://www.oneida-nation.net/BRHISTORY.HTML.

Ong, P. 1993. *Beyond Asian American Poverty: Community Economic Development Policies and Strategies.* Los Angeles: LEAP Asian Pacific American Public Policy Institute.

Ong, P. and E. Blumenberg. 1994. In P. Ong (ed.). *The State of Asian Pacific America: Economic Diversity, Issues, and Policies.* Los Angeles: LEAP and UCLA Asian-American Studies Center.

Ong, P., E. Bonacich, and L. Cheng. 1994. "The Political Economy of Capitalist Restructuring and the New Asian Immigration." In *The New Asian Immigration in Los Angeles and Global Restructuring.* P. Ong, E. Bonacich and L. Cheng, (eds.). Philadelphia: Temple University Press, pp. 3–35.

Ono, H. 2002. "Assimilation, Ethnic Competition, and Ethnic Identities of U.S.-Born Persons of Mexican Origin," *International Migration Review* 36(3): 726–745.

Orfield, G. and J. Yun. 1999. "Resegregation in American Schools." Cambridge, MA: The Civil Rights Project, Harvard University, June. http://www.civilrightsproject.harvard.edu/research/deseg/reseg_schools99.php (accessed April 5, 2005).

Organized Labor. 1906. "Asian Coolie Invasion." Reprinted at www.sfmuseum.org/1906.2/invasion (accessed April 30, 2003).

Ortiz, V. 1996. "The Mexican Origin Population: Permanent Working Class or Emerging Middle Class?" in *Ethnic Los Angeles*, R. Waldinger and M. Bozorgmehr (eds.). New York: Russell Sage Foundation, pp. 247–277.

Orwell, G. 1981. *A Collection of Essays.* New York: Harcourt.

Osorio, J. K. 2001. "What Kind Hawaiian Are You? A moʻolelo about Nationhood, Race, History and the Contemporary Sovereignty Movement in Hawaiʻi." *The Contemporary Pacific Journal of Island Affairs* 13(2): 359–379.

Osorio, J. K. 2002. *Dismembering Lāhui: A History of the Hawaiian Nation to 1887.* Honolulu: University of Hawaiʻi Press.

Pacyga, D. A. 1995. "Chicago's Ethnic Neighborhoods: The Myth of Stability and the Reality of Change." In *Ethnic Chicago: A Multicultural Portrait.* M. G. Holli and P. Jones (eds.). Grand Rapids: MI: William B. Eerdmans Publishing Company, pp. 604–617.

Paisano, R., N. Cobb, D. K. Espey. 2003. "Cancer Mortality Among American Indians and Alaska Natives-United States, 1994–1998." *Morbidity and Mortality Weekly,* August 2003, Vol. 52(30): 704.

Panagopoulos, E. P. 1966. *New Smyrna: An Eighteenth Century Greek Odyssey.* Gainesville: University Presses of Florida.

Park, R. E. and H. A. Miller. 1921. *Old War Traits Transplanted.* New York: Harper & Brothers.

Park, R. and E. Burgess. 1921. *Introduction to the Science of Sociology.* Chicago: University of Chicago Press.

Park, R. E. 1925. "The Concept of Social Distance." *Journal of Applied Sociology* 8: 339–344.

Park, R. E., E. W. Burgess, and R. D. McKenzie (eds.). 1925. *The City.* Chicago: University of Chicago Press.

Park, R. E. 1950. *Race and Culture,* Glencoe, IL: Free Press.

Parker, S. 1989. *Native American Estate: The Struggle over Indian and Hawaiian Lands.* Honolulu: University of Hawaiʻi Press.

Pasquaretta, P. 2003. *Gambling and Survival in Native North America.* Tuscon, AZ: The University of Arizona Press.

Pattillo-McCoy, M. 1999. *Black Picket Fences: Privilege and Peril among the Black Middle Class.* Chicago, IL: University of Chicago Press.

Peach, C. 1980. "Ethnic Segregation and Intermarriage." *Annals of the Association of American Geographers* 70(3): 371–381.

Peake, L. and A. Kobayashi. 2002. "Policies and Practices for an Antiracist Geography at the Millennium." *The Professional Geographer* 54(1): 50–61.

Pearcy, J. N. and K. G. Keppel. 2002. "A Summary Measure of Health Disparity." *Public Health Reports* 117: 280–293.

Peck, J. 1996. *Work Place: The Social Regulation of Labor Markets.* New York: Guilford.

Peet, R. 1997. "The Cultural Production of Economic Forms." In *Geographies of Economies.* R. Lee and J. Wills, (eds.). London: Arnold, pp. 37–46.

Penrose, E. R. 1973. *California Nativism: Organized Opposition to the Japanese, 1890–1913.* San Francisco: R & E Research Associates.

Perkins, M. ʻU. 2005. "O ka ʻĀina ke Ea: The Waitangi Tribunal and the Native Hawaiians Study Commission." *Hūlili Multidisciplinary Research on Hawaiian Well-Being* 2(1): 193–214.

Perle, E. D., H. Bauder, and N. Beckett. 2002. "Accessibility Measures in Spatial Mismatch Models." *Professional Geographer* 54: 106–110.

Perry, B. 1991. *Malcolm X: The Life of the Man Who Changed Black America.* New York: Station Hill Press.

Philpott, T. L. 1978. *The Slum and the Ghetto: Neighborhood Deterioration and Middle Class Reform, Chicago, 1880–1930.* New York: Oxford University Press.

Pinal, J. and A. Singer. 1997. "Generations of Diversity: Latinos in the United States." *Population Bulletin* 52(3): online version, http://www.prb.org/Template.cfm?Section=PRB&template=/ContentManagement/ContentDisplay.Cfm&ContentID=6196.

Pikman, D. 2004. "Southern Appeal on the Rise, Study Finds Evidence of a 'Reverse Migration' Trend for Black Students." *Daily Bruin.* June 1, p. 1.

Pisarski, A. 1996. *Commuting in America II.* Westport, CT: Eno Foundation.

Polednak, A. P. 1996. "Segregation, Discrimination, and Mortality in the U.S. Blacks." *Ethnicity and Disease* 6: 99–108.

Population Reference Bureau. *2004 World Population Data Sheet.* Washington, D.C.

Porter, P. W. and F. E. Lukermann. 1976. "The Geography of Utopia." In *Geographies of the Mind: Essays in Historical Geosophy,* D. Lowenthal and M. J. Bowden (eds.). New York: Oxford University Press, pp. 197–223.

Portes, A., J. M. Clark, and M. M. Lopez. 1981. "Six Years Later, a Profile of the Process of Incorporation of Cuban Exiles in the United States." *Cuban Studies,* pp. 15–57.

Portes, A. and R. L. Bach. 1985. *Latin Journey: Cuban and Mexican Immigrants in the United States.* Berkeley: University of California Press.

Portes, A. and B. Jozsef. 1988. "Contemporary Immigration: Theoretical Perspectives on its Determinants and Modes of Incorporation." *International Migration Review* 23(3): 606–630.

Portes, A. and R. Rumbaut. 1990. *Immigrant America: A Portrait.* Berkeley: University of California Press.

Portes, A. and M. Zhou. 1993. "The New Second Generation: Segmented Assimilation and its Variants." *The Annals of the American Academy of Political and Social Science* 530: 74–96.

Portes, A. 1995. "Children of Immigrants: Segmented Assimilation and its Determinants." In A. Portes (ed.). *The Economic Sociology of Immigration: Essays on Networks, Ethnicity, and Entrepreneurship.* New York, NY: Russell Sage Foundation, pp. 248–280.

Portes, A., and R. G. Rumbaut. 1996. *Immigrant America: A Portrait.* Berkeley, CA: University of California Press.

Portes, A. 1997. "Globalization from Below: The Rise of Transnational Communities" WPTC 98-01, Working Paper, Transnational Communities Programme, Oxford University (www.transcomm.ox.ac.uk).

Potter, R., B. D. Barker, D. Conway, and T. Klak. 2004. *The Contemporary Caribbean.* New York: Pearson/Prentice Hall.

Poulsen, M., R. Johnston, and J. Forrest. 2001. "Intraurban Ethnic Enclaves: Introducing a Knowledge-Based Classification Method." *Environment and Planning A* 33: 2071–82.

Poulsen, M. R. and R. Johnston. 2002. "Plural Cities and Ethnic Enclaves: Introducing a Measurement Procedure for Comparative Study." *International Journal of Urban and Regional Research* 26(2): 229–243.

Prashad, V. 1996. "Desh: The Contradictions of 'Homeland'." In *Contours of the Heart: South Asians Map North America,* S. Maira and R. Srikanth (eds.). New York: The Asian American Writers' Workshop, pp. 225–236.

Preston, V. and S. McLafferty, 1999. "Spatial Mismatch Research in the 1990s: Progress and Potential." *Papers in Regional Science* 78: 387–402.

Price, M. and C. Whitworth. 2004. "Soccer and Latino Cultural Space: The Futbol Leagues in Washington, D.C." in *Hispanic Spaces, Latino Places.* D. Arreola (ed.). Austin: University of Texas Press, pp. 167–186.

Price, M., I. Cheung, S. Friedman, and A. Singer. 2005. "The World Settles in: Washington, D.C. as an Immigrant Gateway." *Urban Geography* 26(2): 61–83.

Public Broadcasting System. 2005. Manifest Destiny: An Introduction. Retrieved on April, 15, 2005 from http://www. pbs.org/kera/usmexicanwar/dialogues/prelude/manifest/d2aeng.html.

Pūkui, M. K., S. Elbert, and E. Moʻokini. 1974. *Place Names of Hawaii.* Honolulu, HI: University of Hawaii Press.

Pūkui, M. K., E. W. Haertig, M.D., and C. A. Lee. 1972. Nānā I ke kumu, Volume I & II. Honolulu, Hawaiʻi: Queen Liliuʻokalani Children's Center.

Pūkui, M. K. 1983. ʻŌlelo Noʻeau: Hawaiian Proverbs and Poetical Sayings. Honolulu: Bishop Museum Press.

Pūkui, M. K. and S. H. Elbert. 1986. *Hawaiian Dictionary.* Honolulu: University of Hawaiʻi Press.

Radelat, A. 2001. "The Year of the Latino Mayor." *Latino Magazine. Com,* July–August, 2001. http://www.Latino magazine.com/2001/julaug/Features/villarraigosa.html.

Raitz, K. B. 1978. "Ethnic Maps of North America." *Geographical Review* 68(4): 335–350.

Raitz, K. B. 1979. "Themes in the Cultural Geography of European Ethnic Groups in the United States." *Geographical Review* 69(1): 79–94.

Ramos, J. 2002. *The Other Face of America: Chronicles of the Immigrants Shaping our Future.* New York: Harper-Collins.

Rapado, J. R. 1981. *Las Migraciones Internacionales de Bolivia.* Organización de los Estados Americanos, Seminario Técnico sobre Migraciones Laborales en el Grupo Andino.

Rapaport, A. 1969. *House Form and Culture.* Englecliff, NJ: Prentice Hall.

Rapaport, M. 1999. *The Pacific Islands: Environment and Society.* Honolulu, HI: Bess Press.

Ravenstein, E. G. 1889. "The Laws of Migration." *Journal of the Royal Statistical Society* 52: 241–305.

Reardon, S. F., J. T. Yun, and T. M. Eitle. 2000. "The Changing Structure of School Segregation: Measurement and Evidence of Multiracial Metropolitan-Area School Segregation, 1989–1995." *Demography* 37(3): 351–364.

Reeve, H. (translator), F. Bowen (revisions), and P. Bradley, A. de Tacqueville (ed.). 1835. *Democracy in America.* Volume 1. New York: Alfred A. Knopf (reprinted in J. Boskin, 1976).

Reisinger, M. E. 2003. "Determinants of Latino Migration to Allentown, PA." In J. W. Frazier and F. M. Margai (eds.). *Multicultural Geographies.* Binghamton: Global Academic Publishing.

Reitz, J. and R. Breton. 1995. *The Illusion of Difference, Realities if Ethnicity in Canada and the United States.* Toronto: CD Howe Institute.

Relph, E. 1976. *Place and Placelessness.* London: Pion Limited.

Repak, T. 1995. *Waiting on Washington: Central American Workers in the Nation's Capital.* Philadelphia: Temple University Press.

Rhodes, R. W. 1990. "Measurements of Navajo and Hopi Brain Dominance and Learning Styles." *Journal of American Indian Education* 29(3). http://jaie.asu.edu/v29/V29S3mea.htm.

Rickford, R. J. 2003. *Betty Shabazz: A Remarkable Story of Survival and Faith Before and After Malcolm X.* Naperville, IL: Sourcebooks.

Riley, R. B. 1997. "The Visible, the Visual, and the Vicarious: Questions about Vision, Landscape, and Experience." In *Understanding Ordinary Landscapes*. P. Groth and T. W. Bressi (eds.). New Haven: Yale University Press, pp. 200–209.

Ringer, B. B. and E. R. Lawless. 1989. *Race-Ethnicity and Society*. New York: Routledge.

Rivera-Batiz, F. 1989. "The Characteristics of Recent Puerto Rican Migrants: Some Further Evidence." *Migration World,* p. 10.

Rivera-Batiz, F. L. and C. E. Santiago. 1996. *Island Paradox: Puerto Rico in the 1990's.* New York: Russell Sage Foundation.

Rivkin, S. 1994. "Residential Segregation and School Integration." *Sociology of Education* 67: 279–292.

Robinson, A. J. 1997. "The Two Nations of Black America: An Analysis of Black Income Groups, 1970–1994." www.pbs.org/frontline (accessed March 1, 2003).

Roediger, D. R. 1991. *The Wages of Whiteness Race and the Making of the American Working Class.* London: Verso.

Rogg, E. M. 1974. *The Assimilation of Cuban Exiles: The Role of Community and Class.* New York: Aberdeen Press.

Root, G. 2003. "Determinants of Migration in Texas Counties: Economics vs. Amenities." Masters Thesis, Southwest Texas State University.

Root, M. P. 2001. *Love's Revolution*: *Interracial Marriage*. Philadelphia, PA: Temple University Press.

Rosales, G., M. D. Navarro, and D. Cardosa. 2001. "Variation in Attitudes toward Immigrants Measured among Latino, African American, Asian, and Euro-American Students" in *Asian and Latino Immigrants in a Restructuring Economy: The Metamorphosis of Southern California,* M. López-Garza and D. R. Díaz (eds.). Stanford, CA: Stanford University Press.

Rosales, R. 2000. *The Illusion of Inclusion: The Untold Political Story of San Antonio.* Austin, TX: The University of Texas Press.

Rose, H. 1971. *The Black Ghetto: A Spatial Behavioral Perspective.* Englewood Cliffs: NJ: Prentice Hall.

Rose, H. M. 1976. *Black Suburbanization: Access to Improved Quality of Life or Maintenance of the Status Quo?* Cambridge: Ballinger.

Rose, H. 2000. "The Evolving Spatial Pattern of Black America." In J. McKee (ed.). *Ethnicity in Contemporary America: A Geographical Perspective,* 2nd edition. NY: Rowman and Littlefield Publishers, Inc.

Roseman, C. C. 1971. "Migration as a Spatial and Temporal Process." *Annals of the Association of American Geographers* 61(3), 589–598.

Roseman, C. 2002. "The Changing Ethnic Map of the United States." In K. Berry and Henderson (eds.). *Geographical Identities of Ethnic Americans.* Reno: University of Nevada Press.

Rosenbaum, E. 1991. "Racial/Ethnic Differences in Home Ownership and Housing Quality." *Social Problems* 43: 403–426.

Rosenfeld, M. J. 2002. "Measures of Assimilation in the Marriage Market: Mexican Americans 1970–1990." *Journal of Marriage and Family* 64(1): 152–162.

Rosie, G. 2000. "What if Scotsmen Had Guns." *New Statesman* 12(599) April 13: 38–39.

Rossell, C. H. and D. Armor. 1996. "The Effectiveness of School Desegregation Plans, 1968–1991." *American Politics Quarterly* 24: 267–302.

Roundtree, L. B. 1996. "The Cultural Landscape Concept in American Human Geography," *Concepts in Human Geography*. London: Rowman & Littlefield Publishers, Inc., pp. 127–159.

Rumbaut, R. G. 1994. "The Crucible within: Ethnic Identity, Self-esteem, and Segmented Assimilation among Children of Immigrants." *International Migration Review* 28: 748–794.

Rutherford, B. M. and G. R. Wekerle. 1988. "Captive Rider, Captive Labor: Spatial Constraints on Women's Employment." *Urban Geography* 9: 116–37.

Said, E. W. 1978. *Orientalism.* New York: Vintage Books.

Sailer, S. 2002. "Who Exactly is an Asian American?" *United Press International,* 11 July.

Sales, Jr. W. W. 1994. *From Civil Rights to Black Liberation: Malcolm X and the Organization of Afro-American Unity.* Boston: South End Press.

Saloutos, T. 1964. *The Greeks in the United States.* Cambridge: Harvard University Press.

Saltman, M. 2002. *Land and Territoriality.* New York, NY: Berg.

Sanabria, H. 1993. *The Coca Boom and Rural Social Change in Bolivia.* Ann Arbor: University of Michigan Press.

Sanders, J. and V. Nee. 1987. "Limits of Ethnic Solidarity in the Enclave Economy." *Americam Sociological Review* 52(6): 745–773.

Santiago, C. E. 1991. "Wage Politics, Employment, and Puerto Rican Migration." In E. Melendez, C. Rodriquez, and J. Barry-Figueroa (eds.). *Latinos in the Labor Force: Issues and Policies.* New York: Plenum.

Saxton, A. 1995. *The Indispensable Enemy Labor and the Anti-Chinese Movement in California.* Berkeley, CA: University of California Press.

Schacter, J. 2001. "Why People Move: Exploring the March 2000 Current Population Survey." *Current Population Reports* P23–204.

Schenker, M. B. 1995. "Farm-Related Fatalities among Children in California, 1980–1989." *American Journal of Public Health* 85(1): 89–92.

Schneider, M. and T. Phelan. 1993. "Black Suburbanization in the 1980's." *Demography* 30(2): 269–279.

Schnell, S. M. 2000. "The Kiowa Homeland in Oklahoma." *Geographical Review* 90(2): 155–177.

Sechler, A. R. 2002. MDH Center for Health Statistics, Liberian births by zip code, 4/27/02.

Selassie, B. 1996. "Washington's New African Immigrants." In *Urban Odyssey: Migration to Washington, D.C.* Frances Carey (ed.). Washington, D.C.: Smithsonian Institution Press, pp. 264–275.

Seminole Tribe of Florida v. Butterworth, 658 F.-2d 310 (1981), cert. denied, 455 U.S. 1020 (1983).

Senior, C. 1965. *Our Citizens From the Caribbean.* New York: McGraw-Hill.

Shain, Y. 1999/2000. "The Mexican-American Disppora's Impact on Mexico." *Political Science Quarterly* 114(4): 661–691.

Shankar, R. 1998a. "Foreword: South Asian identity in Asian America." In *A Part, Yet Apart,* L. D. Shankar and R. Srikanth (eds.). Philadelphia: Temple University Press, ix–xv.

Shankar, R. 1998b. "The Limits of (South Asian) Names and Labels: Postcolonial or Asian American?" In *A Part, Yet Apart,* L. D. Shankar and R. Srikanth (eds.). Philadelphia: Temple University Press, pp. 49–66.

Sheth, M. 1995. "Asian Indian Americans." In *Asian Americans: Contemporary Trends and Issues,* P. G. Min (ed.). Thousand Oaks, CA. Sage Publications, pp. 169–197.

Shiner, C. 1890. *Paterson, New Jersey: Its Advantages for Manufacturing and Residence.* Paterson, NJ: The Printing and Publishing Company.

Silva, N. 2004. *Aloha Betrayed: Native Hawaiian Resistance to American Colonialism.* Durham, NC: Duke University Press.

Silvey, R. and V. Lawson. 1999. "Placing the Migrant." *Annals of the Association of American Geographers* 89(1): 121–132.

Simmons, J. W. 1968. "Changing Residence in the City: A Review of Intra-Urban Mobility." *Geographical Review* 58: 622–651.

Simon, S. 1999. "An Insular Iowa Town, a Jolt of Worldliness: A Torrent of Diversity has been a Shock to Tiny Postville, Iowa," *The Los Angeles Times.* January 26.

Singer, A., S. Friedman, I. Cheung, and M. Price. 2001. "The World in a Zip Code: Greater Washington, D.C. as a New Region of Immigration." Washington, D.C.: The Brookings Institution.

Singer, A. and A. Brown. 2001. "Washington, D.C.," in James Ciment (ed.). *Encyclopedia of American Immigration.* Armonk, NY: M. E. Sharpe.

Singer, A. 2003. "At Home in the Nation's Capital: Immigrant Trends in Metropolitan Washington." Washington, D.C.: The Brookings Institution.

Singer, A. and J. H. Wilson. 2004. "Polyglot Washington: Language Needs and Abilities in the Nation's Capital." Washington, D.C.: The Brookings Institution.

Singer, A. 2004. "The Rise of New Immigrant Gateways." *The Bookings Institution, The Living Cities Census Series.* February, p. 35.

Singh, G. K. and A. Kposowa. 1996. "Occupation—Specific Earnings Attainment of Asian Indians and Whites in the United States: Gender and Nativity Differential Across Class Data." *Applied Behavioral Science Review* 4: 137–175.

Skop, E. 2001. "Race and Place in the Adaptation of Mariel Exiles." *International Migration Review* 35(2): 449–471.

Skop, E. (forthcoming). "Indian Immigrants in the United States: Constructions of Community and Identity." In *Contemporary Ethnic Geographies in America,* I. M. Miyares and C. A. Airriess (eds.). Lanham, MD: Roman and Littlefield.

Skop, E. *Living in the 'Burbs: The Creation of an Indian Immigrant Community.* Center for American Places. (Under Review.)

Skop, E. 2002. "Saffron Suburbs: Indian Immigrant Community Formation in Metropolitan Phoenix." Dissertation, Department of Geography, Arizona State University.

Skop, E. and W. Li. 2003. "From the Ghetto to the Invisiburb: Shifting Patterns of Immigrant Settlement in Contemporary America." J. W. Frazier and F. L. Margai (eds.). *Multi-Cultural Geographies: Persistence and Change in U.S. Racial/Ethnic Geography.* Binghamton, NY: Global Academic Publishing, pp.113–124.

Skop, E. and W. Li. 2006 (forthcoming). "Asians in America's Suburbs: Patterns and Consequences of Settlement." *Geographical Review.*

Smedley, B., A. Stith, and A. Nelson. 2002. *Unequal Treatment: Confronting Racial and Ethnic Disparities in Health Care.* Institute of Medicine: National Academies Press.

Smith, C. J. and J. R. Logan. 2006 (forthcoming). "Flushing 2000: Geographic Explorations in Asian New York." In W. Li (ed.). *From Urban Enclave to Ethnic Suburb: New Asian Communities in Pacific Rim Countries.* Honolulu: University of Hawaii Press.

Smith, D. 2000. *Modern Tribal Development: Paths to Self-Sufficiency and Cultural Integrity in Indian Country.* New York: AltaMira Press.

Smith, G. A. 2002. "Place-Based Education: Learning to be Where we Are." *Phi Delta Kappan* 83(8): 584–94.

Smith, H. A. and O. J. Furuseth (eds.). (forthcoming). *The New South: Latinos and the Transformation of Space.* Burlington, VT: Ashgate Publishing.

Smith, J. M. 2004. Transcript of Interview with 'Brian Ishii.' Conducted March 25, 2004. Little Tokyo, Los Angeles California, p. 10.

Smith, R. C. 2001. "Mexicans: Social, Educational, Economic, and Political Problems and Prospects in New York," in *New Immigrants in New York.* N. Foner (ed.). New York: Columbia University Press, pp. 275–300.

Smitherman, G. 1992. "Talkin and Testifyin: The Language of Black America." Detroit: Wayne State University Press, p. 5.

Sowell, T. 1981. *Ethnic America: A History.* New York: Basic Books.

Sowell, T. 1981. *Markets and Minorities.* New York, NY: Basic Books.

Spickard, P. and R. Fong. 1995. "Pacific Islander Americans and Multiethnicity: A Vision of America's Future?" *Social Forces* (73)4: 1365–1383.

SPLC. 2001. "Blood on the Border." *Intelligence Report,* Issue 101, Spring, 2001. Southern Poverty Law Center. http://www.splcenter.org/intel/intelreport/article.jsp?pid=418.

Stack, C. 1996. *Call to Home.* New York: Basic Books.

Stahura, J. M. 1986. "Suburban Development, Black Suburbanization and the Civil Rights Movement since World War II." *American Sociological Review* 51: 131–144.

Stahura, J. M. 1988. "Changing Patterns of Suburban Racial Composition, 1970–1980." *Urban Affairs Quarterly* 23(3): 448–459.

Stains, L. R. 1994. "Latinization of Allentown, PA." *The New York Times,* 15 May, 1994: 56–62. The New York Times Company.

Staton, R. 2005. "Language Revival: Hawaiian Rates as the Nation's Only Growing Indigenous Tongue." *Honolulu Star-Bulletin,* March 14, 2005, http://starbulletin.com/2005/03/14/news/story7.html.

Statistical Service. 2002. *Census of Population 2001.* Nicosia: Printing Office of the Republic of Cyprus.

Stearman, A. M. 1985. *Cabma and Kolla: Migration and Development in Santa Cruz, Bolivia.* Florida: University of Florida Press.

Stein, E. 2001. "Quantifying the Economic Cost of Predatory Lending." *A Report from the Coalition of Responsible Lending.* Durham, NC.

Stewart, D. J. 1999. "Hot'lanta's Urban Expansion and Cultural Landscape Change." *The Geographical Review* 89(1): 132–140.

St Hilaire, A. 2002. "The Social Adaptation of Children of Mexican Immigrants: Educational Aspirations beyond Junior High School." *Social Science Quarterly* 83(4): 1026–1043.

St John, C. and R. Clymer. 2000. "Racial Residential Segregation by Level of Socioeconomic Status." *Social Science Quarterly* 81(3): 701–715.

Stock, R. D. 2002. "Study of Predatory Lending in Montgomery County, 1994–2000." Dayton, OH: Center for Business and Economic Research, University of Dayton.

Stoll, M. A. 1996. "Distance or Discrimination? The Convergence of Space and Race in Understanding Metropolitan Racial Differences in Employment." *SAGE Race Relations* 21: 3–25.

Stoll, M. A. 1999. "Spatial Mismatch, Discrimination, and Male Youth Employment in the Washington, D.C. Area: Implications for Residential Mobility Policies." *Journal of Policy Analysis and Management* 18: 77–98.

Stoller, P. 2001. "West Africans: Trading Places in New York," in *New Immigrants in New York.* Nancy Foner (ed.). New York: Columbia University Press, pp. 229–249.

Stout, D. 2005. Justices Refuse to Restore Sovereignty to Land Bought by Indians. Retrieved on April 28, 2005 from http://www.law.syr.edu/Pdfs/0Justices%20Refuse%20to%20Restore%20Sovereignty%20-%20March%2030.pdf.

Stowell, J. and D. Oakley. 2002. "Choosing Segregation: Racial Imbalance in American Public Schools, 1990–2000." Lewis Mumford Center for Comparative Urban and Regional Research, SUNY-Albany, March, 2002.

Stull, D. and M. Broadway. 2004. *Slaughterhouse Blues: The Meat and Poultry Industry in North America.* Belmont, CA: Wadsworth.

Sturdevant, P. and W. J. Brennan. 2000. "The Double Dirty Dozen Predatory Mortgage Lending Practices." National Association of Consumer Advocates. http://209.219.154. 214/dirtymortgages1a.htm (2).

Sultana, S. 2003. "Commuting Constraints of Black Female Workers in Atlanta: An Examination of the Spatial Mismatch Hypothesis in Married-Couple, Dual-Earner Households." *Southeastern Geographer* 43(2): 249–259.

Sultana, S. 2005. "Racial Variations in Males' Commuting Times in Atlanta: What Does the Evidence Suggest?" *Professional Geographer* 57(1): 66–82.

Suttles, G. D. 1968. *The Social Order of the Slum: Ethnicity and Territory in the Inner City.* Chicago: The University of Chicago Press.

Sullivan, E. 2002. Personal Interview, 13th September.

Suro, R. and A. Singer. 2002. "Latino Growth in Metropolitan America: Changing Patterns, New Locations." *The Brookings Institution Survey Series, Census 2000.* July. 18 pp.

Taeuber, I. B. 1958. "Migration, Mobility, and the Assimilation of the Negro." *Population Bulletin.* November, pp. 137–138.

Taeuber, K. E. and A. F. Taeuber. 1972. *Negroes in Cities.* New York: Athenaeum.

Takahashi, J. 1997. *Nisei/Sansei: Shifting Japanese American Identities and Politics.* Philadelphia: Temple University Press.

Takaki, R. 1989. *Strangers From a Different Shore: A History of Asian Americans.* Boston: Little, Brown and Co.

Takaki, R. 1998. *Strangers From a Different Shore: A History of Asian Americans,* revised edition. Boston: Back Bay Press.

Tatum, B. D. 1999. *Why Are All the Black Kids Sitting Together in the Cafeteria?* New York: Basic Books.

Taylor, B. D. and P. M. Ong. 1995. "Spatial Mismatch or Automobile Mismatch? An Examination of Race, Residence and Commuting in U.S. Metropolitan Areas." *Urban Studies* 32: 1453–1473.

Taylor, J. and J. Kalt. 2005. *American Indians on Reservations: A Databook of Socioeconomic Change between the 1990 and 2000 Censuses.* Cambridge, MA: The Harvard Project on American Indian Economic Development, Malcolm Wiener Center for Social Policy, John F. Kennedy School of Government, Harvard University.

Tchen, J. 1985. *Towards Building a Democratic Community Culture: Reflections on the New York Chinatown History Project.* Paper delivered at the Fifth International Oral History Conference, March 29–31, 1985. Cited in D. Hayden (1995). *The Power of Place: Urban Landscapes as Public History,* 50. Cambridge, MA: MIT Press.

Tettey-Fio, E. 2003. "Black American Geographies: The Historical and Contemporary Distributions of African-Americans." In *Multicultural Geographies: The Changing Racial and Ethnic Patterns of the United States.* J. W. Frazier and F. M. Margai, (eds.). Binghamton, NY: Global Academic Publishing.

The Economist, "A Survey of Migration," November 2nd, 2002, p. 10.

The Economist, "Immigration: Into the Suburbs," March 13th, 2004, pp. 31–32.

Therrien, M., R. Therrien, and R. Ramirez. 2000. The Latino Population in the United States: March 2000, Current Population Report, pp. 20–535, U.S. Census Bureau, Washington, D.C.

Thiel, H. and A. Finezza. 1971. "A Note on the Measurement of Racial Integration of Schools by Means of Informational Concepts." *Journal of Mathematical Sociology* 1: 187–94.

Thiel, H. 1972. *Statistical Decomposition Analysis.* Amsterdam: North-Holland Publishing Company.

Thomas-Hope, E. 1988. "Caribbean Skilled International Migration and the Transnational Household." *Geoforum* 19(4): 423–432.

Thompson, M. A. 1997. "The Impact of Spatial Mismatch on Female Labor Force Participation." *Economic Development Quarterly* 11: 138–145.

Tinker, H. 1977. *The Banyan Tree: Overseas Emigrants from India, Pakistan, and Bangladesh.* London: Oxford University Press.

Tobler, W. 1995. "Migration: Ravenstein Thornwaite, and Beyond." *Urban Geography* 16: 327–343.

Tolbert, M. 2002. "Census 2000: Chinese Largest Asian Group in the United States." *United States Department of Commerce News CB02-CN* 59. Washington, D.C.: Bureau of the Census.

Trask, H.-K. 1993. *From a Native Daughter: Colonialism and Sovereignty in Hawai'i*. Monroe, ME: Common Courage Press.

Trask, M. 2002. "*Rice* v. *Cayetano*: Reaffirming the Racism of Hawaii's Colonial Past," *Asian-Pacific Law & Policy Journal* 3(2): 352–358.

Trewartha, G. 1926. "Recent Thoughts on the Problem of White Acclimatization in the Wet Tropics." *Geographical Review* 6(4): 467–478.

Trotter, J. W., Jr. (ed.). 1991. *The Great Migration Historical Perspective*. Bloomington: Indiana University Press.

Tuan, Y.-F. 1979. "Space and Place: Humanistic Perspectives," in *Philosophy in Geography*. S. Gale and G. Olsson (eds.). Dordrecht, Holland: D. Reidel Publishing Company.

Tuan, Y.-F. 1979. "Thought and Landscape: The Eye and the Mind's Eye," D. W. Meinig (ed.). *The Interpretation of Ordinary Landscapes*. Oxford University Press, Inc.

Tusitala M. S. 1999. "Here our Words." Ch. 14 in M. Rapaport (ed.). *The Pacific Islands: Environment and Society*. Honolulu: Bess Press.

Tyner, J. A. 2003. "Geography, Ground-Level Reality, and the Epistemology of Malcolm X." *Journal of Geography* 102: 167–178.

Tyner, J. A. 2004. "Territoriality, Social Justice and Gendered Revolutions in the Speeches of Malcolm X." *Transactions, Institute of British Geographers*. NS 29: 330–343.

Tyner, J. A. 2005a. *The Geography of Malcolm X: Black Radicalism and the Remaking of American Space*. New York: Routledge.

Tyner, J. A. 2005b. "Landscape and the Mask of Self in George Orwell's 'Shooting an Elephant.'" *Area* 37(2).

University of Texas at Austin. 2005. *The Handbook of Texas Online*. http://www.tsha.utexas.edu/handbook/online/articles/ (access September 24, 2005).

Ungar, S. 1995. "Getting Down to Business: The Ethiopians and Eritreans." In *Fresh Blood: The New American Immigrants*. Sanford Ungar (ed.). New York: Simon and Schuster, pp. 247–272.

United Nations Population Division. 2002. *International Migration Report, 2002*. New York: United Nations.

U.S. Bureau of the Census. 1973. Vol. 1 Characteristics of the Population. *Census of Population: 1970*. Part 45, Texas – Section 1. Washington, D.C.: Government Printing Office.

U.S. Bureau of the Census. 1983. General Social and Economic Characteristics. *Census of Population: 1980*. Part 45, Texas – Section 1. Washington, D.C.: Government Printing Office.

U.S. Bureau of the Census. 1983. Vol. 1 Characteristics of the Population. *Census of Population: 1980*. Part 45, Texas – Section 1. Washington, D.C.: Government Printing Office.

U.S. Bureau of the Census. 1990. *1990 Census of Population. Supplementary Reports. Detailed Ancestry Characteristics of Groups for States*, CPS-1-2.

U.S. Bureau of the Census. 1990. *Detailed Ancestry Groups for States*, CPH-L-97.

U.S. Bureau of the Census. 1990. *Profiles of Our Ancestry: Selected Characteristics by Ancestry Group*, CPH-L-149.

U.S. Bureau of the Census. 1990. *Profiles of the Foreign-Born Population: Selected Characteristics by Place of Birth*, CPH-L 148.

U.S. Bureau of the Census. 1993. "General Social and Economic Characteristics." *Census of Population: 1990*. Part 45, Texas – Section 1. Washington, D.C.: Government Printing Office.

U.S. Bureau of the Census. 1993. Vol. 1. "Characteristics of the Population." *Census of Population: 1990*. Part 45, Texas – Section 1. Washington, D.C.: Government Printing Office. U.S. Bureau of the Census. 1980. *Ancestry of the Population by State*. PC80-S1-10.

U.S. Bureau of the Census. 2000. *Census of Population and Housing*. Public Use Microdata Sample, United States.

U.S. Bureau of the Census. 2000. *County and City Data Book: 2000*. Washington, D.C.: U.S. Government Printing Office.

U.S. Bureau of the Census. 2000. http://factfinder.census.gov/servlet/DatasetMainPageServlet?_lang=en. Accessed July 15, 2004.

U.S. Bureau of the Census. 2000. *Summary File 4*.

U.S. Bureau of the Census. 2001. *American Indian- and Alaska Native-Owned Businesses: 1997*. Washington, D.C.: United States Department of Commerce.

U.S. Bureau of the Census. 2001. *Profiles of General Demographic Characteristics: 2000 Census of Population and Housing*. Washington, D.C.: (Issued May, 2001).

U.S. Bureau of the Census. 2001. *The Two or More Races Population: 2000. Census 2000 Brief*. Washington, D.C.: U.S. Government Printing Office.

U.S. Bureau of the Census. 2002. *The Asian Population: 2000. Census 2000 Brief.* Washington, D.C.: U.S. Government Printing Office.

U.S. Bureau of the Census. 2003. *2000 Census of Population and Housing*, Public Use Microdata Sample, United States: Technical Documentation.

U.S. Bureau of the Census. 2003. *2000 Census of Population and Housing*, Summary File 1, American FactFinder, Table P 4, "Hispanic or Latino and Not Hispanic or Latino by Race," www.census.gov.

U.S. Bureau of the Census. 2003. *2000 Census of Population and Housing*, Summary File 3, American FactFinder, Table PCT 18, "Ancestry for People with One or More Ancestry Categories Reported," www.census.gov.

U.S. Bureau of the Census. 2003. *2000 Census of Population and Housing*, Summary File 3, American FactFinder, Table PCT 19, "Place of Birth for the Foreign Born Population," www.census.gov.

U.S. Bureau of the Census. 2003. *2000 Census of Population and Housing*, "Technical Documentation," Public Use Microdata Sample, Washington, D.C.

U.S. Bureau of the Census. Online. 2004. *State and County Quick Facts.* Available at http://quickfacts.census.gov/qfd/states/48000.html. Internet. Accessed May 1, 2004.

U.S. Bureau of the Census. 2005a. Census 2000 Summary File (SF 1) 100-Percent Data. Retrieved on April 25, 2005 from American Factfinder at http://factfinder.census.gov/home/saff/main.html?_lang=en.

U.S. Bureau of the Census. 2005b. Census 2000 American Indian and Alaska Native Summary File (AIANSF) – Sample Data. Retrieved on April 25, 2005 from American Factfinder at http://factfinder.census.gov/home/saff/main.html?_lang=en.

U.S. Bureau of the Census. 2005c. Cartographic Boundary Files, Geographic Area Descriptions. Retrieved on April 22, 2005 from http://www.census.gov/geo/www/cob/na_metadata.html.

U.S. Bureau of the Census. 2005d. Statistical Abstract of the United States: 2004–2005. American Indian, Alaska Native Population. Table number 736. Small Business Administration Loans to Small Businesses: 1990 to 2003. Retrieved on April 24, 2005 from http://www/census.gov/statab/www/sa04aian.pdf.

U.S. Department of Commerce. 1963. *U.S. Census of Population: 1960, Volume 1, Characteristics of the Population, Part 34, New York.* Washington, D.C.: U.S. Bureau of the Census.

U.S. Department of Commerce. 1982. *The Journey to Work in the United States: 1979.* Current Population Reports P-23, Special Studies No. 122. Washington, D.C.: U.S. Bureau of the Census.

U.S. Department of Commerce. 1983. *1980 Census of Population and Housing, Buffalo, New York.* PHC80-2-106. Washington, D.C.: U.S. Department of Commerce, Bureau of the Census.

U.S. Department of Housing and Urban Development. 2000. "Curbing Predatory Home Mortgage Lending: A Joint Report." Washington, D.C.

U.S. Department of Housing and Urban Development. April 12, 2002. "Unequal Burden: Income and Racial Disparities in Subprime Lending in America."

U.S. Immigration and Naturalization Service. 2003. *2002 Statistical Yearbook.* Washington, D.C.: U.S. Government Printing Office.

U.S. Immigration and Naturalization Service. 2003. *Statistical Yearbook.*

Valdez, A. 1993. "Persistant Poverty, Crime, and Drugs: U.S.-Mexican Border Region." In *In the Barrios: Latinos and the Underclass Debate,* J. Moore and R. Pinderhughes (eds.). New York: Russell Sage Foundation, pp. 173–194.

Varma, B. N. 1980. "Indians as New Ethnics: A Theoretical Note." In *The New Ethnics: Asian Indians in the United States,* P. Saran and E. Eames (eds.). New York: Praeger Publishers, pp. 29–41.

Wagenheim, K. 1975. *Puerto Rico: A Profile.* New York: Prager.

Waldinger, R. 1989. "Immigration and Urban Change." *Annual Review of Sociology* 15: 211–32.

Waldinger, R. 1996 *Still the Promised City? African-Americans and New Immigrants in Postindustrial New York.* Cambridge, New York: Harvard University Press.

Waldinger, R. and M. Bozorgmehr (eds.). 1996. *Ethnic Los Angeles.* New York: Russell Sage Foundation.

Waldinger, R. and J. Perlmann. 1998. "Second Generations: Past, Present, Future." *Journal of Ethnic and Migration Studies* 24(1): 5–24.

Walen, B. 1991. "A View of Geography." *The Geographical Review* 81(1001), January. (Terkenli, 1995: 326.)

Walen, B. 2002. Lutheran Social Services, Refugee Services and Employment Programs, Provided data on LSS Resettlement Program-Liberians in MN. 6/12/02.

Walker, R. 1997. "California Rages: Regional Capitalism and the Politics of Renewal." In *Geographies of Economies.* R. Lee and J. Wills, (eds.). London: Arnold, pp. 345–355.

Wallace, L. J. D., R. Patel, A. Dellinger. "Injury Mortality Among American Indian and Alaska Native Children and Youth-United States, 1989–1998." *Morbidity and Mortality Weekly.* August 2003, Vol. 52(30): 697.

Walton-Roberts, M. 1998. "Three Readings of the Turban: Sikh Identity in Greater Vancouver." *Urban Geography* 19(4): 311–331.

Ward, D. 1968. "The Emergence of Central Immigrant Ghettos in American Cities: 1840–1920." *Annals of the Association of American Geographers* 58: 343–359.

Ward, D. 1971. *Cities and Immigrants: A Geography of Changes in Nineteenth Century America.* New York: Oxford University Press.

Ward, D. 1982. "The Ethnic Ghetto in the United States: Past and Present." *Transactions of the Institute of British Geographers* 7(3): 257–275.

Ward, D. 1989. *Poverty, Ethnicity, and the American City, 1840–1925: Changing Conceptions of the Slum and the Ghetto.* Cambridge: Cambridge University Press.

Waters, M. C. 1994. "Ethnic and Racial Identities of Second Generation Black Immigrants in New York City." *International Migration Review* 28(4), pp. 795–821.

Welch, F. and A. Light. 1987. *New Evidence on School Desegregation.* Washington, D.C.: U.S. Commission on Civil Rights.

West, R. C. and J. P. Augelli (eds.). 1989. *Middle American: Its Lands and Peoples.* 3rd rev. ed., Englewood Cliffs, NJ: Prentice Hall, Inc.

White, M. J., R. F. Dymowski, and S. Wang. 1994. "Ethnic Neighbors and Ethnic Myths: An Examination of Residential Segregation in 1910." In *After Ellis Island: Newcomers and Natives in the 1910 Census.* Susan Cotts Watkins (ed.). New York: Russell Sage Foundation.

White, M. J. and S. Sassler. 2000. "Judging Not Only by Color: Ethnicity, Nativity, and Neighborhood Attainment." *Social Science Quarterly* 81(4): 997–1013.

White, S. E. 1994. "Ogallala Oases: Water Use, Population Redistribution, and Policy Implications in the High Plains of Western Kansas, 1980–1990." *Annals of the Association of American Geographers* 84(1): 29–45.

Whiteford, S. 1981. *Workers from the North, Plantations, Bolivian Labor and the City in Northwest Argentina.* Austin: University of Texas Press.

Wiese, A. 2004. *Places of Their Own.* Chicago: University of Chicago Press.

Wikipedia. 2005. Indian Reservation. Retrieved on April 17, 2005 from http://en.wikipedia.org/wiki/Indian_reservation.

Wildsmith, E. 2004. "Race/Ethnic Differences in Female Headship: Exploring the Assumptions of Assimilation Theory." *Social Science Quarterly* 85(1): 89–106.

Wilkes, R. and J. Iceland. 2004. "Hypersegregation in the Twenty-first Century." *Demography* 41(1): 23–36.

Williams, D. R. 1997. "Race and Health: Basic Questions, Emerging Directions." *Annals of Epidemiology* 7(5): 322–333.

Williams, K. and V. W. Johnson. 2002. "Eliminating African-American Health Disparity via History-Based Policy." *Harvard Health Policy Review* 3(2).

Williams, L. S., S. D. Alvarez, and K. S. A. Hauck. 2002. "My Name is Not Maria: Young Latinas Seeking Home in the Heartland." *Social Problems* 49(4): 563–584.

Wilson, B. M. 2002 "Critically Understanding Race-Connected Practices: A Reading of W. E. B. DuBois and R. Wright." *The Professional Geographer* 54(1): 31–41.

Wilson, F. D. 1985. "The Impact of School Desegregation Programs on White Public-School Enrollment, 1968–1976." *Sociology of Education* 58: 137–153.

Wilson, J. H. 2003. *Africans on the Move: A Descriptive Geography of African Immigration to the United States with a Focus on Metropolitan, Washington, D.C.* Master's Thesis. Washington, D.C.: The George Washington University.

Wilson, W. J. 1978. *The Declining Significance of Race: Blacks and Changing American Institutions.* Chicago: Chicago University Press.

Wilson, W. J. 1987. *The Truly Disadvantaged: The Inner City, the Underclass, and Public Policy.* Chicago: University of Chicago Press.

Winters, L. and H. Debose. 2004. *New Faces in a Changing America: Multiracial Identity in the 21st Century.* Thousand Oaks, CA: Sage Publications

Wise, M. B. (ed.). 1977. *Desegregation in Education: A Directory of Reported Federal Decisions.* Notre Dame, IN: Center for Civil Rights, University of Notre Dame Law School.

Wolfenstein, E. 1989. *The Victims of Democracy: Malcolm X and the Black Revolution.* London: Free Association Books.

Wolpert, J. 1965. "Behavioral Aspects of the Decision to Migrate." *Papers and Proceedings of the Regional Science Association* 15: 159–69.

Wong, D. W. S. 1999. "An Index of Chinese Residential Segregation." *Urban Geography* 20(7): 635–647.

Wong, D. 1999. "A Geographical Analysis of Multiethnic Households in the United States," *International Journal of Population Geography* 5: 31–48.

Wong, D. W. S. 2000. "Ethnic Integration and Spatial Segregation of the Chinese Population." *Asian Ethnicity* 1: 53–72.

Wong, D. 2002. "Modeling Local Segregation: A Spatial Interaction Approach." *Geographical and Environmental Modeling* 6(1): 81–97.

Woo, D. 1994. *The Glass Ceiling and Asian Americans.* Washington, D.C.: U.S. Department of Labor.

Wood, H. 1999. *Displacing Natives: The Rhetorical Production of Hawai'i.* Lanham, MD: Rowman & Littlefield Publishers, Inc.

Wood, J. S. 2006 (forthcoming). "Making America at the Eden Center." In W. Li (ed.), *From Urban Enclave to Ethnic Suburb: New Asian Communities in Pacific Rim Countries.* Honolulu: University of Hawaii Press.

Wu, F. 2003. *Yellow: Race in America Beyond Black and White.* New York: Basic Books.

Xenos, P., H. Barringer, and M. J. Levin. 1989. *Asian Indians in the United States: A 1980 Census Profile.* Honolulu: East-West Center.

Xie, Y. and K. Goyette. 1997. "The Racial Identification of Biracial Children with One Asian Parent: Evidence from the 1990 Census." *Social Forces* 76(2): 547–570.

Yeoman, B. 2000. "Hispanic Diaspora." *Mother Jones* 25(4): 34+. July/August.

Yokota, K. A. 1996. "From Little Tokyo to Bronzeville and Back: Ethnic Communities in Transition." Unpublished Master of Arts Thesis. University of California, Los Angeles, Department of Asian American Studies.

Yu, S. M., Z. J. Huang, and G. K. Singh. 2004. "Health Status and Health Services Utilization Among U.S. Chinese, Asian Indian, Filipino, and other Asian/Pacific Islander Children." *Pediatrics Vol. 113 #1* January 2004, pp. 101–107.

Zax, J. F. 1990. "Race and Commutes." *Journal of Urban Economics* 28: 336–348.

Zax, J. F. and J. F. Kain. 1996. "Moving to the Suburbs: Do Relocating Companies Leave Their Black Employees Behind?" *Journal of Labor Economics* 14(3): 472–504.

Zelinsky, W. and B. A. Lee. 1998. "Heterolocalism: An Alternative Model of Sociospatial Behaviour of Immigrant Ethnic Communities." *International Journal of Population Geography* 4(4): 281–298.

Zelinsky, W. 2001. *The Enigma of Ethnicity: Another American Dilemma.* Iowa City: University of Iowa Press.

Zhao, X. 2002. *Remaking Chinese America: Immigration, Family, and Community, 1940–1965.* Rutgers Univ. Press.

Zhou, M. 1992. *Chinatown: The Socioeconomic Potential of An Urban Enclave.* Philadelphia: Temple University Press.

Zhou, M. 1997. "Segmented Assimilation: Issues, Controversies, and Recent Research on the New Second Generation." *International Migration Review* 31(4): 975–1008.

Zhou, M. 1999. "Segmented Assimilation: Issues, Controversies, and Recent Research on the New Second Generation," in C. Herschman, P. Kasinitz, and J. DeWind (eds.). *The Handbook of International Migration: The American Experience.* New York: Russell Sage Foundation, pp. 196–211.

Zhou, M. and J. V. Gatewood. 2000. "Mapping the Terrain: Asian-American Diversity and the Challenges of the Twenty-first Century." In M. Zhou and J. V. Greenwood (eds.). *Contemporary Asian America: A Multi-Disciplinary Reader.* New York University Press.

Zhou, Y. 1997. "Segmented Assimilation: Issues, Controversies, and Recent Research on the New Second Generation." *International Migration Review* 31(4): 975–1008.

Zhou, Y. 1998. "How Do Places Matter? A Comparative Study of Chinese Ethnic Economies in Los Angeles and New York City." *Urban Geography* 19(6): 531–553.

Zorn, P. 1989. "Separate and Unequal." *Digest: Clearinghouse on Urban Education,* Vol. 59. Columbia University, p. 1.

Zorn, P. December 21, 2000. "Subprime Lending: An Investigation of Economic Efficiency." Freddie Mac.

About the Authors

Short descriptions of author's affiliations and research interests appear below in the order that authors appear in the text.

John W. Frazier is Professor of Geography and Director of the GIS Core Facility at the State University of New York at Binghamton. His research interests have focused on the applied aspects of geography and racial/ethnic studies. He is the author of books and articles on these topics. He also is the founder of the Race, Ethnicity, and Place Conferences.

Eugene L. Tettey-Fio is Associate Professor of Geography at SUNY-Binghamton. His recent publications have focused on Africa, African Americans, and racial-ethnic inequalities. He is the co-author of **Race and Place**.

James A. Tyner is Associate Professor of Geography at Kent State University. He has authored four books and over forty articles and book chapters on the topics of race, ethnicity, and migration. His latest book is **The Geography of Malcolm X: Black Radicalism and the Remaking of American Space.**

John R. Logan is Director, Spatial Structures in the Social Sciences, and Professor of Sociology at Brown University. He has studied patterns of residential segregation and neighborhood change. His recent work examines the consequences of these processes on education. He is widely published in social science journals.

Deirdre Oakley is Assistant Professor of Sociology at Northern Illinois University. Her publication entitled "The American Welfare State Decoded: Uncovering the Neglected History of Public-Private Partnerships" is forthcoming in *City and Community*. She is also working on a project partially funded by the National Poverty Center at the University of Michigan concerning the effectiveness of the Federal Empowerment Zone and Enterprise Communities initiative.

Jacob Stowell received a Ph.D. in Sociology from SUNY-Albany. Dr. Stowell's research interests focus on racial inequality and crime. Previously, he worked as a research assistant at the Lewis Mumford Center. He currently is Assistant Professor of Criminal Justice at the University of Massachusetts-Lowell.

Audrey Singer is Immigration Fellow at the Brookings Institution Metropolitan Policy Program. Her research focuses on the economic, social, and political incorporation of immigrants. She is currently working on a study of contemporary immigrant settlement and emerging gateways in the United States, including in-depth work on Washington, D.C. She earned a Ph.D. in sociology, with a specialization in demography, from The University of Texas at Austin.

Wei Li is Associate Professor of Geography at Arizona State University. Her research focus is immigration and integration. She also studies the financial sector and community development. She coined the term "*ethnoburb*" to describe some contemporary suburban minority settlements. Currently she conducts empirical studies in the Pacific Rim. Her book, **From Urban Enclave to Ethnic Suburb: New Asian Communities in the Pacific Rim Countries**, will be published in 2006.

Roger Anderson is an MA student at SUNY-Binghamton. His thesis work explores the nature of black return migration to rural and urban South Florida. He is interested in professional planning.

David H. Kaplan is Professor of Geography at Kent State University where he directs the Urban Studies Program. He has published four books, including **Segregation in Cities**, and research articles dealing with urban issues in a wide variety of journals.

Joe T. Darden's interests are urban social geography and residential segregation. His books include **Detroit: Race and Uneven Development** and **The Significance of White Supremacy in the Canadian Metropolis of Toronto**. Dr. Darden is Professor of Geography at Michigan State University.

Louise Jezierski is Associate Professor of Social Relations in the James Madison College of Michigan State University. Dr. Jezierski received a Ph.D. in urban and community sociology and has conducted research in the fields of community development, urban policy, and social stratification (race, ethnicity, social class, and gender).

Ibipo Johnston-Anumonwo is Professor of Geography at SUNY-Cortland. Her research has focused on Africa, gender roles, and transportation issues related to racial-ethnic disparities in American society. Her work has been published in leading journals such as *Urban Geography*.

Selima Sultana is Assistant Professor of Geography at the University of North Carolina, Greensboro. Her research interests in urban and transport geography are based on coupling travel behavior studies with GIS-based methodologies. Her work has been published in leading journals such as *The Professional Geographer*.

Elizabeth Chacko is Associate Professor of Geography and International Affairs at George Washington University. Her work deals with immigrant identity and the creation of ethnic places by immigrant communities. Her recent research focuses especially on the Ethiopian immigrant population in the United States. Among her recent publications on this topic is an article that appears in the *Geographical Review*.

Ivan Cheung was Professor of Geography at George Washington University and currently is Director of GIScience Programs at the Association of American Geographers in Washington, D.C. His specialties include geostatistics and geospatial technologies.

Earl P. Scott is a cultural geographer with a sub-specialty in cultural ecology and regional specialty in Africa. His work involves the ways cultures influence human use and organization of the Earth's surface. He is interested in how ordinary citizens employ small-scale enterprises to advance their own well-being. Dr. Scott is Emeritus Professor of Geography and current Chairperson of the Department of African American & African Studies at the University of Minnesota.

Thomas D. Boswell is Professor of Geography at the University of Miami, Coral Gables. His research and teaching interests are in world population problems, migration, ethnicity, housing segregation and discrimination, and poverty. He was a Research Associate with the Research Institute for the Study of Man in New York City (1973–74), Director of the Policy Center of the Cuban American National Council in Miami (1993–97), and recipient of numerous grants from agencies such as the Ford Foundation. Professor Boswell received the Award for Outstanding Contribution of Affirmatively Furthering Fair Housing in South Florida for the Year 1996. He has published more than 40 articles in refereed journals such as: *Geographical Review, Urban Geography,* and *The Professional Geographer.* He also has authored six books.

Terry-Ann Jones is Assistant Professor of Sociology at Fairfield University in Connecticut. Her recently completed dissertation, "Comparative Diasporas: Jamaicans in South Florida and Toronto," compares Jamaican immigrants in the two metropolitan areas, examining the racial and ethnic setting and labor markets of the two areas, and the immigration policies of the two countries. Her areas of research and teaching interest are in international migration, particularly movement between the Caribbean and North America.

Mark E. Reisinger is Assistant Professor of Geography at Binghamton University. His research interests include U.S. internal migration, urban-economic geography, and racial-ethnic geographies. His recent research has focused on Latinos in America. Professor Reisinger has published in journals such as *The Professional Geographer*.

Keith Galligano received an MA in Geography from SUNY-Binghamton and is currently employed as a senior analyst by Autozone in Memphis, Tennessee. His research has centered on ethnicity and business geography.

Marie Price is Associate Professor of Geography and International Affairs at George Washington University. Her research focuses on Latin America, migration, and the impact of immigrants on cities. In 2006 Dr. Price will be a visiting fellow at the Migration Policy Institute in Washington, D.C.

Richard C. Jones is Professor of Geography at the University of Texas at San Antonio. His research is on the changing spatial patterns of ethnic and immigrant groups in the San Antonio region. Recently, he has studied Mexican-American settlement patterns and issues in a local context. Dr. Jones' research has been published in a variety of social science journals.

Lawrence E. Estaville is an ethnic geographer and Professor of Geography at Texas State University. He is author of a number of books, book chapters, and journal articles. Two of his works have been honored with awards. In 1992, he led the organizational efforts to establish the AAG's Ethnic Geography Specialty Group and was elected as its first chair.

Edris J. Montalvo received an M.S. in Geography from the Department of Geography at Texas State University. He teaches at San Antonio Community College.

Brock J. Brown is a cultural geographer and Associate Professor of Geography at Texas State University. He has been honored with several teaching awards. Professor Brown's work focuses on geographic education issues.

Shawn Malia Kanaʻiaupuni is Director of the PASE program in Honolulu. A Native Hawaiian demographer and sociologist from Pūpūkea, Oʻahu, Dr. Kanaʻiaupuni's research focuses on the status and well-being of Hawaiians. Formerly a faculty member of the Sociology Department at the University of Wisconsin-Madison, Dr. Kanaʻiaupuni also serves on the Race and Ethnic Advisory Committee of the U.S. Census Bureau and the Native Hawaiian Education Council of the U.S. Department of Education.

Nolan J. Malone is a Research Scientist for PASE. His research at PASE focuses on the well-being of Native Hawaiian learners, families, and communities, as well as on developing tools to better monitor and examine Hawaiian well-being over time. Dr. Malone completed his Ph.D. in Demography at the University of Pennsylvania and was formerly employed as a population analyst at the U.S. Census Bureau. He specializes in survey research and quantitative analysis.

James M. Smith is Assistant Professor of Geography at Towson State University in Maryland. Professor Smith's recently completed dissertation examined how social practices and cultural forms become etched onto local landscapes. He conducted fieldwork in Little Tokyo on a number of occasions and remains interested in the importance of ethnic identity to sense of place.

Emily Skop is Assistant Professor of Geography in the Department of Geography and the Environment at the University of Texas at Austin. Her interests include international migration processes, the social and spatial constructions of racial/ethnic/gender identities, and urbanization, segregation, and inequality in the contexts of the United States and Latin America. She has published findings in *International Migration Review*, *Geographical Review*, *Population, Space, and Place*, and *The Professional Geographer*.

Claire E. Altman is an undergraduate in the Department of Geography and the Environment and the Department of Sociology at the University of Texas at Austin. Her interests include identity formation processes for immigrants, social capital, and remittance activity. Ms. Altman uses an interdisciplinary approach to address geographic questions.

Edmund J. Zolnik is Assistant Professor of Geography at George Mason University. As an economic geographer, Dr. Zolnik is interested in how minority status influences the ability to attain and maintain a living wage. He also is interested in ethnic groups' sense of place. His current work considers American Indians. His recently published work, such as in *Urban Geography*, also assesses urban quality of life.

Susan W. Hardwick is Professor of Geography at the University of Oregon. Her recent studies have focused on newly arriving refugees and immigrants, especially those settling in the Pacific Northwest. Professor Hardwick has examined immigrant settlement patterns and adaptations to their new environments. Her work is published in leading journals such as the *Geographical Review*.

Stavros T. Constantinou is Associate Professor of Geography at Ohio State University. His published research has centered on ethnicity, particularly the nature of Greek-American ethnic identity and patterns of Greek-American geography. His work has been published in a number of journals, including the *Annals of the AAG*.

Milton E. Harvey is Professor of Geography at Kent State University and specializes in spatial statistics and ethnicity. He is the author of two books and numerous articles. His work has been published in leading journals such as *Economic Geography*.

Thomas Y. Owusu is an Associate Professor and Chair of Geography at William Paterson University. His research interests include migration, ethnicity, and urban geography. Among his recently published works are those focusing on African immigrant experiences in North American cities.

William Dakan was Professor of Geography at the University of Louisville. He considered himself an urban-cultural and applied geographer. He routinely addressed practical and curiosity-based problems. His most recent research centered on the rapidly changing city of Louisville, especially its rapid ethnic diversification.

Florence M. Margai is Associate Professor and Chair of Geography at SUNY-Binghamton. Her research has addressed environmental pollution sources and health outcomes in host communities. Dr. Margai is the author of two books and a number of journal articles on these topics, including those appearing in *The Professional Geographer* and *Social Science and Medicine*. Professor Margai also is editor of the *African Geographical Review*.